AF844353

PANDEMOCRACY IN EUROPE

This open access book explains why a democratic reckoning will start when European societies win the fight against COVID-19.

Have democracies successfully mastered the challenges of the pandemic? How has the coronavirus impacted democratic principles, processes and values? At the heels of the worst public health crisis in living memory, this book shines a light on the sidelining of parliaments, the ruling by governmental decrees and the disenfranchisement of the people in the name of fighting COVID-19.

Pandemocracy in Europe situates the dramatic impact of COVID-19, and the fight against the virus, on Europe's democracies. Throughout its 17 contributions the book sets the theoretical stage and answers the democratic questions engaged by health emergencies. Seven national case studies – UK, Germany, Italy, Sweden, Hungary, Switzerland and France – show, each time with a pronounced focus on a particular element of democracy, how different states reacted to the pandemic.

Bridging disciplines and uniting a stellar cast of scholars on democracy, rule of law and constitutionalism, the book provides contours and nuances to a year of debates in political science, international relations and law on the impact of the virus on democracies.

The open access edition of this book is available under a CC BY-NC-ND 4.0 licence on www.bloomsburycollections.com.

Pandemocracy in Europe

Power, Parliaments and People in Times of COVID-19

Edited by
Matthias C Kettemann
and
Konrad Lachmayer

• HART •
OXFORD • LONDON • NEW YORK • NEW DELHI • SYDNEY

HART PUBLISHING

Bloomsbury Publishing Plc

Kemp House, Chawley Park, Cumnor Hill, Oxford, OX2 9PH, UK

1385 Broadway, New York, NY 10018, USA

29 Earlsfort Terrace, Dublin 2, Ireland

HART PUBLISHING, the Hart/Stag logo, BLOOMSBURY and the Diana logo are trademarks of Bloomsbury Publishing Plc

First published in Great Britain 2022

Copyright © The editors and contributors severally 2022

The editors and contributors have asserted their right under the Copyright, Designs and Patents Act 1988 to be identified as Authors of this work.

This work is published open access subject to a Creative Commons Attribution-NonCommercial-NoDerivatives 4.0 International licence (CC BY-NC-ND 4.0, https://creativecommons.org/licenses/by-nc-nd/4.0/). You may re-use, distribute, and reproduce this work in any medium for non-commercial purposes, provided you give attribution to the copyright holder and the publisher and provide a link to the Creative Commons licence.

Open Access was funded by Sigmund Freud University, the *Publikationsfonds für Monografien der Leibniz-Gemeinschaft* (OA Publication Fund for Books of the Leibniz Community) and the Leibniz Institut for Media Research | Hans-Bredow-Institut.

While every care has been taken to ensure the accuracy of this work, no responsibility for loss or damage occasioned to any person acting or refraining from action as a result of any statement in it can be accepted by the authors, editors or publishers.

All UK Government legislation and other public sector information used in the work is Crown Copyright ©. All House of Lords and House of Commons information used in the work is Parliamentary Copyright ©. This information is reused under the terms of the Open Government Licence v3.0 (http://www.nationalarchives.gov.uk/doc/open-government-licence/version/3) except where otherwise stated.

All Eur-lex material used in the work is © European Union, http://eur-lex.europa.eu/, 1998–2022.

A catalogue record for this book is available from the British Library.

Library of Congress Cataloging-in-Publication data

Names: Kettemann, Matthias C, editor. | Lachmayer, Konrad, editor.

Title: Pandemocracy in Europe : power, parliaments and people in times of COVID-19 / edited by Matthias C Kettemann and Konrad Lachmayer.

Description: Oxford ; New York : Hart, 2022. | Includes bibliographical references and index.

Identifiers: LCCN 2021042168 (print) | LCCN 2021042169 (ebook) | ISBN 9781509946365 (hardback) | ISBN 9781509946402 (paperback) | ISBN 9781509946389 (pdf) | ISBN 9781509946372 (Epub)

Subjects: LCSH: COVID-19 (Disease)—Law and legislation—Europe. | COVID-19 Pandemic, 2020—Political aspects—Europe.

Classification: LCC KJC6178.5 C68 P36 2022 (print) | LCC KJC6178.5 C68 (ebook) | DDC 344.404/362414—dc23/eng/20211004

LC record available at https://lccn.loc.gov/2021042168

LC ebook record available at https://lccn.loc.gov/2021042169

ISBN: HB: 978-1-50994-636-5
ePDF: 978-1-50994-638-9
ePub: 978-1-50994-637-2

Typeset by Compuscript Ltd, Shannon

To find out more about our authors and books visit www.hartpublishing.co.uk. Here you will find extracts, author information, details of forthcoming events and the option to sign up for our newsletters.

TABLE OF CONTENTS

List of Contributors vii

Introduction and Acknowledgements 1
Matthias C Kettemann and Konrad Lachmayer

PART I
THE THEORY – POWER, PEOPLE AND THE CRISIS

1. *Lawless Extravagance: The Primacy Claim of Politics and the State of Exception in Times of COVID-19* 9
   Paul Gragl
2. *Abuse of Power and Self-entrenchment as a State Response to the COVID-19 Outbreak: The Role of Parliaments, Courts and the People* 33
   Antonios Kouroutakis
3. *Democracy, Death and Dying: The Potential and Limits of Legal Rationalisation* 47
   Konrad Lachmayer

PART II
THE PRACTICE – DEMOCRACIES AND THE PANDEMIC

4. *Virus Governance in the United Kingdom* 71
   Robert Thomas
5. *Germany – Federalism in Action* 91
   Pierre Thielbörger
6. *The Marginalisation of Parliament in Facing the Coronavirus Emergency: What about Democracy in Italy?* 117
   Arianna Vedaschi
7. *Swedish Constitutional Response to the Coronavirus Crisis The Odd One Out?* 135
   Julia Dahlqvist and Jane Reichel

8. *Using Emergency Powers in Hungary: Against the Pandemic and/or Democracy?* 155
Zoltán Szente and Fruzsina Gárdos-Orosz

9. *Switzerland: The (Missing) Role of Parliament in Times of Crisis* 179
Odile Ammann and Felix Uhlmann

10. *The Hyper-Executive State of Emergency in France* 201
Sylvia Brunet

PART III
BEYOND STATES: DEMOCRATIC GOVERNANCE IN TIMES OF COVID-19

11. *Pandemics, Expertise and Deliberation at the International Level* 227
Pedro A Villarreal

12. *EU Response to Fighting the Coronavirus – Coordination, Support, Action – Heeding its Citizens' Calls?* 243
Anja Naumann

13. *Pandemics and Platforms: Private Governance of (Dis)Information in Crisis Situations* 263
Matthias C Kettemann and Marie-Therese Sekwenz

14. *Digital Human Rights Proportionality During Global Crisis* 283
Mart Susi

PART IV
CONCLUSIONS: PANDEMICS, POPULISM AND POWER

15. *The Pandemic and Illiberal Constitutional Theories* 299
Gábor Halmai

16. *Populism versus Democracy during a Pandemic: Some Preliminary Considerations* 315
Jan-Werner Müller

17. *Conclusions: Pandemocracy – Governing for the People, without the People?* 329
Konrad Lachmayer and Matthias C Kettemann

Index 347

LIST OF CONTRIBUTORS

Odile Ammann is Postdoctoral researcher in Public Law at the University of Zurich (Switzerland).

Sylvia Brunet is Associate Professor (Maître de conférences) in Public Law at the University of Rouen Normandie (France).

Julia Dahlqvist is a PhD student in Public Law at the Faculty of Law, Stockholm University (Sweden).

Fruzsina Gárdos-Orosz is director and senior research fellow of the Institute for Legal Studies, Centre for Social Sciences of the Hungarian Academy of Sciences and associate professor in constitutional law at the ELTE Law School (Hungary).

Paul Gragl is Professor of European Law at the University of Graz (Austria).

Gábor Halmai is Professor and Chair of Comparative Constitutional Law and Director of Graduate Studies at the Law Department of the European University Institute in Florence (Italy).

Matthias C Kettemann is Professor of Innovation, Theory and Philosophy of Law at the Institute for Theory and Future of Law at the University of Innsbruck (Austria) and research program head at the Leibniz Institute for Media Research | Hans-Bredow-Institut (HBI). He is co-editor of this book.

Antonios Kouroutakis is Assistant Professor at IE University in Madrid and teaches Constitutional Law and the Regulation of New Technologies and Startups (Spain).

Konrad Lachmayer is Professor of Public Law, European Law and Foundations of Law and Vice-Dean of Research at Sigmund Freud University, Faculty of Law in Vienna (Austria). He is co-editor of this book.

Jan-Werner Müller is Professor at the Department of Politics, Princeton University (United States).

Anja Naumann has written her PhD on European health law. She is a Researcher and Graduate Teaching Associate at Queen Mary, University of London (United Kingdom).

Jane Reichel is Professor in Administrative Law at Stockholm University and vice head of the Department of Law (Sweden).

Marie-Therese Sekwenz is a researcher working on law, regulation and governance of artificial intelligence at the Sustainable Computing Lab at the Vienna University of Economics and Business (Austria).

Mart Susi is Professor of Human Rights Law at Tallinn University and head of its law school (Estonia).

Zoltán Szente is Professor of Public Law at the University of Public Service, Budapest and holds a Research Chair at the Institute for Legal Studies, Center for Social Sciences (Hungary).

Pierre Thielbörger holds a Chair of Public Law and International Law at Ruhr-University Bochum, and is acting Director of the Institute for Peace Research and Humanitarian Law (Germany).

Robert Thomas is Professor of Public Law at the University of Manchester (United Kingdom) and a visiting fellow at the Université catholique de Louvain (Belgium).

Felix Uhlmann holds a Chair for Constitutional and Administrative Law as well as Legislative Studies at the University of Zurich (Switzerland).

Arianna Vedaschi is Full Professor of Comparative Public Law at Bocconi University, Milan (Italy).

Pedro Villarreal is a Senior Research Fellow at the Max Planck Institute for Comparative Public Law and International Law in Heidelberg, where he co-manages the project 'International Health Governance' (Germany).

Introduction and Acknowledgements

MATTHIAS C KETTEMANN AND KONRAD LACHMAYER

The COVID-19 disease occurred suddenly, spread fast and hit hard. After East-Asia, Europe was a region struck early by the pandemic and European governments were woefully unprepared. The virus challenged healthcare systems and impacted every fibre of European lives. With one million European dead at the time this manuscript was finalised (in May 2021, according to numbers from Johns Hopkins University), the effect of COVID-19 will be felt for years to come. Grandparents who died too early, parents to whom children could not say goodbye, middle-aged persons unable to climb steps due to Long-COVID. We are not doctors. We cannot help fight COVID-19 directly. But as international and constitutional law experts, we can diagnose another ill that COVID-19 has brought to Europe's vibrant democracies, having emerged surprisingly strong from the financial and the migration crisis. The impact of governmental responses to COVID-19 reverberated in their societies. COVID-19, as our book shows, challenged Europe and European democracies in more than one way: Europe needs to develop adequate and effective responses, but also to uphold its democratic values.

Together with an experienced team of authors from across Europe we ask whether *democracy* has to be conceptually reimagined as a *pandemocracy*, with other priorities, players and normative goals. Has a new viral-authoritarian age dawned (or were existing illiberal tendencies enhanced), demonstrably, like in Hungary, or more subtly, like in Germany, where the *Bundestag* quickly and controversially passed legislation? Did the European multi-level governance sufficiently support the Member States in the health crisis? What has been the role that internet platforms have taken on? Will democracies also suffer from Long-COVID?

This book focuses on the implications of the fight against COVID-19 for European democracies in times of the pandemic with contributions linking debates in political science, international relations and law. This book includes 17 chapters across four parts, that analyse the democratic implications of the specific challenges of a health-related state of emergency. Part I begins by focusing on theoretical questions concerning the three main aspects engaged by emergencies: politics, power relations and the people. Part II continues with seven case studies that, each with a pronounced focus on a particular element of democracy, show how different states reacted to COVID-19. Part III looks beyond the states, and analyses the international and European impacts as well as the influence of non-state actors on democracy during COVID-19. Part IV finally asks which lessons can be drawn from the crisis and offers important insights regarding nationalism and populism.

In the opening chapter, Paul Gragl discusses the relationship between law and politics during the COVID-19 crisis. He states that this relationship is particularly problematic during times of crisis and emergency, since some believe in the postulate that politics is permitted to do anything, even in violation of the law, if necessary. He concludes that the law cannot be thought of or constructed from the exception, but only from the rule. The power of exception should not be overestimated, but we should include clear rules on how to handle crisis situations in the legal system.

Antonios Kouroutakis focuses on the abuse of power and self-entrenchment as the states respond to the COVID-19 outbreak. While it is the norm in liberal constitutional theory that power lies in the hands of the executive during emergencies, this leads to limiting the functions of the legislative body and gives rise to abuses of power. Furthermore, legitimate and illegitimate ways of self-entrenchment as well as roles of different institutions monitoring the executive are examined.

Concluding the first part, Konrad Lachmayer deals with the role of death in European democracies. He states that death can no longer be understood as an unpredictable destiny anymore, but having an economised dimension, which gives governments the possibility to influence death and dying. Budgetary law can serve as an example for the democratic decision-making about life expectancy. Legal rationalisation contributes to the discussion, especially regarding state obligations to guarantee eg the right to life, social rights, or right to health, which affects the government's decisions about life and death. He claims that it is necessary to understand death and dying as a core issue of public debate in democracies.

Opening Part II, Robert Thomas outlines the impact of the COVID-19 crisis on parliamentary democracy in the United Kingdom. While in the beginning of the crisis extensive powers were delegated to the executive and fast-track legislation weakened the role of the Westminster Parliament, the Parliament reenabled scrutiny of the government. Nevertheless the author claims that a number of constitutional reforms need to be conceived of and adopted, especially regarding a codified constitution, constitutional conventions, less centralisation and the devolution of more power to the regions as well as a reform of the Parliament by turning the House of Lords into a regionally representative chamber.

Looking at Germany's handling of the crisis, Pierre Thielbörger identifies the most relevant legal features for dealing with the pandemic. This includes the federalist structure ('executive federalism' and 'cooperative federalism'), the rules on emergencies in the German Constitution, changes in democratic processes as well as the restrictions of German fundamental rights during the pandemics. The author concludes that federalism can be an enabler rather than an inhibitor in tackling crises such as pandemics, but only if 'executive federalism' is balanced appropriately with 'cooperative federalism'.

Arianna Vedaschi describes how Italy struggles with two main issues arising as a result of the severe COVID-19 crisis. First, the marginalisation of parliament as a typical effect of emergency times resulting in reduced checks of the executive and its activities and, second the impact of executive decrees on individual rights. She concludes that the COVID-19 crisis has impacted not just on representativeness and political accountability, but also on key features such as the protection of rights, constitutional review, transparency and certainty of law. Italian institutions have shown a fragmented and sometimes incoherent attitude, both as regards the relationship between parliament and the executive and, within parliament itself, between majority and opposition political forces.

Julia Dahlqvist and Jane Reichel analyse the Swedish constitutional response, which has differed from the more restrictive approaches of other nations. This is a result of the particularities of Swedish constitutional law and legal culture including the lack of provisions regarding the state of emergency, the principles of legality, objectivity and transparency as well as non-legal factors like values, social trust and a strong tradition of consensus-building in the political sphere. The authors state that the pandemic has shed light on the need for foreseeable, transparent, and accountable procedures when adopting measures affecting all of society, even when the measures in question are non-binding and adopted by the semi-independent public authorities.

Taking a look at Hungary, Zoltán Szente and Fruzsina Gárdos-Oros analyse the reaction to the pandemic in a semi-authoritarian system. Criticising the unconstitutional governmental self-empowerment, they hone in on the lack of parliamentary control of the emergency measures in practice. They conclude that the Hungarian government prepared the legal system for a long-term state of exception, institutionalising extraordinary powers and instruments, which provide wide-ranging empowerment for the executive even under normalcy, in the ordinary constitutional order.

In Switzerland, the COVID-19 pandemic has led to unprecedented regulatory activity on the part of the executive branch. Odile Ammann and Felix Uhlmann analyse the extensive use of the intra-constitutional emergency powers by the federal government. The authors emphasise that the longer an emergency situation lasts, the more pressing it becomes for parliament to play an active part in tackling the emergency situation. They discuss two dimensions of parliament's reaction: first, they provide a critical appraisal of the COVID-19 Act, and secondly, they examine how parliament adjusted its own functioning to COVID-19, and the extent to which it succeeded in maintaining its capacity to act despite the crisis.

Sylvia Brunet completes the analysis of the practice of domestic states in the second part of the book. She deals with the health crisis that has struck France since March 2020 as a result of the COVID-19 pandemic; lockdown periods have been implemented and a new, exceptional, state-of-emergency legal regime has been created. The decisions for such measures, which severely limit rights and freedoms, are not taken by parliament or local elected councils but by the President of the Republic, surrounded by a few ministers and advised by experts. She analyses the management of the crisis as centralised and technocratic. The mode of operation, unprecedented in various ways, disrupts the usual decision-making processes within the executive branch, weakens national and local democratic bodies and undermines the rule of law.

In the third part of the book, Pedro Villareal takes us beyond the nation states. He deals with rapid decision-making on an international level with the example of the WHO's emergency committee. Since the Director General had deferred to the emergency committee's advice concerning the decision whether a specific event as a public health emergency occurs, it is essential to assess how deliberation takes place within the committees. He concludes that a more harmonious balance of the input and output dimensions of pandemic deliberation at the international level is long overdue.

On the one hand the European Union faces criticism for not taking enough action to tackle COVID-19 while on the other hand the Union only has limited competences to do so. Consequently, Anja Naumann discusses whether this sheds a different light on the current, narrow stance on the need for harmonised EU action in the matter and if this will lead to a shift of power towards the EU in terms of health competences post COVID-19. She concludes that, despite the current instruments' positive impact towards addressing the COVID-19 pandemic, there are good reasons for Member States to consolidate the more influential role the EU has taken on during this pandemic in the form of concrete health crisis competences in the treaties to enhance preparedness as well as to allow for a faster response during future crises.

Analysing the role of online platforms in managing and governing information during the pandemic, Matthias C Kettemann and Marie-Therese Sekwenz take a look at how platforms have reacted to the pandemic, how they have supported governmental health measures and how they have de-amplified and countered disinformation about COVID-19. The authors show how platforms have emerged as key actors in the shaping of communication flows in increasingly datafied societies.

In the final chapter of the third part, Mart Susi puts forward the proportionality deficit paradox, which says that social media and blockchain-based QR codes for monitoring travel and vaccination status (or other statuses during future crises) are capable of applying human rights rules, but are not capable of applying human rights principles. He concludes that the COVID-19 crisis confirms the thesis of a negative correlation between e-statehood and fundamental rights. The spread of e-state usage to more and more public administration areas and by more and more public offices invigorates the development aspect without the need to consider how the new developments coincide with human rights related obligations.

The fourth part focuses on populism and power in times of the pandemic. Gábor Halmai demonstrates how old and new illiberal constitutional theories provide normative justification for autocratic measures introduced by certain illiberal regimes as a reaction to the coronavirus. Before dealing with these justificatory theories the chapter provides a short overview of some typical constitutional reactions to COVID-19, paying particular attention to the Hungarian case. The new emergency situation and its normative justification attempts again raise the question whether 'illiberal democracy' or populism are the proper conceptual frameworks to descibe the perils of new authoritarianism.

While many observers rushed to predict that the pandemic would seriously harm the political fortunes of populists, Jan-Werner Müller states that it is yet too early to determine what impact this crisis will have on populism. Since populism is primarily characterised by claiming to represent the 'real people' and putting citizens against each other, much will depend on the frustrations and economic dislocations that are going to arise. The author states that a pandemic is an emergency, but an emergency is not automatically an exception during which all democratic politics must stop. There are good reasons why an opposition should come on board with emergency measures, but it would be entirely unjustified if dissent became delegitimated in the name of some form of 'national unity'.

Finally, the editors offer some conclusions concerning the current challenges of core elements of democracies, especially the role of parliaments and European multi-level governance. We identify different grades of engagement of parliaments in European democracies in the COVID-19 crisis and identify a backlash to multi-level governance in Europe. We conclude that the traditional governmental-based understanding of crises has to be overcome and a democracy-based concept of the state of emergency should be established.

Together, the chapters in this book allow for a deep and complex reappraisal of the distribution of power between parliaments and governments in pandemic times. The challenges to European democracies in the COVID-19 pandemic are analysed and several suggestions for reform and conclusions to build upon in a post-pandemic world are presented.

We are extremely grateful to our terrific authors, that they were not only willing to participate in this project in these difficult times, but also for delivering their contributions perfectly in time. We are honoured by your participation, especially in times like these.

It should be noted that all contributions were substantively finished by April 2021 and updated slightly in July 2021. Since then a number of new coronavirus measures will have been adapted.

We also would like to thank Hart Publishing, especially Kate Whetter and Rosemarie Mearns, for their willingness to publish this edited collection, their tireless support and their patience with the editors, and Claire Banyard for her excellent copy editing. Moreover, we are grateful to the anonymous reviewers for their endorsement as well as their useful comments.

With our social and scientific lives moving online, open access to knowledge has become essential in pandemic times. It will remain so. We are therefore very happy that we can offer this book as an Open Access title thanks to generous support from Sigmund Freud University, the *Publikationsfonds für Monografien der Leibniz-Gemeinschaft* (OA Publication Fund for Books of the Leibniz Community) and the Leibniz Institut for Media Research | Hans-Bredow-Institut.

The publication of books, especially edited collections, involve many people, who support the project in many different ways, including discussion, formal oversight and language review. Thus, we would like to thank in alphabetical order: Tamara Ehs, Susanne Gstöttner, Susanne Karner, Ilse Kettemann, Felicitas Rachinger, Marie-Therese Sekwenz, Johannes Steinböck, and Lukas Wieser for their support.

The COVID-19 pandemic has been a tremendous struggle for families. We would like to thank our families (and our authors' families), who supported the realisation of this book despite the extreme pressure on all of us in these difficult times.

Floreat Europa.

Hamburg/Vienna, July 2021

Matthias C Kettemann and Konrad Lachmayer

PART I

The Theory – Power, People and the Crisis

1

Lawless Extravagance: The Primacy Claim of Politics and the State of Exception in Times of COVID-19

PAUL GRAGL

I. The Plague of Lawlessness

The idea that the law and times of crisis are mutually exclusive is anything but new.[1] It therefore seems that Cicero's aphorism that *silent enim leges inter arma* ('in times of war, the law falls silent')[2] can be as easily applied to other, non-bellicose crises, such as the outbreak of a pandemic, and that *silent enim leges etiam inter germina* ('also in times of plague, the law falls silent'). Classic literature abounds with horrifying tales of the collapse of morals and law in societies faced with the indiscriminate killing of its residents by an invisible foe. Thucydides describes the plague in Athens during the second year (430 BCE) of the Peloponnesian War as a form of 'lawless extravagance' (a colourful translation of the rather sober ἐπὶ πλέον ἀνομίας, which lends itself perfectly as the title of this contribution). No fear of gods or law would restrain the fear-stricken Athenians, since nobody expected to live to be brought to trial for their offences.[3] In his *De rerum natura*, Lucretius continues this story and tells us that for their fear of contagion, the Athenians neglected the necessary funerary rites for their deceased family members, and simply tossed the bodies on funeral pyres.[4] Given both the then customary-religious and positive-legal significance of these rites,[5] the lawlessness of these acts must be considered extraordinary in a dual sense for the ancient Greeks.

[1] See PC Bobbitt, 'Inter Arma Enim Non Silent Leges' (2012) 45 *Suffolk University Law Review* 253, 253.

[2] MT Cicero, 'Pro Milone' in NH Watts (ed and trans), *Cicero: Orations* (Harvard University Press, 1989) IV.11.

[3] Thucydides, *History of the Peloponnesian War*, trans by R Crawley (JM Dent, 1910) 2.53.

[4] Lucretius, *On the Nature of Things* (Harvard University Press, 1989) VI.1247.

[5] See eg, R Garland, 'The Well-Ordered Corpse: An Investigation into the Motives behind Greek Funerary Legislation' (1989) 36 *Bulletin of the Institute of Classical Studies* 1–15; and above all, the tragedy of Antigone, wishing to bury her fallen brother in accordance with divine law, but in violation of Creon's decrees: Sophocles, *Antigone* (Bloomsbury, 2006).

Social distancing, if possible, proved effective, if we are to believe Boccaccio's *Decameron*, and his stories of seven young women and three young men, sheltering in a secluded villa to outlive the horrors of the bubonic plague rampaging through Florence in 1348, entertaining each other in splendid isolation with bawdy tales.[6] However, it should not go unmentioned that before a society, such as ancient Athens or medieval Florence, descends into utter lawlessness in the face of an epidemic, those in power will usually first try to mitigate the looming catastrophe. This is typically done through legal means and by enacting acts that aim at containing the spread of the disease at hand, for instance by way of quarantine measures, which the Venetian senate fixed at 40 (*quaranta*) days in 1448, presenting us with the now famous and wonderful etymology of this word.[7] Speaking of legal means and measures, it then seems to be only natural that in such a situation, we should not ask, as Albert Camus has his Dr Rieux declare in *The Plague*, 'whether the measures provided for under the law are serious, but if they are necessary to prevent half the town being killed'.[8]

II. The Primacy Claim of Politics

What Camus' Dr Rieux appears to allude to here is the ancient Latin maxim that *necessitas non habet legem*, or that necessity has no law,[9] from which follow two successive consequences: the first is, what I call, the *primacy claim of politics*, from which, in turn, follows the concept of the state of necessity, exception, or emergency (used synonymously and interchangeably here and discussed below in section IV). Let me start, in this section, to explain and analyse the first implication.

The current COVID-19 crisis has of course not assumed such horrifying proportions as depicted in the historical scenarios above. The hypothesis under this first implication is nonetheless that such a crisis could and should allow those in power – that is, in brief, abstract, and perhaps simplified fashion: politics – to do what is *necessary* in order to avoid an apocalyptic scenario as in ancient Athens. What is necessary in such a situation is to protect the *good* of human life and health, along the lines of what Markus Gabriel calls the 'virological imperative': act during a confirmed pandemic as if the prognoses of the best virological models alone were guiding your actions in terms of your social contacts.[10] Human life and health thus become the supreme good that requires protection from a

[6] G Boccaccio, *The Decameron* (OUP, 2008) 6 et seq.

[7] See GF Gensini et al, 'The Concept of Quarantine in History: From Plague to SARS' (2004) 49 *Journal of Infection* 257, 259; PS Sehdev, 'The Origin of Quarantine' (2002) 35 *Clinical Infectious Diseases* 1071, 1072.

[8] A Camus, *The Plague* (Penguin Books, 2001) 40.

[9] See Corpus Iuris Civilis, Dig. 1, 10, 1 § 1; M Koller, *Not kennt kein Gebot: Entstehung – Verbreitung – Bedeutung eines Rechtssprichwortes* (LIT Verlag, 2009); Seneca the Elder, *Controversiae*, IV.4.

[10] M Gabriel, *Moralischer Fortschritt in dunklen Zeiten* (Ullstein, 2020) 287.

particular threat, which also demonstrates that this good is not something perennially fixed, but chosen with a view toward what is necessary in an empirically contingent situation.

This argument results in the assumption that it is generally acknowledged that individuals and societies disagree on how this good may be best achieved and problems on the path thereto be best resolved. Should we always act in line with given normative principles, moral or legal, or is it also permissible to transgress these norms for the sake of attaining this supreme moral good? If we choose this latter option, one way to reach a certain moral good is to subordinate anything else (other conceptions of the good, values, principles, etc) to it in line with the famous adage that 'the end justifies the means'.[11] This approach is usually denoted as a teleological view, in which the good is defined independently of the right, and the right is defined as that which maximises the good.[12] In other words, the good and the right are distinct from and yet only instrumentally interrelated with each other, and I can attain a moral good without acting right.[13] Under such teleological thinking, a given society or political system can place any good on the pedestal of the highest good, thus considering any other good or right a mere means to achieving the supreme good and foregoing them in its favour.

It stands to reason that such a teleological view has a deeply intuitive appeal.[14] It is natural to think that it is only moral to maximise the good, perhaps even by ignoring what is right or by simply instrumentalising it for the sake of the good. What is good can not only be ascertained by common sense, but since right is subservient to the good by maximising it, the goodness of things can also be more easily judged without referring to what is right. Social cooperation can thus be achieved by determining the circumstances which allow for achieving the supreme good of a society, and that good is, at the end of the day, ascertained by politics, depending on what the respective circumstances require.

Since politics can (among other definitions) also usefully be conceived as the quest for the good, which – again – is not a fixed and universal conception and thus historically contingent, let us now assume under this teleological hypothesis that politics represents an efficient as well as more or less direct path to achieving the supreme good it has chosen. This is only reasonable, as politics is equivalent to power and can, if we disregard any constitutional restraints for the time being, wield this power to resolve problems and attain any desired ends. Teleology requires that any political actions conform to 'goodness' and are measured in terms of their effects.

[11] Although this saying is widely attributed to N Machiavelli, *The Prince*, trans by P Bondanella (OUP, 2008) chapter XVIII, he never uses these exact words therein. See instead N Machiavelli, *Discourses on Livy*, trans by JC Bondanella and P Bondanella (OUP, 1997) I.9: 'For although the act condemns the doer, the end may justify him.'

[12] J Rawls, *A Theory of Justice*, rev edn (Harvard University Press, 1999) 21–22; WK Frankena, *Ethics* (Prentice Hall, 1963) 13.

[13] See, however, also the interesting discussion by D Parfit, *On What Matters: Volume One* (OUP, 2011) 244–49.

[14] See Rawls (n 12) 22.

Accordingly, the criterion for judging a given political measure either good or bad is whether it contributes to the realisation of a certain good.[15] If we now also deliberately ignore the problem of unjust or immoral law and regard the law, from a liberal-democratic viewpoint, as the normative system that protects individual freedom as well as equality and hence represents that what is right, then the law must serve politics in attaining the supreme moral good for which that society strives, for right and good are distinct from one another, and the latter is prior to the former. Individual freedom and equality may certainly be protected, secured, and fostered under this view, but they are also only secondary and must take a step back if the need arises to maximise the good.

Having said that, it is then also plausible to envisage politics as an instrument in achieving this good which is unduly shackled by the cumbersome and complex procedures of the law. According to this interpretation, the law is a fetter,[16] a mere convention, that impedes the efficient mechanisms of politics, and hence, it should be as free as possible from any legal constraints. For after all, if it is the aim of politics to make the supreme good a reality, then it would be immoral to hinder it in any way by, say, considering the freedom or equality of one single individual. Politics must, in this conception, be above the law to be efficient in attaining what it deems to be good. We may summarise this position in the following argument, namely that it is *for the law to follow politics, and not for politics to follow the law*,[17] which I denote as the 'primacy claim of politics' throughout this contribution.

Given the plethora of problems a society might face, and the significance of a given good for the thriving of a commonwealth, the reader might be inclined to agree with this statement. Carl Schmitt similarly defended the primacy of the political in official decisions over all abstract norms – may they be moral or legal in nature.[18] Especially in times of emergency and political exigency, the Head of State should enjoy wide-ranging constitutional and quasi-dictatorial powers to resolve such situations, even if this entails the suspension of fundamental rights.[19]

[15] See A Huang, 'On the Teleological Interpretation of the Right to a Happy Life' (2020) 19 *The Journal of Human Rights* 24, 29. Note, however, that this author regards this approach as China's key contribution to human rights.

[16] See I Berlin, *Liberty*, ed by H Hardy (OUP, 2002) 170, fn 3.

[17] This particular turn of phrase was used by the then-Austrian Minister of the Interior Herbert Kickl of the right-wing Freedom Party in a TV interview on 22 January 2019 after he had been asked whether curfews for asylum-seekers and speedy deportations of such individuals could be in violation of the rule of law and human rights. He alleged that the greatest danger to the rule of law would be its being abused and accordingly used against itself, politically incapacitating the State and the proper administration of the law. In reference to the European Convention on Human Rights (ECHR), he complained that there were in place 'strange legal structures, sometimes many years old and created under totally different circumstances that prevent us from doing what is necessary. I would like to take on those rules and challenge them, for I still believe it is for the law to follow politics, and not for politics to follow the law.'

[18] See eg C Schmitt, *The Concept of the Political* trans by G Schwab; expanded edn (University of Chicago Press, 2007) 19; C Schmitt, *Verfassungslehre*, 11th edn (Duncker & Humblot, 2017) §§ 3, 8, 11, and 16.

[19] See C Schmitt, *Political Theology* (University of Chicago Press, 2006) 11–12; C Schmitt, *Der Hüter der Verfassung*, 5th edn (Duncker & Humblot, 2016). The relevant provision is Article 48 of the Weimar Constitution.

Times of crisis – regardless whether real, imagined, or faked – always generate a certain tolerance for the 'necessary' to prevail over the law and to cast the 'normative power of the factual'[20] as a cure for any problems.[21]

In conformity with the virological imperative, governments across the world resorted to massive restrictions on the freedom of movement and other fundamental rights of individuals to combat the COVID-19 pandemic. When confronted with the potential illegality or unconstitutionality of the respective legal provisions put in place to do so, the Austrian chancellor Sebastian Kurz replied that when facing looming disaster, one cannot afford to discuss legal sophistries.[22] It would be better, he continued, not to over-interpret legal questions on this matter and to let the relevant courts deal with them in due time.[23] In other words, the time for critical reflection and discussion may come, but not until the emergency is over. We may interpret these words to the effect that, under the primacy claim of politics which places the good before the right, any use of constitutional provisions that constrain the powers of politics can be regarded as an abuse directed against this good itself. Politics, in its quest for this good, would consequently trip over one's own laws and be rendered hamstrung and incapacitated by them. Legal guarantees of freedom, equality, and human rights in general thus prevent politics from doing what is necessary and need to be taken on and challenged.[24]

III. The Dangerous Abnegation of the Law and a Kantian Response

The crucial question that follows from the primacy claim of politics is that if the appeal to the good at the expense of the right is so intuitive and concurrently efficient, why exactly should we even discuss this issue here,[25] or why should we let the law get in the way of politics, if the latter is trying to save us from the COVID-19 pandemic? The answer to these questions is intricately related to the problem of how we can and should interpret the primacy claim of politics, to what connection the good and the right should have toward one another, and in what specific priority we should rank them, from which directly follows the question of what relationship of priority the law and politics should have vis-à-vis each other. Does, according to the teleological approach and the primacy claim of politics the

[20] See G Jellinek, *Allgemeine Staatslehre* (Athenäum, 1900) 338 et seq.

[21] See AJ Noll, 'Corona-Krise: Der Verordnungsstaat' *Der Standard*, 25 March 2020.

[22] Sebastian Kurz, Zeit im Bild 2, TV interview of 6 April 2020, discussing the legal implications of the 2019-2020 COVID-19 pandemic in Austria. See also A Somek, 'Is the Constitution Law for the Court Only?', (*Verfassungsblog*, 16 April 2020) verfassungsblog.de/is-the-constitution-law-for-the-court-only/.

[23] Kritik an Covid-19-Gesetzen: Kurz plant keine Änderung (News ORF, 14 April 2020) orf.at/stories/3161820/.

[24] Kickl, ORF-Report (n 17).

[25] See also C Bezemek, 'Vom Primat des Politischen: Versprengtes' (2019) 27 *Journal für Rechtspolitik* 194, 194.

right (law) follow from the good (politics)? Or does, in line with the deontological approach, the exact opposite hold true, namely that the good (politics) follows the right (law)?

A. Intricate Interweaving

To begin with, it is true, at least at first glance, that law and politics *appear* antithetical to one another. If one defines law in the Aristotelian sense, namely that it 'is passionless' and thus 'reason unaffected by desire',[26] then the law is certainly distinct from politics, as the latter provides an institutional process for the fulfilment or channelling of desire, whilst the law under this definition remains isolated from desire.

In this vein, one might be even tempted to describe law and politics in Nietzschean terms, the law being Apollonian rational and logical thinking, and politics being Dionysian emotional and instinct-driven acting. But if we regard law and politics through this very particular lens, we should also be aware that they are not necessarily rivals, but intertwined with each other.[27] Law and politics are tightly and dialectically interwoven,[28] particularly in the context of law-creation (ie, legislating), where politicians create new law within the institutional setting of a legislative assembly. Thus, it should equally be emphasised that the impact of politics on the law is certainly not always detrimental, since politics constantly changes the law in order to adapt it to an ever-changing world. Politics can have an extremely positive influence on the law, especially when we think about the constructive and reformative influence of progressive politics on areas such as anti-discrimination law, equality rights, societal inclusion of previously marginalised individuals and groups, etc. during the last couple of decades.[29]

Politics only becomes a problematic factor for the law, however, once it starts to claim for itself absolute primacy over the law, and interferes by abnegating it; begins to reverse these reformative and constructive developments mentioned above, becomes regressive, and suspends or abolishes such fundamental rights without due justification or disproportionately. And in terms of judicial law-application, ie within the realm of an independent and impartial judiciary, it goes without saying that any political interference is undesirable and therefore negative from the perspective of the general public, as it results in arbitrariness, nepotism, corruption, and eventually despotism.

[26] Aristotle, *Politics*, (ed and trans J Barnes), *The Complete Works of Aristotle, Vol. 2* (OUP, 1984) 1286a17-18 and 1287a33-34.

[27] See F Nietzsche, *The Birth of Tragedy*, trans Douglas Smith (OUP, 2008).

[28] See also M Cerar, 'The Relationship between Law and Politics' (2009) 15 *Annual Survey of International & Comparative Law* 19–41; M Zamboni, *Law and Politics: A Dilemma for Contemporary Legal Theory* (Springer, 2008).

[29] See eg D Kairys, *The Politics of Law: A Progressive Critique*, 3rd edn (Basic Books, 1998).

B. The Contingency of Good, the Apriority of Right

Politics may also declare something to be the supreme good and pursue it; that certainly is the prerogative of politics lest it become ineffective and useless. Politics, in itself, is neither morally good nor morally bad – although it certainly *should* be both lawful and morally legitimate. This good pursued by politics is historically contingent and will usually also change in accordance to what is required in a specific situation:[30] in the case of a pandemic such as COVID-19, the preservation of life and public health will most likely take the position of the supreme good; in the event of a security crisis, the defence of the State itself will be considered paramount; and during a global recession and financial crisis, the protection of the economy and the banking system will have absolute priority. The good is thus always in flux and cannot be pinned down perennially. As I wrote before, politics may of course pursue the realisation of these diverse goods, but what it cannot and should not be allowed to do is to pursue any good at the expense of right. Right, in my hypothesis, represents the yardstick for all political measures and should, ideally, be realised in the shape of the positive law.

Yet the reader might wonder at this point what right actually is. If good is contingent and dependent on empirical circumstances, is the same not true for right? Aristotle, for example, infamously claimed that some humans were 'by nature slaves' and that it was therefore *right* to keep them in servitude;[31] an assertion, which, I hope, is met with universal disapproval by contemporary readers. Yet, despite our current condemnation of the institution of slavery, the moral relativist could easily use this argument to confirm that right is, as good, equally in flux, since what was right for the Stagirite more than 2,000 years ago is not right anymore; and similarly, something we consider to be right today (say, the equality of women and men) was an idea frowned upon and scorned by the Ancients and throughout human history.

However, this argument is amiss, as slavery now not being right and the equality of women and men now being right have one thing in common, and that is the central concept of freedom. Aristotle can effortlessly establish something as unsettling as natural slavery, because he denies such natural slaves the faculty of reason.[32] In contrast thereto, Immanuel Kant argues that all human beings possess reason as autonomous beings,[33] and from that reason and autonomy follows the

[30] I deliberately disregard at this point that crises usually do not appear in isolation from each other but simultaneously, and that the COVID-19 crisis is, in fact, a poly-crisis of public health, economy, social cohesion, etc. See eg SL Greer, A de Ruijter, and E Brooks, 'The COVID-19 Pandemic: Failing Forward in Public Health' in M Riddervold, J Trondal, and A Newsome (eds), *The Palgrave Handbook of EU Crises* (Palgrave, 2021) 747–64.

[31] Aristotle, *Politics* (n 26) 1254b19-22.

[32] ibid, 1254b23-25.

[33] See I Kant, 'Groundwork of the Metaphysics of Morals' in MJ Gregor (ed and trans), *Immanuel Kant: Practical Philosophy* (CUP, 1996) AA 4:421 and 429 (hereinafter: *GMS*).

very idea of freedom. For him, freedom is the only innate right we have,[34] and as such, any human action is right as long as it can coexist with everybody else's freedom in accordance with a universal law.[35] The Kantian conception of freedom not only provides everyone with 'independence from someone else's necessitating choice',[36] but also gives us a rule to live by, ie the categorical imperative of right, calling upon everyone to 'so act externally that the free use of your choice can coexist with the freedom of everyone in accordance with a universal law'.[37]

This is therefore what is meant by right, particularly here; and since this right amounts to freedom derived from the a priori principles of reason, right cannot be empirically contingent, but is necessarily fixed – at least as long as one follows and applies reason. This also explains why slavery and the discrimination of women are and always have been wrong, namely because they violate this very reason-based freedom. Again, Kant concedes that there are other important conceptions of what is good, such as happiness, but morality – including right – remains the sole unconditional good for human beings.[38] Right, accordingly, is universal, a priori, and thus independent from any empirically contingent circumstances, and – perhaps most importantly – prior to good. And if we assume, following a liberal democratic understanding, that right is reflected in the positive law, and politics can be equated to the quest for good, then what also follows from the priority of right over good is that law is also prior to politics. This principle must of course also apply in handling the COVID-19 pandemic, and cannot simply be brushed aside, because certain measures are deemed to be necessary above anything else.

I must emphasise, nonetheless, that I do not wish to deny that there are forms of good other than right *qua* freedom; these other forms are of course also extremely significant, if we wish to lead a happy, fulfilled, and prosperous life. Having said that, the crucial point remains that allowing these other forms of good to supersede right is in contravention of reason. The concept of freedom *qua* right and reason is, nonetheless, the basis of any successful socialisation of individuals, since it tells us – and politics – to coordinate our actions in a way so that we can attain that what we desire to attain, ie any contingent good, without harming someone else who might desire to attain a different good. Only then, if right is respected, can all individuals partake in what they deem to be good. A good, which is defined by politics to exclude any individuals or groups as such, is no good, but a mere pseudo-good.

I would also like to clarify that I do not doubt that some or most of the legal measures implemented during the COVID-19 crisis were necessary to overcome this medical emergency. Again, what I doubt is that politics can 'dictate'

[34] I Kant, 'Metaphysics of Morals' in Mary J Gregor (ed and trans), *Immanuel Kant: Practical Philosophy* (CUP, 1996) AA 6:237 (hereinafter: *MS*).

[35] ibid, AA 6:230.

[36] ibid, AA 6:237.

[37] ibid, AA 6:231.

[38] Kant, *GMS* (n 33) AA 4:415.

the question of necessity to the effect that the law can be amended or suspended in such a situation, or the task of legislation delegated to the executive branch *in toto*. If such measures are taken, they cannot simply defy or flout the existing law, first and foremost constitutional principles. I do not think that a pandemic must necessarily result in a state of ἀνομία (anomía), or 'lawlessness', or that politics always pursues a supreme good *without* taking into consideration the concept of right or by even (unintentionally or deliberately) violating it. In Hungary, in contrast, the government, in March 2020, usurped parliament's power for an indefinite period on the basis of an emergency law, granting it the authority to rule by decree in order to be able to deal with the COVID-19 crisis as swiftly as possible.[39] Such a teleological view might certainly yield some desired and positive results in the short-run in combatting the pandemic (although even this argument is highly doubtful), but its long-term effect is all the more disastrous, myopic and irrational, as it undermines right, curtails fundamental rights, and ignores the separation of powers.

For such an approach results in extreme consequences and requires a society to pay a considerable moral price for this. It can even become monstrous – a utility monster, as Robert Nozick put it quite vividly – that receives enormously greater sums of utility (or good) from any sacrifice of others than these others lose.[40] What I do not mean here is the 'sacrifice' that young, healthy people offer to protect those more susceptible to the dangers posed by COVID-19, eg by staying home. What I mean here is the sacrifice by a society and legal system based on reason and freedom offered in the name of the supreme good. This means that if the positive law is a mirror-image of right and should give full effect to it, then politics, in its pursuit of a given good in contravention of the law, should certainly not claim primacy nor prevail over the law. In other words: if the positive law already provides for measures to address a crisis, the relevant rules need to be used; and if it does not yet provide for such measures, they ought to be created first in accordance with the relevant constitutional provisions in place, even if time is of the essence. The pursuit of the supreme good, whatever it is, should therefore only be legitimate and lawful within the framework of right. Right and good are not necessarily contradictory, and whatever politics does to achieve this good must not be done in a normative vacuum. Again: the problem is not *that* politics acts against the COVID-19 pandemic, it simply is *how* it sometimes acts.

C. Anomia: Politics without Law

Let me explain this problem by reference to two dimensions of the role of politics as well as its problematic primacy claim in law-creation: first, the formal rank as

[39] See eg I Bar-Siman-Tov, 'Covid-19 Meets Politics: The Novel Coronavirus as a Novel Challenge for Legislatures' (2020) 8 *The Theory and Practice of Legislation* 11, 26–27.
[40] See R Nozick, *Anarchy, State, and Utopia* (Basic Books, 1974) 41.

well as the substance of the affected positive law in question, and secondly, the effect of this interference. From these two dimensions follows a scenario derived by way of interpretation from the abovementioned primacy claim of politics, or – to be more precise in Kantian terms[41] – among the three pivots around which legislation turns, freedom (the law of reason) as well as law (positive law), and lastly force (politics).

It is conceivable that politics might affect the law negatively by completely suspending it, for instance, in a *state of exception*, which a pandemic such as COVID-19 could possibly cause. Hence, under the abovementioned maxim of *necessitas non habet legem*, political measures might be enacted that result in the disapplication or even abolishment of the basic constitutional rules of a State (most importantly, democratic elections, the rule of law as well as the separation of powers, and fundamental rights), because compliance with these rules is deemed impossible or a hindrance to resolving the cause of the emergency, such as a pandemic. Politics has gained full primacy here and any legal provisions left (if they have not been affected by the state of emergency) will have to follow politics.

To explain this in more depth, let us assume that politics affects sub-constitutional law (eg ordinary statutory law, decrees, ordinances, etc) quite regularly, as this is what politics *qua* the legislature usually does and exactly what it is supposed to do. I denote this rank of law as *lex* (in opposition to *jus*), which means that it represents ordinary law of non- or subconstitutional character that is not subject to any super-majorities or other constitutional safeguards to be changed. It can hence, in principle, be more easily amended than constitutional law.[42] Let us also assume that this very constitutional law fully reflects and protects right, which is why I denote the former as *jus positivum* (because it is the positive-legal reflection of right or *jus*) and the latter as *jus rationale* (because non-positive right or *jus* is based on reason). If now, say, politics amends the sub-constitutional *lex* in a way so that is not in line with the respective Constitution and thus with right anymore, the consequence is *irrational law*, as it is in contravention of right and accordingly in contravention of reason – with the *caveat*, however, that such irrationality can only be determined *post hoc* by a court, deciding on whether the law in question was indeed constitutional or unconstitutional. However, the crucial point is that such irrational law may still be repaired from within the system of positive law in the light of constitutional law that reflects right, for instance by the legislature itself or a court with the powers of constitutional review (in the latter case assuming that access to such a court effectively exists). Here, the positive constitutional law and

[41] I Kant, 'Anthropology from a Pragmatic Point of View' in in RB Louden and G Zöller (ed and trans), *Immanuel Kant: Anthropology, History, and Education* (CUP, 2007) AA 7:330 (hereinafter: *Anth*).

[42] A statement which is, more or less, only true for legal systems with a written constitution. In the United Kingdom with its unwritten constitution, for instance, constitutional rules (with the exception of isolated entrenched Acts of Parliament that were adopted by a supermajority) can be easily and flexibly amended by a simple majority. For a critical view, see eg A Psygkas, 'The United Kingdom's Statutory Constitution' (2020) 40 *Oxford Journal of Legal Studies* 449–81.

the law of reason can work as allies and in symbiosis with one another to overcome the irrationality of the sub-constitutional positive law, and the primacy claim can here still be nipped in the bud, as politics *qua* law-creation has to follow the law. In principle, we do not require any legal-philosophical or metaphysical considerations here, as any problem afflicting the positive law can still be resolved from within itself, or from a system-immanent perspective of legal positivism.

However, in a state of emergency, wherein the positive law has been suspended and no *lex* or *jus positivum* is in force that could give effect to the *jus rationale*, and no access to any courts with the powers of constitutional review is possible, the positive law cannot be easily restored, from and within itself, to its former, pre-emergency and right-based state, if the political will to do so is lacking. Philosophical guidance from the law of reason will be required on the way thereto, although some restrictions apply: such guidance in itself can certainly not give effect to this legal restauration, but it will give individuals in quest of their right and freedom a goal according to which the legal and political system in question should be remodelled.

This scenario represents a drastic regressive step toward the state of nature – a Schmittian state of nature, along the lines of this thinker's ideas for a state of emergency[43] (fortunately, I must add, such a situation did not transpire in the COVID-19 pandemic, and thus remains merely a dystopian thought experiment). In this scenario, there still is a government in place that can somehow ensure the security and basic functioning of the State, but there are no noteworthy legal rules in place anymore that could guarantee the application of the categorical imperative of right, freedom, and the law of reason. I will refer to this situation as the *Anomia* scenario, wherein power is, due to the lack or suspension of legal order, exercised arbitrarily and perhaps in a tyrannical fashion:[44] an extravagance of lawlessness that Kant would probably call 'barbarism', wherein force (politics) reigns supreme without law (positive law) and freedom.[45]

IV. The State of Emergency: From Paradoxical Voids to Full Powers

It is now time to turn to the second implication of the *necessitas* maxim mentioned above at the beginning of section II, and what it means for the concept of the state of emergency. In this section, I would like to discuss in particular the following three problems in relation to the state of emergency, or the *Anomia* scenario: the paradoxical nature of the state of emergency; necessity as the alleged source of law; and the shift of power from the legislative toward the executive branch.

[43] See Schmitt, *Political Theology* (n 19) 11–12.
[44] See K Raaflaub, *The Discovery of Freedom in Ancient Greece* (University of Chicago Press, 2004) 55.
[45] Kant, *Anth* (n 41) AA 7:331.

A. Paradoxical Nature

The first problem inherent to a state of emergency is that it constitutes a point of imbalance between law and political fact[46] which is situated – in the same way as civil war, insurrection, and revolution – in an ambiguous limbo at the intersection of the legal and political.[47] This means that if exceptional measures are the result of a crisis, such as a pandemic, and must accordingly be understood on political-factual rather than on legal-normative grounds,[48] then they are deeply paradoxical, as Giorgio Agamben asserts. On the one hand, as legal measures, they cannot be understood in legal terms, as the state of exception appears as the legal form of what cannot have legal form. On the other, if the law itself employs the exception (ie the suspension of itself), then it concurrently releases all legal subjects from its bonds *and* binds them in a no man's land between law and politics.[49]

To resolve this paradox, as Agamben explains,[50] some seek to include the state of exception *within* the sphere of the law, either considering it to be an integral part of positive law (such as the famous Article 48 of the Weimar Constitution),[51] assuming necessity to be an autonomous source of law,[52] or as the State's subjective natural or constitutional right to its own preservation.[53] Others, conversely, regard it as something essentially political and hence external to the law; factual, but nonetheless having legal consequences.[54] Yet the problem with this neat dichotomy is that it appears to be insufficient to describe the phenomenon it claims to explain. If the characteristic property of the state of emergency is a total or partial suspension of the legal order, then it cannot be contained within it; and if the state of emergency is instead a merely factual situation and thus utterly unrelated to law, then it is rather difficult for a legal order to contain a lacuna precisely where the decisive situation is concerned.[55]

Perhaps, the state of emergency simply is neither external nor internal to the law, but a zone where politics and law blur with each other.[56] And by this blurring, fact and law become undecidable; fact is converted into law, and law is suspended

[46] F Saint-Bonnet, *L'état d'exception* (Presses Universitaires de France, 2001) 28.

[47] A Fontana, 'Du droit de résistance au devoir d'insurrection' in J Zancarini (ed), *Le droit de résistance* (ENS, 1999) 16.

[48] F De Martino, *Storia della costituzione romana* (Jovene, 1973) 320.

[49] G Agamben, *State of Exception* (University of Chicago Press, 2005) 1.

[50] ibid, 22–23.

[51] See C Schmitt, *Dictatorship* (Polity Press, 2014).

[52] See eg S Romano, 'Sui decreti-legge e lo stato di assedio in occasione dei terremoti di Messina e Reggio Calabria' in S Romano (ed), *Scritti Minori: Diritto costituzionale, Vol. 1*, reprint (Giuffrè, 1990); M Hauriou, *Précis de droit constitutionnel*, 2nd edn (Sirey, 1929); C Mortati, *L'ordinamento del governo*, reprint (Giuffrè, 2000).

[53] See eg O Ranelletti, *La polizia di sicurezza* (Società Editrice Libraria, 1904); CL Rossiter, *Constitutional Dictatorship: Crisis Government in the Modern Democracies* (Harcourt Brace, 1948).

[54] See eg G Balladore-Pallieri, *Diritto costituzionale* (Giuffrè, 1970); RC de Malberg, *Contribution à la théorie générale de l'État*, Vol. 1 (Sirey, 1920).

[55] Agamben (n 49) 23.

[56] ibid.

and obliterated into fact.[57] This means that we are back where we started, namely at the paradox of anomic law, an emptiness and standstill of the law; a force of law without law,[58] or – in the vein of my overall hypothesis – the eventual primacy of politics over the law. The two positive conclusions we can draw from this is that, first, the state of exception, also during a pandemic, does not necessarily coincide with dictatorship of full powers (although the executive may certainly act in such a manner during a crisis situation and abuse the absence of the law); and that, secondly, the state of exception is not an anarchic state of nature,[59] wherein there is neither law nor politics,[60] because some order still exists, even if it is not a juridical order.[61] The one principal negative conclusion, however, is that such an anomic state is entirely incapable of guaranteeing the aforementioned *jus rationale* and the concept following from it, ie individual freedom. This is therefore certainly not a situation or result with which we should content ourselves, given the detrimental implications for fundamental rights, democracy, and the rule of law.[62]

B. Necessity as a Source of Law

The second problem in this context follows from the first one. If the juridification of a crisis – ie its 'translation' into a legal framework – is impossible, as normativity presupposes normality,[63] then, as Schmitt writes, 'the exception is that which cannot be subsumed; it defies general codification [...]'.[64] Since the application of a legal norm requires a normal quotidian framework of life, such 'situation belongs precisely to its immanent validity. There exists no norm that is applicable to chaos'.[65]

The only norm applicable would be necessity itself, which thus becomes the foundation of the state of exception,[66] or virtually its *Grundnorm*, in Kelsenian terms. The *necessitas* formula is consequently not only interpreted as resulting in or allowing for an anomic state (ie, that necessity has no law), but also to the extent that 'necessity creates its own law'.[67] The principal argument here is that if the law

[57] ibid, 29; G Arangio-Ruiz, *Istituzioni di diritto costituzionale italiano*, reprint (Bocca, 1972) 528.
[58] Agamben (n 49) 39 and 48.
[59] ibid, 6 and 50.
[60] In a slight variation to Kant, *Anth* (n 41) AA 7:330.
[61] Schmitt, *Political Theology* (n 19) 12.
[62] The question remains at this point which States actually experienced such a full-blown state of exception during the COVID-19 pandemic. In general, it seems, that most States simply temporarily suspended some fundamental rights (first and foremost, the right to free movement) in order to constrain the pandemic. And from a doctrinal perspective, the suspension of derogable fundamental rights does not automatically amount to a violation, especially if such a suspension is grounded on a legal basis, and proves to be adequate, necessary, and proportionate.
[63] A Kaiser, *Ausnahmeverfassungsrecht* (Mohr Siebeck, 2020) 25.
[64] Schmitt, *Political Theology* (n 19) 13.
[65] ibid.
[66] Agamben (n 49) 17 and 24.
[67] ibid, 24.

is no longer able to perform its highest task, which is to guarantee public welfare, it must be abandoned in favour of expediency; instead of transgressing it, it is simply cleared away.[68] As Machiavelli suggests, it is the breaking of the existing legal order that saves it,[69] and thereby, it is this act of breaking that becomes the basis of the substituting new order. Again, politics, or political expediency through necessity, claims primacy over the law.

In this vein, the principle according to which necessity defines a unique crisis situation in which the law loses its *vis obligandi* is reversed, becoming the principle according to which necessity constitutes the ultimate ground and very source of the law.[70] Politics *qua* necessity cannot be regulated by previously established norms, and since it has no law, it makes law and can accordingly overrule the existing law.[71] In the same way as a revolution, the introduction of necessity as the fountain of new law is certainly unlawful from the perspective of the previous legal order, but perfectly legal and constitutional from the view of the new 'revolutionary' order.[72]

However, given that this new order simultaneously suspends the hitherto valid law, it also remains controversial how the end of law (that is, the common good), can be obtained without the law, and that whoever intends to achieve the end of law, must also proceed with law.[73] This brings us again to the notion mentioned above that politics might certainly pursue a particular good, such as the protection of public health during the COVID-19 pandemic, but never against or outside the framework of right; and suspending the law that gives effect to right is certainly not in line with this approach, because it amounts to the 'auto-immunisation' of a given society which, due to the traumata of a crisis, destroys the foundations of its own order.[74]

C. The Hour of the Executive

If the state of exception represents a legal void, then this anomic situation must be remedied somehow. This lacuna is usually filled by the executive power whose hour of action dawns with the sunset of the law. The underlying hypothesis is that since constitutions are designed for a state of normative normality, times of emergency necessitate us to move away from the regular separation of powers and to

[68] A Nissen, *Das Iustitium. Eine Studie aus der römischen Rechtsgeschichte* (Gebhardt, 1877) 98.
[69] Machiavelli, *Discourses* (n 11) I.34.
[70] Agamben (n 49) 26.
[71] Romano (n 52) 362 and 364.
[72] Agamben (n 49) 28.
[73] D Alighieri, *De Monarchia* (CUP, 1995) 2.5.22.
[74] See J Derrida, 'Autoimmunisierung, wirkliche und symbolische Selbstmorde' in J Habermas and J Derrida (eds), *Philosophie in Zeiten des Terrors. Zwei Gespräche* (Philo, 2004) 117–18.

concede more competence to the executive.[75] The main argument for this shift in power from the legislative to the executive branch usually is a temporal one, and the claim that crisis situations require rapid and pragmatic action from the government.[76]

The most rigorous and perhaps most famous attempt to construct a theory on executive powers during the state of exception was made by Carl Schmitt, who intended to inscribe these powers within a legal context.[77] In his 1921 book *Dictatorship*, he undertakes this task by distinguishing between commissarial and sovereign dictatorship. In case of the former, there is a difference between norms of law and norms of the realisation of law, and its ultimate function is to create a situation in which the law can be realised through the suspension of its application. Sovereign dictatorship, conversely, is characterised by creating a situation in which it becomes possible to impose a new constitution by applying law which is not (yet) valid.[78] In sum, commissarial dictatorship represents a state of emergency in which the law is not applied, but remains in force; and sovereign dictatorship represents a state of emergency in which law is applied, but not formally in force.[79]

The significance of this distinction only becomes fully visible in Schmitt's 1922 book *Political Theology*, wherein he adds the difference between norm and decision, and thus transforms his theory of the state of exception into a theory of sovereignty.[80] Only the sovereign – in this case the executive or the Head of State – can decide on the state of exception,[81] and they can only do so by concurrently standing outside of the legal order *and* belonging to it.[82] However unsettling this theory is in terms of the possible abuse of full powers during a crisis situation, it becomes even more disconcerting when taking into account the consequence of the sovereign's protean internal-external status, namely the incorporation of the state of exception and *anomia* directly into the person of the sovereign who then begins to free themselves from all subordination to the law and asserts themselves as *legibus solutus*.[83] And as the sovereign, as part of the executive branch and in charge of all political action, accumulates more powers, the people lose these very powers, and remain without legal protection from them.[84]

[75] Rossiter (n 53) 5.
[76] EA Posner and A Vermeule, *The Executive Unbound: After the Madisonian Republic* (OUP, 2010) 8.
[77] WE Scheuerman, 'States of Emergency' in J Meierhenrich and O Simons (eds), *The Oxford Handbook of Carl Schmitt* (OUP, 2016) 547; Agamben (n 49) 32.
[78] Schmitt, *Dictatorship* (n 51) 136–37.
[79] Agamben (n 9) 36.
[80] Schmitt, *Political Theology* (n 19) 13.
[81] ibid, 5.
[82] ibid, 7.
[83] Agamben (n 49) 69.
[84] Rossiter (n 53) 5.

V. A Kantian Approach to the State of Exception

Sections III and IV demonstrated that any application of the *necessitas* formula without consideration for right is highly dangerous and results in an abnegation of the law under the primacy claim of politics. In the section at hand, I would now like to present and examine solutions to this problem based on Kant's moral and legal philosophy. The principal problem, in this regard, remains, however, that Kant has never explicitly mentioned nor discussed the concept of the state of exception, which means that we therefore can only infer from other statements how we can assess this issue in the light of his philosophy. Such other statements include the requirement of right to be exact, which therefore – and in contrast to ethics – cannot allow 'some room for exceptions'.[85]

An alleged right of necessity, which Kant regarded as a conflict between two moral duties (eg, whether to inform on my father who is about to commit high treason, or not, or whether to give in to the temptations of self-preservation in the famous scenario of Carneades' plank),[86] belongs to Epicurus' unknowable intra-atomic regions. It cannot be clearly decided and must consequently be separated from the doctrine of right.[87]

A. Universalisable Principles, Not Exceptions

Kant's philosophy is shaped by principles, not exceptions, above all the categorical imperative in its formula of universal law, namely the moral obligation to 'act only according to that maxim by which you can at the same time will that it should become a universal law'.[88] And the question of what you can will is a question of what you can will without contradiction. The contradiction is that your maxim would be self-defeating if universalised, and your action would become ineffectual for the achievement of your purpose if everyone else tried to use it for that purpose. Since you propose to use that action for that purpose at the same time as you propose to universalise the maxim, you in effect will the thwarting of your own purpose.[89] Relying on an exception from a universal law therefore destroys the rule and the achievement of your goals.

The same universalising rule is true for the law, both for the law of reason and the positive law. In terms of the former, both the categorical imperative in its original manifestation and the categorical imperative of right share the same form and

[85] Kant, *MS* (n 34) AA 6:233.

[86] I Kant, 'On the Common Saying: That May Be Correct in Theory, but It Is of No Use in Practice' in MJ Gregor (ed and trans), *Immanuel Kant: Practical Philosophy* (CUP, 1996) AA 8:300 and note* (hereinafter: *TP*).

[87] Kant, *MS* (n 34) AA 6:233.

[88] Kant, *GMS* (n 33) AA 4:421.

[89] C M Korsgaard, *Creating the Kingdom of Ends* (CUP, 1996) 77–78.

do not prescribe any material content; they merely command us to act in a way that we wish can be normatively universalised.[90] In other words, the categorical imperative of right is a specialised version of the categorical imperative and thus dependent on it.[91] Selfish and intelligent devils may certainly succeed in creating a functional State, but definitely not in establishing a rightful condition, as they will never have security in their use of external freedom,[92] if right is not based on the categorical imperative. In terms of the positive law, this means that the categorical imperative of right denotes the positive law as an idea of reason, since right pervades the legal system, gives it normative character, unifies it, and renders it systematic and comprehensive.[93] Right supplies 'the immutable principles for any giving of positive law'[94] and 'can be cognized a priori by everyone's reason'.[95] The positive law, derived from right, thus also functions as a categorical imperative that we should will to be a universal law without exceptions, and accordingly also without a state of exception.

Exceptions from the positive law can hence only be justified as part of the positive law itself, but not against it, as such exceptions, through a state of emergency, would contradict its programme of legal protection *qua* universalisation.[96] But how is politics then supposed to deal with crisis situations such as the COVID-19 pandemic, if, say, certain legal provisions hinder the implementation of relevant measures? Kant's brief piece *On a Supposed Right to Lie from Philanthropy* is quite instructive in this respect, because it raises the question whether there is, in deviance from the general duty not to lie, a right to lie in exceptional situations, for instance 'to lie to a murderer who asked us whether a friend of ours whom he is pursuing has taken refuge in our house'.[97] Such a lie does not necessarily harm the right of another person, but 'nevertheless humanity generally, inasmuch as it makes the source of right unusable'.[98] Any such right to lie must be rejected from the perspective of the categorical imperative, because it would, as a maxim elevated to the status of a formal universal law, turn out to be contradictory, as it presupposes truthfulness in order to be meaningful. Doing so would directly contradict itself.[99]

Every single one of us might certainly consider it morally justifiable to lie in order to save our friend's life (which is a matter of practical judgement), but you

[90] See G Seel, 'How Does Kant Justify the Universal Objective Validity of the Law of Right?' (2009) 17 *International Journal of Philosophical Studies* 71, 75.

[91] W Kersting, *Wohlgeordnete Freiheit*, 2nd edn (Suhrkamp, 2016) 128.

[92] Seel (n 90) 88.

[93] EJ Weinrib, 'Law as Idea of Reason' in HL Williams (ed), *Essays on Kant's Political Philosophy* (University of Chicago Press, 1992) 15.

[94] Kant, *MS* (n 34) AA 6:229.

[95] ibid, AA 6:296–297.

[96] O Lembcke, 'Regel und Ausnahme. Zu einer Leitunterscheidung der Politischen Ethik' (2007) 36 *Österreichische Zeitschrift für Politikwissenschaft* 49, 51.

[97] I Kant, 'On a Supposed Right to Lie from Philanthropy' in MJ Gregor (ed and trans), *Immanuel Kant: Practical Philosophy* (CUP, 1996) AA 8:425 (hereinafter: *VRML*).

[98] ibid, AA 8:426.

[99] ibid, AA 8:430.

could then be held legally responsible for all consequences arising from that lie, eg if the victim slips out of the house unaware and the murderer then encounters your friend just because of your lie. You could, however, never be held responsible before a court for telling the truth.[100] We could of course also argue that this situation presents us with a moral dilemma, namely to protect the life of our friend versus the prohibition to lie to a stranger, which we could defuse by making exceptions – for instance that it is permissible to lie in certain situations. Yet this manoeuvre destroys the entire moral system, because one could think for every major premise – even for norms such as 'do not torture children' – of an exception,[101] or another moral dilemma as a minor premise, which would then result in the conclusion that the end always justifies the means.[102]

Kant thereby demonstrates that even the least of exceptions, unless provided for by this system itself, makes a normative system (may it be morality or the positive law) 'uncertain and useless'.[103] He argues that the law even covers situations like the already mentioned plank of Carneades wherein the question arises whether one person might push off another person from the last remaining plank after a shipwreck to save their own life.[104] Saving one's own life by pushing another person toward certain death always constitutes an objective wrong, but it might result in subjective impunity for the perpetrator. Under these premises (and Kant even explicitly mentions the *necessitas* formula here), there can be 'no necessity that would make what is wrong conform with law'.[105]

Kant is nonetheless not that unrealistic that he would misjudge the need for two types of exceptions. The first type concerns the level of principles, or the case of a normative conflict as above.[106] Wide legal duties leaving a margin of discretion are not to be taken as permission to make exceptions,[107] but without a clear rule to resolve such conflicts, we must rely on that worldly 'prudence' which can 'adapt the practical rule in accordance with it to the ends of life even tolerably, by making appropriate exceptions'.[108] The second type takes into consideration that there can be political factors which impede the realisation of the law and require exceptions, 'without, however, losing sight of the end'.[109] This is Kant's outmost concession

[100] ibid, AA 8:427.

[101] For example, whether it is morally justified to torture the child of a suspected terrorist to force him to reveal the location of the next attack.

[102] Gabriel (n 10) 152.

[103] Kant, *VRML* (n 97) AA 8:427.

[104] See MT Cicero, 'De officiis' in W Miller (ed and trans), *Cicero on Duties* (Harvard University Press, 1989) 3.89; and also LL Fuller, 'The Case of the Speluncean Explorers' (1949) 62 *Harvard Law Review* 616–45, for a similar scenario.

[105] Kant, *MS* (n 34) AA 6:236.

[106] Lembcke (n 96) 52.

[107] Kant, *MS* (n 34) AA 6:390.

[108] I Kant, 'Critique of Practical Reason' in MJ Gregor (ed and trans), *Immanuel Kant: Practical Philosophy* (CUP, 1996) AA 5:36 (hereinafter: *KpV*).

[109] I Kant, 'Toward Perpetual Peace' in MJ Gregor (ed and trans), *Immanuel Kant: Practical Philosophy* (CUP, 1996) AA 8:347 (hereinafter: *ZeF*).

toward an exception to legal principles, as everything else would undermine his objective of the juridification of politics, namely politics which tends toward making exceptions. This is the reason why he states that '[r]ight must never be accommodated to politics, but politics must always be accommodated to right';[110] or, almost violently painted in the image of a gesture of physical submission to a monarch, that 'all politics must bend its knee before right'.[111] The differences between Kant and Schmitt could not be greater: the latter constructs the law from the viewpoint of the exception which, in contrast to the rule, 'proves everything';[112] for the former, there can be no exception without a rule in the first place. Even a partial suspension of the law would amount to a regression toward the state of nature, which means that only a temporary acceptance of institutionalised or codified exceptions can be permitted.[113]

Therefore, from a Kantian perspective, the state of exception is not necessarily paradoxical. Since the law of reason as a metaphysical construct continues to exist even during a state of exception, a suspension of the law can only be deemed permissible as long as it is in accordance with the *jus positivum* and allows for a return toward a normal state of affairs. The state of exception only becomes paradoxical or self-contradictory if it is a one-way street with no point of return which is, in any case, inadmissible from a reason-based perspective. The rule is prior to the exception, and the latter only possible if the former allows for it. For our situation in a world ravaged by the COVID-19 pandemic, this means that all legal measures adopted must not only be in accordance with the existing positive law, but should also always be scrutinised in the light of right, or the categorical imperative of right. It is, therefore, absolutely appropriate to constrain the freedom of individuals (ie, free movement rights) to protect the freedom of others (ie, their health). However, any measures in place should also always allow for a return to the *status quo ante* once the pandemic is over, as otherwise, the exception would indeed become the rule. And this situation, as I will argue in the following section, would be incompatible with Kant's law of reason.

B. The Law of Reason and the Moral Obligation to Enter a Juridical State

If we assume, with Kant, that the law of reason is the metaphysical foundation for all positive law, then two arguments follow from this: first, necessity can then not possibly constitute the source of law, as has been argued before,[114] because this position is then taken up by the law of reason. And secondly, we would also have

[110] Kant, *VRML* (n 97) AA 8:429.
[111] Kant, *ZeF* (n 109) AA 8:380.
[112] Schmitt, *Political Theology* (n 19) 15.
[113] Lembcke (n 96) 52.
[114] See section IV(B) above.

a moral obligation to leave the state of exception and return to the regular state of positive law. Let me now explain this second point in more detail.

Whilst most philosophers agree that humans should leave the (hypothetical) state of nature, the reasons to do so vary greatly. For Thomas Hobbes, this departure is paramount for self-preservation, survival, and security,[115] and thus purely instrumental. For Kant, conversely, we must leave the state of nature for *moral* reasons, because therein, a legal status can only be provisional or presumptive, as the law of reason cannot be effectively enforced in the absence of a positive-legal system.[116] Morally autonomous individuals can only be treated as such through a public lawful coercion and judges competent to render rightful and enforceable verdicts.[117] However, the establishment of such a positive legal system is only possible in a juridical state, where all human beings are treated as ends, not as mere means, in line with the 'humanity formula' of the categorical imperative.[118] The positive law of the juridical state therefore ensures the exercise of the external freedom of individuals *qua* the positive law.[119]

If we now apply Kant's argument that the departure from the lawless state of nature and the entering into a juridical state (ie, a state of positive law) is a moral obligation, to the state of exception – which is also a lawless state under the primacy of politics – we see the same result: under the law of reason as the foundation of positive law, there is a moral obligation to leave the state of exception (perhaps with the addendum 'as soon as possible after the end of a given crisis such as the COVID-19 pandemic') through the avenues the positive law itself provides for this exit, because human beings cannot be treated as morally autonomous individuals in such a state of legal suspension. In other words, even if the follow the Schmittian argument of necessity being the basis of all positive law, then this reasoning can only be purchased at the high price of abandoning our moral autonomy and external freedom. Yet, as we have seen in the previous section, the exception – or necessity – cannot, for logical reasons, be the fountain of all law, as this would result in a self-contradiction. An alleged right of necessity, as a supposed right to do wrong, is an absurdity,[120] and politics should therefore also diligently adhere to this principle when enacting measures to combat the pandemic.

C. Resistance against Despotism in the State of Exception

In this last section, let me now address the problem I denoted before as the 'hour of the executive' and the potential deteriorating of the state of exception into authoritarian rule, or despotism. The problem that consequently needs to be addressed

[115] T Hobbes, *Leviathan*, revised student edn by R Tuck (CUP, 1996) chapter XIII.
[116] Kant, *MS* (n 34) AA 6:256 and 307–08.
[117] ibid, AA 6:312 and 314–15.
[118] Kant, *GMS* (n 33) AA 4:439.
[119] GP Fletcher, 'Law and Morality: A Kantian Perspective' (1987) 87 *Columbia Law Review* 533, 535.
[120] Kant, *TP* (n 86) AA 8:300.

here is how Kant regarded the question of resistance or rebellion against such a regime and a state of exception, and whether a revolution against such a political system can be justified or not.

In this context, Kant is often accused of inconsistency:[121] while he expressed evident sympathy for the French Revolution as a crucial step in terms of humanity's moral progress (especially through the establishing of a morally good juridical constitution),[122] he also firmly rejected the idea of any right to revolution against the wrongful conduct of the 'legislating head of a State'. A revolution against the highest legislation – ie the current legal system – can never be lawful in Kant's eyes.[123] However, his position is, once correctly understood, fully plausible and consistent,[124] particularly in the context of this chapter. To begin with, to revolt against every individual legal act we deem wrongful or unjust would not only be highly impractical, as this could destroy the entire political-legal system, but also self-contradictory. It is self-contradictory for the simple formal reason that the existence of a highest law containing a provision that it is not the highest, thus allowing the people to revolt against it, would violate both the positive-legal rules of this legal system from internal aspect[125] and the law of reason, as only such a positive-legal system can guarantee it by securing everyone's freedom.[126] One could say, quite provocatively, that any legal system is still better than having none,[127] and within a lawful juridical state, we should therefore seek reform, not revolution, to overcome defective positive law.[128]

The problem with this line of reasoning remains, nevertheless, that – as a purely formal argument – it can be applied to any system whatsoever, to the mafia with Don Corleone as the highest 'legislator', or to a dictatorial system with any despot at the top of the respective regime. Yet, this argument acquires a substantive content once applied to the juridical state.[129] If it is, as discussed above, a moral obligation to leave the state of nature by establishing a juridical state,[130] then it is prohibited to destroy such a state by way of revolution and to return to the state of nature.[131] And since only the juridical state – and not a mob of gangsters or a dictatorial system – can ensure my freedom and other individual rights, it is irrational as well as morally wrong to revolt against it.

This is exactly the crucial point in terms of the state of exception: not every polity that calls itself a 'State' is indeed a juridical state. If a juridical State reverts

[121] See K Flikschuh, 'Reason, Right, Revolution: Kant and Locke' (2008) 36 *Philosophy & Public Affairs* 375, 375.

[122] I Kant, 'The Conflict of the Faculties' in AW Wood and G di Giovanni (eds and trans), *Immanuel Kant: Religion and Rational Theology* (CUP, 1996) AA 7:84–89 (hereinafter: *SF*).

[123] Kant, *MS* (n 34) AA 6:320.

[124] BS Byrd and J Hruschka, *Kant's Doctrine of Right: A Commentary* (CUP, 2010) 90.

[125] ibid, 182; Kant, *MS* (n 34) AA 6:320.

[126] Kant, *TP* (n 86) AA 8:298.

[127] Kant, *ZeF* (n 109) AA 8:373.

[128] Kant, *MS* (n 34) AA 6:340.

[129] Byrd and Hruschka (n 124) 182.

[130] Kant, *MS* (n 34) AA 6:256 and 307–15.

[131] ibid, AA 6:340.

to a non-juridical State, for instance a den of thieves[132] or a despotic State, then I find myself in a state of nature again,[133] wherein resistance is permitted. Against a 'State' which kills or enslaves people, I not only have a right to defend myself, but actually a duty to do so.[134] Resistance against despotism is consequently permitted, and we find despotism in a government that is 'simultaneously lawgiving',[135] ie when the despot as the executive is not bound by the laws that they, as the lawgiver, can change anytime. Without any separate legislator to bind the executive, the latter can implement arbitrary and ad hoc decisions, and legal subjects have no legal basis on which they may challenge these decisions.[136]

Applied to the state of exception, this means that any measures against, say, a pandemic within the bounds of right and external freedom are certainly lawful and do not allow for any resistance from a Kantian perspective. If, conversely, such a state of exception becomes, during the hour of the executive, despotic, and citizens are degraded to mere subjects,[137] this regression to a Schmittian state of nature would certainly permit resistance, may it be 'the freedom of the pen',[138] negative resistance by refusing to accede to the demands of the despot,[139] or even (albeit only implicitly mentioned) active resistance, thereby coercing others to (re-)enter a juridical condition.[140] But again, this is – in the current situation – definitely not the case, and the measures implemented against the COVID-19 pandemic do certainly not allow for a rebellion, especially if we take into account the positive-legal provisions for them, their objective justification, and their proportionality. In conclusion, we might say that the Schmittian sovereign may certainly declare the state of exception, but it does not thereby gain any legal title in the Kantian sense[141] and can therefore be resisted.

VI. Concluding Remarks

I would like to finish this chapter with the following three conclusions: first, the law cannot be thought of or constructed from the exception, but only from the rule – and we can locate this rule in the concept of the categorical imperative of

[132] See also Augustine, *De civitate Dei* (Penguin, 2003) IV.4.
[133] See G Cavallar, *Kant and the Theory and Practice of International Right* (University of Wales Press, 1999) 101.
[134] Byrd and Hruschka (n 124) 91 and 184; J Hruschka, 'Die Notwehr im Zusammenhang von Kants Rechtslehre' (2003) 115 *Zeitschrift für die gesamte Strafrechtswissenschaft* 201, 201 et seq; Kant, *MS* (n 34) AA 6:461.
[135] Kant, *MS* (n 34) AA 6:316.
[136] Byrd and Hruschka (n 124) 184.
[137] Kant, *ZeF* (n 109) AA 8:351; Kant, *MS* (n 34) AA 6:306–307.
[138] Kant, *TP* (n 86) AA 8:304.
[139] Kant, *MS* (n 34) AA 6:322.
[140] ibid, AA 6:256. See also P Capps and J Rivers, 'Kant's Concept of Law' (2018) 63 *American Journal of Jurisprudence* 259, 288.
[141] H Radermacher, 'Zum Problem des Erlaubnisgesetzes bei Kant' (1988) 74 *Archiv für Rechts- und Sozialphilosophie* 42, 49.

right (ie, external freedom) *qua* the law of reason. Otherwise, we will only find ourselves in theoretical dilemmas and practical problems under the primacy claim of politics which may elevate the pursuit of any good over the realisation of and compliance with right. If a certain good is to be pursued, then only within the bounds of right.

Secondly, even in the current crisis, the COVID-19 pandemic, we should not overestimate the power of the exception. A crisis situation may certainly reveal 'our true faces' or the shortcomings of a given political-legal system, but we should not estheticise it to the point that we forget the underlying rules.[142] In fact, any deficit that manifests should represent a lesson to improve the system and make it more robust against any future crises (and it goes without saying that this should not happen at the expense of right).

And thirdly and last, speaking of improvement, a legal system can be made more robust and respectful of right, if it includes clear rules on how to handle crisis situations, especially under what circumstances and to which extent certain legal rules can be suspended, how and when they can and should be re-activated, and how individuals can challenge this suspension of their rights. A blurring of law and facts and situations where the exception becomes the rule can never be accepted, lest 'the juridico-political system', as Agamben quite violently states, 'transforms itself into a killing machine'.[143]

[142] See also Kaiser (n 63) 20–24.
[143] Agamben (n 49) 86.

2

Abuse of Power and Self-entrenchment as a State Response to the COVID-19 Outbreak: The Role of Parliaments, Courts and the People

ANTONIOS KOUROUTAKIS

I. Introduction

The World Health Organization, on 11 March 2020, declared the coronavirus outbreak known as SARS-CoV2 (severe acute respiratory syndrome coronavirus 2) or COVID-19 a pandemic.

The pandemic was spreading across the globe causing an unprecedented amount of pressure on public health systems, while before the end of 2020 more than 1,800,000 people died.[1] While some countries are affected more than others, governments were under pressure to respond as the mortality of the new virus was much higher than the influenza, estimated up to 1 per cent,[2] while the transmission intensity and the spread was much faster compared again with the common influenza.[3] This high mortality rate and transmission intensity in combination with the lack of medicine and preemptive vaccination disrupted ordinary politics and policies.

[1] For more details on the data regarding the infections and the death toll caused by COVID-19 see worldometers, www.worldometers.info/coronavirus.

[2] According to a report published in February 2020, the case fatality ratio (CFR) was estimated in the range 1.2–5.6%. However, the mortality rate from country to country may vary as it depends on the statistical methods used in combination with the sensitivity of the divergent surveillance systems to detect cases of differing levels of severity of the illness. For more details, see I Dorigatti, L Okell, A Cori, et al, 'Report 4: Severity of 2019-novel Coronavirus (nCoV)', www.who.int/docs/default-source/coronaviruse/situation-reports/20200219-sitrep-30-covid-19.pdf?sfvrsn=3346b04f_2.

[3] According to a report published in January 2020 it was estimated that each patient infected 2.6 new people. For more details see N Imai, A Cori, I Dorigatti, et al, 'Report 3 – Transmissibility of 2019-nCoV', www.imperial.ac.uk/mrc-global-infectious-disease-analysis/covid-19/report-3-transmissibility-of-covid-19/.

The common strategy for mitigation of COVID-19 was the so-called policy of social distancing.[4] A plethora of tools were used to that objective, from the mandatory wearing of masks, to general or partial lockdowns depending on the surge of the COVID-19 incidents. For the implementation of such extraordinary measures the emergency frameworks were employed for instance in Italy,[5] in the USA,[6] in Spain[7] etc.

Much ink has been spilled over the risks and the dangers of such emergency provisions. On the one hand concerns have been voiced from a human rights perspective. It is argued that emergency measures unnecessarily and disproportionally infringe human rights.[8] Furthermore, it is argued that emergency measures enacted on a temporary basis are often renewed to become permanent features of the constitutional order.[9]

On the other hand, concerns are expressed that emergency provisions imperil democratic institutions.[10] The claim is that concentration of powers in the executive vis à vis the legislature[11] and dejuridification might lead to democratic backsliding of the type seen in the Weimar Republic.[12]

However, less attention has been paid to the use of emergency provisions for political self-entrenchment purposes.[13] This chapter considers the way COVID-19

[4] See N Ferguson, D Laydon, G Nedjati-Gilani et al, 'Report 9: Impact of non-pharmaceutical interventions (NPIs) to reduce COVID-19 mortality and healthcare demand', www.imperial.ac.uk/mrc-global-infectious-disease-analysis/covid-19/report-9-impact-of-npis-on-covid-19/: '(a) mitigation, which focuses on slowing but not necessarily stopping epidemic spread – reducing peak healthcare demand while protecting those most at risk of severe disease from infection, and (b) suppression, which aims to reverse epidemic growth, reducing case numbers to low levels and maintaining that situation indefinitely'.

[5] As regards Italy see DECRETO-LEGGE 23 febbraio 2020, n 6, www.normattiva.it/uri-res/N2Ls?urn:nir:stato:decreto.legge:2020-02-23;6!vig= and for the list of executive Decrees adopted by the executive see www.governo.it/it/coronavirus-normativa.

[6] As regards the USA see 'Proclamation on Declaring a National Emergency Concerning the Novel Coronavirus Disease (COVID-19) Outbreak', trumpwhitehouse.archives.gov/presidential-actions/proclamation-declaring-national-emergency-concerning-novel-coronavirus-disease-covid-19-outbreak/.

[7] As regards Spain, see the Real Decreto 463/2020, de 14 de marzo, por el que se declara el estado de alarma para la gestión de la situación de crisis sanitaria ocasionada por el COVID-19, www.boe.es/buscar/doc.php?id=BOE-A-2020-3692.

[8] See for instance D Dyzenhaus, *The Constitution of Law: Legality in a Time of Emergency* (CUP, 2006).

[9] JE Finn, 'Sunset Clauses and Democratic Deliberation: Assessing the Significance of Sunset Provisions in Antiterrorism Legislation' (2010) 48 *Columbia Journal Transitional Law* 442, 501.

[10] A Kouroutakis and S Ranchordás 'Snoozing Democracy: The De-juridification of Emergencies' (2016) *Minnesota Journal of International Law* 25.

[11] J Petrov, 'The COVID-19 Emergency in the Age of Executive Aggrandizement: What Role for Legislative and Judicial Checks?' (2020) 8 *The Theory and Practice of Legislation* 71; E Griglio, 'Parliamentary Oversight under the Covid-19 Emergency: Striving against Executive Dominance' (2020) 8 *The Theory and Practice of Legislation* 49.

[12] On the way the executive manipulated constitutional emergency provisions in order to establish an authoritarian regime see A Kouroutakis, 'The Virtues of Sunset Clauses in Relation to Constitutional Authority' (2020) 41 *Statute Law Review* 16, 23 ff.

[13] Political self-entrenchment, which is defined by Levinson and Sachs as the use of tools by which political actors insulate themselves from political change, has been examined from different perspectives

has been used and might be used as an opportunity for political self-entrenchment especially from the executive. In doing so, it will first examine political self-entrenchment both during ordinary conditions and during times of emergency, such as in the case of the pandemic. The second part will focus on the available means to face political self-entrenchment and in particular, it will focus on both political and legal means. By examining the role of the judiciary, the legislature, the media and the people, this chapter will argue that during the pandemic, when the legislatures are suspended or under functioned, the ground is more fertile for abuse of power for self-entrenchment purposes on behalf of the executive. The main conclusion is that democracies are left vulnerable in times of emergencies with less safeguards to secure their orderly function and proper protection against acts of self-entrenchment.

II. Abuse of Power and Political Self-entrenchment During Ordinary Conditions and During Times of Emergency

A. Executive and Political Self-entrenchment

In theory, political self-entrenchment takes place when 'political actors, incumbent politicians, prevailing political parties, and electoral majorities, take advantage of and even abuse their power for self-serving purposes'.[14] Political self-entrenchment is relevant for incumbents in both executive and legislative positions. As Gardbaum puts it, political self-entrenchment is a political failure and it can take different forms, such as government capture of independent agencies or political process.[15]

For instance, political self-entrenchment takes place when parliament changes the electoral law and adopts a new scheme that favours the incumbents, or when the government appoints in the public broadcasting company directors who lack independency and impartiality and thus use their office to promote the government's agenda. Consequently, when political actors in power abuse their power for self-serving purposes, an uneven playing field is formed in the political arena. In particular, political actors without power, and political opponents, face disadvantages, obstacles and possibly barriers to entry.

and provoked scepticism in different sciences. For more details on political self-entrenchment see D Levinson, and B Sachs, 'Political Entrenchment and Public Law' (2015) 125 *The Yale Law Journal* 400; M Klarman, 'Majoritarian Judicial Review: The Entrenchment Problem' (1997) 85 *Georgetown Law Journal* 491.

[14] A Kouroutakis, 'How liberal is a democracy without a level playing field in the political process?' (*U.K. Const. L. Blog*, 21 May 2020) ukconstitutionallaw.org/.

[15] S Gardbaum, 'Comparative Political Process Theory' (2020) 18 *International Journal of Constitutional Law* 1429.

An expression of political self-entrenchment in the executive is the maladministration of state resources. In particular, incumbents who have access to taxpayer-funded resources may manage and transform state resources, such as state-owned enterprises and free airtime, into public subsidies. According to a report from the OECD, 'public subsidies to political parties can take a variety of forms, including tax breaks, free access to public services including airtime, access to public buildings, provision of goods and allocation of financial resources. Considering the impact of resources on political competition the two most important forms of public subsidies are financial support and free airtime'.[16]

In general, in times of normality, a plethora of political self-entrenchment cases are recorded which are divided between legitimate and illegitimate.[17] For instance, a case of legitimate self-entrenchment in executive position was recorded by Nordhaus. Nordhaus, in a ground-breaking article, remarked that governments constantly manipulate monetary policy for re-election purposes and proposed 'to entrust economic policy to persons who will not be tempted by the Sirens of partisan politics'.[18] This paved the way for the independence of central banks. Nowadays, incumbents generally do not have the power to use monetary policy for re-election purposes in a way that harms long-term financial interests.

Furthermore, in relation to the media, the control of the public broadcasting services by the executive is another common situation that exemplifies the maladministration of state resources. In Italy, during the governments of the Prime Minister Berlusconi, who controlled Italy's top three national and private TV channels, known as the Mediaset empire, via the appointment of the director of the national broadcaster, the so-called Radiotelevisione Italiana (Rai), his governments controlled the vast majority of the popular TV networks.[19] As a result, airtime from both the private and the public TV channels was used to promote the government's policies. Likewise, in Hungary, once Viktor Orban won the elections his ruling party Fidesz introduced a new law which gave them control of the public media, and the ability to use this as a platform for the promotion of governmental policies.[20]

Finally, a case of illegitimate self-entrenchment in relation to executive office is recorded in Israel. In 2019, Prime Minister Netanyahu was indicted on corruption allegations. The prosecutor based the charges on allegations that the Prime Minister agreed with Arnon 'Noni' Mozes, the owner of one of Israel's largest

[16] See 'Money in Politics: Sound Political Competition and Trust in Government' (OECD, Paris, 14–15 November 2013) [20], www.oecd.org/gov/ethics/Money-in-politics.pdf.

[17] See A Kouroutakis, 'Legitimate and Illegitimate Political Self-entrenchment and its Impact on Political Equality' (2021) *Vienna Journal on International Constitutional Law* 1.

[18] WD Nordhaus, 'The Political Business Circle' (1975) 42 *The Review of Economic Studies* 169, 188. Nordhaus examined the Phillips curve and argued that before elections, politicians increase inflation with the aim to decrease unemployment, which will lead to increased salaries.

[19] See D Pavli 'Berlusconi's Chilling Effect on Italian Media' (30 March 2010), www.opensocietyfoundations.org/voices/berlusconi-s-chilling-effect-italian-media.

[20] See 'The state of Hungarian media: Endgame', blogs.lse.ac.uk/medialse/2017/08/29/the-state-of-hungarian-media-endgame/.

newspapers, Yedioth Ahronoth, that the latter would offer more favourable coverage of Netanyahu's government, in exchange for the former limiting the circulation of a rival newspaper.[21]

B. Self-entrenchment Cases During the Pandemic

While much ink is spilled on the issue of political self-entrenchment, substantially less ink is spilled on the issue of political self-entrenchment and abuse of power during emergencies. During emergencies, the separation of power is reshaped, and power is concentrated in the hand of the executive. Thus, political self-entrenchment during emergencies in most cases is associated with abuse of power in executive positions.

During the pandemic, the emergency of the public health, that required social distancing from the common people, at the same time imposed the shutdown of the legislatures or the limited function.[22] Likewise, courts' function was affected. For instance, jury by trial was suspended in the US[23] and in a plethora of jurisdictions some trials were operating online.[24] On top of that, it is well known that the judiciary in times of stress shows deference on emergency provisions.[25]

On the one hand, the limited function of the legislatures and on the other hand the operation of courts in an environment of emergency created a fertile ground for the executive to take the lead in the constitutional system. That said a number of questionable executive laws and actions in relation to the pandemic were recorded in which abuse of power is encapsulated.

To begin with, in the US, once Congress passed the COVID-19 relief package and authorised the president to administer this relief package, President Trump decided to print his name 'Trump' in the memo section of the stimulus check granted to millions of Americans.[26] This action, which was prima facie a questionable exercise of power, at the same time signals a clear and outright expression of political self-entrenchment. It goes without saying that the President's name on

[21] O Liebermann and A Carey, 'Israel's Benjamin Netanyahu to be indicted on corruption charges, pending hearing' (CNN, 28 February 2019) edition.cnn.com/2019/02/28/middleeast/israel-benjamin-netanyahu-indictment-intl/index.html.

[22] I Waismel-Manor, I Bar-Siman-Tov, O Rozenberg, A Levanon, C Benoît and G Ifergane, 'COVID-19 and Legislative Activity: A Cross-National Study' (2 July 2020) Bar Ilan University Faculty of Law Research Paper No. 20-12: www.researchgate.net/publication/342514148_Covid-19_and_Legislative_Activity_A_Cross-National_Study.

[23] 'Courts Suspending Jury Trials as COVID-19 Cases Surge' (20 November 2020), www.uscourts.gov/news/2020/11/20/courts-suspending-jury-trials-covid-19-cases-surge.

[24] A Kouroutakis, 'Legaltech in Public Administration: Prospects and Challenges' in *The Cambridge Handbook of Lawyering in the Digital Age* (CUP, 2021) forthcoming.

[25] About deference see TRS Allan, 'Deference, Defiance, and Doctrine: Defining the Limits of Judicial Review' (2010) 60 *University of Toronto Law Journal* 41; B Aditya, 'The Origins of Judicial Deference to Executive Interpretation' (2017) 126 *Yale Law Journal* 908.

[26] In an unprecedented move, the Treasury orders Trump's name printed on stimulus checks (*The Washington Post*, 15 April 2020) www.washingtonpost.com/politics/coming-to-your-1200-relief-check-donald-j-trumps-name/2020/04/14/071016c2-7e82-11ea-8013-1b6da0e4a2b7_story.html.

the stimulus check is free advertisement which was especially valuable a couple of months before the elections.

Interestingly, the appearance of the President's name on an Internal Revenue Service disbursement was a breach of a longstanding practice, and possibly a constitutional convention, as it was the first time such an incident took place.[27]

Moreover, more indirect policies hide self-serving interests, remarkably by inaction. For instance, in the looming elections of November 2020, Democrats were urging their voters to vote by mail due to social distancing reasons. This meant a huge influx of ballots by postal mail that would undoubtedly have burdened ordinary handling by the US Postal Service. In addition, it was expected that more ballots by email would favour in general the Democratic Party, with the exception of some states like Arizona where it is regular for both republicans and democrats to vote by mail.

Thus, the administration of President Trump was opposing the funding of the US Postal Service. CNN reported that 'Trump is fueling allegations that he is trying to manipulate the postal system for political gain. The pandemic has led to record-shattering levels of voting-by-mail, but Trump has tried to restrict the voting method because he says it will hurt his re-election and Republicans across the board.'[28] It was reported that by defunding the US Postal Service, the latter would have been unable to deliver the ballots by mail on time, which would lead to the disenfranchisement of those votes.[29] Moreover, President Trump put forward the idea that votes by postal mail would lead to voting fraud in order to block states from adapting to mail balloting.[30]

Across the ocean, in Europe, Greece successfully contained the spread of the virus during the first wave, in part by executive legislation that promptly shut non-essential businesses and imposed a stay-at-home order. Among the emergency measures adopted, the government was authorised to run an awareness campaign regarding the pandemic. By executive legislation, private and public radio and TV stations were obliged to air for free awareness messages on how to minimise the spread of the virus.[31]

While the awareness campaigns for free is an emergency measure excused by the exigency of the pandemic, interestingly, with another piece of executive

[27] Kouroutakis (n 14).

[28] E Kaufman, M Cohen, J Hoffman and N Robertson, 'Trump says he opposes funding USPS because of mail-in voting' (CNN, 13 August 2020) cnn.com/2020/08/13/politics/trump-usps-funding-comments-2020-election/index.html.

[29] E Bauer, 'Separating Fact From Fiction On Trump And The Post Office – And Why It Matters' (*Forbes*, 16 August 2020) www.forbes.com/sites/ebauer/2020/08/16/separating-fact-from-fiction-on-trump-and-the-post-officeand-why-it-matters/?sh=66c553273d74.

[30] M Wines, 'As Trump Rails Against Voting by Mail, States Open the Door for It' (*New York Times*, 22 May 2020) www.nytimes.com/2020/05/21/us/vote-by-mail-trump.html.

[31] Legislative Content Act of 11.03.2020, 'Urgent measures to address the negative consequences of the occurrence of coronavirus COVID-19 and the need to limit its spread', codified with 4737/2020 (in Greek) www.taxheaven.gr/law/%CE%A0%C'E%9D%CE%A011.03.2020/2020.

legislation, the government was allowed to derogate from the existing national provisions and to run an additional awareness campaign, this time with payment.[32] However, the latter measure became the source of controversy between the government and the parties of the opposition. The government distributed 20 million euros to news websites, printed journals and TV and radio stations, without transparency. There was suspicion that the distribution was 'based on political criteria and whether media were sympathetic towards the government'.[33]

In the case of Greece, the pandemic gave the government the opportunity to deviate from ordinary procedures and direct money to the media. The government, thus, created a fertile ground for positive reception of its policies and a hostile ground for the policy proposals of the opposition. In other words, the government captured the media with state funds. In this way, the press, the so-called Fourth Estate in the political system, loses its capacity of advocacy and its ability to control those in government.

A report issued from Freedom House remarks that 'authoritarian and democratically elected leaders alike have failed to be candid about the impact of COVID-19. In the survey, 62 percent of the respondents said they distrust what they are hearing about the pandemic from the national government in their country of focus'[34] and it further explains that 'governments are also using the outbreak as a justification to grant themselves special powers beyond what is reasonably necessary to protect public health. They have exploited new emergency authority to interfere in the justice system, impose unprecedented restrictions on political opponents, and sideline crucial legislative functions'.[35]

Within this context, abuses especially from the executive during the pandemic were not a rare or an isolated practice, although it seems that it does not attract much attention. This is quite a paradox given the grave consequences on the quality of the democratic system. But the question is the following: how do we safeguard democracy from political actors who during a state of emergency abuse their power for self-serving purposes in order to retain and consolidate their power? What does constitutional law do to face this problem and what more should it do? How do different institutions act and react?

[32] Legislative Content Act of 14.03.2020, 'Urgent measures to address the need to limit the spread of coronavirus COVID-19', codified by 4735/2020 (in Greek), www.taxheaven.gr/law/%CE%A0%CE%9D%CE%A014.03.2020/2020.

[33] 'Greek government exposed over COVID-19 awareness funds' (*Euractiv*, 9 July 2020) www.euractiv.com/section/politics/short_news/athens-greek-government-exposed-over-covid-19-awareness-funds/.

[34] Freedom House, 'Democracy under Lockdown – The Impact of COVID-19 on Global Freedom' (October 2020) freedomhouse.org/article/new-report-democracy-under-lockdown-impact-covid-19-global-freedom.

[35] ibid.

III. The Difficulty of Facing Political Self-entrenchment During the Pandemic

A. The Role of the Courts

During emergencies, the focus lies often on the overreaction with disproportionately limiting human rights, or the expansion of the executive powers at the expense of the legislature.[36] These are obviously important issues that demand scrutiny and sufficient attention; however, it is also crucial to attend to emergency measures aiming to promote political self-entrenchment.

In general, political actors in power are entrusted with the state resources and policies that have direct or indirect financial impacts. Obviously, their role is to administer state resources and policies with the aim of promoting the public good and public interest. In times of crisis, such resources shall be spent with the aim of facing the emergency. However, when incumbents misuse emergency state resources in their favour, turning them into tools with tremendous impact on the political competition, they distort political fair play and the democratic equilibrium.

Ely elaborated on the pathology of the political self-entrenchment, though for times of normality, and remarked that 'in a representative democracy value determinations are to be made by our elected representatives, and if in fact most of us disapprove we can vote them out of office. Malfunction occurs when the process is underserving of trust, when (1) the ins are choking off the channels of political change to ensure that they will stay in and the outs will stay out, or (2) though no one is actually denied a voice or a vote, representatives beholden to an effective majority are systematically disadvantaging some minority out of simple hostility or a prejudiced refusal to recognise commonalities of interest, and thereby denying that minority the protection afforded other groups by a representative system'.[37]

That said, in times of normality Ely remarked on and suggested two cures: the former is political[38] via the mechanism of reelection and the latter is purely legal via the mechanism of judicial review. In particular, Ely argued that if incumbents depend on re-election, this will drive them into self-restraint since in democratic regimes with free and fair elections it is possible that voters would punish the incumbents who abused power for self-serving purposes.

[36] For instance, Dyzenhaus offers a critique on emergency laws hindering civil liberties, see D Dyzenhaus, 'The Permanence of the Temporary – Can Emergency Powers Be Normalized?' in RJ Daniels, P Macklem and K Roach (eds), *The Security of Freedom: Essays on Canada's Anti-terrorism Bill* (University of Toronto Press, 2001) 21. Moreover, Justice Brennan has famously said that '[a]fter each perceived security crisis ended, the United States has remorsefully realized that the abrogation of civil liberties was unnecessary'. See WJ Brennan, Jr, 'The Quest to Develop a Jurisprudence of Civil Liberties in Times of Security Crises' (1988) 18 *Israel Yearbook on Human Rights* 11.

[37] JH Ely, *Democracy and Distrust: A Theory of Judicial Review* (Harvard University Press, 1980) 78.

[38] On political constitutionalism and its virtues see R Bellamy, *Political Constitutionalism: A Republican Defence of the Constitutionality of Democracy* (CUP, 2007).

On the other hand, the mechanism of judicial review relies on judges to oversee the political process. Participants in the political process, such as political parties, or members of the opposition, and even ordinary citizens might challenge governmental decisions and laws that distort the political process.

Although there is no specific framework to regulate the level playing field in the political process, political actors and ordinary citizens seek protection before the courts,[39] based on constitutional provisions such as the provision on equality,[40] and on ordinary laws such as campaign finance laws[41] and ordinary criminal laws.[42] In the frequently cited footnote 4 of the 1938 case of *United States v Carolene Products*, Justice Stone distinguished the level of scrutiny exercised by the courts between statutes dealing with economic and social welfare legislation and those dealing with, among other topics, the political process.[43] In theory, Ely has stressed the paramount role of the Supreme Court Justices to interpret the open ended provisions of the constitution, with an obligation to protect the political process and reinforce participation and representation.[44] In addition, Ginsburg has argued that judicial review is an important tool to safeguard democracy.[45] Furthermore, Pildes discusses in detail a plethora of decisions from courts around the world, such as the US Supreme Court, the European Court of Human Rights, and the Supreme Court of South Africa that have delivered key decisions protecting the political process.[46]

However, the role of the courts to resolve disputes on political issues is not straightforward as judicial review has external and internal limits. To begin with, there are areas that are not subject to judicial review, such as the amendment process[47] or the *interna corporis*.[48] Secondly, courts show deference to the

[39] In addition, in some countries independent agencies and bodies, such as electoral commissions, are entrusted with the role of solving political disputes. See B Ackerman, 'Good-bye, Montesquieu' in S Rose-Ackerman and PL Lindseth (eds), *Comparative Administrative Law* (Edward Elgar, 2010). However, such independent bodies are not always efficient. As Bellamy has put it, 'most states lack a tradition of independent public service, making electoral commissions heavily biased towards the prevailing administration of which they often form a part, either as appointees or as members of the same electoral ticket. Yet, it has been an area where the Court has usually been reluctant to intervene'. Bellamy (n 38) 112.

[40] On equality in the political process, see T Christiano, *The Constitution of Equality: Democratic Authority and Its Limits* (OUP, 2008) and R Dahl, *On Political Equality* (Yale University Press, 2005).

[41] For instance, as regards campaign finance laws in the USA see the Federal Election Campaign Act of 1971 (FECA), Pub.L. 92–225, 86 Stat. 3, and for similar laws in a number of EU countries see Study for the AFCO Committee, Party Financing and Referendum campaigns in EU Member States (Publications Office of the EU 2015).

[42] ie, general bribery offences, fraud, breach of trust and embezzlement.

[43] See *United States v Carolene Products Company*, 304 U.S. 144 (1938), at fn 4.

[44] Ely (n 37) chs 4 and 5.

[45] See T Ginsburg, *Judicial Review in New Democracies: Constitutional Courts in Asian Cases* (CUP, 2003) 22 ff.

[46] RH Pildes, 'The Constitutionalization of Democratic Politics' (2004) 118 *Harvard Law Review* 28, 32ff,

[47] There is a trend, however, for the review of the amendment process, see Y Roznai, *Unconstitutional Constitutional Amendments The Limits of Amendment Powers* (OUP, 2017).

[48] For instance in the UK, courts do not have jurisdiction to review the *interna corporis*, see *Anisminic Ltd v Foreign Compensation Commission* [1968] UKHL 6 at [13].

political branches of the government in some policy areas.[49] Suffice to cite here the dissenting opinion of Justice Stevens in Jones who stated that 'it is not this Court's constitutional function to choose between the competing visions of what makes democracy work – party autonomy and discipline versus progressive inclusion of the entire electorate in the process of selecting their public officials – that are held by the litigants in this case'.[50] In addition, Justice Felix Frankfurter has famously said that 'it is hostile to a democratic system to involve the judiciary in the politics of the people'.[51]

On top of that, in times of emergency such as a pandemic, when the public health is endangered, and technocrats with expertise in medicine decide policy options, courts are prone to show more and wider deference.[52]

Remarkably, cases of political self-entrenchment have not reached the courts in order to test and examine their stance in practice.[53] No complaint was brought on the defunding of the US Postal Services in the US, nor on the imprint of the name of the President on the stimulus checks.

In the Greek situation there has been no case recorded pertaining to the payments made to the media in relation to the pandemic. Possibly, the lack of a coherent framework to regulate political self-entrenchment, the well-known practice of deference shown by the courts during emergencies, or the lack of standing in specific cases have a deterrent effect, keeping challenges away from the courts.

In theory, judicial review is a key aspect of constitutionalism and the courts are entrusted with the safeguarding of the political process.[54] However, when in times of exigency, courts show deference inevitably, political actors with power, incumbents, are allowed de facto to dominate the political arena. Such dominance takes place in a number of forms, for instance by abusing procedures, such as elections, or by maladministering public resources. Such practices entertain self-serving purposes, which may be to consolidate power or enable their reelection.

As the political actors in power abuse their power for self-serving purposes, and courts are silenced, the level playing field is distorted and self-entrenchment

[49] See Allan (n 25); A Bamzai, 'The Origins of Judicial Deference to Executive Interpretation' (2017) 126 *Yale Law Journal* 908.

[50] *California Democratic Party v Jones*, 530 U.S. 567 (2000) at [598].

[51] *Colegrove v Green*, 328 U.S. 549 (1946) at [554].

[52] Regarding deference in emergencies in a number of countries, see G Zhu, *Deference to the Administration in Judicial Review* (Springer, 2019).

[53] However, courts have not shown complete deference on issues of civil liberties. On the contrary, they have examined restrictions case by case and occasionally they have ruled some restrictions as unconstitutional. For instance, the US Supreme Court granted an injunction against New York State's 'very severe restrictions on attendance at religious services in areas classified as "red" or "orange" zones', see *Roman Catholic Diocese of Brooklyn, New York v Cuomo*, 592 U. S. ____ (2020). In addition, the Constitutional Court in Germany has ruled that the Hessian state government infringed Article 8(2) of the Basic Law by adopting a complete ban of assemblies, see BVerfG, decision of the 1st Chamber of the First Senate of 15 April 2020 – 1 BvR 828/20 -, Rn. 1-19, www.bverfg.de/e/rk20200415_1bvr082820.html.

[54] For more details see Ely (n 37).

takes place. Political actors find it difficult to compete with the incumbents and the quality of democracy is at risk.

B. The Political Means; Legislative Scrutiny, the Press, and the People

The previous section has examined the role of the courts during the pandemic and has shown its limitations. Thus, the protection of democracies from political self-entrenchment during emergencies relies more on the political means. In that process, the role of the opposition in the legislature, of the media and of the ordinary citizen is critical to prevent and block self-entrenchment practices.

Interestingly, due to the nature of the pandemic, in some countries, such as in Hungary, parliamentary sessions were suspended, in others such as in Greece and the UK they were either of limited function or conducted virtually via online platforms respectively. Bar-Siman-Tov explains that 'legislatures' very operation is based on the assembly of many people together. Indeed, the idea of gathering or assembling is so fundamental to the identity of legislatures, that it is even reflected in their institutional names.'[55]

Therefore, the ordinary assembly of parliaments was a potential cluster for infections and the safe option was their limited function. Obviously, the temporary suspension meant the gravest impairment of the role of the legislature, with the virtual transposition to be the least impairment, and the under function to lie in between.

However, virtual transformation of assemblies was not possible everywhere due to technological limits.[56] In total, it was estimated that due to the pandemic governments have shut or limited parliaments in countries with 2 billion people.[57] It is argued that the weakening of the legislature in times of emergency such as the COVID-19 pandemic has paramount consequences for three reasons: first 'legislative control over the acts and actions of emergency authorities is of vital importance for safeguarding the rule of law and democracy', secondly 'problems of input and throughput democracy are gaining major significance vis-à-vis law-making practices during the COVID-19 emergency' and thirdly 'emergency legislation adopted through fast-tracked procedures in response to urgent and compelling policy concerns is traditionally regarded as difficult to reconcile with requirements for good quality legislation'.[58]

[55] See I Bar-Siman-Tov, 'Covid-19 meets politics: the novel coronavirus as a novel challenge for legislatures' (2020) 8 *The Theory and Practice of Legislation* 11.

[56] See Bar-Siman-Tov (n 55).

[57] C Provost, N Archer and L Namubiru, 'Alarm as 2 billion people have parliaments shut or limited by COVID-19' www.opendemocracy.net/en/5050/alarm-two-billion-people-have-parliaments-suspended-or-limited-covid-19/.

[58] Griglio (n 11).

Moreover, there is a fourth reason, which is relevant to executive self-entrenchment. Regardless of the system of separation of powers, presidential or parliamentary, the legislature is the forum in which the opposition operates. By deactivating the legislatures, the opposition is shut down as it loses its forum to scrutinise governmental policies, to question executive actions, to record and condemn practices of self-entrenchment and to keep the government accountable. In other words, this limited function of the legislative body has grave implications on the quality of modern democracy as parliamentary scrutiny is restricted, ministerial accountability is distorted and most importantly the voice of the opposition becomes hollower.

With limited parliamentary scrutiny, oversight exercised by the media and ordinary people is therefore critical. To begin with, the role of the media during the pandemic was criticised due to the exaggeration of the risks and disproportionate coverage.[59] However, the media are not considered as the 4th power in the separation of power without good reasons. The media are entrusted with the role of sharing information and such information is critical for the evaluation of governmental policy in the democratic process. Media panels and columns in newspapers can became a forum for unfettered political debate where political actors representing the government and the opposition may discuss the appropriate and more efficient mechanisms to face the pandemic. This is significant especially in times with shut or under functioning parliaments.

Traditional media and the press are essential means of information and transparency in times where legislature and courts are silenced or under functioned. They are well situated to raise awareness on cases of abuse of power, and to stop disinformation campaigns and governmental propaganda. Their potential criticism of executive actions might act as a bulwark to prevent abuse of power.

But in democracies, where sovereignty lies with the people, people have a responsibility. The people choose their representatives during the elections and decide who will govern them. This decision is a transfer of power, though temporary. The people have an obligation as watchdog to oversee the exercise of this power. In modern times, where social media assist the mainstream media, the people have more power, in theory, to control the policies implemented to combat the pandemic, to participate in public debate with proposals for better solutions.

Democracy under no circumstances is allowed to be imperiled. In most democratic constitutions where the sovereignty lies with the people, the people have an obligation to defend the quality of the democratic polity. People should criticise activities of self-entrenchment and penalise with their votes incumbents who take advantage of an emergency by abusing their power for self-serving purposes.

[59] See A Alemanno, 'Taming COVID-19 by Regulation: An Opportunity for Self-Reflection' (2020) *European Journal of Risk Regulation* 1 and Bar-Siman-Tov (n 55).

IV. Conclusions

This chapter examined the pathology of executive self-entrenchment during the pandemic of COVID-19. Most countries have implemented one way or another an emergency framework and power was concentrated in the hands of the executive to face the exigency. While the focus in times of exigency is on human rights violations and the adoption of disproportionate executive measures, less focus is paid to the possibility of executive abuse of power for self-serving purposes. Political self-entrenchment is an old problem and incumbents in power often aim to perpetuate and consolidate their power, however, this seems to be neglected in times of crisis.

The current pandemic has shown a number of self-entrenchment practices. Cases from the US and Greece were mentioned where governments have taken the opportunity given by the pandemic in order to act with self-serving purposes. The key question that was analysed was how different institutions face such problems.

Based on Ely, in theory there are two ways; the legal and the political way. In the legal way, where the courts are in the frontline, it was discussed that in practice and given the conditions of the pandemic, courts are unlikely to diverge from the general stance of deference they show in times of crisis. Moreover, no incident of executive self-entrenchment was brought before the courts.

On the other hand, the role of politics was examined. Given that parliaments around the world were suspended or under functioning, the authority of the political opposition to monitor and scrutinise executive practices of self-entrenchment were limited. It seems that it is left to mainstream media to report and put in the spotlight such incidents and the people to engage with such events. Unfortunately, when democracies are subject to media scrutiny and the peoples' engagement, it means that democracies are vulnerable in times of emergencies with less safeguards to secure their orderly function and proper protection against acts of self-entrenchment.

All in all, times of exigency create a fertile ground for incumbents to take advantage of power for self-serving purposes, while the system of checks and balances is left with less means to face such practices. The critical issue is that self-entrenchment has a long-standing impact on the political arena and the quality of the democracy that outlasts the emergency period.

While self-entrenchment took place in times of exigency with limited control, when normality would be restored, the political system would suffer from each consequence. Political opposition would be disadvantaged in the political arena, and a democracy without a level playing field and without equality is a democracy without quality.

3

Democracy, Death and Dying: The Potential and Limits of Legal Rationalisation

KONRAD LACHMAYER*

I. Introduction

'When I hear that everything else has to step back from the protection of life, then I have to say: That is not right in this absoluteness ... If there is any absolute value in our Basic Law, then it is human dignity. It is inviolable, ... but it doesn't rule out the fact that we have to die.'[1] In April 2020 the President of the German Bundestag stated that it would be wrong to give the protection of life the highest priority in the fight against the coronavirus pandemic, although the state has to guarantee the best healthcare possible for all.

Pandemics that arise and spread necessarily lead to more people dying than without the diseases involved. Societies have dealt with this situation as a condition of nature since the beginning of mankind, at least since people began to settle. While in medieval times, pandemics had to be dealt with on a local level, especially in towns and cities, in a post-Westphalian world the role of states as the relevant actor in dealing with pandemics has become increasingly relevant.[2] Health issues force governments and administrations to implement preventative, provisional and prohibitive measures.

By the end of December 2020, 84 million cases of COVID-19 had been documented around the world and 1.82 m people had died.[3] An estimated 5.3 m people

* The author is thankful to Lukas Wieser for research assistance; I would like to express my gratitude to the discussion group of the SFU Faculty of Law for a valuable and inspiring debate.

[1] Wolfgang Schäuble is President of the German Bundestag (first chamber of German Parliament) see www.zeit.de/politik/deutschland/2020-04/corona-krise-wolfgang-schaeuble-schutzmassnahmen.

[2] Private companies and organisations as well as civil society must also be taken into consideration.

[3] See ourworldindata.org/covid-deaths.

died in the EU in the year 2019; in the year 2020, up to the end of November, 444,300 people died in the EU and UK due to COVID-19, which represents about 8 per cent of the overall deceased persons.[4] One hundred years ago, the Spanish flu led – within three years – to an estimated total of 2.64 m deaths throughout the whole of Europe.

An epidemic (from the Greek 'upon the people')[5] is a disease which affects a large proportion of a population within a short timeframe (more than 15 cases per 100,000 people in two consecutive weeks), and it becomes a pandemic (Greek: 'all the people')[6] when it affects larger regions, continents or the whole world. Since epidemics and pandemics have a dramatic effect on the people, it is also up to the people to decide how to approach their consequences. This perspective already involves the role of death and dying in democracies.

The first part and starting point of the chapter (section II) refers to the shift of the paradigm of death from an unpredictable though inevitable condition of life to the economised timing of death. This rationalised approach has given governments the possibility to influence death and dying. In terms of Foucault's bio-politics, governments not only control the bodies of the people, but also decide upon their life and death. During the COVID-19 pandemic, (European) states have come under pressure to protect the lives of the people and to keep death rates low.

This role of the state in managing death and dying is also expressed in law, which I will focus on in the second part of the chapter (section III). Democratic processes have created the legal framework of life and death (legal thanatology). Budgetary law can serve as an example for the democratic decision-making about life expectancy. As courts strengthen and enhance the effectiveness of rights, they also have an effect on the life and death of human beings. While the discussion on a traditional liberal rights perspective can be understood as an empowerment of the people to decide for themselves about life and death (individual autonomy), state obligations to guarantee liberal rights (eg, the right to life) or social rights (eg, right to health) affect the government's decisions about life and death. The possibilities and limits of the rationalising function of the rights-based case law will be discussed.

In the third part of the chapter (section IV) the effects of legal thanatology in the COVID-19 pandemic will be analysed. Different approaches of European democracies illustrate that decision-making on life and death will lead to different consequences. Moreover, an international perspective demonstrates European privileges as well as European responsibilities in a post-colonial world. In the concluding section V, the necessity to negotiate about death and dying in democratic societies will be addressed.

[4] This percentage does not express the number of excess deaths, which means that the percentage of increased mortality is lower.

[5] ἐπί (epi), δῆμος (demos).

[6] παν (pan), δῆμος (demos).

II. Pre-Requisites of Legal Thanatology

A. The Economised Timing of Death

The Encyclopaedia Britannica defines death as 'the total cessation of life processes that eventually occurs in all living organisms'.[7] The end arrives when total cessation occurs. Life and death are irreconcilably opposed to one another. Death terminates the (human) life and life ends with the occurrence of death. While death cannot be negotiated, it sometimes seems possible to cheat it. Away from such exceptional circumstances, however, human existence is defined and terminated by death.

The randomness of death as an unpredictable though inevitable condition of life is set against the attempts of humanity to prolong life. Human beings have long dreamt of eternal life and victory over death.[8] As an important step towards the prolongation of life, the enlightenment not only rationalised human existence but also led to an analysis of fatal risks, from child mortality and all kinds of diseases to age-related illnesses. The numbers are impressive: in the year 1800, almost 1 billion people were alive on earth, while the figure was 1.65 billion in 1900, 6.14 billion in 2000 and 7.79 billion in 2020.[9] The global child mortality rate has fallen over the last 200 years,[10] while life expectancy has increased significantly (more than doubling from 32 in 1900 to 72.2 in 2015).[11]

The enlightened and rationalised approach has led to manifold scientific and technological advances. The increase in possibilities to prolong life is remarkable: modern hospital management, genetic analysis and data management, diagnostic devices (including the use of artificial intelligence in diagnosis), organ transplants, artificial organs, traditional or alternative therapies and specialised pharmaceuticals or vaccines. If all of these possibilities are available in cases of emergency or severe illnesses, or just as preventive tools, the enormous developments in life-prolonging processes become evident. With these tools, the range of options to keep human beings alive is not only incredibly broad, but also fundamentally linked to the economic dimension of modern medical care.

An enormous amount of resources is already necessary to facilitate a general medical supply on a technologically feasible level. While investment in targeted medical treatment of individuals enables an even higher success rate in keeping humans alive, it is closely linked to exponentially higher investment of resources. This economic dimension of the health system has great relevance regarding the

[7] See www.britannica.com/science/death.

[8] See eg S Knell, *Die Eroberung der Zeit* (Suhrkamp, 2015).

[9] See eg www.worldometers.info/world-population/world-population-by-year/.

[10] See eg ourworldindata.org/child-mortality.

[11] See eg ourworldindata.org/life-expectancy. The leading causes of death globally include ischaemic heart disease, responsible for 16% of the world's total deaths, strokes and chronic obstructive pulmonary diseases, responsible for approximately 11% and 6% of total deaths respectively, as well as lower respiratory infections.

possibilities to postpone death. In the following section, this development will be addressed as the economised timing of death.

The economised timing of death results in many philosophical questions, political possibilities and legal challenges. The state has the possibility to influence and control this economised dimension of death. From a democratic perspective, one would expect an open public debate, but this is lacking or occurs only indirectly. Although death is nowadays much more than a random, uncontrollable incidence, it still often seems to be a taboo subject. From a legal perspective, we can observe detailed judgements on rights-based discussions about individual fates on the one hand, and judgements about state obligations and social rights on the other hand; the democratic discourse on the economised timing of death is missing. Before turning to the legal dimension, it is necessary to analyse the correlation between death and governance in democracies.

B. From Biopolitics to Necropolitics

We have Foucault to thank for drawing attention to the state's power over the human body and the regulation of the population. Starting from the Roman tradition of the *patria potestas*, which included the possibility to rule over the lives of children and slaves, the state gradually took control of human beings' life and death.[12] The death sentence and war represented two varieties of the right of the sword.[13] The state purposes changed and a new era of biopolitics was developed by the state, which included the capability and aim to control birth and death rates as well as the health level of the population; from a neo-liberal perspective, the relevance of human capital became decisive.[14] The state can organise, influence and control the population in general and discipline individuals. Institutions like schools, barracks, and factories were developed and served the aims of capitalism.[15] While epidemics and hunger were reduced in the eighteenth and nineteenth centuries, bio-politics took over control of the human body.[16]

While Foucault's analysis is focused on the development of the government, Giorgio Agamben radicalises the concept and carries it to the extreme.[17] By combining Carl Schmitt's state of emergency with Foucault's biopolitics, the absolute control over the human body became the characteristic of the absolute

[12] M Foucault, *The History of Sexuality: 1: The Will to Knowledge*, transl Robert Hurley (first published 1976, Penguin, 1998) 135.

[13] ibid, 136–37.

[14] ibid, 139–41.

[15] ibid, 139.

[16] ibid, 141–42.

[17] G Agamben, *Homo Sacer. Sovereign Power and Bare Life*, transl Daniel Heller-Roazen (Stanford University Press, 1998).

sovereign or sovereignty itself.[18] The sovereign rules over the bare (sacred) life of the individual (the homo sacer). Agamben chooses the Nazi regime symbolised by the concentration camp ('Lager') as the unique horror and cruelty of the twentieth century to illustrate the total control over the human body, in which the state does not leave anything to the human being, not even the essence of being human.[19] Agamben demonstrates that states of emergency proliferated in democracies and become a regular part of states shifting between democracies and dictatorships.

Agamben shifts the focus towards the negative potential of biopolitics and the end of humanity and human existence having liberty and autonomy taken away by the state. The state is not characterised by state power but by state terror. Agamben's approach reveals the abysses of bio-power. His perspectives make it possible to look through the realisation of the negative potentials of states back to (contemporary) challenges, which makes it clear that brutal state control over the human body is a permanent paradigm of human existence in the institutional setting of a state.

Achille Mbembe[20] based his research on racism and colonialism on Foucault's bio-politics and applies Agamben's perspective of negative state powers to racism and colonialism. Mbembe identified necropolitics as subjugating life to the power of death. He illustrates how Western democracies are deeply involved in necropolitics both in their own territories (racism) and globally (colonialism). He analyses 'the brutality of democracy', which creates various 'forms of violence and irregular forces'.[21] Following Agamben's discussion on Schmitt and Foucault, he states that the 'ultimate expression of sovereignty largely resides in the power and capacity to dictate who is able to live and who must die. To kill or to let live thus constitutes sovereignty's limits, its principal attributes. To be sovereign is to exert one's control over mortality and to define life as the deployment and manifestation of power. This sums up what Michel Foucault meant by biopower: that domain of life over which power has asserted its control'.[22]

Mbembe exemplifies necropolitics in the context of colonial repression and racism including the exploitation of humans and resources. He shows that 'the sovereign right to kill is not subject to any rule in the colonies. In the colonies, the sovereign might kill at any time or in any manner. Colonial warfare is not subject to legal and institutional rules'.[23] Moreover, 'racism is the driver of the necropolitical principle insofar as it stands for organized destruction, for a sacrificial economy, the functioning of which requires, on the one hand, a generalized cheapening of

[18] ibid.

[19] ibid, 166–80.

[20] A Mbembe has been linked to controversy regarding statements and activities concerning the Palestinian conflict, see eg www.dw.com/en/why-achille-mbembe-was-accused-of-anti-semitism/a-53293797.

[21] A Mbembe, *Necropolitics*, Steven Corcoran tr (Duke University Press, 2019) 16.

[22] ibid, 66. Biopower, in Foucault's work, appears to function by dividing people into those who must live and those who must die. Mbembe (n 21) 71.

[23] ibid, 78.

the price of life and, on the other, a habituation to loss'.[24] Necropower also includes a spatial dimension by 'the dynamics of territorial fragmentation'.[25]

Mbembe brings a specific international perspective to the negative side of biopolitics, which goes beyond the specific (especially Northern) nation states and the role of particular vulnerable groups within societies. The racist concept of necropolitics is not limited to nation states, but has further international effects.

The debate around bio- and necropolitics has created an important perspective to understand the economised timing of death in times of the COVID-19 pandemic. The following thoughts, however, will not build upon a Schmittian understanding of the state of emergency, but will bring the constitutional and legal framework back into consideration. Dealing with health crises in liberal democracies cannot be found in concepts beyond constitutional and legal rationalisation, but lies within the legal concept of addressing human rights and debating death and dying in a democratic society.

C. State of Emergency in the COVID-19 Pandemic?

The COVID-19 pandemic has not created a state of emergency as neither states nor state organs have come under threat. Some states, however, have faced a partial breakdown of their healthcare systems. They have faced a loss of control of the governmental bio-power, which includes an uncontrolled dying of human beings. This creates a dangerous situation for governments as societies might change their attitudes towards governments, which can then lead to social upheaval. While society can react to unreasonable governance by using reason and adopting the necessary measures themselves (eg, staying at home), it can also react with anger (eg, violent demonstrations).[26] A constitutional threat which dissolves state orders has so far not emerged.[27] The challenges have turned out to be much more a question of the effectiveness of the administrative state.

Some states declared states of emergency to accumulate power at the governmental level and to limit human rights. The limitation of human rights, however, is always a question of proportionality. Severe situations will require severe measures, which can be justified if dramatic events make them necessary. However, a

[24] ibid, 38.

[25] ibid, 80. Borders are understood as 'dead spaces of nonconnection which deny the very idea of a shared humanity'. Mbembe (n 21) 99.

[26] See KL Scheppele and D Pozen, 'Executive Overreach and Underreach in the Pandemic' in M Poiares Maduro and PW Kahn (eds), *Democracy in Times of Pandemic. Different Futures Imagined* (CUP, 2020) 38–53; M Ignatieff, 'The Reckoning: Evaluating Democratic Leadership' in M Poiares Maduro and PW Kahn (eds), *Democracy in Times of Pandemic. Different Futures Imagined* (CUP, 2020) 89–103; R Gargarella, 'Democracy and Emergency in Latin America' in M Poiares Maduro and PW Kahn (eds), *Democracy in Times of Pandemic. Different Futures Imagined* (CUP, 2020) 66–76.

[27] This, however, shall not relativise the dramatic situations in Italy, New York, Brazil and India, where hospitals were overloaded, and proper funerals for the dead were no longer possible. The organisational health crisis requires quick and decisive action.

suspension of parliamentary and judicial scrutiny can never be justified. A romantic Schmittian call for an emergency situation could not even have been justified in the serious health crisis, which would call for rational measures and not politics unbound. Thus, sovereignty cannot be defined by declaring a state of emergency, but a sovereign in a democratic sense is one who, while not declaring a state of emergency, takes the necessary actions under full parliamentary and judicial scrutiny.

From the perspective of biopolitics, the governments accumulated bio-power during the pandemic to regain their power to decide over life and death, which they had (partly) lost. Death could not be controlled by governments anymore, at least not to the extent they were used to (at least from a European perspective). The biopolitical regime followed the logic of the security state (conceptualised in the post 9/11 responses to counter terrorism[28]). In some countries, the state of emergency was even promoted as a state of war,[29] with the ongoing war a struggle for the control of death.

The security state of the pandemic can be understood as a sanitary state or hygienic state. The population was disciplined from a health perspective. While democracies were typically unprepared and disorganised in their first responses, societies themselves were qualified as undisciplined and confronted with a new regime of obedience. The statistical data of infections and deaths became the guiding concept in imposing discipline on these societies. The spatial dimension of the new regime referred to the closing down of society, roadblocks, travel limitations and restrictions in freedom of movement; borders became a revived paradigm in the pandemic.

The core paradigms of the pandemic, however, have been hospital wards, especially the intensive care units (ICUs). The potential overloading of hospitals and the threat of applying triage to decide on life (hospital care) and death became the guiding impulse behind governmental approaches towards the pandemic.

While the sanitary state focussed on the fight against the pandemic, the existence of many other diseases and health issues was ignored. Like a rabbit sitting mesmerised before the snake, governments chose to prioritise the pandemic and forgot about the short and long-term psychological and physical effects of the measures taken. While death counts related to COVID-19 have dominated, other also deadly factors and effects have been repressed, not only in the implementation of governmental measures, but also within public perception. Other needs and necessities, eg regarding education, culture or work, had to take a back seat and were downgraded in terms of societal importance by the state. The chosen

[28] See eg K Roach (ed), *The 9/11 Effect: Comparative Counter-Terrorism* (CUP, 2011).

[29] See A Jr Golia and others, 'Constitutions and Contagion – European Constitutional Systems and the COVID-19 Pandemic' (2021) 81 *ZaöRV/ HJIL* 147, 156; S Brunet, 'The Hyper-Executive State of Emergency in France', in this book; M-L Basilien-Gainche, French Response to COVID-19 Crisis: Rolling into the Deep, (*Verfassungsblog*, 18 March 2020) verfassungsblog.de/french-response-to-covid-19-crisis-rolling-into-the-deep/.

rationalisation empowered the states to swiftly regain a certain control, which has since been shaken by the occurrence of new waves of infections and variants.

The transformation towards a sanitary state occurred very rapidly. The dominant principle of liberty was exchanged for a principle of protection against the pandemic.[30] The sanitary state proved to be governmentally driven, restricting freedoms and focusing on disciplinary measures to minimise infections and reduce fatalities[31] based on scientific expertise and modelling. The development of governmental reactions started with lockdowns (including penalties for lockdown breaches), added concepts of testing (thereby controlling) societies and was followed up by vaccinations. All three elements are deeply linked to economical and technical preconditions of (European) societies in the twenty-first century.[32]

This chapter is not arguing in favour of an irrational approach towards denying the occurrence of a pandemic. On the contrary, liberal democracies are obliged to address health crises and to find solutions based on proportionate measures. The proportionality of the measure will be reviewed on the basis of the existing constitutional framework (especially from a rights perspective), and within the existing leeway of governance, the democratic process contributes significantly to the decision-making. Thus, the developments towards a sanitary state were confronted with the role of death and dying in the respective legal culture, which created a particular framework of conceptualising life and death.

III. Legal Thanatology: Rationalisations of Life and Death

A. Thanato Law: Governing Life and Death

As analysed in the previous chapter, death and dying are not merely a matter of fatalities anymore. Biopolitics is understood through the state's influence and access to the life and death of the population. In a democratic setting, biopolitics is transformed into state action by parliamentary decision-making. The legislator sets the agenda in bio-law and politics in manifold ways. The most significant and influential decision-making refers to the structural and budgetary dimension

[30] See a critical approach towards positive obligations of the state: L Lavrysen and N Mavronicola, 'Postscript Coercive Human Rights in Times of Coronavirus' in L Lavrysen and N Mavronicola (eds), *Coercive Human Rights: Positive duties to mobilise the criminal law under the ECHR* (Hart Publishing, 2020) 453–56.

[31] Regarding the different approach in Sweden, see J Reichel and J Dahlqvist, 'Swedish Constitutional Response to the Corona Crisis – The Odd One Out' in this book; see also H Wenander, 'Sweden: Non-binding Rules against the Pandemic – Formalism, Pragmatism and Some Legal Realism' (2021) 12 *European Journal of Risk Regulation* 127, 134–42.

[32] The Global South, however, struggled with these measures as the resources have not been available to the same extent; see section IV(B) of this chapter.

of the health system of the respective country. The extent of investment in the healthcare system in general and the geriatric nursing in particular reveals the role of a government's life-prolonging strategies. These measures are general and structural, and do not directly affect the lives of individuals. Their long-term effect on death and dying cannot be overestimated, since the individual possibilities deeply depend on these general decisions. Moreover, the parliamentary decision-making creates the institutional, procedural and social framework which in the end will have an impact on the life and death of individuals.

This economic dimension of the influence of death and dying in a society raises different issues, which are – most of the time – negotiated indirectly but not discussed explicitly, neither in parliament nor in public. Most importantly, life cannot be prolonged at any cost, but only to an economically reasonable extent. But where are the limits of reasonableness when it comes to the prolongation of life or the acceptance of death? The dilemma becomes even more evident when one takes a closer look. Most of the (European) states are struggling with the rising costs of their healthcare systems.[33] The reason for these increased expenses in the national healthcare systems lies in newly developed and exclusive pharmaceuticals or expensive medical equipment, which enables new forms of medical treatments.[34]

If governments would still provide the same level of healthcare as 20 years ago, the costs of the healthcare systems would decrease, since the now outdated technology has become cheaper. The claim of (European) governments is, however, to improve the drugs or treatments provided. The dilemma of too many possibilities, which cannot be provided for the whole society, also involves a significant social problem and challenges of distributive justice (within different groups of patients). The financing of healthcare systems, both by the state and by social security systems, will finally decide on the resources available, which again will directly affect life expectancy and survival probability. Moreover, the role of private financing of the healthcare system is also crucial in many countries.[35]

Although there is a general claim regarding individuals that every life shall be equally protected and prolonged, the opposite happens through general decision-making about the investment of resources in the healthcare system. Due to the enormous capabilities of medical care, the theoretical possibilities to prolong the lives of individuals are significant; the economic limitations, however, lead to a

[33] See T Popic, 'European health systems and COVID-19: Some early lessons' (LSE EUROPP, 20 March 2020) blogs.lse.ac.uk/europpblog/2020/03/20/european-health-systems-and-covid-19-some-early-lessons/; see eg also European Commission, 'The 2018 Ageing Report. Economic & Budgetary Projections for the 28 EU Member States (2016–2070)', ec.europa.eu/info/sites/default/files/economy-finance/ip079_en.pdf.

[34] This is a greatly simplified presentation of the complex reasons for the rising costs in healthcare systems. It cannot, however, be analysed in detail here.

[35] Even in countries like Sweden, the role of private healthcare is on the increase; see eg C Mason, 'Public-private health care delivery becoming the norm in Sweden' (2008) 179(2) *Canadian Medical Association Journal* 129–31.

(complex) process, which prioritises and selects different forms of medical care and their financing. In the end, certain people can live longer based on these decisions, while others will die early. Thus, legislative, governmental and administrative general decision-making in a democracy has a significant impact on the life and death of people through structural, institutional and economic choices at all times.

This decision-making process cannot only be seen as an internal balancing of resources within the healthcare system.[36] Budgetary decision-making includes the entire dimension of budgetary negotiation of the whole government. Distribution issues concern not only the distribution of money within the healthcare system, but also that between different public duties and services. The state's investment in environmental protection, roads or schools competes with funding for new hospitals or intensive care units. The argument could even be accentuated by contrasting a budgetary investment in the healthcare system at the expense of a reduced cultural budget. The opposite is also possible: the increase of the cultural budget to the detriment of the health budget. It becomes clear that not all money can be invested in the healthcare system and that any reduction of the budget will most likely affect the lifetime of human beings in an efficient healthcare system.

Obviously, there are also other factors at play than just the financial dimension (if the money is used inefficiently, an increase in the money available might not have any direct effect on the lives of the people), which become relevant in influencing the effectivity and efficiency of the healthcare system, but the conflict of objectives remains clear. As health is a crucial, but not exclusive objective of states and societies, the political limits of the optimisation of life duration and healthcare have to be accepted. In conclusion, the state has to balance the possibilities of prolonging life with other seemingly minor public objectives. The role of existing resources in each individual case depends on the previously taken general decisions. The optimisation of the healthcare system is limited by the necessity to balance the prolongation of lives with other public interests, even if they cannot be compared from an extension of life perspective. The state is therefore guiding (in a general, not individual, dimension) the lifespans of human beings and their access to healthcare.

Parliament thus decides on life and death, which cannot be avoided; the question arises to what extent the parliamentarian majority must invest in the healthcare system. Again, the possibilities of the state are more complex since different investments in the healthcare system will have different effects. The economised dimension of death creates the necessity for the state to decide on the life and death of the people in general. As will be discussed below, a

[36] Regarding the complex budgetary consideration, see eg D Elson, R Balakrishnan and J Heintz, 'Public Finance, Maximum Available Resources and Human Rights' in A Nolan, R O'Connell and C Harvey (eds), *Human Rights and Public Finance: Budgets and the Promotion of Economic and Social Rights* (Hart Publishing, 2013) 24–55.

(social) rights perspective can contribute to the rationalisation of this decision-making to a certain extent, but remains limited when it comes to a final political conclusion.

B. Thanato Judgements I: Dignity and Autonomy of Death and Dying

Over the last decades, European, constitutional and supreme courts have become more and more involved in deciding about buying death and dying. In a micro-perspective, courts have developed case law with regard to abortion,[37] assisted suicide[38] or weighing lives in terrorist attacks.[39] The courts have decided on the constitutional basis of human and fundamental rights. This rights-based approach (human dignity, right to life, right to a private and family life, general right of privacy, right to equal treatment) has led to a perspective of self-determination and autonomy of individuals to decide for themselves on death and dying;[40] moreover, the balancing of different lives is partly decided (abortion) and partly understood as undecidable (downing of aircrafts). The courts have had to decide in individual cases and in many cases[41] had to consider the specific circumstances of the individuals.

In a rights-optimising way, the lives of the individuals concerned have gained increased protection and the autonomy of the individual to decide about death and dying has been strengthened. Based on this concept of human dignity and autonomy, living and dying should be laid in the hands of the humans concerned.

In a prominent ruling in 2020, the German Constitutional Court decided on the right to a self-determined death, which the Court established on the basis of the general right of personality as an expression of personal autonomy.[42] The judges argued that 'the right to a self-determined death includes the freedom to take one's own life. Where an individual decides to end their own life, having reached this decision based on how they personally define quality of life and a meaningful

[37] See, regarding recent developments, H Guimarães de Oliveira, 'My Body, the Majority's Choice? A Comparative Overview of Abortion Laws in Ireland and Argentina' (*Verfassungsblog*, 3 September 2018) verfassungsblog.de/my-body-the-majoritys-choice-a-comparative-overview-of-abortion-laws-in-ireland-and-argentina/; C Lops, 'What to expect when you're not expecting – Abortion backlash in the US and constitutional standards' (*Verfassungsblog*, 18 May 2019) verfassungsblog.de/what-to-expect-when-youre-not-expecting-abortion-backlash-in-the-us-and-constitutional-standards/; E Łętowska, 'A Tragic Constitutional Court Judgment on Abortion' (*Verfassungsblog*, 12 November 2020) verfassungsblog.de/a-tragic-constitutional-court-judgment-on-abortion/.

[38] See below.

[39] See below.

[40] See eg German Constitutional Court (BVerfG), 26.02.2020, 2 BvR 2347/15; 2 BvR 651/16; 2 BvR 1261/16; Austrian Constitutional Court (VfGH), 11.12.2020, G 139/2019.

[41] In other cases (eg downing of aircrafts case of the German Constitutional Court) courts dealt with generally applicable statutory law and reviewed this act of parliament without a concrete individual complainant.

[42] German Constitutional Court (BVerfG), 26.02.2020, 2 BvR 2347/15; 2 BvR 651/16; 2 BvR 1261/16.

existence, their decision must, in principle, be respected by state and society as an act of personal autonomy and self-determination.'[43] The Court thereby clarified that the individual decision about life and death shall be in the hands of the individual herself.

This perspective on human dignity and autonomy can be supplemented by the example regarding the downing of aircrafts, in which the Court had to decide on the governmental killing of innocent people.[44] The German constitutional court decided that a statutory provision, which enables the downing of civil aircrafts in cases of terrorism, is unconstitutional:[45] 'Even if in the area of police power, insecurities concerning forecasts often cannot be completely avoided, it is absolutely inconceivable under the applicability of Article 1.1 of the Basic Law to intentionally kill persons such as the crew and the passengers of a hijacked plane, who are in a situation that is hopeless for them, on the basis of a statutory authorisation which even accepts such imponderability if necessary. It need not be decided here how a shooting down that is performed all the same, and an order relating to it, would have to be assessed under criminal law [...]. What is solely decisive for the constitutional appraisal is that the legislature may not, by establishing a statutory authorisation for intervention, give authority to perform operations of the nature regulated in § 14.3 of the Aviation Security Act vis-à-vis people who are not participants in the crime and may not in this manner qualify such operations as legal and thus permit them. As missions of the armed forces of a non-warlike nature, they are incompatible with the right to life and the obligation of the state to respect and protect human dignity.'[46]

The German constitutional court refused to accept the weighing of lives in counterterrorism measures under uncertain circumstances and stressed the role of human dignity to protect innocent individuals, even if the risk of greater harm to an even bigger group of people could be avoided.[47] In a constitutional perspective, the statutory authorisation of the active killing of innocent individuals was rejected.

The examples presented illustrate a strong commitment to human dignity and autonomy of individuals, which shall prohibit statutory law and administrative action to risk the life of individuals. The courts claim the necessity of the state to intervene to protect life, and to abstain from an intervention which actively leads to the death of individuals, as long as dying is not part of the individual's autonomy, freedom and self-determination. This foundation of liberal societies can, however, not provide a solution regarding the use and distribution of resources for healthcare.

[43] ibid.

[44] See German Constitutional Court (BVerfG), 15.02.2006, 1 BvR 357/05; O Lepsius, 'Human Dignity and the Downing of Aircraft: The German Federal Constitutional Court Strikes Down a Prominent Anti-terrorism Provision in the New Air-transport Security Act' (2006) 7 *German Law Journal* 761–76.

[45] See German Constitutional Court (BVerfG), 15.02.2006, 1 BvR 357/05.

[46] ibid.

[47] ibid.

C. Thanato Judgements II: Enabling Life, Avoiding Death

i. State's Obligations and Equality Rights

While liberal rights empower the individual to make autonomous decisions, they do not enable the balancing of lives when human dignity prohibits further argumentation. While European states have been hesitant to implement social rights in their constitutions, the Sozialstaat principle[48] has been introduced in many constitutions and the courts have been ready to activate it.[49] Moreover, positive obligations of the state have been used to introduce social rights guarantees. These guarantees include certain minimum requirements to protect life (eg, providing criminal prosecution),[50] prohibit inhumane treatment and enable private life (eg, right to health).[51]

An example can be used to illustrate how rights-based judgements increased the state's responsibility to guarantee a dignified life and limit the possibilities of death and dying. In the case *Paposhvili v Belgium*, the Grand Chamber of the ECtHR unanimously decided that the applicant, an asylum seeker suffering from leukaemia, pulmonary tuberculosis and hepatitis C, could not be legally deported to Georgia in accordance with Article 3 ECHR.[52] The Court stated that in very exceptional cases Article 3 ECHR also protects aliens suffering from an illness against removal on humanitarian grounds: '[…] the applicant had been in greater need of protection owing to his particular vulnerability linked to his state of health, the stakes in terms of his life and physical well-being, his emotional and financial dependency and the existence of his family ties in Belgium. The Belgian State's responsibility under Article 3 of the Convention stemmed from the fact that it was proceeding with the applicant's removal without taking these factors into account, thereby demonstrating a lack of respect for his dignity and placing him at serious risk, in the event of his return to Georgia, of a severe and rapid deterioration in his state of health leading to his swift and certain death'.[53] Although the Georgian government intervened and argued that an extensive programme of universal medical cover had been implemented, the ECtHR introduced a prohibition of deportation due to the health situation of aliens.[54]

[48] See eg W Heun, *The Constitution of Germany: A Contextual Analysis* (Hart Publishing, 2010) 44–45; JA King, 'Social Rights, Constitutionalism and the German Social State Principle' (2014) E-Pública: Revista Electronica de Direito, available at discovery.ucl.ac.uk/id/eprint/1472218/1/J%20King,%20Social%20Rights.pdf.

[49] C O'Cinneide, 'Austerity and the faded dream of a "social Europe"' in A Nolan (ed), *Economic and Social Rights after the Global Financial Crisis* (CUP, 2014) 169, 174–77.

[50] L Lavrysen, 'Positive Obligations and the Criminal Law: A Bird's-Eye View on the Case Law of the European Court of Human Rights', in Lavrysen and Mavronicola (n 30) 62–98.

[51] M-A Kolliniati, *Human Rights and Positive Obligations to Healthcare: Reading the European Convention on Human Rights through Joseph Raz's Theory of Rights* (Nomos, 2019) 167–227.

[52] ECtHR 13 December 2016, *Paposhvili v Belgium*, Application no. 41738/10; see also V Stoyanova, 'How Exceptional Must "Very Exceptional" Be? Non-Refoulement, Socio-Economic Deprivation, and Paposhvili v Belgium' (2017) 29 *International Journal of Refugee Law* 580–616.

[53] ibid, para 148.

[54] ibid.

Going a step further, the right to equal treatment can be understood as a foundation to rationalise distribution issues. The obligation to justify decisions, to create the non-discriminatory availability of and access to medical support or to develop fair distribution of medicine can be derived from the right to equality.[55] It can therefore serve as a legal basis to improve healthcare in countries. It helps to create fairness within a healthcare system, but cannot, however, resolve questions of balancing different budgetary preferences of the parliament (government).

ii. Right to Health in India

State obligations stemming from liberal rights have led to the establishment of social rights case law, which has contributed to the balancing of different state objectives. In other countries, constitutional law already explicitly provides social rights. The case law of India, South Africa and Colombia can be consulted regarding the right to health.

Article 47 of the Indian Constitution contains an obligation of the state to improve public health.[56] Starting with the *Mullin* Case in the 1980s, the Indian Supreme Court derived the right to health from the right to life.[57] The Supreme Court stated the obligation to access pharmaceuticals and treatment which linked Article 47 and the right to life.[58] In the 1990s, the Supreme Court conceded that 'the obligation of the state to provide medical aid to preserve human life could not be disregarded because of financial constraints of the state'.[59] The Indian courts enabled the reduction of costs for HIV medicine (at least to a certain number of people). The judgment has only had a limited effect on the individuals concerned as quantity and access have been severely restricted. The courts enabled reimbursement of medical expenses to employees.[60] It is important to know that '[c]ommunicable diseases, maternal, perinatal, and nutritional disorders are responsible for 38 percent of deaths in India'.[61]

'In Ram Lubhaya Bagga, the Supreme Court looked to balance financial constraints of the state with its obligation to improve public health by facilitating access to quality health care facilities, goods, and services in a private hospital.'[62] The Court, however, recognised that the right to health was subject to the state's

[55] A Grover, M Misra and L Rangarajan, 'Right to Health: Addressing Inequities through Litigation' in CM Flood and A Gross (eds), *The Right to Health at the Public /Private Divide* (CUP, 2014) 445.

[56] ibid, 431.

[57] ibid, 432; *Francis Coralie Mullin v The Administrator*, Union Territory of Delhi, A.I.R. 1981 S.C. 746 (India).

[58] A Grover, M Misra and L Rangarajan, 'Right to Health: Addressing Inequities through Litigation' in Flood and Gross (n 55) 435.

[59] ibid, 437; see *Paschim Banga Khet Mazdoor Samiti v State of West Bengal* (1996) 4 S.C.C. 37 (India).

[60] PB Mehta and S Shankar, 'Courts and Socioeconomic Rights in India' in V Gauri and DM Brinks (eds), *Courting Social Justice: Judicial Enforcement of Social and Economic Rights in the Developing World* (CUP, 2008) 146, 157.

[61] A Grover, M Misra and L Rangarajan in Flood and Gross (n 55) 424.

[62] ibid, 440; *State of Punjab v Ram Lubhaya Bagga* (1998) 1 S.C.R 1120 (India).

'economic capacity and development. Distinguishing this case from Mohinder Singh Chawla, the Court held that as the policy had been reformulated, the respondent employee could not claim benefits under the old policy'.[63] The Court thereby limited 'the right to access of quality treatment based on the state`s alleged financial constraint'.[64] The budgetary limitations of the rationalising effects of social rights became evident. A similar situation could be observed in South African case law.

iii. Social Rights in South Africa

In South Africa in 1998, 40 per cent of the population were under the poverty threshold and 40 per cent were unemployed. Poverty and unemployment levels have become worse since then.[65] 80 per cent of the population were still dependent on the public healthcare sector in 2008.[66] The share of the total government budget spent on the healthcare sector decreased from 11.5 per cent to 8.75 per cent from 2000 to 2010. Life expectancy fell to 43 years and infant mortality increased,[67] with HIV proving to be the main cause for these devastating developments.[68]

Section 27 of the South African Constitution explicitly provides for a right to health, which includes that '[e]veryone has the right to have access to health care services' and the obligation that the 'state must take reasonable legislative and other measures, within its available resources, to achieve the progressive realisation of each of these rights'. In the famous *Grootboom* case, the South African Constitutional Court recognised with regard to the right to access adequate housing (section 26) 'that the state could not be required to do more than available resources permit, and that while resources would determine the content and pace of realization, the government nonetheless should give adequate budgetary support to social rights, and plan and monitor efforts to meet all needs. The Court found that national housing policy fell short of the government's constitutional duties, and declared that section 26 required a comprehensive program to realize the right to access to adequate housing'.[69] In the TAC (Treatment Action Campaign) Case, the Court found that 'state policy to be unreasonable and held that excluding the drug in question in public health care facilities pending study results unreasonably denied a potentially life-saving drug to children born to mostly indigent mothers

[63] A Grover, M Misra and L Rangarajan, 'Right to Health: Addressing Inequities through Litigation' in Flood and Gross (n 55) 441; *State of Punjab v Mohinder Singh Chawla* (1997) 2 S.C.C 83 (1996) (India).

[64] A Grover, M Misra and L Rangarajan, 'Right to Health: Addressing Inequities through Litigation' in Flood and Gross (n 55) 441.

[65] L Forman and JA Singh, 'The Role of Rights and Litigation in Assuring More Equitable Access to Health Care in South Africa' in Flood and Gross (n 55) 291.

[66] ibid 293.

[67] ibid, 300.

[68] ibid, 301.

[69] ibid, 308.

dependent on the state for their health care. The Court focused on the grave suffering and limited survival prospects of these children, and stressed that the case was concerned with newborn babies whose lives might be saved by the administration of simple and cheap intervention, the safety and efficacy of which had been established, and which the government itself was providing in pilot sites in every province'.[70] While the Court in the beginning was willing to extend social rights, the Court's approach in the *Mazibuko* case in 2009, however, raised concerns about whether it was willing to enforce them.[71] The financial dimension of state expenses seemed to become relevant; moreover, the Court limited the extent of state obligations, which seemed to cease at a certain level without the possibility for the individual to gain the relevant resources.

In contrast to these developments in South Africa, the Colombian Constitutional Court went one step further and started to enforce the right to health in a way which significantly affected the state's budget and governmental leeway in deciding about resources.

iv. Colombian Conflicts on the Right to Health

In Colombia, where the right to health was established by the Constitutional Court interpreting the right to life,[72] the Court extended and enforced the right to health to a significant extent. In the Case SU-480/97,[73] the Court 'ruled that a private insurance company had to provide "excluded" antiretroviral medication to a plaintiff living with HIV/AIDS, because his life was at stake'.[74] In its case T-760/2008, the Colombian Constitutional Court outlined the necessary strategy of the legislation and government to resolve structural problems regarding the right to health in Colombia. These reforms refer to the 'baskets of health services, the unification of the subsidized and contributory regimes, and the improvement of the health system's financial arrangements and universal coverage of the social security system'.[75] Consequences have been a unified basket of health services as well as a price-regulation of pharmaceuticals.

This case law led to an escalation of a conflict regarding the budgetary consequences of the right to health between the President and the Constitutional Court. The President declared an 'economic state of emergency' and enacted decrees opposing the Court's case law. The Constitutional Court, however, declared these decrees to be unconstitutional.[76] 'In many cases, the Constitutional Court has

[70] ibid, 309.
[71] ibid, 316.
[72] C Prachniak-Rincón and J Villar de Onís, 'HIV and the Right to Health in Colombia' (2016) *Health and Human Rights Journal*, www.hhrjournal.org/2016/10/hiv-and-the-right-to-health-in-colombia/.
[73] Colombian Constitutional Court, 25 September 1997, SU-480/97.
[74] E Lamprea, 'Colombia's Right-to-Health Litigation in a Context of Health Care Reform' in Flood and Gross (n 55) 131, 143.
[75] ibid, 146.
[76] ibid, 148.

awarded costly pharmaceuticals and procedures despite the fact that there is not enough medical or scientific evidence to conclude that they are the most effective medical treatments for the plaintiffs.'[77] Expenditure on pharmaceuticals increased to 3.15 per cent of GDP in 2009;[78] 20 high-end pharmaceuticals produced by international corporations were responsible for 45 per cent of the overall expenditure. The solution was found in the price regulation of pharmaceuticals.

The Colombian example illustrates the possibilities to enforce the right to health, but also the limits of the possibilities for rationalising the decision-making process of state governments by social rights.

v. The Rationalising Effect of Social Rights and its (Budgetary) Limits

While exemplifying the case law on the right to health, it is important to note that many social rights have an effect on life and death, including rights satisfying basic needs like the right to housing, right to food or the right to water. The impact on life expectancy of an effective right to education can also not be overestimated.

Social rights demand that the state deals with certain issues and develops state programs. They support the rationalisation of social support, eg prioritising the poorest of the poor; social rights strengthen the establishment of state welfare institutions and economic obligations to reimburse the costs of pharmaceuticals. They also help to support certain healthcare measures. They are not limited to matters concerning the state's budget, but primarily influence the compliance of the government with legislative obligations and are able to change the role and possibilities of private actors (eg, pharmaceutical companies).

Social rights first of all provide a bottom line, a minimum level which has to be guaranteed by the state. This minimum level contributes to the rationalisation of basic public services and can develop certain substantial guarantees. The function of social rights is still not to decide upon the entire state budget (instead of the parliament or the government); on the contrary, social rights present a claim to dedicate a certain amount of the budget to certain state objectives. This does not resolve the conflict between different state objectives.

The financial crisis of 2008 followed by austerity programmes, eg in Southern Europe, showed the limits of social rights approaches, which were limited by economic restraints at the expense of the healthcare system.[79] Even without state cuts in the healthcare system, people had to reduce their standard of living, which necessarily affected their health, while the recession also had a negative impact on mental health.[80] Cost-cutting by the state had even greater effects. Spain's

[77] ibid, 151.
[78] ibid, 149.
[79] NJ Lusiani, 'Rationalising the right to health: is Spain's austere response to the economic crisis impermissible under international human rights law?' in Nolan (n 49) 202–33.
[80] ibid, 207.

cutbacks due to an austerity programme in 2012 profoundly affected the healthcare system.[81] The Spanish government excluded non-citizens, such as irregular immigrants, from access to the Spanish healthcare system; 0.5 m people lost access to healthcare.[82] People earning less than €18,000 had to pay 40 per cent of the pharmaceutical costs on their own.[83] The cuts in state expenses had an effect on people's life expectancy, since access to healthcare and pharmaceuticals was limited (especially excluding poor and helpless people in a discriminatory way).[84] People's lives counted for little, when pure economic savings were considered more important. Strong social rights case law could prevent the worst in such situations.[85]

IV. No Bailout – The Role of Death in the COVID-19 Pandemic in Liberal Democracies

A. Different Approaches towards Death in European Democracies

The COVID-19 pandemic has shown that European countries, despite investing billions, cannot resolve this health crisis only financially. Lockdowns combined with enormous state aid, investments in pharmaceutical industries and financial support for businesses are not sufficient to deal with all the challenges posed by pandemics. The COVID-19 pandemic demonstrates that many difficult trade-offs between infections and fatalities on the one side and freedoms and liberties on the other side are necessary. The closure of societies might be a short-term strategy to prevent an explosion in infection rates, but it cannot serve as an overall solution. Parliaments and governments decide on death rates by choosing their responses to the pandemic. Although certain measures did prove to be highly successful (when compared to the possibilities some decades or even centuries ago), the attempts to control a pandemic revealed their limits. Different approaches (eg, Sweden, Germany, Hungary or Italy) illustrate that, during a pandemic, decisions are made that will have effects on life and death of the people.

Avoiding death is not the only objective of a democratic society and it has to be integrated into more comprehensive governmental strategies. Although democracies promise to support the prolongation of citizens' lives, they also have to accept increased fatalities in order to enable other liberties during a pandemic

[81] ibid, 208–09.
[82] ibid, 214, 217.
[83] ibid, 215.
[84] ibid.
[85] See eg the developments in Portugal: M Canotilho, T Violante and R Lanceiro, 'Austerity measures under judicial scrutiny: the Portuguese constitutional case-law' (2015) 11 *European Constitutional Law Review* 155–83.

(eg, education, business, religion, culture or freedom of movement). Interestingly, different European societies enabled different liberties (eg, culture in Spain,[86] religion in Austria,[87] education in Sweden[88]). These prioritisations affected death rates. The question arises to what extent this balancing of objectives has been adequately discussed in public during the COVID-19 pandemic.

Decisions about life and death have to be accepted in democratic societies, but should not be concealed. Negotiating death rates does not create an inhumane society, but simply implies an acceptance of death as a part of life. Concealing these decisions does not mean that they are not made. European societies in the twenty-first century have to learn to accept that the (technological, medial, etc) opportunities which have arisen in the last centuries and decades, also come with the responsibilities to make decisions which will have corresponding consequences.

B. International Perspectives on the COVID-19 Pandemic

While the protection of life and health seem to be the domestic motivation of European governments, the international ambition of European governments to save lives and fight pandemics was already limited before the COVID-19 crisis started. The underfunding of the WHO can be seen just as a symbol.[89] While statistical data for COVID-19 fatalities is observed and presented on a daily basis (including about 1.82 m deaths in 2020),[90] statistics concerning other diseases which are not significantly relevant in Europe are not even known (eg, tuberculosis, which caused about 1.4 m deaths globally in 2019,[91] is responsible for around 100–150 deaths in Germany every year).[92] Although an investment of not even a thousandth of the money spent in COVID-19 times would have helped to prevent millions of deaths from other diseases, this funding was not provided by European governments. While the (post-)colonial bias still exists, the motivation to fight the COVID-19 pandemic is primarily owed to their own people (focussing on domestic democratic considerations, while the focus on human dignity seems of secondary importance and stops at the domestic borders).

But also within the European borders, we turn from thanato- to necro-law during a pandemic by excluding irregular migrants and other people without a

[86] See www.ft.com/content/9e6795d5-438c-410b-ae6d-259b77d639db.

[87] See K Lachmayer, 'Muddling through Mutation Times or the Return of Federalism in Austria: From Covid-19 Response to the Vaccination Campaign, (*VerfBlog*, 8. May 2021) verfassungsblog.de/muddling-through-mutation-times-or-the-return-of-federalism-in-austria/.

[88] See eacea.ec.europa.eu/national-policies/eurydice/content/sweden-keeps-schools-open-during-covid-19-pandemic-results-situation_en.

[89] See eg www.nature.com/articles/d41586-020-01121-1.

[90] See ourworldindata.org/covid-deaths.

[91] See www.who.int/news-room/fact-sheets/detail/tuberculosis.

[92] See www.rki.de/EN/Content/infections/epidemiology/inf_dis_Germany/TB/summary_2018.html; see also L Fiebig and others, 'Tuberculosis in Germany: a declining trend coming to an end?' (2016) 47 *The European Respiratory Journal* 667–70.

valid permit from access to the healthcare system. When intensive care units in hospitals are only open to regular residents and vaccines are only available for such people, the legal system is already choosing between life and death and creates necro-law, in which the irregular migrant is doomed to die if her physical condition is not good enough.[93]

In the COVID-19 crisis, the limited global solidarity was even intensified by a 'nation-first' concept regarding vaccines. Although EU member states created a common approach towards vaccination (one exception is Hungary),[94] the global dimension was represented in a very limited way in the approaches of European governments. While biopolitical decision-making in the EU was concealed, the international effects of European necro-politics were ignored still further. The usual double standards have been applied. While resources of the global south are used by the global north, the vaccine deals are still based on IP law.[95] The economised dimension of the pandemic enabled many[96] European states to use enormous economic resources to fight against the pandemic with huge investments, while other states were left to their own devices. Death and dying in the north therefore differ from in the south.[97]

V. Conclusion

Discussions about death in democratic societies do not mean unleashing politics in an inhumane way, so that each group tries to create benefits for themselves. Creating medical possibilities (based on an economised use of new technologies) requires the assumption of responsibility. Democratic debates about death and dying start with the acceptance of death as a negotiable objective. Discussions about death presuppose discussions about its complex implications. In the COVID-19 pandemic, it means not only looking at COVID-19 fatalities, but at all the other people affected by deadly dangers (such as suicides, homelessness and other diseases) as well.

[93] See M Mallet-Garcia and N Delvino, *Migrants with irregular status during the COVID-19 pandemic: Lessons for local authorities in Europe*, Working Paper 2020, available at www.compas.ox.ac.uk/wp-content/uploads/CMISE-Impact-of-COVID-on-access-to-services-for-irregular-migrants.pdf; Open Society Foundation (2020), 'COVID-19 and Undocumented Workers', available at www.opensocietyfoundations.org/explainers/covid-19-and-undocumented-workers.

[94] See eg www.reuters.com/article/us-health-coronavirus-hungary-russia-idUSKBN29R0WB, www.nytimes.com/2021/03/11/world/hungary-sinopharm-covid.html.

[95] But see the discussion by US president Biden on the suspension of patents of COVID-19 vaccines; see eg www.nytimes.com/2021/05/05/us/politics/biden-covid-vaccine-patents.html.

[96] The different economic and budgetary preconditions of the different European states shall not be ignored.

[97] The Asian developments in the pandemics demonstrate that other experiences with pandemics as well as cultural approaches can also lead to efficient measures. See VV Ramraj and M Little, 'A Short History and Thematic Overview' in VV Ramraj (ed), *Covid-19 in Asia. Law and policy contexts* (OUP, 2021) 3, 14–16.

A public debate on death has to include science and scientific results in the decision-making process, but finally requires a political decision by democratic, accountable institutions.[98] Governments should still act on the basis of acts of legislation which do not decide on individual fatalities, but rather according to general (financial and institutional) preconditions. The limits of political decision-making arise from human rights, especially the concept of the right to health and the protection of the right to life. Learning from the global south will be an indispensable pre-condition to advancement in a European discourse on the rationalisation of these processes. Within these limits, biopolitics in democracies will be revealed, but should uphold the accountability of the decision-makers.

The COVID-19 pandemic illustrates the difference between rationalised and irrational approaches. The economic costs, limitations of freedoms and death rates in countries like Brazil have been even higher.[99] The different approaches of European countries also reveal that there is not only one possible solution to a pandemic. This, however, does not take away the global responsibility of European governments in the post-colonial settings which we still face.

This chapter argues that it is necessary to understand death and dying as a core issue of public debate in democracies, which are not only negotiated by (supreme/constitutional) courts regarding individual rights and liberties, but also as part of a societal *conditio humana*, which is deeply rooted in the particular culture (including the understanding of death, the way of living and resulting legal framework) of death and dying. In that regard, the balancing of liberty and death requires a public debate to reinsure an open society in a liberal democracy.

[98] Death and dying in a democracy are not only about rights and politics, but also about care and compassion; see PW Kahn, 'Democracy and the Obligations to Care: A Demos Worthy of Sacrifice' in M Poiares Maduro and PW Kahn (eds), *Democracy in Times of Pandemic: Different Futures Imagined* (CUP, 2020) 196–207.

[99] See with regard to the executive underreach, KL Scheppele and D Pozen, 'Executive Overreach and Underreach in the Pandemic' in Poiares Maduro and Kahn (n 98) 38, 43–47.

PART II

The Practice – Democracies and the Pandemic

4

Virus Governance in the United Kingdom

ROBERT THOMAS

The virus has posed many social and economic challenges: the immediate risks to health; high rates of unemployment; businesses losing jobs and closing down; and healthcare being subject to intense pressure. As an essay on contemporary constitutional history, this chapter considers the constitutional challenges of pandemocracy in the United Kingdom (UK), and, in particular, what I term 'virus governance', that is, the concentration of power in the executive to respond to the virus. I discuss and consider the constitutional problems raised by virus governance, in particular, executive law-making, limited parliamentary scrutiny, and the impact of the virus on the UK's territorial constitution. Overall, I argue that the virus has further exposed the UK's pre-existing multiple constitutional fault-lines. The UK's ongoing slow-burn constitutional crisis is being accelerated and there is a heightened need to address its deep-seated underlying structural causes.

I. The Constitutional and Political Background

To start off, we have to recognise the particular constitutional setting of the UK's famously uncodified constitution. A constitution that has developed and evolved incrementally over centuries is very different from one that has been deliberately constituted and codified at a particular point of time. Without a formal overarching architecture, the UK Constitution is simply what happens.[1] It is principally a set of political understandings and constitutional conventions between the different governing institutions.[2] To a large extent, these understandings are relatively stable, but are often a source of tension and contention. Constitutional change rarely results from first principles or pure constitutional logic, but is the product of governmental self-interest and political struggle.

[1] JAG Griffith, 'The Political Constitution' (1979) 42 *MLR* 1.
[2] For a detailed account, see M Elliott and R Thomas, *Public Law*, 4th edn (OUP, 2020).

In the overall constitutional framework, power and authority rests principally with UK central government. The government must, of course, be able to defend its policies and their administration in Parliament. Nonetheless, it is always the government that has the right of initiative, for instance, to raise taxes and make legislation. As regards the UK's evolving territorial governance, the unitary and London-centric nature of central government has accommodated a more quasi-federal structure through devolved governments and legislatures in Scotland, Wales, and Northern Ireland. However, centralising tendencies are difficult to suppress; tensions arise when sites of power beyond London disagree with the UK central state. England is one of the most centralised country in Europe.

When viewed from the outside, the formal constitutional veneer of UK governance may seem serene and robust. This unstructured constitution (sort of) works, albeit often inadequately, but the sense of constitutional decline and dissatisfaction has been gaining pace for decades.[3] There was a period of constitutional modernisation during the New Labour Blair years of the late 1990s to the mid-2000s (the Human Rights Act 1998; devolution; and judicial reform).[4] But constitutional dissatisfaction has grown. The immediate post-war generation of constitutional scholars lavished praise on the Constitution; none would do so today. There are deep sources of political tension and fragmentation, the decay of the state, social inequality, distrust of politicians, and dissatisfaction with party politics and the UK's governing arrangements. This is all evidenced by a long accumulation of difficult multi-dimensional problems: the great financial crisis; austerity; the divisive Brexit referendum 2016 and its fraught aftermath; and an increasingly unstable devolution settlement including increased support for Scottish independence. For good reason, the UK has increasingly been seen as a country in a particularly British type of turmoil.[5]

The virus must also be situated within the immediate and unique political context of the Brexiting UK. In July 2019, Boris Johnson became Prime Minister following Theresa May's resignation. May had faced insuperable difficulties in managing the political differences within the Conservative party over Brexit. Following the failed attempt to prorogue Parliament – held to be unconstitutional by the Supreme Court – Johnson then won the December 2019 general election on the basis that he would get Brexit done.[6] Given that the UK governments govern through Parliament, the critical issue is size of their majorities in the House of

[3] N Johnson, *The Search of the Constitution* (Pergamon Press, 1977); A King, *The British Constitution* (OUP, 2007). This is, of course, a wider phenomenon. See TG Daly, 'Democratic Decay: Conceptualising an Emerging Research Field' (2019) 11 *Hague Journal on the Rule of Law* 9.

[4] M Gordon and A Tucker (eds), *The New Labour Constitution: Twenty Years on* (Hart Publishing, 2021).

[5] For wide-ranging social and political reflections, see D Marquand, *Mammon's Kingdom: An Essay on Britain, Now* (Penguin, 2014); M Moran, *The End of British Politics?* (Palgrave Macmillan, 2017); W Davies, *This is Not Normal: The Collapse of Liberal Britain* (Verso, 2020); M Sobolewska and R Ford, *Brexitland: Identity, Diversity and the Reshaping of British Politics* (CUP, 2020).

[6] *R (Miller) v Prime Minister; Cherry v Advocate General for Scotland* [2019] UKSC 41.

Commons. Johnson achieved a Commons majority of 80 Members of Parliament (MPs), the largest Conservative majority since 1987. He had unexpectedly won over many northern 'red wall' areas: traditional Labour constituencies in the north of England – pro-Brexit and socially conservative – that were attracted by promises of improved funding, 'levelling-up', and getting Brexit done.[7] At the end of January 2020, the UK formally exited the EU and entered the transition period.

II. The Virus Arrives

By March 2020, the situation had changed unexpectedly beyond recognition. The virus had struck. The UK had entered lockdown. Furlough and job retention and support schemes had been introduced. In April 2020, Boris Johnson was himself hospitalised with the virus, but later recovered.[8] The early assumption that the virus would disappear in the summer or, at the latest, by the end of the year seemed hopeful and itself soon faded away. Lockdown ended in late June, although various local restrictions were put in place. By November 2020, with the second wave in full flow, a second national lockdown was introduced. In January 2021, there was a third lockdown.

Overall, the Government had been ill-prepared and ill-equipped for the scale of the challenge posed by the virus.[9] Before the first lockdown, large sporting events had been allowed to proceed despite the evident transmission risks. The UK was late in imposing a lockdown compared to other European countries. Even after the lockdown was announced, 95,000 people had been allowed entered the country without additional restrictions.[10] The Government's (now-former) senior adviser, Dominic Cummings, broke lockdown rules, but kept his job and this weakened public confidence.[11] Hospitals became overwhelmed. The National Health Service (NHS) transferred many elderly people with COVID-19 out of hospital back to care homes, despite clear warnings that this would increase transmission.[12]

There were also many policy 'U-turns', for instance, on people working from home, evictions, free school meals, masks in schools, and the NHS contact tracing app.[13] At the traditional end of summer exam results, the Government made

[7] 'Levelling up' refers to raising the standard of living in less affluent areas when compared with the more prosperous London and the south east of England.

[8] 'Coronavirus: Boris Johnson out of intensive care but remains in hospital' *BBC News* (9 April 2020).

[9] 'Covid-19: did the UK government prepare for the wrong kind of pandemic?' *The Guardian* (21 May 2020).

[10] '95,000 have entered UK from abroad during coronavirus lockdown' *The Guardian* (13 May 2020).

[11] 'Dossier alleges Cummings may have perverted course of justice in account of lockdown trip' *The Guardian* (30 October 2020).

[12] 'More than half of England's coronavirus-related deaths will be people from care homes' *The Guardian* (7 June 2020).

[13] 'Boris Johnson's coronavirus U-turns: A timeline of government indecision during the pandemic' *The Independent* (26 August 2020).

a major mess of A-level results.[14] Given social distancing, 18 year old students had not taken exams; their predicted grades were used instead, but the algorithm used to moderate results to avoid grade-inflation meant that many students had been significantly down-graded, thereby jeopardising their futures.[15] The Prime Minister had – absurdly – blamed the fiasco on the 'mutant algorithm', but was in turn accused of shamefully trying to dodge blame for the exam chaos.[16] It had indeed been the relevant minister that had insisted upon using the algorithm to avoid grade-inflation, but he then blamed everyone else for the resulting, and unnecessary, fiasco.

In terms of actually dealing with the virus, there were repeated problems and delays in the operation of the Government's centralised NHS Test and Trace service.[17] Given the preceding decade of austerity, public services entered the pandemic with low levels of resilience. The virus further disadvantaged people who were already 'left behind'.[18]

Overall, the UK's handling of the first year of the virus had been poor. Excess deaths have been amongst the highest in terms of international comparisons. Government blunders are nothing new.[19] A global pandemic is hardly the ideal environment in which to make the best decisions. Nonetheless, there had been too many mistakes. Even at an early stage, it had become clear that a public inquiry would be needed to provide accountability and lesson learning after the event.[20]

As regards the functioning of Parliament, at an early stage it had moved from in-person voting by MPs to remote voting. In June 2020, a return to in-person voting through a system by which MPs were forced to stand in a line more than a kilometre long to queue to vote – satirically dubbed the 'Rees-Mogg Conga' – was declared a farce even by loyal Conservative MPs.[21] Parliament moved to operating on a hybrid basis with a mixture of (socially distanced) in-person and virtual participation.[22] This enabled Parliament to continue its work. However, like all legislatures, Parliament is highly dependent upon informal interactions between its members.[23] With the virus, this has largely been lost and has arguably

[14] A-Levels in England and Wales and Scottish Highers are mostly taken by 18 year olds and the results used to allocate university places.

[15] House of Commons Education Committee, *Getting the Grades They've Earned – Covid-19: the Cancellation of Exams and 'Calculated' Grades* HC 617 (2019–21).

[16] 'Boris Johnson blames exams chaos on "mutant algorithm"' *The Independent* (26 August 2020).

[17] 'Coronavirus: Inside test-and-trace – how the "world beater" went wrong' *BBC News* (20 November 2020).

[18] House of Lords Public Services Committee, *A Critical Juncture for Public Services: Lessons From COVID-19* HL 167 (2019–21).

[19] See generally A King and I Crewe, *The Blunders of Our Governments* (Oneworld, 2013).

[20] House of Commons Public Administration and Constitutional Affairs Committee, *A Public Inquiry into the Government's Response to the Covid-19 Pandemic* HC 541 (2019–21).

[21] 'MPs join 90-minute-long queue to vote to end virtual voting' *The Guardian* (2 June 2020). The idiosyncratic Jacob Rees-Mogg MP, Leader of the House of Commons, has sometimes been described by other MPs as 'the Member of Parliament for the seventeenth century'.

[22] Institute for Government, *The UK Parliament and Coronavirus*, www.instituteforgovernment.org.uk/explainers/uk-parliament-coronavirus.

[23] P Norton, 'Power behind the Scenes: The Importance of Informal Space in Legislatures' (2019) 72 *Parliamentary Affairs* 245.

weakened the ability of Parliament to scrutinise government.[24] There have also been problems with some MPs being prevented from contributing remotely to parliamentary debates thereby creating an unwelcome 'hierarchy of MPs' and suppressing the voice of those unable to attend in person, although the matter is under review.[25]

III. The Johnson Government's Constitutional Record

Turning to the Government's wider constitutional record, during the same period, the Johnson Government had already quickly established a distinctly bad reputation for undermining constitutional norms and conventions. Such conventions are full of gaps and anomalies.[26] The inherent weakness of this style of governance are the lack of enforcement and the risk that governments may well be tempted to bend and exploit the uncertainties within conventions in order to pursue self-serving and politically motivated ends. However, conventions have long operated against the backdrop of the British governing tradition, a set of shared assumptions that government should exercise self-restraint and act in accordance with the spirit of the Constitution.

Over recent decades, the strength of this tradition has weakened as successive governments have pursued their self-serving political ends and none more so than Johnson's populist and tumultuous government. 'Constitutional hardball' aptly describes Johnson's approach toward undermining constitutional norms and standards of good governance.[27] Brexit had promised the restoration of sovereignty and Parliament taking back control, but the Government had sought to shut down Parliament. When the Supreme Court found this unconstitutional, one minister described the court's ruling as a 'constitutional coup'.[28]

Other rule of law concerns have included Brexit-related legislation contravening the withdrawal agreement with the European Union, a governmental review of administrative law prompted, in large part, by the prorogation case, and Home Secretary Priti Patel's populist rhetoric criticising 'activist' lawyers for challenging immigration decisions (despite the inconvenient fact that many such challenges succeed).[29] In other respects, the doctrine of ministerial responsibility has been

[24] P Norton, 'Problems of a hybrid House' *The Norton View Blog* (14 November 2020).

[25] 'Covid-19: Rees-Mogg under fire over Covid Commons rules' *BBC News* (17 November 2020).

[26] See generally M Foley, *The Silence of Constitutions* (Routledge, 1989).

[27] N Barber, 'Playing Hardball with the Queen' *Oxford Human Rights Hub* (31 August 2019). M Tushnet, 'Constitutional Hardball' (2004) 37 *John Marshall Law Review* 523.

[28] 'Attorney General slaps down Jacob Rees-Mogg over claim Supreme Court launched "constitutional coup"' *PoliticsHome* (16 November 2020).

[29] House of Lords Constitution Committee, *Internal Market Bill* HL 151 (2019–2021); 'Brexit strategy risks UK "dictatorship", says ex-president of supreme court' *The Guardian* (7 October 2020); Independent Review of Administrative Law, www.gov.uk/government/groups/independent-review-of-administrative-law; 'Top ministers urged Priti Patel to stop attacks on "activist lawyers"' *The Guardian* (18 October 2020).

weakened by ministers in effect dismissing senior civil servants and evading responsibility for their personal misbehaviour.[30]

All of this collectively illustrates the trends accelerating the UK's intractable slow-burn constitutional crisis. The Constitution's reliance upon conventions and understandings rests upon trust and self-restraint, but this equilibrium breaks down when government acts against convention for reasons of political self-interest. The resulting constitutional damage can be intense, but what is the solution? Real constitutional change can only be brought about by the government. Constitutional reformers dream of a constitutional commission and the holy grail of a codified constitution, but their proposals are often the 'poetry of the politically impotent' that lose their allure when power is gained.[31] Such is the nature of the UK's ongoing constitutional paralysis.

How then would the Constitution handle the challenges posed by the virus? To consider this question, we must first identify the style of governance prompted by the virus.

IV. Virus Governance

'Virus governance' is a variant of 'crisis governance': the expansion of executive power in response to a sudden critical emergency, such as 9/11 and the financial crisis 2007–08.[32] Each crisis differs. Nonetheless, common themes include the concentration of power in the central core executive, its extensive law-making power, and the adoption of a command and control structure through which the executive directs the machinery of government and the wider public sector more generally. All this happens with minimal Parliamentary and judicial scrutiny.

There are advantages to this style of governance. Governing from the centre enables fast and informed decision making by relying upon a small group of ministers and advisers. Getting things done quickly matters when there is a global pandemic killing hundreds of people a day. Yet, there are weaknesses. Having decisions taken by a small group of people induces 'group think' and mistakes. As time passes, it may become apparent that government, or its zealous agents, have exceeded their powers or that government, faced with the scale of the challenge and competing political pressures, has acted incompetently, or that Parliament

[30] R Brazier, 'Contempt for the Constitution?' *UK Constitutional Law Blog* (6 October 2020) (ministerial responsibility now means ministers must not resign for their mistakes, but they can throw civil servants under a bus to take the flak); M Gordon, 'Priti Patel, the Independent Adviser, and Ministerial Irresponsibility' *UK Constitutional Law Blog* (23 November 2020).

[31] F Mount, *The British Constitution Now* (London, Heinemann, 1992) 2. On the unfortunate experience of the Liberal Democrats, a pro-constitutional reform party, as the junior party in the 2010–15 Coalition government, see M Loughlin and C Viney, 'The Coalition and the Constitution' in A Seldon and M Finn (eds), *The Coalition Effect 2010–2015* (OUP, 2015).

[32] EA Posner and A Vermeule, 'Crisis Governance in the Administrative State: 9/11 and the Financial Meltdown of 2008' (2009) 76 *University of Chicago Law Review* 1613.

becomes increasingly concerned at what is happening and demands more of a role to scrutinise the government. A top-down command and control structure may prove inadequate when local or regional knowledge is required. Virus governance has exemplified all of these problems.

V. Virus Law

Let us consider the interlocking issues of law-making and parliamentary scrutiny. By way of background, the UK Parliament is not, and never has been, a legislature in the sense of a body exclusively and specially constituted to make legislation. Almost all legislation originates from government and is then debated, amended, and enacted by Parliament. Normally, the legislative process is a leisurely affair stretching out over a period of some months. Fast-tracking legislation is generally frowned upon.[33] But, there was clearly a good rationale for fast-tracking the Coronavirus Act 2020, a 370-page statute which completed is passage through Parliament in seven days. Whereas most Acts are sponsored by a specific government department, this was very much a cross-government affair. Its purpose was to enable the Government to respond to the emergency and manage the pandemic across almost many areas of government and the wider public sector.

The Coronavirus Act 2020 was then followed by a large number of regulations – secondary legislation or statutory instruments which are normally subject to limited parliamentary scrutiny. The legal basis for the first lockdown, introduced in March 2020, was through secondary legislation, not the Coronavirus Act 2020.[34] The relevant regulations came into force on 26 March 2020, at 1pm and were laid before Parliament at 2.30pm the same day without substantive debate in Parliament. The shock of the crisis was considerable and there was an evident need for the Government to act. At this stage, the Government had strong support from across the mainstream political spectrum, but things soon started to unravel.

There then followed whole sets of detailed and complex regulations which were frequently amended. As of late 2020, the Government had laid 288 coronavirus-related statutory instruments before Parliament (see Figure 4.1).[35] There were differences between the strict letter of regulations and the associated guidance which generated confusion amongst both the public and public authorities. For instance, the requirement to wear masks on public transport was announced in a Downing Street press conference on 4 June, came into force 11 days later, but

[33] House of Lords Constitution Committee, *Fast-Track Legislation: Constitutional Implications and Safeguards* HL 116 (2008–09).

[34] Health Protection (Coronavirus, Restrictions) (England) Regulations 2020 with separate regulations for Scotland, Wales, and Northern Ireland made under the Public Health (Control of Disease) Act 1984.

[35] For details, see the Hansard Society's Coronavirus Statutory Instruments Dashboard, www.hansardsociety.org.uk/publications/data/coronavirus-statutory-instruments-dashboard.

was not debated in the House of Commons until 6 July. Guidance was often more restrictive than the law, but, of course, guidance is not law, it is just guidance. The regulations were frequently amended and introduced without laying a draft before, and approved by a resolution of, each House of Parliament. By convention, regulations are, wherever possible, laid before Parliament at least 21 calendar days before they come into effect. However, of the 200 coronavirus-related regulations laid before Parliament which were subject to the negative procedure, 132 breached the 21-day rule.[36] Many regulations came into effect before being laid before Parliament. Matters were complicated by a system of tiered restrictions that were locally based. All of this was a recipe for public confusion. If senior police officers did not understand the regulations, then the public had no hope.[37]

Figure 4.1 Number of coronavirus and non-coronavirus UK statutory instruments laid before Parliament in 2020

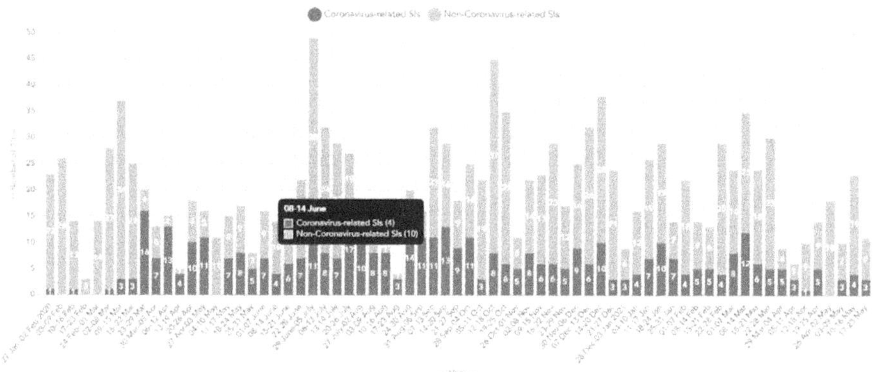

Source: Hansard Society's Coronavirus Statutory Instruments Dashboard, www.hansardsociety.org.uk/publications/data/coronavirus-statutory-instruments-dashboard.

Lawyers were soon raising criticisms of the regulations and guidance by questioning their legal basis, describing them as 'the most illiberal laws imposed in England since at least the second world war', and highlighting the lack of parliamentary scrutiny.[38] The recently retired President of the UK Supreme Court, Lady Hale, argued that Parliament had 'surrendered' its role over emergency laws restricting freedoms amid the pandemic.[39] This combined with criticism of the substance of regulations and their application by the police. The former Supreme Court Justice, Jonathan Sumption, was particularly vocal. Sumption argued that there was no moral or principled justification for these restrictions: 'A society in which the

[36] Ibid.

[37] 'Police chiefs admit even they don't understand Covid rules' *Metro* (22 October 2020).

[38] D Allen Green, 'The significant extension of the Coronavirus restriction on movement – and why it is concerning', *The Law and Policy Blog* (23 April 2020).

[39] 'Parliament surrendered role over Covid emergency laws, says Lady Hale' *The Guardian* (20 September 2020).

Government can confine most of the population without controversy is not one in which civilised people would want to live'.[40] Sumption also criticised the police for their zealous enforcement, such as stopping people from exercising in the countryside; such behaviour risked plunging Britain into a 'police state'.[41]

VI. Parliamentary Scrutiny

Even in normal times, the deeply-embedded constitutional assumption is that 'the first business of government is to govern'; holding it to account being merely 'a sophisticated afterthought compared to the primal need' to govern.[42] In this context, parliamentary 'control' of government assumes a distinctive meaning: it means 'influence, not direct power; advice, not command; criticism, not obstruction; scrutiny, not initiation; and publicity, not secrecy'.[43] Over recent years, a new parliamentary assertiveness has emerged, with MPs more willing to challenge their own government.[44] But the virus firmly reinforced the primal need to govern. From the Government's perspective, in the midst of the emergency and acting in crisis mode, parliamentary scrutiny of secondary legislation barely registered as an issue.

The initial scope for parliamentary scrutiny of virus governance was then very limited, not least because of the cross-party instinct to support the Government. There were numerous government broadcasts and ministerial statements, but little effective scrutiny. However, as the virus dragged on, there was a distinct change of mood, especially toward the autumn. Initial public tolerance and forgiveness toward the Government changed once repeated instances of its incompetence, mistakes, and policy reversals started to pile up. Political divisions within the Conservative party and opposition from other political parties became more pronounced.

Parliamentary scrutiny serves important purposes. The UK Parliament is not the type of legislature that can 'issue commands, conceive long-term strategies or handle a fast-moving crisis', but it is there to be 'wooed, cajoled, consulted, and enthused'.[45] Its main task is 'not to legislate or govern, but to secure discussion and ventilation of all matters'.[46] More specifically, parliamentary scrutiny helps

[40] EP Stringham, 'Lord Sumption: The Lockdown Is Without Doubt the Greatest Interference with Personal Liberty in Our History' *American Institute for Economic Research* (9 May 2020), www.aier.org/article/lord-sumption-the-lockdown-is-without-doubt-the-greatest-interference-with-personal-liberty-in-our-history/.

[41] 'Covid-19: ex-supreme court judge lambasts "disgraceful" policing' *The Guardian* (30 March 2020).

[42] B Crick, *The Reform of Parliament* (London, Weidenfeld, 1968) 1.

[43] ibid, 80.

[44] P Norton, 'Parliament: A New Assertiveness?' in J Jowell, D Oliver, and C O'Cinneide (eds), *The Changing Constitution*, 8th edn (OUP, 2015).

[45] Mount (n 31) 179.

[46] LS Amery, *Thoughts on the Constitution*, 2nd edn (OUP, 1958) 12.

to confer legitimacy upon policy changes made through emergency regulations, particularly when they curtail personal liberty. Scrutiny also enables MPs to raise problems that might arise in the practical operation of regulations and associated guidance. Through parliamentary scrutiny, government by consent is secured: the public can be reassured that their views are represented and government is being held to account.

As time passed, divisions of opinion over the virus come to the fore. On the one hand, scientists expressed the need for caution; on the other hand, there were public protests against the restrictions with fringe elements claiming it was all a governmental conspiratorial grab-power.[47] Parliament went into its usual recess over the summer. By the autumn, the predicted second wave was on its way. The need for Parliament to reassert itself had become increasingly evident, if only to prevent it from becoming entirely supine. The Speaker of the House of Commons, Lindsey Hoyle, criticised government ministers for making major announcements to the media and not Parliament; indeed, some journalists had tweeted the substance of announcements before they were even made by ministers.[48]

VII. The Need for Parliamentary Scrutiny Reasserted

Then, in September 2020, two important developments occurred. First, the House of Commons Public Administration and Constitutional Affairs Committee expressed its concerns at both the scale of legislation and the inability of Parliament effectively to amend virus regulations.[49] It was very difficult even for experts to know what legislation was in effect. There was no means by which Parliament could amend regulations. The system of parliamentary scrutiny in relation to lock-down regulations was unsatisfactory. The Government's use of urgent procedures to introduce regulations had not always been properly justified by the circumstances. The Committee therefore recommended that the Government give higher priority to facilitating parliamentary scrutiny of such legislation.

[47] 'Survey uncovers widespread belief in "dangerous" Covid conspiracy theories: False claims that pandemic is a hoax or was started deliberately are attracting adherents around world' *The Guardian* (26 October 2020).

[48] *Hansard*, HC Vol 679, col 619 (7 September 2020, Mr Speaker): 'It is really not good enough for the Government to make decisions of this kind in a way that shows insufficient regard to the importance of major policy announcements being made first to this House and to Members of this House wherever possible. I have already sent a letter to the Secretary of State. I think the total disregard for this Chamber is not acceptable.' The Speaker is an MP who has been elected by other MPs. The Speaker chairs debates in the Commons and is the chief officer and highest authority of the House of Commons, and must remain politically impartial at all times. During Commons debates, the Speaker keeps order and calls MPs to speak.

[49] House of Commons Public Administration and Constitutional Affairs Committee, *Parliamentary Scrutiny of the Government's Handling of Covid-19* HC 377 (2019–21).

Secondly, Speaker Hoyle weighed in by criticising the Government's 'contempt' for Parliament:

> The way in which the Government have exercised their powers to make secondary legislation during this crisis has been totally unsatisfactory. All too often, important statutory instruments have been published a matter of hours before they come into force, and some explanations why important measures have come into effect before they can be laid before this House have been unconvincing; this shows a total disregard for the House. The Government must make greater efforts to prepare measures more quickly, so that this House can debate and decide upon the most significant measures at the earliest possible point.[50]

In addition, backbench Conservative MPs had become increasingly vocal in raising their concerns about the substance of restrictions and the impact on personal liberty and the economy.[51]

VIII. The Second Lockdown

By October 2020, with the predicted second wave imminent, the Labour opposition had sought to claim the political initiative by calling for a second lockdown to prevent cases and deaths from escalating again. This had been roundly rejected by Johnson, in typically over-the-top rhetorical style, as 'the height of absurdity'.[52] Nonetheless, infection rates continued to rise. Two weeks later, the Prime Minister announced a second lockdown in England – precisely what he had recently dismissed. This time, a parliamentary debate and vote were essential.

The shock of the new, so evident back in March 2020, had now altogether diminished. Boredom and frustration had set in. There were significant concerns about a second lockdown from the Conservative backbench. A senior MP raised concerns about the UK drifting 'further into an authoritarian, coercive state'.[53] Conservative backbench MPs had been wrestling with the impossibly hard choice of protecting public health on the one hand and the economy and personal liberty on the other, and with considerable uncertainty about the consequences and little sense of future direction. There was also growing despair about Johnson's ability to steer the country through the crisis given his Government's incompetence. Government could no longer simply impose its authority on the people and Parliament; much more was required. What about the quality of the Government's

[50] *Hansard*, HC Vol 681, col 331 (30 September 2020, Mr Speaker).

[51] Backbench Conservative MPs refers to those Members of Parliament in the House of Commons who are in the governing party, but are not members of the government. They are part of the government's Commons majority and usually support their government, but they can kick up a fuss when the need arises.

[52] *Hansard*, HC Vol 682, col 1055 (21 October 2020, Boris Johnson MP, Prime Minister).

[53] *Hansard*, HC Vol 683, col 30 (2 November 2020, Charles Walker MP, vice-chair of the Conservative 1922 committee).

modelling of future cases and deaths? What of the impact and costs of a second lockdown?

As the former Prime Minister, Theresa May MP, noted, the figures of predicted deaths used to justify the lockdown appeared to have been 'chosen to support the policy, rather than the policy being based on the figures. We need these proper analyses; we need to know the details behind these models; and we need to be able to assess the validity of the models'.[54] Without any explanation, the regulations had not been accompanied by a detailed impact assessment outlining their costs and benefits. There was, May noted, no data on the costs of the decisions being made in terms of their impact upon non-COVID health care and deaths and the costs in terms of domestic abuse, mental health, the economy, and jobs.

Other Conservative backbench MPs took a more direct pro-liberty constitutional approach. Charles Walker MP argued that the UK government was undermining the rule of law and personal liberty. Government had coerced the public into lockdown. Similarly, Graham Brady MP, the Chair of the influential Conservative backbench 1922 Committee, questioned whether the Government had the moral right to re-introduce a lockdown: 'What troubles me most is that the Government are reaching too far into the private and family lives of our constituents. There is an arrogance – unintended, perhaps – in assuming that the Government have the right to do so'.[55] The lockdown was also viewed as ineffective: 'If lockdowns and blizzards of arbitrary rules were a solution to the problem, we would have solved it months ago'.[56]

Ultimately, the Government won the vote to impose new restrictions in England for 28 days, by a margin of 516 votes to 38, with backing from Labour. Nonetheless, Government whips had to resort to old-fashioned tactics of 'persuading' (ie, bullying) the new intake of 'red wall' MPs 'like mad' in order to win the vote.[57] Questions were also asked about long-term solutions, how to break out of repetitive cycles of lockdowns, and the need for the Government to analyse the effectiveness of restrictions.[58] As regards the many other regulations, more detailed scrutiny was provided by dedicated committees.[59]

Parliamentary scrutiny extends far beyond secondary legislation. In addition to questions to ministers in the Commons chamber, there was also a need for focused scrutiny of the many aspects of the response to the virus through parliamentary committees. The principal parliamentary success story over recent decades has

[54] *Hansard*, HC Vol 683, col 342 (4 November 2020, Theresa May MP).

[55] *Hansard*, HC Vol 683, cols 354–355 (4 November 2020, Graham Brady MP, Chair of the Conservative 1922 Committee).

[56] *Hansard*, HC Vol 683, col 352 (4 November 2020, Philip Davies MP).

[57] 'How a full-scale lockdown rebellion by Tory MPs was called off: Conservative whips "bullied new intake like mad" to get Covid restrictions through Parliament' *The Guardian* (6 November 2020).

[58] House of Lords Secondary Legislation Scrutiny Committee, *34th Report of Session* HL 172 (2019–21), [41].

[59] In particular by the House of Lords Secondary Legislation Scrutiny Committee; see: committees.parliament.uk/committee/255/secondary-legislation-scrutiny-committee/news/115532/scrutiny-of-secondary-legislation-laid-to-tackle-coronavirus-pandemic/.

been the growing stature and authority of select committees.[60] Committee chairs and members used to be selected by the government, even though they scrutinise government. Then, following the 2009 MPs' expenses scandal – MPs were found to have overclaimed expenses for 'essential' items such as garden duck houses – committees were strengthened through appointed chairs.[61]

During the virus, select committees fulfilled their role as the forum for detailed scrutiny of government and pinning down ministers and officials. Appearing before a joint meeting of the House of Commons Health and Social Care Committee and the Science and Technology Committee in November 2020, the head of the NHS Test and Trace, Dido Harding, elicited disbelief from MPs when she told them that the service had been taken by surprise by the increased demand for testing in the autumn.[62] This was despite the obvious risks of heightened transmission posed by children and students returning to schools and universities. A Labour MP, Graham Stringer, was shocked by Harding's inability to explain the failure or the amount of funding spent on local versus national test and trace efforts – the latter was crucial given that the principal issue about the test and trace service has been whether it was better organised locally rather than centrally.

What then of judicial scrutiny of the lockdown? A crowd-funded judicial review had been brought to challenge the lockdown regulations. Given the circumstances, the Court of Appeal was, unsurprisingly, reluctant to find the regulations to be unlawful or irrational. The regulations had been approved by Parliament, albeit some weeks after they were made. Government had to make difficult judgements about medical and scientific issues after taking expert advice. There were powerfully expressed conflicting views about the measures taken by the Government and how to strike the right balance personal liberty and protecting public health. Altogether, the lockdown had been a matter of political judgement for the Government, which is accountable to Parliament, and not suited to determination by the courts.[63]

IX. Devolved Government and Virus Governance

We now turn to consider the impact of virus governance within the UK's developing territorial constitution, the constitutional and governing arrangements

[60] Institute for Government, *Select Committees Under Scrutiny: The Impact of Parliamentary Committee Inquiries on Government* (London, IfG, 2015).

[61] A Kelso, 'Parliament on its Knees: MPs' Expenses and the Crisis of Transparency at Westminster' (2009) 80 *Political Quarterly* 32; House of Commons Reform Committee, *Rebuilding the House* HC 1117 (2009–10); M Russell, "Never Allow a Crisis Go To Waste": The Wright Committee Reforms to Strengthen the House of Commons' (2011) 64 *Parliamentary Affairs* 612.

[62] House of Commons Health and Social Care Committee and Science and Technology Committee, *Coronavirus: Lessons Learnt: Oral Evidence session* (10 November 2020); 'NHS test and trace: Dido Harding says scheme failed to predict demand' *The Guardian* (10 November 2020).

[63] *R (Dolan) v Secretary of State for Health and Social Care* [2020] EWCA Civ 1605, [90].

concerning how political and administrative power is distributed and exercised throughout the UK. As a unitary state, the UK's governing tradition is one of centralisation and the concentration of power within the central state as reflected in constitutional doctrines such as the sovereignty of the Westminster Parliament. But there is something of a mismatch. The unitary tradition is distinctly English in origin and it has long assumed that the rest of UK would also be unitary in nature, but different approaches have existed and are needed in Scotland, Wales, and Northern Ireland.

In the late 1990s, the Labour Government had introduced devolution for the three smaller nations. This has produced a system of 'asymmetrical quasi-federalism': there are devolved governments and legislatures in Scotland, Wales, and Northern Ireland, but not in England.[64] Each scheme of devolution has expanded in response to political pressures. The overall general trend has been toward the greater devolution of power from the UK Government and the process is now de facto irreversible.

But this set up has become increasingly unstable especially given growing support for Scottish independence. Even pre-Brexit, the 'pervasive sense of territorial constitutional crisis, let alone of constitutional unsettlement' was evident.[65] Having narrowly lost the 'once in a generation' 2014 Scottish independence referendum ('indyref'), the fervently pro-independence Scottish Nationalist Party Government has persistently highlighted the material change of circumstances of the 2016 Brexit referendum (Scotland voted remain) as the basis for 'indyref2', a proposal consistently rejected by the Conservative Government.[66]

Brexit has then increased the challenge of trying to hold together the UK's four nations. The repatriation of powers previously exercised at the EU level – not to the devolved governments – but to the UK Government has been seen as an unjustifiable power-grab by the Scottish and Welsh governments. In this context, Johnson's unguarded comment that devolution had been 'a disaster north of the border' (ie, in Scotland) only poured fuel on the bonfire.[67] Even a moderate pro-devolution pro-unionist might well see the biggest threat to the union as not being the Scottish independence movement, but Boris Johnson's behaviour as Prime Minister. The outlook for the future of the union between Scotland and the rest of the UK is now the bleakest it has been for centuries.

In previous crisis governance episodes, there had been no scope at all for devolved governments outside of London to act; both 9/11 and the financial crisis 2007–08 had concerned matters – terrorism and banking – within the reserved competence of the UK Government. The virus was different. Many of

[64] R Rawlings, 'A Coalition Government in Westminster' in Jowell, Oliver and O'Cinneide (n 44) 194.

[65] R Rawlings, 'Riders on the Storm: Wales, the Union, and Territorial Constitutional Crisis' (2015) 42 *Journal of Law and Society* 471.

[66] 'Indyref2: Scottish Secretary rejects new vote "for a generation"' *BBC News* (6 November 2020).

[67] 'Devolution "a disaster north of the border", says Boris Johnson' *The Guardian* (17 November 2020); 'Welsh government calls PM's devolution remarks "shocking"' *The Guardian* 17 November 2020.

the affected policy areas – health, education, social care – are devolved matters. Indeed, the virus has arguably marked the coming of age of devolution through noticeably different approaches between the UK and devolved governments.[68] The Scottish and Welsh publics have had greater confidence in their own First Ministers than the UK Prime Minister. The Scottish Government took its own approach to virus restrictions and lockdowns. For centuries, England and Wales have been homogeneous, but with the virus, Wales went into lockdown separately from England and prevented English residents from crossing the porous border to Wales to prevent transmission.

As regards Northern Ireland, devolved government had been finally restored in January 2020 having collapsed in 2017. Northern Ireland was the first of the four UK administrations to roll out a contact tracing programme and app. The Northern Ireland executive had itself introduced many regulations and restrictions, but only toward the end of 2020 did the Northern Ireland Assembly start to debate them. Such scrutiny was undertaken without the supporting documents that had informed the Minister's recommendations and the Northern Ireland executive's decisions on whether to agree the regulations. Further, scrutiny was undertaken sometime after the regulations had come into effect, and, in some instances, after they had already been superseded.[69]

While devolution allowed for a diversity of responses, effective virus governance also required coordination by the four governments, a feature often notably absent. The Welsh and Scottish First Ministers complained about a distinct lack of engagement from the Prime Minister and highlighted the 'vacancy' at the heart of the UK Government.[70] The Welsh Government only learnt of the second English lockdown from newspaper leaks.[71] There was also a lack of clarity from the UK Government about the availability of furlough support in the context of different lockdowns within the four nations. Through the furlough scheme, the UK Government provided 80 per cent of a worker's wages, up to a maximum of £2,500 a month. When the second lockdown in England was introduced, furlough support was initially available to the devolved nations only for the duration of an English lockdown – not for the period of any lockdown they might unilaterally impose on a different timescale.[72] The Scottish, Welsh, and Northern Ireland Governments argued this was unfair resulting in potentially different treatment as regards different lockdowns in their nations. UK ministers clarified that furlough support would be available to Scotland, Wales, and Northern Ireland if they went into a future lockdown separately from England.[73] The hesitancy stemmed from

[68] G Campbell, 'Covid: How the coronavirus pandemic is redefining Scottish politics' *BBC News* (22 September 2020).

[69] *Hansard*, Northern Ireland Assembly (No 5) Vol 132, 15 (9 November 2020).

[70] 'Welsh and Scottish leaders: Johnson hasn't talked to us for months' *The Guardian* (18 September 2020).

[71] 'Police may be asked to stop England residents escaping to Wales to avoid lockdown' *The Guardian* (2 November 2020).

[72] 'Welsh and Scottish leaders hit out at "unfair" furlough extension' *The Guardian* (1 November 2020).

[73] P Sim, 'Covid in Scotland: What's the furlough scheme row all about?' *BBC News* (3 November 2020).

governmental fiscal caution – otherwise known as HM Treasury – about giving away control over public spending in such uncertain circumstances.[74]

These two episodes played directly into long-standing concerns from the devolved nations about the lack of collaboration from the UK Government and the perception that they are not treated as equals, but only as an after-thought after important policy decisions had already been taken. Over 20 years after the introduction of devolution – and even taking account of the virus – the basic centralising thought processes of UK government had still not fully adjusted to the reality of UK quasi-federalist governance. There is still no 'UK Council of Ministers for the Nations and Regions' to coordinate UK and devolved governance.

Overall, divergent responses to the virus enabled each part of the UK to respond to its local circumstances while effective UK-wide co-ordination and intergovernmental discussion was lacking.[75] There was a joint statement issued by the four government on the virus.[76] However, the lack of regular communication between the four governments is likely to have contributed to the degree of mistrust between the Scottish and UK Governments and to have weakened the ability to ensure a coordinated and evidence-based response to the virus.[77] As the House of Commons Scottish Affairs Committee put it, 'The Covid-19 pandemic has laid bare the weaknesses built into the UK systems of governance. … The four-nations approach that was in place at the beginning of the pandemic needs to be resurrected with regular meetings set up between all four UK nations.'[78]

X. England: The Non-devolved Nation

The UK's largest nation – and 85 per cent of its population – does not have its own devolution scheme. In constitutional terms, England barely even exists. It is more 'a state of mind' than a 'consciously organised political institution'.[79] England has no distinctive governing institutions of its own; it only acquires them by default when the three other countries opt out of UK policies.[80] The question of English devolution has arisen only because devolution has happened elsewhere first.

[74] By instinct and long-established custom, HM Treasury, the UK government's finance and economics department, is a power-hoarding department and, by a long way, the most powerful government department.

[75] J Sargeant, *Co-ordination and Divergence: Devolution and Coronavirus* (IfG, 2020).

[76] *A Joint Statement on Coronavirus (COVID-19) from the UK Government, the Northern Ireland Executive, the Scottish Government, and the Welsh Government* (25 September 2020), www.gov.uk/government/publications/joint-statement-on-covid-19/joint-statement-on-coronavirus-covid-19.

[77] House of Commons Scottish Affairs Committee, *Coronavirus and Scotland* HC 895 (2019–21).

[78] ibid, [66]–[67].

[79] R Rose, *Understanding the United Kingdom* (Longman, 1982) 29.

[80] ibid, 31. For instance, the Department for Education and the Department of Health and Social Care are, in formal terms, UK government departments, but in substance English government departments because these functions are devolved in Wales, Scotland, and Northern Ireland.

Establishing an English executive and legislature separate from those of the UK has long been rejected because of the high degree of overlap and the likely ruinous consequences of institutional conflict.[81] At the same time, the over-centralised model of the UK state has often been highlighted as a distinct source of policy blunders as the London-centric central government has often imposed a 'one-size fits all' approach when diversity and regional nuance have been required. The hoarding of power and money at the centre has often worked to the detriment of English regions, especially those with 'left behind' populations. Indeed, over-centralisation is arguably 'the root cause of regional inequality' in England.[82]

Given England's size, a more regional form of government has been the preferred model. This has been developing ad hoc and piecemeal through 'combined local authorities' led by elected mayors.[83] A combined authority is a group of two or more local authorities that collaborate and take collective decisions on matters that affect the whole area. A number of devolution deals have been agreed with central government on a case-by-case basis.[84] To state the obvious: there is no coherent overall scheme of English regional governance. Repeated calls for devolving more powers to the English regions and accelerating the role of combined authorities have been made, but central government has typically been unwilling to devolve more power and money.[85] Current English governance arrangements remain opaque and deeply confusing thereby illustrating a distinct lack of constitutional vision.

What then of virus governance within England? English councils and city regional mayors were not part of the initial response to the virus. Central government ministers and advisers simply assumed that they could deliver effective responses from London, an assumption that has often been undermined by practical reality. The Government established a centralised test and trace system through the NHS that relied significantly on outsourcing to private contractors, such as Serco. This system was heavily criticised for their poor performance in delivering an effective test and trace system.[86]

The alternative would have been to work with local councils and combined authorities to institute a regionally and locally-based system in which front-line providers had much better knowledge of local conditions. Throughout the virus, it had been argued that decentralised capacity, combined with a constructive

[81] R Hazell, *The English Question* (Manchester University Press, 2006); J Mitchell, *Devolution in the UK* (Manchester University Press, 2009) chs 5 and 9.

[82] Dr Arianna Giovannini of De Montfort University quoted in 'Covid-19: Will the pandemic shift the power balance in England for good?' *BBC News* (6 November 2020).

[83] Cities and Local Government Devolution Act 2016.

[84] See Local Government Association, www.local.gov.uk/topics/devolution.

[85] M Heseltine, *Empowering English Cities* (2019); L Raikes and A Giovannini, *The Devolution Parliament* 20 November 2019, www.ippr.org/public/index.php/blog/the-devolution-parliament; UK2070 Commission, *Make No Little Plans: Acting at Scale for a Fairer and Stronger Future* (2020), uk2070.org.uk/wp-content/uploads/2020/02/UK2070-FINAL-REPORT.pdf.

[86] 'Serco profits surge thanks to Covid-19 test-and-trace contract' *The Guardian* (16 October 2020).

relationship at different levels of governance, was a more effective strategy to deal with the crisis than the habitual 'one size fits all' approach of central government.[87] The Labour party repeatedly called on the Government to allow local public health experts to run test and trace operations, rather than an outsourcing company. Critics questioned why central government was not involving England's 130 local directors of public health to enhance the trace and test system.[88] Local councils were given powers to restrict access to, or close, individual premises, prohibit certain events, and restrict access to, or close, public outdoor places (or types of outdoor public places), but were otherwise largely kept out of the loop.[89] Instead, the Government persisted with its poorly performing centralised test and trace system and private contractors.

XI. 'Northern Republic Now!'[90]

After the lifting of the first lockdown, the Government had introduced a tiered system of local restrictions of increasing severity to respond to local outbreaks and increased transmission rates. With the weakened economy and furloughed employees needing support, a key issue was the amount of financial support when 'tier 3' restrictions were re-imposed ('tier 3' was then the strictest level of restrictions in England akin to a lockdown).

By October 2020, virus cases had increased significantly in northern England, an area already hit hard by a decade of austerity.[91] The Government wanted to impose 'tier 3' local restrictions in Manchester, a city region of 2.8 million people. However, the Mayor of the Greater Manchester Combined Authority, Andy Burnham, a former Labour government minister, had strongly resisted this – not on public health grounds – but because of the inadequacy of the Government's economic support package. The Government's 'generous' offer was furlough support of 67 per cent of people's earnings as opposed to the 80 per cent provided during the first national lockdown. Burnham rejected this: without more support for people and businesses, the tighter restrictions would increase levels of poverty, homelessness, and hardship amongst the region's population. This led to a stand-off between Burnham and the UK Government ending in a spectacular and

[87] J Gaskell and J Stoker, 'Centralised or multi-level: which governance systems are having a "good" pandemic?' *LSE Politics and Policy Blog* (16 April 2020); 'Steven Pleasant: Covid-19 response "better if done through localities"' *Local Government Chronicle* (28 April 2020).

[88] 'Covid-19 unmasks weaknesses of English public health agency' *Financial Times* (22 July 2020).

[89] Health Protection (Coronavirus, Restrictions) (England) (No.3) Regulations 2020.

[90] '"Northern Republic Now" defiant banner appears on one of Manchester's busiest roads amid tier 3 row' *Manchester Evening News* (17 October 2020).

[91] Northern Health Science Alliance, *COVID 19 and the Northern Powerhouse: Tackling inequalities for UK health and productivity* (2020), www.thenhsa.co.uk/app/uploads/2020/11/NP-COVID-REPORT-101120-.pdf; 'Austerity left north of England more vulnerable to Covid, report says' *The Guardian* (11 November 2020).

acrimonious public falling out. Burnham argued that the Government had been willing to spend billions on a test and trace system that did not work, but refused to spend much smaller sums to support people on low incomes.

Ultimately, Burnham was compelled by circumstance to backdown and accept the Government's 'take it or leave it' offer, although he received considerable local political support and was lauded by some as the 'King of the north'.[92] Tellingly, Burnham received some support from Sir Graham Brady, a local senior Conservative MP.[93] The restrictions had been seen as a top-down imposition that would result in the north of England being levelled-down rather than up. Two weeks later the Government introduced the second national lockdown with the 80 per cent furlough support, highlighting its lack of foresight and prompting claims that this confirmed the long-held governmental preference for London and the south east over the north.[94]

In previous instances of central-local tensions, complaints made by local leaders have failed to gain any traction with the national media. Local councils are too provincial; ambitious politicians have long seen getting into Westminster and national politics as the only game in town. But the Manchester stand-off illustrated a growing confidence in the city region as a site of place-based governance and an implicit rejection of the UK central state.

What happens now remains to be seen. There are strong centralising tendencies in UK governance, especially when government is in crisis mode. But the virus had further revealed deep-seated structural weaknesses: the London-centric mindset of central government; the top-down imposition of policy without prior consultation of regional political leaders; the lack of structural representation at the UK level of the devolved governments and English regions. There is a strong perception of people's decreasing affective attachment to a remote UK central state and increasing regional commitment. The longer these issues remain unresolved, then the more pressure for change will accumulate.

XII. Conclusions

The virus has posed enormous challenges across the world in all aspects of life – personal, social, economic, political, and constitutional. All countries have experienced the strain of the enormousness of these challenges and have struggled to deal with them, although some authoritarian states have used the virus as an

[92] The use of *Games of Thrones* imagery in British politics has become more common. For another example, see 'Dominic Raab would not take the knee for Black Lives Matter as he thinks it's from Game of Thrones' *Metro* (18 June 2020).

[93] 'Manchester lockdown: Fury as Boris Johnson provides just £22m support as city faces punishing winter' *The Independent* (22 October 2020); 'Chaos and fury as Boris Johnson forces curbs on Greater Manchester' *The Guardian* (22 October 2020).

[94] 'Greater Manchester businesses "treated with disrespect", say owners' *BBC News* (3 November 2020).

opportunity to further extend governmental control over their own people and weaken democratic liberties. Any initial sense that the virus was only a temporary blip has now passed and it is impossible to know what the longer-term consequences may be. The political uncertainty will almost certainly likely to have constitutional repercussions. And this is against the backdrop of wider political and constitutional instability as evidenced by the development of 'illiberal democracies' in central and eastern Europe and Trump's attempted constitutional coup in Washington on 6 January 2021.

As regards the UK, the virus has highlighted and magnified long-standing structural weaknesses in the UK's constitution. It now seems that that fundamental constitutional reform is needed more than ever. In early 2021, the former Labour Prime Minister, Gordon Brown (2007–10), warned that the UK is at risk of becoming a failed state – only a radical constitutional revolution can stop the UK from unravelling due to nationalism and the alienation felt by people in poorer 'left behind' regions.[95] For things to stay the same, everything must now change. A number of constitutional reforms now need to be developed and adopted: a constitutional convention; a federal UK; regional citizen assemblies; less centralisation; devolving more power to the regions; and reforming Parliament and turning the House of Lords into a regionally representative chamber or senate; and a codified constitution. This is a very wide-ranging project. In the meantime, the virus will continue to affect life for some time – the financial consequences in terms of increased borrowing and future tax rises will has wide-ranging repercussions. Nonetheless, the task of restructuring the UK's constitution is now long overdue.

[95] '"Constitutional revolution" needed to rescue the union, warns Gordon Brown' *The Guardian* (18 January 2020); G Brown, 'How to save the United Kingdom' *New Statesman* (18 November 2020); 'UK at risk of becoming failed state, says Gordon Brown' *The Guardian* (25 January 2021).

5

Germany – Federalism in Action

PIERRE THIELBÖRGER*

I. Introduction

Coronaviruses are not new threats. However, while the most recent two – SARS[1] and MERS[2] – coronavirus related diseases never reached the scale of a pandemic, COVID-19 shook most legal and political systems to their core and caused more than 2.3 million deaths before February 2021.[3] The vast majority of countries was affected, but a variety of factors determined the severity with which states and regions were exposed. These include a region's geography, population density, exposure to tradable sectors and global value chains as well as its economic specialisation, for instance in tourism.[4]

Germany's approach to the pandemic is a particularly interesting one, for mainly three reasons: First, Germany is considered a state not only of enormous economic and financial power (and as a result having offered (albeit very poorly administered) generous measures for struggling businesses during the crisis),[5] but with a strong legal and political tradition of the social state (*Sozialstaatlichkeit*)[6] which should equip Germany well for a public health crisis. This principle is enshrined in Germany's Basic Law (GG) and is one of the inalienable core

* The author is thankful to Vanessa Bliecke, Rouven Diekjobst, Nadine Grünhagen and Ella Schönleben for assistance with research and editing.

[1] Severe Acute Respiratory Syndrome, cf E Rosenthal, 'The SARS Epidemic: The Path' *New York Times* (27 April 2003) www.nytimes.com/2003/04/27/world/the-sars-epidemic-the-path-from-china-s-provinces-a-crafty-germ-breaks-out.html.

[2] Middle East Respiratory Syndrome, cf. WHO, 'Middle East respiratory syndrome coronavirus (MERS-CoV)' www.who.int/news/item/09-07-2013-middle-east-respiratory-syndrome-coronavirus-(mers-cov).

[3] As of 16 February 2021, cf WHO, 'WHO Coronavirus Disease (COVID-19) Dashboard' covid19.who.int/.

[4] OECD, 'The territorial impact of COVID-19: Managing the crisis across levels of government' (10 November 2020) read.oecd-ilibrary.org/view/?ref=128_128287-5agkkojaaa&title=The-territorial-impact-of-covid-19-managing-the-crisis-across-levels-of-government.

[5] V Jentsch, 'Government Responses on Corona and Contracts in Europe: A Compilation of Extraordinary Measures in Times of Crisis', papers.ssrn.com/sol3/papers.cfm?abstract_id=3713699.

[6] cf M Sachs, 'Art. 20' in M Sachs (ed), *Grundgesetz: Kommentar* (CH Beck, 2020) 816f.

principles of the constitution (*Ewigkeitsklausel*, Article 79, paragraph 3 GG).[7] Chancellor Ludwig Erhard coined the idea of social market economy (*Soziale Marktwirtschaft*) in the 1950s;[8] until today this notion forms very much part of German political identity. Along with it comes a supposedly strong healthcare system[9] – even if questions of inequality in that system continue to be raised.[10] So the question is: did the supposedly strong German economy and healthcare systems do as well as we would expect it to do?

Secondly, Germany is, challenged only by France, the political hegemon in the European Union. Economic and financial power are paired with 16 years of Angela Merkel's chancellorship – the most experienced political leader of all 27 EU Member States who has successfully weathered the storms of various European crises (eg, the 'financial crisis', the 'refugee crisis') to become one of the most respected political leaders worldwide. With a new German President of the European Commission and with the political heavyweight of the UK having left the Union, Germany has more power within the EU than ever before. However, did Germany do these high international and in particular European expectations justice?

Thirdly, and most importantly, Germany is explicitly a federal state. The principle of federalism, broadly understood as a mixed form of governance combining a central government with regional/provincial governments,[11] is another one of the inalienable core principles of the GG, of equal constitutional value as the principle of democracy or the rule of law. There is hardly another state within the EU in which the principle of federalism enjoys greater political importance and higher constitutional rank than in Germany[12] – a structure that is certainly in direct contrast to the EU's second most influential state, France, which heavily relies on a centralist form of state organisation. So, has Germany's federalist approach – allowing the *Länder* to set different rules rather than implementing a federal uniform approach – been a more responsive and democratic way of handling the crisis, or has it hampered the effectiveness of the German response?

[7] R Herzog et al (eds), 'Art. 79' in T Maunz and G Dürig (eds), *Grundgesetz: Kommentar* (CH Beck, 2020) para 157.

[8] L Erhard, *Wohlstand für alle* (Anaconda Verlag, 2020).

[9] A Tandon et al, 'Measuring overall Health System Performances for 191 Countries' (*World Health Organization GPE Discussion Paper Series: No. 30*) www.who.int/healthinfo/paper30.pdf; OECD 'State of Health in the EU – Germany, Country Health Profile 2017', www.euro.who.int/__data/assets/pdf_file/0004/355981/Health-Profile-Germany-Eng.pdf.

[10] Out of many: T Lampert et al, 'Health inequalities in Germany and in international comparison: trends and developments over time' (2018) *Journal of Health Monitoring*, edoc.rki.de/handle/176904/3046.

[11] German Federal Constitutional Court (BVerfG), *Neugliederung Hessen*, 11 July 1961, BVerfGE 13, 54 (77 f.); KP Sommermann, 'Art. 20' in H Mangoldt, F Klein and C Starck (eds), *Grundgesetz Kommentar*, 7th edn (CH Beck, 2018), para 28.

[12] Z Desson et al, 'Europe's Covid-19 outliers: German, Austrian and Swiss policy responses during the early stages of the 2020 pandemic' (2020) *Health Policy and technology* 405, 415. For another state with particularly strong federalist features, albeit outside the EU, see O Ammann and F Uhlmann, 'Switzerland: The (Missing) Role of Parliament in Times of Crisis', in this volume.

After giving an overview over the course of the pandemic in Germany including the state's response to it (section II), the analysis proceeds in section III with characterising the German model of federalism, the constitutional rules on state emergencies, democratic power-sharing and the special protection of fundamental rights as well as infectious disease law. It examines the different legal levels – the constitutional framework of the GG, federal laws (mainly the German *Infektionsschutzgesetz (IPA)*[13]) and – to some extent – decrees by the executive at the different levels (*Verordnungen*). In section IV, the strengths and weaknesses of the German (highly federalist) approach are weighed against each other in how far and under which circumstances is the federal state equipped to adapt its institutional set-up and its legislative procedures to adjust to 'crisis mode', and how has the German response played out with regard to the principle of democracy? The chapter concludes with options for legal and policy reform (section V).

II. Germany and the COVID-19 Pandemic in 2020

The first case of COVID-19 in Germany was discovered on 27 January 2020,[14] significantly later than cases in Italy[15] and France. The first two COVID-19 related deaths were reported on 9 March 2020,[16] again much later than in other European States. The 'first wave' (spring to summer 2020) hit Germany later and took a milder course than in other EU States.

When looking at the numbers, Germany did remarkably well compared to other prosperous European States of comparable population size (eg, the UK, France, Italy or Spain),[17] with roughly 2.3 million confirmed cases and an estimated 65,000 COVID-related deaths within the German population of 82 million.[18] Areas in the

[13] Gesetz zur Verhütung und Bekämpfung von Infektionskrankheiten beim Menschen (Infektionsschutzgesetz), 20 July 2000, BGBl. I S. 1045, last amended 21 December 2020, BGBl. I S. 3136.

[14] RKI, 'Epidemiologisches Bulletin 07/2020' (2020) www.rki.de/DE/Content/Infekt/EpidBull/Archiv/2020/Ausgaben/07_20.pdf%3F__blob%3DpublicationFile.

[15] Deutsche Welle, Corona war schon im September 2019 da, auch in Europa, www.dw.com/de/corona-war-schon-im-september-2019-da-auch-in-europa/a-55626017 (first instance in Italy in September 2019); Deutsche Welle, Erster Corna-Fall in Frankreich schon im Dezember, www.dw.com/de/erster-corona-fall-in-frankreich-schon-im-dezember/a-53341847 (first instance in France in December 2019).

[16] RKI, 'Coronavirus Disease 2019 (COVID-19) Daily Situation Report of the Robert Koch Institute, 09/03/2020' (2020) www.rki.de/DE/Content/InfAZ/N/Neuartiges_Coronavirus/Situationsberichte/2020-03-09-en.pdf?__blob=publicationFile.

[17] See R Thomas, 'Virus Governance in the United Kingdom' in this volume; S Brunet, 'The Hyper-Executive State of Emergency in France' in this volume; A Vedaschi, 'The Marginalisation of Parliament in Facing the Coronavirus Emergency: What about Democracy in Italy?' in this volume; J Reichel and J Dahlqvist, 'Swedish Constitutional Response to the Corona Crisis – The Odd One Out', in this volume.

[18] J Schilling et al, 'Disease severity of the first COVID-19 wave in Germany using reporting data from the national notification system' (2020) *Journal of Health Monitoring*, www.rki.de/EN/Content/Health_Monitoring/Health_Reporting/GBEDownloadsJ/JoHM_S11_2020_Disease_Severity_COVID_19.pdf?__blob=publicationFile.

south (Bavaria, Baden-Wuerttemberg, Thuringia and Saxony) were more affected than the north,[19] given, inter alia, the proximity to COVID-19 hotspots in States neighbouring Germany to the south and the east, such as Austria or the Czech Republic. In the west, Germany's region with the highest population density, North-Rhine Westphalia, was also significantly more affected than most rural areas.[20] In this first wave, Germany never reached numbers higher than 7,000 new cases and a death rate of hardly ever over 250 per day – compared to much higher numbers in Italy, Spain, France or the UK, where the daily infection rates were double or triple those in Germany.[21]

During this first wave, Germany was widely considered a poster-child for its approach in tackling the pandemic. Germany managed to establish a very high test rate in the early phase of the pandemic[22] and built a reliable tracing system to follow infection chains.[23] Far-reaching curfews and social distancing rules were introduced in early March 2020.[24] Its modern healthcare system, well-equipped hospitals as well as its highly qualified doctors and hospital personnel, were instrumental in keeping the death rates low.[25] As one caveat, however, some political observers noted already in the first wave that the measures taken had a rather restricting effect on democratic structures, eg the unilateral empowerment of the federal ministry of health at the expense of Parliament.[26]

The second wave (fall/winter 2020/2021) hit Germany significantly harder. While this is true for most, if not all European States, the difference in severity between the first and the second wave in Germany is striking. With infection rates well over 40,000 in December 2020 and regularly reported death rates

[19] A Mense and C Michelsen, 'Räumliche Ausbreitung von COVID-19 durch interregionale Verflechtungen' (2020) Leibniz-Informationszentrum Wirtschaft' (2020) link.springer.com/article/10.1007/s10273-020-2674-7; RKI, 'Daily Situation Report of the Robert Koch Institute 14/03/2020' (2020) www.rki.de/DE/Content/InfAZ/N/Neuartiges_Coronavirus/Situationsberichte/2020-03-14-en.pdf?__blob=publicationFile.

[20] ibid.

[21] *The Economist*, 'Tracking the coronavirus across Europe' (21 January 2020) www.economist.com/graphic-detail/tracking-coronavirus-across-europe.

[22] Bundesministerium für Gesundheit, '"Testen, testen, testen" – aber gezielt' (17 April 2020) www.bundesgesundheitsministerium.de/fileadmin/Dateien/3_Downloads/C/Coronavirus/Faktenpapier_Testen.PDF.

[23] RKI, 'Kontaktpersonennachverfolgung bei respiratorischen Erkrankungen durch das Coronavirus SARS-CoV-2' (18 March 2020) https://cdn.dosb.de/user_upload/Olympische_Spiele/Tokio_2020/Corona/RKI_Kontaktpersonen_Management_COVID-19_1803202.pdf; updated version available under: www.rki.de/DE/Content/InfAZ/N/Neuartiges_Coronavirus/Kontaktperson/Management.html.

[24] T Büthe, L Messerschmidt and C Cheng, 'Policy Responses to the Coronavirus in Germany' in GL Gardini *The World Before and After COVID-19: Intellectual Reflections on Politics, Diplomacy and International Relations* (Stockholm, European Institute of International Studies Press 2020) 97.

[25] F Hattke and H Martin, 'Collective action during the Covid-19 pandemic: The case of Germany's fragmented authority' (2020) *Administrative Theory & Praxis* 614, 616.

[26] Süddeutsche Zeitung, 'Spahn will dauerhaft Sonderrechte' (18 October 2020) www.sueddeutsche.de/politik/jens-spahn-gesetz-pandemie-1.5079500; Bundesministerium für Gesundheit, 'Drittes Bevölkerungsschutzgesetz' (18 November 2020) www.bundesgesundheitsministerium.de/drittes-bevoelkerungsschutzgesetz.html.

of over 1,000 per day,[27] Germany fared worse than many European neighbours. While trying to avoid a second full lockdown, the federal government and the *Länder* agreed in late October 2020 on a 'lockdown light',[28] with educational institutions (schools and kindergartens) as well as essential service-providers (hairdressers) remaining open. Chancellor Merkel had pressed for a more decisive approach and more drastic measures, but was unable to find agreement amongst the Prime Ministers of the *Länder*.[29]

Germany also performed particularly poorly in its mass vaccination strategy since early 2021. While many States had a large part of their population vaccinated by spring 2021, Germany lagged dramatically behind. While, for instance, by mid-February 2021, Israel had vaccinated more than 50 per cent, the United Arab Emirates (UAE) more than 30 per cent and the UK more than 25 per cent of their respective population at least once, Germany had still vaccinated significantly less than 5 per cent of its population at least once at that time.[30] Germany not only started late, but also administered significantly less daily doses of COVID-19 vaccinations[31] than other States such as the UAE, Israel, the US and the UK,[32] even in comparison to other EU States with less advanced healthcare systems such as Malta, Poland, or Spain.[33] The German vaccination campaign was thus late and slow. Reasons for this include insufficient orders of the vaccine by the federal government and the EU in early 2020,[34] but also the lack of coordinated planning strategies of the federal state with the *Länder*.[35]

III. The Relevant German Legal Framework

This section summarises federalist and democratic structures in Germany and highlights how they shaped Germany's response to COVID-19.

[27] eg RKI, 'Daily Situation Report of the Robert Koch Institute 18/12/2020', www.rki.de/DE/Content/InfAZ/N/Neuartiges_Coronavirus/Situationsberichte/Dez_2020/2020-12-18-en.pdf?__blob=publicationFile; see all reports of December here: www.rki.de/DE/Content/InfAZ/N/Neuartiges_Coronavirus/Situationsberichte/Dez_2020/Archiv_Dezember.htm.

[28] Bundesregierung 'Videokonferenz der Bundeskanzlerin mit den Regierungschefinnen und Regierungschefs der Länder am 28. Oktober 2020' www.bundesregierung.de/resource/blob/997532/1805024/5353edede6c0125ebe5b5166504dfd79/2020-10-28-mpk-beschluss-corona-data.pdf?download=1.

[29] Die Zeit 'Jetzt aber schnell' (28 October 2020) www.zeit.de/politik/deutschland/2020-10/ministerpraesidentenkonferenz-coronavirus-zweiter-lockdown-angela-merkel; Süddeutsche Zeitung, 'Teil-Lockdown an Weihnachten befürchtet' (23 November 2020) www.sueddeutsche.de/politik/corona-weihnachten-lockdown-dreyer-1.5123842.

[30] H Ritchi et al, Coronavirus (COVID-19) Vaccinations, www.ourworldindata.org/covid-vaccinations.

[31] 0.13 doses per 100 people, see ibid.

[32] UAE (1.41), Israel (1.12), the UK (0.63) and the US (0.44) per 100 people, see Ritchi (n 30).

[33] Malta (0.37), Poland (0.18) and Spain (0.15), see Ritchi (n 30).

[34] M Becker et al, 'Das Planungsdesaster' *Der Spiegel* (18 December 2020).

[35] S Stalinski, 'Warum so langsam?' (*Tagesschau* 4 January 2021) www.tagesschau.de/inland/gesellschaft/faq-schleppende-impfkampagne-101.html.

A. Federalism in the German Constitution

Both the German federal state as well as the 16 states (*Länder*) hold the basic characteristics of a state (*Staatsqualität*).[36] The *Länder* enjoy, even if in a limited way,[37] what the German constitutional court ('*BVerfG*') termed constitutional autonomy (*Verfassungsautonomie*),[38] emphasising their uniquely strong position within the German legal system.

Federalism is aimed at enabling variety while preserving state unity.[39] It also limits political power over the individual[40] – emphasised also by the central role the German fundamental rights (Articles 1–19 GG) play in the German constitution as a lesson from Nazi history.[41] Federalism enables vertical separation of powers[42] as a central means of checks and balances.

The 16 *Länder* are geographically and economically very different. North-Rhine Westphalia (18 million inhabitants) has 25 times the population of Bremen (0.7 million inhabitants),[43] Bavaria makes up 20 per cent of the German territory while the three city states of Hamburg, Bremen and Berlin combined only hold 0.5 per cent of the territory[44] and the GDP per capita in Hamburg is far more than double that one in Saxony-Anhalt.[45] These conditions are in contrast with the fact that the *Länder* are supposed to be at eye level of each other,[46] given that the constitution postulates comparable living conditions (*gleichwertige Lebensverhältnisse*) for all the *Länder* (Article 72, paragraph 2 GG).

With regard to the democratic principle within these federalist structures, the 'normative programming' in Germany lies firmly in the hand of the federal level.[47] Where the federal state does not hold 'exclusive' legislative powers,[48] it has in many policy fields 'concurrent' legislative powers,[49] which the state has

[36] J Isensee and P Kirchhof, *Handbuch des Staatsrechts VI*, 3rd edn (CF Müller, 2009) § 126, Rn. 4; Sommermann (n 11) 21. Despite this state quality, the Länder remain sub-ordinated to the federal state, see BVerfG, *Zensus 2011*, 19 September 2018, BVerfGE 150, 1 (103f.).

[37] PM Huber, 'Verfassungsautonomie der Länder und Landesverfassungsgerichtsbarkeit' in B Munz and A Uhle (eds), *Der deutsche Verfassungsgerichtsverbund* (Nomos, 2019) 29–51.

[38] BVerfG, *Finanzausgleich*, 24 June 1986, BVerfGE, 72, 330 (388); BVerfG, *Naturschutzgesetz Schleswig-Holstein*, 7 May 2001, BVerfGE, 103, 332 (350f.).

[39] BVerfG, *Studiengebühren Bremen*, 8 May 2013, BVerfGE 134, 1; H Jarass in H Jarass and B Pieroth (eds), *Grundgesetz: Kommentar*, 16th edn (CH Beck, 2020) 544.

[40] BVerfG, *Berufsausbildungsabgabe*, 10 December 1980, BVerfGE 55, 274 (318f.); B Grzeszick, 'Art 20 IV' in R Herzog et al (eds), *Maunz/Dürig Grundgesetz Kommentar* (Issue 92, August 2020), para 20.

[41] H Vorländer, *Die Verfassung. Idee und Geschichte* (CH Beck, 2004) 11.

[42] BVerfG, Telekommunikationsgesetz, 15 July 2003, BverfGE 108, 169 (181f.).; Jarass (n 39) Art 20 GG, p 546, para 32.

[43] Statistische Ämter des Bundes und der Länder, 'Statistikportal, Fläche und Bevölkerung' (2020) www.statistikportal.de/de/bevoelkerung/flaeche-und-bevoelkerung.

[44] ibid.

[45] Statistische Ämter des Bundes und der Länder, 'Statistikportal, Bruttoinlandsprodukt' (2020) www.statistikportal.de/de/vgrdl/ergebnisse-laenderebene/bruttoinlandsprodukt-bruttowertschoepfung/bip.

[46] M Kloepfer, *Verfassungsrecht I* (CH Beck, 2011) § 9, para 90; Grzeszick (n 40) para 113.

[47] J Kersten and S Rixen, *Der Verfassungsstaat in der Coronakrise* (CH Beck, 2020) 113–14.

[48] See the list in Art 73 GG.

[49] See Art 72 and the list in Art 74 GG.

used extensively,[50] minimising legislative powers of the *Länder* de facto to a few selected fields, such as education, culture or police law.[51] The general rule that state powers should primarily be exercised through the *Länder* (Articles 30 and 70 GG) has been reversed for the legislature. As a consequence of this, the devaluation of *Länder* Parliaments has long been observed to be problematic,[52] with a view to the erosion of the democratic principle.

However, where legislative competence lies with the federal level, the *Länder* have nonetheless retained an important role in the legislative process – they are granted, dependent on the substantive matter, either the right to slow down or even veto the process via the upper German house (*Bundesrat*).[53] However, while this indeed promotes the *Länder*'s influence in federal law making, it does not include the *Länder* parliaments in this equation as the *Bundesrat* is made up of representatives of the *Länder* governments, not the *Länder* parliaments.

With respect to administration, Germany's political system takes the form of administrative federalism (*Exekutivföderalismus*).[54] Most federal laws are executed by the *Länder* in their own right (Articles 83 and 84 GG). Only in exceptional cases does the federal state hold the power to execute the laws itself (Article 86 GG). Seldomly does the *Länder* execute the laws on commission of the federal state, giving the federal level an increased power of oversight both in terms of legality and suitability of the chosen measures (Article 85 GG).

Furthermore, the unwritten constitutional notion of mutually faithful federal behaviour (*Bundestreue*) has become increasingly important over the last decades.[55] Both sides have to take each other's interests into account in good faith when exercising their competences.[56] This includes sharing information, consultation or cooperation.[57] Where *Länder* arbitrarily aim at having negotiations with the federal state fail[58] or use own competences to the detriment of the *Bund*,[59] they are in clear violation of said principle. The role of the *Länder* in federal law-making via the *Bundesrat* as well as this duty to cooperate have coined the term of cooperative federalism (*kooperativer Föderalismus*),[60] emphasising the multi-lateral bargaining and consensus-seeking character of German federalism.[61]

[50] Sommermann (n 11), para 31.

[51] A Uhle, 'Art. 72' in Herzog et al (n 40) paras 348ff.

[52] K Stern, *Staatsrecht I*, 2nd edn (CH Beck, 1984) § 19 IV para 3.

[53] MHW Möllers, 'Gesetzgebung' in R Voigt (ed), *Handbuch Staat* (Springer VS, 2018) 1014.

[54] J Kersten and S Rixen, *Der Verfassungsstaat in der Coronakrise* (CH Beck 2020) 113.

[55] BVerfG, *Kalkar II*, 22 May 1990, BVerfGE 81, 310 (337f.); BVerfG, *EG-Fernsehrichtlinie*, 22 March 1995, BVerfGE 92, 203 (234); Schnapp, MüK 11.

[56] BVerfG, *Biblis A*, 9 February 2002, BVerfGE 104, 249 (270).

[57] BVerfG, *numerus clausus II*, 8 February 1977, BVerfGE 43, 291 (348f.); Jarass (n 39) 545.

[58] BVerfG, *Wohnungsbauförderung*, 21 May 1952, BVerfGE 1, 299 (315f.).

[59] BVerfG, *2. Rundfunkentscheidung*, 27 July 1971, BVerfGE 31, 314 (355).

[60] TA Börzel, *States and Regions in the European Union: Institutional Adaptation in Germany and Spain* (CUP, 2001) 45; J Saurer, 'Covid-19 and Cooperative Administrative Federalism in Germany, Comparing Nations Respones to Covid-19' (*The Regulatory Review*, 13 May 2020) www.theregreview.org/2020/05/13/saurer-covid-19-cooperative-administrative-federalism-germany/.

[61] ibid, 48.

Summing up, German federalism is both *executive* (with most legislative powers at the federal level, but the implementation of the federal laws firmly in the hands of the *Länder*) and *cooperative* (obliging the federal state and *Länder* to work together in good faith).

B. Emergency Regulations in the German Basic Law

A specific part of the German constitution (GG) concerns the emergency constitution (*Notstandsverfassung*), largely introduced in 1968 following a wave of left-wing civil society unrest.[62] Until then, the GG had remained silent on emergency regulations, as a result of bad experiences with emergency clauses in the Weimar constitution (Article 48, paragraph 2 of that constitution) and because the Allies had reserved for themselves certain emergency powers in Germany.[63]

Today, these rules of the emergency constitution are spread all through the constitutional text which makes them rather complex and chaotic.[64] Their overarching goal is to protect the state in times of crisis through simplification of procedures and through concentration of powers with the federal executive. The GG sharply distinguishes externally-induced and internal emergency. Cases of externally-caused emergency are the case of self-defence (Article 115 a–i GG) and the case of external tensions (*Spannungsfall*) that are likely to turn into self-defence (Article 80 a GG). The legal consequences of such externally-caused emergencies are competence shifts to the federal government, simplified legislative procedures and possible restrictions in otherwise guaranteed fundamental rights.[65]

Very different is the case of internally-induced emergency (Article 35 GG). This includes special cases of dangers for public security and order as well as the case of catastrophes. In such cases the *Länder* can request help from other *Länder* or the federal state (Article 35, paragraph 2 GG). If several *Länder* are affected, the federal government may instruct the *Länder* governments to place police forces at the disposal of other Länder and may deploy units of the federal border police or the armed forces to support the *Länder* police. The *Bundesrat* is given the power to request that such measures be rescinded (Article 35, paragraph 3 GG).

Going even further, Article 91 GG regulates the case of dangers for the existence or the free democratic basic order of the federal state or at least one of the

[62] M Kenzler, *An den Grenzen der Notstandsverfassung: Ausnahmezustand und Staatsnotrecht im Verfassungssystem des Grundgesetzes* (Duncker & Humblot, 1974) 15 f.

[63] ibid.

[64] P Thielbörger and B Behlert, 'COVID-19 and the Basic Law: On the (Un)suitability of the German Constitutional "Immune System"' (*Blog of the International Journal of Constitutional Law*, 20 March 2020) www.iconnectblog.com/2020/03/covid-19-and-the-basic-law-on-the-unsuitability-of-the-german-constitutional-immune-system/.

[65] For more specific information, see for instance: T Mertins, *Der Spannungsfall. Eine Untersuchung zur Notstandsverfassung des Grundgesetzes unter besonderer Berücksichtigung der Abwehr terroristischer Gefahren* (Nomos, 2013).

Länder. In this case, the *Länder* can request police forces from other *Länder* or the German border police. According to paragraph 2, in such cases the federal executive can even take control over *Länder* police forces, give direct orders to the *Länder* governments or, if the use of police or border police is insufficient, use military forces (Article 87a, paragraph 4 in conjunction with Article 91, paragraph 2 GG).

Pandemics (such as COVID-19) do not classify as externally-induced emergencies, except for scenarios in which viruses would be used against Germany as a weapon by another state. However, they can be understood as internal emergencies such as natural disasters in the sense of Article 35 GG, even if the natural disasters that the authors of GG had in mind were sudden threats such as floods and earthquakes.[66] However, the typical legal consequences of Article 35, paragraphs 1–3 GG (sharing of police forces, the use of the military, etc) are inapt for dealing with a pandemic. Only where it reaches an extreme status (eg, the collapse of the entire healthcare system) which threatens the existence of the nation in the sense of Article 91 GG, might some of the legal consequences (eg, the possibility of giving direct order to *Länder* governments) become relevant. However, such a state of emergency was not proclaimed at the federal level, but only occurred in very few *Länder* (eg, Bavaria) and municipalities (eg, Halle) where regional cases of emergency were proclaimed at certain peak times of infections.[67]

Thus, altogether while the German constitution is rather well equipped for making necessary changes if an externally-induced emergency (such as an armed attack), it provides hardly any tools for the federal level to react to an internal emergency (such as a pandemic).

C. The Role of Parliament

The *Bundestag* is Germany's main legislative organ, the heart of German democracy. Like any Parliament, it has an important 'integrative function through representation':[68] not only decision-making through majority, but also the exchange of different views give the *Bundestag*'s acts a higher degree of legitimacy than the acts of government.[69]

Unlike in other States (eg, Poland), the *Bundestag* is elected for 48 months with no possibility to postpone elections (Article 39 GG), for instance

[66] P Thielbörger and B Behlert, 'COVID-19 und das Grundgesetz – Zur (Un)tauglichkeit des verfassungsrechtlichen „Immunsystems"' (*Verfassungsblog*, 19 March 2020) www.verfassungsblog.de/covid-19-und-das-grundgesetz/.

[67] T Frasch and M Grunert, 'Bayerns Katastrophe' (*Frankfurter Allgemeine Zeitung*, 16 March 2020) www.faz.net/aktuell/gesellschaft/gesundheit/coronavirus/massnahmen-gegen-coronavirus-bayerns-katastrophe-16682097.html.

[68] HM Heinig, 'Parlamentarismus in der Pandemie: Beobachtungen und Thesen' (*Verfassungsblog*, 25 November 2020) www.verfassungsblog.de/parlamentarismus-in-der-pandemie/.

[69] ibid; W Merkel, 'Wer regiert in der Krise? Demokratie in Zeiten der Pandemie' in *WSI-Mitteilungen*, pp 445–53.

during times of emergency.[70] Some of the *Länder* theoretically foresee the possibility of emergency Parliaments,[71] but none of them made use of this possibility during COVID-19.[72] For the *Bundestag*, the *Gemeinsame Ausschuss* (Article 53a GG) can take over certain functions in the case of an external emergency, not during internally-induced emergencies. While some academics[73] as well as the President of the Parliament had suggested including a similar possibility for the *Bundestag* also in case of pandemics (*Notfallausschuss*), this proposal was largely criticised and rejected.[74] Instead, the different party groups agreed informally that the quorum of more than half of the members of the *Bundestag* (§ 45 of the rules of procedure (GOBT) of the German *Bundestag*), if not reached, should not be challenged.[75] Eventually, in March 2020, the *Bundestag* changed and introduced a new § 126a GOBT.[76] § 126a GOBT allows for online meetings and voting of the committees (*Ausschüsse*), but not of plenary meetings, although this possibility was discussed by political observers.[77] Moreover, the *Bundestag* can now vote on issues when one fourth of its members are present, as a direct reaction to the pandemic.

During COVID-19, there were many debates in the *Bundestag* on the topic of the pandemic. These debates, however, remained remarkably uncontroversial with most party groups supporting the same political solutions at least during the first wave,[78] with the role of members of Parliaments largely being reduced to political bystanders.[79] The *Bundestag* never challenged any of the governmental proposals concerning the crisis, including the far-reaching reforms of the IPA which caused a dramatic shift of power from the legislative to the executive branch.

[70] M Friehe, 'Die Demokratie muss immun bleiben' (*Verfassungsblog*, 21 May 2020) www.verfassungsblog.de/die-demokratie-muss-immun-bleiben/.

[71] cf Art 62 I of the Constitution of Baden-Württemberg; Art 113 I of the Constitution of Saxony.

[72] Heinig (n 68).

[73] P Thielbörger and B Behlert, 'COVID-19 und das Grundgesetz: Neue Gedanken vor dem Hintergrund neuer Gesetze' (*Verfassungsblog*, 30 March 2020) www.verfassungsblog.de/covid-19-und-das-grundgesetz-neue-gedanken-vor-dem-hintergrund-neuer-gesetze/.

[74] *Sueddeutsche Zeitung* (4 April 2020) www.sueddeutsche.de/politik/corona-grundgesetz-aenderung-wolfgang-schaeuble-1.4868353; *Legal Tribune Online*, www.lto.de/recht/nachrichten/n/bundestag-corona-grundgesetz-aenderungen-notparlament-fraktionen-ablehnung-schauble-vorschlaege/.

[75] Thielbörger and Behlert (n 73).

[76] § 126a GOBT was initially intended to be in force only until 30 September 2020, but is still in place until 30 June 2021, dip21.bundestag.de/dip21/btd/19/275/1927529.pdf.

[77] R Roßmann, 'Wie der Bundestag virtuell tagen könnte' (*Süddeutsche Zeitung*, 13 April 2020) www.sueddeutsche.de/politik/virtueller-bundestag-corona-schaeuble-digitaler-1.4874777.

[78] R Roland, 'Demokratie und Bürgerbeteiligungs in Zeiten von COVID-19' (Opuscula 141, Maecenata Institut für Philantropie und Zivilgesellschaft Berlin, 2020) nbn-resolving.org/urn:nbn:de:0168-ssoar-68889-1.

[79] See for instance H Aden, C Arzt and J Fährmann, 'Gefährdete Freiheitsrechte in Krisenzeiten – Lehren aus der COVID-19-Pandemie' (2020) *Zeitschrift für Bürgerrechte und Gesellschaftspolitik* 99–111 who list measures that were in their view too far-reaching with respect to freedom of assembly, freedom of movement and data protection, 116.

Some observers have therefore mourned the 'self-disempowerment'[80] or 'uncritical, subservient attitude'[81] of the Parliament during the COVID-19 crisis.

D. The Centrality of German Fundamental Rights

The founding mothers and fathers of the GG put fundamental rights at the very beginning of the GG (Article 1-19 GG)[82] signaling their utmost importance for the new German state. Starting with Article 1 GG (human dignity), the list includes a variety of fundamental rights. For our purpose most importantly, these include personal freedoms (Article 2 GG), freedom of expression, arts and sciences (Article 5 GG), freedom of assembly (Article 8 GG), freedom of association (Article 9 GG), freedom of movement (Article 11 GG) as well as occupational freedoms (Article 12 GG). The state has not only the obligation to respect ('negative obligation'), but also to ensure these rights ('positive obligation').[83] Restrictions are generally allowed, but according to Article 19, paragraph 1 GG, laws must specify the fundamental right they affect, and under no circumstance may the essence (*Wesensgehalt*)[84] of a basic right be touched (Article 19, paragraph 2 GG). Any restriction of fundamental rights must be prescribed by law (*Vorbehalt des Gesetzes*), rules below the rank of the law are not sufficient. While Article 80 GG allows the federal government, a federal minister or the *Länder* governments to issue statutory instruments below the level of the law (*Verordnung*), their content, purpose and scope of the authority conferred must be specified at the level of the law itself. These rules are important safeguards for the principle of democracy in Germany as they put the Parliaments at centre stage when it comes to protecting fundamental rights.

Furthermore, any provisions of the constitution must be understood in light of international law (*Völkerrechtsfreundlichkeit des GG*)[85] which is important for German fundamental rights given that they are closely mirrored in international human rights treaties such as the International Covenant on Civil and Political Rights, the International Covenant on Economic, Social and Cultural Rights or the European Convention on Human Rights and Fundamental Freedoms, which even

[80] C Möllers, 'Parlamentarische Selbstentmächtigung im Zeichen des Virus' (*Verfassungsblog*, 26 March 2020) www.verfassungsblog.de/parlamentarische-selbstentmaechtigung-im-zeichen-des-virus/.

[81] Merkel (n 69).

[82] Grundgesetz für die Bundesrepublik Deutschland vom 23 Mai 1949, BGBl. p 1 (Nr 1).

[83] In detail: M Cornils, *Die Ausgestaltung der Grundrechte: Untersuchungen zur Grundrechtsbindung des Ausgestaltungsgesetzgebers* (Mohr Siebeck, 2005) 561 f.

[84] On the concept of essence, see in general: P Thielbörger, 'The "Essence" of International Human Rights' (2019) 20 *German Law Journal* 924; On the German case specifically, see J Bernstorff, 'Die Wesensgehalte der Grundrechte und das Verhältnis von Freiheit und Sicherheit unter dem Grundgesetz' in F Arndt et al (eds), *Freiheit – Sicherheit – Öffentlichkeit* (Nomos, 2009 40ff.

[85] The „Völkerrechtsfreundlichkeit" is a well-established principle in the jurisprudence of the German Federal Constitutional Court, see eg BVerfG, *Bodenreform III*, 26 October 2004, BVerfGE 112, 1 (25).

enjoys special gravity when interpreting German fundamental rights.[86] As in most other States, fundamental rights and the principle of democracy find themselves in a multi-faceted relationship in the German system: they enable and restrict democratic decision-making at the same time.[87]

E. Challenges to the Legal Regime of Infectious Diseases

i. Amendments of the German Infection Protection Act

The legal regime for the protection against infectious diseases is a typical case of the 'work-share' between *Bund* legislative and *Länder* administration. The *Bundestag* enacted a statutory law in 2000, the Infection Protection Act (IPA) (*Infektionsschutzgesetz*)[88] under Article 74, No 19 GG in the form of concurrent legislation, whose execution lies in the hands of the *Länder* in their own right. The IPA entitles the competent *Länder* authorities to adopt measures for the prevention and control of infectious diseases. Such measures must be ordered by the *Länder* or local authorities within them; the federal state can neither issue directives nor give orders to the *Länder*.

Possible measures under the IPA aim at monitoring (§§ 6 ff. IPA), prevention (§§ 16 ff. IPA) and fighting the disease (§§ 24 ff. IPA). Quarantines can be ordered – at home or in medical isolation units – (§ 30 IPA), professional activities banned (§ 31 IPA), care facilities for minors like kindergartens or schools can be closed (§ 33 IPA), events or other gatherings of a large number of people can be restricted or banned (§ 28, paragraph 1, sentence 2 IPA). Of particular importance is § 28, paragraph 1, sentence 1 IPA which broadly allows the administration to take '*all necessary measures*'. Curfews or the closing of shops or universities were, in the absence of a more specific regulation, regularly based on this general clause of § 28 IPA.[89]

[86] cf Scientific Services of the *Bundestag*, 'Bedeutung der Europäischen Konvention für Menschenrechte und der Entscheidungen des Europäischen Gerichtshofs für Menschenrechte für die deutsche Gesetzgebung' (2016) www.bundestag.de/resource/blob/436800/8e288ab7acd739fcad24630 17ad44b08/wd-3-162-16-pdf-data.pdf; BVerfG, EGMR-Entscheidungen, 24 October 2004, BVerfGE 111, 307 (315f).

[87] J Isensee, 'Staat und Verfassung' in Isensee/Kirchhof (eds), *Handbuch des Staatsrechts*, 2nd edn (CF Müller, 2004) § 15 Rn 4.

[88] Infektionsschutzgesetz of 20 July 2000, BGBl. I, p 1045.

[89] Out of many, curfew in Bavaria: § 4 Allgemeinverfügung Vorläufige Ausgangsbeschränkung anlässlich der Corona-Pandemie Bekanntmachung des Bayerischen Staatsministeriums für Gesundheit und Pflege, Az. Z6a-G8000-2020/122-98 (20 March 2020) www.bayern.de/wp-content/uploads/2020/03/20-03-20-ausgangsbeschraenkung-bayern-.pdf; closure of shops in the city of Bottrop: § 2 Allgemeinverfügung zum Zwecke der Verhütung und Bekämpfung der Ausbreitung des Coronavirus SARS-CoV-2, Amtliche Bekanntmachung der Stadt Bottrop 2020/027 – Allgemeinverfügung Schließung Einzelhandel und Restaurants (18 March 2020) www.bottrop.de/rathaus/bekanntmachungen/2020/2020-026_218369.php; closure of universities in NRW: § 6 Verordnung zum Schutz vor Neuinfizierungen mit dem Coronavirus SARS-CoV-2 (Coronaschutzverordnung – CoronaSchVO) (7 January 2021), www.land.nrw/sites/default/files/asset/document/210212_coronaschvo_ab_14.02.2021_lesefassung_mit_markierungen.pdf.

The competent authorities can implement measures in relation to specific individuals (*Verwaltungsakt*) or issue administrative acts of a more general nature (*Allgemeinverfügung*). The health ministers of the *Länder* can also employ even more broad ordinances (*Rechtsverordnungen*).

Early in the first wave, academics[90] and politicians[91] demanded a reform of the IPA. Some critiqued that the IPA did not give the federal state the competencies it needed for effective disease control,[92] others argued that § 28 IPA was not specific enough to justify intense forms of restrictions of fundamental rights,[93] such as curfews or the closing of businesses.

From March 2020 onwards, the IPA was amended multiple times.[94] The most important amendments were based on three bills. In March 2020,[95] the *Bundestag* introduced a bill to amend the IPA giving new powers to the federal health ministry, which now, according to the new § 5 IPA, has the power to establish ordinances in case of epidemics of national significance. The competence to enact such ordinances in § 5, paragraph 2 IPA explicitly left out the involvement of the *Bundesrat*, thereby not only strengthening the federal government as a collective organ, but one single ministry.[96] Even the scientific services of the *Bundestag* concluded in examining the legality of the new bill that this amendment was alarming, arguing that given the democratic principle Parliament should decide upon such intrusive measures.[97] The possibility to enact ordinances without the support of the *Bundesrat* was also seen as problematic,[98] both with regard to the principles of federalism and democracy. This was only made worse by the vagueness of § 5 IPA, putting its constitutionality in light of Article 80 GG altogether in question.[99]

[90] A Klafki, 'Coronavirus und Reformbedarf des „Pandemierechts"' (*Verfassungsblog*, 5 March 2020) www.verfassungsblog.de/coronavirus-und-reformbedarf-des-pandemierechts; Thielbörger and Behlert (n 80); A Kießling, 'Offene Fragen der (Massen)Quarantäne' (*Verfassungsblog*, 2 July 2020) www.verfassungsblog.de/offene-fragen-der-massenquarantaene/.

[91] cf 'Corona trifft Föderalismus' (*Tagesschau*, 04 March 2020) www.tagesschau.de/inland/coronavirus-297.html.

[92] Klafki (n 90).

[93] A Klafki, 'Corona-Pandemie: Ausgangssperre bald auch in Deutschland?' (*JuWiss*, 19 March 2020) www.juwiss.de/27-2020/; A Edenharter, 'Freiheitsrechte ade? Die Rechtswidrigkeit der Ausgangssperre in der oberpfälzischen Stadt Mitterteich' (*Verfassungsblog*, 19 March 2020) www.verfassungsblog.de/freiheitsrechte-ade/; Möllers (n 80).

[94] See overview at www.buzer.de/gesetz/2148/l.htm.

[95] Gesetz zum Schutz der Bevölkerung bei einer epidemischen Lage von nationaler Tragweite of 28 March 2020, BGBl. I p. 587 (Nr 14).

[96] This was criticised by most commentators, see for instance Möllers (n 80) and Thielbörger and Behlert (n 73).

[97] Scientific Services of the *Bundestag*, 'Staatsorganisation und § 5 Infektionsschutzgesetz' (2020) www.bundestag.de/resource/blob/690262/cb718005e6d37ecce82c99191efbec49/WD-3-080-20-pdf-data.pdf.

[98] ibid.

[99] T Kingreen, 'Comment to the proposed change of the IfSG' (2020), www.bundestag.de/resource/blob/694844/0b2af0e61b45ddbfe1311c78557720ee/19_14_0160-27-_ESV-Prof-Dr-Kingreen_2-Bevoelk-schutzg--data.pdf.

In the second bill[100] of May 2020, the federal ministry of health was given an even broader competence to enact ordinances, again excluding the involvement of the *Bundesrat*. Experts criticised that the proposed further amendment could even amount to a violation of the separation of powers, which is not only an important element of the rule of law,[101] but yet another safeguard for protection of the principle of democracy.[102]

The third bill of November 2020[103] finally introduced a definition of the term '*epidemische Lage von nationaler Tragweite*' in § 5, paragraph 1, sentence 4 IPA, made significant changes in the data protection regime (§ 14 IPA) and introduced a new § 28a IPA, which allowed for a set of *specific* measures to be enacted. These measures include specific rules for social distancing in public as well as an obligation to wear masks in public. Some experts argued again that the new bill did not meet the required standards concerning clarity of the law and the separation of powers, denying the *Bundestag* one of its core competences (*Parlamentsvorbehalt*),[104] thus yet again not paying tribute to the principle of democracy. Fundamental rights had also not been given sufficient importance.[105] The proposal to bind the *Länder* to agree on uniform federal measures (§ 28, paragraph 2, sentence 6 IPA in its proposed form) was seen by experts as outright illegal.[106] For this, an entirely new competence of the federal level to issue ordinances (*Verordnungsermächtigung für den Bund*) would have been needed. Neither *Länder* nor the districts nor the cities could be obliged to agree on uniform measures nationwide.[107] In light of this criticism, the relevant passage in the proposed bill was eventually entirely dropped.

[100] Zweites Gesetz zum Schutz der Bevölkerung bei einer epidemischen Lage von nationaler Tragweite of 19 May 2020, BGBl. I, p 1018 (Nr 23).

[101] Kingreen (n 99).

[102] cf German Federal Constitutional Court, Order of 17 July 1996–2 BvE 2/93, paras 42–45.

[103] Drittes Gesetz zum Schutz der Bevölkerung bei einer epidemischen Lage von nationaler Tragweite of 18 November 2019, BGBl. I,. 2397 (Nr 52).

[104] Kießling, *Comment to the proposed change of the IfSG*; A Klafki, 'Stellungnahme als geladene Einzelsachverständige für die öffentliche Anhörung im Gesundheitsausschuss des Deutschen Bundestages am 12.11.2020' (*Ausschussdrucksache* 19(14)246(9), 10 November 2020); A Kießling, 'Stellungnahme als geladene Einzelsachverständige für die öffentliche Anhörung im Gesundheitsausschuss des Deutschen Bundestages am 12.11.2020' (*Ausschussdrucksache* 19(14)246(7), 10 November 2020).

[105] ibid; H Wißmann, 'Sachverständige Stellungnahme zum Gesetzentwurf der Fraktionen von CDU/CSU und SPD für ein „Drittes Gesetz zum Schutz der Bevölkerung bei einer epidemischen Lage von nationaler Tragweite", BT-Drs. 19/23944 und weiteren Anträge der Fraktionen des Bundestags' (10 November 2020) www.jura.uni-muenster.de/de/institute/kommunalwissenschaftliches-institut/stellungnahmebt4/.

[106] Kießling (n 90) 7.

[107] ibid; C Möllers, 'Stellungnahme zum Entwurf eines Dritten Gesetzes zum Schutz der Bevölkerung bei einer epidemischen Lage von nationaler Tragweite Drucksache 19/23944 und begleitende Anträge' (*Ausschussdrucksache* 19(14)246(15), 11 November 2020) 9, www.bundestag.de/resource/blob/805682/90775997933c613cc334fd5065cded6e/19_14_0246-15-_ESV-Prof-Dr-Moellers-3-BevSchG-data.pdf.

ii. Institutional Perspective

From an institutional perspective, the Robert Koch Institute (RKI) deserves special mention, whose position was significantly strengthened in the first bill.[108] The Robert Koch Institute is a federal scientific authority, which reports to the federal health ministry, but also provides medical information to the *Länder* and issues epidemiological recommendations (§ 5 IPA). Political decision-makers follow the recommendations by the RKI almost word for word, without such findings being challenged or questioned (eg, through a committee of the *Bundestag*).

The federal level and the *Länder* have also developed several modes of institutionalised cooperation, most importantly regular meetings of the Prime Ministers with members of the federal government.[109] The purpose of such meetings is coordination, but also to find a joint political strategy. However, the implementation of the agreed measures is then up to the *Länder*. In the past, *Länder* have regularly deviated from the agreed standards, for instance by opening *kindergardens*, schools or other public institutions earlier or by allowing less restrictive social distancing rules than agreed, or interpreting general terms (eg, bans on 'large' assemblies) very loosely compared to other *Länder*.

IV. Critical Evaluation of the German Legal Regime for Pandemics

Germany faces a conundrum: while the pandemic is a problem of national scale, the execution of the federal laws such as the IPA lies firmly with the *Länder*. The literature has assessed Germany's 'federal approach' to fighting the pandemic very differently.

A. Germany's Federalist Approach as 'Inhibitor' to Fight the Pandemic Effectively

i. Fragmentation Through Federalism

Some authors argue that federalism made it difficult for Germany to tackle COVID-19 effectively as centralised regulations are believed to be more effective

[108] See eg § 4, paragraph 1 and paragraph 1a, § 5, paragraphs 2, 6 and 7 IPA.

[109] For a good summary of the different forms of meetings, see A Klafki, 'Legal Harmonization Through Interfederal Cooperation: A Comparison of the Interfederal Harmonization of Law Through Uniform Law Conferences and Executive Intergovernmental Conferences' (2018) *German Law Journal* 1437, 1437 ff.

than decentralised regulations.[110] A possible more decisive uniform response of federal state and *Länder* action was repeatedly reduced to a minimum common denominator, in favour of political autonomy and individual responsibility of the *Länder*.[111] Some have called the authority of Germany fragmented and insisted that Germany's hesitant approach has highlighted the weakness of the German decentralised authority.[112] The lack of a decisive uniform federal response was made even worse by the lacuna displayed at the same time by European Union law in the field of disease control.[113] Some see a weak institutional link between the federal level and the *Länder* as cause for the lack of a more decisive federal answer[114] arguing that the connection between the delegating and the receiving authority was too loose.[115]

Content-wise the German approach was also critiqued for relying on bans and restrictions, without even giving alternative approaches (like the Swedish one based on incentives and voluntary self-restriction),[116] a chance.[117] While federalism in theory should have enabled the trying of different measures, the variance of attempted measures in practice remained small, as a virtually singular public discourse, largely influenced by the unchallenged expert opinion of the RKI,[118] pressured the *Länder* to adopt measures already taken by other *Länder*, creating fragile cohesion rather than real deliberation.[119]

ii. The Disempowerment of Parliament

Another major criticism relates to the role of parliaments in Germany's COVID-19 response. Governments of *Bund* and *Länder*, not representatives of their parliaments, were involved in the regular meetings between *Bund* and *Länder*.[120] This problem was made worse by the fact that usually only the Prime Ministers

[110] U Münch, 'Beiträge zum Deutschen Föderalismus: Wenn dem Bundesstaat die Stunde der Exekutive schlägt: der deutsche (Exekutiv-)Föderalismus in Zeiten der Coronakrise' (2020) *Jahrbuch des Föderalismus* 209, 217–18; patrially in agreeement: HP Aust, 'Im Auftrag des Bundes, Ein Vorschlag zu einer föderalismusfreundlichen Zentralisierung des Infektionsschutzes' (*Verfassungblog*, 15 December 2020) www.verfassungsblog.de/im-auftrag-des-bundes/.

[111] ibid.

[112] M Bartsch et al, 'Inside Germany's Piecemeal Response to Corona' (*Der Spiegel*, 13 March 2020) www.spiegel.de/international/germany/inside-germany-s-piecemeal-response-to-corona-a-f376b3f9-625f-4a6a-8e7d-04bd48be20b2.

[113] ibid.

[114] J Saurer (n 60).

[115] ibid.

[116] See J Reichel and J Dahlqvist, 'Swedish Constitutional Response to the Corona Crisis – The Odd One Out?' in this book.

[117] M Frommel, 'Corona-Politik 2020 – ein schmaler Grat zwischen kluger Einschränkung und überzogener Panik' (2020) *NK Neue Kriminalpolitik* 123, 124.

[118] ibid.

[119] Büthe, Messerschmidt and Cheng (n 24).

[120] S Harbarth, '„Grundrechte sind keine Privilegien"' (*Rheinische Post*, 10 February 2021) www.rp-online.de/politik/deutschland/praesident-des-verfassungsgerichtes-grundrechte-sind-keine-privilegien_aid-56152945; see also: JM Dostal, 'Governing Under Pressure: German Policy Making During the

of the *Länder* were involved in these meetings, not representatives of all governing parties in the *Länder*. This led to an over-representation of the two big German parties (conservatives and labor) and an under-representation of the smaller parties (ie, greens, liberal, left-party as well as the populist 'Alternative for Germany'), compared to their relatively stronger representations in the Parliaments of *Bund* and *Länder*.

In replacing federal laws by amending the IPA several times in 2020, executive decrees of the federal minister of health took central stage more and more. The rule (law) – exception (executive decree) relationship was essentially reversed with dramatic consequences for federalism[121] as well as the principle of democracy. Given the importance of executive decrees under the new IPA for the exercise of fundamental rights, the disempowerment of the Parliament was found to be highly problematic. In most cases, not even the consent of the *Bundesrat* is required for these decrees – another significant devaluation of Germany's upper house, the *Bundesrat*, representing the *Länder*.[122]

iii. Complex Federalism and the Need to Act Fast

Yet another concern relates to the complexity of federalism. Some observers have argued that an already diffuse situation was made even more protracted through the complexities of federalism.[123] The coordination in federal systems is described to be time-consuming while in a pandemic the state typically has to act fast.[124]

iv. Different Treatment of Fundamental Rights in Different Länder

Limitations of fundamental rights varied in terms of their intensity and duration in the different *Länder*,[125] with such distinctions not always being justified through equally different infectious rates in the *Länder*. This caused unequal treatment[126] in partially similar (if not equal) situations. For instance, the German approach has led to rather erratic outcomes concerning border management,[127] a sensitive

Coronavirus Crisis' (2020) *The Political Quarterly* 542, 549; J Schnabel, 'The Covid-19 crisis and German federalism' (2020) *Cuadernos Manuel Giménez Abad* 71, 73.

[121] Münch (n 110), 212.

[122] ibid.

[123] R Arnold, 'Pandemia and constitutional law: some reflections on the German experience' (2020) *University of Pitesti Journal Legal and Administrative Studies* 33; in this sense, F Palero points out in: 'Is there a space for federalism in times of emergency? What is at stake? Federalism as part of constitutionalism' (*Verfassungsblog*, 13 May 2020) www.verfassungsblog.de/is-there-a-space-for-federalism-in-times-of-emergency/, that federalism is a 'accelerator': it can increase efficiency when this is already given, but it also adds to confusion when this is the prevailing mood.

[124] S Kropp, 'Zerreißprobe für den Flickenteppich?' (*Verfassungsblog*, 26 May 2020) www.verfassungs-blog.de/zerreissprobe-fuer-den-flickenteppich/.

[125] Arnold (n 123) 47.

[126] Münch (n 110) 217.

[127] L Coatleven, F Hublet and T Rospars, 'Subsidiary crisis management in the COVID-19 pandemic. Germany's federalist experiment in transborder perspective' (2020) *Groupe d'études géopolitiques* 10.

issue not only because of the Schengen regime, but also from the perspective of German and European fundamental rights.[128] The erratic treatment of fundamental rights in the different *Länder* is even more dramatic given that the long-term consequences for the economic and mental wellbeing of the incurred fundamental rights restrictions are still unknown.[129]

v. Strengthening Federal Oversight

Some authors have criticised the IPA for putting measures in the realm of the administration of the *Länder in their own right*. Instead, some authors have suggested to make measures under the IPA a case of execution *on federal commission* (*Bundesauftragsverwaltung*).[130] This rather rare form of administration in the German system would constitute a middle ground between administration through the federal state and through the *Länder* on their own, which would give the *Bund* higher levels of control than currently, in particular not limiting such control to the legality, but expanding it to the suitability of the chosen measures.

vi. Clarifying Constitutional Regulations

Other authors have highlighted that Germany's constitution itself is 'unfit' for a pandemic.[131] On the one hand, while procedural simplifications for the constitutional bodies (eg, voting procedures in Parliament) exist for the case of externally-induced emergencies, they exist much less for internal emergencies – during which they would be equally needed.[132] Given how uniquely strict the restrictions of fundamental rights during COVID-19 were,[133] more explicit rules at the level of the German basic law itself for derogation from and restrictions of fundamental rights during internal emergencies would also be desirable.[134] This would make the GG more proactive in terms of warning against fundamental rights restrictions and limiting them in substance and time, as many international human rights treaties already do.[135] The legislator should not have attempted 'quick fixes' at the level of the IPA and the statute of the *Bundestag*, but have engaged in the discussion of constitutional reform to create clearer rules on the limitation

[128] See in detail: M Dawson and P Thielbörger, 'EU Law in the 'first wave' – The Legality of National Measures to tackle the COVID-19 crisis' (8 December 2020) www.greens-efa.eu/en/article/document/eu-law-in-the-first-wave, 39ff.

[129] Desson (n 12).

[130] Aust (n 110).

[131] Thielbörger and Behlert (n 64); Thielbörger and Behlert (n 66).

[132] ibid.

[133] See for instance Aden, Arzt and Fährmann (n 79), 99–111 who list measures that were in their view too far-reaching with respect to freedom of assembly, freedom of movement and data protection.

[134] Thielbörger and Behlert (n 64); Thielbörger and Behlert (n 66).

[135] Ibid.

and derogability of fundamental rights as well as the simplification of legislative procedures rather than putting the rule-making outright into the hands of the executive.[136]

B. Germany's Federal Approach as 'Enabler' to Fight the Pandemic Effectively

i. Coordinated and Cooperative Collective Action

Other authors have emphasised the very positive role of federalism in Germany's response to COVID-19.[137] Decentralised systems governing public (and private) organisations on multiple levels of authority are seen to be more resilient and more capable of collective action during a crisis.[138] These authors argue that a coordinated and cooperative collective action early in the first wave of the pandemic was made possible precisely through the federalist structures, driven by a shared sense of urgency and recognition based on reliable information.[139] The level of variance in the *Länder* responses was adaptable to the severity of the crisis, expressing a successful compromise between the highly decentralised structure of the governmental system and the demand for uniform federal action during more severe stages of the pandemic.[140] Germany is considered to have managed the balancing act between the preservation of the lives and the preservation of democracy particularly well,[141] at least during the first wave of COVID-19.

ii. Scientifically-informed and Transparent Decision-making

Some authors have described the German approach as a hybrid (federal and *Länder*) response, highlighting in particular the key role of scientific advice via the RKI.[142] Coordination was strengthened by increasing the frequency of high-level meetings of the federal government and *Länder* Prime Ministers, taking the scientific advice into account, while making the decision processes transparent through joint press conferences.[143] These high level meetings have, according to some, led

[136] Thielbörger and Behlert (n 73).
[137] S Kropp, 'Demokratie im Ausnahmezustand, Hat sich der bundesdeutsche Föderalismus in der Krise bewährt?' library.fes.de/pdf-files/dialog/16456.pdf; MB Siewert et al, 'A German Miracle? Crisis Management during the COVID-19 Pandemic in a Multi-Level System' (2020) *PEX Special Report on the Coronavirus Outbreak, Presidents' Responses, and Institutional Consequences*.
[138] Hattke and Martin (n 25) 616.
[139] ibid, 628.
[140] S Kuhlmann, 'Between Unity and Variety: Germany's Responses to the COVID-19 Pandemic' in P Joyce, F Maron and PS Reddy (eds), *Good Public Governance in a Global Pandemic* (2020) 291, 294.
[141] C Stelzenmüller, 'COVID-19 Is a Severe Test for Germany's Postwar Constitution' (*Lawfare*, 16 April 2020) www.lawfareblog.com/covid-19-severe-test-germanys-postwar-constitution.
[142] ibid.
[143] ibid, 624.

to better informed, more proportional and more transparent decision-making, allowed for comparison between different approaches and fostered political action closer to the field.[144] The German approach is altogether described as consensus-orientated and deliberative, carried by a high level of public support.[145]

iii. Proven Ability of Federal Level to Gain Influence

While the execution of the measures lies with the *Länder*, the Federal state found ways to increase its influence during the crisis, for instance by making several decisive changes to the IPA,[146] but also by making more federal financial aid available.[147] The partial shift of power to the federal executive by the reform of the IPA is highlighted by some as not being permanent, but stressed to be evaluated within a year by *Bundestag* and *Bundesrat* (or it would otherwise expire).[148] This is a sign of the federalist structures having been able to find a workable short-term, non-permanent solution, in order to strengthen the federal level.

iv. Faster and Better Targeted Adaption Giving Room Also to the Local Level

The competition between the *Länder* gave federal and local actors space to assess conditions and possibilities.[149] In particular, the importance of local actors has been highlighted by some authors, as local actors, more so than *Bund* or *Länder*, could often adapt faster to changing local conditions than actors on higher levels.[150] In this way, Germany's federalist structure altogether allowed for a faster and better targeted adaptation.[151] It focused on local crises so that measures could be tailored to regions where they were most needed,[152] thereby avoiding unnecessary restrictions of fundamental rights in less affected areas.[153] One of the key advantages of federal over unitary systems is one of mutual learning and exchanging best practices,[154] which, according to some, proved very successful during the COVID-19 crisis in Germany.[155]

[144] ibid, 618.
[145] Stelzenmüller (n 141).
[146] G Milbradt, 'Federalism and the COVID-19 crisis: A perspective from Germany' (*Forum of Federations*) www.forumfed.org/2020/04/federalism-and-the-covid-19-crisis-a-perspective-from-germany/.
[147] Aden, Arzt and Fährmann (n 79), 107.
[148] Siewert et al (n 137).
[149] ibid.
[150] Kropp (n 124).
[151] Coatleven, Hublet and Rospars (n 127).
[152] Kropp (n 137).
[153] Münch (n 110) 217.
[154] On the value of understanding country studies mutual learning in the EU specifically, see analysis at L Hantrais, *Comparing and Contrasting the Impact of the COVID-19 Pandemic in the European* Union (Routledge, 2021).
[155] Kropp (n 124); Kropp (n 137).

v. *Importance of Federal Courts*

The federal court system, as one important aspect of federalism, gave citizens a web of multi-layered judicial protection.[156] Claimants were indeed rather often successful with their claims,[157] in several cases forcing policy change in the different *Länder* through the courts.

vi. *Financial Inter-regional Solidarity*

Finally, from a financial and economic perspective, Germany's system of interstate revenue equalisation transfers (*Länderfinanzausgleich*)[158] deserves special attention. While the crisis hit some regions significantly harder than others, this facet of German federalism is seen to help to equally distribute the COVID-19 related revenue shortfalls across all the *Länder* over time.[159] This signals strong inter-regional solidarity as a special dimension of German federalism.

V. The Way Forward: Options for Legal and Political Reform in Germany

A. Assessing the Role of Federalism

Altogether, the management of the COVID-19 pandemic combined decentralised decision-making, given the constitutional distribution of powers, with intergovernmental coordination, mainly instigated through the regular Prime Ministers Conferences.[160] When assessing the literature, it shows that the majority of authors gave Germany a slightly more positive than negative review for its performance in the COVID-19 crisis, although it must be noted that the literature so far concentrates on the first wave which Germany mastered rather well.

I generally concur with this finding, but would suggest some important caveats to keep in mind, before praising the role federalism played in Germany's COVID-19 all too hastily.

[156] ibid.

[157] eg BVerfG, 15 April 2020, Az. 1 BvR 828/20; VGH Baden-Württemberg, 5 February 2021, 1 S 321/21; VG Aachen, 8 February 2021, 6 L 82/2; OLG NRW, 10 February 2021, 13 B 1932/20.NE. Also several claims to the BVerfG were successful, see regarding the high number of cases: www.lto.de/recht/nachrichten/n/bverfg-bundesverfassungsgericht-corona-covid19-krise-pandemie-eilantraege-rekordwert-2020-verfassungsbeschwerde/.

[158] Bundesministerium der Finanzen, 'Länderfinanzausgleich', www.bundesfinanzministerium.de/Content/DE/Standardartikel/Themen/Oeffentliche_Finanzen/Foederale_Finanzbeziehungen/Laenderfinanzausgleich/laenderfinanzausgleich.html.

[159] OECD (n 4) 31.

[160] Schnabel (n 120).

Empirical studies do not support the broader thesis that federal States generally do better than unitary States in coping with pandemics. This is in line with the finding that the state which did the worst of all during the pandemic (the USA) is a highly federalist state, while other federalist states performed rather well, for instance Canada or Australia.[161] It is a variety of many factors, such as geographical, political, economic and cultural ones that determine the performance of a state during a pandemic – its federal or unitary character per se is of secondary importance.

In this regard, it is important to note, that the first wave of COVID-19 hit Germany at a time of political calmness, financial stability and economic prosperity. There was neither a particularly important upcoming election nor a sharp political conflict between government and opposition. The German Government was led by a Grand Coalition continuously since 2013. In the year 2020, 14 out of the 16 German *Länder* were spearheaded by a Prime Minister being member in one of the two parties constituting also the federal government. Not a single of the *Länder* had a government without the involvement of at least one of the two governing parties at the federal level. To put it rather cynically, the crisis hit Germany during a time of political monotony. Politicians during the first wave levels concentrated on finding constructive solutions, with little incentive to make immediate political gains with the pandemic. Cooperative federalism only very occasionally turned into an overly competitive or dualistic[162] form of such federalism.[163]

In the second wave, the tables turned. The German economy was significantly compromised and the financial situation became stable,[164] with federal elections coming up in fall 2021[165] and with several Prime Minister of the *Länder* having high political personal ambitions in this election. It comes as no surprise that the tone between *Bund* and *Länder*, and between different political parties, roughened up. The political 'good will', praised during the first wave, had started to erode.

[161] MJ Rozell and C Wilcox, 'Federalism in a Time of Plague: How Federal Systems Cope With Pandemic' (2020) *The American Review of Public Administration*: factors for the particularly poor performance of the US discussed here include the high number of States, neoliberal welfare policies (including the lack of universal healthcare), partisan polarisation and the failure of national political leadership. Also see: T Büthe et al, 'Patterns of Policy Responses to the COVID-19 Pandemic in Federal vs. Unitary European Democracies', papers.ssrn.com/sol3/papers.cfm?abstract_id=3692035.

[162] N Behnke, 'Föderalismus in der (Corona-)Krise? Föderale Funktionen, Kompetenzen und Entscheidungsprozesse' (*Bundeszentrale für politische Bildung*, 21 August 2020) www.bpb.de/apuz/314343/foederalismus-in-der-corona-krise.

[163] R Sturm, 'Der deutsche Föderalismus in Corona-Zeiten, Blog des Institut für Föderalismus' (*Institut für Föderalismus*, 18 May 2020) www.foederalismus.at/blog/der-deutsche-foederalismus-in-corona-zeiten_236.php?&title=der-deutsche-foederalismus-in-corona-zeiten&id=236.

[164] M Clemens et al, 'Zweite Corona-Infektionswelle: Deutsche Wirtschaft wird zum Jahresende schrumpfen' (2020), *Deutsches Institut für Wirtschaftsforschung*, www.diw.de/de/diw_01.c.801919.de/publikationen/diw_aktuell/2020_0055/zweite_corona-infektionswelle__deutsche_wirtschaft_wird_zum_jahresende_schrumpfen.html.

[165] Der Bundeswahlleiter, 'Wahl zum 20. Deutschen Bundestag am 26. September 2021', www.bundeswahlleiter.de/bundestagswahlen/2021.html.

If we assume that the effectiveness of responses is proportional to the political, institutional, and procedural quality of the cooperation among the different levels of government,[166] one cannot assume that Germany will perform equally well in future public health crises. This will be highly dependent on the political climate during which a new pandemic will hit. We have witnessed such under-performance of the German system already during the second and the third wave, and particularly with regard to the poorly-performing national vaccination campaign. This shows that the German federalist model can, but will not automatically, function well in times of crisis.

Of crucial importance is the balanced interplay of two developed features of German federalism: executive federalism and cooperative federalism. It is a dangerous development if the federal state restricts the role of the *Länder* and the *Bundesrat* (as in the recent IPA reforms) severely from the perspective of executive federalism. It is, however, an equally dangerous development, from the perspective of cooperative federalism, if the *Länder* either deviate from agreements with the federal state or portray their compliance as pure political goodwill rather than an obligation as part of their unwritten, but nonetheless binding *Bundestreue*.

In order to ensure the balance between executive federalism and cooperative federalism in future crises, certain legal and policy reforms should be considered.

From the perspective of federalism, the format of high-level meetings of the federal government with the Prime Minister of the *Länder* remains highly unregulated. Given the enormous de facto power this institution enjoys, it needs public discussion and a transparent regulation of how these meetings are constituted, who can participate in these meeting and how the body makes decisions. For instance, the role of governmental units below the level of the *Länder*, eg districts and free cities, should be strengthened. They often carry some of the harshest (financial) burdens during times of crisis – but they are not at the table, as they are seen as part of the *Länder*, while they have their very own set of interests and experiences. Additionally, in the preparation of such meetings, more institutionalised exchange formats with representatives of particularly affected groups (for the current crisis, eg representatives of the elderly, children, patients or medical personnel) should be established in order to have the interests and needs of these groups more clearly articulated before making decisions.

B. Assessing the Future Role of the Constitution and the Parliaments During Pandemics

The constitution lacks suitable provisions on the derogability and restrictability of fundamental rights during times of pandemics. Such provisions should be established at the level of the constitution, not to enable more frequent or more

[166] Palero (n 123).

severe restrictions, but rather to contain them to the minimum necessary level and continuously remind policy makers of their exceptional character. Equally, rules for slimmer, faster or even remote/virtual forms of law-making in the *Bundestag* are almost entirely absent.

Thus, more explicit rules for internal state emergencies (both with regard to the temporary restrictability of rights and the temporary simplification of the legislative process) must be established, preferably at the level of the constitution. So far, the constitution holds comparable rules on externally-induced emergencies, but remains silent on internal emergencies (such as pandemics). This is inapt, as both scenarios are in many ways comparable in their effects on citizens and state organs.

Such new rules to enable slimmer legislative procedures must, however, not be misunderstood as rules in which the legislature is replaced by the executive. This was the unfortunate effect of some of the 2020 IPA reforms. These changes are equally problematic with regard to the separation of powers and the principle of democracy. Any forms of law-making circumventing the Parliament (eg, by widening the competencies of individual ministers to make them a de facto legislator in times of crisis) should not be part of any future reform efforts. In fact, some of the changes of the recent IPA reforms must be reversed.

If future reforms of the IPA should aim to strengthen the federal level further, as Chancellor Merkel audaciously announced at the beginning of the third wave[167] in order to avoid a future cacophony of *Länder* responses, such reform must empower not only the federal executive, but also the federal legislative.

The authorisation to issue statutory instruments (*Verordnungsermächtigung*) could, for instance, be made subject to the approval of the *Bundestag*, if the federal government (or even a single ministry) is given the competence to issue statutory instruments that interfere directly with the exercise of fundamental rights. Such intensive state measures require a high level of democratic legitimisation – a level that is not satisfied if the government or a ministry alone take such decisions.

A second beneficial change would be to strengthen the democratic legitimacy of the meetings of the Prime Ministers with the federal government. Even if it is an unofficial state organ that cannot create binding decisions, the platform has gained an enormous amount of de facto power. Much more than the *Bundestag*, the meetings of the Prime Ministers with the federal government have made the most crucial decisions for Germany during the crisis. Therefore, the stronger involvement of democratically elected representatives appears necessary (eg, via the chair(wo)men of the groups (*Fraktionen*) in the *Bundestag*, selected representatives of the *Länder* Parliaments or via members of the *Bundestag*'s Health Committee). This would also ensure a more balanced representation at the meetings as representation through heads of governments alone largely favours big parties.

[167] cf 'Merkel zur Pandemiebekämpfung' (*Tagesschau*, 29 March 21) www.tagesschau.de/inland/corona-lage-merkel-soeder-101.html.

Altogether, while a shift to the federal level in times of emergency is needed (but must be established clearly and transparently), strengthened democratic safeguards are all the more essential in these times. Otherwise the separation of power is loosened on both ends of the equation: in its vertical dimension (where power shifts from the *Länder* to the *Bund*) and in its horizontal dimension (where power shifts from the legislative to the executive). Both such shifts *at the same time* must be avoided.

6

The Marginalisation of Parliament in Facing the Coronavirus Emergency: What about Democracy in Italy?

ARIANNA VEDASCHI*

I. Introduction

The outbreak of the coronavirus (COVID-19), a new disease which quickly turned into a pandemic[1] (still ongoing while this chapter is being written), can be included among the major emergencies of (at least) the last 100 years.[2]

It is widely known that, when an emergency takes place, legal measures to react to the crisis are necessary, and these responses always imply temporary departure from what is usually called 'normalcy'.[3] As a consequence, emergency tools have both an institutional impact – ie on the ordinary relationship and balance between state powers – and an effect on the enjoyment of rights and freedoms – which can be limited during 'times of stress'.[4]

* The author would like to express her gratitude to Chiara Graziani for research assistance.

[1] COVID-19 was labelled a pandemic by the World Health Organization (WHO) on 11 March 2020. WHO Director-General, 'Opening Remarks at the Media Briefing on COVID-19' (11 March 2020) www.who.int/dg/speeches/detail/who-director-general-s-opening-remarks-at-the-media-briefing-on-COVID-19---11-march-2020.

[2] If one looks at data about death from COVID-19, it emerges that, up to 26 December 2020, 1,744,235 people passed away from the virus. See World Health Organization, 'WHO Coronavirus Disease (COVID-19) Dashboard (26 December 2020) COVID19.who.int/.

[3] As well known, several theories justify the resort to emergency powers. Carl Schmitt referred to decisionism, meaning that a sovereign body – in Schmitt's view, the President of the Reich within the institutional background of the Weimar Constitution – should be entitled to decide in times of exception, exercising a discretion that could even amount to arbitrariness, if necessary. C Schmitt (1921), *Die Diktatur* (Duncker & Humblot, 2015). Another theory is based on necessity as a source of law, from which emergency measures stem. The latter theory can be traced back to the thought of Santi Romano and, then, of Carlo Esposito. S Romano, 'Sui decreti-legge e lo stato d'assedio in occasione del terremoto di Messina e di Reggio-Calabria' (1909) *Rivista di diritto pubblico* 251; C Esposito, 'Decreto-legge' in *Enciclopedia del diritto* 1 (Giuffrè, 1962).

[4] M Rosenfeld, 'Judicial Balancing in Times of Stress: Comparing the American, British, and Israeli Approaches to the War on Terror' (2006) 27 *Cardozo Law Review* 2079.

The COVID-19 emergency did not represent an exception in this regard, since almost all countries of the world – although not with the same timings and mechanisms – enacted legal measures trying to prevent the spread of the virus and to protect their citizens.[5]

This chapter focuses on the reactions to COVID-19 in Italy. Italy has been one of the Western countries that have been most and earliest hit by COVID-19, setting itself, during the so-called first wave of coronavirus, as the 'model' to which other states looked in order to put in place their own lockdown strategies. Yet what have been the consequences of legal responses to COVID-19 on the Italian democratic framework? To what extent can some principles at the very core of democracy be put under tension in order to safeguard public health? Could the 'Italian approach' to COVID-19 be improved in terms of compliance with such principles without losing its effectiveness? Ultimately, what about democracy in Italy?

With a view to trying to answer these challenging questions, touching upon the heart of Italian constitutional foundations, this chapter is structured as follows.

Section II shows how Italy handled COVID-19, starting from earliest legal reactions. First, this section explains that, differently from other jurisdictions in the comparative scenario, Italy lacks a fully-fledged 'emergency constitution', ie a set of constitutional provisions specifically settling how to tackle political and non-political emergencies.[6] Second, once the constitutional background is clarified and placed in a comparative context, Italian concrete measures taken from the beginning of the crisis are described, pointing out the main legal issues arising from them.

Section III discusses the implications of Italian anti-COVID-19 measures on democracy. In order to do so, this section takes into account both the representative dimension of democracy and the substantive one. Therefore, the analysis digs into the role of the Houses of the Italian Parliament (ie the Chamber of Deputies and the Senate of the Republic) during the crisis, assessing whether they have been (excessively) marginalised and what could be the resulting effects on representativeness and, more in general, on the balance among powers. Afterwards, this section examines substantive aspects of democracy, studying how restrictions imposed during the pandemic may clash with fundamental principles that give shape to the Italian democracy; and actually that are at the roots of Western liberal democracies. Among them, one can list the protection of rights and freedoms, and the possibility to have measures restricting rights reviewed by a judicial body, transparency and (consequent) accountability of public powers, not to mention certainty of law.

[5] For a comparative overview of legal reactions to COVID-19, A Vedaschi, 'Il COVID-19, l'ultimo stress test per gli ordinamenti democratici: uno sguardo comparato' (2020) 2 *DPCE Online* 1453.

[6] In the present chapter, the word 'political' is used to define emergencies that are triggered by some political factors (eg, international or domestic terrorism), while 'non-political' ('neutral' or again 'technical') emergencies are those that are caused by non-political events (eg, public health emergencies such as COVID-19, natural disasters etc). A Vedaschi, *À la guerre comme à la guerre? La disciplina della guerra nel diritto costituzionale comparato* (Giappichelli, 2007) 266.

Some concluding remarks take into consideration the resulting background and draw up some guidelines that might be helpful to ensure, in the future, effective responses to global and long-lasting emergencies (as COVID-19 is) without sacrificing values and principles that are crucial in a democratic context.

II. Early Legal Reactions to the COVID-19 Crisis in Italy

The Italian legal reaction to COVID-19 can be traced back to 31 January 2020, ie the day after the World Health Organization (WHO) declared a public emergency of international concern under the International Health Regulations of 2005.[7] From that day onward, a number of legal measures were adopted, amended, repealed and replaced to face this unprecedented health crisis.

Before examining in detail the legal tools employed by the Italian Government to address this new disease, it is useful to analyse the Italian constitutional framework regarding regulation and use of emergency powers.

A. Emergency Powers in the Italian Constitution and in the Comparative Scenario

Looking at the comparative scenario and focusing only on the constitutions of Western liberal democracies, two main 'macro-models' of emergency can be identified.[8]

The first macro-model consists of all those constitutions that do regulate the resort to emergency powers, either in general terms, the so-called general clause model, or more in detail, the so-called rationalised model. An example of the general clause model is the French Constitution of 1958. Its Article 16 gives very undefined (and, so, highly discretionary) powers to the President of the Republic, who, in case of (especially) political distress, is entitled to 'take measures required by these circumstances',[9] meaning any action the President deems appropriate to restore the *status quo ante*.

[7] World Health Organization, 'Statement on the second meeting of the International Health Regulations (2005) Emergency Committee regarding the outbreak of novel coronavirus (2019-nCoV)' (30 January 2020) www.who.int/news/item/30-01-2020-statement-on-the-second-meeting-of-the-international-health-regulations-(2005)-emergency-committee-regarding-the-outbreak-of-novel-coronavirus-(2019-ncov).

[8] Vedaschi (n 6).

[9] Official translation by the French Conseil Constitutionnel, www.conseil-constitutionnel.fr/sites/default/files/as/root/bank_mm/anglais/constiution_anglais_oct2009.pdf. Art 16 French Const is modelled on Art 48 of the 1919 Weimar Constitution. According to Art 48, para 2 of the Weimar Constitution, 'the President of the Reich can, if public safety and peace of the Reich are seriously endangered or threatened,

Constitutions belonging to the rationalised model, instead, regulate emergency more in-depth. For example, the 1949 German *Grundgesetz*, after a constitutional amendment of 1968,[10] provides for several emergency regimes. The choice among them is determined by the intensity of a threat arising from a same source of danger; therefore, the German paradigm can be defined as a 'growing intensity model'. Other constitutional texts designed different emergency patterns that do not depend on the intensity of a threat stemming from a same cause, but on what circumstances triggered the emergency itself. For instance, Article 116 of the 1978 Spanish Constitution envisages the 'state of alarm', the 'state of exception' and the 'state of siege', which can be applied in the case of neutral emergencies (such as an epidemic), political emergencies and state of war, respectively.[11] Thereby, Spanish emergency powers can be qualified as a model based on 'parallel levels', since the intensity of the threat does not affect the choice of the emergency regime to be invoked, which hinges on the very nature of the crisis.

The second macro-model might be more appropriately defined as a 'non-model', as it includes all those constitutions that do not provide an explicit and systematic regulation of emergency.[12] This model is inspired by European constitutions of the Liberal age.[13]

The current Italian Constitution, which entered into force in 1948, falls within this second macro-model. The reason why the Italian Constituent Assembly decided not to embody any extensive and precise regulation of emergency situations in the new constitutional text can be traced back in its history. The Italian Constitution was drafted in the aftermath of World War II, when awful memories of the Fascist regime, which oppressed Italy for 20 years, were still fresh. Consequently, the Constituent Assembly opposed the centralisation of power in the hands of a single body, especially of the executive, fearing resurgence of past authoritarian drifts.

Therefore, the only emergency to be explicitly (though vaguely) addressed by the Italian Constitution is war (in its conventional meaning). Article 78 Italian Constitution states that 'Parliament has the authority to declare a state of war and

take the necessary measures to restore public safety and peace, and, when necessary, he can resort to armed forces' (translated by the author). On the Weimar Constitution, T Ginsburg and A Huq, *How to Save a Constitutional Democracy* (The University of Chicago Press, 2018) 80.

[10] Act (No 17) to amend the Basic Law of the Federal Republic of Germany, DEU-1968-L-18187), 24 June 1968.

[11] The Spanish constitutional regime of emergency is complemented by *Ley Orgánica* no 4 of 1 June 1981.

[12] For the sake of completeness, it is necessary to mention – without going into its details, given the focus of this chapter – an 'ambiguous' model, which can be referred to the United States (US) and can be considered as a 'halfway' paradigm between the two analysed macro-models. Art 1, para 9, cl 2, US Const only enables the suspension of habeas corpus 'when in Cases of Rebellion or Invasion the public Safety may require it'. Thus, there is no procedural rule on emergency, nor is the body vested with emergency powers explicitly spelled out, albeit, according to some theories, these powers are entrusted to the US President. For more information on this model, see Vedaschi (n 6) 327.

[13] For example, the Belgian Constitution of 1831 or the Italian Statuto Albertino of 1848. They both did not provide any systematic regulation of emergency, and such choice depended on the historical-political backdrop, based on a compromise between the Monarch and the representative Assembly.

vest the necessary powers into the Government'.[14] In other and clearer terms, the Italian Government[15] has substantive powers in time of war, following the decision to resort to *bellum* taken by the Houses of the Italian Parliament and, pursuant to Article 87 Italian Constitution, proclaimed by the President of the Republic.

War is for sure the most traditional, but not the sole form of emergency. Other situations of crisis – terrorist attacks, financial turmoil, epidemics, etc – are not governed by any explicit and specific norm of the Italian Constitution. Nonetheless, emergencies different from war can be dealt with through Article 77 Const, a clause that can be applied to cases 'of necessity and urgency'.[16] For this reason, it can be said that the Italian Constitution is 'silent', but not 'mute' as far as emergency is concerned.[17]

According to Article 77 Italian Constitution, the Council of Ministers, under its own responsibility, can adopt decrees with the same legal force as ordinary law (for this reason they are called 'decree laws') to address extraordinary and pressing situations. These acts are then issued by the President of the Republic, who orders their publication in the Official Journal of the Italian Republic.

Although decree laws enter into force the same day of their publication, they have to be immediately submitted to the Houses of Parliament to be converted into a law called 'conversion law'. If the Houses do not pass a law converting the decree within 60 days of the latter's publication, the decree retroactively loses its effects (ie, from the time of its adoption, as if it had never existed). Otherwise, in case the decree is converted into law by the Houses, the 'conversion law' replaces the decree as if the latter had never come to light.[18]

Some scholars argue that decree laws can indeed be considered as a fully-fledged emergency constitution.[19]

Actually, the Constituent Assembly had conceived Article 77 Italian Constitution as a provision to deal with natural catastrophes (for example, floods, earthquakes etc). However, praxis in Italy shows that these decrees are frequently used by the Government (and, often, converted by the Houses of Parliament) in a much wider range of circumstances, some of them falling outside of the very definition of 'emergency'.[20] Of course, they were also resorted to during actual emergencies, eg to address international terrorism in the aftermath of 9/11, when

[14] English translation of the Italian Constitution by the Italian Senate, www.senato.it/documenti/repository/istituzione/costituzione_inglese.pdf.

[15] ie, the body called 'Council of Ministers', made up of a President of the Council of Ministers and of all the Ministers of the Italian Republic. Art 92 It Const.

[16] English translation of the Italian Constitution (n 14).

[17] As highlighted by M Luciani, 'Il sistema delle fonti del diritto alla prova dell'emergenza' (2020) *Rivista AIC* 1.

[18] A phenomenon called '*novazione della fonte*' in Italian constitutional law.

[19] Luciani (n 17).

[20] Decree laws were and are used, inter alia, to regulate the price of oil and other fuels, to amend rules on housebuilding and to introduce new taxes, to the point that many Italian scholars talked about 'abuse' of decree laws. See, among others, F Modugno and A Celotto, 'Rimedi all'abuso del decreto-legge' (2002) 39 *Giurisprudenza costituzionale* 3232.

a decree law amended the Criminal Code's provisions on terrorism,[21] and after subsequent attacks that hit Europe.[22] In these cases, due to the very fact that they were converted into law, they contributed to a worrisome phenomenon of 'normalisation of emergency'.[23] From this perspective, there is no doubt that decrees adopted pursuant to Article 77 Italian Constitution differ, to some extent, from temporary emergency regimes, since, at least potentially, they can be turned into permanent law (in case of conversion).

At the same time, specific legislation was approved in Italy to tackle natural disasters. In particular, Legislative Decree no 1/2018,[24] (so-called Civil Protection Code) was enacted to deal with these situations. Pursuant to Article 76 Italian Constitution, legislative decrees are, like decree laws, acts with the same force of law adopted by the Council of Ministers. Differently from decree laws, they are not converted into law *ex post* by the Houses of Parliament, but the latter play an *ex ante* role, delegating the Government, through a 'delegation law', to adopt the legislative decree.

B. Legal Reactions to COVID-19: The (Head of the) Executive as the 'Dominus' of the Pandemic Emergency

Against this constitutional and legislative background, the Italian Government has addressed the COVID-19 crisis.

Despite not being an act precisely conceived to cope with health emergencies, Legislative Decree no 1/2018 was the first legal tool to be triggered when Italy was faced with COVID-19.

On 31 January 2020, the Council of Ministers, pursuant to Articles 7 and 24 of Legislative Decree no 1/2018, declared a 'national state of emergency'. Originally,

[21] Decree Law no 374 of 18 October 2001, converted into Law no 438 of 15 December 2001.

[22] After attacks perpetrated in Paris in 2015, Decree Law no 7 of 18 February 2015, converted into Law no 43 of 17 April 2015, was adopted. Further measures against international terrorism enacted through decree laws and the ones that partially conflate counter-terrorism strategy with immigration policies. See Decree Law no 144 of 27 July 2005, converted into Law no 155 of 31 July 2005 (introducing a new ground of expulsion from the Italian territory, on a decision of the Minister of Interior or of the Prefect, based on alleged links to international terrorism). See also Decree Law no 113 of 4 October 2018, converted into Law no 132 of 1 December 2018 (providing for the revocation of Italian citizenship in case a naturalised citizen is convicted on a terrorist offence). On legal issues arising from citizenship stripping as a counter-terrorism strategy, A Vedaschi and C Graziani, 'Citizenship Revocation in Italy as a Counter-Terrorism Measure' (*Verfassungsblog*, 29 January 2019) verfassungsblog.de/citizenship-revocation-in-italy-as-a-counter-terrorism-measure/.

[23] On this topic in Italy, G de Vergottini, *Guerra e costituzione. Nuovi conflitti e sfide alla democrazia* (il Mulino, 2004) 212.

[24] Legislative Decree no 1 of 2 January 2018. This legislative decree replaces an older piece of legislation, dating back to 1992.

this state of emergency was set to last up to 31 July 2020, then it was extended several times.[25]

The mentioned provisions of Legislative Decree no 1/2018, empowering the Council of Ministers to declare a state of emergency, do not vest the Italian Government with well-defined powers. For instance, they do not list a number of rights and freedoms that can be limited during the emergency, nor explain which acts have to be passed to set out concrete measures.

In this context, and also in the light of the quick increase in the number of COVID-19 cases, on 23 February 2020 the Italian Government adopted Decree Law no 6/2020.[26] This Decree Law, recognising the seriousness of the threat posed by the virus and acknowledging the need to limit some everyday activities in order to try to contain its quick spread, was still very vague. It deferred the adoption of further measures aimed at curtailing individuals' rights and freedoms, enshrined in the Constitution, to 'one or more decrees of the President of the Council of Ministers'.[27] And this is exactly what happened in Italy. All provisions enacting very severe lockdown measures and curbing a wide number of rights and freedoms, such as personal freedom,[28] freedom of movement,[29] freedom of assembly,[30] freedom of worship,[31] freedom to conduct businesses,[32] and many others were taken by decrees of the President of the Council of Ministers (DPCMs). Albeit Decree Law no 6/2020 was repealed and replaced by other decree laws,[33] as the factual situation evolved and new measures were required, the scheme is always the same: a decree law is enacted, it gives further DPCMs the power to limit basic rights and personal freedoms, then DPCMs are adopted.[34]

At this point, it is essential to shed light on the legal tool called decree of the President of the Council of Ministers and on its position within the hierarchy of Italian sources of law. First of all, DPCMs are decrees adopted by the sole President of the Council of Ministers (PCM, ie the Head of the Italian executive), and not by the whole Council of Ministers (as it happens, according to Article 77 Italian Constitution, with decree laws). Moreover, while decree laws are issued by the

[25] The state of emergency was extended, on the decision of the Council of Ministers, on 29 July 2020 up to 15 October 2020; on 7 October 2020 up to 31 January 2021; on 13 January 2021 up to 30 April 2021; on 21 April 2021 up to 31 July 2021; on 23 July 2021 up to 31 December 2021.

[26] Decree Law no 6 of 23 February 2020, converted into Law no 13 of 5 March 2020.

[27] Decree Law no 6/2020, Art 3. Translated by the author.

[28] Art 13 It Const.

[29] Art 16 It Const.

[30] Art 17 It Const.

[31] Art 19 It Const.

[32] Art 41 It Const.

[33] Decree Law no 19 of 25 March 2020, converted into Law no 35 of 22 May 2020, repealed and replaced this Decree Law.

[34] It should be noticed that, due to the troubles it raised, the use of DPCMs has been considerably reduced starting from February 2021, when a new executive was sworn in. Nevertheless, this chapter was written between December 2020 and January 2021, so it takes into account the approach to the pandemic from February 2020 to January 2021.

President of the Republic[35] – who, in doing so, ensures a *lato sensu* check on the constitutionality of decrees – DPCMs are issued by the PCM, without any check by the President of the Republic. Additionally, DPCMs are not submitted to the Houses of Parliament to ask for their conversion into law as is the case for decree laws. All these features mean that no parliamentary nor presidential[36] oversight is carried out on DPCMs.

Looking at the Italian hierarchy of legal sources, DPCMs have a lower rank than laws, while decree laws are equated to them. As a consequence, the constitutionality of DPCMs cannot be reviewed by the Italian Constitutional Court, which is only entitled to rule on the compliance of statutory laws and acts having the same legal force (ie, decree laws and legislative decrees) with the Constitution.[37]

The use of DPCMs to face a major emergency such as COVID-19 is an unprecedented approach in Italy. Wide resort to DPCMs is a blatant sign of concentration of powers in the hands not of the whole executive, but of his Head alone, which is very uncommon in the Italian parliamentary form of government. The described setting is unquestionably a peculiar and challenging one and it has significant implications on democracy in Italy. This is the object of analysis developed in section III.

III. The Impact of Reactions to COVID-19 on Democracy in Italy

In order to examine the impact of the backdrop presented in the previous section on Italian democracy in a thorough and comprehensive way, two sides of the Italian concept of democracy (which can be extended to most of Western legal systems) have to be taken into account.

First, Italian democracy is a so-called representative (or indirect) democracy. In other words, sovereignty, belonging to the people according to the Constitution,[38] is exercised by the Houses of Parliament. The latter are made up of representatives of the Nation,[39] expressing the will of people. Consequently, Parliament plays a pivotal role in the Italian democratic context.

Second, the Italian democracy has a substantive side, meaning that at its very core there are some crucial principles that have to be respected. Among them, one can list the protection of rights and freedoms, judicial review, transparency and accountability and certainty of law.

[35] Pursuant to Art 87 It Const.

[36] In the Italian legal system, the President of the Republic is considered to be a 'neutral' body, not directly involved in politics and tasked with ensuring the respect of constitutional legality.

[37] Art 134 It Const.

[38] Art 1 It Const.

[39] Art 67 It Const.

The Italian legal response to COVID-19 impacts on both these limbs, which deserve separate analysis.

A. The Marginalisation of Parliament: The Italian Case in the Comparative Context

The Italian approach to the COVID-19 pandemic, revealing a key role of the Head of the executive, resulted, at least at first, in the blatant marginalisation of Parliament.

In emergency circumstances, a certain degree of prevalence of executive bodies to the detriment of Legislatures is a common factor, since Executives, by their very nature, are better placed to deal with 'exceptional' times.[40] Nevertheless, the risk of thwarting the role of the parliamentary institution was made even worse by the peculiar traits of the COVID-19 emergency. With social distancing being the main way to contain the effects of the disease (and consequent banning of major gatherings and minimisation of people meeting), convening the Houses of Parliament to carry out their activities entailed many risks, especially at the beginning of the pandemic.

Yet at the same time – particularly in a parliamentary form of government, as Italy is – hindering the activity of Parliament might seriously endanger the relationship among powers as well as political accountability. In a parliamentary system, there is a confidence relationship between the political majority sitting in Parliament and its Government, so that the Legislative should be able to continuously check the activity of the executive (through tools that the Constitution and the standing orders of each House provide), holding it politically accountable if necessary.

Political accountability is not the sole reason why marginalising Parliament might be troublesome. In the Italian system, the Houses of Parliament are tasked with exercising 'collectively'[41] the legislative function. And there are matters (eg, the limitation of some rights and freedoms) that, according to the Constitution, have to be governed by laws of Parliament (or primary sources, meaning acts with the same force as law, like decree laws). This mechanism – called statutory limit (*riserva di legge*) in Italian constitutional law – is aimed at ensuring that some sensitive issues are only addressed by the bodies (the Houses of Parliament) that guarantee the widest possible representation of Italian people, while the executive represents just the temporary political majority.

[40] This is due to the fact that the executive's action is usually quicker than potentially long parliamentary procedures. Moreover, it is easier, for executive bodies, to deal with technical measures and with the involvement of experts in decision-making. On the role of the executive in times of emergency, AV Dicey (1885), *Introduction to the Study of the Law of the Constitution* (McMillan, 1979).

[41] Art 70 It Const.

At first, marginalisation of Parliament is exactly what happened in Italy. On 5 March 2020, the Heads of parliamentary groups of the Chamber of Deputies suspended the work of the lower House of the Italian Parliament, with the exception of undeferrable acts. The Heads of parliamentary groups of the Senate of the Republic did the same on 9 March 2020. This situation could not last long, since it seriously undermined the Italian form of government.

Italy has not been the only jurisdiction to face the problem of how to convene Parliament and ensure that it can carry out its activities in times of COVID-19 without fuelling the spread of the virus. Other countries have had to deal with similar issues while struggling against the pandemic.

In this regard, a comparative overview shows that, in some cases, remote voting has been identified as a possible solution. Not just at the domestic level – for instance, in Spain and in the United Kingdom[42] – but also within the European Union,[43] distance voting procedures have been enacted to keep the functions of representative bodies alive while averting the risks deriving from large gatherings of people.

To make compliance with social distancing rules easier, in Germany, parliamentary standing orders have been amended so as to reduce the *quorum* requirements of members who have to be present in order to validly adopt new laws or take any other decisions.[44]

Another arrangement that has been made is the introduction of reduced formats for parliamentary sittings combined with proxy voting, as happened in France.[45]

In Italy, the possibility to resort to remote voting and, thus, to the use of technology in parliamentary activity[46] has given rise to a lively debate among both

[42] In Spain, the Congreso de los Diputados (ie, the lower House of the Spanish Parliament) opened to the possibility of distance voting as of March 2020, then extended also to the Senado (ie, the upper House). In the United Kingdom, on 21 April 2020, the House of Commons adopted a system called 'hybrid Parliament', meaning that some members of the House are physically present, while others resort to remote voting. On the British approach, see the chapter by R Thomas, 'Virus Governance in the United Kingdom' in this volume.

[43] On 26 March 2020 the European Parliament resorted for the first time to an extraordinary remote voting procedure to approve urgent measures to fight the pandemic.

[44] A temporary amendment of the Bundestag's standing orders provided that valid decisions can be taken when more than one quarter of the members of the German lower House are present (before this change, the quorum was more than one half). *Beschlussempfehlung und Bericht des Ausschusses für Wahlprüfung, Immunität und Geschäftsordnung*, Drucksache 19/18126, 25 March 2020.

[45] In France, a specific working method was adopted: only three members per political group can sit in the Assemblée Nationale, but each member can cast vote (by proxy) for all the members of his/her political group. On the French situation, see S Brunet, 'The Hyper-Executive State of Emergency in France', in this volume.

[46] To the point that someone talked about 'virtual parliaments' in times of COVID-19. D Natzler, 'Building a "virtual parliament". How our democratic institutions can function during the coronavirus' (*The Constitution Unit*, 20 April 2020) constitution-unit.com/2020/04/20/building-a-virtual-parliament-how-our-democratic-institutions-can-function-during-the-coronavirus; A Williamson, 'Virtual Members: Parliaments During the Pandemic' (2020) *Political Insights* 40. See also L Sciannella, 'La crisi pandemica da Covid-19 e la "trasformazione digitale" dei Parlamenti. Un'analisi comparata' (2020) 2 *DPCE Online* 2509.

political parties and scholars. Pros and cons of the use of distance voting and the feasibility of such procedure within the Italian constitutional framework have been widely examined.

On the one side, some are in favour of remote voting during public health crises, maintaining that it would be a feasible option to ensure representativeness without impairing the right to health.[47] They can be divided into those who argue that distance voting should be introduced through a change of the standing orders of the Houses of Parliament[48] and those who hold that the current drafting of the procedural rules would already allow e-voting practices, which could be legitimised by a mere authorisation of the Presidents of the Houses.[49]

On the other side, there are some stances against remote voting. First, in some scholars' opinion, the provisions of the Italian Constitution regarding the activity of members of Parliament unequivocally refer to physical attendance. And, according to this literal reading, even if the Constitution were amended and the requirement of physical presence removed, such a change would seriously jeopardise the very concept of 'political representativeness', since the idea of 'representativeness' exactly means to give voice to those who are absent.[50] Not to mention that distance voting would frustrate debate in the Houses and transparency of parliamentary sessions, which instead are crucial in representative democracies.[51] Second, someone claims that remote voting would be dangerous, since it would end up being used also outside of emergency contexts. In other terms, distance voting during the pandemic might turn out to be a dangerous precedent, and the duty to physically sit in the premises of the Houses of Parliament would be neglected even in ordinary times.[52]

It is worth highlighting that this reluctance towards remote voting has been shared also by the Presidents of the two Houses of the Italian Parliament and by some political forces.[53] As a consequence, no distance voting mechanism has ever

[47] Among others, S Curreri, 'Il Parlamento nell'emergenza' (2020) 3 *Rivista AIC* 214; N Lupo, 'Perché non è l'art. 64 Cost. a impedire il voto "a distanza" dei parlamentari. E perché tale voto richiede una "re-ingegnerizzazione" dei procedimenti parlamentari' (2020) *Osservatorio Costituzionale* 23. Among political parties, Partito Democratico, Movimento 5 Stelle and Liberi e Uguali.

[48] S Ceccanti, 'Verso una regolamentazione degli stati di emergenza per il Parlamento: proposte a regime e possibili anticipazioni immediate' (2020) 2 *BioLaw Journal* 1. See also the proposal for a reform of the standing orders of the Chamber of Deputies, submitted by Stefano Ceccanti, stefanoceccanti.it/lo-stampato-della-proposta-di-riforma-regolamentare-per-il-parlamento-a-distanza-con-le-104-firme.

[49] S Curreri, 'Voto a distanza in Parlamento: i precedenti non lo impediscono affatto' (*La Costituzione.info*, 16 March 2020) www.lacostituzione.info/index.php/2020/03/16/voto-a-distanza-in-parlamento-i-precedenti-non-lo-impediscono-affatto/.

[50] R Calvano, 'Brevi note su emergenza Covid e voto dei parlamentari a distanza. Rappresentanza politica, tra effettività e realtà virtuale' (2020) 21 *Federalismi* 45.

[51] V Lippolis, 'Parlamento a distanza? Meglio di no' (*Il Foglio*, 1 April 2020).

[52] M Luciani, at the debate: 'Parlamento aperto: a distanza o in presenza? (II appuntamento)', organised on Facebook on 3 Aprile 2020 by the President of "Commissione Affari Costituzionali" of the Italian Chamber of Deputies, www.radioradicale.it/scheda/602453/parlamento-aperto-a-distanza-o-in-presenza-ii-appuntamento.

[53] Among these political forces, Fratelli d'Italia, Italia Viva, Lega.

been introduced in Italy. Rather, to lower the risk of spreading the virus, as of the end of March 2020, parliamentary sittings started to be held using all spaces available (including those usually reserved for journalists) to allow as many members of the Houses as possible to attend without breaching social distancing rules. In some cases – for example, when the increase of budget deficit to tackle the emergency needed to be voted on – Heads of parliamentary groups even made agreements to ensure that no more than half of the members of each Houses sat in Parliament.

Hence, after a first moment – coinciding with the very beginning of the pandemic – of real marginalisation of Parliament, it cannot be said that the Italian Houses have been completely excluded from decisions regarding the COVID-19 pandemic.[54] However – and this is the most questionable aspect – even when they played a role in the handling of the pandemic, not always did they do so in an effective way. Some examples can be made.

First, thanks to described ploys enabling voting without violating anti-COVID-19 safeguards, the Houses have converted into law many decree laws dealing with the emergency, but without fixing main problems arising from them. Among others, excessive discretion left to the PCM.[55]

Second, an improvement in the relationship between the Parliament and the (Head of) Government is due to a provision of Decree Law no 19/2020,[56] according to which, before adopting DPCMs aimed at managing the pandemic, the PCM (or a Minister delegated by him) has to inform both Houses of forthcoming measures on which the Houses can pass a resolution.[57] This mechanism was applied also when the state of emergency, declared pursuant to Legislative Decree no 1/2018 and originally set to expire on 31 July 2020, was extended up to 15 October 2020 and then up to 31 January 2021, as both Houses passed their own resolutions. However, Decree Law no 19/2020 does not ensure full participation of the Houses. As a matter of fact, in some cases, the PCM resorted to a clause – contained in the same Decree Law – permitting him to adopt measures and, after doing so, merely inform the Houses *ex post*; as a result, the Houses cannot vote a resolution, but only engage in an *ex post* debate.

In sum, available tools were not always appropriately used by the Houses themselves to fully exercise their role (reference is to failure to amend decree laws during the conversion procedure). And even newly established procedures aimed at reintroducing Parliament (at least to some extent) in the decision-making process do not ensure a significant voice of the Houses on actions to be taken. Actually, they can simply pass resolutions and, furthermore, the PCM can choose

[54] On whether the marginalisation of Parliament was 'real', see also G Zagrebelsky, 'Chi dice Costituzione violata non sa di cosa sta parlando' interview published by *Il Fatto Quotidiano*, 1 May 2020, www.vasroma.it/zagrebelsky-chi-dice-costituzione-violata-non-sa-di-cosa-sta-parlando/.

[55] The Houses could have done so because, when they convert a decree law into law, they have the possibility to make amendments to the substantive content of the act.

[56] Decree Law no 19 of 25 March 2020, Art 2, para 5.

[57] In the Italian parliamentary system, a resolution is a tool that each House can pass – usually after a debate – in order to direct governmental action (although not being legally binding).

to trigger the *ex post* clause embodied in Decree Law no 19/2020, depriving them of this possibility. It might be argued that these improvements in the relationship between the Legislature and the executive in times of emergency are just apparent or, at least, their outcome highly depends on the two branches' will to engage in a cooperative behaviour.

B. The Pandemic's Effect on Human Rights and Personal Freedoms

Moving to the effects of anti-COVID-19 measures on 'substantive' aspects of democracy, it is worth considering that, albeit abovementioned tools have been introduced to ensure involvement of Parliament, acts concretely used to face the health emergency have still been taken by the executive (rather, by its Head).

Consequences on basic principles of democracy are manifold and they touch upon at least four main areas.

A first point concerns effective protection of rights and freedoms, which is an essential feature of any democratic context. As is widely known, protecting rights and freedoms does not necessarily mean that all of them must be considered as 'absolute' and so subject to no limitations. Rather, in many cases, limitations may be legitimate in a democracy, when they are necessary to safeguard other competing rights or interests and a balancing effort is needed. However, the restriction of rights and freedoms is a very sensitive matter and, thereby, the Italian Constitution prescribes that some of these limitations can only be set by a law or an act having the same legal force.

As said, DPCMs are not laws, nor do they have the same legal force. Although they are not primary sources, they do have impact on rights and freedoms that can exclusively be limited by the law, according to the Constitution.[58] In this regard, some Italian scholars maintain that there has been no violation of the Italian Constitution. They say that, even though concrete measures are established by DPCMs, such acts find their legal basis in previous decree laws, whose legal force is the same as laws. In their view, this would be sufficient to legitimise limitations of personal freedom and freedom of movement.[59] Other stances, instead, argue that this legal basis is too vague and undefined, so, in practice, the powers of the PCM are excessively wide.[60]

[58] eg, Art 13, para 2, It Const (restrictions of personal freedom); Art 16, para 1, It Const (restrictions of freedom of movement).

[59] Luciani (n 17). On the legitimation of emergency measures based on decree laws, see also G Azzariti, 'I limiti costituzionali della situazione di emergenza provocata dal COVID-19' (*Questione Giustizia*, 2020) www.questionegiustizia.it/articolo/i-limiti-costituzionali-della-situazione-d-emergenza-provocata-dal-COVID-19_27-03-2020.php.

[60] S Cassese, 'La pandemia non è una guerra. I pieni poteri al governo non sono legittimi' (*Il Dubbio*, 14 April 2020) www.ildubbio.news/2020/04/14/cassese-la-pandemia-non-e-una-guerrapieni-poteri-al-governo-sono-illegittimi; Vedaschi (n 5).

A second point is strictly related to the first one. Given that the possibility to challenge the constitutionality of acts limiting rights and freedoms before a court is another key element of democracy, the lack of constitutional review of DPCMs is a problem. Pursuant to Article 134 Italian Constitution, the Italian Constitutional Court – ie the sole body in Italy mandated with constitutional adjudication – can review the constitutionality of laws and acts with the same legal force, declaring their invalidity if they violate the constitutional standards. Therefore, DPCMs are excluded from any chance of constitutional review.

There is, indeed, a possibility of judicial (not constitutional) review of these acts in the Italian legal system. DPCMs are considered to be administrative acts and, consequently, administrative courts are in charge with reviewing their legality and, if necessary, declaring them null and void. And there have been cases in which DPCMs dealing with the COVID-19 crisis have been challenged before administrative courts, with the applicants claiming that they left too much discretion to the PCM. Yet, in these circumstances, there have been two main issues, a procedural and a substantive one.

The procedural issue is that, since the coronavirus pandemic situation evolves rapidly, DPCMs are quickly replaced by other following ones. Rules governing the procedure before Italian administrative courts require dismissal of the case, if the administrative act that has been challenged loses its effects. Thus, since the beginning of the pandemic, judges have frequently had to abstain from ruling on the content of the acts, since the DPCM under review was no longer in force.[61] A way to overcome this situation might be conceivable, but would entail a partially innovative attitude of Italian administrative courts. More specifically, a possible solution might be that administrative courts decided to review the DPCM in force, if it shows the same flaws that characterised the expired one. This would recall a well consolidated case law of the Constitutional Court regarding decree laws,[62] but Italian administrative courts have not taken this approach yet.

The substantive point can be explained as follows. Even when administrative courts have assessed the merit of DPCMs (and also of acts issued by lower levels of government in Italy, such as the presidents of regional executives and even mayors) containing anti-COVID-19 measures, they have very often ruled that these acts pursued a legitimate aim, ie the protection of public health, and, therefore, they were fully legitimate. In other words, courts did not engage in an in-depth scrutiny of whether (or not) the limitative measures, in safeguarding public health – which is for sure a legitimate purpose – were appropriate and proportionate.[63] Rather, they have merely made sure that reviewed acts did not lack any rational basis.

[61] See, among others, Regional Administrative Court for Lazio, order no 3453/2020, 4 May 2020.

[62] For more details, see Vedaschi (n 5).

[63] See, inter alia, Regional Administrative Court for Campania, decree no 416, 18 March 2020; Regional Administrative Court for Friuli, order no 61, 10 April 2020; Regional Administrative Court for Veneto, decree no 205, 21 April 2020. In Italian administrative law, this approach is called 'extrinsic scrutiny'.

A third reason of concern regarding the substantive dimension of democracy has to do with the principle of transparency. Transparency is at very roots of any democratic environment and is the precondition for accountability.[64] The executive must be held accountable before Parliament (in parliamentary forms of government, as Italy), but also before public opinion, as citizens have a right to know choices made and actions taken by governmental bodies and rationales behind them.

Transparency issues in the COVID-19 emergency can be addressed under both the perspective of scientific evidence and the viewpoint of the use of mass communication.

As far as scientific knowledge is concerned, DPCMs aimed at tackling the pandemic have often been adopted on the basis of analyses carried out by a 'Comitato Tecnico-Scientifico' (Technical-Scientific Committee), specifically set up at the beginning of the COVID-19 crisis. Reports and other documents of this Committee, on which Italian anti-COVID policies have been grounded, remained confidential for a long time, and just recently they have become public, after judicial litigation and a huge political and media debate.[65]

The problem of transparency of technical and scientific information on which political decisions in times of the coronavirus emergency are based affected other jurisdictions, too. For instance, in France, the Assemblée Nationale created an ad hoc parliamentary enquiry commission to investigate on how executive authorities, supported by a 'Conseil Scientifique' (Scientific Council) with functions that are similar to those of the Italian Committee, are handling the pandemic. This step might be desirable in Italy, too, as it would probably result in further involvement of Parliament in the struggle against the pandemic.

Regarding the perspective of communication from public authorities to the general public (mass communication), it should be noticed that the PCM has taken a peculiar stance, which the history of the Italian Republic had never witnessed before, in the relationship with citizens and the media. As a matter of fact, prior to the entry into force of new anti-COVID-19 measures, the PCM has directly addressed citizens in press conferences, broadcast on TV. Usually, only the President of the Republic, and in very limited circumstances, directly speaks to Italian people. Yet, such a media exposure of the Head of the executive does not automatically result in ensuring transparency in its proper sense, since there is no guarantee that all available and correct information is shared with citizens.

[64] JJ Rousseau (1762), *The Social Contract*, trans M Cranston (Penguin Books Ltd, 2008); J Bentham (1791) in J Bowring (ed), *Panopticon; or The Inspection House* (Russel & Russel, 1962); I Kant (1795) in B Orend (ed), *Perpetual Peace*, trans W Hastie (Broadview Press, 2015); N Bobbio, *La democrazia e il potere invisibile* (1980) 10 *Rivista italiana di scienza politica* 181.

[65] More specifically, some plaintiffs asked the Regional Administrative Court for Lazio to order the Civil Protection Department of the Council of Ministers to disclose reports of the Committee. The Court granted their request (Regional Administrative Court for Lazio, judgment no 8615 of 13 July 2020). Although, on appeal, the Council of State had temporarily suspended the execution of the lower court's ruling (Council of State, decree no 4573 of 31 July 2020), the Civil Protection Department decided to autonomously disclose the documents, perhaps due to the media hype that had been raised.

A fourth and last point needs to be addressed, representing another very peculiar aspect of the handling of the COVID-19 crisis. As the content of DPCMs is sometimes unclear, a new practice was established according to which, a few hours after publication of a new DPCM imposing restrictions on citizens' rights and freedoms, the website of the Presidency of the Council of Ministers published a set of Frequently Asked Questions (FAQs) clarifying the most common doubts. However, even these FAQs raise several questions as to their binding nature. Undoubtedly, leaving the interpretation of tools limiting rights and freedoms to non-binding guidelines seriously undermines the principle of certainty of law, another foundational aspect of democracy.

IV. Concluding Remarks

The analysis carried out throughout this work brought to light some points that have a significant impact on Italian democracy.

First, this chapter proved that there is a close link between effects of emergency on the representative dimension of democracy and effects on its substantive limb. As seen, marginalising Parliament – in a first moment – and endowing it with weak participation tools – during the so-called second wave of COVID-19 – has impacted not just on representativeness and political accountability, but also on key features such as – among others – the protection of rights, constitutional review, transparency and certainty of law. As a matter of fact, DPCMs escape a number of checks: by the whole Council of Ministers, being adopted by its Head alone; by the President of the Republic, not being issued by him; by the Houses of Parliament, not being converted into law; by the Constitutional Court, not falling within its jurisdiction. And although, in theory, they can be scrutinised by administrative courts, this review has not proven effective, due both to procedural issues (timing) and to administrative judges' deferential approach.

Second, the handling of COVID-19 in Italy has shown that, even when mechanisms ensuring a certain degree of participation of Parliament have been arranged in the midst of the pandemic, state powers have not cooperated much. Italian institutions have shown a fragmented and sometimes incoherent attitude, both as regards the relationship between Parliament and the executive and, within Parliament itself, between majority and opposition political forces. On the one side, the executive often labelled anti-COVID-19 measures to be taken as 'urgent', so as to exclude any *ex ante* discussion in the Houses of Parliament and the possibility for them to adopt their own resolutions. On the other side, majority and opposition have frequently disagreed on crucial aspects (among others, whether or not to resort to remote voting), without setting a cohesive response plan. This situation, indeed, mirrors the condition of political fragmentation that Italy was already going through before the beginning of the pandemic emergency. The latter has done nothing but emphasise this framework and its drawbacks, as COVID-19 has been exploited to fuel political antagonism. This situation is undesirable, since, in circumstances of crisis, loyal cooperation among state bodies and political forces would be essential.

A third and particularly important aspect concerns the legal framework to deal with an emergency in Italy. Albeit abovementioned loyal cooperation efforts on the political scene would be helpful in stressful times, they might not be enough, as they might need to be complemented by a new constitutional framework to address emergency. The choice, made by the Italian Constituent Assembly, not to introduce any systematic and detailed regulation of emergency in the Italian Constitution was based on precise historical reasons, and can be considered as a thoughtful and reasonable one in a post-World War II Italy. Nonetheless, the historical and political scenario has changed and, most of all, emergencies have been transformed. Society is now facing emergencies characterised by a global reach and by a considerable amount of time, to the point that the requirement of temporary nature, traditionally considered to be one of the main features of emergency, is increasingly ebbing away. COVID-19 is a blatant example of a global and long-lasting crisis, but the same can be said with regard to pre-existing emergencies, such as the threat posed by international terrorism, which has permanently loomed over democracies since 11 September 2001.[66]

Against this backdrop, it might be necessary to reconsider the decision, made in the aftermath of World War II, to have a 'silent' Constitution on emergency. Whether or not it is time for the Italian Constitution to 'speak up' on emergency is something that needs at least to be discussed, both at the political and academic level, once the coronavirus crisis is over.

[66] A Vedaschi, 'The Dark Side of Counter-Terrorism: *Arcana Imperii* and *Salus Rei Publicae*' (2018) 66 *American Journal of Comparative Law* 877.

7

Swedish Constitutional Response to the Coronavirus Crisis
The Odd One Out?

JULIA DAHLQVIST AND JANE REICHEL*

I. Introduction

The Swedish response to the coronavirus crisis has, at least initially, deviated from those in most other comparable countries and the Swedish strategy has gained attention worldwide.[1] Only a few binding restrictive measures have been enacted and the Swedish model has, at least initially, been to mostly rely on informal and voluntary measures based on recommendations from the Public Health Agency (PHA). No lockdowns, as in mass quarantines or stay-at-home orders, or mandatory mask wearing have, as of February 2021, been introduced. However, during the 'second wave' of the pandemic, in Autumn 2020, the strategy somewhat changed and new restrictions have gradually been introduced. The development brought to light the need for new legislative tools and at the beginning of 2021 the Swedish Parliament, the Riksdag, enacted the temporary COVID-19 Act, delegating further powers to the Government.[2] It may be submitted that the constitutional framework, in essence, has been respected. However, the strong position of Swedish public authorities in the area of communicable diseases, together with the vast delegation of powers to the Government, has in practice impacted on the traditional division of tasks for implementing policies in a manner unprecedented in modern Swedish constitutional history.

* We would like to extend our warmest gratitude to Tim Holappa, Mark Klamberg, Andreas Knutsson, Jaan Paju, Lena Sandström, Mauro Zamboni and Karin Åhman, all at the Faculty of Law at Stockholm University, and to Henrik Wenander at the Faculty of Law, Lund University, for their insightful comments.

[1] See eg C Andersson and HP Libell, *New York Times*, 'In the Coronavirus Fight in Scandinavia, Sweden Stands Apart' www.nytimes.com/2020/03/28/world/europe/sweden-coronavirus.html.

[2] Lag (2021:4) om särskilda begränsningar för att förhindra spridning av sjukdomen covid-19 (The COVID-19 Act).

The Swedish Constitution is not a single document, instead comprising four different *fundamental laws*: the Instrument of Government (IG), the Act of Succession, the Freedom of the Press Act, and the Fundamental Law on Freedom of Expression.[3] The principles for democracy are set out in the IG and, in accordance with its opening paragraph, all public power proceeds from the people. In modern times, Sweden has not taken part in any war and thus has developed its democracy and welfare state during mostly stable and peaceful times. This has affected the constitutional framework, and the IG from 1974 has been influenced by a high level of trust and belief in the state and the work of politicians.[4] This was reiterated in relation to COVID-19, with the Government on its website stating that '[p]eople in Sweden have a high level of trust in government agencies. This means that a large proportion of people follow government agencies' advice. In the current situation, people in Sweden are on the whole acting responsibly to reduce the spread of infection by, for example, restricting their social contacts'.[5]

In this contribution, the Swedish response to the coronavirus crisis is analysed against the Swedish constitutional and administrative model, taking into account non-legal factors such as social trust and a tradition of consensus-building in the political sphere. The main focus of this chapter is to analyse the Swedish constitutional framework and illustrate how the structure of power and democracy may have influenced the Swedish approach to COVID-19 – and how well these structures have been maintained during the pandemic. The Swedish approach is illustrated in actions relating to restrictions for private citizens, eg, of the freedom of movement and freedom of assembly, and some restrictions against companies. As the pandemic remains ongoing, the strategies and actions continue to change and develop at the time of writing.

II. Swedish Legal Responses to the Coronavirus Crisis

A. An Overview

Even though the 2021 COVID-19 Act allows for further binding measures to be introduced, Swedish policies still mainly favour non-binding measures. Some binding measures were, however, enacted in spring 2020, in accordance with

[3] Chapter 1, Section 3, IG. Changing a fundamental law is however relatively easy and as of 2020 a parliamentary committee has been assembled to investigate the process and whether it should be changed – the purpose being to strengthen the basic protection of democratic structures, see Dir 2020:11.

[4] J Nergelius in A Alen and D Haljan (eds), *IEL Constitutional Law* (Kluwer Law International BV, 2018), Reviewed October 2014), kluwerlawonline.com.ezp.sub.su.se/EncyclopediaChapter/IEL+Constitutional+Law/CONS20190048, 11.

[5] Article from the Prime Minister's Office, 'Strategy in response to the COVID-19 pandemic' (6 April 2020) www.government.se/articles/2020/04/strategy-in-response-to-the-covid-19-pandemic/.

delegated powers based on existing or amended acts of law: restrictions on public gatherings (including freedom of assembly and demonstrations), a requirement for venues serving food and drink at tables to ensure social distancing among costumers, and a general ban on visiting homes for the elderly. Prisons and other institutions have also adopted provisions banning visitors. Universities and schools, with pupils aged 13–19 years, have been given legal tools to move to web-based teaching, based on recommendations from the PHA. Since November 2020, alcohol cannot be served past 10 pm, later changed to 8 pm.[6] Entry bans into EU via Sweden from countries outside the EU or Schengen have been in place since March of 2020. As of 6 February, due to the mutations of the virus spreading, stricter regulations were enacted by the Government and all foreign citizens who want to travel into Sweden must present a negative COVID-19 test upon entry.[7] Three principles guide Swedish crisis management: the principles of responsibility, subsidiarity and equivalence. The principle of responsibility means that no specific crisis organisation has been introduced, but the organisation of tasks rests on the party responsible for a particular activity under normal circumstances. The principle of subsidiarity entails that the crisis is to be handled where it occurs and on as low a level as possible. The principle of equivalence means that no bigger changes in the organisation than the situation requires should be made and that activities during a crisis should function as close to normal as possible.[8]

It may also be noted that the Riksdag during 2020, until the ordinary budget proceedings, enacted 11 amending budgets containing financial support to the cultural sector, businesses, etc as well as several acts of laws relieving requirements for social insurance, business, etc.[9]

B. General Governance in Relation to Communicable Diseases

The main Swedish Act of law regulating management of infectious diseases is the Communicable Diseases Act (CDA) of 2004.[10] This Act is focused on voluntary and preventive measures, placing the responsibility to prevent transmissions of communicable diseases on individuals.[11] The PHA is given the mandate to take

[6] ibid.

[7] Förordning (2020:127) om tillfälligt inreseförbud till Sverige (Ordinance on a temporary entry ban to Sweden). Some exceptions apply.

[8] P Bergling, J Engberg, M Naarttijärvi, E Wennerström and ME Wimelius, Krisen, myndigheterna och lagen: krishantering i rättens gränsland (The crisis, the authorities and the law: crisis management in the legal borderland) (Gleerups Utbildning, 2016), 24 f.

[9] See further Sveriges Riksdag (The Swedish Parliament), 'The Riksdag's work in connection with the coronavirus' www.riksdagen.se/en/the-riksdags-work-in-connection-with-the-coronavirus/.

[10] Communicable Diseases Act (2004:168).

[11] Chap 2, ss 1–2 CDA and H Wenander, 'Sweden: Non-binding Rules against the Pandemic – Formalism, Pragmatism and Some Legal Realism' (2021) 38 *European Journal of Risk Regulation* 127–42 et seq.

initiatives as to effective infection control, as well as to coordinate the work at a national level, whereas the regions are responsible for ensuring that control measures are taken regionally.[12] With mandate provided in the CDA, the PHA has adopted the '[PHA] regulations and general recommendations on the responsibility of all to prevent infection by Covid-19, etc'.[13] The recommendations include advice to, eg, ensure social distancing, move meetings to web-based tools, and for individuals to take a personal responsibility by washing their hands carefully for at least 20 seconds, avoid public transport and parties, weddings, etc. No sanctions are proscribed. For a period of time during spring 2020, the Government, together with the PHA, made recommendations against travelling distances longer than a two-hour car drive.[14] In October 2020, when the spread of COVID-19 again started to rise, the PHA enacted general recommendations, advising individuals to, eg, refrain from visiting indoor locations, go to meetings or concerts, and have physical contact with persons from other households.[15] The Government and the Prime Minister have during autumn and winter 2020 repeatedly advised the public to refrain from new social contacts outside their household or a close circle of friends.

C. Temporary Prohibitions and Delegation of Further Norm-making Powers to the Government

One of the first measures adopted by the Government was to introduce temporary restrictions on public gatherings, based on norm-making powers already existing in the 1993 Public Order Act, including to limit the constitutionally protected right to assembly and demonstration. The prerequisites for limiting these fundamental rights are given in the IG,[16] eg that the Government in certain situations can limit them through ordinance after previous delegation in law, and in the Public Order Act the Riksdag has specified the relevant requirements. Further involvement of the Riksdag was thus not necessary.

During spring 2020, the Government however anticipated the need to enact further restrictions. By using the flexibility in the regular legislative procedure to the fullest, the Parliament enacted an amendment to the CDA in an extraordinarily

[12] Chap 1, ss 7–8 CDA.

[13] HSLF-FS 2020:12.

[14] 'Reseavrådan förlängs – nya råd för resor inom landet, (Advice against travels extended – new advice for travels within the country)' sverigesradio.se/sida/artikel.aspx?programid=83&artikel=7472677.

[15] Folkhälsomyndighetens beslut den 29 oktober 2020: Införande av lokala allmänna råd enligt HSF-FS 2020:12 i Stockholms län (The Public Health Agency's decision of 29 October 2020: Introduction of local general recommendations in Stockholm County).

[16] Chap 2, ss 1, 20, 21 and 24 IG and Chap 2, s 15 Public Order Act (1993:1617) and Förordning (2020:114) om förbud mot att hålla allmänna sammankomster och offentliga tillställningar (Ordinance on a prohibition against holding public gatherings and events).

swift legislative process in April 2020, allowing the Government to, eg, close down commercial and cultural locations as well as measures to redistribute drugs and medical supplies from private healthcare providers.[17] However, these delegated powers could not be used to limit fundamental rights protected by the IG and were only applicable for a period of two and a half months, from 16 April until 30 June 2020. In the end, the delegated powers were never used, but if a government ordinance had been enacted, it had to be placed before the Riksdag as soon as possible after enactment. The Riksdag could then revoke the ordinance if its content was not considered appropriate.

It should be emphasised that the initial proposal from the Government gave the Government a wider mandate. The sphere of application of the act was formulated in a more general manner and the requirement on placing ordinances enacted before the Riksdag allowed the Government a more generous time frame.[18] The changes were made after criticism from both the Council on Legislation[19] and the Riksdag's Committee on the Constitution, who found the delegation to be too far-reaching.[20]

In the 2021 COVID-19 Act, the Government has been given tools to enact targeted measures adjusted to the specific conditions of different activities to, eg, limit public gatherings and public events, access to places for cultural activities, marketplaces, public transport, and domestic air transport, and use or renting of places for private gatherings. The COVID-19 Act, unlike the previous delegated powers in the amendment to the CDA, includes the possibility to limit fundamental rights in accordance with the IG: the freedom of assembly and demonstration, the right to ownership and the freedom of trade.[21] During the preparation of the Act, the Council of Legislation and the Parliamentary Ombudsman raised objections. The Ombudsman especially issued strong critique, eg in regards to the vast scope of application and the limited control mechanisms.[22] After the preparation some changes were made, the time for the entry into force was changed from 15 March 2021 to 10 January 2021, and the timeframe for placing an ordinance before the Riksdag was shortened from one month to a week, thus a wider timeframe than the previous powers in the temporary amendment to the CDA. The Act is set to expire on 30 September 2021.

So far, the measures taken by the Government under the Act have mostly targeted businesses and not individuals. The measures include a limit of people

[17] Sections 6–6 c Act (2020:241) amending the CDA.

[18] Utkast till lagrådsremiss: Ett tillfälligt bemyndigande i smittskyddslagen med anledning av det virus som orsakar covid-19 (Draft bill for the Council on Legislation: A temporary authorisation in the Communicable Diseases Act by reason of the virus that causes covid-19).

[19] The Council on Legislation consists of current and former justices (from both the Supreme Court and the Supreme Administrative Court) and is tasked with giving opinions on draft legislation, Chapter 8, Section 20–22 IG.

[20] Opinion of the Legislative Council 6 April 2020 and Report 2019/20:SoU20, app 3, 43.

[21] See The COVID-19 Act and Prop. 2020/21:79.

[22] JO, Dnr R 144-2020, Yttrande över promemorian Covid-19-lag (Statement over the memorandum Covid-19 Act) (S2020/09214), 2020-12-18.

allowed in shops (calculated based on 10 square meters of store space per customer), an obligation to specify how many people can visit the store at once and a maximum limit of eight people for events – including some private events outside the residence. In preparation for the school break in February 2021, the Government announced that actions would be taken to limit the spreading of the virus on long-distance traffic, eg trains and buses, and the restrictions came into force on 14 February.[23] Measures directed towards individuals to a large extent remain in the form of recommendations. If regulations directed towards individuals are enacted, violations of some of the regulations can be met with a fine.[24]

III. Legislative Institutions and the Judiciary: Parliamentary Sovereignty

A. The Constitutional Framework, a Division of Functions

The Swedish Constitution and governance is based on a division of functions, rather than a division of power. This is made clear by the principle of popular sovereignty (eg, that all public power proceeds from the people), whereas power is not something divided between the state organs. Furthermore, there are two types of public bodies (decision-making political assemblies and public authorities; the Riksdag is an example of the former and the Government and the courts of the latter).[25] The Riksdag is the foremost representative of Sweden, and thereby of the Swedish people. The strong commitment to parliamentarianism and popular sovereignty is manifested in, eg, the absence of control over the Riksdag's activities, such as the lack of a constitutional court and a traditionally weak judiciary and that the Riksdag is considered the final arbitrator of the constitution.[26] The Government governs the realm, but it is accountable to the Riksdag in accordance with the principle of parliamentarism.[27] Furthermore, Sweden has authorities at the local and regional levels which enjoy a constitutionally protected partial self-governance.[28]

The Swedish Constitution has mostly been developed and changed lawfully,[29] although it has not always been respected as a written document. In 1974, a new

[23] Förordning (2021:8) om särskilda begränsningar för att förhindra spridning av sjukdomen covid-19 (The limitations ordinance for COVID-19). HSLF-FS 2021:2.

[24] Section 24 The COVID-19 Act, Riksåklagarens föreskrifter om ändring i Riksåklagarens föreskrifter (1999:178) om ordningsbot för vissa brott (The Prosecutor General's regulations on revisions of the Prosecutor General's regulations on fines for certain crimes), Utfärdad den 18 januari 2021.

[25] Chapter 1, s 1 IG; W Warnling Conradson, H Bernitz, L Sandström and K Åhman, *Statsrättens grunder* (*Foundations of Constitutional Law*), 6th edn (Norstedts Juridik, 2018) 42 ff.

[26] See eg Prop. 2009/10:80, 148.

[27] Chapter 1, s 6 IG.

[28] See Chapter 14 IG.

[29] See Nergelius (n 4) 11.

IG replaced the IG from 1809. Between approximately the start of the 1920s up until when the new IG came into force, a time that has been referred to as the half-century without a constitution, the constitutional system was based on constitutional customs instead of on a written constitution. One of the aims of the 1974 reform was to codify these practices.[30]

B. Legislation and Norms: Actors within the Norm-making Procedures

The Riksdag is the only body that can enact laws and make decisions as to the use of state funds. However, the Riksdag has a minor office with few staff and a weak investigatory capacity. Legislation is prepared by the Government, traditionally after a report has been drafted by Government commissions of inquiry (which may include members of parliament).

Chapter 8 of the IG contains the provisions on statutory acts of law. This is supplemented by Chapter 2 of the IG regarding fundamental rights and freedoms, where the preconditions for limiting such rights by acts of law or ordinances are provided. Some rights are absolute, eg, the prohibition on capital punishment, and cannot be limited by other laws, whereas other rights are relative and can be limited, eg, the right to freedom of assembly and the right to free movement.[31] However, limitations can only be made under certain conditions, eg, to satisfy a purpose that is acceptable in a democratic society, and may not go further than what is necessary in relation to the intended purpose – they need to be proportionate.[32] Generally, a limitation also needs to be made by an act of law, but as noted above, the freedom of assembly and demonstration can also be limited by government ordinances in certain situations, for example to combat an epidemic.[33] It should be noted that recommendations have to be in line with the judicial system as a whole and cannot run contrary to legislation or the basic laws.

In essence, there are different levels of regulation in the Swedish system – ie, legislation enacted by the Riksdag's vote, ordinances issued by the Government, and statutory instruments enacted by public and local authorities.[34] The Riksdag enacts most of its decision by simple majority, in accordance with Chapter 4, Section 7 IG. Before a vote is held, any matter raised by the Government or a member of parliament is to be prepared within the relevant parliamentary committee.[35] The Riksdag can authorise the Government to adopt provisions relating to various

[30] F Sterzel, *Författning i utveckling: tjugo studier kring Sveriges författning* (*A constitution in development: twenty studies on Sweden's constitution*), 2nd edn (Iustus, 2009) 18 ff.

[31] See Chapter 2, Sections 1, 4 and 8 IG.

[32] See Chapter 2, Sections 20–25 IG.

[33] Chapter 2, Sections 20 and 24 IG.

[34] See Chapter 8 IG.

[35] Chapter 4, Section 5 IG, unless otherwise stipulated in the IG.

issues (although this does not prevent the Riksdag from enacting laws on the same issue).[36] When the Government prepares its legislative bills and other matters, there is a procedural requirement in Chapter 7, Section 2 IG on gathering necessary information and opinions from the public authorities concerned. Regions, municipalities, organisations and individuals may also be given an opportunity to express opinions on the matter.[37] The Riksdag or the Government may authorise other authorities to adopt provisions, although such authorisation needs to be established in an act of law or ordinance. It is not uncommon that such delegation occurs, and it is well in line with the constitutional tradition and framework.[38] This is also what has made the more intrusive measures undertaken in the pandemic possible.

Furthermore, there are two main categories of non-binding measures in Swedish public law: general recommendations (*allmänna råd*) and a wider category of other guidance documents, such as recommendations and guidelines.[39] General recommendations are formalised in the Ordinance on Official Gazettes.[40] They are to be printed or otherwise made available to the public.[41] A general recommendation must relate to a specific binding act of law or ordinance, whereas other guidance documents are independent and can be issued in various forms. Since general recommendations can be formulated in a broad manner, their contents may overlap with areas covered by other acts. For example, the PHA has adopted regional general recommendations under the CDA, advising people to avoid visiting indoor locations, attending meetings, concerts, etc.[42] Effectively, however not formally binding, the general recommendation thus supplements temporary ordinances adopted under the Public Order Act, which restricts public gatherings.

On 16 March 2020, the group leaders for the political parties in the Riksdag reached an agreement to reduce the number of members to be present for votes – this was voluntary, as there are no regulations on the matter. All 349 members of parliament are still in service, but only 55 of them are to be present when there is a vote in the Chamber. Each party decides which members are to represent them before the vote (ie, it is not always the same 55 members who are present). As of 16 April, there is also free seating in the Chamber, to ensure that physical distance can be kept.[43] The Riksdag has thus been flexible and able to adapt swiftly to the

[36] See Chapter 8, Section 8 IG. What can be delegated is limited – some matters can only be regulated in legislation enacted by the Riksdag, see Chapter 8 IG.

[37] Chapter 7, Section 2 IG.

[38] See eg Chapter 8, Sections 10–11 IG.

[39] U von Essen, A Bohlin and W Warnling Conradson, *Förvaltningsrättens grunder* (*Foundations of Public Administrative Law*), 4th edm (Norstedts Juridik, 2020), 66 and Wenander (n 11) 133.

[40] Författningssamlingsförordning (1976:725) (Ordinance on Official Gazettes).

[41] Section 6 Ordinance on Official Gazettes.

[42] See (The Public Health Agency's decision of 29 October 2020: Introduction of local general recommendations in accordance with HSF-FS 2020:12 in Stockholm County).

[43] Sveriges Riksdag, 'The Riksdag's work in connection with the coronavirus', www.riksdagen.se/en/the-riksdags-work-in-connection-with-the-coronavirus/; SVD, 'Riksdagen drar ner – 55 ledamöter i omröstningar (The Parliament cuts back – 55 Members of parliaments in votes)', www.svd.se/riksdagen-drar-ner--endast-55-ledamoter-i-omrostningar.

current situation. Without political will and flexibility, this would probably not have been possible, as the adaptation relies on political solutions and trust rather than binding regulations.[44] A parliamentary committee, with an impartial Chair, has been appointed to follow up on the Riksdag's work during the pandemic and it remains to be seen whether the 'Corona-Riksdag' will be met with any criticism.[45]

In terms of the legislative procedure, both the Government and the Riksdag have minimised the time needed for preparing matters substantively. For example, the entire legislative process for enacting the temporary amendments in the CDA lasted only 10 days, from the time the Government referred its proposal to the procedure for consultation under Chapter 7, Section 2 IG, until the Riksdag enacted the law. However, the very short time period for the consulting procedure – 24 hours beginning on a Saturday afternoon – and the limited number of actors consulted, were criticised by the Council on Legislation.[46] The Constitutional Committees, on the other hand, have previously found the IG to allow for a flexible procedure when needed – and in this instance referred the question to the preparatory committee.[47]

C. The Courts and Judicial Review

In recent decades, Swedish courts have undergone important changes, primarily due to influences of European law. The position of the courts was strengthened in the 2011 reform of the IG, including by a widening of the possibilities to conduct judicial review and by providing more independent procedures for appointing judges.[48] The courts have, however, so far not played any specific role in the response to the pandemic. The courts have historically taken a comparatively restrained position in the Swedish constitutional culture. Several factors have contributed to this.[49] For example, Sweden does not have a constitutional court

[44] This is also the case with the notion of pairing. The procedure is based on constitutional practice (and is hence not regulated), where the parties amongst themselves agree to let one member abstain from voting when a member from another party is unable to participate (this is used in relation to occasional absences). This is a way to ensure balance in the chamber and the procedure is voluntary – not all parties take part in the pairing. See S Riksdag, 'The economic conditions of the members', www.riksdagen.se/en/test-sidor/the-economic-conditions-of-the-members/ and Warnling Conradson et al (n 25) 83. The concept has similarities with the War delegation, consisting of 50 members of parliament and the speaker. The War delegation is to replace the Riksdag if circumstances so warrants during war or danger of war, see Chapter 15, Sections 2–3 IG.

[45] Direktiv för en parlamentarisk utredning om riksdagens arbete under coronapandemin (Directive for a parliamentary inquiry into the work of the Riksdag during the corona pandemic), Dnr 608-2020/21, 2020-12-09.

[46] Opinion of the Council on Legislation 6 April 2020, 2.

[47] Report 2019/20:SoU20, app 3, 43. See further A Jonsson Cornell, Författningsberedskap i praktiken – en kommentar med anledning av lagen om ändring i smittskyddslagen (Anticipatory statutorification – a comment on the amendment to the Communicable Diseases Act), SvJT, 2020, 379–81.

[48] Prop. 2009/10:80, 119, 126, 130 and 141.

[49] Compare M Zamboni, 'The Positioning of the Supreme Courts in Sweden – A Democratic Oddity?' (2019) 4 *European Constitutional Law Review* 668–90, 676 et seq.

and it is the Riksdag that is the main interpreter of the IG.[50] All the courts and the administrative authorities have the mandate to disapply legislation if it is found contrary to higher norms, meaning that the power is not provided to one single court or institution. The possibility of judicial review can only be used in relation to a specific case; there is no way to declare regulation as null or void in full.[51] Sweden has an *ex ante* control of legislation via the Council on Legislation which is tasked with giving opinions on draft legislation.[52] Although not formally binding, the opinions of the Council on Legislation are usually observed. If they are not, this could be argued to increase the probability of judicial review in later cases where the legislation would be applicable.[53] As seen above, the Council has during the pandemic raised concerns about proposed legislation, and the criticism has to a large extent been taken into account.[54]

IV. The Executive Branch: Command, Control and Delegation

A. Local Government and the Swedish Administrative Model

The organisation of the Swedish executive branch is highly influenced by two specific traits: the dualism of the Swedish administrative model and that a large part of Swedish welfare is implemented at the local level, with traditionally strong local self-government.

Starting with the latter, it may be noted that the Swedish state is organised into three political and administrative levels. Each level is governed by a democratically elected body: the Riksdag at the national level as well as regional and municipal councils at the regional and municipal levels, respectively. Regions and municipalities function under the constitutionally protected principle of local self-government and any restriction in local self-government should be proportionate.[55] Implementation of the majority of Swedish welfare policies is allocated to the regions and municipalities, which are responsible for, eg, healthcare, local public transport, social services, housing and education (in primary and secondary schools). With the principle of responsibility in Swedish crisis management, all parties remain responsible for their normal tasks, which in practice has

[50] See eg Prop. 2009/10:80, 148.
[51] Chapter 11, Section 14 and Chapter 12, Section 10 IG.
[52] See Chapter 8, Section 20–22 IG.
[53] See also Nergelius (n 4) 117 ff.
[54] See Prop. 2019/20:155 and Prop. 2020/21:79.
[55] Chapter 14, Sections 2–3 IG.

meant that recommendations have varied between regions and that vaccinations and testing schemes have differed.[56]

The dualism within the executive branch of the Swedish administrative model differs from what is seen in most western-style democracies. Even though public authorities function under the executive branch, there is a division between the Government and the public authorities. Authorities are organisationally and legally separated from the Government, regional and municipal councils, respectively, and enjoy a partial independence.[57] The minister in charge cannot singlehandedly take actions to command and control the public authorities sorting under his or her cabinet, since government decisions must be adopted by the Government collectively.[58] Ministerial control of public authorities by an individual minister is thus forbidden, and authorities are instead accountable to the Government as a whole.[59] According to the principle of independence '[n]o public authority, including the Riksdag, or decision-making body of any local authority, may determine how an administrative authority shall decide in a particular case relating to the exercise of public authority vis-à-vis an individual or a local authority, or relating to the application of law'.[60] The Public authorities thus enjoy a partial independency, both towards the Government and towards each other. Hence, the administration is to be governed by law and other general guidelines, not by political decrees in individual cases. There is to be a separation between policy-making and administrative decision-making. In regard to organisation, government offices have traditionally been comparably small, whereas the public authorities are large in terms of staff and budget.

Public authorities thus hold a strong position in Sweden, and historically there has not been a strict constitutional division between courts and public authorities.[61] It is also notable that the principle of objectivity and impartiality in the IG applies equally to courts and public authorities.[62] The principle of transparency and the right to access official documents guarantees insight into public authorities, as documents used in the decision-making process are available to the public.[63]

[56] Information on the regional measures is collected on a national website: www.krisinformation.se/detta-kan-handa/handelser-och-storningar/20192/myndigheterna-om-det-nya-coronaviruset/regional-information-om-coronaviruset.

[57] von Essen et al (n 39) 115, and P Hall, 'The Swedish Administrative Model' in J Pierre (ed), *The Oxford Handbook of Swedish Politics* (OUP, 2015, pub online 2016).

[58] Chapter 7, Section 3 and Chapter 12, Section 1 IG.

[59] S Ahlbäck Öberg and H Wockelberg, 'The Public Sector and the Courts' in Pierre (n 57) 4.

[60] Chapter 12, Section 2 IG.

[61] T Bull and F Sterzel, *Regeringsformen: en kommentar* (*The Instrument of Government: A commentary*), 3rd edn (SNS förlag, 2015) 259, 275 et seq. As seen above, in section III(C), courts and administrative authorities both have the mandate to disapply legislation contrary to higher norms, Chapter 11, Section 14 and Chapter 12, Section 10 IG, respectively.

[62] See Chapter 1, Section 9 IG.

[63] See further J Hirschfeldt, 'Free Access to Public Documents – A Heritage From 1766' in AS Lind, J Reichel and I Österdahl (eds), *Transparency in the Future – Swedish Openness 250 Years* (Ragulka Press, 2017) 21–28, 21.

B. Instruments to Steer the Administration

The main instrument to steer the semi-independent administration is statutory law. The principle of legality, laid down in Chapter 1, Section 1 IG, is reiterated in Section 5 of the Administrative Procedure Act.[64] An authority may thus act only in areas within its field of competence, under a relevant legal basis. The principle of a law-bound administration is to a certain extent mediated by the fact that the authorities produce a fair share of the norms within their respective policy area. Swedish sector-specific administrative law often takes the form of a framework act of law, delegating norm-making power to the Government, regions or municipalities, as well as to the public authorities.[65] Public authorities may also adopt non-binding guidance documents within their respective areas, without formal delegation.[66] These have been instrumental to the Swedish strategies to combat the pandemic.[67]

The Government can also give an authority a specific assignment, for example to perform a study or to draft guidance documents for a specific situation. For example, the National Board of Health and Welfare (*Socialstyrelsen*) has been commissioned to provide guidance, coordinate and support regions and municipalities in their handling of COVID-19 and to produce plans for further initiatives.[68]

V. Questions of Accountability for the Executive Branch

The structure of accountability for the Government in Swedish constitutional law is provided mainly in Chapter 13 of the IG. The main function of control is the Committee on the Constitution (*konstitutionsutskottet*). The Committee is tasked with examining ministers' performance of their official duties and their handling of government business. Various measures and mechanisms can be enacted to ensure accountability, such as interpellations and questions, a declaration of no confidence or prosecution of a minister.[69] During spring 2020 the Committee decided to postpone its annual examination due to the pandemic, a decision to resume was however taken on 2 July. Furthermore, on 26 July the Committee announced that it would examine the Governments' handling of the coronavirus crisis and that the

[64] Administrative Procedure Act (2017:900).

[65] F Sterzel, *Författning i utveckling: konstitutionella studier* (*Constitution in development: constitutional studies*) (Iustus, 1998) 59, 89 et seq.

[66] Prop.1983/84:119, 7 and Wenander (n 11) 135.

[67] See section II.

[68] Parts of the assignments have been reported in Socialstyrelsens plan inför eventuella nya utbrott av covid-19 (The National Board of Health and Welfare's plan for potential new outbreaks of covid-19). Socialstyrelsens rapportering av uppdrag (S2020/05825/FS (delvis)).

[69] Chapter 13, Sections 1–5 IG.

focus would be on how governmental powers have been exercised from a broad constitutional perspective.[70]

The Government is ultimately responsible to the Riksdag for everything that the public authorities do, except where the administration's duty of obedience to the Government does not apply (ie, pursuant to Chapter 12, Section 2 IG).[71] In order for the Government to be able to answer to the Riksdag, the Government must be able to exercise control over the administration. Moreover, it is the Government's responsibility to ensure that the public authorities are well-equipped to perform their duties in an efficient manner.[72] A survey assessing the functions of the Swedish administrative model during the pandemic has found that, in practice, the sectorisation of the administration at national level as well as local self-government challenge the Government's ability to govern coherently.[73]

The main political tool for the Government to use against a public authority is to remove the Director General from his or her post.[74] The Director General of the Swedish Civil Contingencies Agency left his post in December 2020, after media reports that he during autumn 2020 twice spent family vacations abroad, against the recommendations of the Government and the PHA to avoid unnecessary travels. This was not done in his official capacity, but rather his private sphere.[75]

Within their respective areas of independent decision-making, the authorities are solely responsible for measures undertaken. Administrative decisions may generally be appealed to courts.[76] Actions may also be taken vis-à-vis individual officials, in the form of criminal charges for misconduct in office or disciplinary action. Further, the administration is under the supervision of the Chancellor of Justice and the Parliamentary Ombudsman.

VI. Extraordinary Measures in Times of Crises

A. Peace or War, no Inbetween

In other countries, proclamation of a state of emergency is a possible way to shift the power during a time of crisis, eg, giving the executive branch unrestricted

[70] KU granskar regeringens hantering av coronakrisen (The Committee on the Constitution reviews the Governments handeling of the Corona crisis) (26 June 2020), www.riksdagen.se/sv/press/pressmeddelanden/2020/jun/26/ku-granskar-regeringens-hantering-av-coronakrisen/.

[71] J Reichel, *Ansvarsutkrävande – svensk förvaltning i EU* (*Accountability – Swedish administration in the EU*) (Jure, 2010) 90 et seq and SOU 2007:75, 39.

[72] See eg DS 2018:6.

[73] Statskontoret, Förvaltningsmodellen under coronapandemin (The administrative model during the coronavirus pandemic), 2020, 62 et seq (English summary).

[74] Sections 32–33 lag (1994:260) om offentlig anställning [The Public Employment Act] and lagen (1982:80) om anställningsskydd (Swedish Employment Protection Act).

[75] Dagens Nyheter, Dan Eliasson begär att få lämna sitt uppdrag (Dan Eliasson requests to be dismissed from his assignment) 6 January 2021.

[76] Section 41 Administrative Procedures Act.

power. The Swedish approach is different. The IG does not contain any provisions regarding the proclamation of a state of emergency in peacetime. It knows only two situations: peace and war.[77] Any extraordinary measures to be taken in times of a peacetime crisis should thus be in compliance with the regular legal framework.[78] Propositions have previously been made to include regulations regarding emergency powers in peacetime in the IG.[79] The constitutional law inquiry proposed the creation of a regulation meaning that the Government, in a peacetime crisis and under certain conditions, could issue regulations that would usually fall under the Riksdag's mandate – however, the proposal was rejected by the Government.[80] The Committee on the Constitution, in its response to the temporary amendment to the CDA, underlined that the bill gave reason to consider a review of the prerequisites for legal actions in peacetime crises.[81]

Even though the Swedish Constitution does not contain any provisions on emergency powers in peacetime, Chapter 8 of the IG provides the possibility to shift regulatory power relatively quickly, which has been considered to decrease the need to regulate extraordinary powers in peacetime within the constitution.[82] The pandemic seems to have challenged this notion, at least from a political view, and on 22 December 2020 the Government announced that a parliamentary committee will be formed and tasked with reviewing the Government's powers to, for example, legislate in place of the Riksdag during exceptional situations in peacetime.[83]

B. Anticipatory Statutorification (*Författningsberedskap*)

Instead of constitutional regulation and the possibility to proclaim a state of emergency in case of a peacetime crisis, the Swedish legislator has chosen to use anticipatory statutorification – meaning an effort to provide relevant legislation (statutes) with provisions relating to emergencies beforehand and during stable times, including delegations etc. This is inter alia based on the idea that the rule of

[77] Emergency powers in times of war or risk of war are found in Chapter 15 IG.

[78] It is up to the Government, under constitutional responsibility, to interpret the notion of war, see Prop 2009/10:80, 204. This means that a crisis in peacetime would not be enough to invoke Chapter 15 IG.

[79] See SOU 1963:16, SOU 2008:61, Prop. 2009/10:80.

[80] However, the Government noted that the matter should be evaluated further and required more consideration, see Prop. 2009/10:80, 207.

[81] Konstitutionsutskottets yttrande (Statement by the Committee on the Constitution), 2019/20:KU8y.

[82] See eg E Wennerström, 'Inget undantag utan regel – den konstitutionella nödrätten och Sverige' (No rule without exception – Constitutional necessity and Sweden) in J Hirschfeldt (ed), *Vänbok till Sten Heckscher* (Iustus, 2012) 365.

[83] Digital pressträff med statsministern 22 December (Digital press conference with the Prime Minister) 2020, (22 December 2020) www.regeringen.se/pressmeddelanden/2020/12/digital-presstraff-med-statsministern-22-december-2020/.

law should not be disregarded in times of crisis.[84] Thus, the Swedish approach has been prior enactment of new regular legislation, or specific provisions, relating to crises.

After previous crises, eg, the 2004 Indian Ocean earthquake and tsunami (which affected many Swedes), attempts have been made to improve practical management and to increase the preparedness with new legislation – so that similar events could be handled within the existing legal framework in the future.[85] However, it seems unlikely that the legislator is able to foresee all serious events or future crises that may occur, and there will probably be situations where the legislation intended to be used could prove to be insufficient. This was made apparent during the COVID-19 pandemic, both when previously existing regulations in, eg, the CDA, were feared to be insufficient and with the enactment of the new COVID-19 Act.[86]

If actions that are deemed necessary are not legally available, the Government can rely only on the debated principle of constitutional necessity. Constitutional necessity is a principle that means that state agents, in an emergency situation where society is in jeopardy, can disregard the Constitution and still claim to have acted lawfully.[87] With the introduction of the 1974 IG, arguments were made against accepting constitutional necessity, as it was considered a too 'uncertain basis' for actions in times of crisis. Other arguments against constitutional necessity have been that it is considered to be in conflict with the rule of law and that decisions made on this basis run the risk of not being respected or being considered illegitimate.[88]

In an investigation following the 9/11 attacks, it was stated that the Swedish state to a large extent had rejected the notion of constitutional necessity. The investigation subsequently stated that there might nevertheless be a (limited) scope for the use of a customary rule of constitutional necessity in addition to the Constitution – but the reach of such a rule was considered unclear.[89] Since then, similar statements have also been made in other preparatory works.[90] The role of constitutional necessity therefore remains uncertain, and whether or not a decision taken in conflict with the Constitution due to necessity is to be accepted has been left to *post facto* assessment by the Committee on the Constitution.[91]

[84] See eg SOU 2005:104, 56 and 314; A Jonsson Cornell and J Salminen, 'Emergency Laws in Comparative Constitutional Law – The Case of Sweden and Finland' (2018) 19(2) *German Law Journal* 219–50.

[85] See eg lag (2010:813) om konsulära katastrofinsatser (Act of consular disaster aid), enacted after the 2004 Indian Ocean earthquake and tsunami and the situation in Lebanon in 2006, Prop. 2009/10:98, 7.

[86] See section II.

[87] H Jermsten, Konstitutionell nödrätt (Constitutional necessity), (Stockholm Juristförlaget, 1992) 9; SOU 2005:104, 57.

[88] See eg Prop. 1987/88:6, 16; SOU 2003:32, 96; SOU 2008:61, 93 f.

[89] SOU 2003:32, 96.

[90] See eg SOU 2005:104, 57; Prop. 2005/06:111, 40 f; SOU 2008:125, 525.

[91] Compare Chapter 13 IG and Betänkande 2005/06:KU8.

VII. Constitutionalism, Governance, Social Trust and Consensus-building

A. Constitutional Limitations or Governance Culture as the Decisive Argument?

During autumn 2020, a debate arose whether the IG would hinder further actions – for example a lockdown – from being taken.[92] As shown by the 2021 COVID-19 Act, the Riksdag has accepted at least some further restrictive measures. In our opinion, the reason for Sweden's deviating approach to the pandemic is not so much a result of constitutional limitations, but on the trust-based, consensus-oriented and decentralised governance culture that has been guiding the Swedish welfare state.[93] Sweden's legal framework on communicable diseases is based on voluntary and preventive measures, under the coordination and control of the PHA.

The Swedish constitutional culture places the authorities and regional and local municipalities in the centre of interpreting, supplementing and enforcing sector-specific administrative law. The IG and the manner in which it has been applied throughout Swedish history thus favours a decentralised decision-making model.[94] As held by political scientists Jacobsson and Sundström, Swedish politicians trust the officials to do their best to act in accordance with what they believe is the will of their political superiors or else hand over the issues to the politicians.[95] This response is in line with the constitutional tradition where the Riksdag enacts the basic components of the sector-specific policy areas in acts of law, and delegates further norm-making power to the Government and the partially independent public authorities and local municipalities. This governance approach is seen in the two acts of law that have been most central during the pandemic: the CDA and the Public Order Act. Furthermore, as noted by Wenander, it is common that public authorities issue non-binding rules within their fields of competence.[96] However, neither the Swedish constitutional model nor its administrative model hinder the Government from taking the lead in policy-making. The Swedish administrative model aspires to separate general policy-making from decision-making in

[92] See eg Sveriges Radio, Podcast, Det politiska spelet (The political game) – 315: 'Här syns SD:s studentikosa humor' (19 November 2020) sverigesradio.se/avsnitt/1622105.

[93] N Edling in H Haggrén, J Rainio-Niemi, J Vauhkonen (eds), 'The Primacy of Welfare Politics. Notes on the language of the Swedish Social Democrats and their adversaries in the 1930s, Multi-layered Historicity of the Present: Approaches to social science history' (University of Helsinki, 2013) 1, 125–50, 125.

[94] B Jacobsson and G Sundström, 'Governing the State, in J Pierre (ed), *The Oxford Handbook of Swedish Politics*, DOI: 10.1093/oxfordhb/9780199665679.013.20, 12–13 and L Jonung and J Nergelius, 'Grundlagen sätter ramarna för Sveriges coronastrategi (The Fundamental Law sets the framework for Swedens coronastrategy)', DN Debatt, Dagens Nyheter, 1 August 2020.

[95] Jacobsson and Sundström (n 94) 1–17, 13.

[96] Wenander (n 11) 141 et seq.

individual cases, granting authorities a protected sphere in the latter, but not in the former. As discussed above, the Government may steer authorities via general measures and is responsible for ensuring that the authorities are well-equipped to perform their duties in an efficient manner.

B. Has the Swedish Administrative Model Been Too Soft?

In the light of the aforementioned, it is interesting to take a closer look at the amendment to the CDA in spring 2020, with its temporary delegation of further norm-making power to the Government to shut down theatres, restaurants, traffic, etc. In essence, the same measures that were initially controversial from a constitutional point of view when the Government was to adopt them as binding instruments, were later introduced by the Government or the PHA via non-binding measures. As the pandemic continued, this hesitance subsided and in the 2021 COVID-19 Act the Government has been conferred powers to enact stricter measures, preferably against businesses and organisations. However, as seen, even with the new act, the emphasis on voluntary measures remains the main rule, placing the responsibility on the individual to act with due care. The 2021 COVID-19 Act thus comes closer to corresponding with the Swedish constitutional foundation, with the Riksdag being the final arbitrator of the basic law and the foremost norm-maker, by setting the frame for what restrictions the Government may enact. However, the pragmatic tradition favouring flexible and soft measures vis-à-vis individuals remains.

Furthermore, during the pandemic, the non-binding measures have often been treated as binding in the public debate. Non-binding measures are used as complements in areas not covered by binding law. The Government has explicitly stated that the binding restrictions on public gatherings are to be normative in all social situations – regardless of whether they are covered by the legislation 'in purely formal terms'.[97] The statement is peculiar. When presenting non-binding regulations together with binding ones, there is a risk that the non-binding ones are perceived as being binding, which risks blurring important legal distinctions. A binding measure may, for example, produce legal effects in relation to third parties and can provide a legal basis for agreements (eg, insurance), whereas non-binding measures generally cannot. As criticised by Jonung and Nergelius, even the Prime Minister referred to the recommendation of the PHA not to travel more than two hours by car as a 'travel ban'.[98] The fact that even representatives of the Government issue statements that make the non-binding regulations appear to be

[97] Article from the Prime Minister's Office, 'A maximum of eight participants should be normative for all of society' (20 November 2020) www.government.se/articles/2020/11/a-maximum-of-eight-participants-should-be-normative-for-all-of-society/.

[98] Jonung and Nergelius (n 94).

binding is troubling. In a society where social trust is strong, there is a relationship between citizens' trust in each other and in societal institutions, on the one hand, and their willingness to accept what are perceived as professional and objective measures taken by representatives of the state, on the other.[99] Given how trust in state agents has affected the Swedish system, this is also something that could be exploited. Had the recommendation been an actual ban, this would have entailed a limitation to the right of free movement within the state and the right to leave it, which could be created only in accordance with the special procedures laid down in Chapter 2 IG, including performance of a test of proportionality. In regular parliamentary legislative procedures, even when these are not related to the limitation of fundamental rights, there are mechanisms in place to ensure transparency and participation of important actors. As seen above, these include compulsory consultation with administrative authorities and the public, involvement of the Council on Legislation and, where relevant, the Committee on the Constitution. In this sense, the 2021 COVID-19 Act constituted a step forward, providing more transparency and insight into the Government strategies. Furthermore, legal requirements, especially if they include sanctions, are reviewable *ex post* by courts, which is not the case with non-binding recommendations. Non-binding measures are not even published in any regulated manner. For example, the non-binding measures announced by the PHA during spring 2020 are no longer available the authority's website. This obstructs the means of control.

C. Effects on the Constitutional Setting

It may be submitted that the Swedish constitutional framework, both in regard to norm-making powers and the role of the executive, has been respected throughout the pandemic. The Riksdag has maintained its role and the strong position of the administration is grounded in the IG. In the end, the initial Swedish strategy was found to be insufficient and the need for legally enforceable rules based on an act of law apparent. The question may be asked why it took so long.

As of now, there are no other mechanisms in the IG that allow the Government to act without the support of the Riksdag. The IG does not allow for a state of emergency, shifting the power to the executive branch, and the principle of constitutional necessity has never been actualised in relation to legislative actions, only in relation to executive actions.[100] Since the IG provides for swift means for enacting regulations (which have been upheld by the Riksdag throughout the year 2020),

[99] T Bull, 'Global Governance; Need for a New Theory or the Return of an Old Friend?' in AS Lind and J Reichel (eds), *Administrative Law Beyond the State: Nordic Perspectives* (Brill – Nijhoff, 2013) 235.

[100] J Hirschfeldt, 'Svensk krishantering i fredstid – De konstitutionella aspekterna och en framåtblick (Swedish crisis management in peacetime – The constitutional aspects and a look forward)' (2020) SvJT, 1148.

and the possibility to delegate further powers to the Government, it is unlikely that arguments of necessity from the Government would be accepted. Furthermore, the COVID-19 pandemic perhaps could be classified as an enduring crisis, and the possibility for reflections and changes as the situation evolves would be considered greater than it might be in other situations, ie a terror attack or a tsunami – limiting the need for such extraordinary powers in this instance. Furthermore, the principle of parliamentary supremacy remains strong in the Swedish fundamental law, presupposing that the Government and opposition agree on the basic prerequisites of the decision-making process and the need for a speedy procedure in the situation at hand. If there is a difference of opinion on: (a) whether something in fact constitutes a crisis, and (b) if actions should be taken, cooperation will be more difficult. Next to the soft governance culture, and how the pandemic has been viewed by the PHA, this reason may explain the fact that it took Sweden 10 months to arrive at the conclusion that at least a partial lockdown might be necessary.

The fact that the Riksdag has been able to be flexible and continue its work throughout the pandemic points to the respect of parliamentarism and the principle of popular sovereignty. However, the flexibility and the fact that only 55 members of parliament attend each vote arguably also challenge the same notions. The members of parliament usually follow the party line but they are not obliged to do so, and the results may thus differ based on who is attending the vote. Furthermore, members of parliament can be elected based on personal votes.[101] It is noteworthy that the possible democratic implications of the Corona-Riksdag have gained relatively little attention in the public and legal debate so far. The fact that a committee has been tasked to evaluate the work of the Riksdag is in this regard welcome and might diminish questions about the legitimacy of the Corona-Riksdag. Even though the constitutional framework in essence has been respected there are thus aspects that warrant attention.

VIII. Concluding Thoughts: Does the Swedish Strategy Lead to an Accountability Deficit?

Arguably, there are risks connected with leaning heavily on non-binding measures that in practice have important effects in society. Even if the prominent position conferred on the PHA in the relevant legislation is in line with the Swedish administrative model, it must be submitted that the pandemic has caused challenges out of the ordinary. It is clear that the pandemic calls for delicate political balancing, given that the lack of effective measures in a pandemic risks the health and lives of the population. The Swedish strategy, to combat the pandemic via a combination of limited binding rules and non-binding measures, adopted by the Government

[101] See vallag (2005:837) (The Elections Act).

in close collaboration with the PHA, has in practice brought the Swedish administrative model far away from its main idea – that the administration is to be governed by law and general guidelines. Even though the 2021 COVID-19 Act was a step forward from this perspective, the emphasis on voluntary measures remain. The lack of clear norm-making procedures with built-in tools for participation and scrutiny make it hard to establish which party is responsible and on what grounds a measure has been enacted. There are mechanisms to hold both the Government and the public authorities accountable, as seen above, but the responsibility of each actor becomes diluted under the current Swedish strategies. The Swedish administrative model renders accountability difficult, when the Government and the Public Authorities collaborate closely within the broad framework of acts of law, and with independent regions and municipalities.

Sweden has come a long way since the 'half-century without a constitution', and has gone through a process where constitutional law has gradually hardened.[102] Some further measures have already been initiated. For example, the process for changing fundamental laws is being reviewed, an attempt to strengthen the protection of democratic structures. On 30 June 2020, the Government appointed a commission tasked with evaluating the measures taken both by the Government and by the relevant administrative authorities, regions and municipalities to limit the spread of COVID-19.[103] The commission issued an interim report on 15 December 2020, focusing on the spread of infection within elder care facilities, where criticism eg was made against the organisational structure. The commission stated inter alia that the 'ultimate responsibility for these shortcomings rests with the Government in power – and with the previous governments that also possessed this information'.[104]

The pandemic has shed light on the need for foreseeable, transparent and accountable procedures when adopting measures affecting all of society, even when the measures in question are non-binding and adopted by the semi-independent public authorities. Time will tell whether new ordinary legislation will be enacted based on lessons learned in the pandemic, in line with the tradition of anticipatory statutorification, or if the Swedish approach to crises in peacetime will be revised and a new system enacted – and whether this in fact will strengthen or weaken the constitutional framework.

[102] Zamboni (n 49) 683 and T Bull, 'Rättighetsskyddet i Högsta förvaltningsdomstolen' (The protection of rights in the Supreme Administrative Court) (2017) SvJT, 216.

[103] Dir. 2020:74.

[104] SOU 2020:80, Summary in English, coronakommissionen.com/wp-content/uploads/2020/12/summary.pdf. See also Statskontoret, Förvaltningsmodellen under coronapandemin (The administrative model during the coronavirus pandemic) 2020, 62 et seq (English summary).

8

Using Emergency Powers in Hungary: Against the Pandemic and/or Democracy?

ZOLTÁN SZENTE AND FRUZSINA GÁRDOS-OROSZ

I. Introduction*

In terms of the political consequences and constitutional implications of the COVID-19 pandemic, the case of Hungary received special attention both in international politics and the media, partly because Hungary was one of the first countries to introduce an extraordinary legal order, and partly because the declared state of danger provided, in principle, unlimited powers for the Government. It made the legal treatment of the COVID-19 pandemic even more interesting in that there is a widespread view among the international public and a significant proportion of the political science and constitutional literature that Hungary has been systematically undermining the rule of law since the 2010 change of government.

It may therefore be of particular interest to see how the extraordinary powers provided by the two emergency situations announced so far have affected the constitutional system and democracy of a country which is frequently characterised as a 'populist',[1] 'illiberal',[2] 'hybrid'[3] or 'semi-authoritarian'[4] regime. These

* The research is funded by project 129018 FK, The responsiveness of the legal system, funded by the National Research Development and Innovation Office.

[1] M Anselmi, *Populism. An Introduction* (Routledge, 2018) 90; G Halmai, 'A Coup Against Constitutional Democracy. The Case of Hungary' in MA Graber, S Levinson and M Tushnet (eds), *Constitutional Democracy in Crisis?* (OUP, 2018) 243; N Walker, 'Populism and constitutional tension' (2019) 17(2) *International Journal of Constitutional Law* 515–35, at 521, 524; T Fournier, 'From rhetoric to action, a constitutional analysis of populism' (2019) 20(2–3) *German Law Journal* 362–81; S Chambers, 'Democracy and constitutional reform: Deliberative versus populist constitutionalism' (2019) 45(9–10) *Philosophy and Social Criticism* 1116–31, at 1117; B Bugarič, 'Central Europe's descent into autocracy: A constitutional analysis of authoritarian populism' (2019) 17(2) *International Journal of Constitutional Law* 597–616.

[2] C Pinelli, 'Populism and Illiberal Democracies: The Case of Hungary' in Z Szente, F Mandák and Z Fejes (eds), *Challenges and Pitfalls in the Recent Hungarian Constitutional Development. Discussing*

labels are given special weight by the fact that the need to manage and resolve crisis situations is often taken as a source of legitimacy for populist or authoritarian regimes, because an external threat gives populist leaders or autocrats the opportunity to legally break free from the limits of power.[5] Some authors presume that such politicians sometimes invent or exacerbate a crisis situation themselves, because citizens are more tolerant or even supportive of authoritarian measures in times of crisis that threaten their security.[6]

Below, we present a constitutional analysis of the introduction of the two special legal orders in March and November 2020, the legislative authorisation of the Government to exercise extraordinary powers to fight the coronavirus pandemic, and the emergency decrees of the Government. Our primary intention is to examine how the executive has used the emergency powers during a real crisis situation in a country that has been so frequently characterised as a semi-authoritarian or populist regime.

II. The Constitutional Landscape of Emergency Situations in Hungarian Law

The general elections of 2010 brought about a landslide victory for the conservative parties that had been in opposition for the previous eight years. Owing to the disproportionate election system, the main government party, Fidesz, and its satellite coalition partner, the Christian Democrats, gained a two-thirds parliamentary majority. The new coalition government immediately started to change the constitutional landscape of the country; after they had come to power, in less than a year, they amended the Constitution of 1949/89[7] 12 times, and adopted a new constitution in April 2011 named the 'Fundamental Law' with the votes of the government party MPs.

the New Fundamental Law of Hungary (L'Harmattan, 2015) 211–19; T Drinóczi and A Bień-Kacała, 'Illiberal Constitutionalism: The Case of Hungary and Poland' (2019) 20(8) *German Law Journal* 1140–66.; R Uitz, 'Can you tell when an illiberal democracy is in the making?' (2015) 13 *International Journal of Constitutional Law* 279–300.

[3] A Bozóki and D Hegedűs, 'An externally constrained hybrid regime: Hungary in the European Union' (2019) 25(7) *Democratization*.

[4] B Bugarič and T Ginsburg, 'The Assault on Postcommunist Courts' (2016) 27(3) *Journal of Democracy* 69–82, at 70.; B Bugaric and A Kuhelj, 'Varieties of Populism in Europe: Is the Rule of Law in Danger?' (2018) 10(3) *Hague Journal on the Rule of Law* 21–33 at 25.

[5] S Levitsky and D Ziblatt, *How Democracies Die* (Crown Publishing, 2018) 93.

[6] Levitsky and Ziblatt (n 5) 94, 208, JW Müller, *What Is Populism?* (University of Pennsylvania Press, 2016) 43, S Blombäck, 'Populism as a Challenge to Liberal Democracy in Europe' in A Bakardjieva, EN Bremberg, A Michalski and Lars Oxelheim (eds), *The European Union in a Changing World Order. Interdisciplinary European Studies* (Palgrave Macmillan, 2020) 223.

[7] Hungary was the only post-communist country in Central and Eastern Europe where, after the defeat of communist rule, no new constitution was adopted. However, during the period of democratic transition, the communist constitution, originally adopted as the Act XX of 1949, was substantially revised by a constitutional amendment (Act XXXI of 1989), which is why it was frequently referred to in this way after 1989.

The new Constitution thoroughly changed the rules on the special legal order, even though it adopted several provisions almost verbatim from the previous one. These provisions are included in a separate part (*special legal orders*). The Fundamental Law defines six different forms of the special legal order[8] in a unique way in Europe, in particular if we take into account two other emergency situations, the so-called 'crisis situation caused by mass immigration',[9] and the 'health crisis situation'[10] introduced by legislative measures.

Since the entry into force of the Fundamental Law, the state of danger has been a separate form of special legal order; previously, in similar cases, ie in the event of an emergency caused by a natural or industrial disaster, the more general state of emergency could be declared. According to Article 53 (1) of the Fundamental Law, a state of danger may be declared 'in the event of a natural disaster or industrial accident endangering life and property, or in order to mitigate its consequences'. It is worth noting that neither the term 'danger' nor the definition of the circumstances under which this kind of special legal order can be declared are precise. Beyond this, this type of emergency can only be introduced in the event of a disaster (natural or man-made) that has already occurred (not in the case of a potential danger), and moreover, it must not only 'endanger' life and property, but must also have already caused serious damage to them when it occurred. The rules of the special legal orders must be very clear and precise, and should be interpreted narrowly because they provide extraordinary power to the executive and allow unusual restrictions to fundamental rights that otherwise would be unacceptable.

A state of danger may be declared by the Government, according to Article 53 of the Fundamental Law, which endows it with special powers. As part of this, the Government

- may introduce emergency measures defined by cardinal law, and
- may adopt decrees by means of which it may, as provided for by a cardinal act, suspend the application of certain legislative acts, derogate from the provisions of acts, and take other extraordinary measures.

These are special empowerments and apply to the adoption of decisions that the Government would not otherwise be able to make. However, even if the power of emergency legislation is wide-ranging, it is not unlimited. First, it can be exercised only within the framework specified in a cardinal law, that is as a delegated power, and furthermore, the cardinal law itself that gives this special legislative power may cover only the legal provisions necessary to eliminate the consequences of an emergency.

The Government decrees issued at the time of the state of danger may have *contra legem* effects, which means that temporarily they may substitute for effective

[8] In December 2020, the National Assembly adopted the Ninth Amendment to the Fundamental Law which restructured the constitutional rules on special legal orders, establishing three.

[9] See Art 80/A-80/K of the Act LXXX of 2007 (on Asylum).

[10] See Arts 228-254/E of the Act CLIV of 1997 (on Public Health).

parliamentary laws. Over time, however, this legal rank of the emergency decrees becomes conditional, because they can remain in force beyond 15 days only with the consent of the National Assembly. Formally, the extension of the temporal effect of emergency decrees is the competence of the Government, but it can be exercised only on the basis of the authorisation of the Parliament. Consequently, in times of a state of danger, the National Assembly is obliged to hold sessions, otherwise it could not control and approve the emergency decrees of the Government. Besides this, the Government's political responsibility to Parliament cannot be suspended, even during a state of danger. In addition, the continuous operation of the National Assembly is not affected by the rules of the special legal order, since Article 54 Section (2) of the Constitution states that 'the application of the Fundamental Law may not be suspended'. The same consequence arises from the fact that in some other cases of special legal orders the Fundamental Law allows the suspension of the operation of Parliament and even determines the circumstances.

The state of danger can be terminated only by the Government, this being, in principle, a constitutional obligation rather than a power, since it is the duty of the Government to cease the special legal order 'if the conditions for its promulgation no longer exist'. Emergency decrees[11] issued by the Government at the time of a state of danger automatically cease on the same day the special legal order is terminated, even if Parliament has previously agreed to extend their temporal effect. Nevertheless, the National Assembly may adopt a law(s) with the same content as the repealed Government decree(s) (as happened after the termination of the first state of danger).

III. Declaring the First State of Danger

On 11 March 2020, the Government declared a state of danger in the whole territory of Hungary according to Article 53 of the Fundamental Law due to the disease caused by COVID-19 being 'a mass human pandemic endangering the safety of life and property', and 'in order to protect the health and lives of Hungarian citizens'.[12] The declaration of this kind of special legal order provided the Government with an extraordinary power to respond with emergency decrees to the emergency caused by the pandemic.

The governmental decree declaring the state of danger raised constitutional issues and took several reasons into consideration, but, remarkably, in the absence of a constitutional legal basis, none of the Government decrees issued during this emergency situation met constitutional standards.

First, according to the Fundamental Law, as we have seen, the Government can declare a state of danger only in the event of a 'natural or industrial disaster'

[11] It can be observed that the Fundamental Law does not use the term 'emergency decrees' but refers simply to (Government) decrees.

[12] Government decree 40/2020 (III. 11.).

that endangers the safety of the lives and property of the citizens. In the absence of an effective vaccine against COVID-19, and also taking into account the number of documented deaths due to the pandemic, the risk to 'safety of life' can be considered justified. With regard to the rapidity of the spread of infection and its spatial extent, the extension of the state of danger to the whole country can also be corroborated. It also seems clear that the threat to the 'safety of property' is widespread, because, as a result of the coronavirus, a number of companies have ceased or restricted their economic activities, resulting in job losses and significant loss of income or wealth.

However, the state of danger was unconstitutional because it was declared on account of a 'human pandemic causing a mass illness'. In Hungarian law, a human pandemic neither falls within the conceptual scope of a natural disaster, nor can it be interpreted as an industrial catastrophe.[13] In Hungary, since the democratic transition of the country, the concept of natural disaster has always been understood in the traditional sense, ie as signifying an unavoidable event caused by natural forces, and it was distinguished from other dangers that could also pose a threat to human life, health and the safety of property. Human epidemics have never been classified as natural disasters in law.[14]

Human pandemics have not been considered a natural or industrial disaster by the Disaster Management Act[15] which specifies the detailed rules of emergency situations. Although this law contains only an illustrative list of dangers, it classifies 'human epidemic causing a mass illness' or 'threat of an epidemic' in the group of 'other hazards', distinguishing it from natural disasters (as 'natural hazards') and industrial catastrophes (as 'civilizational hazards'). It means that this statutory law, adopted in 2011, did not lead to any new interpretation of natural or industrial disasters (ie, classifying human pandemics as such), but added to them new sources of danger. This makes sense, because this law has a special significance, since it is the cardinal law within the framework of which the Government may use extraordinary measures or decrees in an emergency situation. The Disaster Management Act clearly considers a 'human epidemic causing a mass illness' and an 'epidemic threat' as an 'event' that can serve as a basis for declaring a state of danger. However, this is an arbitrary extension of the circumstances on the basis of which a state of danger can be declared, far beyond the conditions defined by the Fundamental Law, for which Parliament did not have authority.

[13] Notably, epidemics are generally not classified as natural disasters in international scholarship, but there is a significant literature on post-natural disaster epidemics, as there is a strong correlation between the two phenomena (ie, natural disasters often lead to infectious diseases). See, on this, JE Suk, EC Vaughan, RG Cook and JC Semenza, 'Natural disasters and infectious disease in Europe: a literature review to identify cascading risk pathways' *European Journal of Public Health*, ckz111, doi.org/10.1093/eurpub/ckz111.

[14] Z Szente, 'A 2020. március 11-én kihirdetett veszélyhelyzet alkotmányossági problémái' (2020) LXI(3) *Állam- és jogtudomány* 115–39.

[15] Act CXXVIII of 2011.

This extension is, therefore, clearly unconstitutional because it goes beyond the definition of the Constitution. It should be noted here that it does not follow from the Fundamental Law that a human pandemic cannot be included in the conceptual scope of natural disasters. However, the Disaster Management Act was not amended correctly, for example by including epidemics in the conceptual scope of a natural disaster, and merely considered the pandemic as a possible reason for the state of danger. As a result, the declaration of the state of danger on 11 March, 2020 did not have any constitutional basis, and, consequently, all emergency decrees issued on the grounds of this declaration, must also be unconstitutional inasmuch as they suspended the application of certain laws, deviated from statutory provisions or enacted other extraordinary measures which, according to the Fundamental Law, are the exclusive statutory subjects. Even if their content did not violate the Constitution, they were formally flawed, because they were based on an incorrect constitutional basis in that, according to the existing constitutional text, a human pandemic could not have been a legitimate reason for declaring a state of danger.

IV. The First Authorisation Act

A. The Scope of Authorisation and the Legislative Guarantees

On 30 March 2020, Parliament adopted an Act on protection against the coronavirus pandemic.[16] The purpose of the statutory act as stated in its preamble was to ensure that the Government could take any emergency measures necessary 'to prevent and manage the consequences of the human pandemic of COVID-19 in 2020' (hereinafter: the Authorisation Act). To this end, Parliament gave its prior consent to any emergency decree beyond the scope of measures specified in the Disaster Management Act by stating that the Government must use this authorisation only for a specific purpose, to the extent necessary and proportionate to the aim pursued. In addition to confirming Government decrees issued since the declaration of the state of danger, the Act also authorised the Government to extend the temporal effect of all subsequent emergency decrees until the end of the emergency.

The Act contained several safeguarding provisions. On the one hand, it stipulated that the Government must regularly inform Parliament of the measures taken on the basis of the authorisation, and, on the other hand, the National Assembly reserved its power to withdraw this special empowerment.

Finally, it laid down particular rules to avert the danger and manage the consequences of the pandemic. For example, it postponed the holding of by-elections and national and local referendums until the end of the emergency. In addition, the

[16] Act XII of 2020.

Authorisation Act added a new kind of crime, that of 'obstruction of the protection against the pandemic', with accompanying punishments, to the Criminal Code, and amended the previous Article on the dissemination of scaremongering, clarifying its wording and supplementing it with a new statement of facts on scaremongering in a special legal order, as any action 'which is likely to impede or thwart the effectiveness of the defense'. The Act classified some of its own parts as 'cardinal'.[17]

B. Constitutional Concerns of the Act

The Act raises several constitutional issues.[18]

First, Article 2 of the Authorisation Act, which provides an unlimited authority for the Government to issue emergency decrees, is unconstitutional. This Article expressly states that its authorisation confers a special legislative power 'beyond the exceptional measures and rules specified in the Disaster Management Act'. Pursuant to Article 53 Section (2) and Article 54 (4) of the Fundamental Law, the National Assembly has the right to define the framework of such regulations in a cardinal Act, as had been done in the Disaster Management Act. Parliament may change, narrow, or expand the frames defined by this Act. However, the National Assembly has no constitutional power to refrain from defining the legislative framework of the emergency power of the Government; otherwise the use of extraordinary powers by the Government cannot be evaluated by Parliament in its compulsory control function. The Authorisation Act, however, did precisely this; referring only to the purposefulness of emergency decrees, which is nothing more than a repetition of the relevant constitutional text in other words. It did not specify which emergency measures could be taken beyond what was required by the Disaster Management Act. The unlimited power of the delegated legislation is particularly striking in the light of the fact that Parliament waived ex-post control of all emergency decrees.

Secondly, Article 3 Section (1) of the Authorisation Act must also be qualified as contrary to the Fundamental Law; it authorised the Government to extend the scope of emergency decrees until the end of the state of danger. In this way, the Hungarian legislature really did 'commit suicide': it waived the right to the subsequent control of emergency decrees in such a way that made the exceptional authorisation an irrevocable process. Although the Act ostensibly reserved the right of the National Assembly to revoke this blanket authorisation 'before the end of the emergency' (Article 3 Section (2)), it – intentionally or accidentally – forgot to provide protection for this guarantee. For example, the authorisation

[17] The 'cardinal acts' form a special group of acts of Parliament. The adoption or amendment of this kind of law requires the votes of two-thirds of the members of the National Assembly present.

[18] See, on this, Szente (n 14) 115, 132; T Drinóczi and A Bień-Kacała, 'COVID-19 in Hungary and Poland: extraordinary situation and illiberal constitutionalism' (2020) 8(1–2) *The Theory and Practice of Legislation* 171–92.

of the Government did not preclude the amendment of the Act on the National Assembly, which ensures the continuous operation of the Parliament, or even the modification of the Authorisation Act. Consequently, the Government could theoretically exclude the operation of Parliament with its own emergency decrees. This extraordinary power of the Government was limited only by the Fundamental Law to the extent that it contains provisions on the date of the next general election (no later than in 2022), ie the authorisation did not cover the postponement or cancellation of the next parliamentary elections.

Thirdly, the Act was also unconstitutional in that it authorised the Government to extend the temporal effect of emergency decrees without any limit or parliamentary control. As has been noted above, the Government decrees issued during the state of danger may remain in effect beyond 15 days only with parliamentary approval. The Authorisation Act extended this special authority to emergency decrees to be made in the future, that is, it granted the authority in advance. However, the extension of the temporal effect of legislation that has not yet been enacted is conceptually flawed, as the temporal effect of legislation that has not yet started cannot be extended.

Fourthly, it is also questionable from a constitutional point of view that Parliament consented to extend the validity of all emergency decrees issued by the Government from the promulgation of the state of danger until the adoption of the Act, in a single package, without any investigation. Although the Fundamental Law does not explicitly stipulate that the Parliament should give its consent to each emergency decree separately, the only meaning and function of this constitutional provision is to ensure continuous parliamentary control over the extraordinary measures. A general approval, without any examination of the necessity, proportionality or effectiveness of these extraordinary measures, renders the whole parliamentary procedure meaningless. As the subsequent parliamentary control of emergency decrees is a constitutional obligation, the Parliament obviously cannot waive it. Any constitutional omission of the National Assembly cannot be defended in itself, but is especially serious if it results in giving a blank authority to the exceptional power of the Government during a special legal order, in other words, resigning from any control. There can be no acceptable reason for this, in particular when, as in this case, Parliament is otherwise sitting continuously, that is, it is able to perform its tasks and functions.

V. Crisis Management with Government Decrees

A. On the Nature of the Decrees

Between 11 March and 18 June 2020, in the almost 100 days of the state of danger, 149 Government decrees based on the Fundamental Law and on the Authorisation Act were issued over 'the entire territory of Hungary for the elimination of the consequences of the human epidemic endangering life and property and causing massive disease outbreaks, and for the protection of the health and lives of Hungarian citizens' or 'for the protection of the national economy'.[19] In this period, 94 ordinary Government decrees were enacted, so 61.32 per cent of the Government's activity was based on the emergency situation, which means that a broad and extensive regulation was adopted to deal with the state of danger.[20] Until the first Authorisation Act, the Government decrees were primarily issued for introducing emergency, immediate and temporary measures to prevent and slow down the spread of the COVID-19 pandemic within the country. The normative content of these Government decrees designated the strategy and means used by the Government for the entire duration of the first months of the emergency. As was originally described in Government decree 41/2020 of 11 March 2020 on the declaration of the state of danger, the major restrictions on liberty in this period were related to the control of borders, and other free movement restrictions, such as the obligatory 14-day quarantine, the closing of many state and private institutions (schools, restaurants, swimming pools, etc), social distancing and the ban on gatherings including assemblies, as in many other European countries. Most of these rules were temporal in nature, with some of them declared only for some days or for special occasions such as Easter. In the worsening economic and social situation caused by the restrictions on liberty, the Government introduced extraordinary measures in order to help individuals and firms, for example within the framework of the Economy Protection Action Plan,[21] which were beneficial for many market players. Debate focused more on the extent of these Government measures and less on their necessity.

Social matters, protection of the economy and security were the focus of the governmental decisions and many of the decrees allowed alterations from the regular statutory rules in order to create a better legal environment for comprehensive protection. In May, proceeding towards the end of the first state of danger, by and large the Government lifted or eased restrictions by various decrees. Apart from some outstanding examples of the misuse and abuse of the emergency powers (see below), the Government acted in accordance with its authorisation and used its power to diminish or eliminate the disadvantages caused by the epidemic. The outstanding examples show, however, that when in some cases the Government measure was not necessary to achieve legitimate goals, or when the action was not proportionate to the aim pursued, there were neither institutional nor procedural barriers to these actions; it was impossible to strike down such a decree or at least claim its unconstitutionality effectively within the state organisation.

[19] As stated in the preambles to these decrees.

[20] L Rácz gives a detailed analysis of all Government decrees in *Rendeleti kormányzás és különleges jogrend*. in F Gárdos-Orosz and V Lőrincz (eds), *Jogi diagnózisok* (L'Harmattan, 2020).

[21] See the official summary of the programme at abouthungary.hu/news-in-brief/coronavirus-update-pm-orban-announces-five-new-economy-protection-programs/.

From the perspective of constitutional (and rule of law) standards, we have identified objectionable measures, and classified them into three groups based on their flaws: those which suffer from a lack of necessity, a lack of proportionality, and a lack of normative clarity. Subsequently, we describe how far the Constitutional Court was able to progress in the constitutional review of emergency measures.

B. The Lack of Necessity

In some cases, although the decree's preamble contained the usual reference to the state of danger and the necessity of diminishing loss of life, health or wealth, the Government decree or some of its provisions could in fact hardly be justified by the need to take effective steps in such a situation. It is one of the requirements of the necessity-proportionality test of rights-limitations, as contained in Article I Section (3) of the Fundamental Law, that the measures imposed should not only serve a legitimate, constitutional goal but should also be factually able to achieve that legitimate goal. The means should be strictly related to the legitimate end.[22] The Government is therefore not completely free to choose adequate measures to reach the legitimate aim pursued. The rationally reasoned and factually based adequacy is subject to constitutional control in any of its forms.

From this point of view, one of the most disturbing decrees refers to the introduction of special economic zones.[23] Under this regulation, industrial establishments of significant regional economic importance could be qualified as special economic zones by the Government. The business taxes paid by the companies on such territories are transferred from the local authorities to the county local authorities. In fact, this implies an expropriation of a very large income from the municipalities in whose territories these economic zones are located. While many additional tasks in the fight against COVID-19 were distributed to local authorities,[24] the necessity of reorganising the ownership of the real estate used by these important investments and the new tax rules introduced in accordance with this does not seem to be necessary to achieve a better protection against COVID-19. The county authorities, unlike the local authorities in Hungary, do not, as yet, have significant competencies in organising a public response to a pandemic.

Immediately after the adoption of the decree, another decree declared one particular area in the city of Göd, where there was a large industrial plant, a special economic zone. It is worth noting that it is an exceptionally extraordinary measure

[22] F Gárdos-Orosz, 'Alapjogok korlátozása' in J András (ed), *Az alkotmány kommentárja* (Századvég, 2009).

[23] Government decree 135/2020 of 17 April 2020.

[24] I Balázs and I Hoffman, 'Közigazgatás koronavírus idején, A közigazgatási jog rezilienciája' (Administrative law in times of coronavirus – the resilience of the administrative law), *MTA Law Working Paper* 2020/21.

that had never occurred before. The municipality of Göd is an opposition-run local authority, whereas the county level authority has a governing party majority. The opposition-led local authority submitted a constitutional complaint[25] to the Constitutional Court claiming that the decree violates the local authority's right to property and, furthermore, is discriminative in nature. The Court has not yet decided on the case. In a related case concerning the constitutionality of the general decree that made it possible to create these special economic areas, 59 opposition MPs turned to the Constitutional Court in an abstract ex post facto review procedure, also claiming that the decree violates international treaties. The Constitutional Court refused to examine the case on the merits, because the time of its effectiveness had passed, and the decree was not in force in October at the time of the decision.[26]

The Government decree 128/2020 of 17 April 2020 ordered the state supervision of Kartonpack, a public company, as a company of strategic importance in the defence against COVID-19, and replaced the company's directors and supervisory board members. Although the Government decree 128/2020 has become ineffective,[27] the transitional rules[28] extended the application of its provisions until 15 August 2020 at the latest. This small but public company could not affect the efficacy of the defence against the virus, so it was unnecessary to intrude upon the existing private law relations, something which was needed in order to settle long-lasting disputes between the different owners, one of which is the Hungarian state. A constitutional complaint was not initiated in the case, because the situation did not make it possible, as it was not in the interest of the new management appointed to contest this rule.

By decree 233/2020 of 26 May 2020 the asylum procedure was incorporated into the state of danger and prolonged by Act LVIII on transitory measures. Those present on Hungarian territory or at the border crossing points cannot apply for asylum in Hungary and are directed to the nearest Hungarian embassy. There is a separate decree that defines precisely at which embassies the statement of intent to make an application for asylum can be submitted. Following the submission of a statement of intent, authorities may conduct remote interviews before issuing a single-entry permit to make an application for asylum. It is no longer possible to apply for asylum on Hungarian territory, nor at the border crossing points. This is another example of unnecessary measures where Government policy does not follow the goals of the emergency. To outsource the beginning of the procedure is not relevant to the question of how to fight the virus, but rather ties in with the general refugee policy of the Government.

[25] IV/00839/2020 CC decision.
[26] 3388/2020 (X. 22.) CC decision.
[27] In accordance with Art 53(4) of the Fundamental Law.
[28] Act LVIII on transitory measures, Art 162.

C. Disproportionate or Discriminatory Measures

Besides the above examples of the ultra vires decrees and the lack of effective control, we find legal measures in this period which are in line with the goal of fighting against the effects of the virus but are not proportionate with this goal.

Immediately after the declaration of the state of danger, a Government decree effectively put the hospital system under military management. Military commanders as 'hospital commanders' were placed in hospitals, and they make management decisions in a hierarchical military structure that reaches up to the Government, according to Article 45 of the Fundamental Law.[29] The use of the military in companies of strategic importance was quite unusual and apparently disproportionate to the situation existing in spring 2020 in Hungary; it surprised public opinion as, according to Article 45 of the Fundamental Law, the primary function of the Hungarian military is to protect the territory of the Hungarian state, the independence of the state and the border and to commit itself to peacemaking and ensuring international military cooperation. None of its major goals are related to fighting against a pandemic; therefore, even if lawful, because a state of danger was declared on 11 March based on the (unconstitutional) qualification that the 'epidemic is a natural disaster' and Article 45 Section (3) of the Fundamental Law allows the military to take part in the prevention of disasters and in the relief and elimination of their consequences, it seemed to be disproportionate for precisely the same reasons as with the declaration of the state of danger.[30]

The Government decree 179/2020 of 4 May 2020 was also disproportionate because it postponed the procedures and suspended the decisions for the disclosure of public data until the end of the state of danger. Furthermore, public bodies do not have to answer individual claims in cases in which the information is published on the Internet in a general form. Additionally, in cases in which providing the information would prevent the authority from performing its duties, it can refuse to provide the information until 45 days have elapsed (which can be extended by 45 days with due reason). This applies instead of the usual 15-day deadline for access to public data.

The Government initiated tax breaks, including for a number of small businesses, and specific tax breaks for affected sectors such as tourism, and introduced reduced rates for certain social security taxes for employers. According to the reasoning of the Government decree, in order to successfully complete the Economy Protection Action Plan and to receive income for the Epidemic Fund,

[29] Government decree 72/2020 of 29 March 2020. See a more detailed analysis in C Győry and N Weinberg, 'Emergency Powers in a Hybrid Regime. The Case of Hungary' (2020) *Theory and Practice of Legislation* 329–53.

[30] I Vörös, a former member of the Constitutional Court of Hungary warns of this in: I Vörös, 'A felhatalmazási törvénytől az egészségügyi válsághelyzetig és tovább' in F Gárdos-Orosz and V Lőrincz (eds), Jogi diagnózisok (L'Harmattan, 2020).

banks and other credit institutions were ordered to pay extra taxes according to Government decree 108/2020 of 14 April 2020 to contribute to dealing with the pandemic. The Government also imposed a special tax on retail companies. This was formulated in such a way that it disproportionately affects large international corporations, and does not apply to Hungarian-owned smaller corporations. This raises discrimination concerns as well; these are questions of competition law and state aid law which are decided by the European Commission. EU decisions, however, have not yet been made regarding these national protectionist tax policies.[31]

It is also typical of the discriminatory measures that certain interest groups received exemptions from the general rule, including in subject areas of minor interest. Some sports activities, for example, received exemptions from the general framework, while Decree 116/2020 of 15 April 2020 enacted a quite restrictive ban on gatherings, affecting assemblies.

The problems of non-proportionate or discriminatory rulings were not explored by review procedures; therefore these – at the moment – are simply concerns raised in constitutional scholarship[32] and also in the media and public discourse. The constitutional review was initiated in the case of the prolongation of the access to public information, but the Constitutional Court waited and then refused to examine the case on the merits, because the rule was no longer valid at the time of the decision.[33] It is a procedural problem of the constitutional review in the state of danger that the statutory deadlines for the procedures have not adapted to the rapid regulatory activity necessary in such an exceptional situation. If the procedure is not amended by shortening the deadlines by Government decree, as happened in Hungary, the Constitutional Court can avoid making timely decisions in sensitive cases.

D. Legal Certainty Problems

While the number of decrees is high, not all of them are original legislation; many are amendments of earlier decrees, some of which needed to be amended because of the evolving situation, while others simply corrected drafting mistakes. The quality of these decrees varies. Some are extremely poorly drafted, which can be attributed to the urgency of the situation. In some cases it is clear that the

[31] M Papp, M Varju, 'Tax policies and populism', manuscript, submitted to *the Journal of Central and East European Law* special issue forthcoming in 2021.

[32] C Győry and N Weinberg, 'Emergency Powers in a Hybrid Regime. The Case of Hungary' (2020) *Theory and Practice of Legislation* 329–53; T Drinóczi, 'Hungarian Abuse of Emergency Regimes, also in the light of the COVID-19 Crisis', *MTA Law Working Papers* 2020/13; I Balázs and I Hoffmann, A közigazgatási jog rezilienciája – koronavírus idején in F Gárdos-Orosz and V Lőrincz (eds), *Jogi diagnózisok* (L'Harmattan, 2020).

[33] 3413/2020. (XI. 26.) CC decision.

political decision was taken quickly and the draft was transformed into law too fast, without much attention being given to the legal formulation.[34] However, in this hurried law-making activity, the problems were sometimes not only those of poor codification.

Although Government decrees were mostly adopted to control the situation, in some cases the Chief Medical Officer as an administrative authority played an important role in order to avoid legal uncertainty, although, at the same time, this caused legal uncertainty on a more general level.

As the first 15 days of the Government decree issuing the state of danger expired some days before 1 April when the Government received the authorisation from the Parliament to extend the temporal effect of its emergency decrees, the Hungarian state reacted with a normative order to solve this problem issued by the Chief Medical Officer that kept in force all emergency measures for these intervening days, by overstepping the textual interpretation of its competencies.

In another emblematic case, specific rules on the operation of the justice system were imposed, such as an extraordinary 'justice break'.[35] A 'justice break' is a period when courts do not sit, apart from adjudicating urgent matters, such as cases of custody. The decree ordering the break due to COVID-19 failed to include regulations governing the procedural consequences of such a break; therefore the situation was completely uncertain. It was not clear whether the break affected deadlines and other administrative matters. Access to justice became unstable for some days, so the head of the National Office of the Judiciary quickly issued a normative order regulating these matters.[36] The problem is again that under Hungarian law this type of internal regulation only relates to personnel in the justice system, and does not address ordinary citizens. The Government finally resolved the situation with a decree issued two weeks later, the longest and most exhaustive of all decrees issued.[37]

As far as legal uncertainty is concerned, temporality is a crucial question. While in most cases it was clear that the rearrangement of certain questions was temporary, in other questions the new measures were not only prolonged by Act LVIII on transitory measures until August or until the end of the year, but due to the declaration of the new health emergency situation and later the second state of danger, strict temporality became a quite abstract concept. Many of the health protection measures and the social and economy protection measures are still valid in some form and if we have learnt the lessons of democracy in 2020 we can easily expect the introduction of a new emergency situation after the pandemic is over to allow the Government to freely rebuild and rearrange the economy and

[34] See, for further analysis, Győry and Weinberg (n 32).

[35] Government decree 45 /2020 of the 15 March 2020. Section (1).

[36] Orders of the Head of the National Office of the Judiciary Nrs. 35 (III.15), 36 (III.16.), 37 (III.17.), 38 (III.17.), 40(III.24.), 42 (III.26), 47(IV.1.) of 2020.

[37] See, in more detail, Győri and Weinberg (n 32); see also Government decree 74/2020 of 31 March 2020.

society without the usual institutional oversights, which are considered to be not too effective anyway.[38]

E. The Role of the Constitutional Court

In the state of danger, the Constitutional Court remained in session, following the constitutional provision that the Constitutional Court cannot be suspended in any state of exception.[39] Thus, the Constitutional Court is positioned to rule on the constitutionality of Government decrees or of the Authorisation Act or of the Act on the transitory measures, upon proper motions (ie, not *ex officio*). Whether this control could be effective is unclear and debatable, as the Constitutional Court is widely known to be deferential to the Government, especially in the extraordinary situations such as the financial crisis, migration issues etc;[40] however, it is the only forum where constitutional review can be initiated.

First, the lack of proper motions in many of these outstanding matters is indicative, although in some cases there is a procedural (partly competence) burden of the review. So far, the Constitutional Court has not brought any decisions assessing Government emergency acts as unconstitutional, but it has already stated in one of its decisions, in general terms, that the Government should decide on the necessity of the regulative measures in this situation and the Constitutional Court is not qualified and therefore not authorised to review any related decision.

One case that the Constitutional Court examined on the merits concerned a Government decree which classified the intention to extend the Central European Press and Media foundation to be of national strategic importance. The motion claimed that defining this exceptionally protected merger as of 'strategic importance' was against the concept of plural media communications. The Constitutional Court found the decree constitutional, stating that the Government can freely decide on the necessity of qualifying such an action as of strategic importance for the defence against the pandemic situation.[41]

In another case the Constitutional Court decision was also quite deferential, but it drew attention to the dangers of a new piece of legislation, and therefore stated – in a constitutional requirement with binding force – how to interpret it. At the beginning of the state of danger, Parliament adopted an amendment to the Criminal Code on scaremongering, the essence of which was that these rules should become more severe during a pandemic and other dangers. The motion claimed that the new regulation restricts the freedom of speech disproportionately and is uncertain, as it does not concretely define the conduct which is against the

[38] Z Szente, *The Constitutional Law in Hungary* (Kluwer International, 2021).

[39] Art 54 Section (2) of the Fundamental Law.

[40] Z Szente and F Gárdos-Orosz, *New challenges to Constitutional Adjudication in Europe* (Routledge, 2018).

[41] 16/2020. (VII. 8.) CC decision.

law. This new rule is contrary to the former practice of the Court and the constitutional requirements of the criminal law. The Constitutional Court ruled in its decision that the provision is not to be annulled because it has a constitutional meaning. The Court said that it is a constitutional requirement that the criminal act, or scaremongering, can only be committed in a case in which the perpetrator makes a statement which he/she knows is incorrect, or which is explained tentatively in an incorrect manner, and which is thus capable of hindering or preventing the defence against the pandemic. This is the only constitutional interpretation of the new rule according to the Constitutional Court.[42] Although this decision did not strike down the amendment as required by the petitioner, according to experts in penal law the constitutional requirement was convincingly sufficient because penal law doctrine does not allow an extensive interpretation of the provision.[43]

There were no other substantive reviews[44] of major relevance regarding this period of the first state of danger, which is a telling demonstration of the operation of Hungarian democracy and the relevance of the possibility of the constitutional review in practice.

VI. The Management of the Legal Consequences of the Emergency Situation

During the state of danger, which lasted for about four months, several members of the Government indicated the possibility that some of the provisions made under the special legal order had worked so well that they should be maintained after the emergency. This was a somewhat surprising argument, since legislation enacted during a special legal order specifically reflects, in principle, extraordinary circumstances and solutions. Nevertheless, these ideas were largely realised when Parliament adopted in June an act which enacted a number of emergency provisions as statutory law.

Just before the adoption of this law, Parliament passed Act LVII of 2020 on the abolition of the state of danger. It is notable that the title of this Act is misleading because the National Assembly did not actually terminate the special legal order (as this is the exclusive power of the Government under the Fundamental Law) but merely asked the Government to do so. It is worth adding that the bill was submitted by the Government, so in fact the Government itself suggested to Parliament that it call on the Government to end the special legal order. Beyond this, the

[42] 15/2020. (VII. 8.) CC decision.

[43] I Ambrus: A koronavírus járvány és a büntetőjog, MTA Law Working Papers 7:5, 1–22., 22, (2020) 13–14.

[44] There were two other cases in which the Constitutional Court refused to examine the case on the merits, because the Government decree was no longer in force at the time of the decision. One concerned the alteration of the Labour Code (3326/2020 (VIII. 5) CC decision, upon a motion initiated by 52 MPs), and the other the so-called vehicle tax (3234/2020 (VII. 1.) initiated by 54 MPs).

Act only expresses its intention to repeal the Authorisation Act, but it contains, in a very confusing way, two different dates for this: on the one hand, it says that the Authorisation Act ceases when the state of danger ends (a point in time defined by the Government), but on the other hand, it states also that this date will be determined by an individual resolution of the Prime Minister promulgated in the Official Gazette. Although this contradictory regulation had no practical effect, it clearly illustrates the constitutional confusion over the handling of the state of danger. It also shows the complete subordination of the legislature to the executive, which went so far that the date of the repeal of an act of Parliament that provided extraordinary powers for the Government was determined by the individual decision of the Prime Minister. Indeed, this is how it happened: the Government declared the end of the state of danger from 18 June,[45] and the Prime Minister on the same day issued his own resolution determining the date of the termination of special legal order accordingly.[46]

Notwithstanding, another act of Parliament, the Act on the transitional rules related to the abolition of the state of danger and the declaration of the new health crisis situation,[47] has had much greater significance. This law is expected to have important and longstanding effects on the legal system. As a matter of fact, this Act is a 'super salad law' of great length (having 410 articles) and diverse subject matters (amending dozens of laws), but without any internal coherence.

The provisions of this Act can be classified into three groups. First, it contains a number of technical rules by providing, in particular, for the legal consequences of the specific legal order for various legal relationships. Thus, for example, it has extended the debtors' payment moratorium prescribed by an emergency decree until the end of the year, allowed delays for tax obligations, maintained certain exemptions and benefits, and lifted some restrictions (eg, by-elections and referendums can once again be held and initiated). From a constitutional point of view, most of these rules have become necessary in order to ensure legal security, as well as to return to the normal legal order. Among them, the only objectionable measures are those which granted financial advantages for certain economic activities without objectively defined criteria; the Act simply enumerates the economic sectors or activities entitled to legal advantages (the list covers, for example, breweries or wine-makers, but not language teachers).

The second group of legal provisions contain or prolong restrictions of rights. Thus, the Act introduced a two-step asylum procedure until the end of 2020. Under the new rules, asylum seekers have to inform, in person, the National Directorate-General for Alien Policing that they intend to enter Hungary in order to submit an application for asylum. In case of approval, the asylum authority may designate accommodation for the asylum-seeker in a closed host institution.

[45] Government decree 282/2020 (VI. 17.).
[46] Prime Ministerial Resolution 41/2020 (VI. 17).
[47] Act LVIII of 2020.

Another provision of the Act empowers the Government to determine special rules for staying at the venue of public assemblies or demonstrations.

Finally, there is a number of rules that appear to exploit the special circumstances of the post-emergency situation to promote other policy aims.

During the period of the state danger, as we described above, it attracted widespread attention that a private company, the Kartonpack Company, was placed under direct state supervision, following which the government commissioner appointed to head the company dismissed the members of its governing bodies. The Act on the transitory provisions abolished direct state control, but the previous management could not return to its duties. Other provisions have extended the validity of final building, installation and demolition permits, which expired during the state of danger, for another year. Compared to the four-month-long period of the special legal order, this is a very generous advantage, which can probably be explained by the intention to support Government investment projects, or the fact that the construction industry is a priority in Government policy. The measures necessary for the protection of companies based in Hungary were also included in the scope of the protection against the COVID-19 pandemic. According to these rules, the competent minister has to be notified about the most important decisions taken by the companies classified by the Government as 'strategic companies' (primarily in the energy, transport and telecommunication sectors) by 30 June 2021. In fact, these decisions (including the sale, transformation, merger or division of these companies, or the acquisition of an ownership share of over 10 per cent in such a company) need to be approved by the minister. Although a ministerial ban can be challenged in court, the minister's discretion is so wide-ranging (he or she decides in the interest of the state) that judicial protection is of no more than symbolic importance.

The Government exploited the opportunity offered by the management of the consequences of the pandemic by introducing the so-called health crisis situation immediately after the termination of the state of danger. This new legislation has resulted in a quasi-special legal order outside the Constitution, allowing the Government to restrict basic rights and overruling acts of Parliament by decrees without constitutional obstacles.

By amending the 1997 Act on Public Health,[48] Parliament stated that 'the government, on the proposal of the National Chief Medical Officer, and on the basis of the initiation of the Minister, may declare a health crisis situation in a Government decree if it is necessary in the event of an epidemiological emergency', or 'in any event, usually unexpected, which endangers or damages the life, physical integrity or health of the citizens or the operation of healthcare providers'. In addition, such a health crisis situation may be promulgated 'in the event of any circumstance which seriously and directly impedes the provision of the healthcare

[48] Act CLIV of 1997.

of the population', provided that the provision of care to the population 'would be disproportionately difficult'.

In this situation, the Government can take almost any measure that could be previously used only under the special legal order. Thus, it may limit or prohibit:

- the operation of any institution, the attendance and organisation of events and activities which may contribute to the spread of the epidemic;
- the operation and opening hours of shops;
- domestic and international travel;
- public transport;
- the transportation of livestock or goods.

In addition, the Government may prescribe lockdowns and quarantine, may issue orders relating to the sale, consumption, or purchase of certain foodstuffs and products, the consumption of drinking water, the supply of medicines and medical aids and the procedure for accessing health services. For specific purposes, it may use the help of the army and the police, and it can put military commanders in charge of hospitals.

The health crisis situation may last up to six months, but may be extended by the Government as many times as it wants, provided that the conditions for its promulgation are met.

The new legislation does not contain any guarantees against the abuse of this extremely wide-ranging empowerment. Although the National Chief Medical Officer must continuously monitor the existence of the conditions of the health crisis situation and, if these conditions are no longer met, he or she has to initiate a request to the Minister to propose to the Government that the health crisis situation be repealed, the Government has full discretionary power to assess whether the conditions are met or not. Only the Health Committee of the National Assembly must be informed about the prolongation of the health crisis situation, and while these emergency measures may, to a large extent, take the form of individual decisions, neither Parliament nor the Constitutional Court may control them.

The Government immediately took advantage of this opportunity when, in parallel with the termination of the state of danger, it introduced the health crisis situation[49] until 18 December 2020 and prolonged it by six more months until mid-2021.

The new legislation introducing the health crisis situation would have been justified by the need not to declare a special legal order with almost unlimited authorisation of the executive power, but instead to supply more narrowly tailored instruments and tools to eliminate specific risks such as a human epidemic. However, the legal construction of the health crisis situation raises some constitutional concerns.

[49] Government decree 283/2020. (VI. 17.).

Whereas the state of danger is a form of the special legal order defined in the Constitution, the health crisis situation is based on a statutory authorisation and therefore, in principle, can be declared by the executive power as part of the normal legal order. In terms of the scope of the authorisation, a health crisis situation differs from a state of danger only in that the Government decrees and measures issued under this empowerment can only be taken to avert health risks, while in special legal orders the Government can generally derogate laws (in the areas, for example, of economic or social policy). In fact, this newly-established health crisis situation, as has been noted above, is a quasi-special legal order with the possibility of extensive, extraordinary restrictions of fundamental rights, liberties and properties, but without any constitutional authorisation. The Government's authority in such a situation, for example as far as the restriction of fundamental rights is concerned, goes far beyond what is usual and acceptable in the normal legal order. Beyond this, the necessary conditions of the declaration of a health crisis situation are too general and vague, which hardly provides a legal basis for any control body to override the Government's decision concerning it.

Based on past experience, the unchecked power of the Government to declare and abolish the health crisis situation is also troubling. It is worth noting that since 2016, the Government has consistently maintained another, also extra-constitutional, quasi-special legal order, the crisis situation caused by mass immigration, so that its legal conditions (eg, the number of immigrants arriving in the country) have not been met for years.

Nonetheless, as the situation caused by the COVID-19 became more severe from the fall of 2020 and the Government also had to handle the unfolding economic crisis, the authorisation provided by the new health crisis situation was no longer sufficient.

VII. State of Danger Reloaded

A. The Context

The second state of danger was declared in a much more serious situation than the first had been in March. When the Government first declared the special legal order in spring 2020, there were only a total of 13 identified infected people in Hungary, and no confirmed deaths had occurred due to COVID-19. In contrast, when the second state of danger was introduced on 2 November, there were approximately 64,000 infected individuals in the country and the daily mortality rate was around 80–90.[50] While the introduction of the first state of danger actually

[50] The source of this data is the official Government site www.koronavirus.gov.hu.

served to prevent the spread of the pandemic, or at least to prepare for the impending health crisis, in the meantime, society had learned to live with the pandemic, and the legal empowerment provided by the health crisis situation may have been sufficient. However, the reason for the declaration of the second special legal order in late autumn was presumably to reduce the economic downturn; at least the key phrase in the governmental campaign which ran in summer and early fall was that 'life can't stop'. In support of this, the Government organised a 'national consultation',[51] the unsubstantiated results of which allegedly proved that the majority of the population also opposed the introduction of stricter rules (especially social distancing or school closures).

B. The Declaration of the Second State of Danger and the New Authorisation Act

Due to the exacerbation of the coronavirus pandemic, the Government declared the state of danger again on 3 November 2020.[52] The spread of the pandemic and the increase in the mortality rate justified this step. Nevertheless, since this Government decree relies on the same constitutional foundations and has a largely similar content as on the first occasion, it shares its constitutional problems too. This is not changed by the fact that the Disaster Management Act has, in the meantime, been amended,[53] because the amendment only confirmed the unconstitutional parts of the Act. Thus, for example, it extends the reasons for the declaration of state of danger provided by the Fundamental Law to human epidemics which cause a mass illness that endangers the safety of life and property. Since Article 53 Section (1) of the Fundamental Law has not changed, this extension explicitly goes far beyond the cases defined by the Constitution in which this kind of special legal order could be declared. The Government decree again declared the state of danger for an indefinite period, and only stated that it would keep the need for the special legal order under review.

Interestingly, neither this Government decree nor subsequent decrees put an end to the health crisis situation declared in the summer, so this is in force in parallel with the special legal order.

Just a few days later, Parliament passed a new Authorisation Act,[54] with more or less the same content as before. The National Assembly again relinquished the compliance of its constitutional obligation to review governmental emergency decrees, and, through this law, approved, without any scrutiny, any Government

[51] National consultations are general surveys organised by the Government. The results of the surveys do not have any legal effect. The survey on the coronavirus pandemic has been the ninth national consultation since 2012.

[52] Government decree 478/2020 (XI. 3.).

[53] Act LVIII of 2020.

[54] Act CIX of 2020.

decrees issued since the introduction of the second state of danger, and any subsequent decrees the Government deems necessary to adopt in the future.

In assessing the current state of Hungarian democracy, it is important to be aware that the parliamentary opposition, which had often protested in the past against the unlimited empowerment of the Government provided by the first Authorisation Act, this time voted unanimously for the same authorisation. Although the Act again included a stipulation that it could revoke the authorisation for the fully-fledged emergency management, its own preamble justified the necessity of this Act by stating that 'the session of the National Assembly may be suspended due to the second wave of the coronavirus pandemic'. Yet, this time too, Parliament did not provide any constitutional guarantee for its own continuous functioning.

In summary, in autumn 2020, from a constitutional point of view, the new declaration of the state of danger and the adoption of the second Authorisation Act was enacted in the same unconstitutional manner as had occurred in March. The only significant difference is that this time, the temporal effect of the parliamentary authorisation does not depend on the decision of the Government, but has been set at 90 days.

When the temporal effect of the second Authorisation Act expired, the Government, although not obliged to do so, terminated the special legal order declared in November 2020,[55] but immediately re-proclaimed it with another Government decree[56] without any deadline (and a new Authorisation Act).

In addition, it is worth noting that, in December 2020, the National Assembly passed the Ninth Amendment to the Fundamental Law which provides indirect evidence of the constitutional flaws of the practice of applying a special legal order which seeks to remedy the constitutional problems of the first two declarations of the state of danger. According to the modification, the Government may, in the future (from 2023), declare a state of danger in a case of 'a serious incident endangering the safety of life and property', and a human epidemic is no longer excluded from this list, as events such as natural or industrial disasters are only examples of reasons for a declaration of state of danger. In addition, the state of danger can only be declared for thirty days, after which the Government can extend its duration only with the authorisation of the National Assembly.

VIII. Conclusions

While it could be argued that the extraordinary power of the Government is not unlimited because Parliament has stipulated that it can revoke the full authorisation

[55] Government decree 26/2021. (I. 29.).
[56] Government decree 27/2021. (I. 29.).

at any time and, moreover, the Constitutional Court is constantly functioning and able to review the constitutionality of emergency decrees, in practice, Parliament did not control the emergency measures and the Constitutional Court has been silent on almost all constitutional issues despite the constitutional objections raised and explained in this chapter.

It is true that the Constitutional Court cannot act *ex officio* in such matters, that is, if a constitutional review of a piece of legislation is not initiated by an authorised body, it is completely toothless, but even when opposition MPs initiated the procedure, the Court refused to take the case on the merits, with reference being made to procedural obstacles. However, it is questionable whether the Court, which consists exclusively of members supported by the government majority, could oppose any serious intention of the Government, even if it had a formal opportunity to do so.

Parliament's inactivity is even more problematic, as the legislature has failed to perform its constitutional duty to control the executive branch in both states of danger, although the extraordinary power of the Government would have justified a strict parliamentary oversight. It is worth noting that in Hungary, Parliament was in continuous operation and had an active legislative programme during both special legal orders (in 2020 the National Assembly passed more laws than in the previous two years), yet it kept itself removed from the management of the health crisis caused by the coronavirus. Under such circumstances, when the legislature is working continuously without any hindrance, the extraordinary law-making power of the executive branch is questionable, but even if it is acceptable given the speed and flexibility of governmental decision-making, failure to exercise parliamentary scrutiny of emergency decrees cannot be defended for any reason.

It seems that the often-voiced assumption of political and constitutional studies that semi-authoritarian regimes prefer to use extraordinary powers in times of crisis can be justified in the case of Hungary. As a matter of fact, the outbreak of the COVID-19 pandemic in March 2020 in Hungary led to the possibility of a continuous, long-term quasi state of emergency with almost unlimited Government rule and very weak if not non-existent institutional control mechanisms, both in law and in practice with the introduction of the new health crisis situation. Furthermore, the Ninth Amendment to the Fundamental Law made it easier to declare a state of emergency as a special legal order too. It is important to remember that the pandemic has indeed caused a serious health and economic crisis that requires special instruments to be managed. However, even such a serious situation does not justify the evasion of the fundamental constitutional rules and a waiver of the constant parliamentary and judicial control of the executive branch authorised to exercise extraordinary power.

The Government's populist policy making has exploited the well-known effect by which when the people 'panic they support policies that are unwise and excessive'.[57] As we have described, in this situation the Government prepared the legal system for a long-term state of exception, institutionalising certain extraordinary powers and instruments, which provide wide-ranging empowerment for the executive even under normalcy, in the ordinary constitutional order. All these are in contrast with the exceptional nature of the special legal orders, which should have the function to act 'only to resolve the emergency and restore the normal legal order'.[58]

[57] EA Posner and A Vermeule, 'Accommodating Emergencies' (2003) 56(3) *Stanford Law Review* 609.

[58] J Ferejohn and P Pasquino, 'The law of the exception: A typology of emergency powers' (2004) 2(2) *International Journal of Constitutional Law* 223.

9

Switzerland: The (Missing) Role of Parliament in Times of Crisis

ODILE AMMANN AND FELIX UHLMANN*

I. The COVID-19 Pandemic, a Shutdown of Swiss Democracy?

Swiss legal scholars have described the COVID-19 pandemic as giving rise to an 'extraordinary extraordinary situation' in Switzerland from a regulatory perspective,[1] an expression that alludes to the Swiss Federal Epidemics Act's[2] distinction between 'normal', 'special', and 'extraordinary' epidemiological situations, and to the fact that the pandemic was so unprecedented that it was more than just 'extraordinary'. COVID-19 does not only have severe health, economic, and social implications: it also has an impact on democratic institutions, including in Switzerland.[3] In spring 2020, the press noted that Swiss democracy had 'paused';[4] some legal scholars even talked about a 'shutdown of direct democracy' after the adoption, on 20 March 2020, of the Ordinance on the Standstill of Deadlines for Federal Popular Votes.[5]

* The authors thank Martin Wilhelm, MLaw, for his help with the editing of this chapter, and Konrad Lachmayer for his thoughtful suggestions and comments.

[1] F Brunner, M Wilhelm, and F Uhlmann, 'Das Coronavirus und die Grenzen des Notrechts: Überlegungen zu einer ausserordentlichen ausserordentlichen Lage' (2020) 29 *Aktuelle Juristische Praxis* 685, 691–92.

[2] Bundesgesetz über die Bekämpfung übertragbarer Krankheiten des Menschen vom 28. September 2012 (SR 818.101).

[3] M Andina, 'What Remains of Swiss Democracy After Covid-19 Measures?' *swissinfo.ch* (Bern, 22 May 2020) www.swissinfo.ch/eng/democracy-lab_what-remains-of-swiss-democracy-after-covid-19-/45773496.

[4] C Lenz and P Loser, 'Die Demokratie macht Pause' *Tages-Anzeiger* (Zurich, 16 March 2020) 5; Y Pauchard and B Wuthrich, 'La démocratie Suisse se met en mode pause' *Le Temps* (Geneva, 18 March 2020) www.letemps.ch/suisse/democratie-suisse-se-met-mode-pause; D Ryser and O Würgler, 'Wir haben ihn so geliebt, den Rechtsstaat' *Republik* (Zurich, 17 April 2020) www.republik.ch/2020/04/17/wir-haben-ihn-so-geliebt-den-rechtsstaat.

[5] Verordnung über den Fristenstillstand bei eidgenössischen Volksbegehren vom 20. März 2020 (SR 161.16). See G Biaggini, 'Der coronavirusbedingte Fristenstillstand bei eidgenössischen Volksbegehren – eine Fallstudie zur Tragfähigkeit von Art. 185 Abs. 3 BV' (2020) 121 *Schweizerisches Zentralblatt für*

While the Swiss government – the Federal Council – had already used its intra-constitutional[6] emergency powers before the outbreak, it had never done so in such an extensive, all-encompassing, and rapidly evolving way.[7] At the time of writing (end of 2020), Switzerland is being severely hit by a second wave of COVID-19 infections, which in turn is triggering a new wave of emergency measures. The federal government's unprecedented regulatory activity provides 'a touchstone for the existing emergency law clauses and for the transposition of the measures taken into ordinary law'.[8] Unsurprisingly, the Federal Council's emergency ordinances have been and continue to be hotly debated in the scholarly literature.[9]

What impact has the pandemic had on Swiss democracy? Many issues and Swiss peculiarities could be discussed in response to this vast question, such as the powers of the Federal Council versus Parliament in the context of emergencies,[10] the (dis)advantages of Swiss federalism,[11] and the consequences of the federal and cantonal governments' measures for direct democracy[12] and fundamental rights, especially communicative and political rights. In this chapter, we focus on how the Swiss Parliament – the Federal Assembly – has been reacting to the pandemic.[13]

Staats- und Verwaltungsrecht 277, 277. See also R Trümpler and F Uhlmann, 'Problemstellungen und Lehren aus der Corona-Krise aus staats- und verwaltungsrechtlicher Sicht' in *COVID-19: Ein Panorama der Rechtsfragen zur Corona-Krise* (Helbing & Lichtenhahn, 2020) 567, 590. At the time of writing (end of 2020), the ordinance was no longer in force.

[6] Extra-constitutional emergency powers are – as the term suggests – exercised outside the constitutional framework. Whether it is appropriate to use the expression 'emergency powers' to describe intra-constitutional measures is contested. See (besides many other examples) D Rechsteiner, *Recht in besonderen und ausserordentlichen Lagen* (Dike, 2016) para 34 ff. Still, most legal scholars rely on this terminology because it has gained currency in public discourse. See eg Brunner, Wilhelm, and Uhlmann (n 1) 688.

[7] A Stöckli, 'Regierung und Parlament in Pandemiezeiten' (2020) Sondernummer *Zeitschrift für Schweizerisches Recht / Revue de droit suisse* 9, 11–12.

[8] Brunner, Wilhelm and Uhlmann (n 1) 686.

[9] eg D Wyss, 'Sicherheit und Notrecht: Ein Überblick über die Anwendung des Epidemiengesetzes und das konstitutionelle Notrecht des Bundesrats in der COVID-19-Krise und im Allgemeinen' (*Jusletter*, 25 May 2020) jusletter.weblaw.ch/juslissues/2020/1025/sicherheit-und-notre_4e888001e7.html. See also the references provided in O Ammann, 'Regulatory Uncertainty Over Emergency Powers in Switzerland' (2020) *The Regulatory Review* www.theregreview.org/2020/05/29/ammann-regulatory-uncertainty-over-emergency-powers-switzerland.

[10] For a critique, see A Kley, '"Ausserordentliche Situationen verlangen nach ausserordentlichen Lösungen." – Ein staatsrechtliches Lehrstück zu Art. 7 EpG und Art. 185 Abs. 3 BV' (2020) 121 *Schweizerisches Zentralblatt für Staats- und Verwaltungsrecht* 268. See also A Kley, 'Pandemie und exekutive Selbstermächtigung' *Neue Zürcher Zeitung* (Zurich, 18 May 2020) 8 (condemning a 'self-empowerment by the executive').

[11] eg F Bernard, 'La répartition des compétences entre la Confédération et les cantons en situation de pandémie' (2020) Sondernummer *Zeitschrift für Schweizerisches Recht/Revue de droit suisse* 55; Ammann (n 9); F Bergamin and S Mazidi, 'Kompetenzabgrenzung zwischen Bund und Kantonen bei der Bekämpfung von Epidemien: Erste Einschätzungen unter besonderer Berücksichtigung der COVID-19-Verordnungen' (*Newsletter IFF, 7 April 2020)* www3.unifr.ch/newsletter/archive/mail.php?lang=de&y=2020&id=2567. Depending on the viewpoint, Swiss federalism is described negatively as a 'patchwork rug', or positively as a 'mosaic'. See eg 'Die Kantone müssen jetzt Massnahmen zur Eindämmung des Virus treffen', *NZZ am Sonntag* (Zurich, 5 July 2020) 8; Wyss (n 9) para 5.

[12] Biaggini (n 5).

[13] For a detailed chronology of the measures adopted by Parliament since the beginning of the pandemic, see Parliamentary Services, Factual Report, 'Die Bundesversammlung und die Covid-19-Krise: Ein chronologischer Überblick', status as of 18 December 2020 (Appendix VIII: status as of

It is well known that the executive power usually moves centre stage in times of crisis,[14] and Switzerland is no exception in this regard. The Swiss Parliament is slower to react due to its size, bicameral system, and heterogeneous composition. Moreover, the Federal Assembly is a non-professional ('militia') legislature which only holds four ordinary three-week sessions per year.[15] Yet, the longer the pandemic lasts, the more pressing it becomes for Parliament to play an active part in tackling it. This is even more important in States like Switzerland, where the judicial review of executive measures is limited.[16]

In this chapter, we discuss two dimensions of Parliament's reaction to the pandemic. We first provide a critical appraisal of the COVID-19 Act, which the Federal Assembly adopted in September 2020 in order to establish a statutory legal basis for the Federal Council's numerous emergency ordinances (section II). We then examine how Parliament adjusted its own functioning to COVID-19, and the extent to which it maintained its capacity to act despite the crisis (section III). In both cases, our goal is to determine whether the Swiss legislature acted appropriately, a question which must be examined in light of Parliament's constitutional status as 'supreme authority of the Confederation',[17] and of its institutional duty to keep the federal executive and administration in check.[18] By shedding light on the Swiss example, our chapter contributes to a rapidly growing legal and political science scholarship on the implications of COVID-19 for parliamentary lawmaking, both in Switzerland[19] and elsewhere.[20]

8 February 2021) www.parlament.ch/centers/documents/de/Faktenbericht-Bundesversammlung%20in%20der%20Covid-19%20Krise-d.pdf (hereinafter: 'Factual Report'). See also 'Bericht des Bundesrates über die Ausübung seiner Notrechtskompetenz und die Umsetzung überwiesener Kommissionsmotionen seit Beginn der Krise' (27 May 2020) www.bk.admin.ch/bk/de/home/dokumentation/gesetzgebung/berichtnotverordnungen.html.

[14] This also applies to the Federal Council, mainly due to its capacity to meet and to act swiftly in a situation that requires almost immediate action. Moreover, the executive branch has a head start over the Federal Assembly when it comes to knowledge and information, as it can easily draw on the federal administration's expertise and resources. For a historical and political theory perspective, see Stöckli (n 7) 9, 13 ff.

[15] See Art 151(1) of the Federal Constitution of the Swiss Confederation of 18 April 1999 (SR 101; hereinafter: 'Cst.') and Art 2(1) of the Federal Act on the Federal Assembly of 13 December 2002 (SR 171.10, hereinafter: 'ParlA'), which merely prescribe that the Councils meet 'regularly'. Parliament can also hold special or extraordinary sessions (see Art 2(2) and (3) ParlA).

[16] This is especially due to the absence of abstract (direct) judicial review of federal ordinances: Swiss Federal Tribunal [BGer], judgment 2C_280/2020 of 15 April 2020; BGer, judgment 2C_776/2020 of 23 September 2020. On remedies against COVID-19 measures in general, see Stöckli (n 7) 45 ff. It is important to add that federal acts adopted by the Swiss Parliament are immune from judicial review (Art 190 Cst.), but that ordinances of the Federal Council can in principle be reviewed by courts in particular cases.

[17] Art 148(1) of the Swiss Constitution. On this topic, see G Rutz, 'Motion 18.4050, Die Verwaltung als oberste Gewalt im Staate?', 28 September 2018.

[18] G Biaggini, 'Demokratie in Zeiten des Coronavirus: Dürfen Parlamente nur tagen, wenn die Regierung es will?' (2020) 23(2) *Parlament – Parlement – Parlamento* 14, 14.

[19] See eg the issue dedicated to the 'Rights of Parliaments and Their Organs in Situations of Crisis' (2020) 23(2) *Parlament – Parlement – Parlamento*.

[20] See the other contributions in this volume, and the forthcoming volumes in this book collection. See also 'Legislatures in the Time of Covid-19' Special Issue (2020) 8(1–2) *The Theory and Practice of*

Three caveats are in order. First, our chapter only focuses on the Federal Assembly, although it goes without saying that similar difficulties to those faced by the Swiss parliament can be witnessed in the federal subunits, ie in the cantonal and municipal legislatures. It is important to note that the cantonal constitutions offer different solutions to the interplay between the executive and the legislative branch in times of crisis, hence creating what can be described as a federalist laboratory – not unlike US Supreme Court Justice Louis Brandeis' famous depiction of the US States as laboratories of democracy. Secondly, this chapter does not aspire to an exhaustive analysis of the impact of COVID-19 on Parliament; for reasons of scope, we only discuss selected facets of the Swiss case that call for further scrutiny. Thirdly, our chapter reflects the state of the law and practice in Switzerland as of the end of 2020. Considering the rapidly changing epidemiological situation, further analysis will be needed in the months (and perhaps even years) to come.

II. From Executive Emergency Ordinances to Parliamentary Emergency Legislation: Parliament's Adoption of the COVID-19 Act

A. The Swiss Legal Framework Governing the Adoption of Emergency Regulation

The Swiss constitutional framework pertaining to emergency situations mostly took shape in the two decades preceding and following World War II.[21] The emergency measures it provides for fall into three main categories: (1) emergency ordinances and rulings ('Verfügungen') adopted by the Federal Council (Articles 184(3) and 185(3) of the Swiss Constitution (Cst.)),[22] (2) emergency parliamentary ordinances and decrees (Article 173(1)(c) combined with Article 173(1)(a) and (c) Cst.), and (3) emergency (parliamentary) legislation (Article 165 Cst.). Since our focus is on Parliament, we will not dwell on the first category; rather, our interest lies in the instruments which are at Parliament's disposal.

First, as Article 173(1)(c) Cst. states, the Federal Assembly has the power, '[i]f extraordinary circumstances require, [to] issu[e] ordinances or simple federal decrees in order to fulfil its duties under letters (a) and (b).' While Article 173(1)(a) Cst. enables Parliament to adopt 'measures to safeguard external security and the independence and neutrality of Switzerland', Article 173(1)(b) Cst. allows it to act in

Legislation; 'National and European Parliamentary Involvement in the EU's Economic Response to the COVID Crisis' Special Issue (2020) N° 36 *EU Law Live Weekend Edition*.

[21] T Gächter, 'Demokratie und Dringlichkeit: Gedanken zu Geschichte und Anwendung des Dringlichkeitsrechts der schweizerischen Bundesverfassung' in I Häner (ed), *Nachdenken über den demokratischen Staat und seine Geschichte – Beiträge für Alfred Kölz* (Schulthess, 2003) 75, 77.

[22] Federal Constitution of the Swiss Confederation of 18 April 1999 (SR 101).

order to 'safeguard internal security'. These ordinances are not subject to a referendum, nor is their validity limited in time. However, they must be abrogated as soon as the emergency is over. Emergency parliamentary ordinances are of limited practical relevance because their adoption is no less cumbersome than the enactment of emergency legislation.[23] Such ordinances primarily provide an 'amendment and cancellation right' to Parliament with regard to emergency ordinances adopted by the Federal Council,[24] although some scholars stress that for reasons of legal certainty, the legislature should be wary of making use of this possibility.[25]

Secondly, Article 165(1) Cst. provides that '[f]ederal acts whose coming into force cannot be delayed (emergency federal acts) may be declared urgent by an absolute majority of the members of each of the two Councils' – the two chambers of Parliament, the National Council and the Council of States – 'and be brought into force immediately'. It also states that '[s]uch acts must be of limited duration'.[26] Article 165(1) Cst. does not require that specific public interests ('Polizeigüter', such as public health or public safety) be at stake; it only presupposes a situation that does not suffer any delay. As soon as this urgency fades away, Parliament must adopt ordinary legislation. Moreover, a referendum can be launched against an emergency federal act after its entry into force (Article 165(2) Cst.). Emergency acts need not have a basis in the Constitution; if such a basis is lacking, the act is subject to a mandatory referendum if it stays in force for more than one year (Article 165(3) Cst.). As long as the Federal Assembly is in a position to adopt emergency legislation, the Federal Council is barred from adopting emergency ordinances.[27]

Besides these constitutional provisions, several statutory norms are equally relevant. First, in a 'special' epidemiological situation, the Federal Council can adopt emergency measures after having consulted the cantons (Article 6(2) of the Epidemics Act (EpA)).[28] In an 'extraordinary situation', it can even enact such measures for the whole country or for selected regions without any consultations (Article 7 EpA). Most scholars consider that Article 7 EpA has declaratory character, ie that it simply restates the content of Article 185(3) Cst.[29]

[23] Gächter (n 21) 96.

[24] U Saxer, 'Art. 185 BV' in B Ehrenzeller, B Schindler, and R J Schweizer (eds), *Die schweizerische Bundesverfassung: St. Galler Kommentar*, 3rd edn (Dike, 2014) para 63.

[25] Stöckli (n 7) 35 f, 50. See also M Häfliger, 'Wir machen viele Parlamentarier hässig', Interview with Hans Stöckli, *Tages-Anzeiger* (Zurich, 27 March 2020) www.tagesanzeiger.ch/nach-verfassung-ist-das-parlament-die-oberste-gewalt-im-bund-450043086249.

[26] The Federal Council has stated that in practice, the period of validity usually amounts to two to six years. See Federal Council, 'Botschaft zum Bundesgesetz über die gesetzlichen Grundlagen für Verordnungen des Bundesrates zur Bewältigung der Covid-19-Epidemie (Covid-19-Gesetz) (12 August 2020) BBl 2020 6563 (hereinafter: 'COVID-19 Dispatch'), 6616.

[27] Brunner, Wilhelm, and Uhlmann (n 1) 689.

[28] Federal Act on the Control of Communicable Human Diseases of 28 September 2012 (SR 818.101).

[29] Brunner, Wilhelm, and Uhlmann (n 1) 693 f. For an overview of the different positions, see B Waldmann, 'Staatsrechtliche Herausforderungen' in F Uhlmann and S Höfler (eds), Notrecht in der Corona-Krise (Dike, 2021) 3, 13 fn 54. See also Stöckli (n 7) 21 f. In the dispatch regarding the revision of the EpA, the Federal Council explicitly noted that Art 7 EpA has 'declaratory character'. See Federal Council, 'Botschaft zur Revision des Bundesgesetzes über die Bekämpfung übertragbarer Krankheiten des Menschen (Epidemiengesetz, EpG) vom 3. Dezember 2010' BBl 2010 311, 365.

Another important provision is Article 7d of the Government and Administration Organisation Act (GAOA).[30] Amongst other things, its second paragraph states that a Federal Council ordinance pursuant to Article 185(3) Cst. loses its validity after six months if the government has not submitted a bill to Parliament within this time frame, with the goal of creating either a statutory legal basis for the Federal Council's ordinance, or a parliamentary ordinance replacing the government's ordinance. However, Article 7d GAOA does not mean that an emergency ordinance lapses automatically after six months.[31] This has been criticised by some authors, who regret that under the current regime, Parliament is under no duty to adopt a corresponding legal basis.[32]

B. The COVID-19 Act of 25 September 2020

In light of the Federal Council's frenetic regulatory activity, many voices quickly pressed Parliament to adopt legislation in order to place the Federal Council's measures on firmer – ie more democratically legitimate – ground[33] (on Parliament's reaction to the crisis before the adoption of such a legal basis, see below, III.B. and III.C.). On 19 June 2020, the federal government opened the consultation procedure on its bill for a COVID-19 Act. While the consultation period usually lasts for at least three months,[34] the government shortened it to three weeks to ensure that Parliament could deliberate on the bill as soon as possible.[35]

On 12 August 2020, the Federal Council presented its dispatch on a draft emergency law to Parliament. By doing so, it ensured that its emergency ordinances did not lose their validity after six months, as stated in Article 7d(2)(a) GAOA (above, A.). Based on the consultations, the Federal Council had proceeded to several adjustments, which included shortening the period of validity of the Act by one year, ie until 31 December 2021.[36] In its dispatch, it requested Parliament to

[30] Government and Administration Organisation Act of 21 March 1997 (SR 172.010). Art 7d GAOA, which pertains to Federal Council ordinances pursuant to Art 184(3) Cst., and Art 7e GAOA, which concerns rulings ('Verfügungen') of the Federal Council, are of limited relevance to our analysis.

[31] Brunner, Wilhelm, and Uhlmann (n 1) 699 f. This solution was adopted based on legal certainty considerations. See 'Parlamentarische Initiative Wahrung von Demokratie, Rechtsstaat und Handlungsfähigkeit in ausserordentlichen Lagen, Bericht der Staatspolitischen Kommission des Nationalrates' (5 February 2010; hereinafter: 'PIC-NC Report') 1582.

[32] A Glaser and K Gfeller, 'Das Ringen des Parlaments um mehr Macht: Rückschlag infolge der Corona-Pandemie?' (*Jusletter*, 5 October 2020) jusletter.weblaw.ch/fr/juslissues/2020/1039/das-ringen-des-parla_3ae3ddfeb2.html para 43.

[33] eg Brunner, Wilhelm, and Uhlmann (n 1).

[34] See also Art 7(3) of the Federal Act on the Consultation Procedure of 18 March 2005 (SR 172.061). However, Art 7(4) of this Act provides that this period may exceptionally be shortened '[i]f the project may not be delayed'.

[35] Federal Chancellery, Letter to the Political Parties, the Umbrella Organizations for the Communes, Cities, and Mountain Regions, the Umbrella Organisations for the Economic Sectors, and Interested Groups, 19 June 2020.

[36] COVID-19 Dispatch (n 26) 6587.

debate the bill and to legitimise its measures as swiftly as possible.[37] This occurred shortly thereafter, in the autumn parliamentary session, where Parliament discussed the bill under great time pressure. Eventually, on 25 September 2020, the legislature adopted the Federal Act on the Statutory Principles for Federal Council Ordinances on Combating the COVID-19 Epidemic (COVID-19 Act),[38] which entered into force on the next day.[39] The Council of States approved the Act unanimously; in the National Council, the statute was adopted by 153 votes to 36, with six abstentions.

Article 1 of the COVID-19 Act, titled 'Subject matter and principles', is the most important provision for our purposes. Initially, this provision only had three paragraphs. Amongst other things, it established a duty for the Federal Council to only adopt measures 'to the extent that they are required to respond to the COVID-19 epidemic' (Article 1(2)). Article 1 did not mention Parliament, nor did the rest of the bill.

The version eventually adopted by Parliament encompasses six paragraphs. Article 1(2) COVID-19 Act now also states that the Federal Council 'shall not use these powers if the same objective can be achieved using regular or emergency legislative procedures'. Importantly, Article 1(4) provides that the government 'shall inform Parliament regularly, in good time and comprehensively about the implementation of this Act', and 'consult the relevant committees beforehand about planned ordinances and amendments to ordinances'. Another relevant provision is Article 1(5), which requires that in an emergency, the federal government must inform the presidents of the relevant parliamentary committees, which in turn must swiftly inform the committee members. At this point in time, it is too early to assess whether this provision has indeed led to a greater – and especially more meaningful – inclusion of Parliament. The interaction between the Federal Council and Parliament was certainly intense during the second half of 2020.

While additional clarity is provided on Parliament's role in the context of emergency measures, the involvement of the legislature remains modest. The bill had already been criticised for mainly containing delegation norms in favour of the executive[40] as well as discretionary clauses ('Kann-Vorschriften'), two problems which the revised version does not address. The emphasis on the subsidiary role of executive measures vis-à-vis parliamentary ones constitutes an improvement. Yet, it does not modify the existing institutional arrangements in any way.

The duty of the government to inform Parliament and to consult the relevant committees before adopting or amending ordinances certainly goes in the right

[37] COVID-19 Dispatch (n 26) 6622–23.

[38] Federal Act on the Statutory Principles for Federal Council Ordinances on Combating the COVID-19 Epidemic of 25 September 2020 (SR 818.102).

[39] See Art 165(1) Cst., which states that emergency legislation is 'brought into force immediately', and Art 21(2) COVID-19 Act; see however Art 21(3) COVID-19 Act.

[40] T Sägesser and D Kettiger, 'Fragwürdiges Covid-19-Gesetz' *Neue Zürcher Zeitung* (Zurich, 3 September 2020) 7.

direction. However, Article 1 of the Act does not give Parliament an actual veto right, nor does it contribute to streamlining the procedure through which the committees are consulted. In particular, the Act does not establish an ad hoc (COVID) delegation, as some scholars had suggested.[41] Such a delegation could have been tasked with assisting the government before the measures are adopted, with reviewing its measures (eg from the perspective of their proportionality), and potentially even with adopting emergency measures itself. The fact that the legislature must merely be consulted also means – as Parliament has already repeatedly emphasised in the past[42] – that it does not assume any political responsibility for the emergency measures.

Another constitutional problem is that the delegation clauses of the COVID-19 Act remain too vague for ordinary legislation, and that even if the Act is considered emergency legislation, it creates a form of empowerment vis-à-vis the government that lacks a constitutional basis. It is also doubtful whether Parliament may lower the bar for emergency regulation by the Federal Council – which it effectively does if one compares the requirements of the Act with those provided for in Article 185(3) Cst.

In 2010, the Political Institutions Committee of the National Council proposed the creation of a six-member 'delegation for extraordinary situations'[43] before making a U-turn and abandoning this proposal. The idea also failed to garner support in the Council of States.[44] The Federal Council disagreed with it categorically, stating that a duty of the executive to consult such a delegation before adopting emergency ordinances would lead to conflicts of competence, and that it lacked flexibility and practicability.[45]

Ten years later, the COVID-19 Act confirms this assessment. This is surprising, given the considerable power shift towards the executive triggered by the pandemic at the expense of parliamentary involvement. The President of the Council of States highlighted that an *ad hoc* committee would side-line the expertise of Parliament's standing committees, and that its decisions would not enjoy broad enough political support.[46] While this view reflects a commendable commitment to the equality of MPs and to democratic legitimacy, it also endorses a weak position of Parliament vis-à-vis the executive. Indeed, it prevents Parliament from

[41] eg Stöckli (n 7) 49. On this topic, see also C Forster, 'Das Parlament benötigt eine Corona-Impfung' *Neue Zürcher Zeitung* (Zurich, 30 April 2020) 10.

[42] eg PIC-NC Report (n 31) 1564, 1579, 1586, 1588.

[43] PIC-NC Report (n 31) 1579, 1586 ff. Pursuant to this proposal, such a delegation would merely act in a consultative capacity.

[44] The Council of States considered that creating a new body would lead to conflicts of competence, and that the existing institutional structures were sufficient. See the statement of then Council of States member (now Federal Councillor) Alain Berset, '09.402 Parlamentarische Initiative SPK-NR. Wahrung von Demokratie, Rechtsstaat und Handlungsfähigkeit in ausserordentlichen Lagen' (1 December 2010) AB 2010 S 1062.

[45] 'Parlamentarische Initiative Wahrung von Demokratie, Rechtsstaat und Handlungsfähigkeit in ausserordentlichen Lagen, Bericht vom 5. Februar 2010 der Staatspolitischen Kommission des Nationalrates, Stellungnahme des Bundesrates' (21 April 2010) 2808–2809.

[46] Häfliger (n 25). See also, in the same vein, Glaser and Gfeller (n 32) para 44.

being immediately involved and from reacting swiftly and autonomously in situations of crisis. Moreover, it is inconsistent with the significant powers enjoyed by the Finance Delegation (FinDel), which is composed of six members of the finance committees (three per committee),[47] and which can veto urgent expenses decided by the Federal Council.[48] More generally, this assessment does not cohere with Parliament's past and current intention to strengthen its own position vis-à-vis the executive branch.[49] Andreas Glaser and Katja Gfeller have argued that the FinDel mechanism – a short-term approval reservation – should apply with regard to all emergency ordinances of the Federal Council, and that it should be extended to Parliament as a whole, instead of being limited to a delegation.[50] Several Swiss cantons already follow this approach.[51]

As an emergency statute with a period of validity that exceeds one year, the COVID-19 Act was subject to a facultative referendum (see Article 165(1) and Article 141(1)(b) Cst.). After a referendum request was submitted, Swiss citizens voted on the COVID-19 Act on 13 June 2021. The Act was approved by 60.21 per cent of voters.

III. Parliamentary Lawmaking in Times of COVID-19: The Swiss Federal Assembly's Adjustment to the Pandemic

Since the first case of COVID-19 was confirmed in Switzerland on 25 February 2020, Parliament has also had to adjust its own working methods to the pandemic. We first provide a cursory overview of the main organs of the Federal Assembly (A.). We then highlight two aspects of Parliament's activity which were affected by the pandemic, namely the meetings of both chambers (the Councils) (B.) and of the parliamentary committees (C.).

A. The Federal Assembly and Its Organs

Article 31 of the Federal Act on the Federal Assembly (ParlA) lists eight parliamentary organs,[52] several of which played an active part in adjusting Parliament's

[47] Art 51(1) ParlA.

[48] See Art 28(1) and Art 34(2) of the Financial Budget Act of 7 October 2005 (SR 611.0; hereinafter: 'FBA').

[49] On this trend, see Glaser and Gfeller (n 32). See also PIC-NC Report (n 31) 1565 (stating that Parliament should not be presented with a *fait accompli*).

[50] Glaser and Gfeller (n 32) para 51 f.

[51] ibid, para 53.

[52] Namely, a. the National Council, b. the Council of States, c. the United Federal Assembly, d. the Presiding College, e. the Offices, f. the Conference for Coordination and the Administration Delegation,

mode of functioning in the pandemic. Before we discuss these adjustments (below, sections B and C), additional clarifications as to these organs' roles are in order.

Each Council has a Presiding College, which is composed of the Council President and two Vice-Presidents.[53] Among other tasks, the President chairs the Council's meetings and has a representative function.[54]

Each chamber also has 'an office to deal with its administration and other related matters',[55] which is composed of the members of the Presiding College, several tellers, and representatives of the parliamentary groups.[56] All three authoritative linguistic versions of the ParlA (ie the German, French, and Italian versions) suggest that the Offices 'lead' the Councils ('für seine *Leitung*'; 'chargé de sa *direction*'; 'per la propria *direzione*'; emphasis added).[57] Yet while the Offices play, without a doubt, an important role in facilitating and structuring the Councils' activities,[58] most scholars emphasise that this role is primarily administrative.[59]

Taken together, the two Offices constitute the Conference for Coordination,[60] which takes care of a range of tasks, including scheduling the ordinary and extraordinary sessions, helping the Councils to coordinate themselves, and serving as an intermediary between them and the Federal Council.[61]

Parliament also has an Administration Delegation. The Delegation counts six members of the two Offices (three each)[62] and is tasked with 'the overall management of Parliament',[63] eg as regards the use of the parliamentary premises (except for the two Council rooms).[64] It also has a residual administrative competence.[65] In practice, its members are the same as those of the two Offices.[66] As Boris Burri

g. the parliamentary committees and their subcommittees and delegations, and h. the parliamentary groups ('Fraktionen').

[53] Art 152 Cst.; Art 34 ParlA.

[54] Art 7(1) of the Standing Orders of the National Council of 3 October 2003 (SR 171.13; hereinafter: 'SO-NC'); Art 4(1) of the Standing Orders of the Council of States of 20 June 2003 (SR 171.14; hereinafter: 'SO-CS').

[55] Art 35(1) ParlA.

[56] Art 8(1) SO-NC; Art 5(1) SO-CS.

[57] See also M Graf, 'Die Büros des Nationalrates und des Ständerates: Hierarchisch vorgesetzte Parlamentsleitungen oder Organe der Selbstorganisation des Rates?' (2015) 18(2) *Parlament – Parlement – Parlamento* 14, 14.

[58] B Burri, 'Art. 35 ParlG' in C Theler, M Graf, and M von Wyss (eds), *Parlamentsrecht und Parlamentspraxis der Schweizerischen Bundesversammlung: Kommentar zum Parlamentsgesetz (ParlG) vom 13. Dezember 2002* (Helbing & Lichtenhahn, 2014) 301 ff, para 15 ff.

[59] F Uhlmann and M Wilhelm, 'Kurzgutachten zuhanden der sozialdemokratischen Fraktion der Eidgenössischen Räte betreffend die Durchführung von Sessionen und Kommissionssitzungen in ausserordentlichen Lagen (Coronavirus)' (2020) publikationen.sgp-ssp.net, paras 49 ff.

[60] Art 37 ParlA.

[61] Art 37(2)(a) and (b) ParlA.

[62] Art 38(1) ParlA.

[63] Art 38(2) ParlA.

[64] Art 69(1) ParlA.

[65] Art 20(2)(f) Verordnung der Bundesversammlung zum Parlamentsgesetz und über die Parlamentsverwaltung vom 3. Oktober 2003 (SR 171.115).

[66] B Burri, 'Art. 38 ParlG' in C Theler, M Graf and M von Wyss (eds), *Parlamentsrecht und Parlamentspraxis der Schweizerischen Bundesversammlung: Kommentar zum Parlamentsgesetz (ParlG) vom 13. Dezember 2002* (Helbing & Lichtenhahn, 2014) 323, para 5.

notes, the decisions of the Administration Delegation should not disproportionately interfere with the competences and activities of other parliamentary organs, which should be consulted in cases of doubt.[67]

Last but not least, '[e]ach Council forms committees from its members'.[68] The parliamentary committees are crucial from the perspective of parliamentary lawmaking. They fulfil a range of functions, including 'conduct[ing] a preliminary discussion of the business referred to them for the attention of their council', 'consider[ing] and decid[ing] on the business referred to them for final decision', and 'draw[ing] up proposals relevant to their areas of responsibility'.[69] They also have the right to submit parliamentary initiatives to the Federal Assembly.[70] Each chamber appoints standing committees (12 for the National Council, 11 for the Council of States)[71] and, 'in exceptional circumstances', special committees.[72]

Having clarified the main responsibilities of these parliamentary organs, we now turn to two aspects of Parliament's lawmaking activity that were affected by the pandemic, namely the meetings of the Councils (section B) and those of the committees (section C). Scope precludes an in-depth analysis of the numerous and complex issues involved; instead, we highlight the main difficulties which arose in this context.

B. The Meetings of the Councils

Article 151(1) Cst. states that the two Councils 'convene in session regularly'.[73] The pandemic had three consequences for these meetings. First, on 15 March 2020, the Offices decided to interrupt Parliament's (three-week) spring session after two weeks.[74] Secondly, in early May 2020, the Councils convened for an extraordinary session outside the Federal Palace, in two halls inside Bernexpo, a trade fair and exhibition centre located in Bern.[75] The summer session of June 2020 also took place on these premises. Thirdly, the question arose as to whether the Councils' physical meetings could be replaced by virtual ones. We discuss each of these three issues in turn.

A first difficulty that has been discussed in the scholarly literature pertains to *the legality of the Offices' unanimous decision to interrupt the ordinary spring session.*

[67] ibid 325, para 13.
[68] Art 153(1) Cst.
[69] Art 44(1)(a) and (b) ParlA.
[70] Art 160(1) Cst. See also Art 45(1)(a) ParlA, which states that the committees may 'submit parliamentary initiatives, parliamentary procedural requests and proposals and compile reports'.
[71] Art 42(1) and 43 ff ParlA, Art 10 SO-NC, Art 7 SO-CS.
[72] Art 42(2) ParlA.
[73] See also Art 2(1) ParlA, which restates this requirement for ordinary sessions.
[74] 'Keine dritte Sessionswoche der Frühlingssession der Bundesversammlung', press release (15 March 2020) www.parlament.ch/press-releases/Pages/mm-vd-2020-03-15.aspx.
[75] On extraordinary sessions, see Art 151(2) Cst. and Art 2(3) ParlA. Art 2(2) ParlA also enables the Council 'to convene special sessions if the ordinary sessions are not sufficient to deal with the volume of business'.

At the beginning of the same week, on 9 March, MP Thomas Aeschi's request to interrupt the session had been overwhelmingly rejected by the National Council by 155 votes against 13 votes in favour and 8 abstentions, and on 13 March, the Administration Delegation had endorsed the same view, while adopting stricter measures aiming to prevent the virus from spreading inside Parliament.[76] The Offices' unanimous decision to eventually interrupt the session on 15 March was based on the rapid increase in cases in the previous days, on the need to protect MPs and their family members belonging to high-risk groups,[77] but also, as the press noted, on growing public pressure on Parliament.[78] For the first time in its history, Parliament was unable to complete its ordinary session.[79]

It is widely accepted that the executive branch cannot prevent Parliament from convening.[80] This position was also defended by the Presidents of the two Councils.[81] However, disagreement arises with regard to Parliament's internal division of competences: in light of the Offices' administrative function (above, section A), several scholars have expressed doubts about the legality of this interruption.

The Offices are indeed tasked with convening the Council meetings[82] and even with defining the items of business to be discussed, although the Councils may modify the agenda items.[83] Yet, the law does not explicitly state that the Offices may *interrupt* a session. Andrea Caroni and Stefan G Schmid argue that the principle of parallel forms should be observed: if the Offices are in charge of convening the meetings, they should also be able to interrupt them.[84] By contrast, according

[76] 'Mit weiteren Massnahmen gegen das Coronavirus in die dritte Sessionswoche', press release (13 March 2020) www.parlament.ch/press-releases/Pages/mm-vd-2020-03-13.aspx.

[77] According to F Schäfer, eight MPs are older than 65 and therefore likely to be particularly at risk; moreover, while their exact number is not known, other MPs are vulnerable due to a pre-existing medical condition: 'Zuerst wollte das Parlament die Session durchziehen – doch dann kam die Einsicht' *Neue Zürcher Zeitung* (Zurich, 15 March 2020) 9.

[78] ibid.

[79] A Caroni and SG Schmid, 'Notstand im Bundeshaus: Die Rolle der Bundesversammlung in der (Corona-)Krise' (2020) 23 *Aktuelle juristische Praxis* 710, 710.

[80] eg F Uhlmann and E Scheifele, 'Legislative Response to Coronavirus (Switzerland)' (2020) 8(1–2) *The Theory and Practice of Legislation* 115, 122–23; M Würmli, 'Auswirkungen der COVID-19-Verordnung 2 auf die Versammlungsfreiheit der Parlamente' (2020) 23(2) Parlament – Parlement – Parlamento 42, 43; F Uhlmann and M Wilhelm, 'Kurzgutachten zuhanden der sozialdemokratischen Fraktion der eidgenössischen Räte betreffend Sessionsabbruch und Einberufung zu einer ausserordentlichen Session' (2020) publikationen.sgp-ssp.net, para 23; Caroni and Schmid (n 79) 717. Würmli also comes to this conclusion based on a teleological and systematic interpretation of the Ordinance on Measures to Combat the Coronavirus (COVID-19 Ordinance 2) of 13 March 2020 (SR 818.101.24, no longer in force) and based on the principle of proportionality: Würmli (above) 45 f. He therefore argues that even if parliamentary meetings were 'events' pursuant to the COVID-19 Ordinance 2, it would be inappropriate to require parliaments to obtain a derogation from a third party: ibid 46 f. See also Stöckli (n 7) 40. See further Legal Service/Secretariat of the Finance Committees/Secretariat of the Political Institutions Committees, 'Powers of Parliament and the Federal Council in Extraordinary Situations: Note to the Presidencies of the Councils (25 March 2020), www.parlament.ch/centers/documents/de/notiz-kompetenzen-parlament-und-bundesrat-in-ausserord-lagen-d.pdf.

[81] Uhlmann and Wilhelm (n 59) n 15.

[82] Art 33(1) ParlA.

[83] Art 9(1)(a) SO-NC and Art 6(1)(a) SO-CS.

[84] Caroni and Schmid (n 79) 719.

to Felix Uhlmann and Martin Wilhelm, it is unclear why the Councils should not be able to correct the decision of the Offices to interrupt the session if they may do so as regards the agenda items.[85] Andreas Glaser and Katja Gfeller submit that Parliament should be able to veto the Offices' decision or, by the same token, that this decision should be validated by a qualified majority of the legislature.[86] Moreover, while it seems acceptable for the Offices to interrupt a session in the event of an extreme emergency,[87] it can be doubted that in mid-March, the situation was such that the Councils could by no means be given the opportunity to meet one more time in order to decide themselves whether or not to interrupt the session.[88] At any rate, a suspension of the session would have been more proportionate than a complete interruption.[89]

A second issue pertains to the Offices' and Administration Delegation's *decision of 26 March 2020 to hold an extraordinary session in the Bernexpo building starting on 4 May 2020*.[90] This location was chosen in order to ensure compliance with the Federal Office of Public Health's recommendations in terms of hygiene and physical distancing. The extraordinary session would be devoted to the emergency credits decided by the Federal Council.

Strikingly, the Federal Council was the first to request that such an extraordinary session be held.[91] It did so on 23 March 2020, invoking Article 34(4) of the Federal Financial Budget Act (FBA). Only afterwards, on 25 March, did 31 members of the Council of States ask that Parliament be convened for an extraordinary session as well, a request that can thus be described as symbolic. Twelve members of the National Council submitted an equivalent request demanding that an extraordinary session be held in April, but the required quorum of one quarter of the members of the National Council was not reached.[92]

The ParlA (not the Constitution) provides that '[t]he Federal Assembly meets in Bern'.[93] Given that the ParlA does not mandate meeting in the Federal Palace, holding the extraordinary session at Bernexpo in May 2020 was unproblematic from the perspective of parliamentary law.

The Offices' and Administration Delegation's decision of 26 March can be criticised on several counts. First, scheduling the beginning of the extraordinary session on 4 May 2020 – six weeks after the Federal Council had declared the

[85] Uhlmann and Wilhelm (n 80) para 28. See also M Wilhelm and F Uhlmann, 'Herausforderungen für Parlamente in der Corona-Krise – Versuch eines Überblicks' (2020) 23(2) *Parlament – Parlement – Parlamento* 4, 10.

[86] Glaser and Gfeller (n 32) para 42.

[87] Uhlmann and Wilhelm (n 80) para 32.

[88] ibid, para 33 f.

[89] ibid, para 35.

[90] 'Corona-Krise: Das Parlament tagt Anfang Mai in der Bernexpo', press release (26 March 2020) www.parlament.ch/press-releases/Pages/mm-information-2020-03-26.aspx.

[91] Art 151(2) Cst., Art 2(3) ParlA.

[92] Factual Report (n 13) 27 f.

[93] Art 32(1) ParlA.

existence of an extraordinary situation – did not enable a swift enough reaction to the federal government's measures.[94] To describe this extraordinary session as a 'rebirth of democracy'[95] therefore seems exaggerated: as rightly noted by Glaser and Gfeller, Parliament largely stood in front of a *fait accompli*.[96] The authors argue that whenever the executive adopts an emergency ordinance, Parliament should have the *duty* to immediately meet for an extraordinary session.[97]

Secondly, and importantly, Article 34(4) FBA requires that if an extraordinary session is requested for the subsequent approval of urgent supplementary credits, the session should take place 'in the third calendar week following the filing of the request', a requirement which was disregarded.

Thirdly, the question arises as to whether the Councils should be able to meet virtually, something that many voices (including MPs) have called for.[98] Indeed, for MPs belonging to a high-risk group, the decision as to whether to attend the Bernexpo session was not self-evident.[99] Currently, an explicit legal basis for virtual Council meetings is lacking. Article 151(1) Cst. and Article 2(1) ParlA merely state that Parliament 'convenes', while Article 32(1) ParlA provides that it 'meets'. Moreover, as per Article 159(1) Cst., '[t]he Councils are quorate if a majority of their members is present'. Article 10 ParlA creates a duty for MPs to attend the meetings of the Councils.

Legal scholars consider that Article 159(1) Cst. requires being physically present in the Council rooms.[100] This requirement applies not only to the voting stage, but also to the deliberations.[101] In practice, however, it is only followed in

[94] eg Glaser and Gfeller (n 32) para 41. Some members of the Council of States criticised this state of affairs: 'Ständerat gibt sich zu Beginn der Sondersession selbstkritisch' (*SDA*, 4 May 2020) www.parlament.ch/de/services/news/Seiten/2020/20200504180605119194158159041_bsd162.aspx. The President of the Council of States defended this decision by stating that Parliament needed to be well-prepared: Häfliger (n 25). This is in line with the Federal Council's observation that a three-week deadline is too short to allow for meaningful preparation, especially when the topic is complex. See 'Parlamentarische Initiative Wahrung von Demokratie, Rechtsstaat und Handlungsfähigkeit in ausserordentlichen Lagen, Bericht vom 5. Februar 2010 der Staatspolitischen Kommission des Nationalrates, Stellungnahme des Bundesrates' (21 April 2010) 2810–2811.

[95] 'La renaissance de la démocratie' *Le Temps* (Geneva, 4 May 2020) www.letemps.ch/suisse/renaissance-democratie.

[96] Glaser and Gfeller (n 32) para 48.

[97] ibid, para 56.

[98] eg Forster (n 41); T Brunner, 'PaIv 20.423, Situationsgerechte Flexibilisierungsmöglichkeiten für den Parlamentsbetrieb bei aussergewöhnlichen Umständen' (5 May 2020); K Christ, 'PaIv 20.425, Schaffung der rechtlichen Grundlagen für einen digitalen Parlamentsbetrieb respektive die digitale Teilnahme am physischen Betrieb' (6 May 2020); PIC-NC, 'PaIv 20.437, Handlungsfähigkeit des Parlamentes in Krisensituationen verbessern' (29 May 2020); PIC-NC, 'PaIv 20.438, Nutzung der Notrechtskompetenzen und Kontrolle des bundesrätlichen Notrechts in Krisen' (29 May 2020).

[99] M Surber, 'Parlament kann per Videokonferenz tagen' *Neue Zürcher Zeitung* (Zurich, 9 April 2020) 11.

[100] Caroni and Schmid (n 79) 719; Glaser and Gfeller (n 32) para 31; Giovanni Biaggini, 'Art. 159 BV', *BV Kommentar: Bundesverfassung der Schweizerischen Eidgenossenschaft*, 2nd edn (Orell Füssli, 2017) para 2.

[101] Stöckli (n 7) 41.

relation to voting.[102] According to Moritz von Wyss, this flexibility is appropriate given that the Federal Assembly is a non-professional parliament.[103] Moreover, while violations of Article 10 ParlA could in theory be sanctioned pursuant to Article 13 ParlA, this does not happen in practice.[104] Still, Caroni and Schmid argue that *de lege lata*, virtual meetings are not an option as long as Parliament can use another physical meeting place in Switzerland.[105] Uhlmann and Wilhelm likewise consider that virtual meetings are not envisaged by, and might even conflict with, constitutional law, as well as with the requirement for Parliament to meet in Bern.[106]

On the one hand, several authors believe that online meetings would have a negative impact on, or at least modify, the quality of the deliberative process.[107] For this reason, Caroni and Schmid argue that Article 159(1) Cst. would need to be amended to allow for virtual meetings.[108] This position was also adopted by the Offices in September 2020.[109] Relatedly, it is often argued that parliamentary lawmaking requires direct human contact in order to generate trust, and for compromises to eventually be reached.[110] As a matter of fact, it is generally accepted that trust emerges in the context of face-to-face – but not virtual – interactions.[111]

On the other hand, and as Uhlmann and Wilhelm stress, given that the duty of attendance is handled loosely in practice, 'it seems questionable to apply excessive demands of deliberation to telephone or video conferences'.[112] Deliberation, they emphasise, also takes place in the lobby of Parliament, and it seems unclear why it should not be allowed to happen online.[113] Moreover, and crucially, the rationale

[102] M von Wyss, 'Art. 10 ParlG' in C Theler, M Graf, and M von Wyss (eds), *Parlamentsrecht und Parlamentspraxis der Schweizerischen Bundesversammlung: Kommentar zum Parlamentsgesetz (ParlG) vom 13. Dezember 2002* (Helbing & Lichtenhahn, 2014) 84, para 6; Caroni and Schmid (n 79) 719; Glaser and Gfeller (n 32) para 31; Stöckli (n 7) 41.

[103] von Wyss (n 102) 85 para 9.

[104] ibid 85, para 11.

[105] Caroni and Schmid (n 79) 720.

[106] Uhlmann and Wilhelm (n 59) para 33.

[107] von Wyss, 'Wie virtuell kann ein Parlament sein?' (2020) 23(2) *Parlament – Parlement – Parlamento* 16, 18 ff. See also the opinion of the Office of the National Council regarding D Fiala, 'Interpellation 20.3098, E-Parlament als eine mögliche Antwort auf Notsituationen wie infolge des Coronavirus' (11 March 2020); Wilhelm and Uhlmann (n 85) 11. See also Uhlmann and Wilhelm (n 59) para 29. More nuanced: Stöckli (n 7) 51.

[108] Caroni and Schmid (n 79) 720.

[109] See the response of the Offices of 10 September 2020 to M Binder-Keller, 'Motion 20.3904, Dringliche Schaffung der gesetzlichen Grundlagen für die virtuelle Teilnahme an Parlamentssitzungen', 19 June 2020.

[110] von Wyss (n 107) 20. In the same vein: J Malloy, 'The Adaptation of Parliament's Multiple Roles to COVID-19' (2020) 53 *Canadian Journal of Political Science* 305, 308; R Koop, K Blidook, and LA Fuga, 'Has the COVID-19 Pandemic Affected MPs' Representational Activities?' (2020) 53 *Canadian Journal of Political Science* 287, 288. See also Forster (n 41), describing physical meetings as the 'lubricant of parliamentary operations'.

[111] O O'Neill, *A Question of Trust* (CUP, 2002) 83 ff.

[112] Uhlmann and Wilhelm (n 59) para 36.

[113] ibid.

pursued by the requirement of physical presence is that the required quorum be reached, ie that the Councils retain their capacity to act.[114] This, in turn, increases the democratic legitimacy of the deliberations and decisions; in other words, physical presence is not an end in itself.[115] Glaser and Gfeller even argue that the quorum of Article 159(1) Cst. should be lowered to one quarter of all members in the event of an emergency.[116] Importantly, this constitutional provision only requires being present, and not being *physically* present.[117]

Still, in light of the indeterminacy of existing legal provisions, and given that parliamentary law is currently tailored to physical meetings,[118] the Councils would be well-advised to adopt an emergency statute or an emergency ordinance on phone and video meetings.[119] Virtual meetings would resolve the issue of a discriminatory exclusion of specific MPs due to their age or a pre-existing medical condition.[120] Moreover, the exclusion of *any* MP is problematic from the perspective of political representation. The importance granted to the fact that MPs can represent their constituents by attending parliamentary meetings is reflected in several provisions of parliamentary law.[121]

Of course, the committees tasked with drafting such an emergency statute or ordinance would need to reflect upon 'the implications of a virtual Council meeting, eg for the principle of publicity and the representative function of Parliament, but also for the media and interest representatives'.[122] Moreover, the security requirements of virtual Council meetings must be high in order to avoid abuse, such as illegal substitutions.[123] Finally, even in a virtual setting, MPs' rights and

[114] von Wyss (n 102) 84 para 5. On the importance of this element ('Verhandlungsfähigkeit', ie of the Council being 'quorate'), see Uhlmann and Wilhelm (n 59) para 9. See also Art 31 SO-CS; Art 38 SO-NC.

[115] Wilhelm and Uhlmann (n 85) 11. See also Uhlmann and Wilhelm (n 59) paras 10, 34.

[116] Glaser and Gfeller (n 32) para 57. The authors highlight that the requirement of physical meetings is 'rigid', and that unlike Germany and Austria, Switzerland does not have an 'emergency parliament' that would be able to adopt decisions in a situation of crisis. See ibid, para 38.

[117] Stöckli (n 7) 41 fn 201.

[118] See especially provisions pertaining to the 'Right to use Assembly chambers and access to the Parliament Building' (art. 69 ParlA) and to house rules (Art 61 f SO-NC and 47 f SO-CS), as well as individual provisions (eg stating that members of the National Council vote from their desks if they are rapporteurs, or from their seats in all other cases, Art 56(4) SO-NC; see also Art 44(1) SO-CS, providing that members of the Council of States vote from their desks).

[119] Uhlmann and Wilhelm (n 59) para 33. See also Uhlmann and Scheifele (n 80) 125; Stöckli (n 7) 41–42.

[120] Uhlmann and Scheifele (n 80) 124–25.

[121] See eg Art 11(3) ParlA (no duty of recusal for MPs even in the event of a conflict of interests); Art 20 ParlA (session attendance guarantee in relation to criminal proceedings pertaining to acts not covered by an MP's immunity).

[122] Opinion of the Office of the National Council regarding D Fiala, 'Interpellation 20.3098, E-Parlament als eine mögliche Antwort auf Notsituationen wie infolge des Coronavirus' (11 March 2020). See also the opinion of the Office of the National Council of 10 September 2020 regarding M Binder-Keller, 'Motion 20.3904, Dringliche Schaffung der gesetzlichen Grundlagen für die virtuelle Teilnahme an Parlamentssitzungen' (19 June 2020).

[123] Uhlmann and Wilhelm (n 59) paras 10, 34.

the applicable parliamentary procedural norms must be respected to the extent possible (eg the duty to hold minutes): 'this is certainly a high, but not an insuperable hurdle'.[124]

C. The Meetings of the Committees

COVID-19 also has an impact on the activities of the parliamentary committees. First, the interruption of the spring session equally affected the meetings of the committees. Indeed, by deciding to interrupt the spring session, the Offices also cancelled all committee meetings set to take place in the third week of the session and until the next session.[125] A second aspect pertains to whether parliamentary committees should be able to hold meetings over the phone or using videoconferencing software.

On 19 March 2020, the Offices announced that until the May and June session, only committee meetings devoted to urgent matters (ie, connected to the extraordinary situation) would be allowed.[126] These meetings would take place in the Federal Palace or in the Bernerhof, an adjacent government building. The Offices declared that if necessary, informal exchanges pertaining to urgent matters could be held via phone or videoconferences. However, these exchanges were not 'committee meetings' and MPs could not claim any compensation for them. Other committee meetings were, as mentioned, prohibited.

This decision remained applicable until 19 April 2020. Eventually, on 6 April 2020, the Offices declared that the parliamentary committees would be given the opportunity to meet for half a day from 20 April 2020 onwards. Moreover, they decided to allow videoconferences for ordinary meetings and not only for informal ones, provided that: (1) the President and the majority of the committee agreed to a videoconference; (2) the matters to be discussed were appropriate for a videoconference, eg 'hearings or the deliberation of proposals'; (3) that Skype for Business was used, taking into account that classified topics could not be discussed.[127]

On 21 April 2020, for the first time in the history of the Swiss Parliament, a parliamentary committee – the Environment, Spatial Planning, and Energy Committee of the National Council – held a meeting via videoconference. In total, 13 committee meetings were held in the National Council, and 11 in the Council of States. Three took place virtually.[128] Finally, on 23 April 2020, all restrictions

[124] ibid.
[125] Caroni and Schmid (n 79) 717–18.
[126] 'Schweizer Parlament bleibt in der Krise handlungsfähig', press release (19 March 2020) www.parlament.ch/press-releases/Pages/mm-bue-n-s-vd-2020-03-19.aspx.
[127] 'Kommissionen arbeiten in der ausserordentlichen Lage weiter', press release (6 April 2020) www.parlament.ch/press-releases/Pages/mm-information-2020-04-06.aspx.
[128] Factual Report (n 13) 31.

applicable to committee meetings were lifted.[129] The committees met again to deliberate before the summer session, which began on 2 June 2020.

Were the Offices competent to interrupt all committee meetings? The Offices play an important role when it comes to coordinating the committees' work. In particular, they are in charge of defining 'the remit of the standing committees', 'schedul[ing] the meetings of the committees for the year', and 'handl[ing] all other issues of organisation and procedure in the Council'.[130] However, analogously to what applies to the Councils (see above section B), scholars argue that due to the committees' prominent status by virtue of constitutional and statutory law (above section A),[131] the Offices mainly fulfil an administrative role vis-à-vis the committees. This administrative – as opposed to 'hierarchical' – function of the Offices is also derived from their statutory tasks and the equality of MPs.[132] Therefore, according to Caroni and Schmid, a decision of the Offices 'to restrict the committees' activity for a prolonged period of time would violate the Constitution and statutory law'.[133] This has also been acknowledged by the Parliamentary Services, which however stated that the Offices and the Administration Delegation must organise and plan the meetings in a way that is safe for all participants.[134]

One problem noted by Caroni and Schmid is that the committees 'do not have an (emergency) power to convene meetings despite contrary decisions by the Offices'.[135] When requesting that an extraordinary session be held, the 31 members of the Council of States had also asked that the relevant committees be given the possibility to discuss COVID-19-related matters beforehand. Because it is not formally covered by Article 2(3) ParlA, this second request constituted 'a mere wish directed at the Offices'.[136] When it comes to emergency situations, the regular instruments at the disposal of the committees (eg parliamentary initiatives, procedural requests, and proposals[137]) are not particularly helpful, which leads Caroni and Schmid to conclude that the decisions of the Offices created *faits accomplis*.[138] Uhlmann and Wilhelm too concede that, as is the case with the meetings of the Councils, the Offices seem 'particularly able to cancel or postpone committee meetings in the event of a serious, immediate threat to the committee members',

[129] ibid, 30.

[130] Art 9(1)(b), (e), and (j) SO-NC; Art 6(1)(b), (f), and (j) SO-CS.

[131] See Art 153 Cst., Art 160(1) Cst., and Art 42 ff ParlA.

[132] Uhlmann and Wilhelm (n 80) para 14. See also Graf (n 57) 14 ff.

[133] Caroni and Schmid (n 79) 717. See also Uhlmann and Wilhelm (n 59) paras 51, 58; Glaser and Gfeller (n 32) para 42.

[134] Parliamentary Services, 'Kommissionssitzungen und Corona-Krise: Beilage für die Sitzung der Koordinationskonferenz vom 6. April 2020', (30 March 2020) www.parlament.ch/centers/documents/de/kommissionssitzungen-und-coronakrise-d.pdf.

[135] Caroni and Schmid (n 79) 717.

[136] ibid, 718.

[137] Art 45(1)(a) ParlA.

[138] Caroni and Schmid (n 79) 718.

and that 'a cancellation of committee meetings by the Offices or the Conference for Coordination appears to be permissible only, but at least then when it is necessary to ensure the safety of the committee members'.[139] This is why Caroni and Schmid argue that the option of enshrining an explicit right of the committees to hold meetings should be examined, eg by amending Article 2(3) ParlA.[140]

This brings us to our second point, namely virtual committee meetings. Indeed, the committees' incapacity to act arises from the lack of an explicit legal basis for virtual meetings (which again mirrors the situation in the Councils, see above section B). It is doubtful whether the committees could themselves decide to hold a meeting via phone or videoconference, given that, as already mentioned, there is no emergency ordinance competence of the committees.[141]

Just like what applies to the meetings of the Councils, attending committee meetings is mandatory for MPs.[142] However, Council and committee meetings are not comparable in every respect. First, no quorum applies to the latter, but for two narrow exceptions.[143] Secondly, such meetings do not need to take place in Bern. Thirdly, committee meetings are confidential,[144] which means that if virtual meetings are allowed, security requirements must be even stricter than for Council meetings. Fourthly, committee members who cannot attend a meeting can be replaced by another member of their parliamentary group.[145] Finally, the fact that circular resolutions ('Zirkularbeschlüsse') have been practised without an explicit legal basis[146] further suggests that there is no duty for committee members to *physically* attend the meetings. According to Caroni and Schmid, videoconferences should be possible as long as the various provisions governing the activities of the committees are respected.[147]

Still, it seems appropriate for the possibility and modalities of virtual committee work to be enshrined in parliamentary law.[148] At present, online meetings are still being held on the basis of ad hoc regulation,[149] which weakens the position of Parliament. When adopting such a legal basis, the specificities of committee meetings should be accounted for. Moreover, a solution needs to be found in order to allow committees to discuss classified topics, especially in light of the fact that all committee meetings are confidential anyway.

[139] Wilhelm and Uhlmann (n 85) 10.
[140] Caroni and Schmid (n 79) 718.
[141] Uhlmann and Wilhelm (n 59) para 47.
[142] Art 10 ParlA.
[143] ie when the competent committee decides whether to lift an MP's immunity (Art 17(a)(3) ParlA), or with regard to a conciliation committee (Art 92 ParlA).
[144] Art 47(1) ParlA.
[145] Art 18(1) SO-NC; Art 14(1) SO-CS.
[146] Caroni and Schmid (n 79) 718. This practice is simply based on Art 16 SO-NC and Art 12 SO-CS.
[147] ibid. See also Wilhelm and Uhlmann (n 85) 11.
[148] Caroni and Schmid (n 79) 718.
[149] Forster (n 41).

IV. Conclusion: COVID-19 as a Missed Opportunity for the Swiss Parliament?

As this chapter has shown, the pandemic has unveiled several weak spots in Swiss parliamentary and constitutional law. Through our analysis, our goal is not to criticise past decisions that were made under very difficult circumstances, but rather to adopt a prospective approach.[150] Such an approach is needed in light of the fact that Switzerland is currently facing a second wave of infections, and that others are likely to follow in the future as long as no highly effective vaccine is widely available to and used by the population. The present crisis has shown that in the future, Parliament will need to fulfil its decisional, legitimising, and control function even more.[151]

As regards the COVID-19 Act, it is comprehensible for Parliament to be focused on addressing the pandemic's consequences, and not primarily on its own role. Yet strengthening Parliament's position in times of crisis would constitute neither unwarranted narcissism nor an abuse of authority. Importantly, Parliament should not shy away from its political responsibility. Instead, it should strive to confer democratic legitimacy on the measures.

Handling the pandemic involves taking many unpopular decisions, as shown by the many protests against COVID-19 measures throughout the world, including in Switzerland. These measures require Parliament to intervene in order to deliberate and to ensure that citizens are adequately represented. Parliament reflects a wider spectrum of views than the government, even if in Switzerland, the federal government consists in a broad coalition; moreover, in contrast to the Federal Council, Parliament's plenary deliberations are public. If necessary, the legislature must contest the measures adopted by the executive. MPs should not be 'degraded to head nodders'.[152] During the extraordinary session, however, they did not attempt to modify the measures adopted by the Federal Council.[153]

Given the protracted crisis we are still experiencing, it seems particularly crucial for Parliament to adopt a legal basis for virtual Council and committee meetings. One of the main reasons why it is assumed that the executive is best able to react swiftly is that it can meet more quickly than the legislature. Yet as stated by the Political Institutions Committee of the National Council, 'modern means of communication make it possible for a decision of the [six-member] Finance

[150] See, in the same vein, M von Wyss, 'Die Demokratie ist eine Baustelle, auch 246 Jahre nach Philadelphia' (2020) 23(2) *Parlament – Parlement – Parlamento* 1, 2.

[151] Biaggini (n 18) 15.

[152] See the statement of then Council of States member (now Federal Councillor) Simonetta Sommaruga in the parliamentary deliberations surrounding the UBS safety package adopted by the Federal Council in 2010: '08.077 Massnahmenpaket zur Stärkung des schweizerischen Finanzsystems' (9 December 2008) AB 2008 S 924.

[153] Glaser and Gfeller (n 32) para 40.

Delegation to be taken within a short time'.[154] There is no reason why this assessment should not apply to larger committees and potentially even to Parliament as a whole. As Glaser and Gfeller rightly note, Parliament's status of 'supreme authority of the Confederation' (Art 148(1) Cst.) is not a mere privilege: it also means that Parliament must step in, including and perhaps all the more so in times of crisis.[155]

[154] PIC-NC Report (n 31) 1588.
[155] Glaser and Gfeller (n 32) para 45.

10

The Hyper-Executive State of Emergency in France

SYLVIA BRUNET

I. Introduction: Chronology of the Management of the Health Crisis

While some people were probably infected with the COVID-19 virus in December or even November 2019, it was not until 24 January 2020 that the first cases were confirmed on French soil. On 13 February 2020, the plan to organise the health system response was activated. Faced with an increase in the number of COVID-19 cases, phase one of the response plan to the coronavirus epidemic was triggered ten days later by the Minister of Health. On 29 February, the first defence council and an exceptional Council of Ministers were held under the authority of the President of the Republic. The health plan also moved from phase one to phase two. Gatherings of more than 5,000 people in an enclosed space were forbidden.[1] This measure proved to be late and insufficient, as more than 2,000 people participating in a religious gathering in Mulhouse in February 2020 would then spread the virus throughout France.

It was, therefore, particularly at the beginning of March that Prime Minister Edouard Philippe and the ministers concerned adopted numerous measures via orders, decrees, circulars and press releases in order to slow down the spread of the virus. Admittedly, on 12 March 2020, the Prime Minister brought together the presidents of the two Houses of Parliament (the National Assembly and the Senate), the presidents of parliamentary groups, party leaders and the presidents of associations of local elected representatives, but it was not a question of involving them in the decision-makings. At most, it was a question of informing them of the decisions that had already been taken at the highest level of the State and that were announced the same evening by President Emmanuel Macron in a televised speech.[2]

[1] Order of 4.03.2020 and Decree 2020-191 of 4.03.2020.

[2] Address to the French (12 March 2020) www.elysee.fr/emmanuel-macron/2020/03/12/adresse-aux-francais.

There was, indeed, an urgent need for action. On 14 March 2020, there were 4,500 confirmed cases (a figure that doubled in 72 hours) and 91 deaths in hospitals.[3] The Prime Minister announced the passage to phase three of the plan, which meant that it had become an epidemic. However, the first round of the municipal elections on 15 March was maintained, which was incomprehensible to many in the population and led to a participation rate of only 44 per cent (36 per cent in major cities). The maintaining of the elections was even more criticised because the following day, during his second televised speech,[4] the President reinforced the measures, hammering home several times that 'France is at war'. Non-essential shops and businesses were required to close, the second round of municipal elections (scheduled for 22 March 2020) was postponed[5] and, if the President did not pronounce the term 'lockdown', he warned that from 17 March and for at least 15 days, all travel would be reduced to a strict minimum. A certificate for derogatory travel needed to be presented to justify the need for travel, failing which the fine would be at least €135.[6] The Prime Minister's Decree 2020-260 of 16 March 2020, which added to the measures taken by the Minister of Health – in particular his Order of 14 March[7] – thus introduced a general lockdown of the population from 17 to 31 March 2020.

In an abrupt and unpredictable manner, the legal framework for the management of the crisis then changed. On 18 March 2020, the Prime Minister tabled an emergency bill to deal with the COVID-19 epidemic in the Senate. In addition to organising the postponement of the second round of the municipal elections, that Act of Parliament, on the one hand, introduced a brand new 'state of emergency' system, ie, a new exceptional regime, that could be imposed by a Council of Ministers' decree in the event of a health disaster. On the other hand, it empowered the Government to legislate by 'ordinance' (*ordonnance*), without parliamentary debate, in order to take emergency economic and adaptive measures to combat the COVID-19 epidemic. In addition to that statutory law, there was an Institutional Act (*loi organique* – supplementing the Constitution). Its purpose was surprising as this Act suspended the deadlines for examining an 'application for a priority preliminary ruling on the issue of constitutionality' (*question prioritaire de constitutionnalité – QPC*).[8] The two statutes were adopted and promulgated in record time, the Government having triggered the accelerated procedure.[9] The new

[3] 'Coronavirus: la secrétaire d'Etat Brune Poirson testée positive; un premier cas en prison' *Le Monde* (14 March 2020).

[4] Address to the French (16 March 2020) www.elysee.fr/emmanuel-macron/2020/03/16/adresse-aux-francais-covid19.

[5] Decree 2020-267 of 17.03.2020. The second round took place on 28 June 2020. The departmental and regional elections, scheduled for March 2021, were also postponed to June 2021, as recommended in the 'Debré Report', submitted to the Prime Minister on 13 November 2020.

[6] Decree 2020-264 of 17.03.2020.

[7] Order on the closure of places that open to the public, the prohibition of gatherings of more than 100 people or the closure of schools and universities.

[8] See fn 62 concerning the *QPC*'s procedure.

[9] Statutory law 2020-290 of 23.03.2020 and Institutional Act 2020-365 of 30.03.2020.

legal framework was of immediate application, with Article 4 of the statutory law proclaiming a state of emergency for a period of two months.

It was not really this new regime, but rather the more concrete issues, such as the lockdown, that were of concern to the French people. The latter was extended to 15 April 2020, then 11 May, the date on which a progressive ending of the lockdown[10] began according to sectors of activity (restaurants, schools …) and regions (green, orange or red colours indicating the level of ending of the lockdown by department). The (first) general lockdown of the population thus lasted 55 days, from 17 March to 11 May 2020, and until 2 June 2020 and even beyond for Mayotte and French Guiana. Even if certain constraints remained in force (obligation to wear a protective mask on public transport, limitation of travel to a radius of 100 kilometres from home, etc.), with the ending of the lockdown, freedom was once again the rule – travelling without a certificate in particular – and police restriction was the exception.

As for the state of emergency that was imposed on 23 March, it remained in force for almost 16 weeks until 10 July 2020.[11] Then, statutory law 2020-856 of 9 July 2020 implemented a transitional regime to end the state of emergency,[12] authorising the Government to continue to take exceptional measures until 31 October to deal with the epidemic. However, in view of the resumption of the active circulation of the virus after the summer and the 'second wave' of the epidemic, the state-of-emergency regime was once again activated[13] for one month, starting on 17 October 2020. It allowed the introduction of a night curfew policy[14] over a large part of the country. It was not, however, enough to stop the epidemic and a new national lockdown was decreed[15] from 30 October and at least until 1 December 2020, a less strict lockdown than the first so as not to paralyse the economy[16] or aggravate social disparities[17] (keeping schools, businesses and public services open, then reopening shops, etc), but which was to last until 15 December, the date on which a night curfew has been re-imposed.[18] As a result, Parliament had to authorise the extending of the state of emergency.[19] The bill was tabled on 21 October and adopted on 7 November 2020, again in record time,

[10] Decree 2020-548 of 11.05.2020.

[11] Extended by statutory law 2020-546 of 11.05.2020.

[12] Except in French Guiana and Mayotte, where the state of emergency was extended until the end of October 2020.

[13] Decree 2020-1257 of 14.10.2020.

[14] Decree 2020-1262 of 16.10.2020.

[15] Decree 2020-1310 of 29.10.2020.

[16] As of 9 April 2020, the emergency plan to support the economy, which was initially €45 billion, was increased to €100 billion.

[17] One million French people have fallen into poverty during the health crisis.

[18] Decrees 2020-1582 of 14.12.2020 (night curfew from 8 PM to 6 AM) and 2021-31 of 15.01.2021 (from 6 PM to 6 AM). The curfew was then lightened and finally ended on 20 June 2021 (Decree 2021-782 of 18.06.2021).

[19] Statutory law 2020-1379 of 14.11.2020.

but not without tensions.[20] The statutory law extends the state of emergency by three months until 16 February 2021. The senators wanted to reduce the deadline to 31 January 2021 and impose a Parliamentary vote if the lockdown extended beyond 8 December 2020, but they were unsuccessful. The statutory law of 14 November 2020 also extends the transitional regime for ending the state of emergency until 1 April 2021. The senators had abolished the extending of the post-state of public health emergency regime, but the National Assembly reinstated it. Like in March 2020, a series of authorisations to take economic and social measures by way of ordinance completes the statutory law. The senators had reduced the authorisations requested by the government from 70 to 30, but they were not followed by the deputies.[21] With the virus continuing to spread rapidly and the vaccination campaign evolving slowly in France, statutory law 2021-160 of 15 February 2021 has again extended the state of emergency until 1 June 2021. Lastly, statutory law 2021-689 of 31 May 2021 implemented a transitional regime to end the state of emergency, authorising the Government once more to continue to take exceptional measures until 30 September 2021. This gives the executive a free hand to govern the country without parliamentary debate for several more months.

II. Management of the Health Crisis within the Executive

While it is true that the executive leads the dance, it is at the cost of an impaired functioning, as decisions are taken by the highest levels of State on the advice of experts, with the Council of Ministers marginalised.

A. The Council of Ministers, an Echo Chamber

i. The Role of Experts

Interestingly, two councils play a fundamental role in the management of the crisis: A scientific council and the Defence Council.

a. A Scientific Council

At the request of the President of the Republic, a 'COVID-19 Scientific Council' was created on 11 March 2020 by the Minister of Health to inform public

[20] After the failure of the joint committee, the two Houses did not adopt the same text and the statutory law was, therefore, definitively passed by the National Assembly under Article 45, paragraph 4, of the Constitution.

[21] Statutory law 2020-1379 of 14.11.2020 authorising the extension of the state of health emergency and establishing various measures for managing the health crisis, www.legifrance.gouv.fr/dossierlegislatif/JORFDOLE000042452030/.

decision-making on the management of the health situation linked to the coronavirus. This informal council (comprised above all of medical doctors) was added to existing bodies such as the National Public Health Agency, the High Authority for Health, the High Council for Public Health, the Operational Centre for Regulation and Response to Health and Social Emergencies of the Ministry of Health, and the Academy of Medicine. The new scientific council was also backed by another council of experts – some of whom are on both councils – the 'Analysis Research and Expertise Committee', which was created on 24 March 2020 by the Government to advise the public authorities on the follow-up to be given to proposals for innovative scientific, technological and therapeutic approaches.

The scientific council has been criticised because its functioning did not have any legal basis and it lacked legitimacy and transparency. For this reason, the statutory law of 23 March 2020 gave it legislative existence[22] and then the statutory law of 14 November 2020 provided that the council's opinions, formed in application of the two new regimes – the state-of-emergency regime and the regime for ending the state of emergency – were required to be communicated simultaneously to the Prime Minister and the presidents of the National Assembly and the Senate and be published without delay. Since decisions at the highest levels of the State are taken on the basis of those opinions, they are, at the very least, required to be sent to the public institution decision-makers.

b. The Defence Council

The 'National Security and Defence Council' is an inter-ministerial body that reports directly to the presidency of the Republic, as provided for in Article 15 of the Constitution, pursuant to which the President, as head of the armed forces, 'presides over the higher councils and committees of national defence'. The Council was created by decree in 2009,[23] replacing the 'Internal Security Council'. A priori, its role is not to manage a health crisis, as it is competent in matters of national defence. However, the 2009 decree broadened its name and competences.[24]

The Council has three configurations:[25] a plenary configuration, composed of the President of the Republic, the Prime Minister, the Minister of Defence, the Interior, the Economy, the Budget and Foreign Affairs; a restricted configuration, composed of ministers concerned by the agenda; and specialised configurations in specific areas: the national intelligence council, the nuclear armaments council, the ecological defence council (since 2019) and the health defence council, which brings together the ministers of health, of economy and of labour, the director-general of health and the chairman of the scientific council, as well as the President and the Prime Minister. It is within this National Security and Defence Council,

[22] Article L.3131-19 of the Public Health Code (*Code de la santé publique – CSP*). A Decree of 3 April 2020 appointed the chairman and members of the 'committee of scientists'.

[23] Decree 2009-1657 of 24.12.2009.

[24] Art R.1122-1 of the Defence Code ('Planning responses to major crises').

[25] Art R.1122-2 of the Defence Code.

which has met (in restricted or specialised configurations) more than 60 times since February 2020, that the President of the Republic's decisions are taken to combat the coronavirus pandemic.

This mode of operation is criticised, essentially for two reasons. On the one hand, it departs from the usual decision-making process. Draft bills or regulations are, in principle, discussed collegially in the Council of Ministers, under the Presidency of the Republic (Article 9 of the Constitution), and a report is then drawn up by the government spokesperson, in complete transparency and under the control of Members of Parliament and citizens. However, the Council of Ministers no longer plays its role and has become the echo chamber of the National Security and Defence Council. On the other hand, the latter remains first and foremost a Defence Council. The proof of this is that its participants are bound by defence secrecy: nothing is filtered out and no reports are drawn up. Admittedly, the decisions taken are then formally enacted by the Government (decree, order, circular) or by parliament (statutory law), and defence secrecy can also be lifted at the request of a court, as provided for in the Code of Criminal Procedure, but there is no mechanism for political accountability with regard to the justification of what is decided within the Council. The Defence Council has therefore become the principal crisis management tool of the Head of State, but outside the usual institutions of the political system.

ii. Hyper-presidentialism

a. An Isolated President

Surrounded by experts – the members of the two councils above mentioned – who guide him with their opinions and recommendations, Emmanuel Macron has isolated himself and arbitrates alone,[26] outside the Council of Ministers that he presides over and out of touch with his parliamentary majority. He decides on his own and then communicates his decisions to the French people, under the fire of the media.

b. A Powerful President

In substance, he grants himself a competence that he does not have in principle. In the French system, health is within the competence of the Prime Minister and the dedicated minister, not the President. But recourse to the Defence Council allows Emmanuel Macron to circumvent that principle in order to take care of health security himself and thus further strengthen the preponderance of the Head of State – 'hyper-presidentialisation' or 'monarchisation' – already inherent in the spirit of the Fifth Republic since its inception in 1958. In normal times, and even

[26] E Favereau, 'Pour le Président, des avis à tout-va puis des décisions en solo, *Libération* (13 April 2020).

more so in times of crisis, it is not the Prime Minister but the President who 'determines and conducts the policy of the Nation', contrary to what is stated in the wording of Article 20 of the Constitution. The Prime Minister intervenes only in the wake of the President. This is no doubt also why Jean Castex was appointed Prime Minister in July 2020, replacing Edouard Philippe. This high-ranking civil servant has never been a Member of Parliament or a Minister and as merely a locally elected representative and behind-the-scenes coordinator of the strategy for the ending of the lockdown in April 2020, he was totally unknown to the French people. He was, however, required to take on the role of Head of a Government the role of which was to play by ear an unprecedented health crisis.

B. The Proliferation of Government Measures

i. Regulation-making Power and Authorisation to Legislate

The Prime Minister is, at the national level, the principal authority that holds regulatory power (*pouvoir réglementaire*), as 'the Government shall have at its disposal the civil service' (Article 20 of the Constitution) and he is the Head of Government (Article 21[27]). The COVID-19 crisis has increased the regulatory power of the Prime Minister and certain ministers[28] through the acknowledgment of a specific regulatory power in the Prime Minister and some ministers and the authorisation by Parliament for the government to pass measures by ordinance that are normally the preserve of statutory law.

a. Autonomous Regulatory Power and Regulatory Power to Implement Statutory Laws

The decrees and orders issued in March 2020 by the executive before the adoption of the statutory law instituting the public health emergency were based on dual legal grounds.

Article L.3131-1 of the Public Health Code (*Code de la santé publique – CSP –*) allows the Minister of Health to adopt emergency health measures in the event of a serious health threat, such as an epidemic, for example.[29] At the beginning of the crisis, measures were taken pursuant to orders by the Minister of Health on that basis. As the policing powers required are not general but specific, on 13, 14 and 15 March 2020 we witnessed a series of orders by the Minister of Health, with the Prime Minister simply implementing the orders by way of decree. In other

[27] 'The Prime Minister shall direct the action of the Government. […] he shall exercise regulatory power […]'.

[28] See eg JM Pontier, 'La crise sanitaire de 2020 et le droit administratif' (2020) *AJDA* 1692.

[29] See eg D Truchet, 'Covid 19: point de vue d'un administrativiste sanitaire', *Blog Jus Politicum* (27 March 2020).

words, important measures were formally enacted by a minister and not by the most important, ie the Prime Minister.

The process was so inconsistent that the Prime Minister finally issued the lockdown decree of 16 March 2020. The 'theory of exceptional circumstances', shaped by administrative courts during war,[30] which authorises the executive branch to free itself from compliance with the legislation under certain conditions, forms the legal basis of that decree. But the foundation is fragile, which is why the statutory law of 23 March would give the decree a legal basis.

In Articles 2 and 3 of the statutory law of 23 March 2020,[31] the legislator created a specific 'state of public health emergency' (*état d'urgence sanitaire*) regime within the *CSP*.[32] This state of emergency can be declared by decree of the Council of Ministers – on the basis of scientific data and a report by the Health Minister – for all or part of the country in the event of a health disaster that, by its nature and seriousness, endangers the health of the population. In order to guarantee public health, the Prime Minister can then, by decree, take a series of measures that derogate from the law applicable in normal circumstances and that are particularly prejudicial to rights and freedoms (Articles L.3131-12 to 20 of the *CSP*). This extension of the Prime Minister's regulatory power was implemented by the new Article L.3131-15.[33] Between 23 March and 10 July 2020, then from 17 October and until 1 June 2021, the Government measures were taken under that state-of-emergency regime.

As stated above, between these two periods and then from June 2021, another, transitional, regime takes over, namely that of the 'ending' of the state of emergency. It allows the Prime Minister to take numerous binding measures to combat the spread of the COVID-19 epidemic.

b. Authorisation to Legislate by Ordinance (Ordonnance)

With the statutory laws of 23 March, 17 June and 14 November 2020, the Government is largely empowered to adopt 'measures by ordinance that are normally the preserve of statutory law' (Article 34 of the Constitution) in accordance with the procedure in Article 38 of the Constitution.[34] By the end of March 2020,

[30] *Conseil d'État (CE)*, 28 June 1918, No 63412, *Heyriès*.

[31] Statutory law amended by statutory law 2020-546 of 11.05.2020.

[32] See below.

[33] See below.

[34] 'In order to implement its programme, the Government may ask Parliament for authorisation, for a limited period, to take measures by ordinance that are normally the preserve of statutory law. Ordinances shall be issued in the Council of Ministers, after consultation with the *Conseil d'État*. They shall come into force upon publication, but shall lapse in the event of failure to table before Parliament the bill to ratify them by the date set by the authorisation statutory law. They may only be ratified in explicit terms.

At the end of the period referred to in the first paragraph hereinabove ordinances may be amended solely by a statutory law in the subjects that are the preserve of statutory law.'

37 ordinances had already been adopted by the Council of Ministers in the context of the public health emergency. Those ordinances significantly changed many areas of law and daily life (working hours, part-time work, exceptional aid, public procurement, budgetary law, operation of local authorities, justice, criminal law, civil service, competitive examinations and tests, etc). Parliament is thus deprived of its power to enact statutory laws in a scope constitutionally reserved to it.

ii. The Question of the Effectiveness of the Management of the Crisis

a. Criticism of the Policies of the Executive

The action of the Head of State and his Government is criticised not only by the political opposition but also by numerous others.[35] The media have also highlighted various barometers indicating a 'strong mistrust' towards the Government by the French due to its management of the pandemic.[36]

Three major issues arose during 2020.[37] The necessary equipment was not available in sufficient quantities (shortages of protective masks and hydro-alcoholic gel during the 'first wave' of the epidemic, lack of screening tests, respirators, hospital beds, etc), which was not made clear to the French; all available resources were not immediately mobilised (private clinics and laboratories in particular); and official communications were fluctuating, even inconsistent, particularly with regard to the 'test, trace,[38] isolate' method[39] and the wearing of masks by the general public (of no use and then compulsory). Even France's highest administrative court, the *Conseil d'État*, had to adapt and be pragmatic. For example, with regard to the obligation decreed by mayors or prefects (State representatives in the local authorities) to wear masks, in April 2020, the Court considered that such a decision was not possible in the absence of specific local circumstances.[40] In September, on the other hand, the Court considered that the wearing of masks could be imposed in public in widely delimited areas.[41]

[35] See eg the report of the Firefighters' Federation, *Le Monde* (5 July 2020).

[36] J Imad, 'Gestion de crise: pourquoi les Français sont-ils plus défiants à l'égard de leur gouvernement que leurs voisins ?' *Figaro Vox* (20 April 2020).

[37] Others arise in early 2021, in particular concerning the vaccination campaign, with fewer than one million French people vaccinated mid-February 2021: www.covidtracker.fr/vaccintracker/ (updated figures).

[38] '*StopCovid*' (Decree 2020-650 of 29.05.2020) was a failure. The purpose of the application was to inform its users of the risk of contamination in case of proximity with other users who tested positive for COVID-19. Only 2.6 million people downloaded this application in four months. Another application ('*TousAntiCovid*') was, therefore, implemented from October 22 (with a legal basis only as from the Decree 2021-157 of 12.02.2021). More than 12 million people have downloaded the new application in February 2021.

[39] Method that, on 24 November 2020, becomes (in the televised speech by the President): 'test, alert, protect, care': Address to the French (24 November 2020) www.elysee.fr/emmanuel-macron/2020/11/24/adresse-aux-francais-24-novembre.

[40] *CE ord* (summary order), 17 April 2020, No 440057.

[41] *CE ord*, 6 September 2020, Nos 443750 and 443751.

The unpreparedness of the French State was compared to the more effective crisis management carried out simultaneously in Germany or Japan. More broadly, the health crisis revealed the inadequacies of our health system, which had been undermined by budgetary reforms over the past 20 years, and France's over-dependence on a globalised economy.

b. Criminal Proceedings

In addition to the dozens of complaints filed against government bodies (ministries, Public Health France, etc) for involuntary homicide and injury, endangering the lives of others and failure to fight against a disaster, nearly 100 complaints were filed against ministers and former ministers[42] in the Court of Justice of the Republic (*Cour de Justice de la République*), which is responsible for judging the criminal liability of ministers for acts carried out in the exercising of their duties (Part X of the Constitution). The Court will have to determine whether their management of the public health crisis linked to the pandemic includes criminal offences. In particular, the ministers are accused of concealing the shortage of masks and maintaining the first round of the municipal elections. As part of the judicial investigation commenced by the Court, on 15 October 2020 the ministries as well as the homes of former Prime Minister, Edouard Philippe, the current Minister of Health, Olivier Véran, his predecessor in that position, Agnès Buzyn, the former government spokesperson and the Director General of Health were searched by police from the central office for the fight against environmental and public health damage.

These actions, spectacular and the focus of media attention, illustrate a current trend in society, that of the criminalisation of public life. Criminal law is over-solicited, based on the logic that the same law should apply to everyone; ministers are thus treated as 'vulgar common criminals'.[43] These criminal charges are, however, not appropriate. On the one hand, according to the principle of the division of powers, justice should not prevent the executive branch from functioning and the 'representatives of the State' should be given specific protection.[44] On the other hand, the dysfunction of a Government in the management of public affairs must be subject to political accountability. In other words, political accountability and criminal liability should not be confused, which is why the charges against the ministers will most likely be dismissed by the Court.

The mode of governance within the executive is unprecedented and raises many substantive and procedural questions. Democratic life is the other

[42] However, the President benefits from political and legal immunity (Art 67 of the Constitution).

[43] See eg O Beaud, 'Mal gouverner est-il un crime? Réflexions critiques sur les perquisitions effectuées dans le cadre de l'enquête judiciaire relative aux ministres impliqués dans la gestion de l'épidémie du Coronavirus' *Blog de Jus Politicum* (21 October 2020).

[44] O Beaud, 'La responsabilité administrative de l'État comme modèle de la responsabilité de droit public' in D Chagnollaud (ed), *Responsabilité pénale et vie publique en France et à l'étranger* (LGDJ, 2002) 89.

collateral victim of the methods used to manage the public health crisis, insofar as Parliament, in particular, but also locally elected representatives, are marginalised and downgraded.

III. Putting Democracy in Parentheses in Times of Crisis

Already under normal circumstances, Parliament is weakened, and the decentralised authorities often lack the resources to exercise their powers. This structural tendency in the Fifth Republic is accentuated in this period of public health crisis.

A. The Weakening of Parliament

Article 24 of the Constitution provides that Parliament fulfils two main tasks. On the one hand, it 'shall pass statutory laws'. On the other hand, it 'shall control the actions of the Government' and 'assess public policies'. These two missions have been undermined, however, because Parliament has been doubly sidelined since the beginning of the epidemic.

i. The Deprivation of the Power to Create Statutory Laws

In the framework of the state-of-emergency regime, in addition to empowering the government to legislate by ordinance, Parliament transfers all prescriptive power to the executive.

a. Existing Bases were Possible but Rejected

Although clearly the legislature had to intervene to enable the executive to act as a matter of urgency, the issue arises, and will no doubt arise for a long time to come, of the need, and even the usefulness, of creating a new emergency regime.[45] Two existing legislative bases[46] could have been indeed exploited.

The Members of Parliament could have relied on statutory law 55-385 of 3 April 1955 on the 'state of emergency'[47] – even if they had to amend it again – because one of its two conditions, in addition to that of 'imminent risk resulting

[45] See eg S Renard, 'L'état d'urgence sanitaire: droit d'exception et exceptions au droit' (2020) *RDLF* 13.

[46] But none constitutional bases: neither Art 16 (presidential exceptional powers in the event of other serious threats), nor Art 36 (state of siege in the event of foreign war or armed insurrection, which implies a transfer of various powers from the civilian to the military authority) of the Constitution were adapted to the 2020 health crises.

[47] This exceptional regime had been adopted to counter the Algerian insurrection. It was applied in Algeria in 1955 and 1961-62, in France in 1958, in New Caledonia in 1985, in Wallis and Futuna in 1986, in Polynesia in 1987, in 25 departments in 2005 during the civil riots in the suburbs, then

from serious breaches of public order', is the existence of 'events that, by their nature and seriousness, have the characteristics of a public calamity'. And a pandemic is indeed such an event.

The legislator could also have relied on Art. L.3131-1 of the *CSP* cited above – which was only slightly amended by the statutory law of 23 March 2020 – under which it is incumbent on the Minister of Health, 'in the event of a serious health threat requiring emergency measures', to 'prescribe, in the interest of public health, any measure that is proportionate to the risks involved and appropriate to the time and place in order to prevent and limit the consequences of possible threats to the health of the population'. The legislator could have supplemented that Article by specifying, for example, that jurisdiction was now shared with the Prime Minister in the event of a health disaster. Such a reform of the *CSP* would have been a way to remedy the exclusive competence of the Minister of Health in health emergencies and legal consolidate the Prime Minister's lockdown decree of 16 March 2020. However, the Members of Parliament preferred to establish a brand-new legal basis for action.

b. The New Basis for Action

Under pressure of Government and in an emergency situation, the legislator chose to create a new legal basis for major crisis. In other words, the health emergency police – the specific police powers of the Minister of Health – is supposed to be a police dedicated to the prevention of a mere health 'threat'. Furthermore, the state of public health emergency – the specific police powers of the Prime Minister – is supposed to be applied when the threat is no longer a 'threat' and the 'disaster' endangering the health of the population (new Article L.3131-12 of the *CSP*) is proven, thus opening the way to more restrictive measures which are prejudicial to rights and freedoms.[48] However, there is nothing to prevent the Minister of Health from taking, before or after the state of emergency, measures that are equivalent (lockdown, isolation, quarantine, etc) to those that could be imposed by the Prime Minister in the framework of the state of emergency. More precisely, the

between November 2015 and November 2017 following the terrorist attacks in Paris; the 1955 statutory law was then amended by statutory laws 2015-1501 of 20 November 2015 and 2016-987 of 21 July 2016. Afterwards, a new anti-terrorism legislation was adopted (statutory law 2017-1510 of 30 October 2017), which created a de facto permanent state of emergency. See eg O Beaud and C Guérin-Bargues, *L'état d'urgence. Étude constitutionnelle, historique et critique* (LGDJ, 2016, 2nd edn, 2018). The work shows not only how the state of emergency affects relations between public authorities, with administrative power dominating the legislative and jurisdictional branches, but also how it affects freedoms in ways that, under normal circumstances, would be contrary to law.

[48] This is also the justification put forward by the *Conseil d'État* in the opinion (*avis*) No 399873 of 18 March 2020: 'the existence of a health disaster makes it useful to have a special state-of-emergency regime in order to have an organised and clear framework for intervention in such cases'.

scope of the new Chapter I *bis*, entitled 'state of public health emergency' (Articles L.3131-12 to 20 *CSP*) is twofold. Article 7 of the statutory law of 23 March 2020 provides that that Chapter is applicable until 1 April 2021 – then until 1 June 2021 since the statutory law 2021-160 of 15 February 2021 – in the current specific context of the COVID-19 crisis, with numerous Government authorisations to adopt adaptation measures by way of ordinance. But the mechanism governing the new specific state of emergency is also and above all now permanently codified in the legislation. The issue therefore arises as to whether it is possible to multiply *ad infinitum* emergency regimes, the aim of which is to transfer all prescriptive power to the executive for the resolution of crises.[49]

ii. *Restraints on Political Control Over the Government*

a. Insufficiently Reinforced Oversight

Logically, parliamentary oversight should be strengthened during a state of emergency. This is, moreover, what is provided for in Article 4-1 of the statutory law of 3 April 1955 cited above, with an increased obligation for the Government and the administrative authorities to inform the National Assembly and the Senate. In addition, and to emphasise the abnormal and necessarily temporary nature of the state of emergency, which may be declared by a decree of the Council of Ministers, Article 2 provides that after a period of 12 days, a statutory law must authorise its extension.[50]

The health emergency bill of 2020 was presented by the political majority as being inspired by that 1955 statutory law. The text adopted therefore clearly provides for increased parliamentary oversight, with both Houses having to be informed 'without delay of the measures taken by the Government' under the state of emergency and being able to 'request any additional information in the context of the oversight and evaluation of those measures' (new Article L.3131-13 of the *CSP*). However, that control is less stringent than that provided for in the 1955 statutory law.[51] Article 4 of the new law states that a state of emergency 'is declared throughout the national territory for a period of two months' (a derogatory duration in the current case) from the entry into force of the statutory law. After these two months, Parliament must authorise its extension. And as regards the future, the general 'state of public health emergency' system does not envisage any such intervention by Parliament before the (long) one-month period has elapsed: the

[49] See eg P Cassia, 'L'état d'urgence sanitaire, remède, placebo ou venin juridique?' *Mediapart* (24 March 2020).

[50] This is also the case with regard to the extension of another specific exceptional regime, the 'state of siege cited above' (Art 36 of the Constitution).

[51] What is most surprising is that it was the *Conseil d'État* which, in the opinion on the bill, recommended changes unfavourable to political control over the government by Parliament.

new Article L.3131-13 of the *CSP* provides that a state of emergency 'is declared by decree of the Council of Ministers' and that its extension 'beyond one month' must be authorised by legislation, after consultation with the scientific council.[52] Thus, in the event of a health disaster, Parliament is excluded for a period (one month) that is longer than in the event of terrorism or war (12 days).

b. Parliamentarians' Attempt to Respond

Deputies and senators reacted and immediately seized the tools at their disposal in order to inform themselves and exercise political control over the governmental action. In addition to question sessions with the Government, the most effective tool is that of commissions of enquiry. Since the constitutional reform of 23 July 2008, their existence has been enshrined in Article 51-2 of the Constitution, which provides that 'committees of enquiry may be set up within each House to gather […] information'. In addition, since a review of the Rules of Procedure of the National Assembly in 2003, the Conference of Presidents may create 'temporary fact-finding missions' on a proposal by the President of the National Assembly. A fact-finding mission was thus set up on 17 March 2020 in the National Assembly on the management and consequences of the COVID-19 epidemic. From 2 June, it was given the prerogatives of a committee of enquiry for six months. The Senate also set up its committee of enquiry on 30 June 2020 to evaluate public policies in the face of major pandemics in the light of the COVID-19 health crisis and its management. The ministers, including the former and new prime ministers, and other public decision-makers and experts have thus been convoked to explain to Members of Parliament their management of the health crisis.

It should, however, be emphasised that these parliamentary initiatives were clearly in competition with an initiative by the President of the Republic who, on 25 June 2020, entrusted a 'fact-finding mission' to a Swiss expert, who, together with other scientists, were instructed to analyse how the French executive had managed the COVID-19 crisis.[53] His mission, therefore, exactly overlapped that carried out by the national representative body under the Constitution. By the way, the fact-finding mission of the National Assembly was suddenly dissolved on 27 January 2021, a very criticised decision taken by the political majority, qualified as a 'democratic sinking' or a 'democratic treason' by all opposition parties.[54] Here again, the formal institutions and procedures are bypassed, in favour of an expertise commissioned by the Head of State.

[52] However, if the public health emergency ceases to exist, it can be terminated by decree of the Council of Ministers before its expiry.

[53] The final report was published in March 2021: www.vie-publique.fr/sites/default/files/rapport/pdf/279851.pdf.

[54] M Darame, 'Les oppositions protestent contre la dissolution de la mission d'information de l'Assemblée nationale sur le Covid-19' *Le Monde* (28 January 2021).

B. Centralised Management of Local Affairs

i. A Uniform Policy Throughout the National Territory

a. The Centralisation/Decentralisation Dialectic

France is a unitary State, an 'indivisible Republic' that 'shall ensure the equality of all citizens before the law'. But its organisation is 'decentralised' (Article 1 of the Constitution). Consequently, the principle of self-government by local authorities (communes, departments, regions) through their elected councils (Article 72 of the Constitution) multiplies the decision-making centres and local specificities.[55]

The health crisis has accentuated an already strong trend over the last 15 years, that of the recentralisation of power, such recentralisation being particularly marked in the field of health.[56] Thus, the State alone directed the management of the coronavirus crisis without relying on local democracy.

b. Crisis Management and Centralism

The centralised and uniform exceptional law on health emergencies prevents local initiatives or coordinates them with those of the State.[57] In particular, while a municipality could present itself as a priority area in order to ensure the exercising of the policing powers in the event of an epidemic, mayors are largely excluded.[58] More broadly, local authorities are not able to use the regulatory power conferred on them by the Constitution (Article 72) to take appropriate local measures. From the very first months of the health crisis, local authorities did take action, often symbolic, at their own level, for example by ordering masks for their inhabitants[59] or by providing material or financial assistance. Some mayors went further and tightened the lockdown (Paris, Nice, Perpignan) or imposed the wearing of masks in the city centre (Strasbourg) by municipal order – on the basis of the general police powers of the mayor – but still under the authority of prefects – on the basis of the specific police powers of the State in the event of a health crisis – and under the control of the administrative courts.[60]

No commune, department, region or metropolis was, therefore, able to play a significant role in the fight against the pandemic, which caused incomprehension

[55] In addition, since 2010, decentralisation has been coupled with a policy of inter-communalisation (notably with the creation of metropolises). The result is a complex institutional superimposition, a vector of duplication and heaviness, described as a 'multi-layered system' (*millefeuille territorial*).

[56] Social competences were indeed transferred to the departments in 1982, but a recentralisation took place in 2004. The State became 'solely responsible for campaigns to prevent and combat major diseases', for reasons of 'efficiency' and in order to guarantee 'equal access to care': J-M Pontier, 'La santé, entre centralisation et décentralisation' (2019) 4 *RDSS* 669.

[57] B Faure, 'Théorie et pratique des compétences des collectivités territoriales face à la crise sanitaire' (2020) *AJDA* 1727.

[58] See eg O Renaudie, 'La police administrative aux temps du coronavirus' (2020) *AJDA*, 1704.

[59] Action that was possible after the State had lifted its ban (Decree 2020-285 of 21 March 2020).

[60] See above (case law on the obligation to wear a mask).

among the population and might have partly explained the high abstention rate during the municipal (2020), departmental and regional (2021) elections.

ii. A Minimalist Differentiation

a. During the Crisis

Although various decisions were made on a territorial basis, they were not taken by elected representatives of local authorities. It was the central State that, on the ending of the first lockdown for example, established zones (green, orange or red) depending on the speed of circulation of the virus in the different areas. And it was the prefects, the State representatives in the departments and regions, who were empowered to adopt 'more restrictive measures' where required by 'local circumstance'. For example, on the basis of Article 2 of the Decree of 16 March 2020 on the first lockdown, on 21 March 2020, the prefect of the *Alpes-Maritimes* decreed a night curfew throughout the department.

b. After the Crisis?

Once the health emergency is over, the role of local authorities and metropoles will undoubtedly be especially important when it comes to implementing locally adapted economic, social, cultural and tourism policies to manage the consequences of the crisis and attempt to mitigate its impacts. But they still need to have the financial resources to do so.

Faced with a weakened democracy at both national and local level, checks and balances to executive power could come from the courts. However, the jurisdictional guarantee of legality and freedoms does not seem to play the full role it should have, and the rule of law is consequently weakened.

IV. Distorting the Rule of Law in the Name of the State of Emergency

Due to the 'specific circumstances' linked to the pandemic, even the constitutional judges (*Conseil constitutionnel*) did not censure (ex ante review) new legislative provisions that were nonetheless contrary to the Constitution. It remains to be seen what their position will be when they rule (ex post review) on the applications for a priority preliminary ruling on the issue of constitutionality (*QPC*, Article 61-1 of the Constitution[61]) on provisions that are potentially prejudicial to rights and freedoms.

[61] The application for a priority preliminary ruling on the issue of constitutionality, introduced under the constitutional reform of 23 July 208, is 'the right for any person who is involved in legal

A. The Breaching of the Constitution

The Institutional Act of 30 March 2020 was referred prior to enactment (ex ante) to the *Conseil constitutionnel* pursuant to Article 46, paragraph 5, and Article 61, paragraph 1, of the Constitution (mandatory referral). In the decision 2020-799 *DC* of 26 March 2020, the Act is declared to be in conformity with the Constitution, which may come as a surprise.

i. *Suspension of the Time Limits for the Examination of a QPC*

a. Subject

In terms of substance, the single Article of the Institutional Act, which is not directly linked to the prevention of the spread of COVID-19, suspends until 30 June 2020 the two time limits that are, in principle, required for the examination of a *QPC*: the first (mandatory) three-month period at the end of which the highest non-constitutional administrative and judicial courts (*Conseil d'État* and *Cour de cassation*) must transmit a *QPC* to the *Conseil constitutionnel*,[62] and the second (indicative) three-month period, during which the latter is invited to rule on the issue.[63]

b. Purpose

The aim is to suspend the time limits for the highest non-constitutional courts at a time when the courts are placed on standby due to the lockdown because, after three months, those courts must automatically (*ipso jure*) transmit the *QPC* that they have not ruled to the constitutional judges. A failure to suspend the three-month period might, therefore, have led to a possible bottleneck in the *Conseil constitutionnel*, which is why the *Conseil constitutionnel* validated in the 26 March 2020 decision the suspension of the time limits. However, the issue remains as to whether such suspension is not directly contrary to Article 61-1 of the Constitution, which provides that a 'determined time limit', in this case that required by the ordinance of 7 November 1958, must be respected.

Moreover, the interest of suspending the time limit for the examination of the *QPCs* before the *Conseil constitutionnel* is less understandable, as a failure to comply with the said time limit does not entail any consequences or sanctions.

proceedings before a court to argue that a statutory provision infringes rights and freedoms guaranteed by the Constitution'. The *Conseil constitutionnel*, 'to whom the application will have been referred by the *Conseil d'Etat* or the *Cour de cassation*, will give its ruling and, if need be, repeal the challenged statutory provision', www.conseil-constitutionnel.fr/en/selection-of-qpc-decisions.

[62] Article 61-1 of the Constitution requires a 'determined time limit' (but without further specification).

[63] These two deadlines are referred to in ordinance 58-1067 of 7 November 1958 on *Conseil constitutionnel*.

Lastly and more generally, the issue may arise as to whether such exceptional suspension of the two deadlines was truly necessary and urgent.

ii. Unconstitutionality of the Procedure

a. Breach of the Constitution

With regard to the procedure for adopting the Institutional Act, the *Conseil constitutionnel* did not sanction the breach, however manifest, of paragraph 2 of Article 46 of the Constitution. Where the accelerated procedure has been initiated under the conditions provided for in Article 45 paragraph 2, which was the case here, that Article 46 paragraph 2 provides that the bill 'cannot be submitted for deliberation by the first House to which it is referred before the expiry of a period of fifteen days after its submission'. That deadline was not, however, respected, as the bill was tabled on 18 March 2020 and voted on by the Senate and the National Assembly in the following three days.

b. Justification

The *Conseil constitutionnel* considered that the 'specific circumstances in the instant case' preclude a finding of unconstitutionality. The reasoning (the indirect reference to the theory of exceptional circumstances in administrative law) and the wording (the constitutional judges seem to imply that they are judges of facts, whereas their review of the legal rules is abstract) are very curious and questionable. The constitutional judges confuse their role with that of the administrative courts and in so doing, moreover, allow themselves not to apply the Constitution, which is their legal rule of reference. They implicitly assert (on what basis?) that their decisions have a higher value than that of the Constitution that they are supposed to be the guardian of. Thus, in that incomprehensible decision, the *Conseil constitutionnel* breached the Constitution and created an irreversible breach in the rule of law.

B. Breaches of Rights and Freedoms

The new state of emergency extends the specific policing powers of the Prime Minister, the Minister of Health and the prefects. It defines a regime that is very restrictive in terms of civil liberties, which is justified by the courts. In particular, the *Conseil d'État* validates the fact that the state-of-emergency regime, which is 'useful' in the event of a proven health disaster, gives 'the Prime Minister the possibility of taking the most restrictive measures for freedoms'.[64]

[64] Opinion No 399873 of 18 March 2020.

i. The Choice of Extended Policing Powers Potentially Prejudicial to Freedoms

Periods of major crisis inevitably lead to restrictions on rights and freedoms and there cannot be any real objection to the principle of inevitable restrictions. The question is how far they can go. With regard to the COVID-19 pandemic, the difficulty is to know how to reconcile the 'objective' set by the *Conseil constitutionnel* (*objectif de valeur constitutionnelle*) of the protection of health with the respect for fundamental freedoms. The measures taken in France by the Minister of Health and the Prime Minister from March 2020 onwards may, however, have sacrificed the substance of the latter.[65]

a. The Concerns of the Senators

Article 2 of the statutory law of 23 March 2020 refers to 'exceptional circumstances' that justify the restriction of rights and freedoms. However, the Senate sought to provide a better framework for the prerogatives granted to the Prime Minister. While the bill merely stated that the declaration of the state of emergency gave him the power to take 'general measures limiting the freedom to come and go, the freedoms to act and meet and allowing him to proceed with the requisition of all necessary goods and services', an exhaustive list of possible regulatory measures was introduced by the senators. That list now appears in Article L.3131-15 of the *CSP*. Pursuant to that Article, the Prime Minister can, on the basis of a report by the Minister of Health and 'for the sole purpose of guaranteeing public health':

1. restrict or prohibit the movement of persons and vehicles in the places and at the times fixed by decree;
2. prohibit people from leaving their homes, subject to travel that is strictly necessary for family or health needs;
3. order measures that are for the purpose of quarantining [...] persons likely to be affected by the virus;
4. order measures for the placement and maintenance of the affected persons in isolation [...], in their homes or any other suitable accommodation;
5. order the temporary closure of one or more categories of establishments receiving the public as well as meeting places, with the exception of establishments providing essential goods or services;
6. limit or prohibit gatherings in public and meetings of any kind;
7. order the requisition of all goods and services necessary for the fight against the health disaster as well as any person necessary for the functioning of such services or the use of such goods [...];
8. take temporary measures to control the prices of certain products in order to prevent or correct tensions observed for certain products on the market [...];
9. if necessary, take any measure to ensure that patients have access to appropriate medicines to eradicate the health disaster.

[65] See eg P Wachsmann, 'Les libertés et les mesures prises pour lutter contre la propagation du COVID-19: sanctuariser le noyau dur des libertés' *Le club des juristes* (13 May 2020).

The list validated by the Senate contains considerable powers that are, therefore, limited to these nine points.

b. Government Requirements

Under pressure from the Government the deputies adopted an amendment that adds a very general, imprecise and open tenth point to that list, according to which the Prime Minister can 'where necessary, decree any other regulatory measure limiting the freedom to act'.[66] Admittedly, such measures can be taken only 'for the sole purpose of ending the health disaster' and must, therefore, comply with the requirements of administrative and constitutional case law, that means be strictly adapted and proportionate. The statutory law thus supplemented gives actually the Head of government policing powers on a scale not seen since the Act on Health Police of 3-9 March 1822, which was enacted to counter the yellow fever epidemic. This is evidenced by the fact that the National Consultative Commission for Human Rights and the Defender of Rights published an opinion on the former[67] and a letter addressed to Members of Parliament on the latter[68] expressing their concerns about the impact of the state of emergency on democratic life and freedoms.

In addition, the Government retains significant policing powers when the state of emergency is 'lifted', as provided for in the statutory law of 9 July 2020.[69] This transitional regime, which links the emergency regime and the ordinary-law regime, allows the Prime Minister and prefects to adopt restrictive measures to curb the spread of the coronavirus epidemic: limiting movements (lockdown is therefore possible) and gatherings of people in public and in places open to the public, regulating the opening of establishments receiving the public or requiring travellers using public air transport to or from France to present a negative COVID-19 test.

ii. Litigations on the State of Emergency and the Protection of Rights and Freedoms

Faced with this unprecedented factual and legal context, the courts have already had the opportunity to decide certain issues but, above all, they will be creating a body of case law that is sure to be abundant in the months and years to come.

[66] Moreover, such regulations do not prevent complementary measures adopted by the Minister of Health (Art L.3131-16 *CSP*) or the prefects. The latter may be empowered to take all general or individual measures appropriate for the implementation of national decisions (Art L.3131-17 *CSP*) and may even, in the event that the state of emergency only concerns a limited area not exceeding the area of a department, be empowered to initially intervene in order to take the measures listed in points 1 to 9 of Art L.3131-15.

[67] 'État d'urgence sanitaire et État de droit', *JORF* 0108 (3 May 2020) text No 49.

[68] Letter of 2 May 2020, www.defenseurdesdroits.fr/sites/default/files/atoms/files/courrier_au_parlement_-_3_mai_2020_-_prorogation_de_letat_durgence_sanitaire_0.pdf.

[69] Statutory law validated by the *Conseil constitutionnel* in the decision 2020-803 *DC* of 9 July 2020.

a. The Position of the *Conseil Constitutionnel*

The *Conseil constitutionnel*, to which the statutory law of 23 March 2020 was not referred in the context of the ex ante review, can censor it on the occasion of a *QPC*, as the *Conseil* did with regard to legislative provisions on the 'state of emergency' provided for in the 1955 statutory law.[70] The judges may also be called on to rule on the conformity of various ordinances with the rights and freedoms guaranteed by the Constitution, in particular ordinances that have made significant changes to court procedures, such as the extension of time limits.[71]

The 2020 statutory law extending the new state of emergency was, nonetheless, referred to the *Conseil constitutionnel* just after its adoption. In the decision 2020-800 *DC* of 11 May 2020, the *Conseil* attempts to reconcile the requirements of public health order with a respect for rights and freedoms. With regard, for example, to the use of digital technology for health purposes – the 'tracing' of people affected by COVID-19 and their contacts – the judges strongly emphasise the importance of the right to privacy and medical confidentiality.[72]

b. The Case Law of the Administrative Courts

For the time being, it is principally the administrative courts that arbitrate under urgency in order to determine whether various rights (to privacy, expression, etc) and freedoms (to come and go, meet, demonstrate, worship, act, etc) are sufficiently respected within the framework of the state of emergency. Article L.3131-18 of the *CSP* specifies that the measures taken in the event of a health emergency may be the subject of summary proceedings (temporary suspension – *référé-suspension* – or safeguarding freedom – *référé-liberté* –) in the administrative courts. Appeals immediately flooded in and the summary proceedings judge at the *Conseil d'État* issued numerous decisions, which can be easily consulted online as the Court has classified them in chronological order on its website.[73]

In some cases, the *Conseil d'État* has decided in favour of public health order. Thus, at the beginning of the first lockdown, the *Conseil* rejects an application by a union of young doctors for a total lockdown of the population but forces the Government to provide details concerning the certificate for derogatory travel

[70] Six total or partial censorships out of nine *QPCs*. See eg decision 2017-684 *QPC* of 11 January 2018: the *Conseil constitutionnel* notes the lack of a balanced reconciliation between the need to protect public order and the freedom to come and go, as the statutory law, due to its imprecision, has allowed a prefect to establish a 'protection zone' around a migrant camp.

[71] eg, two *QPCs* have been sent to the *Conseil constitutionnel* by the *Cour de cassation* on 3 November 2020 concerning the automatic extension of pre-trial detention provided for in Art 16 of ordinance 2020-303 of 25 March 2020. The *Conseil constitutionnel* considers (decision 2020-878/879 QPC of 29 January 2021) that this Article is contrary to the prohibition on arbitrary detention and individual freedom guaranteed by Art 66 of the Constitution in that it automatically extends the effects of pre-trial detention orders without court intervention.

[72] See also decision 2020-808 *DC* of 13 November 2020 on the statutory law of 14 November 2020.

[73] 'Dernières décisions (référés) en lien avec l'épidémie de covid-19', www.conseil-etat.fr/.

(travel for 'health reasons' and 'short' commutes).[74] The judges also reject an application from sports professionals who want sports facilities to reopen[75] and do not suspend the closure of bookshops.[76] They also reject an application against curfews[77] and refuse to suspend restrictions on gatherings in places of worship during the second lockdown.[78] It should also be noted that the *Conseil d'État*, to which was referred the merits of an application for annulment of a provision in decree 2020-293 of 23 March 2020 prescribing the general measures necessary to deal with the epidemic, considered that the lockdown was not in the nature of an individual deprivation of liberty within the meaning of Article 66 of the Constitution. In other words, lockdown is not house arrest.[79]

In other decisions, the *Conseil d'État* ensures that rights and freedoms are protected, the limitation of freedoms being possible only if it respects the principles of strict necessity, an adaptation to the circumstances of time and place, proportionality to the health risks incurred and non-discrimination. For example, the judges protect the right to asylum by requiring the re-registration of asylum applications, especially for vulnerable persons.[80] They protect the freedom to cycle by asking the Government to clearly specify the possibility of the use of a bike for authorised travel during lockdown.[81] In other notable decisions, they protect the fundamental freedom to demonstrate in public. They suspend the obligation to obtain prior authorisation before organising demonstrations.[82] They also sanction the general and absolute ban on demonstrations imposed by a decree that prohibited gatherings, meetings or activities involving more than 10 people in public areas: a demonstration could be banned only in the event of a breach of public order, including public health order (absence of 'protective gestures'), or when particular circumstances so required, which was not the instant situation as the circulation of the virus was at the time decreasing.[83] Lastly, a summary order should be cited in which the *Conseil d'État* orders the State to immediately cease police surveillance by drone on the grounds that the capturing of images by drone constitutes the processing of personal data and must be accompanied by sufficient guarantees.[84]

[74] *CE ord*, 22 March 2020, No 439674. See the criticisms by X Dupré de Boulois: 'On nous change notre .... référé-liberté' (2020) *RDLF* chron. No 12.

[75] *CE ord*, 16 October 2020, Nos 445102, 445186, 445224, 445225.

[76] *CE ord*, 13 November 2020, Nos 445883, 445886, 445899.

[77] *CE ord*, 23 October 2020, No 445430.

[78] *CE ord*, 7 November 2020, Nos 445827 et al (21 applications). On 18 May 2020 (Nos 440361-440511, 440366 et seq, 440512, 440519), on the other hand, the court protects the freedom of worship by ordering the Government, at the beginning of the (first) ending of the lockdown, to lift the general and absolute ban on assembly in places of worship and enact measures strictly proportionate and appropriate to the health risks.

[79] *CE*, 22 July 2020, No 440149, *Cassia et al.*

[80] *CE ord*, 30 April 2020, Nos 440250 and 440253.

[81] *CE ord*, 30 April 2020, No 440179.

[82] *CE ord*, 6 July 2020, Nos 441257, 441263 and 441384.

[83] *CE ord*, 13 June 2020, Nos 440846, 440856 and 441015.

[84] *CE ord*, 18 May 2020, Nos 440442, 440445.

V. Conclusion

The French management of the health crisis disrupts since March 2020 the usual democratic decision-making processes, in so far as neither the Members of Parliament nor locally elected representatives, but various experts (scientific council, Defence Council, Swiss expert, private consulting firms[85] …) without any democratic legitimacy surround President Macron, who decides on his own what measures must be taken by ministers and by the political majority in Parliament. The President of the Republic has further decided to create from 16 January 2021 an additional new tool, the 'Citizens' Collective' – made up of 35 citizens selected at random – in charge of sharing preoccupations and proposals concerning the vaccination campaign against the COVID-19. The question arises as to whether the 233 members of the 'Economic, Social and Environmental Council' (Title XI of the Constitution) designated by various bodies and who have practically set up the 'Collective' couldn't have themselves taken on this role.

Under the pretext of an exception, not only democracy but also the Constitution and the guarantee of rights and freedoms have been undermined. The robustness of a democracy and the rule of law can, in particular, be assessed in exceptional circumstances, which test the coherence of a legal, political, economic, social and sanitary system. From this point of view, it is fairly obvious that France was not prepared to face and manage a health crisis of such magnitude.[86] In an emergency a hyper-centralised response outside the normal functioning of the institutions has been improvised.

The risks are the normalisation of emergency regimes and the permanency of exceptional measures within the standardised rule of law, so that these regimes and measures remain insidiously in force even without any emergency nor exceptional circumstances. That's why it remains to be seen whether the legislator and the courts will take back control in the coming months so that the ending of exceptional regimes can lead to a return to a more balanced, shared and protective decision-making system. It also remains to be seen whether the lessons drawn from the crisis and its haphazard management will be learnt, both politically and legally.

[85] eg, the American firm McKinsey is in charge of the French vaccination strategy, *ie* a sovereign function: R Besse Desmoulières 'Vaccination contre le Covid-19: le gouvernement a fait appel à quatre cabinets de conseil', *Le Monde* (7 January 2021).

[86] The figures prove this: more than 5,7 million confirmed COVID-19 cases, more than 111,000 deaths and not even 24,900 million people full vaccinated as of 7 July 2021, www.santepubliquefrance.fr/dossiers/coronavirus-covid-19/coronavirus-chiffres-cles-et-evolution-de-la-covid-19-en-france-et-dans-le-monde. The measures implemented have led to a stabilisation in the number of new positive cases in March 2021, but a third wave occurred in May, and a fourth one in summer 2021.

PART III

Beyond States: Democratic Governance in Times of COVID-19

11

Pandemics, Expertise and Deliberation at the International Level

PEDRO A VILLARREAL

I. Introduction

On 22 and 23 January 2020, a group of 19 people gathered in a conference room in Geneva, Switzerland, some in person and some online, where a closed-door meeting was held. These people have a professional background in medicine, public health or closely related areas.[1] A couple of weeks prior, a new virus had been identified in humans in Wuhan, China, causing major epidemics throughout the country.[2] There were reports that people had been infected in other countries as well. Against this backdrop, the group of 19 had to deliberate on whether an emergency should be declared or not, and what type of health measures were the most appropriate for constraining the spread of the virus. It would serve as a warning for the international community of states, namely that there is a risk of cross-border spread of the virus requiring a coordinated response. Preliminary guidance on the best ways to deal with the threat was also at stake.

Yet the decision by these people also carried pitfalls. Unnecessarily sounding the alarm or recommending excessive measures might lead to a plethora of negative consequences, including fearmongering and an overreaction by authorities from other states. It could unnecessarily disrupt international travel and trade, triggering major economic damage and altering peoples' mobility.

The two-day meeting in Geneva did not yield a definitive result. For reasons initially undisclosed to the public, opinions on the matter were almost evenly split. A slight majority favoured refraining from raising the alarm, mostly because they considered that they didn't have sufficient information to reach a final outcome. Instead, the attendants requested additional data from Chinese authorities.

[1] See the list of attendants at the meeting at www.who.int/groups/covid-19-ihr-emergency-committee.

[2] C Wang, P Horby, F Hayden and G Gao, 'A novel coronavirus outbreak of global concern' (2020) 395 *The Lancet* 470, 470–71.

At a press conference, an announcement was circulated stating that the meeting would reconvene one week later.[3]

On the scheduled date for resuming the Emergency Committee's work, 30 January 2020, more information was available. The virus continued to spread to other countries. The members now unambiguously affirmed in unison: the spread of the new coronavirus should be declared a public health emergency of international concern. They issued this recommendation to the person with the authority to issue the formal declaration, the World Health Organization (WHO)'s Director-General. He correspondingly heeded the Committee's advice and issued the corresponding declaration, a legal power granted by the International Health Regulations (IHR) of 2005.[4] The world was now formally facing a public health emergency of international concern due to the spread of a new coronavirus.

The process of deliberation described above depicts the workings of the WHO's Emergency Committee. It is composed of a handpicked group of experts with the legal mandate to give advice to the Director-General. Although they do not have the ultimate say, in practice their views have been followed without exception.[5]

As proven by the catastrophic events of COVID-19 during 2020, the subject matter is unquestionably one of global concern. Yet the proceedings of the WHO's Emergency Committee raise key questions related to multiple political elements of the decision-making process. Given how Committee members are tasked with such a consequential matter, their engagement with the public at large begs for scrutiny. One of the major questions is whether democratic principles play any role at all. Considering the WHO is a specialised agency of the United Nations, and that its main foundational treaty – the Constitution of the WHO[6] – is the outcome of ratifications by Member States, the link to the public at large is more distant than that of national authorities. Consequently, they may seem not only physically, but also politically remote from most individuals in the world. Yet it is manifest how the ramifications of the subject matter of their deliberations may be felt in the most distant places.

This chapter aims at addressing certain elements of the process of deliberation within the WHO's Emergency Committees. The analysis focuses on the legal dimension, which undergirds deliberations as part of expert decision-making at the international level regarding health emergencies. One caveat is that, although the analytical starting point is legal, the subject of analysis is a consultative ad hoc body not fully equivalent to deliberation within adjudication. Therefore, the

[3] WHO, *Statement on the first meeting of the International Health Regulations (2005) Emergency Committee regarding the outbreak of novel coronavirus (2019-nCoV)* 23 January 2020, www.who.int/news/item/23-01-2020-statement-on-the-meeting-of-the-international-health-regulations-(2005)-emergency-committee-regarding-the-outbreak-of-novel-coronavirus-(2019-ncov).

[4] International Health Regulations (Geneva, 23 May 2005), Art 12.

[5] L Mullen et al, 'An analysis of International Health Regulations Emergency Committees and Public Health Emergency of International Concern Designations' (2020) 5 *BMJ Global Health* 1, 1–9.

[6] Constitution of the World Health Organization (New York, 22 July 1946).

descriptive and the normative premises should not be equated to those of other legal operators, such as judges. Instead, the current text tackles the internal deliberations of an ad hoc expert body which is not the ultimate decision-maker, but rather fulfills a consultative purpose.

II. Unpacking the Mandate of WHO Emergency Committees

WHO Emergency Committees exercise their mandate under the IHR, a legally binding instrument approved by the World Health Assembly in 2005 by its Member States – 194 in total. As they did not explicitly express their opposition ('opt out'), the contents of the IHR became binding for all of them.[7] Another two non-WHO members, Liechtenstein and the Holy See, adhered to the IHR later. The total stands at 196 states parties, which represents a very high degree of inclusiveness. Unlike other international treaties, no ulterior ratification procedure is required, as these regulations enter into force after a designated period of time – in the particular case at hand, after 18 months.[8]

Broadly speaking, the IHR poses three types of legal functions: (1) it creates obligations for states, particularly to notify diseases to the WHO[9] and enhance their national capacities for pandemic surveillance and response;[10] (2) it grants specific rights to persons, mainly travellers, vis-à-vis states, although these rights are not directly actionable under the IHR itself;[11] and (3) it gives the WHO and its ad hoc bodies a specific set of legal powers. For the purposes of this chapter, the focus on the legal mandate of the Emergency Committee means the third legal output is the guiding thread.

In terms of allocation of powers, the IHR's provisions enshrine the leading role of the WHO's Director-General in emergency decision-making.[12] S/he has the maximum authority – ie the last word – to declare a public health emergency of international concern and issue so-called temporary recommendations.[13] As a procedural requirement, before doing so s/he must summon an Emergency Committee and ask for its advice.[14] These are ad hoc bodies composed of

[7] Art 22 IHR.

[8] Art 59 IHR.

[9] Art 6 IHR.

[10] Art 5 IHR.

[11] Arts 32 and 40 IHR.

[12] On the key role of Director-Generals in steering the WHO's policies, T Hanrieder, *International Organization in Time. Fragmentation and Reform* (OUP, 2015) 143–44.

[13] Arts 12 and 15 IHR.

[14] GL Burci and C Feinäugle, 'The ILC's Articles Seen from a WHO Perspective' in M Ragazzi (ed), *Responsibility of International Organizations: Essays in Memory of Sir Ian Brownlie* (Martinus Nijhoff Publishers, 2013) 187.

persons selected from a Roster of Experts which, in turn, is drafted by the WHO Director-General. While not explicitly mentioned in the IHR, the criteria for selecting such a Roster are formulated in WHO regulations and rules on the matter.[15]

The legal mandate of these Committees is further described as: providing views on whether a public health emergency of international concern should be declared; whether the latter ought to be terminated; and proposing temporary recommendations.[16]

Even though, legally speaking, Committees' advice may be disregarded as the Director-General may go her/his own way, in practice this has never occurred. Thus, the advisory body arguably enjoys a very high degree of deference.[17] Conversely, both the summoning and the composition of Emergency Committees fall within the discretion of the WHO Director-General. If s/he does not consider it is necessary to invoke a meeting, or if s/he deems a group of persons to be the most suitable and not others, there is no legal path to challenge this choice. Nevertheless, summoning an Emergency Committee, and declaring a public health emergency of international concern or issuing a particular set of temporary recommendations, is not necessarily an automatic process. On past occasions, Emergency Committees have explicitly recommended not to raise the alarm.[18] To a certain extent, this shows a degree of independence from the WHO Director-General's own assessments of the situation. Therefore, Emergency Committee members are not subject to any restraints related to a preferred outcome. Conversely, the main limitation for decision-making, as seen below, is related to the amount of information provided by the WHO Director-General and states parties.

Declaring an emergency does not lead to mandatory action from its addressees, ie states parties. But the effects of these declarations, as well as their omissions, have been documented in the past, with both hastiness and belatedness being a source of condemnation.[19]

As for the actual proceedings within Emergency Committee meetings, from the outset, the list of agenda items for the meetings is prepared by the WHO Director-General,[20] thus allowing her/him to choose what shall be discussed. Consequently, the Committee does not have a full, self-standing autonomy in how it processes the substantive input. Moreover, the state where the event in question has taken place must be notified of the meeting's date in advance.[21]

[15] WHO, *WHO Regulations for Expert Advisory Panels and Committees.*

[16] Art 48(1) IHR.

[17] Av Bogdandy and P Villarreal, 'Critical Features of International Authority in Pandemic Response. The WHO in the COVID-19 Crisis, Human Rights and the Changing World Order' (2020) *MPIL Research Paper Series No. 2020-18,* 11, papers.ssrn.com/sol3/papers.cfm?abstract_id=3600058.

[18] L Mullen et al, 'An analysis of International Health Regulations Emergency Committees and Public Health Emergency of International Concern Designations' (2020) 5 *BMJ Global Health* 1, 1–9.

[19] A Kamradt-Scott, 'WHO's to blame? The World Health Organization and the 2014 Ebola outbreak in West Africa' (2016) 37 *TWQ* 401, 409.

[20] Art 49(2) IHR.

[21] Art 49(4) IHR.

The internal proceedings of Emergency Committee are, for the most part, not subjected to external scrutiny. As established in the corresponding rules of procedure, closed-door meetings are a general feature which can be sidelined by the Director-General.[22] As it is a matter of evolving practice, there would no legal impediments for shifting to public deliberations. It is rather a question of policy preferences.

III. Assessing WHO Emergency Committee Deliberations: Between Input and Output

When a collegiate body is entrusted with powers to interpret the application of norms to specific facts, it begs the question of how to assess the ensuing deliberative process. In line with institutional theories,[23] the normative focus can be divided into input and output. Though they are addressed separately, below it is argued how, in actual practice, these two dimensions operate jointly.

In terms of input, the composition of a body is a key determinant of whether the voices that ought to be taken into account are actually heard or not.[24] The lack of participation by major stakeholders is a central issue in representative democracies, where decisions affecting a number of people in very relevant ways are taken by a few. In the case of international organisations composed of states, their distance from individuals in terms of representation is further increased.[25]

As for output, the result of deliberation processes, ie the decision, is the main subject of analysis. It reflects how the role of expertise is taken by public authorities at all levels of governance as a means to justify their own decisions.[26] The question becomes whether such a decision manages to satisfy the expectations of the public at large regarding the goals set upon the body entrusted with legal powers. For instance, if a decision has the input of all relevant stakeholders, but leads to adverse or possibly even counterproductive consequences than what was originally attempted, there is an output deficit. Needless to say, as achieving a particular

[22] Rule 1, *WHO Rules of Procedure for Expert Committees*, Rule 1. The so-far opaque nature of internal WHO meetings has already criticised at length in M Eccleston-Turner and A Kamradt-Scott, 'Transparency in IHR emergency committee decision making: the case for reform' (2019) 4 *BMJ Global Health* e001618.

[23] See the seminal work by F Scharpf, *Governing in Europe: Effective and Democratic?* (1999) 7–9; on a typology of input and output legitimacy in the case of intergovernmental organizations, JA Sholte and J Tallberg, 'Theorizing the Institutional Sources of Global Governance Legitimacy' in J Tallberg, K Bäckstrand and JA Scholte (eds), *Legitimacy in Global Governance. Sources, Processes, and Consequences* (OUP, 2018), 58–65; on the need for input-based democracy in international organizations, C Kreuder-Sonnen, *Emergency Powers of International Organizations* (OUP, 2019) 202–03.

[24] V Rittberger and B Zangl, *International Organization. Polity, Politics and Policies* (Palgrave Macmillan, 2006) 60–61.

[25] S Marks, 'Democracy and international governance' in JM Coicaud and V Heiskanen (eds), *Legitimacy of International Organizations* (United Nations University Press, 2001) 50–52.

[26] S Jasanoff, *Science and Public Reason* (Routledge, 2012) 163.

result is dependent on multiple variables, often beyond decision-makers' control, normative output analyses requires an ex post empirical assessment which may not be immediately available when a decision is taken.

Both of these dimensions, input and output, converge in the case of the WHO Emergency Committees in concrete manners. The WHO's regulations on expert bodies explicitly describe the two core, and at times conflicting, goals related to deliberation in health emergencies at the international level: the need for efficient and expedited decision-making in the face of pressing circumstances, on one hand, and the need for incorporating a diversity of views capable of reflecting multiple local insights to the largest extent possible, on the other hand.[27] Here, two major requirements are stated by the IHR and the regulations: expertise and geographical representation. These two elements are understood in a relatively open matter, as there are no concrete criteria to fulfil.

In terms of expertise, the WHO Emergency Committee is an ad hoc body that shifts its composition each time it is summoned. Nevertheless, all Committees must be composed of persons with 'expertise and experience',[28] though it is not further specified how this can be ascertained. It reflects a technocratic setup, since a person is entitled to have a say if, and only if, s/he holds certain credentials. However, there is no clear-cut definition of expertise for the purposes of Committee Members' mandatory qualifications. The requirement of expertise would seem to exclude alleged 'laypersons', such as elected public officials or civil society representatives without technical credentials, from participating in the decision-making process. But more critical assessments have pointed towards both the oft-unclear distinction between 'experts' and 'non-experts', as well as the element of exclusion per se.[29] Research on expertise as a social construct has shown how there may be different, equally valid perspectives towards the epistemic bases that are given preference.[30] The degree of inclusion will depend on how broadly the question of the needed expertise is formulated.

The goal of broader geographical representation strives for enhanced inclusiveness. It may be posited that it somehow makes up for the initial exclusion created by the expertise clause. When combined with the latter, geographical diversity addresses the need for a more heterogenous composition of Emergency Committees. Such criterion falls in line with growing calls for diversification at the international level. Moreover, the geographical element is visible in the fact that states affected by a disease event have the right to propose their own expert to participate in the deliberations.[31] It reinforces the claim that the potential impact

[27] See above n 15.

[28] Art 48(2) IHR.

[29] D Innerarity, *The Democracy of Knowledge* (Bloomsbury 2013) 90–93.

[30] Jasanoff (n 26) 267–69.

[31] Art 48(2) IHR. According to data from 2020, though all regions of the world are represented in the WHO's IHR Roster of Experts, the highest number of state-appointed experts continues to be from Europe (41% of the global sum). WHO, *Annual report on the implementation of the International Health Regulations (2005). Report by the Director-General*, A73/14, 12 May 2020, para 25.

of decisions by the Emergency Committee on the interests of a state asks for ways to guarantee that the voice of addressees will be heard.

The element of geographical representativeness carries an epistemic relevance as well. It is a tenet of public health that knowledge from factual, on-the-ground circumstances is key for devising proper responses. Therefore, persons with a homogenous geographical origin would be at high risk of missing out central features of diverse settings, whilst taking their own epistemic standpoint for granted. This could result in myopic disregard of factual considerations relevant for public health insights.

In terms of how each Committee Member may weigh in the deliberations, although there is a Chair, there is no formal hierarchy between them. When it comes to the ultimate decision, it is a horizontal process that mostly takes place without a vote, rather through consensus.[32]

The decision itself has so far been unitary, as the Committee speaks to the public in 'one voice' and separate opinions are not set on the record.[33] Even though a divergence of views between members may be reflected on the resulting statement, it is unclear whether disagreements by one or a few of them with the final decision could prevent a decision from being taken. When coupled with the closed-door nature of their deliberations, Emergency Committees effectively operate as a 'black-box'[34] where no insight on their internal proceedings is provided.

IV. Inside the Black-Box: Technocracy and Health Emergencies

Since the entry into force of the IHR in 2005 and at the moment of writing, Emergency Committees have been summoned to face nine different disease events.[35] In turn, public health emergencies of international concern have been declared for six of those events, with accompanying temporary recommendations for every instance.[36] Afterwards, Emergency Committees meet regularly for a status update, since temporary recommendations expire after three months after they are issued.[37] If Emergency Committees are summoned but do not consider an emergency must be declared, they may nevertheless reconvene again if and when the WHO Director-General considers it necessary. In the aegis of COVID-19, the Emergency Committee met on a total of five occasions in 2020.[38]

[32] Rule 6, WHO Rules of Procedure for Expert Committees.
[33] J Heath, 'Global Emergency Power in the Age of Ebola' (2016) 57 *Harvard Intl LJ* 1, 17.
[34] M Eccleston-Turner and A Kamradt-Scott, 'Transparency in IHR emergency committee decision-making: the case for reform' (2019) 4 *BMJ Global Health* e001618.
[35] Mullen et al (n 5) 2.
[36] ibid.
[37] Art 15(3) IHR.
[38] www.who.int/groups/covid-19-ihr-emergency-committee.

The overview of the input and output elements of WHO Emergency Committees posed above can be used for a retrospective analysis of how deliberations have taken place. Expanding upon the metaphor of a 'black box', deliberations taking place within these Committees are based on the input provided by the WHO Director-General – who, in turn, relies heavily upon information furnished by states parties or, exceptionally, to unofficial sources. The deliberations lead to an outcome which must be communicated to all WHO states parties.[39]

The process is mired with opacity. The largest part of information furnished by states parties is generally unavailable to the public at large. Consequently, it is difficult to ascertain what type of data was used to justify a decision. This became ostensible during the first meeting of the Emergency Committee on the then-novel coronavirus in 23 January 2020, where the postponement of the decision until 30 January was based on insufficient information.[40] Yet there was no clear indication of what exactly the missing data was. Instead, the reasons were further expanded through external sources, ie once certain Committee members were interviewed by the media.[41]

As for the outcome, although the decision itself must be communicated, it is not the case of the reasons for its adoption. Here, institutional practice has evolved ever since the IHR entered into force. Since deliberation takes place behind closed-doors, a more extended exposition of the core reasons justifying a decision is all the more important, since deliberation take place behind closed doors. The decision's criteria of validity may not be appraised.

The first summoning of an Emergency Committee occurred at the onset of the H1N1 influenza pandemic in 2009. As there was no pre-established procedure, it fell upon the WHO Director-General, Margaret Chan, to decide how to deal with certain matters related to input and output. As the regulations were not explicit in the matter, a decision was made not to disclose the names of the Members of the Emergency Committee to shield them from potential external influence. Given the stakes at hand, namely that declaring an emergency could benefit pharmaceutical companies, it was deemed to be a reasonable solution. But the choice backfired, in so far as it raised suspicions of concealing potential conflicts of interest.[42] Moreover, considering the criticisms related to the decision to raise the alert,[43]

[39] Art 49(6) IHR.

[40] WHO, *Statement on the first meeting of the International Health Regulations (2005) Emergency Committee regarding the outbreak of novel coronavirus (2019-nCoV)*, 23 January 2020, www.who.int/news/item/23-01-2020-statement-on-the-meeting-of-the-international-health-regulations-(2005)-emergency-committee-regarding-the-outbreak-of-novel-coronavirus-(2019-ncov).

[41] A Joseph, 'WHO postpones decision on whether to declare China outbreak a global public health emergency', *STAT*, 22 January 2020, www.statnews.com/2020/01/22/who-postpones-decision-on-whether-to-declare-china-outbreak-a-global-public-health-emergency/.

[42] D Cohen and P Carter, 'Conflicts of interest. WHO and the pandemic flu "conspiracies"' (2010) 340 *BMJ* c2912.

[43] However, criticisms were raised both against the Emergency Committee's decisions as well as the WHO Director-General's own pandemic declaration, which are two different acts. P Villarreal, 'Pandemic Declarations of the World Health Organization as an Exercise of International Public Authority: The Possible Legal Answers to Frictions Between Legitimacies' (2016) 7 *Goettingen Journal of International Law* 95, 129.

input choices on hiding Members' identities 'tainted' the output as well. The H1N1 episode attested the inextricable link between both dimensions, considering how shortcomings in one spill over to the other.

As for output, the H1N1 emergency declaration displayed the institutional learning curve in applying the IHR. The explanation given for why the decision was made did not clarify why the event fulfilled the legal definition of a public health emergency of international concern.[44] Since deliberations took place behind closed doors, there was no way to ascertain why the spread of the disease constituted a public health emergency of international concern. The legal reasoning related to the interpretation of the IHR's provisions were not sufficiently clear.

In subsequent occasions, despite explicit institutional or legal reforms, the names of members of the Emergency Committee have consistently been disclosed. In a similar vein, more detailed explanations became available on why certain situations did or did not merit declaring an emergency. This shows responsiveness by the WHO and its Director-General, deriving from the amount of discretion when modifying these practices.

Although the input dimension regarding the Emergency Committee has arguably improved after the H1N1 controversy, further criticisms on the output – or, rather, lack thereof – have nevertheless risen. At the beginning of the West African Ebola crisis in 2014, the WHO Director-General's decision not to summon an Emergency Committee after initial reports in March of that year was met with widespread criticism.[45] It is both an input- and output-related problem, referring both to the absence of a Committee deliberating in the first place (input), as well as to a decision which should have been issued earlier (output).

In a similar vein, the Ebola outbreak in the Democratic Republic of the Congo (DRC) of 2018–19 was the subject of stark disagreements amongst commentators in terms of the Emergency Committee's output, particularly its legal interpretation. In three of its meetings, the Committee advised the WHO Director-General not to declare a public health emergency of international concern.[46] The justification provided was not particularly convincing to legal analysts, as it seemed to have departed from the elements comprising the definition of a public health emergency of international concern.[47]

[44] WHO, *Swine influenza. Statement by WHO Director-General, Dr Margaret Chan*, 25 April 2009, www.who.int/mediacentre/news/statements/2009/h1n1_20090425/en/.

[45] WHO, *Implementation of the International Health Regulations (2005). Report of the Review Committee on the Role of the International Health Regulations (2005) in the Ebola Outbreak and Response* (2016), A69/21, paras 99–103; S Moon et al, 'Will Ebola Change the Game? Ten essential reforms before the next pandemic. The report of the Harvard-LSHTM Independent Panel on the Global Response to Ebola' (2015) 386 *The Lancet* 2204, 2210.

[46] A Kamradt-Scott, 'The International Health Regulations (2005). Strengthening Their Effective Implementation and Utilisation' (2019) 16 *IOLR* 242, 262–64.

[47] Art 1 IHR. See on this matter D Fidler, 'To Declare or Not to Declare: The Controversy Over Declaring a Public Health Emergency of International Concern for the Ebola Outbreak in the Democratic Republic of the Congo' (2019) 14 *Asian Journal of WTO & International Health Law and Policy* 287.

The mandate to give advice on temporary recommendations for states regarding health measures is another instance where the interplay between input and output is at stake. These recommendations are supposed to reflect the expertise of the members of Emergency Committees. Wrongful guidance can undermine the WHO's own credibility as an authority in matters of health.[48] An overarching challenge is how to issue advice amidst a scenario of insufficient data related to a particular disease. Without the latter, reflecting best practices with sufficient accuracy is too tall an order. One notable example was the Zika epidemic in the Americas of 2016. Both the WHO Director-General's decision to declare an emergency itself, as well as the recommendations, reflected both known and unknown facts regarding the disease's effects.[49] For instance, as it was clear that human-to-human transmission was not a major source of contagion, no travel restrictions were recommended.[50]

As espoused below, insufficient scientific data was determinant in recommendations for states regarding COVID-19.

The elements described above shed light on the premises of expert deliberation, namely that the interpretation of available information ought to be undertaken by persons fulfilling a series of personal features. The potential of expertise is thus contingent upon having a robust input dimension consisting of finding 'the right persons' and gathering the best data. Otherwise, the cogs within the black box do not turn. In so far as existing procedures can ensure that both will be available, the decision-making process may be more resilient to criticisms in case of disagreements with the outcome.

V. COVID-19 and the Future of International Deliberation in Health Emergencies

In terms of magnitude, none of the previous public health emergencies of international concern declared by the WHO Director-General can be comparable to the COVID-19 pandemic. With a global death toll in the millions, its dramatic nature is hard to overstate. The dire outlook has put institutional decision-making processes at the international level in the spotlight. As the events were first reported in China, and later spread globally, a looming question is whether something could have been done differently.

[48] As established in Art 2 of the Constitution of the WHO.

[49] D Heymann, 'Zika virus and microcephaly: why is this situation a PHEIC?' (2016) 387 *The Lancet* 719.

[50] WHO, *WHO statement on the first meeting of the International Health Regulations (2005) (IHR 2005) Emergency Committee on Zika virus and observed increase in neurological disorders and neonatal malformations, 1 February 2016*, www.who.int/news/item/01-02-2016-who-statement-on-the-first-meeting-of-the-international-health-regulations-(2005)-(ihr-2005)-emergency-committee-on-zika-virus-and-observed-increase-in-neurological-disorders-and-neonatal-malformations.

The beginning of the pandemic was characterised by the WHO's particularly deferent approach towards the Chinese government.[51] Several possible explanations come to the fore. The organisation had to deal with the delicate balance between asserting its mandate as the international authority in global health, as well as procuring the necessary data for its own decision-making despite the absence of coercive powers.[52]

The episode also demonstrates how different viewpoints on deliberation may be at stake. While an increasing call for transparency and accountability at the international level is directly linked to the normative elements of authority,[53] it also risks falling out of tune with national-level processes where such practices are not as widespread. When facing settings of very limited guarantees of access to information at the national level, the pendulum shifts between promoting democratic principles through enhanced transparency and ensuring the participation of key stakeholders, namely Chinese authorities possessing first-hand information on the virus. Even though it is an international law obligation,[54] the institution tasked with collecting it, the WHO, lacks the means to enforce it.[55]

Insufficient information on the 'new' coronavirus shaped the recommendations issued by the WHO Director-General, on the advice of the Emergency Committee. A core purpose of the IHR is to serve as the legal instrument for devising health responses that are not more restrictive of international travel and trade than what is necessary.[56] Such an estimation can only be done on a case-by-case basis and by assessing the available medical-epidemiological data regarding a particular disease. Whereas some diseases may merit travel or trade restrictions due to their way of transmission, in others these measures have been considered to be counterproductive.[57]

In the case of COVID-19, a temporary recommendation issued at the beginning stood out, namely that all states should abstain from imposing any type of travel restriction.[58] No scientific-epidemiological evidence was quoted for justifying the decision, either because it was not available, due to considerations towards the Chinese government – which would have been the main country at the

[51] P Renninger, 'The "People's Total War on COVID-19": Urban Pandemic Management Through (Non-)Law in Wuhan, China' (2020) 30 *Washington International Law Journal* 63, 85 and 90.

[52] The dilemma is described in P Villarreal, 'The 2019–2020 novel coronavirus outbreak and the importance of good faith for international law' *Völkerrechtsblog*, 28 January 2020, voelkerrechtsblog.org/the-2019-2020-novel-coronavirus-outbreak-and-the-importance-of-good-faith-for-international-law/.

[53] M Zürn, M Binder and M Ecker-Ehrhardt, 'International Authority and its Politicization' (2012) 4 *International Theory* 69; S Quack, 'Expertise and authority in transnational governance' in R Cotterrell and M Del Mar (eds), *Authority in Transnational Legal Theory* (Edward Elgar, 2016) 365.

[54] Art 6 IHR.

[55] GL Burci, 'The Legal Response to Pandemics. The Strengths and Weaknesses of the International Health Regulations' (2020) 11 *Journal of International Humanitarian Legal Studies* 204, 216.

[56] Art 2 IHR.

[57] The Emergency Committee consistently advised against travel restrictions for limiting the spread of Ebola in West Africa. WHO, *Report of the Review Committee on the Role of the International Health Regulations (2005) in the Ebola Outbreak and Response*, A69/21, 13 May 2016, para 69.

[58] See above n 40.

receiving end of such restrictions – or perhaps both.[59] Soon after the WHO issued this advice, a growing list of countries imposing some form of restriction to the cross-border mobility of persons grew exponentially. Eventually, even the Chinese government would impose restrictions of its own.[60] Impediments to travel became the rule, the absence thereof the exception.[61]

Research in the field of medicine and public health has provided empirical evidence on the effectiveness of COVID-19-related travel restrictions – though with several caveats, including their coexistence with other measures.[62] Only a few days after the recommendation had been issued, the WHO revised its formulation.[63] By the next meeting of the Emergency Committee on 30 April 2020, the temporary recommendation to refrain from any sort of travel restriction was modified, now having a more qualified wording.[64]

As time went by, the WHO's declaration of 30 January regarding travel was subjected to increasing scrutiny. National governments with the highest rates of success in mitigating the spread of the virus had also resorted to travel bans from countries with a high rate of virus transmission.[65] Even though deviating from the WHO's recommendations is not a violation of international law per se,[66] such a lack of observance by the addressees undermines the organisation's authority. Taken to the extreme, the goal of sharing 'best practices' may be undermined when these are not accepted as such.

Another hypothesis has to do with the role of non-scientific considerations. While public health and epidemiology should always be at the helm of recommendations issued under the IHR, the *lato sensu* political dimension of measures related to international travel and trade cannot be sidelined. States have a major interest in not being at the receiving end of these restrictions. They are likelier to stop cooperating with the system of disease surveillance if they perceive that the institution, on the basis of the underlying legal regime, does not pay heed to their

[59] 'America and China take their rivalry to the World Health Organisation' *The Economist*, 17 May 2020.

[60] D Fidler, 'COVID-19 and International Law: Must China Compensate Countries for the Damage?' *JustSecurity*, 27 March 2020, www.justsecurity.org/69394/covid-19-and-international-law-must-china-compensate-countries-for-the-damage-international-health-regulations/.

[61] An account of travel restrictions imposed due to COVID-19 during the course of 2020, though without naming states imposing them, is visible in WHO, *Implementation of the International Health Regulations (2005). Report by the Director-General*, A74/17, 12 May 2021, para 21.

[62] M Chinazzi et al, 'The effect of travel restrictions on the spread of the 2019 novel coronavirus (COVID-19) outbreak' (2020) 368 Science 395, 395–400.

[63] WHO, 2019 Novel Coronavirus (2019-nCoV): Strategic Preparedness and Response Plan, 4 February 2020, 10.

[64] WHO, 'Statement on the third meeting of the International Health Regulations (2005) Emergency Committee regarding the outbreak of coronavirus disease (COVID-19)', www.who.int/news/item/01-05-2020-statement-on-the-third-meeting-of-the-international-health-regulations-(2005)-emergency-committee-regarding-the-outbreak-of-coronavirus-disease-(covid-19).

[65] Notable examples include China, Taiwan, Singapore and New Zealand. See above n 62.

[66] But see a stronger formulation in R Habibi et al, 'Do not violate the International Health Regulations during the COVID-19 outbreak' (2020), 395 *The Lancet* 664, 664–66.

interests in the matter.[67] This concern is at the helm of the relationship between the WHO and its Member States.

Despite the stakes involved in temporary recommendations under the IHR, which legally require taking into account the interests of affected states in terms of input, the structures of accountability are not equivalent to those at the national level.[68] Being the result of state consent through its representatives,[69] the WHO's officials only indirectly respond to the population at large. As the entity with personality under international law, states overtake oversight functions, including political ones. They may vote every five years on the election of the Director-General,[70] thus having the possibility to steer institutional changes, particularly in the Secretariat. It is a mild form of accountability. Furthermore, although Staff Regulations foresee certain types of disciplinary action in case of wrongdoings,[71] there is no general framework for holding legal responsibility in case states are not satisfied with one of the decisions. If there are claims of a potential breach of international law obligations, a claim could be made that the WHO qua organisation could be legally responsible under the Articles on the Responsibility of International Organizations (ARIO).[72] But this would require reaching an even higher threshold of demonstrating the breach of a legal obligation attributable to the organisation.[73] As long as the procedure is respected, disagreements on the substance would seldom lead to ulterior legal consequences.

VI. Conclusion: Towards Enhanced Pandemic Deliberation at the International Level

When decision-making at the international level rests on the basis of expertise,[74] an ensuing challenge is how to uphold a minimum of democratic principles, a 'thin' conception. Conversely, a 'thick' idea of democracy would include, inter alia,

[67] See already P Dorolle, 'Old Plagues in the Jet Age' (1968) 4(5634) *British Medical Journal* 789, 792.

[68] S Wheatley, 'A Democratic Rule of International Law' (2011) 22 *EJIL* 525, 547–48.

[69] T Christiano, 'Is democratic legitimacy possible for international institutions?' in D Archibugi, M Koenig-Archibugi and R Marchetti (ed), *Global Democracy. Normative and Empirical Perspectives* (CUP, 2012) 80–81.

[70] Rule 108, World Health Assembly Rules of Procedure.

[71] Rules 1075.1 and 110.8, World Health Organization Staff Regulations and Staff Rules.

[72] The argument has been made in M Eccleston-Turner and S McArdle, 'The Law of Responsibility and the World Health Organisation: A Case Study on the West African Ebola Outbreak' in M Eccleston-Turner and I Brassington (eds), *Infectious Diseases in the New Millennium* (Springer Nature, 2020) 106–07.

[73] Article 4, Articles on the Responsibility of International Organizations (New York, 9 December 2011).

[74] W Wouter, 'The politics of expertise: applying paradoxes of scientific expertise to international law' in M Ambrus, K Arts, E Hey and H Raulus (eds), *The role of 'experts' in international and European decision-making processes* (CUP, 2014); O Jacob Sending, *The Politics of Expertise. Competing for Authority in Global Governance* (University of Michigan Press, 2015) 44–62.

both equal representation of, and public deliberation by decisions' addressees.[75] Since very few, if any, intergovernmental organisations fulfil this ideal type, the remaining task is how to adjust the normative expectations held towards their role. As the literature on the democratic deficit of international institutions has long underscored, calls for more robust mechanisms of participation therein are by no means recent.[76]

Considering the wide variety of Member States represented therein, a major hurdle is how to find a standard of democratic deliberation in the exercise of international organisations' legal powers that is acceptable to all of their members.[77] Arguments on the agnostic view of international law towards democracy emphasise the need for inclusiveness and non-interference with internal issues in light of sovereignty.[78] Countries lacking democratic credentials at the national level might think twice about joining international institutions adopting standards which they explicitly refuse for themselves.

While the logic of international law's agnosticism towards democracy refers mostly to national political procedures, a similar perspective can be used regarding the functioning of international organisations. As states are still largely the ones at the steering wheel, it begs the question of whether they would be willing to advocate for enhancing the democratic pedigree of international institutions, and to what extent.

Normative debates on pandemic deliberation at the international level face the conundrum of which models would be more acceptable for a larger number of states. Without their acquiescence, the entire global system of pandemic surveillance and response risks collapsing. The high level of inclusiveness leads to a difficult task for creating a sufficient majority supporting any reform. If the likelihood of countries 'opting out' of the IHR regime increases, more ambitious proposals may be discarded.

Lastly, formalising the proceedings of Emergency Committees by instituting rules of procedure would address some pitfalls but create others. It would contribute towards increasing the acceptability of Committees' decisions in the eyes of external observers. But, at the same time, it could lead to creating backdoor deliberations where members are able to sideline procedural constraints.[79] It might inhibit discussions in the pre-scheduled official meetings, as the participants

[75] C Kreuder-Sonnen and B Zangl, 'Which post-Westphalia? International organizations between constitutionalism and authoritarianism' (2015) 21 *European Journal of International Relations* 574–75.

[76] D Archibugi and D Held, 'Editors' Introduction' in D Archibugi and D Held (eds), *Cosmopolitan Democracy* (Polity Press, 1995) 13.

[77] JM Coicaud, 'International organizations, the evolution of international politics, and legitimacy' in JM Coicaud and V Heiskanen (eds), *Legitimacy of International Organizations* (United Nations University Press 2001) 520–21.

[78] T Ginsburg, 'Authoritarian International Law?' (2020) 114 *AJIL* 221, 226 and 259–60.

[79] S Chambers, 'Behind Closed Doors: Publicity, Secrecy, and the Quality of Deliberation' (2004) 12 *The Journal of Political Philosophy* 389, 409–10.

might not express their views as openly.[80] At the very least, ensuring a franker debate amongst all Committee members and not only smaller groups enhances the value of their consensus. The IHR itself recognises the need to maintain confidentiality. Whatever the case, multiple arguments have been made in favour of increased consistency of the Emergency Committee's interpretation of the IHR, a matter concerning both input – regarding the need to incorporate legal expertise – and output – by issuing certain types of arguments justifying their decisions.[81]

Beyond the path chosen for upcoming improvements – either legal reforms or discretionary shifts in institutional policies – the COVID-19 pandemic has led to core questions of how to ensure that future responses at the international level will not be hampered by eschewed institutional processes. A more harmonious balance of the input and output dimensions of pandemic deliberation at the international level is long overdue.

[80] For empirical insights on this phenomenon, see D Statsavage, 'Does Transparency Make a Difference? The Example of the European Council of Ministers' in C Hood and D Heald (eds), *Transparency: The Key to Better Governance?* (Proceedings of the British Academy, vol 135, 2006) 165 and 177.

[81] See above, n 18.

12

EU Response to Fighting the Coronavirus – Coordination, Support, Action – Heeding its Citizens' Calls?

ANJA NAUMANN

I. Introduction

After the SARS-CoV-2 virus hit Europe in March 2020 and EU Member States started to introduce national measures to address the virus and the illness COVID-19 causes,[1] calls became louder for the EU and its institutions to start taking distinct EU-level action to address the pandemic. EU citizens expressed their views on inter alia European Action taken in response to the pandemic[2] in an official survey conducted on behalf of the EU Parliament (Parliament Survey).[3]

Notably with regard to this volume's focus on democratic relationships, decision-making structures, and respective changes prompted by COVID-19, surveyed citizens expressed that 'the EU should have more competences to deal with crises such as the Coronavirus pandemic'.[4] The citizens' calls for broader EU competences aligned with similar ones from newspapers, who called out the EU's response as too slow and condemned Member States' individual approaches as 'selfish', fighting the crisis against, rather than with each other.[5] It was frequently

[1] For an overview of some of the bigger Member States see S Price, 'COVID-19 in the EU Member States' (*Health Europa*, 10 August 2020) www.healtheuropa.eu/covid-19-in-the-eu-member-states/102019/.

[2] European Parliament and Kantar, 'Uncertainty/ EU/Hope – Public Opinion in Times of COVID-19 – Public Opinion Survey' (2020) 22 et seq www.europarl.europa.eu/at-your-service/files/be-heard/eurobarometer/2020/public_opinion_in_the_eu_in_time_of_coronavirus_crisis/report/en-covid19-survey-report.pdf.

[3] European Parliament and Kantar (n 2). The results were published in June 2020. The information was gathered from 23 April to 1 May 2020 from 21,804 respondents in 21 EU Member States.

[4] 23% strongly agreed and 46% 'tended to agree' ibid 8, 30 et seq.

[5] See eg P Müller et al, 'The EU Struggles for Relevance in the Fight against Coronavirus – DER SPIEGEL – International' *Der Spiegel* (23 March 2020) www.spiegel.de/international/europe/corona-the-eu-struggles-for-relevance-in-the-fight-against-coronavirus-a-83052f57-ed42-4a69-85fd-61e6795a4d20; J Rankin, 'Coronavirus Could Be Final Straw for EU, European Experts Warn' *The Guardian* (1 April 2020) www.theguardian.com/world/2020/apr/01/coronavirus-could-be-final-straw-for-eu-european-experts-warn; SL Greer, 'Opinion | How Did the E.U. Get the Coronavirus So Wrong?' *The New York Times* (6 April 2020) www.nytimes.com/2020/04/06/opinion/europe-coronavirus.html.

pointed out from early on in the pandemic that the EU can only address COVID-19 within the boundaries set by its formal competences, which determine the scope of EU action and decision-making.[6] Nevertheless, arguments that the EU as supranational organisation was in a prime position to address this health-crisis across EU national borders in a more unified and faster way are hard to ignore. In the Parliament Survey, citizens from every participating Member States stated that the EU's top priority should be to ensure sufficient availability of medical supplies in all Member States.[7] The second highest priority for the EU should be, in the citizens' view, for the EU to support research to develop a vaccine.[8] Further, 57 per cent of survey respondents submitted that they were generally unsatisfied with the solidarity shown between Member States.[9] Scholars similarly argued in favour of Member States transferring more powers to the EU to allow it to be better prepared for future health crises and to assume a more central role in the response to such health crises, eg regarding preventive procurement to build a stockpile of medical supplies before the outbreak of a future public health crisis and the centralised distribution of protective and medical equipment as well as vaccines and medicines.[10]

Beyond that and somewhat akin to other, previous crises in which EU action arguably stretched the limits of its competences,[11] some scholarship has further suggested that there is scope for the EU to use existing competences and a broad interpretation particularly of the concepts of proportionality and solidarity to take more action to address COVID-19.[12] It argues that this way, it could be possible to regulate eg restrictions of freedom of movement of (medical) goods or border control measures regarding the free movement of people more centrally through the EU, despite the Member States as such having competence in these areas[13]

[6] See eg N Nielsen, '[Analysis] Coronavirus: What EU Can and Can't Do' (*EUobserver*, 25 March 2020) euobserver.com/coronavirus/147865.

[7] European Parliament and Kantar (n 2) 8, 33 et seq; three top priorities could be chosen from a list of eight possible answers.

[8] ibid.

[9] ibid, 21 et seq.

[10] A de Ruijter, 'Give the EU More Power to Fight Epidemics' *POLITICO* (26 March 2020) www.politico.eu/article/coronavirus-eu-power-pandemic/; AM Pacces and M Weimer, 'From Diversity to Coordination: A European Approach to Covid19' (2020) 11 *European Journal of Risk Regulation* 292; DG Dimitrakopoulos and G Lalis, 'The European Union's Reaction to the COVID-19 Pandemic – a Preliminary Assessment' (*EUROPP*, 27 March 2020) blogs.lse.ac.uk/europpblog/2020/03/27/the-european-unions-reaction-to-the-covid-19-pandemic-a-preliminary-assessment/; A Renda and R Castro, 'Towards Stronger EU Governance of Health Threats after the COVID-19 Pandemic' (2020) 11 *European Journal of Risk Regulation* 273, 281.

[11] Compare eg in relation to the Financial Crisis *Case C-493/17 Proceedings brought by H Weiss and Others [2018] ECLI:EU:C:2018:1000*; but also note *German Federal Constitutional Court, Judgment of the Second Senate of 5 May 2020 – 2 BvR 859/15.*

[12] See Arts 122, 222 TFEU and KP Purnhagen et al, 'More Competences than You Knew? The Web of Health Competence for European Union Action in Response to the COVID-19 Outbreak' (2020) 11 *European Journal of Risk Regulation* 297, 304–06.

[13] ibid, 304–06, also see Art 36 TFEU; and Regulation (EU) 2016/399 of the European Parliament and of the Council of 9 March 2016 on a Union Code on the rules governing the movement of persons across borders (Schengen Borders Code) OJ L 77/1 2016 Particularly Arts 25 et seq.

and indeed having made use of such competences during the COVID-19 crisis. Such an approach, however, involves a new interpretation of those norms and goes beyond the current understanding expressed in legislative practice or case law.[14] If used, it would remain to be seen whether such an approach would remain unchallenged by the Member States and could find the approval of the EU courts if brought before them. Further, it seems doubtful whether the Member States would ultimately be willing to formalise such an approach in the form of EU competences explicitly sanctioning such broad scope for EU action. In any case, so far, the EU seems to have remained within the acknowledged limits of its competences and no changes in official EU competences have taken place with regard to the EU's powers in a health crisis situation yet.

Since the first calls for more EU action on COVID-19 arose, the EU has taken action in a range of policy areas.[15] It is beyond the scope of this chapter to examine all those measures in detail as to their current and future implications for the decision-making powers or structures in the EU. Some of these instruments, which eg facilitate EU joint procurement and which have been inter alia relied on to procure medical countermeasures[16] in this pandemic, existed before the outbreak of the current pandemic, namely the EU Civil Protection Mechanism strengthened by the 2019 RescEU reserve[17] and the 'Joint Procurement Agreement' for health-threat situations (JPA).[18] Their content and limitations have been extensively discussed in academic literature elsewhere.[19] The main shortcomings pointed out regarding these instruments are that contribution to and participation in these instruments is voluntary for Member States and that their scope is too limited to fully address a crisis such as the current pandemic.[20]

Instead, in order to examine changes COVID-19 specifically made, or could make, to the EU's decision-making powers in relation to health, this chapter will focus on two instruments which were proposed or adopted specifically in response

[14] Purnhagen et al (n 12) 305.

[15] For an overview see eg European Commission, 'Timeline of EU Action on COVID-19' ec.europa.eu/info/live-work-travel-eu/health/coronavirus-response/timeline-eu-action_en.

[16] Meaning 'any medicines, medical devices, other goods or services that are aimed at combating serious cross-border threats to health', Art 2(a) 'Joint Procurement Agreement to Procure Medical Countermeasures' ec.europa.eu/health/sites/health/files/preparedness_response/docs/jpa_agreement_medicalcountermeasures_en.pdf.

[17] Decision No 1313/2013/EU of the European Parliament and of the Council of 17 December 2013 on a Union Civil Protection Mechanism (OJ L 347/924) 2013; Decision (EU) 2019/420 of the European Parliament and of the Council of 13 March 2019 amending Decision No 1313/2013/EU on a Union Civil Protection Mechanism (OJ LI 77/1) 2019.

[18] Decision No 1082/2013/EU of the European Parliament and of the Council of 22 October 2013 on serious cross-border threats to health and repealing Decision No 2119/98/EC (OJ L 293/1) 2013; 'Joint Procurement Agreement to Procure Medical Countermeasures' (n 16).

[19] see eg SL Greer and A de Ruijter, 'EU Health Law and Policy in and after the COVID-19 Crisis' (2020) 30 *The European Journal of Public Health* 623; Pacces and Weimer (n 10); A de Ruijter et al, 'EU Solidarity and Policy in Fighting Infectious Diseases: State of Play, Obstacles, Citizen Preferences and Ways Forward' (2020) *Cesifo Working Papers*.

[20] Greer and de Ruijter (n 19); Pacces and Weimer (n 10); de Ruijter et al (n 19).

to COVID-19: the proposed EU4Health Programme[21] and the Emergency Support Instrument (ESI).[22] It will draw some parallels to the instruments existing pre- COVID-19 where the Member States' participation in the new instruments indicates a changing stance on more centralised EU action, but will not discuss RescEU and the JPA in detail.

Further, in keeping with this volume's focus on changes of democratic structures and of the relationship between power and people, this chapter will focus on the citizens, whose preferences are, after all, the ones ultimately meant to be represented in the EU,[23] and adopt their opinions on EU action as expressed in the Parliament Survey as framework for its analysis.

While the economic and the health-impacts of COVID-19 are closely intertwined, in keeping with the focus on the EU citizens' main opinions as expressed in the Parliament Survey, this chapter will not examine EU actions which are ultimately not focused on addressing health aspects, such as the measures to address the economic crisis caused by the pandemic.[24]

The relevant aspects of the Parliament Survey as highlighted above, concerned citizens' views on the EU's competences, its medical supply and vaccine-measures, and health solidarity. The chapter will ask whether the citizens' calls regarding the EU response to COVID-19 are being heeded and how necessary and likely a bigger role for the EU is in light of the EU new instruments directly prompted by COVID-19.

To answer this question, this chapter will first provide a brief overview of the EU's limited current health-competences in section II(A). Section II(B). will then briefly discuss the process of broadening such competences, as endorsed by the EU citizens in the Parliament Survey, and point out the Member States' reasons behind the EU's limited health-competences.

Section III will examine the two new instruments proposed or already used for the procurement of medical supplies and for the support of vaccine-research as part of the EU's COVID-19 response: the proposed EU4Health Programme and particularly the ESI. The section will give a brief overview of the instruments

[21] European Commission – Proposal for a Regulation of the European Parliament and of the Council on the establishment of a Programme for the Union's action in the field of health – for the period 2021–2027 and repealing Regulation (EU) No 282/2014 ('EU4Health Programme') (COM(2020) 405 final) 2020.

[22] Council Regulation (EU) 2020/521 of 14 April 2020 activating the emergency support under Regulation (EU) 2016/369, and amending its provisions taking into account the COVID-19 outbreak [2020] OJ L 117/3 2020 521.

[23] Art 10(1) TEU; shortcomings and issues of democracy at EU level and a 'democratic deficit' of the EU have been extensively discussed, compare eg Giandomenico Majone, 'Europe's "Democratic Deficit": The Question of Standards' (1998) 4 *European Law Journal* 5; A Moravcsik, 'Reassessing Legitimacy in the European Union' (2002) 40 *JCMS: Journal of Common Market Studies* 603; A Follesdal and S Hix, 'Why There Is a Democratic Deficit in the EU: A Response to Majone and Moravcsik' (2006) 44 *JCMS: Journal of Common Market Studies* 533.

[24] See eg European Commission, 'Recovery Plan for Europe' ec.europa.eu/info/live-work-travel-eu/health/coronavirus-response/recovery-plan-europe_en.

and will analyse them against the backdrop of the citizens' calls and the Member States' reservations against broader EU competences as described in section II(B). It will also discuss further arguments which particularly the Member States' participation in the ESI could raise to support the introduction of broader EU health-competences to address health crises in the future. Section IV concludes.

II. The EU's Health-Competences – Limits, Changes, and Concerns

A. Limited EU Health-Competences

In terms of competences to adopt legal measures, the EU's explicit health-competences are considered limited.[25] The respective Treaty provisions corroborate this impression. Article 4(2)(k) of the Treaty on the Functioning of the European Union (TFEU) sets out that the EU shares competences with the Member States regarding 'common safety concerns in public health matters, for the aspects defined in this Treaty'. Article 6(a) TFEU makes it clear that the EU's role regarding the 'protection and improvement of human health' is limited to measures supporting, coordinating, or supplementing Member States measures. When the EU chooses to act pursuant to these shared competences, it is subject to the principle of subsidiarity[26] and must therefore prove that taking action at centralised EU-level provides added value and that 'the objectives of the proposed action cannot be sufficiently achieved by the Member States'.[27]

Article 168 TFEU elaborates further on the EU's competences and measures on health. It allows for some harmonising EU measures on health within clearly demarcated boundaries. For instance, the EU can set binding minimum quality and safety standards for several substances of human origin, or for medical products and devices, and adopt measures in 'veterinary and phytosanitary fields which have as their direct objective the protection of public health'.[28] While the

[25] See eg M Guy and W Sauter, 'The History and Scope of EU Health Law and Policy' in TK Hervey, CA Young and LE Bishop (eds), *Research Handbook on EU Health Law and Policy* (Edward Elgar Publishing, 2017) 19; Pacces and Weimer (n 10) 286; the possibility for EU health measures based on other than explicit health-competences is generally acknowledged in the literature and the EU's options to take measures impacting health based on other than its explicit health-competences will be explained later in this section.

[26] As well as the principle of proportionality, which is, however, less relevant in context of 'power shifts' through changes to the EU's health-competences.

[27] Art 5(3) TEU, European Commission, 'Annual Report 2019 on the Application of the Principles of Subsidiarity and Proportionality and on Relations with National Parliaments [2020] COM(2020) 272 Final' 4; Kieran St C Bradley, 'Legislating in the European Union' in C Barnard and S Peers (eds), *European Union Law*, 2nd edn (OUP, 2017) 112.

[28] See Art 168(4) TFEU.

EU can also adopt 'incentive measures' regarding a range of health aspects,[29] it is important to point out that these are not binding on Member States regarding the specific actions these must adopt.[30]

Overall, Article 168 TFEU re-affirms that EU action on health should 'complement national policies' and that EU action should facilitate and support cooperation between Member States.[31] The limited scope for EU action and the focus on the Member States' autonomy regarding health is once again reiterated in Article 168(7) TFEU, which explicitly sets out that the EU must respect the Member States' responsibilities regarding the 'definition of their health policy and for the organisation and delivery of health services and medical care'.

However, the EU does not only affect health through explicit health-measures based on its health-competences. The EU taking measures based on other, broader than explicit health-competences which ultimately have an effect on health could indeed be witnessed even before the introduction of the first explicit health-competences and predecessors of Article 168 TFEU. Examples for the EU including health objectives in other measures early on can eg be found in EU measures which were as such aimed at the integration of the internal market and EU market-related policies, such as inter alia with regard to the health of workers[32] or regarding the inclusion of human health concerns in context of agricultural legislation.[33] This use of 'creeping competences'[34] to adopt measures having an effect on health was indeed one of the initial reasons for the introduction of explicit health-competences. The Member States hoped that health-competences would provide an explicit, clearly demarcated frame for EU action on health.[35]

Despite the introduction of clearly demarcated health-competences, EU action affecting health via other competence-bases can still be observed and has been accepted by the CJEU,[36] provided that these competences are not merely 'used as a legal basis in order to circumvent the express exclusion of harmonisation laid

[29] Art 168(5) TFEU.

[30] SL Greer et al, *Everything You Always Wanted to Know about European Union Health Policies but Were Afraid to Ask* (European Observatory on Health Systems and Policies, 2019) 64 at n 7.

[31] Art 168(1)(2).

[32] See eg 'Community Charter of the Fundamental Social Rights of Workers of 9 December 1989' www.eesc.europa.eu/resources/docs/community-charter--en.pdf Article 19 and throughout; European Commission, 'From the Single Act to Maastricht and beyond: The Means to Match Our Ambitions Communication from the Commission (COM(92) 2000)'; J Delors, '1992: A Pivotal Year: Address by Jacques Delors, President of the Commission, to the European Parliament, Strasbourg, 12 February 1992'; also see Guy and Sauter (n 25) 23 et seq.

[33] See eg Council Directive 70/524/EEC of 23 November 1970 concerning additives in feeding-stuffs [1970] OJ L 270/1 1970 particularly Arts 6(2b), 7(1); Regarding the history of EU action on health, including before the introduction of explicit health-competences, see TK Hervey and JV McHale, *European Union Health Law: Themes and Implications* (CUP, 2015) 30 et seq.

[34] TK Hervey and JV McHale, 'Community Competence in the Field of Health' in TK Hervey and JV McHale (eds), *Health Law and the European Union* (CUP, 2004) 80.

[35] ibid.

[36] eg Case C-376/98 *Federal Republic of Germany v European Parliament and Council of the European Union* [2000] ECLI:EU:C:2000:544 at [78].

down in [now Article 168 TFEU]',[37] the aim pursued by the respective measure is still mainly within the subject matter of the non-health-competences relied on, and the impact on health is necessary to achieve the measure's primary, non-health aim.[38] In context of COVID-19, it has been argued that the EU can, despite its limited health-competences, take a more active role than is generally perceived because of the possibility and obligation to address health impacts in conjunction with other issues.[39] Indeed, section III will examine inter alia the ESI, which is based on Article 122(1) TFEU, aiming at solidarity[40] and economic support, rather than on explicit health-competences and will show that nevertheless this instrument could support arguments towards the introduction of new EU health-crisis competences.

B. Conferring Health-Competences – Mechanism and Concerns

First, it is important to outline the process of introducing new EU-competences, as well as the Member States' main concerns regarding broader EU action on health. Whether new health-crisis competences would be explicitly rooted in a health, or in another context, the EU's new powers will likely only be adopted if the political process can be successfully navigated and if the Member States' past concerns relating to EU action touching on health-measures can be mitigated.

The EU can only act 'within the limits of the competences conferred upon it by the Member States in the Treaties'.[41] Conveying broader health-competences to the EU therefore requires a Treaty amendment for which unanimous consensus between all 27 EU Member States is required[42] – something which is not a given considering the current political inner-EU struggles surrounding the EU's financial recovery package and the 2021–27 budget[43] or the 'rule of law' proceedings against Hungary and Poland.[44] Whether the citizens' calls for broader EU

[37] ibid, 79.

[38] see eg Case 300/89 *Commission of the European Communities v Council of the European Communities* [1991] ECLI:EU:C:1991:244 at [10]; Case C-376/98 *Federal Republic of Germany v European Parliament and Council of the European Union* [2000] ECLI:EU:C:2000:544 (n 36) para 77 et seq.

[39] Purnhagen et al (n 12).

[40] A similar approach focusing on facilitating solidarity can be found in Art 222 TFEU, which is related to the Civil Protection mechanism mentioned above; see 2014/415/EU: Council Decision of 24 June 2014 on the arrangements for the implementation by the Union of the solidarity clause OJ L 192/53 2014; de Ruijter et al (n 19) 6, 13; Purnhagen et al (n 12) 298.

[41] Art 5(2) TEU.

[42] Art 48 TEU.

[43] J Chalmers and G Baczynska, 'EU Leaders Struggle with "mission Impossible" at Deadlocked Recovery Summit' *Reuters* (20 July 2020) www.reuters.com/article/us-eu-summit-idUSKCN24K094; European Council, 'Special Meeting of the European Council (17, 18, 19, 20 and 21 July 2020) – Conclusions (EUCO 10/20)'.

[44] See eg Art 7 TEU and European Parliament, 'Press Release – Rule of Law in Poland and Hungary Has Worsened' (16 January 2020) www.europarl.europa.eu/news/en/press-room/20200109IPR69907/rule-of-law-in-poland-and-hungary-has-worsened.

health-crisis competences do indeed lead to such a change depends on the Member States governments' willingness to heed their citizens' calls and on their ability to find political consensus for such a Treaty change among all 27 governments.

As can be seen from the current health-competences set out in Articles 4, 6, and 168 TFEU, the Member States have adopted a restrictive stance regarding the EU's health-competences in the past. Currently, some Member States still demonstrate this cautious stance on the EU's health-competences. For instance, the Czech Republic voiced concerns that the recent proposal for a new EU health programme[45] did not sufficiently respect the Member States' competences regarding their own healthcare systems.[46]

The internal documents surrounding past Treaty revisions involving health-competences are not available to the public.[47] Nevertheless, the Member States' interest to keep their autonomy over laws affecting their national social welfare budgets and, accordingly, the shaping and financing of their national healthcare systems has been accepted in the literature as the main reason for the limited scope of the EU health-competences as set out in the Treaties.[48]

Currently, there seems to be no political hunger on part of the Member States' governments for a change in EU health-competences. The political hurdles of extending these competences should not be underestimated. Nevertheless, the next section will argue that certain aspects of the EU's response to COVID-19 seem to alleviate some of the Member States' concerns regarding health-competences or shed a new light on the question of EU health-competences and might after all facilitate the debate in favour of broader health-competences in the nearer future.

III. The EU4Health Programme and the Emergency Support Instrument – Answering Citizens' Calls and Paving the Way for New EU Competences?

Taking the EU citizens' responses that the availability of medical supplies and research-funding for a COVID-19 vaccine should be the EU's top priorities as frame,

[45] EU4Health Programme (n 21).

[46] ES Nicolás, '[Coronavirus] EU Commission Ready to Play Bigger Role in Health Sector' (*EUobserver*, 15 June 2020) euobserver.com/coronavirus/148640 accessed 18 August 2020.

[47] Hervey and McHale (n 34) 74.

[48] ibid, 80; M McKee, TK Hervey and AB Gilmore, 'Public Health Policies' in E Mossialos et al (eds), *Health Systems Governance in Europe: The Role of European Union Law and Policy* (CUP, 2010) 237; A de Ruijter, 'A Silent Revolution: The Expansion of EU Power in the Field of Human Health: A Rights-Based Analysis of EU Health Law & Policy' (PhD, University of Amsterdam, 2015) 33; ME Földes, 'Member State Interests and European Union Law' in Marton Varju (ed), *Between Compliance and Particularism: Member State Interests and European Union Law* (Springer International Publishing, 2019); M Guy, 'Towards a European Health Union: What Role for Member States? (First View Version)' (2020) *European Journal of Risk Regulation* 1, 2; B Przywara, 'Projecting Future Health Care Expenditure at European Level: Drivers, Methodology and Main Results' (Directorate-General for Economic and Financial Affairs 2010) 4 et seq.

this section will give an overview of the two instruments proposed or adopted in direct response to COVID-19 and demonstrate that the current approach indeed goes some way to answers the citizens' calls. It will further analyse whether the use of these instruments in response to the pandemic mitigates the Member States' concerns regarding their national health-budgets and, in that, strengthens the case for the introduction of new EU health-crisis competences in the future, eg regarding broader up-front powers for the EU to engage in procurement and distribution of protective equipment, medicines, vaccines, and other supplies, or supporting research. It will show that the scale and use of these instruments indeed support arguments for the introduction of broader EU competences.

From a democratic point of view, it is notable that, while these instruments do not give the EU broader legislative powers, particularly the ESI attributes significant decision-making powers in relation to taking financial measures to the Commission. It serves to note that the members of the Commission are chosen by Member States and appointed,[49] but that the Commission is the EU institution with arguably the least amount of democratic legitimisation, compared to the Council, consisting of members of the nationally elected governments, or the directly elected EU parliament.[50] Accordingly, the following sections will also comment on the legitimisation, democratic control, and transparency of the powers these instruments confer to the Commission.

A. The Proposed EU4Health Programme

Joint procurement of medical supplies, as well as investment in vaccine and other relevant research will be possible under the new 'EU4Health' Programme.[51] The EU's role under the EU4Health Programme is to support and coordinate the actions of Member States, in line with the limits of the EU's health-competences and the subsidiarity principle,[52] and particularly to distribute and manage the budget available under the programme.[53] The programme has been proposed by the European Commission and is being discussed in the Council and its preparatory bodies at the time of writing.

It should not be underestimated how significant the existence of this proposal is. There were no plans for a new, fourth specific health-programme before

[49] Art 17 TEU.

[50] Arts 14 (2), (3), 16(3) TEU.

[51] eg Recital 10, Arts 8, 10 EU4Health Programme (n 21).

[52] ibid, 5.

[53] Arts 8 et seq EU4Health Programme (n 21); Regulation (EU, Euratom) 2018/1046 of the European Parliament and of the Council of 18 July 2018 on the financial rules applicable to the general budget of the Union, amending Regulations (EU) No 1296/2013, (EU) No 1301/2013, (EU) No 1303/2013, (EU) No 1304/2013, (EU) No 1309/2013, (EU) No 1316/2013, (EU) No 223/2014, (EU) No 283/2014, and Decision No 541/2014/EU and repealing Regulation (EU, Euratom) No 966/2012 (OJ L 193/1) 2018.

COVID-19. Rather, health was to form a part of the new ESF+ programme,[54] which merged several social, employment, and aid funding programmes.[55] After having previously adopted three dedicated consecutive health programmes,[56] the inclusion of health in the ESF+ could only be seen as a step back for the EU's role regarding health. This step back will now be reversed by giving health its own EU programme after all and providing it with a significantly strengthened budget. While health had been allocated 413 million EUR under the ESF+ proposal,[57] the proposed EU4health programme sets out a budget of 9.4 billion EUR.[58] The budget had been cut to 5.1 billion EUR by the EU governments, but the Commission has committed early on to funding the remaining amount itself through other avenues.[59]

While not in itself extending the competences of the EU, the EU4health programme demonstrates the Member States'[60] acknowledgement of the role the EU has to play in health-matters. Furthermore, the significantly increased budget and particularly the EU's willingness to provide a large part of it through the EU budget, could arguably mitigate some of the Member States' concerns regarding their national health budgets, as will be further discussed below.

In the EU4health programme, both transparency mechanisms as well as provisions safeguarding Member States representation are in place. According to Article 16(4) of the Regulation, the Commission must annually inform the Parliament of the work programme and priorities it intends to adopt. It must further seek the views of relevant stakeholders when drawing up its annual work programmes in which it determines the priorities for the funding provided under the EU4Health programme.

The programme ensures the involvement of the Member States through a Steering Group, consisting of the Commission and representatives appointed by the Member States.[61] This Steering Group is asked to consult on the EU's planned work programmes and the priorities pursued therein. The programme further entails the EU Commission being assisted by a dedicated Committee, comprising

[54] EU4Health Programme (n 21) 7; Proposal for a Regulation of the European Parliament and of the Council on the European Social Fund Plus (ESF+) (COM(2018) 382 final) 2018, part III, chapter II; Annex III.

[55] Explanatory Memorandum p. 1 EU4Health Programme (n 21).

[56] Decision No 1786/2002/EC; Decision No 1350/2007/EC; Regulation (EU) No 282/2014.

[57] ESF+ Proposal p 12.

[58] Art 5 EU4Health Programme (n 21).

[59] European Parliament, 'Press Release – Compromise on Long-Term EU Budget' (10 November 2020) www.europarl.europa.eu/news/en/press-room/20201106IPR91014/compromise-on-long-term-eu-budget-ep-obtains-EU16-billion-more-for-key-programmes; G Fortuna, 'Commission Promises to Remedy Health Cuts Made by EU Leaders' (*www.euractiv.com*, 16 September 2020) www.euractiv.com/section/health-consumers/news/commission-promise-to-remedy-health-cuts-made-by-eu-leaders/; European Commission, 'New EU4Health Programme' ec.europa.eu/commission/presscorner/detail/en/qanda_20_956.

[60] Represented in the Council of the EU.

[61] Art 16 Proposal for a Regulation of the European Parliament and of the Council on the establishment of a Programme for the Union's action in the field of health for the period 2021–2027 and repealing Regulation (EU) No 282/2014 ('EU4Health Programme') (COM(2020) 405 final) 2020.

representatives of the Member States and of the Commission without whose opinion the Commission may not adopt the respective implementing acts pursuant to the EU4health programme.[62] Regarding the democratic legitimisation of the rules and powers set out by the EU4Health programme, one must also note that this Regulation was adopted both by Parliament and Council, both accordingly endorsing the extent of the EU's powers under this programme.

B. The Emergency Support Instrument (ESI)

The pandemic prompted the activation of the ESI for the purpose of addressing COVID-19, as the existing mechanisms mentioned above alone were deemed insufficient to address the financial needs arising to address the COVID-19 pandemic.[63] Through the ESI, the EU can engage in a range of measures addressing the pandemic,[64] inter alia joint procurement of medical supplies, vaccines, and support of vaccine research.[65] It is based on a 2016 Council Regulation[66] set up to address disasters within the EU and to strengthen the EU's solidarity response and capacities, as eg the Civil Protection Mechanism was deemed potentially lacking by having to rely on voluntary contributions from Member States.[67] The ESI operates with a much larger budget than RescEU, with 2.7 billion EUR available through the ESI compared to just 300 million EUR through RescEU capacities.[68] It applies in parallel to eg RescEU and the JPA and is intended to be complementary to the other EU instruments and the Member States' individual responses.[69]

The ESI is inter alia used for the purpose of support research into vaccines, as was one of the citizens' requests for EU action.[70] It is further used for securing vaccine doses once a successful vaccine is found.[71] In order to do so, the Commission centrally and on behalf of all Member States enters into so-called 'advanced purchase agreements' (APAs) with vaccine-manufacturers.[72] Based on these APAs, the EU uses parts of the ESI budget for up-front financing in return

[62] Art 23 EU4Health Programme (n 21); Recital 6, Art 3(2) Regulation (EU) No 182/2011 of the European Parliament and of the Council of 16 February 2011 laying down the rules and general principles concerning mechanisms for control by Member States of the Commission's exercise of implementing powers OJ L 55/13 2011.

[63] Recital 4 ESI.

[64] ibid, Art 3(3).

[65] ibid.

[66] Council Regulation (EU) 2016/369 of 15 March 2016 on the provision of emergency support within the Union [2016] OJ L 70/1 2016.

[67] ibid, Recital 5.

[68] European Commission, 'EU Solidarity for Health Initiative' ec.europa.eu/commission/presscorner/detail/en/qanda_20_577.

[69] Recital 8, Art 3(1) ESI.

[70] European Parliament and Kantar (n 2) 8, 33 et seq.

[71] Commission Decision of 18.6.2020 approving the agreement with Member States on procuring COVID-19 vaccines on behalf of the Member States and related procedures (C(2020) 4192 final) 2020.

[72] ibid, Recital 3, Article 1(1).

for the right for all EU Member States to purchase a certain amount of dosages and as an advance payment for purchases the Member States might later carry out.[73] With this up-front financing, the EU hopes to decrease the risk for vaccine manufacturers and, in this, support and accelerate the development of a successful vaccine.[74] While there is no formal obligation to join, all EU Member States participate in the APAs.[75] Under the APA Framework Agreement, the Member States commit not to negotiate unilaterally with the same vaccine manufacturers.[76] Even though an explicit opt-out option exists and the Member States can still negotiate individually with other manufacturers,[77] this commitment signifies a difference to the Member States' right to negotiate separately despite joint procurement contracts which form eg part of the JPA.[78] This arguably mitigates some of the criticism raised in academic literature regarding the voluntary nature of joint public procurement,[79] at least with regard to the ESI.

From a democratic perspective, it is notable that the ESI and its activation legislation are Council Regulations, with no involvement of the EU Parliament, which is, after all, the EU institution most closely representing all EU citizens.[80] Article 122 TFEU does provide the Council with the competence to adopt measures in response to Member States experiencing difficulties, particularly vis-à-vis the supply of certain products, as it has done in the ESI and its activation Regulation. Despite this power being conferred explicitly to the Council, the absence of Parliament involvement in the APAs based on the ESI is noteworthy.

With regard to the representation of the Member States' views and their involvement, the ESI and the APAs concluded on its basis do not significantly differ from the EU4Health programme in that a focus is put on involving representatives named by the Member States. The APA Decision provides for a Steering Board to advise and assist the Commission in evaluating the APAs, comprising of representatives of the Commission as well as of each of the participating Member States. Experts from six Member States are further appointed to assist the Commission in negotiating the APAs, though not in a capacity to represent the Member States as such.[81] Nevertheless, it must be noted that the focus of the decision-making

[73] Art 2, Annex p 4 Annex to the Commission Decision on approving the agreement with Member States on procuring COVID-19 vaccines on behalf of the Member States and related procedures (C(2020) 4192 final ANNEX) 2020.

[74] Decision on procuring COVID-19 vaccines (C(2020) 4192 final) Recital 3; Decision on procuring COVID-19 vaccines, Annex – APA Framework Agreement Annex p 4.

[75] European Commission, 'Draft Amending Budget N°8 to the General Budget 2020 – Increase of Payment Appropriations for the Emergency Support Instrument to Finance the COVID-19 Vaccines Strategy and for the Impact of the Corona Response Investment Initiative Plus (COM(2020) 900 Final)' 3.

[76] Art 7 Decision on procuring COVID-19 vaccines, Annex – APA Framework Agreement.

[77] ibid.

[78] Art 1(5) 'Joint Procurement Agreement to Procure Medical Countermeasures' (n 16).

[79] Compare above.

[80] Art 14 TEU.

[81] Recital 5, Art 2(1) Decision on procuring COVID-19 vaccines (C(2020) 4192 final); Decision on procuring COVID-19 vaccines, Annex – APA Framework Agreement 3, 4.

powers is given firmly to the Commission which 'retains exclusive responsibility over the [APA evaluation] process'[82] and which[83] is in charge of the final decision as to which of the APAs should be concluded.[84]

While the focus on the views of the Member States rather than the EU citizens more directly through the Parliament therefore does not seem to be out of the ordinary with regard to research funding and procurement, the lack of transparency safeguards towards Parliament in the ESI, its activation, and the APAs is remarkable.

The ESI and its activation make no mention of duties to report to or inform the EU Parliament. The Annex to the Commission Decision vis-à-vis the centralised procurement of vaccines through the EU requires to inform the Council's integrated political crisis response (IPCR) at least once every two weeks 'for full transparency',[85] but both the Decision as well as the Annex equally do not entail any requirement to inform the Parliament. This has already attracted criticism in practice. Indeed, with regard to the contracts for the procurement of vaccines, the EU Parliament has criticised the Commission for its lack of transparency and clarity.[86] As will be further discussed below, such shortcomings may to some extent be addressed by the introduction of new, explicit health-crisis competences.

C. A Budding Competence-Change?

The EU has not tired of underlining its role as supporting and coordinating Member States action in these instruments.[87] Nevertheless, despite the EU's reassurances, calls for more competences from EU institutions and academics are not abating, but only growing stronger. Commission President von der Leyen explicitly raised the issue of extended EU health-competences and endorsed an EU Health Union in her 2020 State of the Union speech.[88] Further, President von der Leyen set the issue out as a topic for the Conference on the Future of Europe and announced a Global Health Summit in Italy 2021 convened by the EU Commission.[89]

[82] Recital 5 Decision on procuring COVID-19 vaccines (C(2020) 4192 final).

[83] Albeit assisted by the Steering Board.

[84] Out of those to which at least four Member States in principle agreed, Decision on procuring COVID-19 vaccines, Annex – APA Framework Agreement 4.

[85] ibid.

[86] 'COVID-19 Vaccinations: More Solidarity and Transparency Needed | News | European Parliament' (19 January 2021) www.europarl.europa.eu/news/en/headlines/society/20210114STO95642/covid-19-vaccinations-more-solidarity-and-transparency-needed; 'COVID-19 Vaccines: MEPs Call for More Clarity and Transparency | News | European Parliament' (12 January 2021) www.europarl.europa.eu/news/en/press-room/20210111IPR95308/covid-19-vaccines-meps-call-for-more-clarity-and-transparency.

[87] See eg Art 1(2) Health Threats Decision No 1082/2013/EU; Civil Protection Mechanism Decision 1313/2013/EU eg Recitals 1, 14, Art 3(1) and throughout; 'RescEU' Decision (EU) 2019/420 Recital 2; European Commission, 'EU Solidarity for Health Initiative' (n 68); European Commission, 'New EU4Health Programme' (n 59).

[88] U von der Leyen, 'State of the Union Address by President von Der Leyen' ec.europa.eu/commission/presscorner/detail/en/SPEECH_20_1655.

[89] ibid.

The abovementioned political hurdles needed to bring about the necessary Treaty change aside, there are hints that such a change might be more realistic now, due to the COVID-19-response, than before. Two main aspects of the EU4health programme and the ESI, as well as the Member States' participation in the latter, suggest that a change in the Member States' attitude towards EU health-competences, at least with regard to health crises, might come about due to the current pandemic: (a) in the way in which the crisis has exemplified the need for and advantages of joint action centralised at EU level, and (b) in the involved financial contributions from the EU, mitigating some of the Member States' health-budget concerns.

i. A Stronger Endorsement of Centralised Action and a Bigger Role for the Commission

The sheer possibility of the EU4health programme as a separate health programme can only be seen as an endorsement by the Member States of the important role the EU has to play regarding health. Despite the current budget discussions involving the health programme, the existence of this programme as such has not in itself attracted criticism by the Member States. While the EU must still reassure Member States that the health programme itself does not exceed the EU's competences, the inherent acknowledgement of the necessity and advantages of health action at EU level may well influence future discussions towards the introduction of explicit EU health crisis competences.

The ESI, which has, after all, been joined by all Member States, equally signifies such an endorsement of the central and strengthened role the EU can play in relation to health, particularly with regard to research and procurement. The ESI explicitly points out the 'utmost importance to extend the possibilities for the Commission to purchase supplies or services on behalf of Member States' in its preamble.[90]

While the benefits of joint action, such as a stronger negotiation position, solidarity, risk-sharing, or resource-pooling, were well-known before the COVID-19 pandemic and influenced eg the joint procurement instruments which already existed before COVID-19,[91] the current pandemic has provided an undeniable example which underlines the need for solidarity and joint crisis responses to a yet unprecedented extent. In response to COVID-19, the EU's role has already been strengthened, particularly through the ESI, and its role endorsed by the Member States' participation in the ESI. For instance, the list of possible actions which the EU can support under the ESI is explicitly non-exhaustive,[92] empowering the EU

[90] ESI Recital 15.

[91] See eg 'Joint Procurement Agreement to Procure Medical Countermeasures' (n 16) Recital 6; Health Threats Decision No 1082/2013/EU Recital 13; 'RescEU' Decision (EU) 2019/420 Recitals 9, 11, 18.

[92] Art 3(3) ESI, added Annex to; Council Regulation (EU) 2016/369.

and giving it discretion to choose to support COVID-19-responses beyond those explicitly mentioned.

Further, the ESI allows the EU to engage in procurement as wholesaler to then resell or even donate the procured countermeasures to Member States or other organisations.[93] This option is already generally contained in the financial rules on the EU budget in cases where the EU awarded contracts on its own account.[94] However, the ESI mentions this possibility explicitly in response to COVID-19 and adds the possibility for donation of the procured goods. There is currently no information available whether the Commission has made use of this option. Nevertheless, it arguably provides the opportunity for a much more central role for the EU with more central decision-making powers, eg which Member States it deems in need, as well as whether and to whom it chooses to donate procured goods. There are further examples of the strengthened decision-power and influence the EU has been given regarding public procurement in response to COVID-19 through the ESI. Due to the urgency of the situation, grants under the ESI can be awarded by the Commission without the usual prior call for proposals and under the conditions set out by the Commission itself.[95] The ESI also allows the Commission to modify existing contracts or framework contracts without a separate procurement procedure, as well as for several derogations from the JPA, the Civil Protection Mechanism, and the respective Regulation on the financial budget rules.[96]

The Member States' acceptance of a stronger, more central role for the EU also becomes clear in light of the ESI-mechanism to fund and procure vaccines.

Once the EU approach to joint vaccine development and procurement had been adopted, the Member States gave up more individual approaches to vaccine procurement, eg by France, Germany, the Netherlands and Italy, who had formed the 'Inclusive Vaccine Alliance'.[97] Instead they asked the Commission to take on contracts they had already concluded for a broader, joint European response.[98] Joining the ESI and the APA Framework Agreement, the Member States further accepted the need for a strong, united approach and accepted that the option to bilaterally negotiate in addition to joint procurement, as forms part of the JPA,[99]

[93] Art 4 ESI.

[94] Regulation (EU, Euratom) 2018/1046 Annex I, Section 32.1.(a).

[95] ESI Recital 20; 'Commission Decision of 24.4.2020 on the Financing of Emergency Support under Council Regulation (EU) 2016/369 (C(2020) 2794 Final)' Recital 3, Art 5; 'Annex to the Commission Decision on the Financing of Emergency Support under Council Regulation (EU) 2016/369 (C(2020) 2794 Final ANNEX)', point 1; also see Arts 195, 197 Regulation (EU, Euratom) 2018/1046.

[96] Art 4 ESI; also see Art 172 Regulation (EU, Euratom) 2018/1046.

[97] Y Natsis, 'Getting It Right: COVID19 Vaccines Procurement – EPHA' (*European Public Health Alliance*) epha.org/getting-it-right-covid19-vaccines-procurement; Nicolás (n 46).

[98] European Commission, 'Communication from the Commission to the European Parliament, the European Council and the European Investment Bank – EU Strategy for COVID-19 Vaccines (COM/2020/245 Final)' 3; J Bauomy, 'Once a COVID-19 Vaccine Is Found, What Happens Next?' *euronews* (1 August 2020) www.euronews.com/2020/08/01/once-a-covid-19-vaccine-is-found-what-happens-next. Note, however, that Member States are still free to negotiate with vaccine-manufacturers not part of the EU's joint approach.

[99] See above.

is excluded under the ESI. This endorsement of joint actions should arguably address subsidiarity concerns or potential Member States' doubts as to the need for centralised EU action in this regard.

ii. Financial Contributions from the EU Budget

With regard to the potential introduction of new, broader EU health crisis competences, one should recall the reasons behind the Member States' decidedly cautious stance on EU health-competences, ie their aim to retain control of their national healthcare-related budgets and spending.[100]

The current EU measures touching on the health-emergency response do not negatively impact, but rather even support the national healthcare budgets.

Through the ESI and, once adopted, the EU4health-Programme, the EU is not only able to engage in further public procurement, but as pointed out above is also willing to rely to a significant degree on its own budget to do so. Through joint procurement of medical countermeasures, the negotiation and purchasing position of the Commission acting on behalf of Member States is strengthened vis-à-vis the respective manufacturers. This is sought to facilitate the procurement of the countermeasures at more favourable terms and prices,[101] which can ultimately positively affect how much money the Member States have to direct at the purchase of the countermeasures from their national budgets. Further, the EU's financial contributions as part of the vaccine APAs in part function as advance payment for potential later purchases by the Member States, explicitly reducing the financial burden of the Member States if they enter into a purchase agreement.[102] At the same time, this measure leaves the Member States' regular healthcare spending untouched.

It is important to remember that these arguments arise primarily in context of a health-crisis. The EU citizens explicitly endorsed health-crisis competences,[103] even though this is the case because of the way the respective statement in the Parliament Survey was pre-formulated.

New competences would likely only concern a limited and, (hopefully) infrequent occurrence. They would therefore likely only apply to strictly limited situations, complementing and supporting the Member States' exercise of their regular, national health-competences.[104] If such new, explicit health-crisis competences were tied to a reliance on the EU budget rather than impacting the national ones, one could argue that the Member States' main concern regarding

[100] See above at n 32.

[101] 'Joint Procurement Agreement to Procure Medical Countermeasures' (n 16) Recital 6; Health Threats Decision No 1082/2013/EU Recital 13; 'RescEU' Decision (EU) 2019/420 Recital 18.

[102] Article 2, Annex p 4 Decision on procuring COVID-19 vaccines, Annex – APA Framework Agreement.

[103] European Parliament and Kantar (n 2) 8, 30 et seq.

[104] Also compare Pacces and Weimer (n 10) 292.

health-competences seems to be alleviated and that, in conjunction with the proven need for central EU action, new competences should be introduced.

iii. The Case for Explicit Competences – Boundaries, Speed, and Solidarity

The previous sections have shown that the citizens' calls seem to have been answered to a large extent by using existing competences and instruments. In light of this and despite the Member States' endorsement of a stronger role for the EU in a health-crisis and the mitigation of their health-budget concerns, is the introduction of new, broader EU health-crisis competences, as the citizens demanded, even necessary? There are three main reasons for the Member States to do so: setting informed boundaries for EU action, facilitating a faster response in future crises, and decisively addressing criticism as to the lack of solidarity between EU Member States.

With regard to the advantage of explicit competences as setting boundaries, it serves to recall one of the reasons behind the initial introduction of explicit health-competences in the Treaties, the issue of 'creeping competences'.[105] The Member States sought to provide an explicit frame and explicit boundaries to EU action on health taking place based on other legal norms.

While EU action impacting health based on other competences is still happening, as eg the ESI shows, some of these instruments are very broadly phrased and, in theory, allow for an even more central role than the EU has currently taken on under this pandemic.[106] The ESI itself is time-limited. However, its use is likely to prove instructive to which extent EU-led action truly is useful and necessary in response to a major health-crisis.

Consolidating the broader EU decision-making powers, which prove useful based on the current use of the ESI in the form of official competences, could facilitate EU measures towards preparing for a future health crisis or even towards extending such preparatory measures to the yearly flu-epidemics – measures which of course cannot be based on a strictly time-limited instrument. At the same time, explicit competences would allow the Member States to set evidence-based boundaries. Drawing from the experiences with the COVID-19 instruments discussed in this chapter, explicit competences could limit EU action to only where it has indeed proven necessary and useful, but also prevent EU action from going beyond this on the basis of emergency instruments. This does not preclude the option to retain emergency mechanisms such as the ones relied on in the current pandemic to allow flexibility where health crisis competences prove insufficient in the future.

[105] Hervey and McHale (n 34) 80, compare section II(B) above.

[106] See section III(C)(i).

Related to the advantage of allowing more extensive, evidence-based preparation for a potential future health crisis, adopting a fixed set of official health-crisis competences further has the advantage of facilitating timely EU-action, skipping the need for bureaucratic procedures necessary to eg activate and amend the ESI only after some time has passed and the explicit needs of EU-action have become clear. In a crisis situation, time is of the essence and the EU's initial lack of possibility to engage in procurement as a matter of urgency rightfully drew criticism.[107] Such criticism could be relieved by new crisis-competences informed by the COVID-19 experience, which could allow more immediate and to some extent preventive procurement and measures.

With regard to the time sensitivity of crisis responses, introducing eg EU competences allowing the strategic stockpiling of medical countermeasures in preparation for possible future health crises further allows the introduction of transparency mechanisms and further democratic safeguards.

While the current response for the most part seems to achieve its aims, as raised above, criticism has arisen particularly from members of the EU parliament regarding a lack of transparency in the Commission's decision-making, particularly with regard to the details of the contracts with vaccine manufacturers, the Commission concluded.[108] The Commission has published, partially redacted, some of its vaccine contracts, but had initially been reluctant to do so. Introducing clearer, more explicit competences regarding the procurement of eg vaccines or other medical countermeasures could allow binding transparency safeguards to be put into writing while also enhancing the preparedness of the EU. Further, providing the EU with central powers of procurement and distribution of medical supplies in times of crisis allows the integration of democratic safeguards akin to or going beyond those relied on in the EU4Health Programme or the ESI,[109] such as supervisory or comitology procedures under which the Commission's procurement decisions can be reviewed and approved by the Council or committees consisting of representatives of the Member States.[110] Such safeguards are likely to further alleviate Member States' concerns regarding their representation in health matters. Further, conferring explicit competences on the EU allows the procedures and structures for such safeguards to be in place, facilitating a swifter decision-making process to accommodate the time-sensitivity of a crisis situation.

With regard to building a pre-emptive stockpile of medical supplies, similar or even stronger democratic safeguards could be built into the respective processes. Introducing explicit competences in this regard with the respective transparency and democratic safeguards included, similar or going beyond those contained in the EU4Health programme, and regarding Member States representation, the

[107] de Ruijter et al (n 19) 14.

[108] See eg 'COVID-19 Vaccines: MEPs Call for More Clarity and Transparency | News | European Parliament' (n 86).

[109] Compare sections III(A) and (B) above.

[110] Compare C Barnard and S Peers (eds), *European Union Law*, 2nd edn (OUP, 2017) 130.

ESI could contribute to better preparedness for future crises without decisively compromising the Member States' or other bodies representing the EU's citizens' influence on the process.

Lastly, introducing explicit health crisis competences has the power to send an important political signal to EU citizens regarding the solidarity between Member States, which citizens had criticised.[111] Permanent health crisis competences for the EU, inspired by the current EU-action based on the principle of solidarity,[112] could rely on the EU as the 'facilitator' of solidarity between Member States and underline their fundamental willingness to act together and for each other through the EU in times of crisis. Pre-empting the EU having to fall back on the solidarity-competence once a crisis has hit, perhaps partly for lack of other ways to address an ongoing crisis at EU level, but instead setting out concrete competences inspired by the experience of the current health crisis and the response based on solidarity, can send an important political signal of forward thinking solidarity between EU Member States.

IV. Conclusion

Returning to the citizens whose views on EU action in response to the COVID-19 pandemic framed this chapter: have their calls been answered? If not, will they in the future?

Starting from the limited EU health-competences and the Member States' cautious stance on EU action regarding health, the chapter has shown that vis-à-vis the more concrete priorities the citizens endorsed, EU involvement in the procurement of medical equipment and EU funding for vaccine research,[113] the EU uses what health, but also what non-health-competences and instruments it has to support the Member States' actions in the COVID-19 pandemic. Indeed, the EU has taken on a central, albeit not exclusive, role both in the actual procurement as well as in the funding of medical countermeasures and vaccine-research. EU action seems, for the most part, to have made a significant contribution to the attainment of these two citizen-priorities.

This chapter has shown that the Member States' participation in and acceptance of the EU as a central actor via these instruments and of the use of the EU budget in response to the COVID-19 crisis already illustrates a bigger endorsement of a more centralised role for the EU regarding health crises, which strengthens the case for more extensive health crisis competences in the future. Further, this chapter has argued that, despite the historically cautious stance of the Member States towards EU health-competences, the extent to which the EU is willing

[111] European Parliament and Kantar (n 2) 21 et seq.
[112] The activation of the ESI based on Art 122(1) TFEU, compare above.
[113] European Parliament and Kantar (n 2) 8, 33 et seq.

to mobilise its own budget to financially contribute to the pandemic-response could significantly alleviate Member States' concerns that broader EU health-competences might negatively impact their authority vis-à-vis their national health budgets, if those competences are tied to contributions from the EU budget.

Lastly, the chapter has argued that, despite the current instruments' positive impact towards addressing the COVID-19 pandemic, there are good reasons for Member States to consolidate the more influential role the EU has taken on during this pandemic in the form of concrete health crisis competences in the Treaties to enhance preparedness as well as to allow for a faster response during future crises, while also establishing transparency and democratic safeguards.

One must hope that at a later stage in the pandemic, or after it has successfully been overcome, a detailed review of the action taken, both with regard to more immediate health measures as well as other aspects of EU action, such as a centralised management of free movement restrictions and controls,[114] will be carried out. Such a review will certainly be instructive and essential for an evidence-based future debate on the need for and advantages of centralised EU action in response to major health crises. However, to rely on extensive, robust evidence, this should be reserved for a later stage of the pandemic.

This pandemic has brought a lot of uncertainty in many regards, but what can be said with certainty is that with the upcoming Conference on the Future of Europe and a 2021 Global Health Summit, the COVID-19 pandemic has undoubtedly given calls for more EU health-crisis competences more teeth and we may see a transfer of health decision-making powers from the Member States to the EU yet.

[114] Compare eg Purnhagen et al (n 12) 201 et seq; Pacces and Weimer (n 10) throughout; de Ruijter et al (n 19) 14 et seq and throughout.

13

Pandemics and Platforms: Private Governance of (Dis)Information in Crisis Situations

MATTHIAS C KETTEMANN AND MARIE-THERESE SEKWENZ

I. Introduction

What role do online platforms play in managing and governing information during the pandemic? Chinese platforms cooperated substantially with the governments' message (and message control) on the coronavirus, but also US-based platforms like Twitter and Facebook that had employed a hands-off approach to certain types of disinformation in the past invested considerably in the tools necessary to govern online disinformation more actively. Facebook, for instance, deleted Facebook events for anti-lockdown demonstrations while Twitter had to rely heavily on automated filtering (with human content governance employees back at home). This chapter will assess these practices, their impact and permanence in light of the author's research on the important role of intermediaries as normative actors, including their establishment, through terms of service and content governance practices, of a private order of public communication.

II. State Responsibilities and Private Duties Regarding Online Communication

Online just as offline, states have an obligation to respect, protect and ensure human rights for everyone on their territory or under their control.[1] This extends the duties states have from the analogue world into the digital one, especially as

[1] This section draws on M Kettemann and W Benedek, 'Freedom of expression online' in M Susi (ed), *Human Rights, Digital Society and the Law. A Research Companion* (Routledge, 2019) 58–74 and W Benedek and M Kettemann, *Freedom of Expression on the Internet* (Council of Europe, 2014, 2nd edn, 2020).

being 'online' is now the new normal and the internet of platforms and contents is enriched by an internet of things (like smart cars) and an internet of bodies (like intelligent wearables). Even as new approaches to norm entrepreneurship online emerge,[2] rights that people have offline are still their rights in online environments.

Online just as offline, states have a primary responsibility and ultimate obligation to protect human rights and fundamental freedoms.[3] But what are these requirements international law imposes on states to ensure rights online? A key international legal basis for freedom of expression is Article 19 of the Universal Declaration of Human Rights, which is largely considered to reflect customary law. In addition, in 1976 the International Covenant on Civil and Political Rights (ICCPR) was adopted, which in its Article 19 reiterates the text of the Universal Declaration and then clarifies (in para 2) that everyone 'shall have the right to freedom of expression; this right shall include freedom to seek, receive and impart information and ideas of all kinds, regardless of frontiers, either orally, in writing or in print, in the form of art, or through any other media of his choice'.

Accordingly, the right goes beyond the freedom of the press and the freedom of the media to include individual expression in the widest sense. However, the right, with the exemption of the freedom of opinion, is not absolute or without limits. Under certain clearly defined conditions it can be restricted. In its biannual resolution on human rights on the internet in 2012, 2014 and 2016, the Human Rights Council affirmed, with references to Articles 19 of the UDHR and the ICCPR, the special role of freedom of expression online: 'the same rights that people have offline must also be protected online, *in particular freedom of expression*, which is applicable regardless of frontiers and through any media of one's choice [...]'.[4]

An evaluation of freedom of expression standards in international law from a European perspective (must) also consider similar regional standards such as the protections of Article 10(1) of the European Convention on Human Rights (ECHR), enshrining 'the right to freedom of expression. This right shall include the freedom to hold opinions and to receive and impart information and ideas without interference by public authority and regardless of frontiers'. Note the reference to the non-interference 'by public authority': States are obliged to protect freedom of expression both as a free-standing right and as an essential 'enabler' of other rights through the internet. As former UN Special Rapporteur for Freedom of Expression, Frank La Rue, wrote, 'by acting as a catalyst for individuals to exercise their right to freedom of opinion and expression, the internet also facilitates the realisation of a range of other human rights'.[5]

[2] R Mares et al, 'Normfare: Norm entrepreneurship in internet governance' (2021) 45(6) *Telecommunications Policy*, doi.org/10.1016/j.telpol.2021.102148.

[3] Just see European Court of Human Rights, *Beizaras and Levickas v Lithuania* (Application no. 41288/15), 15 January 2020.

[4] Human Rights Council Resolution 32/13, The promotion, protection and enjoyment of human rights on the Internet, UN Doc. A/HRC/RES/32/13 of 18 July 2016, para 1 (emphasis added).

[5] Report of the Special Rapporteur on the promotion and protection of the right to freedom of opinion and expression, UN Doc. A/HRC/17/27 of 16 May 2011, paras 22 and 23. But the internet also brings about new challenges to these same human rights.

The ECtHR case of *KU v Finland*[6] confirms that states have an obligation, under the European Convention of Human Rights, to ensure that the human rights of persons under their jurisdiction are protected – offline just as online. If social network service providers fail to introduce safeguards (in the case of *KU v Finland*, to protect the privacy rights of a child), states need to enforce a legal protection framework.[7] Just as real as the primary responsibility of states, however, is the observation that a lot of the discourse relevant for the constant opinion-forming work of democratic modernity takes place in private spaces.

The key questions regarding how to enable, moderate and regulate speech today therefore have to be asked and answered with a view to digital and private spaces.

The vast majority of communicative spaces on the internet are privately held and owned.[8] This is due to the powerful role of intermediaries, companies that enable our online activity.[9] States are therefore not the only actors in ensuring human rights online. As the 2018 Recommendation of the Council of Europe on internet intermediaries notes, a

> wide, diverse and rapidly evolving range of players, commonly referred to as 'internet intermediaries', facilitate interactions on the internet between natural and legal persons by offering and performing a variety of functions and services. Some connect users to the internet, enable the processing of information and data, or host web-based services, including for user-generated content. Others aggregate information and enable searches; they give access to, host and index content and services designed and/or operated by third parties.[10]

Network effects and mergers have led to the domination of the market by a relatively small number of key intermediaries. As the 2018 Recommendation warned, these few companies have growing power: '[the] power of such intermediaries as protagonists of online expression makes it imperative to clarify their role and impact on human rights as well as their corresponding duties and responsibilities, including as regards the risk of misuse by criminals of the intermediary's services and infrastructure'.[11]

Internet intermediaries have duties under international and national law. In line with the UN Guiding Principles on Business and Human Rights and the

[6] ECtHR, *KU v Finland* (2 December 2008), Application No. 2872/02.

[7] See W Benedek and M Kettemann, *Freedom of Expression on the Internet* (Council of Europe, 2014, 2nd edn, 2020) 92, 110.

[8] On why we would need public social media, too, see LB Wieser, 'Social Media im demokratischen Verfassungsstaat – Warum wir öffentlich-rechtliche soziale Medien brauchen' in M Becker et al (eds), *Gesellschaftliche Herausforderungen – Öffentlich-rechtliche Möglichkeiten* (Verlag Jan Sramek) 239–88.

[9] cf M Kettemann and W Schulz, 'Setting Rules for 2.7 Billion. A (First) Look into Facebook's Norm-Making System: Results of a Pilot Study' (Working Papers of the Hans-Bredow-Institut, Works in Progress # 1, January 2020), leibniz-hbi.de/uploads/media/Publikationen/cms/media/5pz9hwo_AP_WiP001InsideFacebook.pdf.

[10] Council of Europe, Recommendation CM/Rec (2018) 2 of the Committee of Ministers to member States on the roles and responsibilities of internet intermediaries, preambular para 4.

[11] ibid, preambular para 7.

'Protect, Respect and Remedy' Framework, intermediaries should respect the human rights of their users and affected parties in all their actions. This includes the responsibility to act in compliance with applicable laws and regulatory frameworks. Internet intermediaries also develop their own rules, usually in form of terms of service or community standards that often contain content-restriction policies. This responsibility to respect within their activities all internationally recognised human rights, in line with the United Nations Guiding Principles on Business and Human Rights, exists independently of the states' ability or willingness to fulfil their own human rights obligations.[12]

States have also misused intermediaries in the past to introduce filters and enforce laws that violate international human rights commitments. Therefore, as the Recommendation notes, any norms applicable to internet intermediaries, regardless of their objective or scope of application, 'should effectively safeguard human rights and fundamental freedoms, as enshrined in the European Convention on Human Rights, and should maintain adequate guarantees against arbitrary application in practice'.[13]

Due to the multi-layered nature of the regulatory framework governing services provided by or through intermediaries, their regulation is challenging. As they operate in many countries and data streams, especially for cloud-based services, and often cross many countries and jurisdictions, different and conflicting laws may apply.[14] This is exacerbated by, as the 2018 Council of Europe recommendation identified, 'the global nature of the internet networks and services, by the diversity of intermediaries, by the volume of internet communication, and by the speed at which it is produced and processed'.[15]

In line with the UN Guiding Principles on Business and Human Rights and the 'Protect, Respect and Remedy' Framework ('Ruggie Principles'), a convincing approach posits that intermediaries need to behave in a certain way to keep their 'social licence' to operate the quasi-public sphere. Such a 'licence' necessitates commitments to human rights of their users and affected parties in all their actions (including the formulation and application of terms of service) in order to address and remedy negative human rights impacts directly. For example, in order to identify and prevent adverse human rights impacts, business enterprises need to carry out human rights-due diligence. This should involve meaningful consultation with potentially affected groups and other relevant stakeholders, taking appropriate action, monitoring the effectiveness of the response and communicating their action as part of their accountability obligations.[16]

[12] ibid, para 2.1.1.

[13] ibid, para 2.1.2.

[14] ibid, preambular para 6.

[15] ibid, preambular para 9.

[16] See J Ruggie (7 April 2008), Human Rights Council, Report of the Special Representative of the Secretary-General on the issue of human rights and transnational corporations and other business enterprises, Protect, respect and remedy: a framework for business and human rights, UN Doc. A/HRC/8/5 and Guiding principles on business and human rights, implementing the United Nations

There is substantial literature on the duties of private entities in international law, especially with regard to the duties of transnational corporations[17] and private military contractors.[18] Much of it is applicable to internet standard-setters, but also to internet content companies, such as search engine providers and social networking services.[19]

III. Platforms in Pandemic Times

In a study[20] and subsequent analysis[21] of platform behaviour during the year of the rising COVID-19 pandemic 2020, we have identified a number of key shared commonalities among more than 40 states. Dominant platforms have been able to defend, or even solidify, their position, but communicative practices on those platforms are changing. State authorities increasingly use platforms to communicate and inform, and platforms support these approaches willingly. In the following, we look specifically at selected platforms and study their reaction to (dis)information related to the coronavirus to assess whether we can see an emergence of a cross-platform commitment to counter coronavirus-related disinformation.

A. Facebook

During the pandemic Facebook continued to remain one of the leading platforms with its two point seven billion daily users on its main platform alone.[22] With data traffic for messaging services, video and voice calls throughout the time of

'Protect, respect and remedy' framework, Annex to the Final Report of the Special Representative to the Human Rights Council, UN Doc. A/HRC/17/31 and adopted by the Human Rights Council (16 June 2011) by Resolution 17/4, Guidelines 17–21. See Benedek et al (n 7) 85f.

[17] Especially after the adoption of the UN Guiding Principles on Business and Human Rights. See R Mares (ed), *The UN Guiding Principles on Business and Human Rights. Foundations and Implementation* (Nijhoff, 2011); and, for a comprehensive analysis, W Cragg (ed), *Business and Human Rights* (Edward Elgar, 2012). For the international trade dimension relevant for aspects of ICTs, see AM Macleod, 'Human rights and international trade: normative underpinnings' in ibid, 179–96.

[18] cf L Cameron and V Chetail, *Privatizing War. Private Military and Security Companies under Public International Law* (CUP, 2013) 288–382 (arguing that PMSCs can be bound both as companies and as the sum of their individual employees). See also the body of scholarship cited in ibid, 269, n 22.

[19] Council of Europe, Committee of Ministers (4 April 2012), Recommendation CM/Rec(2012)3 on the protection of human rights with regard to search engines and Recommendation CM/Rec(2012)4 on the protection of human rights with regard to social networking services.

[20] M Kettemann and M Fertmann, 'Viral Information: How States and Platforms Deal with Covid-19-related Disinformation: an Exploratory Study of 18 Countries' (Verlag Hans-Bredow-Institut, 2021), GDHRNet Working Paper #1, 126.

[21] Kettemann et al, 'Healthy Conversations? Selected Trends in Covid-19-Related (Dis)Information Governance on Platforms' in M Kettemann and M Fertmann (eds), *Viral Information: How States and Platforms Deal with Covid-19-related Disinformation: an Exploratory Study of 18 Countries* (Verlag Hans-Bredow-Institut, 2021), GDHRNet Working Paper #1.

[22] J Clement, 'Facebook MAU Worldwide 2020' (*Statista*, 2020) www.statista.com/statistics/264810/number-of-monthly-active-facebook-users-worldwide/.

the pandemic was an important space for online speech during the pandemic.[23] Before the pandemic, Facebook claimed not wanting to be an 'arbiter of truth'.[24] While this was never accurate, and Facebook has always influenced how online communication takes place on this platform, the reaction to COVID-19 was much stronger than any other single issue addressed by automated and human content moderation.

According to the report by 'Avaaz' Facebook projected three point eight billion pieces of content that were classified as misleading health content to its users.[25] While the amount of content on the platform has increased, its content moderation was more difficult during the pandemic.[26] Because of global lockdown constraints, Facebook had to rely even more on automated content moderation.[27] Facebook also changed the community standards and defined content related to anti-vaccine statements,[28] or advertising claims for medical face masks, hand sanitiser, disinfectant wipes and COVID-19-test kits, as forbidden by its terms of service, which also can be seen as a shift in the company's approach.[29]

In March 2020, Facebook introduced an 'Information Hub'[30] for most users to provide health information by trusted authorities like the 'Center for Disease Control and Prevention' or the 'World Health Organization,' matched with content from hand-picked journalists and politicians, or other selected content about the pandemic. Facebook makes also use of pop-ups as a user-interface-design decision to additionally remind users to wear facemasks or to provide further information about the pandemic. Another information-related action was the investment of 100 million dollars to support fact-checking and journalism on the coronavirus crisis.[31] The financial support by Facebook also included donations

[23] K Khan et al, 'The COVID-19 Infodemic: A Quantitative Analysis Through Facebook' (Cureus, 2020) ncbi.nlm.nih.gov/pmc/articles/PMC7719473.

[24] T McCarthy, 'Zuckerberg Says Facebook Won't Be "arbiters of Truth" after Trump Threat' *The Guardian* (28 May 2020) www.theguardian.com/technology/2020/may/28/zuckerberg-facebook-police-online-speech-trump.

[25] See 'Facebook's Algorithm: A Major Threat to Public Health' *AVAAZ*, secure.avaaz.org/campaign/en/facebook_threat_health/.

[26] Facebook, 'Community Standards Enforcement Report, November 2020' (*About Facebook*, 19 November 2020) about.fb.com/news/2020/11/community-standards-enforcement-report-nov-2020/.

[27] 'Keeping People Safe and Informed About the Coronavirus – About Facebook' about.fb.com/news/2020/10/coronavirus/.

[28] Jin Kang-Xing, 'Supporting Public Health Experts' Vaccine Efforts' (*About Facebook*, 19 October 2020) about.fb.com/news/2020/10/supporting-public-health-experts-vaccine-efforts/.

[29] Facebook, 'Information about Ads about Social Issues, Elections or Politics and COVID-19' (*Facebook Business Help Center*, 2020) www.facebook.com/business/help/213593616543953 and Facebook, 'Banning Ads and Commerce Listings for Medical Face Masks' (6 March 2020) about.fb.com/news/2020/12/coronavirus/.

[30] Salvador Rodriguez, 'Facebook Is Encouraging Everybody to Take Social Distancing Seriously' *CNBC* (18 March 2020) www.cnbc.com/2020/03/18/coronavirus-facebook-launches-information-center-at-top-of-news-feed.html.

[31] Facebook, 'Investing $100 Million in the News Industry' (30 March 2020) about.fb.com/news/2020/12/coronavirus/.

for relief efforts,[32] healthcare workers,[33] small businesses[34] or supporting health crisis helplines.[35]

According to Kahn et al 22.3 per cent of their investigated Facebook posts contained misinformation about COVID-19.[36] Facebook furthermore opened some data silos to the public and researchers[37] as part of the 'Data for Good' programme.[38] To increase the use of this data Facebook had to further adapt its terms of service to the situation.[39] This data-support includes a COVID-19 map and dashboard with data about global symptom surveys, as well as information about datasets that mirror the movement range or other mobility-related information of Facebooks users. This data can be used for research that eg takes a close look at the friendship-boundaries of Facebook users in two countries to predict the likelihood of the creation of coronavirus hotspots.[40]

Facebook had to send home content moderators on 16 March 2020.[41] This situation caused by the lockdown led to a high increase in artificial intelligence supported content moderation.[42] While the old moderation system was going through the amount of content chronologically, the use of a variety of algorithms (this includes machine learning approaches, filtering, ranking and sorting) now uses criteria[43] to sort through the content and prioritise it.[44] This change within the moderation system should help remove harmful content more quickly than the chronological system did.

Nevertheless, Facebook remained a key platform for the spread of misinformation.[45] This claim is based on the high number of interactions related

[32] Facebook, 'Matching $20 Million in Donations to Support COVID-19 Relief Efforts' (13 March 2020) about.fb.com/news/2020/12/coronavirus/.

[33] Facebook, 'Donating $25 Million to Support Healthcare Workers' (30 March 2020) about.fb.com/news/2020/12/coronavirus/.

[34] Facebook, 'Investing $100 Million in Small Businesses' (17 March 2020) about.fb.com/news/2020/12/coronavirus/.

[35] Facebook, 'Connecting People to Well-Being Tips and Resources' (9 April 2020) about.fb.com/news/2020/12/coronavirus/.

[36] K Khan et al (n 23).

[37] Facebook, 'Data for Good: New Tools to Help Health Researchers Track and Combat COVID-19' (*About Facebook*, 6 April 2020) about.fb.com/news/2020/04/data-for-good/.

[38] Facebook, 'Our Work on COVID-19' (*Facebook Data for Good*) dataforgood.fb.com/docs/covid19/.

[39] Facebook, 'Protecting Privacy in Facebook Mobility Data during the COVID-19 Response' (*Facebook Research*, 3 June 2020) research.fb.com/blog/2020/06/protecting-privacy-in-facebook-mobility-data-during-the-covid-19-response/.

[40] T Kuchler et al, 'The Geographic Spread of COVID-19 Correlates with the Structure of Social Networks as Measured by Facebook' (2020), arXiv:2004.03055, 1.

[41] 'Keeping People Safe and Informed About the Coronavirus – About Facebook' (n 27).

[42] J Vincent, 'Facebook Is Now Using AI to Sort Content for Quicker Moderation' (*The Verge*, 13 November 2020) www.theverge.com/2020/11/13/21562596/facebook-ai-moderation.

[43] The criteria used are: virality, severity and how likely it is for the content to violate the Facebook Community Standards.

[44] S Majó-Vázquez et al, 'Volume and Patterns of Toxicity in Social Media Conversations during the Covid-19 Pandemic' (Reuters Institute, 2020) 12.

[45] A Knuutila et al, 'Covid-Related Misinformation on Youtube' (Oxford Internet Institute, 2020) demtech.oii.ox.ac.uk/wp-content/uploads/sites/93/2020/09/YouTube-misinfo-memo.pdf, 7.

to the content in question compared to other platforms. A study also highlighted the connection between YouTube and Facebook, which are more strongly correlated through content shares than other platforms. The authors therefore come to the conclusion that misinformation is more likely to become viral if it is shared through Facebook.

B. Twitter

The company reports a total reach of its monetisable daily active users (mDAU) of 164 million in the first quarter of 2020, which is a growth of 23 per cent in comparison to the corresponding values in 2019.[46]

While the traffic on the platform has risen in numbers, the problems via moderation, misinformation and fake news became even more problematic for COVID-19 related content.[47] Twitter took several measures to overcome the challenges of the pandemic. It supported verified information sources and tried to make them easy to access[48] in order to protect the debate on its platform.[49] Twitter strengthened its organisation-relationships and fostered public engagement on its platform.[50] Twitter also focussed on the research aspects as a fourth pillar of handling the pandemic.[51] Furthermore, Twitter decided to focus on the safety of partners and employees.[52] In order to provide valuable information to its users Twitter developed a COVID-19 tab in its 'Explore'[53] function. Here users have easy access to reliable sources and hand-picked page highlights from public health experts. Through the use of verified accounts misleading speech or misinformation should be tackled on the microblogging platform.[54]

[46] Statista, 'Twitter Global MDAU 2020' (*Statista*) www.statista.com/statistics/970920/monetizable-daily-active-twitter-users-worldwide/ and S Rosenberg et al, 'The Twitter Pandemic: The Critical Role of Twitter in the Dissemination of Medical Information and Misinformation during the COVID-19 Pandemic' (22 Canadian Journal of Emergency Medicine, 2020) 418.

[47] A Gruzd and P Mai, 'Going Viral: How a Single Tweet Spawned a COVID-19 Conspiracy Theory on Twitter' (2020) journals.sagepub.com/doi/full/10.1177/2053951720938405 and Rosenberg, Syed and Rezaie (ibid).

[48] Twitter, 'Helping People Find Reliable Information: Staying Safe and Informed on Twitter' (18 May 2020) blog.twitter.com/en_us/topics/company/2020/covid-19.html.

[49] Twitter, 'Protecting the Public Conversation' (14 July 2020) <https://blog.twitter.com/en_us/topics/company/2020/covid-19.html> accessed 1 May 2021.

[50] Twitter, 'Partnering with Organizations and Public Engagement' (10 April 2020) blog.twitter.com/en_us/topics/company/2020/covid-19.html.

[51] Twitter, 'Empowering Research of COVID-19 on Twitter' (29 April 2020) and Twitter, 'Twitter Developer Labs' (2020) developer.twitter.com/en/products/labs; blog.twitter.com/en_us/topics/company/2020/covid-19.html.

[52] J Christie, 'Keeping Our Employees and Partners Safe during #coronavirus' (12 May 2020) blog.twitter.com/en_us/topics/company/2020/keeping-our-employees-and-partners-safe-during-coronavirus.html.

[53] Twitter, 'Coronavirus: Staying Safe and Informed on COVID-19 Tab in Explore' (18 May 2020) blog.twitter.com/en_us/topics/company/2020/covid-19.html.

[54] Twitter, 'COVID-19 Account Verification' (20 March 2020) blog.twitter.com/en_us/topics/company/2020/covid-19.html.

Pulido et al. found out that during the pandemic misinformation increased online, but was retweeted less often compared to scientific or evidence-based content, which created more engagement in the online environment.[55] The COVID-19 search prompt is another design decision Twitter took in order to curb the spread of misinformation.[56] This search prompt should also correct misspellings within the search function and promote search results from credited sources like the 'World Health Organization' in relation to COVID-19.[57] The second cluster of actions against the pandemic amplified the need of clarifying statements about misleading information and how the company deals with it.[58]

Twitter published its three key questions which are taken into consideration for COVID-19 content removal decisions, an important element of justification governance. First, 'Is the content advancing a claim of fact regarding COVID-19?' Secondly, 'Is the claim demonstrably false or misleading?' The third question risen by Twitter is: 'Would belief in this information, as presented, lead to harm?'

The first question demands the existence of more than an opinion and rather seeks for content that covers some degree of factual truth. The expression has to have the power to influence the behaviour of other users on the platform in order to fulfil the criteria Twitter has set. The second question analyses the degree of truth of the statement or otherwise it will classify the Tweet as misleading.[59] The Tweet either contains already falsified information[60] or the claim could confuse users through the process of visibility and sharing pattern.[61] The third question tries to minimise the harm that misinformation could cause through its platform. Twitter explicitly names content that could increase the likelihood of exposure to the virus or information that could lead to capacity bottlenecks within the public health system. When a Tweet meets all three of the forementioned questions and criteria, Twitter grants itself the right to block or remove the content in question.

On 11 May 2020 Twitter updated its 'Terms of Service' for the placement of warning labels on Tweets that come with a reduced visibility for others.[62] Twitter's

[55] C M Pulido et al, 'COVID-19 Infodemic: More Retweets for Science-Based Information on Coronavirus than for False Information' (2020) 35 *International Sociology* 377.

[56] Twitter, 'Global Expansion of the COVID-19 Search Prompt' (4 March 2020) blog.twitter.com/en_us/topics/company/2020/covid-19.html.

[57] World Health Organization, 'World Health Organization (WHO) (@WHO)/Twitter page' (*Twitter*, 2020) twitter.com/WHO.

[58] Twitter, 'Broadening Our Guidance on Unverified Claims' (22 April 2020) blog.twitter.com/en_us/topics/company/2020/covid-19.html and Twitter, 'Clarifying How We Assess Misleading Information' (14 July 2020) blog.twitter.com/en_us/topics/company/2020/covid-19.html.

[59] An example given by Twitter includes statements like: 'The National Guard just announced that no more shipments of food will be arriving for two months – run to the grocery store ASAP and buy everything' or '5G causes coronavirus – go destroy the cell towers in your neighbourhood!'.

[60] This process of falsification is supported by subject-matter experts.

[61] Twitter gives the following examples: 'Whether the content of the Tweet, including media, has been significantly altered, manipulated, doctored, or fabricated; Whether claims are presented improperly or out of context; Whether claims shared in a Tweet are widely accepted by experts to be inaccurate or false.'

[62] Y Roth N Pickles, 'Updating Our Approach to Misleading Information' (11 May 2020) blog.twitter.com/en_us/topics/product/2020/updating-our-approach-to-misleading-information.html and

ads policy had to be renewed in order to meet the COVID-19 needs on the platform. The update restricted content that could cause panic, and content that could influence prices or the advertising of products that might be short in stock like face masks or hand sanitisers. Twitter also widened its understanding of harm on its platform.[63] Now the term also addresses speech that directly challenges the guidance from authoritative sources that contain public health information.

The first layer of the moderation process of Twitter is automated and Twitter's systems questioned one and a half million accounts that were under suspicion of amplifying COVID-19 discussion through spamming or other manipulative behaviours. Tasks related to judgement of the content itself had to be changed due to the pandemic. Twitter clarified its use of automated systems on 16 March 2020.[64] Twitter reported the automated surfacing of the uploaded content on its platform through the help of data trained on previous moderation decisions taken by its human moderation team. While misleading or false claims around COVID-19 often demand additional context, the human moderation team of Twitter will take review decisions 'by hand'.[65] Twitter also informs its users of longer waiting periods for content moderation, while also giving the user a right to appeal.[66] Furthermore, Twitter announced to change its hierarchy of the global 'content severity triage system'. It now prioritises content that might be classified as a rule violation, because this contravention is attributed as the highest risk by the platform to cause harm to its users.[67] The company also reported to have implemented a daily assurance check of its moderation system.[68] On 3 March 2020, Twitter also reminded its users of the 'zero-tolerance approach' the platform has towards manipulation.[69]

The third category of measures include the Twitter questions and answers that supported public engagement and promoted actions like 'Clapping for our healthcare heroes'[70] or '#AsktheGov',[71] where elected leaders were able to answer

'Tweets that are labelled under this expanded guidance will have reduced visibility across the service. Reducing the visibility of Tweets means that we will not amplify the Tweets on a number of surfaces across Twitter. However, anyone following the account will still be able to see the Tweet and Retweet'.

[63] Twitter, 'Broadening Our Definition of "Harm"' (1 April 2020) blog.twitter.com/en_us/topics/company/2020/covid-19.html.

[64] Twitter, 'An Update on Our Content Moderation Work' (23 March 2020) blog.twitter.com/en_us/topics/company/2020/covid-19.html.

[65] Twitter, 'Coronavirus' (n 53).

[66] Twitter, 'Appeal an Account Suspension or Locked Account' (*Help Center*, 2020) help.twitter.com/forms/general.

[67] @Vijaya and M Derella, 'An Update on Our Continuity Strategy during COVID-19' (16 March 2020) blog.twitter.com/en_us/topics/company/2020/An-update-on-our-continuity-strategy-during-COVID-19.html.

[68] ibid.

[69] Twitter, 'Our Zero-Tolerance Approach to Platform Manipulation' (4 March 2020) blog.twitter.com/en_us/topics/company/2020/covid-19.html.

[70] Twitter, 'Clapping for Our Healthcare Heroes' (7 April 2020) blog.twitter.com/en_us/topics/company/2020/covid-19.html.

[71] Twitter, '#AsktheGov & #AsktheMayor Twitter Q&As' (2 April 2020) blog.twitter.com/en_us/topics/company/2020/covid-19.html.

questions of Twitter users. Twitter announced a global software solution hackathon to fight the pandemic.[72] The company also donated one million dollars to the 'Committee to Protect Journalists' and the 'International Women's Media Foundation'.

As a further response to the crisis, Twitter tried to keep the public conversation alive while also using valuable information about the pandemic through the user data. In order to do that, Twitter created 'Twitter Developer Labs'[73] to grant access of real-time data to developers and researchers. Open research data is used for projects that take a closer look at trends and COVID-19 related discriminatory conversation.[74] There are other examples of valuable insight through Twitter's data to determine the amount or magnitude of misinformation.[75]

Kouzy found that 24.8 per cent of tweets contained misinformation, while not only the tweet is of interest but also its author. Kouzy found that the rate of misinformation increased to 33.8 per cent when the author was an informal individual or posted within a group account setting. This finding is also mirrored within the usage of verified accounts, where 31.0 per cent of the unverified accounts were classified as misinformation, while only 12.6 per cent of verified accounts contained misinformation. The company also focussed on parameters like site reliability in the pandemic due to an increase in service demand.[76] Metrics can provide a valuable insight into numbers and statistics or in this case of sentiment analysis. According to Ordun et al[77] the information related to COVID-19 was about 50 minutes faster retweeted compared to other Chinese networks.

Kruspe,[78] Mustafa et al[79] and Proharel[80] used Twitter data to employ a sentiment analysis of the tweets to find out more about people's moods. But not only

[72] DEVPOST, 'COVID-19 Global Hackathon 1.0' (*COVID-19 Global Hackathon 1.0*, 2020) covid-global-hackathon.devpost.com/.

[73] Twitter, 'Twitter Developer Labs' (n 51).

[74] MR Jimenez-Sotomayor et al, 'Coronavirus, Ageism, and Twitter: An Evaluation of Tweets about Older Adults and COVID-19' (2020) 68 *Journal of the American Geriatrics Society* 1661.

[75] MD Kearney et al, 'The Twitter Origins and Evolution of the COVID-19 "Plandemic" Conspiracy Theory' (Harvard Kennedy School Misinformation Review, 2020) 1; R Kouzy et al, 'Coronavirus Goes Viral: Quantifying the COVID-19 Misinformation Epidemic on Twitter' (Cureus, 2020) 12; Q Kruspe et al, 'Cross-Language Sentiment Analysis of European Twitter Messages during the COVID-19 Pandemic' in *Proceedings of the 1st Workshop on NLP for COVID-19 at ACL 2020* (Association for Computational Linguistics, 2020) www.aclweb.org/anthology/2020.nlpcovid19-acl.14; RJ Medford et al, 'An "Infodemic": Leveraging High-Volume Twitter Data to Understand Early Public Sentiment for the Coronavirus Disease 2019 Outbreak' (Open Forum Infectious Diseases, 2020) 7 academic.oup.com/ofid/article/7/7/ofaa258/5865318; A Mustafa and S Balla, 'Public Reaction to COVID-19 on Twitter: A Thematic Analysis' (EPRA International Journal of Multidisciplinary Research, 2020 (IJMR)) 2455. GK Shahi et al, 'An Exploratory Study of COVID-19 Misinformation on Twitter' (*ArXiv*, 2020); K Sharma et al, 'COVID-19 on Social Media: Analyzing Misinformation in Twitter Conversations' (2020) arXiv:2003.12309 [cs].

[76] @Vijaya and Derella (n 67).

[77] C Ordun et al, 'Exploratory Analysis of Covid-19 Tweets Using Topic Modeling, UMAP, and DiGraphs' (*ArXiv*, 2020) 1.

[78] Kruspe et al (n 75).

[79] Mustafa et al (n 75).

[80] BP Pokharel, 'Twitter Sentiment Analysis During Covid-19 Outbreak in Nepal' (Social Science Research Network, 2020) SSRN Scholarly Paper ID 3624719, papers.ssrn.com/abstract=3624719.

ordinary Twitter users are under investigation – Rufai and Bunce analysed tweets from leaders of G7 countries, where the majority of tweets were classified as 'informative' content (82.8 per cent) by the researchers while the G7 leaders also used their twitter accounts to boost the morale of their citizens (9.4 per cent).[81]

Twitter reported to have taken into account several measures to support its employees' safety through mandatory[82] work from home whenever possible, while also assuring contractual fulfilment in cases where home office solutions are not possible.[83] In order to smoothen the change in working conditions the company also provided reimbursement toward home office related costs and additional resources for parents in the form of financial help for COVID-19 related additional daycare expenses.

C. YouTube

YouTube has a current user base of two billion that consumes one billion hours of content daily.[84] YouTube had some prior knowledge and experience of how to deal with pandemics.[85] Misleading information amounts to a fourth of classified COVID-19 related misleading content, which reached up to 62 million users around the globe.[86]

YouTube uses a search algorithm coupled with a recommendation system that makes use of 'collaborative filtering' in order to individually sort content according to user preferences.[87] Research in user behaviour sheds light on the importance of the ranking order of YouTube's search results. Gudivada et al found out that users usually only consider the top 20 search results for consumption, therefore the algorithmic recommendation of YouTube is responsible for approximately 70 per cent of content consumed by users on their platform.[88] Furthermore, Li et al claim that during the coronavirus crisis the content of credited sources on the platform are under-represented compared to other content creators.[89]

[81] S Rufai and C Bunce, 'World Leaders' Usage of Twitter in Response to the COVID-19 Pandemic: A Content Analysis' (2020) *Journal of Public Health* 1.

[82] Twitter reported on the *Updated April 1, 2020 to Send home content moderators.*

[83] For contractors and hourly workers who are not able to perform their responsibilities from home, Twitter will continue to pay their labor costs to cover standard working hours while Twitter's work-from-home guidance and/or travel restrictions related to their assigned office are in effect (11 March 2020).

[84] YouTube, 'YouTube in Numbers' (2020) www.youtube.com/intl/en-GB/about/press/.

[85] K Bora and others, 'Are Internet Videos Useful Sources of Information during Global Public Health Emergencies? A Case Study of YouTube Videos during the 2015–16 Zika Virus Pandemic' (2018) 112 *Pathogens and Global Health* 320.

[86] H Li et al, 'YouTube as a Source of Information on COVID-19: A Pandemic of Misinformation?' (2020) 5 *BMJ Global Health* 1.

[87] J Davidson et al, *The YouTube Video Recommendation System* (2010).

[88] VN Gudivada et al, 'Understanding Search-Engine Optimization' (2015) 43 *Computer* 48.

[89] H Li et al (n 86); N Marchal et al, 'Coronavirus News and Information on YouTube', 5 and N Marchal and H Au, '"Coronavirus EXPLAINED": YouTube, COVID-19, and the Socio-Technical Mediation of Expertise' (2020) 6 *Social Media + Society* 19.

YouTube used several measures to curb the spread of coronavirus-related disinformation on its platform. YouTube implemented the following key strategies: authoritative voices, providing helpful information, boosting remote learning, removing misinformation, reducing the spread of borderline content through the creation of a COVID-19 'Medical Misinformation Policy', while also providing infrastructure to its users to stay connected.[90]

With YouTube's efforts for making authoritative voices more visual, the company displayed information panels of health organisations connected to search results related to COVID-19 queries. According to YouTube, this promoted content had around 100 billion views.[91] COVID-19 related content also has high engagement, while content that also is politicised raises on average around 9,000 comments for a video and factual content gained 3,000 comments on average.[92] Furthermore, the consumption of news (compared to the numbers of the previous year) on the platform soared up to 75 per cent.[93] Marchal et al found out that four-fifths of channels on YouTube sharing information are professional news agencies.[94] Nevertheless, content containing misinformation reached high volumes of shares on social media platforms and amounted to the sum of shares of the five biggest English media and news sites.[95]

The company also increased the visibility of non-profit organisations and governments through free ad inventory. Another change in the user interface is the news shelf for COVID-19 related information to highlight news from authoritative sources and health agencies[96] while also building a fact-checker network that can place warning labels on content that also reduces the visibility of the video.[97]

On 13 July 2020, YouTube first launched a feature called 'Depression and Anxiety Information Panels'[98] that uses information and guidelines provided by the 'Centre for Disease Control' (CDC).[99] One of the latest changes to YouTube's information channels on 17 November now also corners content about misinformation on vaccines for COVID-19.[100] The platform started in 2019 to limit

[90] YouTube, 'Youtube Response During Coronavirus – How YouTube Works' (*Youtube Response During Coronavirus – How YouTube Works*, 2020) www.youtube.com/howyoutubeworks/our-commitments/covid-response/.

[91] ibid.

[92] Marchal et al (n 89).

[93] C Newton, 'How YouTube's Moderators Are Keeping up with Changing Guidance around COVID-19' *The Verge* (29 April 2020) 19 www.theverge.com/interface/2020/4/29/21239928/youtube-fact-check-neal-mohan-interview-misinformation-covid-19.

[94] Marchal et al (n 89).

[95] Knuutila et al (n 45).

[96] YouTube, 'Youtube Response During Coronavirus – How YouTube Works' (n 90) and Newton (n 93) 19.

[97] ibid and Knuutila et al (n 45).

[98] YouTube, 'Health Information Panels' (2020) support.google.com/youtube/answer/9795167.

[99] YouTube, 'Update to COVID-19 Information Panels' (11 June 2020) support.google.com/youtube/answer/9777243?hl=en-GB.

[100] YouTube, 'Update to COVID-19 Information Panels' (17 November 2020) support.google.com/youtube/answer/9777243?hl=en-GB.

its recommendation for borderline content.[101] Borderline content makes up for around one per cent of the content on YouTube and describes cases that almost meet the criteria of deletion according to the 'Community Guidelines'.[102] Furthermore, YouTube promotes content for fundraising through a specific tag and a donation button.[103]

According to YouTube almost eight million videos were removed by the platform between July and September 2020.[104] The platform now exercises more intensive oversight and strives to limit the reach of content that contains medical misinformation or discredits authoritative health authority's guidance in one of the following categories: treatment,[105] prevention,[106] coronavirus diagnostics[107] and/or transmission.[108]

YouTube, in contrast to Facebook, monetises COVID-19 related content.[109] This is a change in the platform's monetarisation approach that prohibited the utilisation of sensitive events.[110] On 16 March 2020, the company announced that it will

[101] YouTube, 'Continuing Our Work to Improve Recommendations on YouTube' (*blog.youtube*, 2019) blog.youtube/news-and-events/continuing-our-work-to-improve/.

[102] YouTube, 'YouTube Community Guidelines & Policies – How YouTube Works' (*YouTube Community Guidelines & Policies – How YouTube Works*, 2020) www.youtube.com/howyoutubeworks/policies/community-guidelines/.

[103] S Perez, 'YouTube Launches a Suite of Fundraising Tools' (*TechCrunch*, 2018) social.techcrunch.com/2018/08/30/youtube-launches-a-suite-of-fundraising-tools/ and YouTube, 'Youtube Response During Coronavirus – How YouTube Works' (n 90).

[104] 'YouTube Community Guidelines Enforcement – Google Transparency Report' transparencyreport.google.com/youtube-policy/removals?hl=en.

[105] YouTube gives the following examples: 'Content that encourages the use of home remedies in place of medical treatment such as consulting a doctor or going to the hospital, Content that encourages the use of prayer or rituals in place of medical treatment, Content that claims that there's a guaranteed cure for COVID-19, Claims about COVID-19 vaccinations that contradict expert consensus from local health authorities or WHO, Content that claims that any currently-available medicine prevents you from getting the coronavirus' or 'Other content that discourages people from consulting a medical professional or seeking medical advice'.

[106] YouTube gives the following examples: 'Claims that there is a guaranteed prevention method for COVID-19, Claims that an approved COVID-19 vaccine will cause death, infertility, or contraction of other infectious diseases, Claims that an approved COVID-19 vaccine will contain substances that are not on the vaccine ingredient list, such as fetal tissue, Claims that an approved COVID-19 vaccine will contain substances or devices meant to track or identify those who've received it, Claims that an approved COVID-19 vaccine will alter a person's genetic makeup, Claims that any vaccine causes contraction of COVID-19, Claims that a specific population will be required (by any entity except for a government) to take part in vaccine trials or receive the vaccine first'.

[107] YouTube gives the following example: 'Content that promotes diagnostic methods that contradict local health authorities or WHO'.

[108] YouTube gives the following examples: 'Content that claims that COVID-19 is not caused by a viral infection, Content that claims COVID-19 is not contagious, Content that claims that COVID-19 cannot spread in certain climates or geographies, Content that claims that any group or individual has immunity to the virus or cannot transmit the virus, Content that disputes the efficacy of local health authorities' or WHO's guidance on physical distancing or self-isolation measures to reduce transmission of COVID-19'; see also YouTube, 'COVID-19 Medical Misinformation Policy – YouTube Help' support.google.com/youtube/answer/9891785?hl=en.

[109] YouTube, 'Monetising COVID-19-Related Content' (2 April 2020) support.google.com/youtube/answer/9777243?hl=en-GB see also Marchal and Au (n 89).

[110] S Perez, 'YouTube Warns of Increased Video Removals during COVID-19 Crisis' techcrunch.com/2020/03/16/youtube-warns-of-increased-video-removals-during-covid-19-crisis/.

use more automated content moderation and informed its platform users about the fact that more false positives and false negatives will be visible.[111] According to their enforcement report, YouTube removed 99 per cent of comments[112] through automated filtering.[113] Furthermore, YouTube defines exceptions for removal in cases of educational, documentary, scientific or artistic settings. The platform grants itself the power to remove content that violates a provision of its 'Community Guidelines', where YouTube also informs the uploading-user of the content removal per mail. Users that violate the company's rules for the first time will only be warned, while YouTube will strike against the user's channel for further violations. When a user has reached three strikes, YouTube will delete the channel.[114]

According to Priyanka et al users are a central player in the creation or sustainment of misinformation. The authors argue that independent user content, which accounts for 11 per cent of total video content, is seven times less likely useful information about COVID-19 compared to academic institution content.[115]

The platform is a popular host for remote learning. YouTube launched 'Learn@ Home', an extension to its 'Learning Hub' and is supported by several educational content creators and services like eg 'Khan Academy'.[116]

The removal of content on the platform is one way to target misinformation, but here the technological eco-system is more entwined than expected. In the deletion process of a video, YouTube had a longer removing time of several hours that was also viral on Facebook and Twitter. According to Knuutila et al YouTube needed 41 days to remove misleading videos that gained 149,825 views on average according to their sample.[117] As mentioned in section III(A), the authors describe that the audience for misleading content of COVID-19 on YouTube is closely correlated[118] to (and on a large scale caused by) Facebook shares.

This entwined ecosystem was studied by Cinelli et al for several platforms, including YouTube.[119] The authors discovered that users have a specific timing pattern for content consumption. Furthermore, 'mainstream social media' only amounted to a small fraction of interaction to questionable content.[120] The questionable content on the platform can reach different degrees of visibility. In order

[111] ibid; see also YouTube, 'Actions to Reduce the Need for People to Come into Our Offices' (*Google*, 16 March 2020) blog.google/inside-google/company-announcements/update-extended-workforce-covid-19/.

[112] The total amount of comments removed between July and September this year add up to 1,140,278,887 comments on the platform.

[113] 'YouTube Community Guidelines Enforcement – Google Transparency Report' (n 104).

[114] YouTube, 'Community Guidelines Strike Basics' (2020) support.google.com/youtube/answer/2802032.

[115] P Khatri et al, 'YouTube as Source of Information on 2019 Novel Coronavirus Outbreak: A Cross Sectional Study of English and Mandarin Content' (Travel Medicine and Infectious Disease, n 1) 35.

[116] Khan Academy, 'Khan Academy' (2020) www.youtube.com/user/khanacademy.

[117] Knuutila et al (n 45).

[118] With a positive correlation of 0.7 for the variables 'views on YouTube' and 'Shares on Facebook'.

[119] The authors investigated: Twitter, YouTube, Gab, Reddit.

[120] M Cinelli et al, 'The COVID-19 Social Media Infodemic' (2020) *Scientific reports* 10.

to compare the platform's approach, the authors used the coefficient of relative amplification.[121] According to their findings, YouTube amplifies unreliable content less compared to reliable content with a ratio of four out of ten.

D. Telegram

Telegram is a Russian instant messaging service and was founded in 2013 by Pavel Durov.[122] Pavel Durov also founded the Russian social network 'VKontakte', which can be seen as a *pendant* to Facebook.[123] The service has more than 200 million[124] active users. Germany, Austria and Switzerland together account for eight million users on a daily basis.[125] The service's popularity can be explained through the one-to-many messaging option which also provides for the creation of groups reaching up to 200,000 members. Messages sent within those groups can only be seen if searched for or appear within the group for every user.[126] A user can stay anonymous while posting to other users. Telegram therefore can create a wide reach for an individual user, while the user's personality can be hidden. Furthermore, the platform, in contrast to Facebook or Twitter, does not use a recommendation system nor an algorithmic timeline.[127]

The service is available within the EU or the United Kingdom for users that are 16, according to the company's terms of service.[128] Telegram's terms of service are very brief. A user has to avoid practices that 'Use our service to send spam or scam users, promote violence on publicly viewable Telegram channels, bots, etc. or post illegal pornographic content on publicly viewable Telegram channels, bots, etc.'.[129]

Through this open formulation of the online behaviour of users, Telegram grants its online population an ample understanding of free speech. Telegram therefore is an *El Dorado* for extremist groups like the Islamic State[130] or the

[121] The coefficient of amplification is a metric to capture the amplification on a platform for the fraction of average engagement for unreliable posts to reliable posts.

[122] A Baydakova, 'Telegram CEO Donates 10 BTC to Pandemic Relief Effort' (*CoinDesk*, 28 May 2020) www.coindesk.com/telegram-ceo-donates-10-btc-to-pandemic-relief-effort.

[123] Katsiaryna Baran and Wolfgang Stock, 'Facebook Has Been Smacked Down. The Russian Special Way of SNSs: Vkontakte as a Case Study' (ECSM, 2015).

[124] M Singh, 'Telegram, Nearing 500 Million Users, to Begin Monetizing the App' (*TechCrunch*, 23 December 2020) social.techcrunch.com/2020/12/23/telegram-to-launch-an-ad-platform-as-it-approaches-500-million-users/.

[125] BR, 'Hildmann, Naidoo & Co., 'Warum Verschwörungsfans Telegram nutzen' (*BR24*, 8 May 2020) www.br.de/nachrichten/netzwelt/hildmann-naidoo-and-co-warum-verschwoerungsfans-telegram-nutzen,RyOCmN4.

[126] A Knuutila et al, 'Junk News Distribution on Telegram: The Visibility of English-Language News Sources on Public Telegram Channels' (Oxford Internet Institute, 2020) 1.

[127] ibid.

[128] Telegram, 'Terms of Service' (*Telegram*) telegram.org/tos.

[129] ibid.

[130] A Shehabat et al, 'Encrypted Jihad: Investigating the Role of Telegram App in Lone Wolf Attacks in the West' (2017) 10 *Journal of Strategic Security* 1; A Yayla and A Speckhard, 'Telegram: The Mighty Application That ISIS Loves' (2017) *International Center for the Study of Violent Extremism (ICSVE)* 10.

far right.[131] Nevertheless, Telegram announced cooperation with the EUROPOL to counter terrorist propaganda online.[132] Because of the *laissez-faire* approach the company has towards content moderation and fake news, it poses a serious threat for COVID-19 misinformation.[133]

Telegram has a much less strict approach to governing COVID-19 information than other major platforms. Yet, Pavel Durov started to promote verified channels[134] on his platform.[135] Those channels can be verified if an active official channel, bot or a public group is concerned and another platform (Twitter, Facebook, Instagram or YouTube) already has verified a similar account.[136] If the user has no verified account on any of those platforms, an undisputed page on Wikipedia that is in accordance with its 'Notability Guidelines'[137] is also accepted by Telegram. Ordinary user accounts cannot be verified. These are reserved for 'big and active official channels and bots'.[138] Therefore, Telegram expands their cooperation with worldwide[139] health ministries.[140] Telegram also allowed for notification of users by verified channels to address COVID-19.[141]

Hui Xian Ng and Loke Jia were researching group behaviour and misinformation on Telegram in relation to COVID-19.[142] Most activity could be measured at midday or between eight to ten pm. According to them zero point zero five per cent of overall content could be classified as misinformation. The corresponding answers to misinformation on the platform express scepticism to overall zero point four per cent. The authors found that activity within the group increased

[131] A Bovet and P Grindrod, 'The Activity of the Far Right on Telegram v2.11' (2020) 11, researchgate.net.

[132] EUROPOL, 'Europol and Telegram Take on Terrorist Propaganda Online' (*Europol*, 2019) www.europol.europa.eu/newsroom/news/europol-and-telegram-take-terrorist-propaganda-online.

[133] Knuutila et al (n 126).

[134] Telegram, 'Telegram Channels' (*Telegram*, 29 January 2018) telegram.org/tour/channels.

[135] E Hacking News, 'Pavel Durov: The World Will Not Be the Same after the COVID-19 Pandemic' (*E Hacking News – Latest Hacker News and IT Security News*) www.ehackingnews.com/2020/04/pavel-durov-world-will-not-be-same.html.

[136] Telegram, 'Page Verification Guidelines' (*Telegram*) telegram.org/verify?setln=en.

[137] Wikipedia, 'Notability', *Wikipedia* (2020) en.wikipedia.org/w/index.php?title=Wikipedia:Notability&oldid=995288718.

[138] Telegram, 'Page Verification Guidelines' (n 136).

[139] Ministerio de Salud Pública de Cuba, 'Canal Oficial Del Ministerio de Salud Pública de La República de Cuba Para Ofrecer Información Sobre La #COVID19.' (*Telegram*) t.me/MINSAPCuba; Ministry of Georgia, 'StopCoV.Ge □□' (*Telegram*) t.me/StopCoVge; German Federal Ministry of Health, 'Corona-Infokanal Des Bundesministeriums Für Gesundheit' (*Telegram*) t.me/Corona_Infokanal_BMG; Government of India, 'MyGov Corona Newsdesk' (*Telegram*) t.me/MyGovCoronaNewsdesk; Italy Ministry of Health, 'Ministero Della Salute' (*Telegram*) t.me/MinisteroSalute; Italy Ministry of Health, 'Ministero Della Salute' (*Telegram*) t.me/MinisteroSalute; Russian Ministry of Health, 'СТОПКОРОНАВИРУС.РФ' (*Telegram*) t.me/stopcoronavirusrussia.

[140] Telegram, 'Coronavirus Info Telegram' (*Telegram*, 26 March 2020) t.me/s/corona?before=20, and L Dymples, 'Responding to COVID-19 with Telegram' (*East Asia Forum*, 1 May 2020) www.eastasiaforum.org/2020/05/01/responding-to-covid-19-with-telegram.

[141] Telegram, 'Coronavirus News and Verified Channels' (*Telegram*, 2020) telegram.org/blog/coronavirus.

[142] LH Xian Ng and YL Jia, 'Is This Pofma? Analysing Public Opinion and Misinformation in a COVID-19 Telegram Group Chat' (*Arxiv*, 2020).

when government announcements were made, whereas the soar in confirmed COVID-19 cases did not influence the activity level upon the platform that much. Hui Xian Ng and Loke Jia also found that the sentiment of the users' content could be labelled within a rather negative spectrum which correlates to governmental communication.

IV. Conclusion and Outlook

A. Private Ordering of Coronavirus-related Content

During the pandemic all of the platforms mentioned above took some measures related to COVID-19 while the amount of action differs. Telegram is based on a very broad understanding of free speech. Its one-to-one and one-to-few communication channels are rightly protected by law, but the groups and other one-to-many communication facilities leave room for largely unregulated online speech which can turn problematic.[143] This gap between Telegram and the other platforms grew when measures and moderation on other social networks or messaging services became stricter. Facebook, Twitter and YouTube all have taken a selection of different means to tackle COVID-19.

The 'Organisation for Economic Co-operation and Development' (OECD) provides four recommendations to handle the pandemic: first, 'supporting a multiplicity of independent fact-checking organisations'; secondly, 'ensuring human moderators are in place to complement technological solutions'; thirdly, 'voluntarily issuing transparency reports about COVID-19 disinformation'; fourthly, 'improving users' media, digital and health literacy skills'.[144]

The first recommendation was *in nuce* supported by Facebook, Twitter and YouTube. The second recommendation was only partly deployed through the platforms and was not implemented when lockdowns were in place. The third recommendation was of special importance, because only with increased transparency can the phenomenon of misinformation be studied properly and tackled across platforms. The fourth recommendation was also partly employed by Facebook, Twitter and YouTube.

The European Commission also provided recommendations to digital companies.[145] It stressed the visibility of trusted content by authoritative sources,

[143] M Kettemann and M Fertmann, 'Viral Information: How States and Platforms Deal with Covid-19-related Disinformation: an Exploratory Study of 18 Countries' (Verlag Hans-Bredow-Institut, 2021), GDHRNet Working Paper #1, 126.

[144] OECD, 'Combatting COVID-19 Disinformation on Online Platforms' (*OECD*, 3 July 2020) www.oecd.org/coronavirus/policy-responses/combatting-covid-19-disinformation-on-online-platforms-d854ec48/.

[145] European Commission, 'Disinformation: EU Assesses the Code of Practice' (*European Commission – European Commission*, 10 September 2020) ec.europa.eu/commission/presscorner/detail/en/ip_20_1568.

the awareness of users for content that is displayed to them, the detection of harmful content and the reduced advertising for disinformation.[146] Platforms largely incorporated the recommendations.

Misinformation can only be tackled effectively if measures are taken coherently upon platforms. With a general increase in users and views this year the platforms have a severe duty to protect users from harm through their offered services. This increase in numbers also will lead to a gain in profit for most of the platforms. Content moderation is at the core of a company's service and has changed for Facebook, Twitter and YouTube. The working conditions for moderators at Facebook are problematic especially during the pandemic. Most had to work from home or were unable to work. That is why the usage of automated systems for content moderation soared for Facebook, Twitter and YouTube. Automated systems have drawbacks compared to human content moderation and could foster the spread of misinformation online. On average 25 per cent of content relating to COVID-19 could be classified as misleading on all platforms.[147] This amount further increased up to 31 per cent when the users stayed anonymous.[148]

The recommendation algorithms employed by the platforms act as 'digital curators' on platforms and are responsible for most of the content consumed by users.[149] In the business model platforms employ user engagement is an important key performance indicator, misleading content with high engagement and visibility can increase the company's profit.[150] This relation between profit and polarising content can also explain why YouTube is monetising COVID-19 content after it has banned it only a month before. Trusted sources are still under-represented and should be promoted even more on the platforms. It is important to give authoritative sources and trusted healthcare content a loud voice in the pandemic to keep misinformation at bay.

B. Outlook

Platforms are here to stay. Their communicative role is likely to remain influential and to even grow, especially in developing states. Private ordering, that is the application of private norms in online spaces through which they are constituted as normative orders, will continue to be a useful concept to understand platform behaviour. States and platforms both have different duties and responsibilities vis-à-vis freedom of expression. As we have shown, private ordering has its limits: Public law is necessary in order to control public values. Privately constructed normative orders often lack a socially responsible finality. Even carefully constructed

[146] ibid.
[147] Kouzy and others (n 75).
[148] ibid.
[149] Gudivada et al (n 88).
[150] S Boberg et al, 'Pandemic Populism: Facebook Pages of Alternative News Media and the Corona Crisis -- A Computational Content Analysis' (2020) arXiv:2004.02566, 21, 11.

quasi-judicial entities, meant to increase legitimacy of platform law, suffer from flaws.

A basic problem of content moderation cannot be solved by even the most cleverly crafted law. It is this: While the primary responsibility for safeguarding individual spheres of freedom and social cohesion rests with states, it is platforms that have the primary power (in the sense of effective impact) to realise and influence rights and thereby cohesion. They set the rules, they design the automated tools, they delete and flag. Platforms have started to do better in terms of protecting rights, but they are still far off – in normative terms – when it comes to ensuring social cohesion.

Currently, all major platforms follow the approach of leaving as much 'voice' online as possible (though overblocking happens), deleting only dangerous postings (eg, death threats) and adding counter-statements (eg, warnings) to problematic speech (eg, disinformation). COVID-19 has gradually changed this, as we have seen above. For the first time, a cross-platform phenomenon has become visible: the recognition that mostly lawful speech could be highly corrosive of societal values (like public health) and that platforms needed to use all tools in their normative arsenal, automatic filtering, downranking, deleting, counterinformation, flagging, to support efforts to fight the coronavirus. If it worked overall rather well for fighting platform-based disinformation narratives on the coronavirus, the one question which remains is this: What about protecting other societal values against less well-designed threats? Here both more rights-conscious and more authoritarian futures are possible and continued engagement in critical platform research is essential.

14

Digital Human Rights Proportionality During Global Crisis

MART SUSI

I. The Proportionality Deficit Paradox

The impact of the COVID-19 crisis on human rights reveals the triumph of practice over theory. This means departure from the established pattern of human rights normative development as we know since the aftermath of World War II, that is, as long as human rights have been cards in the international arena. Little can be added to the understanding that the development of human rights law and practice is gradual and incremental, passing through the stages of rhetoric, epistemic and ontological conceptualisation, and finally regional or global recognition.[1] This pattern was abandoned in 2020 in connection with COVID-19 and human rights. Within less than one year the absence of foreseeability and transparency as inherent characteristics of private online content governance were tacitly accepted by the civil societies and governments around the world.[2] Social media platforms are now expected to conduct factual control of information related to the disease, and governments and public authorities are no longer reluctant to rely on social media communication for conveying 'official' messages. At first glance this seems to strengthen citizen democracy, at least diversify the 'ownership' of democracy.

The Estonian Government is vigorously advancing the idea of QR code, which is presented as an instrument for a 'return to normality' through tracing infection routes and individual behaviour in connection with testing and vaccination.[3]

[1] The concept of human rights law and practice gradual development is one of the pillars in the seminal book about new human rights, see: A von Arnaud, K von der Decken and M Susi (eds), *Cambridge Handbook on New Human Rights of the 21st Century: Rhetoric, Recognition and Novelty* (CUP, 2020).

[2] See recent comparative study undertaken by the Global Digital Human Rights Network: MC Kettemann and M Fertmann (eds), *Viral Information: How States and Platforms Deal with COVID-19-related Disinformation: an Exploratory Study of 20 Countries* (Verlag Hans-Bredow- Institut, 2020), GDHRNet Working Paper #1.

[3] By the time this chapter is published there may be several other comparable initiatives, or perhaps the QR code will already be accepted or be en route to being accepted within the EU. Due to the likelihood of discussions about initiatives of conditioning travel and enjoyment of several human rights upon certain individual medical steps taken and consent to electronic monitoring of these steps, mere reference to the likely new control method has to suffice here.

We are about to witness social acceptance of the proposed medical and vaccination individual coding because of the same rhetoric as mass surveillance of electronic communication has been accepted to increase national and global safety. Social acceptance of the maturity of social media networks and willingness to succumb to medical coding has happened without significant contestations from theory and practitioners simply because one year is too short a period for theoretical debates and practical 'testing'. By analogy, when the production of new medicine and vaccines usually takes around 10 years, but due to the pandemic was shortened to less than one year, the digital technologies were turned into tools of countering the spread, effects and the day-after impact of the pandemic. Questions not related to goal-efficiency were abandoned.

The preponderant social interest of not succumbing to the COVID-19 pandemic at all costs rolls across economic and psychological spheres into human rights. Even if by the time this chapter is published the pandemic crisis is in retreat and social life is en route to pre-pandemic 'normality', the dichotomous nature of human rights landscape in the digital domain, that is, generally speaking, more freedom in private and less freedom in public digital domains, has become more solidified without recourse to pre-pandemic status. I would coin this as the 'normalisation' of such dichotomy, where two simultaneously ongoing processes find broad social acceptance because the public is suddenly and understandably more concerned with the outcome than the assessment process and threats. These processes are the widening of human rights in private online platforms and narrowing of human rights in government controlled online environments. This chapter views the impact of the COVID-19 crisis on digital human rights on the basis of participant observation from Estonia. It will explore whether the recently elsewhere articulated five caveats of digital human rights and e-statehood[4] are/were magnified due to the pandemic. Before launching the review of these caveats, some additional introductory remarks are in order to set the stage for the discussion.

Among several objections often raised in pre-pandemic times against the capability to protect fundamental rights in the digital domain was the fluctuation and unpredictability of the scope of traditional rights originating from and conceptualised in an offline environment. In other words, the boundaries of traditional fundamental rights either become broader or narrower once transposed into the digital context. This appears in two different contexts, is led by different actors and leads to opposite images. The first image reflects the broadening of fundamental online rights and is related to social media's incapability of securing comparable protection of fundamental rights such as privacy or freedom of expression in comparison with traditional media. At the extreme corner of this image the claim is posited that social media portals are capable only of detecting hate speech and leaving the rest for user-unregulated territory. The second image

[4] M Susi, 'The image of human rights in e-state' (2020) 1 *Journal of the Belarusian State University. International Relations* 62–68.

reflects the narrowing of fundamental rights once online and is related to technologies developed for e-governance and e-public administration, such as blockchain. The perpetual memory inherent in an e-governance technological approach leads to algorithmic traps and magnifies governmental and private surveillance and monitoring capabilities.

The present chapter will show that both images which at first sight appear almost opposite to one another (the first based on almost total freedom and the second on almost total absence of freedom) are explainable through one distinct feature, which can be coined as the proportionality deficit paradox. This is a theoretical conclusion arrived at via an accelerated pace due to the pandemic pressure, which might otherwise have taken years. Verification or possible rejection of this thesis would happen in the future through contestation and non-pandemic pressure. The proportionality deficit paradox is based on the norm-theoretic distinction between rules and principles.[5] Social media and blockchain technologies are capable of applying human rights rules but have yet to be able to apply human rights principles. The reason for such an incapability, in the case of social media, is the practical impossibility to articulate arguments during content moderation, whereas application of rules through subsumption stays within social media reach and is reflected in content moderation outcome of deleting or retaining certain words, expressions or images. The reason for such incapability in the case of blockchain technology is related to this technology's essence. Proportionality application means optimisation and is therefore incompatible with technology which is based on definite solutions and opposed to infinite outcomes of similar input resulting from proportionality assessment.

The 2020 pandemic crisis accelerated the development of practices related and leading to the concretisation of both of these images. These two images appear more solidified in comparison with the pre-pandemic period. This means that the process of contestation and criticism usually associated with the development of new legal concepts and claims simply did not happen due to time pressure. Social media is now a recognised means to disseminate 'official' information about the crisis threatening the well-being of entire nations. Governments and public entities have accepted the utility and efficiency of social media for communication with the public. The Estonian Government has often used social media for disseminating urgent information about pandemic-related restrictions. Similarly, the blockchain technologies enabling the creation of databases of individuals across the globe on the basis of vaccination acceptance or rejection are seen as necessary and beneficial.

A sketch below illustrates the proportionality deficit paradox. The curve shows the capability level of proportionality assessment via argumentation. The y-axis indicates the level of proportionality assessment capabilities and the x-axis the level of normativity as opposed to arbitrariness and absence of foreseeable standards.

[5] R Alexy, *A Theory of Constitutional Rights* (OUP, 2010).

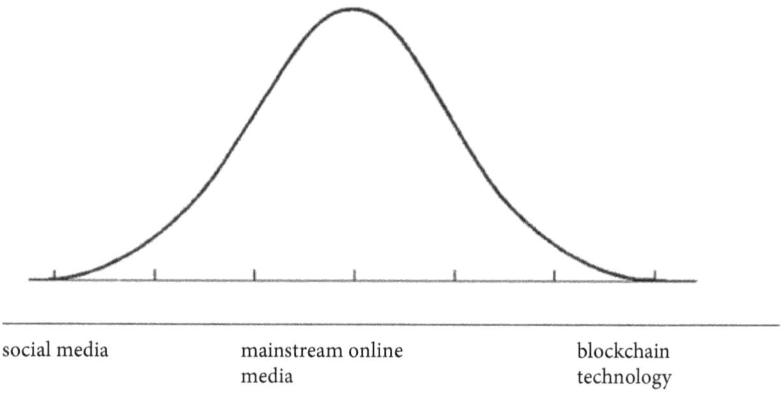

How if at all has this accelerated reliance on digital technologies taken into account the fundamental rights aspect? I will now apply the five caveats identified for e-state towards both images at the margins of digital human rights which became vivid during the pandemic crisis.

II. The Five Caveats and the Pandemic

A. The First Caveat: Rhetoric

The first caveat is related to an almost complete absence of human rights rhetoric from e-state goals and strategic commitments. This observation is subjectively cognitive and is based on reading Estonia's strategy documents, observing administrative practices and political rhetoric when Estonia's success story as an e-governed state is presented either domestically or internationally. The author's hypothesis claims that the countries which rely on a higher number of e-solutions for the purpose of public administration resort primarily to rhetorical arguments when the issue of safeguarding human rights through these solutions is raised. This safeguarding is theoretical and illusory. The countries which have quickly and on a large scale resorted to e-state solutions demonstrate at a relatively lower degree how exactly these solutions are in line with the obligation to protect human rights. The author's observations and discussions with researchers and practitioners in the field reveal an endemic absence of human rights goals from e-state strategy and practice. The new concepts of human rights by design and human rights by default,[6] when applied to human rights protection mechanisms in digital vertical

[6] See the UN Guiding Principles on Human Rights and Business, and the Report of the Special Rapporteur on the promotion and protection of the right to freedom of opinion and expression, UN General Assembly 6 April 2018.

relations, are indicative that human rights are engrafted into e-state strategy and solutions, which means they were not part of the e-state philosophy in the first place.

A similar pattern is clearly visible in the images of social media and of potential QR solutions planned for the future in the context of the pandemic. The recently conducted comparative study[7] reveals that social media platforms are expected to conduct and present fact checking of possible misinformation related to COVID-19. The matter of standards to be applied for this fact-checking and number of arguments expected when presenting the conclusions remains negligent at best. The rhetoric surrounding the QR or other technical solutions, aimed at controlling individual status of vaccination, and leading to the restoration of one's fundamental rights has so far mentioned only at a very general level the need to consider the human rights aspect during the development and implementation phases. It would be a mistake to expect that the absence of human rights rhetoric, which is already an established feature of e-state solutions, is reversed in the pandemic crisis. To the contrary – the crisis provides a justification for considering such absence as normal.

We are trained to think that human rights are connected to social development.[8] Many examples could be given, well known to readers of the subject of human rights, of how the interests of vulnerable groups were enhanced because of the human rights argument. Contemporary human rights discourse seems to accept the proposition that social development and human rights work in tandem. The non-coherence theory of digital human rights suggests that something must be at variance from this picture from offline dimension when reflected into online dimension. Elsewhere I have proposed the non-coherence theory of digital human rights, which is paradigmatically different from the practice-dependency-independence framework.[9] The digital dimension of human rights can be described via a novel principle that is termed the variance principle. This dimension is characterised by a consistent condition of unpredictability and lack of clarity on whether human rights norms, their realisation, related obligations, and remedies against violations as established in the offline world, continue to exist undistorted online. If distortion is established then the question emerges about the degree and consequences of such distortion, or whether these principles are replaced by online-specific elements. The variance principle claims that ontic and epistemic aspects of human rights from the offline domain may be at variance with these aspects in the online sphere. It is perhaps more accurate to state that offline rules and principles may apply sporadically, but there exists no predictability about

[7] See n 2.

[8] P Alston, 'Ships Passing in the Night: The Current State of the Human Rights and Development Debate Seen through the Lens of the Millennium Development Goals' (2005) 27(3) *Human Rights Quarterly* 755–829.

[9] M Susi, 'Human rights in the digital domain: the idea of non-coherence theory' in M Susi (ed), *Human Rights, Digital Society and the Law: A Research Companion* (Routledge Publishing, 2019) 3–13.

the circumstances under which they apply and exactly how. In some cases, they may apply, such as in relation to some concrete online service providers, or in some countries, or regarding some specific rights – and in other instances they may not.[10] The variance principle leads to the non-coherence theory of digital human rights, which claims that human rights law and its application online is characterised by a decrease in transparency, legal certainty and foreseeability.

I claim for the purpose of the present chapter, that this variance concerns the transformation of the development and tandem argument. In the offline world social and perhaps economic development is enhanced or accelerated when taking into account human rights component. In the online world's e-state development, to the contrary, human rights transform from enhancing factor into impediment. Instead of pushing forward with more and new e-state solutions and expanding the e-statehood into new public administration areas, the developers now would need to add an element which is not functionally indispensable. Another way to formulate the first caveat is to say that the human rights factor has not yet been integrated into e-state to the extent that it becomes a functional part of the e-state organism. There is no specific vulnerable group which would gain some competitive advantage if pressure upon e-state design would be channelled into e-state solutions taking into account human rights concerns. This is because of the notion of internet vulnerability – we are all vulnerable in front of the internet, which leads to the collective vulnerability thesis. This impediment is clearly visible in the potential of QR solutions enabling the 'return to normality'. This normality, conditioned on giving up privacy and medical confidentiality rights and allowing consistent monitoring with potential sanctions, would be based on non-applicability of human rights principles and could therefore be coined only as 'new normality'. Elaboration of this concept can easily lead to recognition that human rights considerations from the offline past are incompatible with the proposed solutions. The same can be said about the development of social media's role as a governmental communication channel and fact-verification instrument of user-posted information. Consideration of human rights has rarely been a strategic modus operandi of social media networks and is/was perhaps a means to acquire social, normative and constitutional legitimacy. COVID-19 enabled a jump across the process of acquiring such legitimacy and social media found itself unexpectedly behind the finish line. Further empirical and comparative research is needed to verify or oppose the proposition that due to the COVID-19 crisis social media

[10] See eg similar propositions. Schaumburg-Müller writing: 'I am not arguing that life online and offline is always completely the same and ought to be regulated in precisely the same manner in all details. What I am arguing is that they are not fundamentally different either' (S Schaumberg-Müller, 'Liability regimes for online human rights violations' in Susi (n 9); or Kulesza writing: 'Does the internet's transboundary nature, scale, speed of communication, automation, interconnectivity and invisibility change the way in which we view and protect fundamental rights (privacy, data protection, non-discrimination, due process, presumption of innocence and free speech)? Are human rights online exactly the same as offline or are they modified by the internet-specific circumstances, possibly impacting their very core?' J Kulesza, 'Multistakeholderism – meaning and implications' in Susi (n 9) 117–32.

is now in a position to reject concern for human rights principles (which does not mean rejecting the concern for human rights rules). If the proposition is correct, then the tandem argument of social development and human rights is incorrect in the digital domain, which in turn shows the correctness of the non-coherence theory.

The problem originating from this caveat is the strong possibility that, when making further choices about the development of e-state strategy and practical solutions like QR coding, and when further legitimising social media with new semi-public roles, regard for human rights simply is not a relevant criterion for assessing the justifiability of proposed measures. This caveat reduced by default constitutional legitimacy of social media as fact-controller and e-governance solutions like QR codes, since proportionality assessment is an inseparable aspect of constitutional adjudication.

B. The Second Caveat: Justification of E-state Success

The second caveat is related to the absence of conclusive justification about e-state success in social context. It claims that there exists little or no evidence to comprehensively assess the benefits or failure of the e-state project. This can be a continuous condition, at least as long as data emerges to either support or reject the positive social impact of the e-state project. This caveat is magnified in connection with social media new post-pandemic status and the potential of QR code-based surveillance. This caveat boils down to the reproach that the e-state raises expectations which it cannot fulfil. This reproach is carried over to the two images under review in this article, that is, entrusting social media with a fact checking role and establishing global controls like QR codes are likely to enhance social discontent. Social media can present results of facts checking but cannot show how exactly the facts were checked.

While the e-state doctrine remains subject to scientific and practical contestations, it can be explored whether any relationship exists between happiness and high development of e-state, that is, whether there is some causal relationship between happiness and/or unhappiness and e-state development in a given country. By analogy the findings, even if remaining provisional and intuitive, can be applied to the subject of this article.

The World Happiness Report 2019 refrains from presenting correlational conclusions between unhappiness and the time spent on digital media, yet it refers to studies that people who limit their time on social media improve their well-being.[11] In short, the report concludes that adolescents who spend more time on electronic devices are less happy, and adolescents who spend more time on most

[11] JM Twenge, *The Sad State of Happiness in the United States and the Role of Digital Media*, ch 5, World Happiness Report 2019, worldhappiness.report/ed/2019/the-sad-state-of-happiness-in-the-united-states-and-the-role-of-digital-media/.

other activities are happier. The World Happiness Report 2020 explores why people in the Nordic countries seem to be happier than in other countries.[12] Among other observations it refers to a cross-sectional study over 2005–12 which links improvements in government quality to improvements in well-being. When government quality is divided into democratic and delivery quality, it is the latter which is more strongly related to citizen happiness. These short brushstrokes, while not establishing that more e-state means less happiness, do not establish the contrary either. Yet it remains a question why Estonia as the 'most advanced digital society in the world'[13] is ranked only 51st in the 2020 World Happiness Report. When viewing usage of e-state solutions as part of individual digital habits, and comprehending that more digital time usage means less happiness, then digital public services can be viewed as part of the more general behaviour from the individual's perspective. If the former is correct, then more e-state and time spend on the Internet means less happiness. Should social media retain the function of a fact controlling instrument with a possible silent mandate from public authorities, then forthcoming surveys should address the question whether the 'status change' of social media influences users' happiness. While happiness is not a matter of direct interest from the perspective of human rights law, because of the non-exchangeability of happiness to morality, the following aspect is.

This is the matter of algorithmic prisons or algorithmic 'gatekeepers' which influence access to various social services and may lead to insurmountable barriers on behalf of the state power.[14] When in face-to-face situations between humans' administrative misunderstandings or issues often can be resolved, there is nobody to talk to in many e-state solutions. This second caveat means that the economic or rhetorical 'success' of e-statehood can easily overshadow reliable data on how e-state affects people's daily lives and well-being. Should the QR code materialise, it can become not only a gatekeeper to social services, but it can become the key to access to fundamental rights. Those who get approval by the QR coding system get full access to these rights, and those who do not get approval do not get access. It might be objected that this division is necessitated by the promise of a return to normality and is of temporary existence. The broader conclusion from the second caveat is an increase in utility-based considerations regarding human rights at times of societal crisis. It means, inter alia, possible change towards complicating the simple weight scale of absolute versus relative human rights. This observation has to suffice for the purpose of the present chapter and will be followed up on elsewhere in the future.

[12] F Martela, B Greve, B Rothstein and J Saari, *The Nordic Exceptionalism: What Explains Why the Nordic Countries are Constantly Among the Happiest in the World*, ch 7, World Happiness Report 2020, worldhappiness.report/ed/2020/the-nordic-exceptionalism-what-explains-why-the-nordic-countries-are-constantly-among-the-happiest-in-the-world/#fnref28.

[13] A rhetorical statement often used in reference to Estonia's digitalisation and e-governance, see eg e-estonia.com/.

[14] HY Liu, 'The digital disruption of human rights foundations' in Susi (n 9) 75–87.

C. The Third Caveat: Horizontal or Vertical Governance?

It is claimed that in the digital sphere fundamental rights protection is more comprehensively expected and realised under horizontal than under a traditional vertical governance model. The non-coherence theory posits that several core fundamental rights principles change once transposed from the offline domain into the online domain. To justify or reject the third caveat our interest turns to the question of whether there are any significant differences between public and private digital domains vis-à-vis the meaning of human rights and mechanisms for protection? This question can be explored from the normative perspective, through practice and the capabilities approach. On first observing, the previously formulated proportionality deficit paradox rejects this third caveat.

From the normative side the growth of soft law instruments is calling upon the private internet service providers to respect fundamental rights.[15] Private entities themselves are developing and publishing *modus operandi*, or original terms of service.[16] The terms of service of the public sector, *a contrario*, originate from the offline environment and appear transposed for providing in the online domain the 'same services' as in the offline realm. The variance therefore lies in the origin of the operation models for protecting fundamental rights in the digital domain: the private online service providers rely on original design meant for the online environment, whereas the public service providers, eg the e-state, uses a model which is necessary to manage the offline public domain. Despite contestations against the foreseeability of the terms of service used by the online service providers,[17] the fact remains that generically they are meant for the digital environment and thereby strengthen the online service providers per se, whereas the goal of the e-state is not to strengthen e-state applications, but concrete real-world political and power-oriented processes.

Against this background the COVID-19 images at the digital human rights painting reconfirm the observations and allow us to draw even further conclusions.

[15] At the European level, the primary efforts are undertaken by the Council of Europe and the EU. Various instruments exist at the Council of Europe level, such as the Internet Governance strategy 2016–19, or the 'Recommendation CM/Rec(2018)2 of the Committee of Ministers to member states on the roles and responsibilities of internet intermediaries'. The European Commission has adopted the EU Human Rights Guidelines on Freedom of Expression Online and Offline. At the global level the UN Guiding Principles on Business and Human Rights and the 'Protect, Respect and Remedy' Framework are pertinent.

[16] In recent years, the main global social media actors have published community standards regarding their anticipated actions towards online content. The focus of these standards is against hate speech and/or clearly illegal content, but there are also guidelines for when legal content affecting someone's privacy can be removed or blocked. These standards neither refer to the international normative human rights architecture, nor do they address the matter of the sameness of online and offline rights. When YouTube writes in its standards that it 'reserves the right to make the final determination of whether a violation of its privacy guidelines has occurred', this reflects the doctrine of law as practice. We may use terms like *Lex Facebook, Lex Twitter*, etc, which means that the origin of digital human rights law has, strictly speaking, a private character.

[17] T Wischmeyer, 'The role and practices of online stakeholders' in Susi (n 9).

Social media portals acquired more legitimacy during the COVID-19 situation without specific efforts to internally strengthen their normative basis. Nor was there normative pressure connected with COVID-19, from the outside, that is the norm-creating public establishments. This was because the end mattered/matters, that is the utilitarian goal of combat against worldwide urgency, and the means were of secondary importance. For human rights on the other hand, as we know from the offline domain, the process is often more important that the end. The provisional conclusion towards social media as evidenced through COVID-19 driven practice says that human rights are not trumps for social media, but an unnecessary burden, which can be given up once a legitimate justification can be advanced. COVID-19 offered such justification.

The main epistemic question related to the practice of social media portals, and e-state applications is what exactly these two realms are set to accomplish. Here, a wide discrepancy exists. The private online portals have their whole business model focusing on increasing the economic efficiency of digital solutions, whereas the e-state solutions have the clear target to make public administration more effective, including in the economic aspect. The difference in goals leads to difference in expectations. Elsewhere I have shown that although private online enterprises are capable of balancing fundamental rights, the balancing entails a high degree of arbitrariness due to the incapability of these portals to attach reasons for the balancing decisions.[18] This is evident from the so-called community standards of major internet companies, as well as from individual notification to portal users, where the decision to block or delete information posted by the user is explained by mere reference to non-compliance with the community standards.[19] The calls for balancing instruments can thus be viewed as a burden for social media. To use an analogy, like a burden for a child who practices piano because the parents say so. Many children who had the piano learning obligation imposed on them never sit behind the instrument once they have grown up. The same applies to social media – it has grown up during the pandemic crisis and does not need to care about the burden of balancing any longer.

E-state on the other hand has no requirement to balance conflicting rights, since the collusions of conflicting rights of individual rights-holders having the same weight are excluded. This is because the e-state is not a place where private individuals and/or companies can advance their rights claims towards one another, it is the platform for exercising state vertical power. When various private stakeholder groups' fragmentation can be categorised through focus

[18] M Susi, 'Balancing Fundamental Rights on the Internet – the Proportionality Paradigm and Private Online Capabilities' in M La Torre, M Susi and L Niglia (eds), *The Quest for Rights: Ideal and Normative Dimensions of Law* (Edward Elgar Publishing, 2019).

[19] Consider the recommendation of the Google Advisory Council, which was set up after the Goolge judgment of the CJEU – Case C-131/12 *Google Spain SL and Google Inc. v Agencia Española de Protección de Datos (AEPD) and Mario Costeja González* (13 May 2014). The council suggested in its report at para 19, that Google should not attach reasons to individual decisions of blocking or deletion, but should rather publish statistics.

to process-driven,[20] substance-oriented[21] and issue-oriented[22] initiatives, such fragmentation does not emerge in the e-state context. The main fundamental rights concern for e-statehood is whether the e-state solutions by themselves have secret doors enabling the arbitrary usage of data, which is a matter concerning the following two caveats. The previous has led me to advance the hypothesis that fundamental rights are non-essential for justifying nor the realisation of e-state solutions. Another way to formulate the same idea is to suggest that e-state does not need fundamental rights, or even more bluntly – fundamental rights disturb the development of e-state. This conclusion becomes stronger and perhaps primary in relation to the proposed QR code enabling the following and storing of individual behaviour regarding vaccinations and travel. Analysis of the human rights impact of such solutions and accommodation of various safeguards decreases/would decrease the efficiency of the planned solutions. Human rights observers see that large-scale emergencies and disturbances threatening the well-being of entire nations are like a wind which blows away from the rock landscape the sand of human rights. This is a disturbing image.

D. The Fourth Caveat: Meaning of Privacy

It is related to the dichotomy of the meaning of privacy in the digital domain, and to the perpetual digital memory. The non-coherence theory is based on the recognition that the meaning of human rights norms changes once transposed into the digital domain. The following can be said about the change of the meaning of privacy through digital transposition. The COVID-19 crisis can serve as the practical test for the correctness of the theoretical statement. The doctrine of privacy fatalism is advanced as a persistent contemporary phenomenon to characterise the distortion of the traditional meaning of privacy online.[23] Privacy online has been declared 'dead' or 'dying',[24] or as the founder of Facebook Mark Zuckerberg says, 'privacy is no longer a social norm'.[25] The concerns related to intrusions into privacy by contemporary media, traced to the seminal article by Warren and Brandeis introducing the modern concept of privacy (Warren and Brandeis[26]

[20] The Global Network Initiative.

[21] Manila Principles.

[22] Google Advisory Council.

[23] C Mims, 'Privacy Is Dead. Here's What Comes Next' (*Wall Street Journal*, 6 May 2018) and A Tan, 'Privacy is dead' (*The Business Times*, 9 June 2018) and K Bonnell, 'Privacy is Dead and We All Helped Kill It' (*Ottawa Citizen*, 2 April 2018) and CF Kerry, 'Why protecting privacy is a losing game today and how to change the game' (*Brookings*, 12 July 2018) www.brookings.edu/research/why-protecting-privacy-is-a-losing-game-today-and-how-to-change-the-game/.

[24] N Richards, 'Four Myths of Privacy' in A Sarat (ed), *A World Without Privacy: What the Law Can and Should Do* (CUP, 2015).

[25] B Johnson, 'Privacy no longer a social norm, Facebook founder says' (*The Guardian*, 11 January 2010).

[26] SD Warren and LD Brandeis, 'The Right to Privacy' (1890) 4 *Harvard Law Review* 193.

for example critiqued 'the press' which was 'overstepping in every direction' beyond common decency and engaging in 'vicious' and 'unseemly' gossip[27]), have possibly reached an extreme in modern internet-driven technology. It is suggested that the internet has given birth to modern privacy rights, as proposed by several scholars focusing on new technology and associated data practices and threats and challenges to privacy, particularly the development of new computing and data-based technologies.[28] The result of this process is that defining and conceptualising privacy has become an increasingly complex and complicated task,[29] which has led to the notion of privacy being divided up and segmented into numerous categories; for example, physical or spatial, decisional, and informational privacy.[30] It has been argued that today nobody appears 'to have any very clear idea what privacy is'.[31] The difficulties associated with defining privacy online may have the 'chilling effect' of deterring people from exercising their rights and freedoms on the internet.[32] These brushstrokes have to suffice here when painting privacy in the digital domain.

This fourth caveat has led previously to the conclusion that the notion of privacy is considerably more difficult to define in a private digital domain in comparison with the public digital domain, including e-state. This conclusion needs a revision due to the proportionality deficit paradox. This paradox shows that the right to privacy can be advanced in social and legal contexts which enable proportionality assessment. In e-state applications, such as the QR code, or in social media networks, the right to privacy starts to evaporate.

The private online digital domain is influenced by time and forgetting, whereas the e-state is not and blockchain never forgets. There is no corresponding entitlement in the public sphere to the right to be forgotten which obligates private online search engines[33] under certain conditions to block access to information which is not relevant for the public. A well-known statement – which is part of popular and scientific folklore – that the Internet knows you better than you know yourself can be proven both for the private online sphere and for blockchain technology. Only when the private internet companies may be compelled to enable forgetting, the blockchain by design is unable to yield to this command. The possible QR code for

[27] See also DJ Glancy, 'Invention of the Right to Privacy' (1971) 21 *Arizona Law Review* 1.

[28] J Rosenberg, *The Death of Privacy*, (Random House, 1969) and PM Regan, *Legislative Privacy: Technology, Social Values, and Public Policy* (University of North Carolina Press, 1995) and M Froomkin, 'The Death of Privacy?' (2000) 52 *Stanford Law Review* 1461 and S Garfinkel, *Database Nation: The Death of Privacy* (O'Reilly Media, 2000).

[29] E Lin, 'Prioritizing Privacy: A Constitutional Response to the Internet' (2002) 17 *Berkeley Technology Law Journal* 1088.

[30] J Kang, 'Information Privacy in Cyberspace Transactions' (1998) 50 *Stanford Law Review* 1193.

[31] JJ Thomas, 'The Right to Privacy' in FD Schloeman (ed), *Philosophical Dimensions of Privacy: An Anthology* (CUP, 1984).

[32] JW Penney, 'Chilling Effects: Online Surveillance and Wikipedia Use' (2016) 31 *Berkeley Technology Law Journal* 117.

[33] U Pagallo and M Durante, 'Human rights and the right to be forgotten' in Susi (n 9) 197–209.

travel and vaccination manifests in practice the theoretical proposition. No matter which status one gets in the QR coding system, it is likely to affect this person's enjoyment of fundamental rights forever – like travel, family rights, freedom of movement, access to services. Blockchain or non-human technology determines a matter which should remain the prerogative of the human mind.

E. The Fifth Caveat: Police State

Fifth and finally, there is a threat – which at the time of its formulation in 2019 was considered primarily theoretical, of the e-state transforming into a police state. I put forward such a threat because blockchain and the Internet generate many tools which enable such a transformation, remaining unnoticed and disguised under the veil of economic and technological efficiency. Such a transformation would be accompanied by the rhetoric of trading protection of privacy for increased international and national security.[34] It is sufficient to claim under this fifth caveat that with the expansion of e-state the possibility of police statehood measures increases. This threat moves from a theoretical one into a realistic one if the QR technology as a gateway to enjoyment of some fundamental rights was to find practical implementation. The elements for such a transformation are clearly visible at the image we are looking at. First, there is a worldwide crisis. Secondly, there is rhetoric that the QR code for travel will enable 'return to normality'. Against this background, it can be easily argued, the price of giving up some of our fundamental rights and entrusting the technology with the power to determine the degree of enjoyment of the fundamental rights is not too high. This completes the creation of the police state. As soon as AI through the QR code tells you whether you can leave your home, how far you can go on foot, whom you can and whom you cannot meet – you live in a police state. At the time of writing this chapter it is not yet clear what safeguards to eliminate or minimise this threat will be built into the design and what is their projected effectiveness. These possible safeguards have the capacity to soften the image of the police state.

III. Conclusion

The COVID-19 crisis has revealed certain ontological and epistemic features of human rights in the digital domain, which without the crisis-driven impetus might have remained only theoretical and contestable through the absence of practice argument. These features are not only connected to the 2020 medical global emergency but can be viewed as digital human rights inherent characteristics of

[34] For discussion about this matter, see J Waldron, 'Security and liberty: the image of balance' (2003) 11 *Journal of Political Philosophy* 191.

any global emergency with unpredictable economic and social consequences. The chapter has put forward the proportionality deficit paradox, which says that social media and a blockchain based QR code for monitoring travel and vaccination status (or other statuses during future crises) are capable of applying human rights rules, but are not capable of applying human rights principles. This leads to an absence of mechanisms for protecting privacy rights in social media and blockchain technology. The theoretical conclusion from the pandemic crisis of 2020–21 clarifies the image of privacy, that is, the fundamental right to privacy is conditional on co-existence of social and legal contexts enabling the proportionality assessment. The label of privacy is still usable in social media and a blockchain based QR code, but it is at variance with privacy as we know it – the right to be left alone.

The five caveats shown above as general considerations and as applied to the COVID-19 crisis lead to the thesis about negative correlation between e-statehood and fundamental rights. The spread of e-state usage to more and more public administration areas and by more and more public offices invigorates the development aspect without the need to consider how the new developments coincide with human rights related obligations. The COVID-19 crisis has added another anchor to justify this thesis – the development aspect is seconded by the duty to protect aspect. The stronger the e-state, the more the human rights factor is withering. This leads to reflection about the relationship between fundamental rights and democracy. Traditionally, democracy and human rights have been regarded as two different phenomena, human rights belonging to the international sphere and democracy to the national sphere as an internal matter under the sovereign prerogative of the respective state.[35] The entitlement to fundamental rights originates from international law and national law defines the corresponding obligations. These two phenomena have existed in equilibrium, which surprisingly the e-state development has shaken. The ongoing crisis demonstrates how the phenomena of fundamental rights and e-democracy are on diverging paths, which is not yet the course towards non-compatibility.

[35] S Wheatle, 'Democracy in International Law' (2002) 51 *International and Comparative Law Quarterly* 225; D Beetham, *Democracy and Human Rights* (Polity Press, 1999).

PART IV

Conclusions: Pandemics, Populism and Power

15

The Pandemic and Illiberal Constitutional Theories

GÁBOR HALMAI

I. Emergency Measures by Illiberal Regimes

I use 'illiberalism' in this chapter as a critical reaction to liberalism. The main theoretical objects of this illiberal critique are the values of political liberalism: human rights, justice, equality and the rule of law, its commitment to multiculturalism and tolerance, ideas of Isaiah Berlin's 'negative liberty', Karl Popper's 'open society', John Rawls' 'overlapping consensus', or Ronald Dworkin's equality as the 'sovereign virtue'. From an institutional point of view, and this will be more visible in the legal reactions to COVID-19, illiberalism challenges liberal democracy, which is not merely a limit on the public power of the majority, but also presupposes rule of law, checks and balances, and guaranteed fundamental rights.

No one reasonably disputes that emergency situations, like the coronavirus pandemic, require special legal and constitutional measures even in fully-fledged liberal democratic systems.[1] These measures have to take into account various aspects, among them health and economic considerations, which can lead to different balancing outcomes between certain legitimate public interests, like public health, public order, security and fundamental rights, such as right to human dignity, right to life, freedom of movement, right to education, freedom of information and expression, privacy, etc. Even decisions of democratic legislators and governments potentially reviewed by independent judicial bodies can lead either to 'under-' or 'overreaction' to the pandemic.

[1] Among the very few exceptions are Slavoj Zizek, Giorgio Agamben and Peter Sloterdijk, who even warned of the dangers of any emergency power in stable liberal democracies. J Joffe, 'Die Corona-Krise offenbart auch eine Krise der Meinungsmacher: Ihnen fällt nicht allzu viel Kluges ein' (2020) *Neue Zürcher Zeitung* 11.04, www.nzz.ch/feuilleton/die-corona-krise-ist-auch-eine-krise-der-intellektuellen-ld.1551336. Agamben in his fear of every kind of emergency power went as far as to call the coronavirus a 'supposed pandemic' and suggested that emergency measures were 'absolutely unwarranted'. See A Berg, 'Giorgio Agamben's Coronavirus Cluelessness' (2020) *CHRON. HIGHER. ED*, www.chronicle.com/article/Giorgio-Agamben-s/248306.

As Francis Fukuyama argues, the type of regime involved does not determine why some countries have done better than others in dealing with the crisis so far.[2] Some democracies have performed well, but others have not, and the same is true for autocracies. Therefore, Fukuyama considers the factors responsible for successful pandemic responses to have been state capacity, social trust, and leadership.[3] Indeed, one can think of old democracies, such as the US and the UK, which did not perform well due to lack of state capacity and/or effective leadership. That being said, all the states he mentions which have used the crisis through overreaction to give themselves emergency powers, thus moving them still further away from democracy, happen to be non-democracies. Tom Ginsburg and Milla Versteeg, after surveying 106 countries in the world to see whether the executive is bound by either judicial, legislative or supranational oversight in their pandemic responses, came to the conclusion that in no fewer than 82 per cent of the countries in their data at least one of these checks and balances could be observed.[4] They found that only in six democratic countries out of the 106 surveyed could no oversight be detected: Australia, Botswana, Jamaica, Switzerland,[5] Peru, and Guyana. Of course, this does not necessarily indicate that the executive's reactions have been problematic, and conversely the formal oversight by non-independent bodies does not exclude the misuse of executive power in non-democratic regimes. This is because the lack of independence means the executive power is not bound by the oversight bodies. This is why the unbound character of the executive power cannot be equally assessed in democratic and autocratic systems.[6] The overall positive picture of the Ginsburg-Versteeg survey was not confirmed by the report of Freedom House, which found that since the start of the pandemic, the state of democracy

[2] F Fukuyama, 'Pandemic and Political Order' (2020) *Foreign Affairs*. www.foreignaffairs.com/articles/world/2020-06-09/pandemic-and-political-order.

[3] Of course one can think of many other important factors Fukuyama fails to mention, such as the cultural traditions of societies. For instance, in Asia, certain social behaviours already require distancing and the experience with different viruses in the last decades has also led to further preventive concepts in Africa. The age composition of the population also seems to be a crucial factor, as does the possibility to seal off the country (eg, New Zealand).

[4] In 52% of the countries (68% of democratic and 30% of autocratic ones) the legislatures, in 41% of them the judiciary (in 55% of the democracies, compared with 27% of autocracies) and in 34% (in 40% of democracies as compared with 28% of autocracies) subnational bodies have become involved in the decisions of the executive. See T Ginsburg and M Versteeg, 'The Bound Executive: Emergency Powers During the Pandemic' (2020) 52 *Virginia Public Law and Legal Theory Research Paper*. University of Chicago, Public Law Working Paper No 747, 26.

[5] See O Ammann and F Uhlmann, 'Switzerland: The (Missing) Role of Parliament in Times of Crisis', in this volume.

[6] Another comparative constitutional study comparing four European liberal democracies' (Germany, France, the UK and Italy) efficiency in tackling the pandemic comes to the conclusion that the main difference is not between bound or unbound executives, between Madisonian or Schmittian models, but rather whether the 'compulsion to legality' triggers virtuous or vacuous circles. See A Golia, L Hering, C Moser and T Sparks, 'Constitutions and Contagion. European Constitutional Systems and the COVID-19 Pandemic' (2020) *Max Planck Institute for Comparative Public Law & International Law (MPIL) Research Paper No 42*, papers.ssrn.com/sol3/papers.cfm?abstract_id=3727240. But how can this comparison possibly prove that the unbound character of the executive does not play any role in the efficiency of the reaction if none of the four selected countries has ever implemented the Schmittian model?

and human rights, which tells us a lot about the unbound character of the executive, has worsened in at least 80 countries out of the 192 nations surveyed by them.[7]

In addition to the lack of oversight, authoritarian regimes in Bangladesh, Belarus, Cambodia, China, Egypt, El Salvador, Syria, Thailand, Turkey, Uganda, Venezuela and Vietnam have all detained critics, health workers, journalists and opposition members, and implemented strong tools against the pandemic, including harsh censorship and even criminal sanctions against social media posts related to COVID-19, as an excuse to grab more power.[8] On the other hand, countries with competent governments which performed well in containing the virus can be considered as stable democracies, such as Australia, New Zealand, Germany, Japan or Taiwan.[9] Some democracies have managed to adapt faster. For instance in South Korea the disease was tamed by extensive tracing and widespread surveillance of possible carriers, because the regime there had recent experience to draw on from its handling of the Mers outbreak of 2015, an event which also shaped the collective memory of the citizens. But it is true that COVID-19 infected the world with an ultimate uncertainty at a time in which democracy was already under threat. As David Runciman argues, the distinction between democracies and authoritarian regimes has been blurred: 'Under the lockdown, democracies reveal what they have in common with other political regimes: here too politics is ultimately about power and order'.[10]

One of Tom Daly's four categories of how governments deal with COVID-19 is preserved for 'autocratic opportunists', such as the Hungarian Government. The second one, the 'fantasists' who denied the scientific facts of the pandemic, consists of autocracies, like China, illiberal states, such as Brazil, and traditional democracies with huge leadership problems, like the US.[11] His two remaining categories of country are rather considered as democracies: the 'effective rationalists,' like New Zealand, and the 'constrained rationalists', such as South Africa, whose constraint has been their limited state capacity.

Given the importance of strong state capacity and action to slow the pandemic, it is hard to argue against greater state involvement during a national emergency.

[7] 'Democracy Under Lockdown. The Impact of COVID-9 on the Global Struggle for Freedom, Special Report 2020', Freedom House, freedomhouse.org/report/special-report/2020/democracy-under-lockdown?utm_campaign=wp_todays_worldview&utm_medium=email&utm_source=newsletter&wpisrc=nl_todayworld.

[8] See an overview of these countries' emergency measures: 'Would-be Autocrats Are Using COVID-19 as an Excuse to Grab more Power' (*The Economist*, 23 April 2020) www.economist.com/international/2020/04/23/would-be-autocrats-are-using-covid-19-as-an-excuse-to-grab-more-power.

[9] See L Diamond, 'Democracy Versus the Pandemic, The Coronavirus Is Emboldening Autocrats the World Over' (*Foreign Affairs*, 13 June 2020) www.foreignaffairs.com/articles/world/2020-06-13/democracy-versus-pandemic.

[10] See D Runciman, 'Coronavirus has not suspended politics – it has revealed the nature of power' (*The Guardian*, 27 March 2020) www.theguardian.com/commentisfree/2020/mar/27/coronavirus-politics-lockdown-hobbes?CMP=Share_iOSApp_Other.

[11] T Daly, 'Democracy and Global Emergency – Shared Experiences, Starkly Uneven Impacts' (*Verfassungsblog*, 15 May 2020) verfassungsblog.de/democracy-and-the-global-emergency-shared-experiences-starkly-uneven-impacts/.

According to Ivan Krastev and Mark Leonard, the virus also strengthened rather than weakened national sovereignty.[12] Interestingly enough, challenges to the state's 'pandemic power' have come from groups and movements, ranging from far-right populists or radical ecologists to wellness fanatics and left-wing populists, all united by claims to 'personal sovereignty', 'bodily autonomy' and 'bodily rights'.[13] Even the Dutch Prime Minister Mark Rutte described the Netherlands as a 'grown-up country', whose citizens did not need to be treated like children 'to behave responsibly', unlike in other European countries.[14] But despite these rather minority views, most governments have assumed executive powers considered to be broadly necessary to contain the health crisis, and it remains uncertain whether these will entail long-term restrictions on democratic rights.[15] Ivan Krastev calls it one of the coronavirus-paradoxes that, when people realise the threat to fundamental rights, they are rather inclined to reject authoritarian rule.[16] This was the case in Belarus, where one of the reasons for the 'Revolution of Dignity'[17] which started in the summer of 2020 was that the people realised that absolute power did not provide security against COVID-19, but rather posed a threat to their lives.

The 'semi-liberal'[18] constitutional system of Israel has an in-built 'overreach' element, because a state of emergency already existed before the COVID-19 crisis: in Israel, the Basic Law. The Government states that the Knesset 'may, of its own initiative or, pursuant to a Government proposal, declare that a state of emergency exists'. This state of emergency was declared upon the establishment of the State of Israel, and has been extended yearly ever since. Using the pandemic crisis, the government sought to employ surveillance technology to track those who tested positive for coronavirus. But unlike in more authoritarian illiberal systems, the Supreme Court in Israel blocked measures,which disproportionately limited fundamental rights.[19]

[12] I Krastev and M Leonard, 'Europe's pandemic politics: How the virus has changed the public's worldview' (*ECFR*, 20 June 2020).

[13] See L Bialasiewicz and HL Muehlenhoff, '"Personal sovereignty" in pandemics: or, why do today's "sovereignists" reject state sovereignty?' (*openDemocracy*, 30 June 2020) www.opendemocracy.net/en/can-europe-make-it/personal-sovereignty-in-pandemics-or-why-do-todays-sovereignists-reject-state-sovereignty.

[14] See L Bialasiewicz, 'National stereotypes in times of COVID-19: the "frugal four" and the "'irresponsible South'" (*openDemocracy*, 13 July 2020) www.opendemocracy.net/en/can-europe-make-it/national-stereotypes-in-times-of-covid-19-the-frugal-four-and-the-irresponsible-south/.

[15] cf a report of Carnegie Europe, carnegieeurope.eu/2020/06/23/how-coronavirus-tests-european-democracy-pub-82109.

[16] I Krastev, 'Sieben Corona-Paradoxien – es ist nicht leicht zu begreifen, was das Virus mit unserer Welt gemacht hat, während wir in unserem Zuhause festsassen' (*Neue Zürcher Zeitung*, 16 June 2020) www.nzz.ch/meinung/sieben-corona-paradoxien-was-das-virus-mit-uns-gemacht-hat-ld.1557102?reduced=true.

[17] See this phrase used by Adam Michnik. See S Sierakowski, 'Belarus's Revolution of Dignity, Interview with Adam Michnik' (*Project Syndicate*, 21 August 2020) www.project-syndicate.org/onpoint/belarus-revolution-of-dignity-by-adam-michnik-and-slawomir-sierakowski-2020-08.

[18] Gila Stopler defines the state of the current Israeli constitutional system as 'semi-liberal constitutionalism'. cf G Stopler, 'Constitutional Capture in Israel' (2017) *Int'l J. Const. L. Blog* www.iconnectblog.com/2017/08/constitutional-capture-israel.

[19] See a detailed report: TH Brandes, 'Israel's Perfect Storm: Fighting Coronavirus in the Midst of a Constitutional Crisis' (*Verfassungsblog*, 7 April 2020) verfassungsblog.de/israels-perfect-storm-fighting-coronavirus-in-the-midst-of-a-constitutional-crisis/.

In illiberal regimes, all reactions can be motivated by the rulers' authoritarian pursuits, in other words they can use the crisis situation as a pretext to strengthen the autocratic character of their systems. In some cases this needed an 'underreach', like the extreme ignorance of the virus expressed by President Bolsonaro of Brazil, or in the United States, where President Trump, after his first failed claim to have 'absolute power', responded insufficiently and incompetently with 'executive underreach'[20] to the pandemic. This meant that the US had an appalling lack of emergency measures deployed at federal level. Similarly, the illiberal Polish government insisted on the presidential election taking place despite the health risks, since it was important to entrench the power of the governing party's incumbent.[21]

In many more illiberal states, an 'overreach' has served the purpose of power grabbing, like in India, where the Modi Government used the pandemic chaos to suppress nationwide protests against the efforts of the Hindu Nationalist ruling party to marginalise religious minorities, which had been held two months before the coronavirus broke out, an example of these protests being the peaceful sit-in spearheaded largely by Muslim women in the Shaheen Bagh section of Delhi.[22] There was also a new law restricting foreign NGOs from giving money to Indian ones, which had the potential to get rid of civil organisations providing checks on the increasingly authoritarian government.[23]

II. Hungary as a Model Case: From 'Illiberal Democracy' to Autocracy

Hungary represents a special case.[24] Since the landslide victory of Viktor Orbán's Fidesz party in the 2010 parliamentary election, the country, according to Prime Minister Orbán's own definition, has become an 'illiberal democracy',[25] with a new

[20] See the term used by J Gould and D Pozen, 'How to Force the White House to Keep Us Safe in a Pandemic' (*Slate*, 6 April 2020) slate.com/news-and-politics/2020/04/nancy-pelosi-white-hous e-covid-19-supplies.html. Kim Lane Scheppele uses the term 'underreaction' to describe the same phenomenon, KL Scheppele, 'Underreaction in a Time of Emergency: America as a Nearly Failed State' (*Verfassungsblog*, 9 April 2020) verfassungsblog.de/underreaction-in-a-time-of-emergency-america-as-a-nearly-failed-state/. See also the joint study of D Pozen and KL Scheppele, 'Executive Underreach, in Pandemics and Otherwise' (2020) *American Journal of International Law* forthcoming (posted on SRRN 15 July).

[21] See T Drinóczi and A Bien-Kacala, 'Illiberal Constitutionalism at Work' (*Verfassungsblog*, 31 March 2020) verfassungsblog.de/illiberal-constitutionalism-at-work/.

[22] theconversation.com/coronavirus-versus-democracy-5-countries-where-emergency-powers-risk-abuse-135278.

[23] See A Kazmin, 'Indian charities battle for survival after government crackdown' (*Financial Times*, 30 September 2020) www.ft.com/content/41e65a46-1ca3-4cfa-b1db-c7a1b7273996.

[24] The previously quoted Ginsburg-Versteeg survey also distinguishes Hungary among the 106 countries surveyed, with measures there violating all three rule of law principles (temporally limited responses, judicial and legislative oversight, non-discriminatory application). See Ginsburg and Versteeg (n 4) 51.

[25] Based on Fareed Zakaria's use of the term 'illiberal democracy' (F Zakaria, *The Future of Freedom. Illiberal Democracy at Home and Abroad* (WW Norton and Company, 2003)) it was PM Orbán of

constitution motivated by the 2008–09 financial crisis, and enacted with the exclusive votes of the governing party. In 2015, at the height of the migration crisis, the Parliament bestowed upon the government the power to declare a 'state of migration emergency' which allowed authorities to hunt down and detain asylum seekers, punish those who assisted them and to use draconian new standards for rejecting asylum claims. The 2015 emergency law included sunset conditions that should have ended the state of emergency when the flow of refugees stopped. But some five years later with hardly a new refugee in sight, these emergency powers are still in place, with the government having renewed them continuously up to the present day. Since both the 2014 and the 2018 parliamentary election results renewing Fidesz's two-thirds majority were manipulated, some scholars have started to question even the formal democratic character of the regime.[26]

This is the political background against which Hungary hit by COVID-19. After the very first cases of contagion, in a clear overreaction to the actual danger, the government introduced an unlimited emergency power. To make matters worse, the legal presumption on which both the initial emergency decree 40/2020 and the subsequent emergency statute (the Enabling Act) rest itself violated even Fidesz' own illiberal constitution, the Fundamental Law of 2011, because it did not provide constitutional authorisation either for the decree or for the Enabling Act. The Enabling Act was not even needed either to cope with the crisis, since the existing ordinary laws would have provided ample powers for dealing with a pandemic. The Parliament again unconstitutionally authorised the government to define the end of the pandemic, and limited its own power to control the government's power of decree.[27] There was also no chance that the Constitutional Court would have questioned the constitutionality of the emergency measures, which discredited local governments and opposition parties, and limited freedom of expression, data protection, freedom of information and labour rights.[28]

Hungary who first proudly characterised his regime as such in his speech at the 28th Bálványos Summer Open University and Student Camp, 28 July 2018. Tusnádfürdő (Băile Tuşnad), www.miniszterelnok.hu/prime-minister-viktor-orbans-speech-at-the-29th-balvanyos-summer-open-university-and-student-camp/.

[26] Larry Diamond, for instance, called the Hungarian system a 'pseudo-democracy'. See L Diamond, 'How Democratic Is Hungary?' (2019) *Foreign Affairs*. Similarly, Steven Levitsky and Lucan Way argued that 'Orbán's Hungary is a prime example of a competitive autocracy with an uneven playing field'. S Levitsky and L Way, 'How autocrats can rig the game and damage democracy' (*The Washington Post*, 4 January 2019). See also A Bozóki and D Hegedűs, 'An externally constrained hybrid regime: Hungary in the European Union' (2018) *Democratization* 1173. In 2015, Hungary was also reclassified from a consolidated democracy to a semi-consolidated democracy by Freedom House's Nations in Transit report, freedomhouse.org/sites/default/files/2020-02/FH_NIT2015_06.06.15_FINAL.pdf. In its 2020 report, Freedom House went further, declaring that Hungary had sunk from the status of a semi-consolidated status to that of a hybrid regime of democracy and authoritarianism, < freedomhouse.org/country/hungary/freedom-world/2020.

[27] The Italian Government did exactly the opposite: without having such a ruling in the constitution, it adopted a new decree law that included important safeguards, such as an obligation to report to Parliament every two weeks.

[28] Concerning the details of the emergency measures of the Hungarian Government, see, in addition to the Hungarian chapter of this book, G Halmai and KL Scheppele, 'Don't Be Fooled by Autocrats!

However, in mid-June 2020, the Hungarian Parliament repealed the law that gave outsized powers to the government, allowing it to override laws by decree with no time limit. The Hungarian Government was facing EU budgetary sanctions so it gave way. But on the same day that Parliament repealed the law giving the government those extraordinary powers, it passed another law that gave back the same powers, with even fewer constraints.[29] With these regimes still being in force on 3 November 2020, after the severe second wave of the pandemic hit the country, the government again declared the state of danger,[30] and a week later Parliament adopted Enabling Act III, unconstitutionally providing authorisation for future governmental decrees until 22 May 2021.[31] On 19 May 2021 the Parliament adopted an amendment to the Enabling Act III.[32] According to this the emergency measures will be in force until September 2021.

Even a less destructive outbreak of COVID-19 in Hungary provided a pretext for the Orbán Government to dismantle the remnants of democratic character in its already 'illiberal' state. In this rather autocratic state, the government seems also to have the power to suspend parliamentary elections, or change their rules at will as long as the emergency lasts. And if there are no regular and fair elections, then we cannot talk in terms of a democracy and must refer instead to 'institutionalised uncertainty', a political system in which parties can lose elections.[33] Together with losing its democratic character, the system, while violating its own constitution, made huge rhetorical efforts to maintain its 'authoritarian legalist'[34] image.

Assessing the reactions of the Hungarian Government to the challenges of the pandemic, the European People's Party (EPP) President and former Polish Prime Minister Donald Tusk was right when he claimed that Adolf Hitler's jurist and prominent Nazi legal scholar Carl Schmitt would be proud of Hungarian Prime Minister Viktor Orbán.[35] Carl Schmitt famously defended Hitler's emergency

Why Hungary's Emergency Violates Rule of Law' (*Verfassungsblog*, 22 April 2020) verfassungsblog.de/dont-be-fooled-by-autocrats/?fbclid=IwAR1y2QoJktMihGxcp5G5QGkR8NZ9WerG6z3fHj808QDiHMPPym1XEB-x3cM and G Halmai and K L Scheppele, 'Orbán Is Still the Sole Judge of his Own Law' (*Verfassungsblog*, 30 April 2020) verfassungsblog.de/orban-is-still-the-sole-judge-of-his-own-law/?fbclid=IwAR03paK8fBl6pkRyUFCDKJBUInyP3q7dEGK30jErSxNeJqHCMfoUxuQOEA0.

[29] See a detailed analysis of the new emergency power written by KL Scheppele, G Mészáros and G Halmai, 'From Emergency to Disaster' (*Verfassungsblog*, 30 May 2020) verfassungsblog.de/from-emergency-to-disaster/?fbclid=IwAR3gVwcgZ9NEzd8B67YHIUWL_s1ZA_RdULDSsS-N4R3EzvB-C3y86z7Nd2c.

[30] ejf.hu/hireink/a-kormany-4782020-xi-3-korm-rendelete-a-veszelyhelyzet-kihirdeteserol.

[31] See G Halmai, G Mészáros and K L Scheppele, 'So It Goes – Part I' (*Verfassungsblog*, 19 November 2020). verfassungsblog.de/so-it-goes-part-i/.

[32] Act XL of 2021 on amending the Act I of 2021 on Protecting against the Global Pandemic, the text of the law in the National Gazette: https://magyarkozlony.hu/dokumentumok/131c0a0d4454de6ee3ae55d11a26ea9b47ddac05/megtekintes.

[33] See this epigrammatic definition of democracy in A Przeworski, 'Some Problems in the Study of the Transition to Democracy' in GA O'Donnell, P-C Schmitter and L Whitehead (eds), *Transition from Authoritarian Rule: Comparative Perspectives* (The John Hopkins University Press, 1986) 58.

[34] See the term used by KL Scheppele, 'Autocratic Legalism' (2018) 85 *University of Chicago Law Review* 545.

[35] rmx.news/article/article/hungarian-government-outraged-after-donald-tusk-claims-prominent-nazi-would-be-proud-of-pm-orban.

measures by saying: 'The Führer protects the law. And that situation has been introduced by Viktor Orbán's Ermächtigungsgesetz'.[36] This does not mean a completely lawless situation, since the constitution and laws are still in force, just as the Weimar Constitution was not formally abolished during the Nazi era.[37]

III. Old and New Normative Justifications for Authoritarian Use of Emergency Power

The authoritarian illiberal Hungarian and Polish constitutional systems were based on Carl Schmitt's critique of liberal constitutionalism and its conception of the rule of law even before the pandemic, ever since coming to power in 2010 and 2015 respectively.[38] Although Schmitt never used the terms 'illiberal' or 'illiberal democracy', he did merely consider liberalism as an indecisive parliamentary system, and his anti-pluralism and the concept of homogeneity as a precondition for a plebiscitarian, charismatic democracy (Führerdemokratie) is very similar to the idea of 'illiberalism' à la Viktor Orbán.

As David Dyzenhaus convincingly proves, Schmitt argued prior to 1933 that in times of fractious pluralism and political partisanship, only the chief executive can rise above the political fray, excluding the 'enemies' and governing by law which is loyally interpreted by a homogeneous group of judges. In his Political Theology, written in 1922, Schmitt famously argues that 'the sovereign is: He who decides on the exception'.[39] This exception seemed to be law-governed.[40] In another publication from the same year, Schmitt differentiates between 'sovereign' (legally unbound) dictatorship and 'commissarial' (legally bound) dictatorship.[41] Two years later, he specified the commissarial dictatorship with Article 48, the emergency powers section of the Weimar Constitution, by arguing that the president could not violate the essential organisational structure of the constitution in

[36] G Halmai, 'How COVID-19 Unveils the True Autocrats: Viktor Orbán's Ermächtigungsgesetz' (2020) *Int'l J. Const. L. Blog* at www.iconnectblog.com/2020/04/how-covid-19-unveils-the-true-autocrats-viktor-orbans-ermachtigungsgesetz/.

[37] See Jiri Priban's interview after the start of the coronavirus crisis: www.e15.cz/rozhovory/obdobi-prosperity-ceske-spolecnosti-prave-konci-mini-sociolog-jiri-priban-1369589.

[38] As Heiner Bielefeld demonstrates, Carl Schmitt systematically undermines the liberal principle of the rule of law. See H Bielefeld, 'Deconstruction of the Rule of Law. Carl Schmitt's Philosophy of the Political' (1996) 82 *Archiv für Rechts- und Sozialphilosophy* 379–96."

[39] 'Souverän ist, wer über den Ausnahmezustand entscheidet': C Schmitt, *Politische Theologie: Vier Kapitel zur Lehre von der Souveränität* (Berlin, 1990).

[40] See D Dyzenhaus, *Legality and Legitimacy. Carl Schmitt, Hans Kelsen, and Hermann Heller in Weimar*, (OUP, 1997) 44.

[41] C Schmitt, *Die Diktatur: Von den Anfängen des modernen Souveränitätsgedankens bis zum proletarischen Klassenkampf* (Berlin, 1989). The term 'commissarial dictatorship' originates from the Roman Republic, which is also the basis of Machiavelli's description of dictatorship, later used by Jean Bodin. See J Bodin, *On Sovereignty: Four Chapters from the Six Books of the Commonwealth,* edited and translated by JH Franklin (CUP, 1992). Quoted by Z Bretter, 'Carl Schmitt, "Az illiberális demokrácia kottája"' [The Music Sheet of Illiberal Democracy], Manuscript with the author.

exercising this power, because he is not a legislature.[42] In his book on Constitutional Theory (*Verfassungslehre*) published in 1928, he is still talking about the concept of law based on rule of law ('*rechtsstaatlicher Gesetzesbegriff*') and sharing of powers ('*rechtsstaatliche Gewaltenunterscheidung*') between the legislature and the executive, where the former is responsible for general law-making, and the latter is in charge of implementation of the law (*Massnahmenhandel*).

It was only in 1932, right before the collapse of the Weimar Republic, that Schmitt in 'Legality and Legitimacy' ('Legalität und Legitimität') raised the possibility of an anti-liberal democracy, in which the President, the dictator or the Führer may legitimise breaches of legality with political realisation of right.[43] This political stance, on which such a legal order is based, was based on the distinction between friends and enemies elaborated in *The Concept of the Political*, also written in 1932.

In other words, during the Weimar period, Schmitt respected 'authoritarian legalism', though this ended on 24 March 1933, when Hitler's Ermächtigungsgesetz was enacted. In August 1934, Schmitt published his infamous article 'Der Führer schützt das Recht' retroactively legalising the murders of Hitler's rivals in the Nazi Storm Troopers (SA) during the Night of the Long Knives on 30 June 1934. One of the most important sentences says that 'in a Führerstate other than in a liberal state governed by the rule of law, the legislator, the executive and the judiciary cannot distrustfully control each other'.[44]

The question is whether the described distinction between the legally bound 'commissarial dictatorship' and the unbound 'sovereign dictatorship' represents a change in Schmitt's concept, or whether he merely reacted to the different stages of German development from the Weimar era until Hitler's Nazism. I agree with David Dyzenhaus that there is an essential continuity in Schmitt's work dating roughly from 1922 onwards.[45] This applies from his already mentioned anti-pluralism and homogeneity concept to his consequent Hobbesian decisionism. Prior to 1933, he saw the role of the law and the constitution differently. The idea in his Verfassungslehre that the core of the constitution should not be subject to constitutional amendments was even instrumental in introducing an eternity

[42] 'Der Reichspräsident ist kein Gesetzgeber'. C Schmitt, 'Die Diktatur des Reichspräsidenten nach Artikel 48 der Weimarer Verfassung' (first published in 1924).

[43] C Schmitt, 'Legalität und Legitimität' in *Verfassungsrechtliche Aufsätze* (Berlin, 1958). See R Mehring, 'Carl Schmitt und die Pandemie. Teil II.' (*Verfassungsblog*, 12 May 2020) verfassungsblog.de/carl-schmitt-und-die-pandemie-teil-ii/.

[44] 'In einem Führerstaat, in dem Gesetzgebung, Regierung und Justiz sich nicht, wie in einem liberalen Rechtsstaat, gegenseiting misstrauisch kontrollieren.' C Schmitt, 'Der Führer schützt das Gesetz' (1934) *Deutsche Juristen-Zeitung* 1. László Kövér, co-founder of Fidesz, speaker of the Hungarian Parliament has spoken several times in a similar vein by saying that the 'concept of checks and balances is a nonsense' (index.hu/belfold/2019/10/23/kover_laszlo_valasztas_ellenzek_rendszervaltas) and 'the judiciary cannot be independent from the state' nepszava.hu/3033652_kover-laszlo-a-biroi-fuggetlenseg-napjan-kovetelt-engedelmesseget-a-biroktol.

[45] See Dyzenhaus (n 40) 39.

clause to the 1949 Grundgesetz, though from the publication of his *Political Theology* he stood by his conviction that the basis of law is the sovereign's decision, which can always result in a new constitution. The aim of this work is not to answer the question raised by many scholars, about whether Schmitt was an eternal Nazi or just an opportunist. His concept of homogeneity of the people certainly changed in 1933 and again after 1945: before and after these dates, he considered homogeneity as a political requirement, while during the Nazi era he also saw it as a racial one. One can even interpret his support of the Führer against the SA as his way of greeting the abandonment of the 'second', social revolution earlier promised by Hitler. On the other hand, some people argue that behind the friend-enemy dichotomy can be detected his well-known anti-Semitism.[46] In this matter I also tend to agree with David Dyzenhaus, who argues that it is a mistake to describe Schmitt as a 'Nazi legal theorist', because his most important contributions were made during the Weimar Republic, when he was allied to conservative forces deeply opposed to the Nazis.[47]

Even though Carl Schmitt's sovereignty concept is not based on the emergency situation related to the Spanish flu,[48] it is no surprise that his ideas about the executive branch as being the proper locus of sovereignty emerge again in the time of the recent emergency situation, and that there are new followers of him who use his concepts to normatively legitimise authoritarian misuse of the pandemic. Maybe Schmitt's truest believers are Eric Posner, a professor at the University of Chicago Law School, and Harvard Law professor Adrian Vermeule, who articulated the descriptive and normative theory of 'unbound executive' in times of emergency (at least in the US, but also beyond) in several of their works.[49]

It is certainly no coincidence that Adrian Vermeule published an article with an argument in keeping with post-1933 Schmittian ideas the day after Viktor Orbán's Parliament enacted his version of the Enabling Act.[50] Vermeule presents his concept of a 'substantive moral constitutionalism' as an alternative to 'left-liberal' constitutionalism, which prefers 'an illiberal legalism that is not "conservative"

[46] See R Gross, 'The "True Enemy": Antisemitism in Carl Schmitt's Life and Work' in J Meierheinrich and O Simons (eds), *The Oxford Handbook of Carl Schmitt* (OUP, 2017).

[47] D Dyzenhaus, 'Lawyer for a Strongman' (*Psyche*, 12 June 2020) aeon.co/essays/carl-schmitts-legal-theory-legitimises-the-rule-of-the-strongman.

[48] R Mehring, 'Carl Schmitt und die Pandemie' Teil I. (*Verfassungsblog*, 11 May 2020). <https://verfassungsblog.de/carl-schmitt-und-die-pandemie-teil-i/> accessed 1 May 2021.

[49] Their first joint book is *Terror in the Balance* (2007), which brought Schmitt's insights into the context of the contemporary American war on terror, while the second is *Executive Unbound: After the Madisonian Republic* (2011), which inspired Tom Ginsburg and Milla Versteeg's comparative study on emergency powers during COVID-19. In their critique they refer to the theory of Posner and Vermeule as 'neo-Schmittian'. See Ginsburg and Versteeg (n 4) 26. 5.

[50] A Vermeule, 'Beyond Originalism. The Dominant Conservative Philosophy for Interpreting the Constitution Has Served its Purpose, and Scholars Ought to Develop a More Moral Framework' (*The Atlantic*, 31 March 2020) www.theatlantic.com/ideas/archive/2020/03/common-good-constituti onalism/609037/.

at all, insofar as standard conservatism is content to play defensively within the procedural rules of the liberal order'. In other words, Vermeule considers liberalism as a set of purely destructive tools and procedures. The central aim of this 'common-good constitutionalism' is not to 'protect liberty' as an end in itself, but to promote good rules, and 'police power', which 'despite its misleading name refers to the general power of state governments to protect health, safety, order, and public morality'. In another essay titled 'Integration from Within', published in 2018 in the conservative journal *American Affairs*, Vermeule dreams of a world in which we will 'sear the liberal faith with hot irons' in order 'to defeat and capture the hearts and minds of liberal agents'. For this purpose, he asserts, 'coercion' ought to be on the table.[51] As David Dyzenshaus rightly points out, it is a mystery why Vermeule thinks that one can have an illiberal legalism that is not 'content to play within the procedural rules of the liberal legal order', and abandons the constitution altogether as an agreed basis for legal arguments.[52] Viktor Orbán did violate his own 'illiberal' Fundamental Law while introducing the unlimited emergency power, because under Article 53.3 of Hungary's current constitution, decrees issued in a state of emergency lose their legal force after 15 days unless Parliament affirmatively approves their continuation. But in the Enabling Act, the Parliament relinquished that power. But Orbán still attempted to appear to be constrained, because Schmitt's unbound sovereign is so clearly recognised as a danger now, especially within the European Union, a value community of liberal democracies.

IV. Conclusion

As has been shown, beyond the choice between economic and health considerations also applied in liberal democratic countries, which have led either to 'under-' or 'overreaction' to the pandemic, certain illiberal regimes have used the crisis situation as a pretext to strengthen the autocratic character of their systems. In some cases, this required an 'underreach', such as in Poland, where the authorities insisted on the presidential election taking place in order to entrench the power of the governing party's incumbent, despite the health risks. Elsewhere an 'overreach' has served to increase the government's power, a good example being Hungary, where unlimited emergency powers for the government were introduced after the very first cases of infection. Based on Carl Schmitt's critique of liberal democracy, new theories on the 'unbound executive' or 'common good constitutionalism' have emerged to legitimise the necessity of authoritative rule by (wannabe) autocrats.

[51] See this interpretation of Vermeule's essay: J Chappel, 'Nudging Towards Theocracy: Adrian Vermeule's War on Liberalism' (*Dissent*, spring 2020) www.dissentmagazine.org/article/nudging-towards-theocracy.

[52] See D Dyzenhaus, 'Schmitten in the USA' (*Verfassungsblog*, 4 April 2020) verfassungsblog.de/schmitten-in-the-usa/.

The measures taken by illiberal governments as pretexts for further power grabs have demonstrated that liberalism in these cases is not besieged by democracy run amok,[53] or by populism for that matter, but rather by simple authoritarianism. Hence, neither the concept of 'illiberal democracy' nor that of populism can serve as an analytical tool to understand the motivations of those would-be autocrats using COVID-19 for their own interests.

Let me start with 'illiberal democracy', which is an oxymoron, because there is no democracy without liberalism, and there also cannot be liberal rights without democracy.[54] In this respect, there is no such thing as an 'illiberal or anti-liberal democracy', or 'democratic illiberalism'[55] for that matter. Those who perceive democracy as liberal by definition also claim that illiberalism is inherently hostile to values associated with constitutionalism, as an institutional aspect of liberal democracy: separation of powers, constraints on the will of the majority, human rights, and protections for minorities. Therefore, the equally oxymoronic 'illiberal' or 'populist' constitutionalism[56] is necessarily authoritarian in character.[57]

[53] See D Luban, 'Among the Post-Liberals' (*Dissent*, winter 2020) www.dissentmagazine.org/article/among-the-post-liberals.

[54] cf J Habermas, 'Über den internen Zusammenhang von Rechtsstaat und Demokratie' in U Preuss (ed), *Zum Begriff der Verfassung. Die Ordnung der Politischen*, (Fischer, 1994) 83–94. For the English version, see J Habermas, 'Rule of Law and Democracy' (1995) *European Journal of Philosophy* 3. Also Juan José Linz and Alfred Stepan assert that if governments, even those freely elected, violate the rights of individuals and minorities, their regimes are not democracies. See JJ Linz and A Stepan, 'Toward Consolidated Democracies' (1996) 7(2) *Journal of Democracy* 14, 15. Similarly, János Kis claims that there is no such thing as non-liberal democracy, or non-democratic liberalism. See J Kis, 'Demokráciából autokráciába. A rendszertipológia és az átmenet dinamikája' [From Democracy to Autocracy. The System-typology and the Dynamics of the Transition] (2019) 1 *Politikatudományi Szemle* 45–74. Those critics who argue that liberalism, as a 300-year-old concept, predates liberal democracy forget that not only democracy but also liberalism presupposes general and equal suffrage.

[55] Takis S Pappas defines modern populism as democratic illiberalism, and calls the current Hungarian regime an 'illiberal democracy'. TS Pappas, 'When Populists Come to Power' (2019) 30(2) *Journal of Democracy* 70.

[56] For instance, Paul Blokker considers 'populist constitutionalism' as an alternative, conservative understanding of the constitutional order, which is, among other things, a reaction to injustices resulting from liberal democratic politics, to unbalanced emphasis on formalistic liberal institutions, rights, and norms, and an aggressive institutionalisation of a liberal understanding of law in the post-1989 transformation. See P Blokker, 'Populist Constitutionalism,' in C de la Torre (ed), *Routledge Handbook of Global Populism* (Routledge, 2018); P Blokker, 'Populism As a Constitutional Project' (2019) 17(2) *ICON*. Using Isaiah Berlin's terminology on 'false populism' I argue elsewhere that this 'authoritarian populist constitutionalism' is only a rhetoric, and not a real populist appeal to the 'people'. See G Halmai, 'Populism, Authoritarianism and Constitutionalism' (2019) 20(3) *German Law Journal*.

[57] Following Juan José Linz's classical categories, authoritarianism lies in between democratic and totalitarian political systems. See JJ Linz, *Totalitarian and Authoritarian Regimes* (Lynne Rienner, 2000). Writing about Franco's Spain, Linz has already outlined the following four main characteristics of authoritarianism: limited, not responsible political pluralism, without elaborate and guiding ideology, without political mobilisation, and with formally ill-defined, but quite predictable limits of power. See JJ Linz, 'An Authoritarian Regime: the Case of Spain' in E Allard and Y Littunen (eds), *Cleavages, Ideologies and Party Systems* (Helsinki, 1970). About the constitutional markers of authoritarianism as a pretence of democracy, such as the lack of procedural rights, institutional guarantees and public discourse, see GA Tóth, 'Constitutional Markers of Authoritarianism' (2018) *Hague Journal on the Rule of Law*, published online 10 September 2018.

What the coronavirus has done is to make the autocrats show their authoritarianism more openly.[58]

But using an undifferentiated concept of populism does not help us understand all governmental reactions to COVID-19 either.[59] For instance, the Italian Government, led by the populist Five Star Movement (after a terrible start due mostly to the regions of Lombardy and Veneto led by the far-right League party) has been successful in flattening the curve and containing the pandemic.[60] Not all populists are autocrats who abhor restraints on the political executive;[61] moreover, economic populism can be justified against discretionary monetary policy or beneficial treatment of foreign investors without democratic deliberation by both national and transnational executives.[62] For the same reason, blaming the people cannot help us understand the crisis of democracy also deepened by COVID-19.[63]

In his recent book, *The Tyranny of Merits* (2020), Michael Sandel argues that populism is a reaction to the liberal left's pursuit of meritocracy. In an interview, he claims that the only way out of the crisis to dismantle the meritocratic assumptions that have morally rubber-stamped a society of winners and losers. Referring to the COVID-19 pandemic, he believes that the new appreciation of the value of supposedly unskilled, low-paid work offers a starting point for renewal: 'This is a moment to begin a debate about the dignity of work; about the rewards of work both in terms of pay but also in terms of esteem. We now realise how deeply

[58] Similarly, J-W Müller, 'One Damn thing After Another. The Long Roots of Liberal Democracy's Crisis' (*The Nation*, May 18/25 2020) www.thenation.com/article/culture/sheri-berman-adam-przeworski-democracy-dictatorship-crisis-book-review/.

[59] See such a view in A Weale, 'Anti-Populist Lessons of Coronavirus' (2020) 13(62) *Global-e* www.21global.ucsb.edu/global-e/september-2020/anti-populist-lessons-coronavirus?fbclid=IwAR0l4PdngkjfyFk67yoTEHTC0LjHFJAr2WdDlos-7cGBxH1m9zVCChrv4uw.

[60] Paul Krugman compared the Italian success in weathering the coronavirus with the failure of the US to do the same. See P Krugman, 'Why Can't Trump's America Be Like Italy?' (*The New York Times*, 23 July 2020).

[61] Among the many critics of anti-populism, see the book by T Frank, *The People, NO, A Brief History of Anti-Populism* (Metropolitan Books, 2020), which praises the 'real' populism of the American People's Party in the 1890s, as well as FDR's New Deal in the 1930s. He argues that the 'empty culture-war fight' of the GOP and Trump (or Fidesz and Orbán in Hungary for that matter) is 'false populism'. See an interview with him: P MacDougald, What's the Matter With Populism? Nothing' (*The Intelligencer*, 1 September 2020) nymag.com/intelligencer/2020/09/whats-the-matter-with-populism-nothing.html?fbclid=IwAR1CJYiPF_6uFalCGgHB9TKlDTk-ppcu3ZFnfAPpyoZYxGaSE5ccpugcCnw.

[62] See D Rodrik, 'In Defense of Economic Populism' (*Social Europe*, 18 January 2018) www.social-europe.eu/defense-economic-populism.

[63] See Eric Posner's book, *The Demagogue's Playbook*, which blames the American people for Trump's rise, criticised by Yale Law School historian, S Moyn, 'The Guardians. Does "The Resistance" Actually Want More Democracy or Less' (*The Nation*, 24 August 2020) www.thenation.com/article/culture/eric-posner-demagogues-playbook/. Similarly, Joseph Weiler blamed the Hungarian people for supporting Orbán. JHH Weiler, 'Editorial' (2020) 18(2) *ICON* www.iconnectblog.com/2020/08/icon-volume-18-issue-2-editorial/?utm_source=feedburner&utm_medium=email&utm_campaign=Feed%3A%20I-CONnect%20(I-CONnect%20Blog)&fbclid=IwAR1CJYiPF_6uFalCGgHB9TKlDTk-ppcu3ZFnfAPpyoZYxGaSE5ccpugcCnw. See a critique by V Kazai, 'Blaming the People is not a Good Starting Point' (*Verfassungsblog*, 8 August 2020) verfassungsblog.de/blaming-the-people-is-not-a-good-starting-point/?fbclid=IwAR1CJYiPF_6uFalCGgHB9TKlDTk-ppcu3ZFnfAPpyoZYxGaSE5ccpugcCnw.

dependent we are, not just on doctors and nurses, but delivery workers, grocery store clerks, warehouse workers, lorry drivers, home healthcare providers and childcare workers, many of them in the gig economy. We call them key workers and yet these are oftentimes not the best paid or the most honoured workers.'[64]

It is also misleading to distinguish between antidemocrats, nativists and populists, as the main challengers of political liberalism and liberal democracy.[65] The illiberals are all antidemocrats who delegitimise representative democracy's normative foundation, nativists who protect the interests of the native-born or established inhabitants against those of immigrants, and they are populists, referring to the 'pure people' against the 'corrupt elite', or during the pandemic crisis against experts, like virologists.[66] As Rogers Brubaker convincingly argued in 2017, several independent crises, like the financial crisis, the refugee crisis, the security crisis caused by terror attacks, and lately the crisis of public knowledge of fake news and alternative facts – and today we can add the coronavirus crisis – have converged and created a 'perfect storm' conducive to populism.[67] But autocrats' populism is 'false'[68] and they only use populist rhetoric, which does not necessarily correspond with populists' practice.[69] In other words, we can answer the

[64] www.theguardian.com/books/2020/sep/06/michael-sandel-the-populist-backlash-has-been-a-revolt-against-the-tyranny-of-merit?CMP=Share_iOSApp_Other.

[65] See TS Pappas, 'The Specter Haunting Europe: Distinguishing Liberal Democracy's Challengers' (2016) 27(4) *Journal of Democracy* 22–36.

[66] While in my view all illiberals nowadays are populists, not all populists are necessarily illiberals, for instance some of the left populists are not. Even in East-Central Europe the populism of the Czech Prime Minister, Andrej Babis, is lacking strong illiberal components. Contrary to my understanding, Andrew Arato and Jean Cohen, analysing the normative theory of left populism by Ernesto Laclau and Chantal Mouffe respectively claim that left populism also cannot avoid illiberal authoritarianism inherent in the strategy and logic of populism despite the inclusionary and democratising projects of the left-wing movements it attaches to and despite the democratic socialist rhetoric of left populist leaders and their organic intellectuals. See A Arato, 'Political Theology and Populism' (2013) 80(1) *Social Research* and JL Cohen 'What's Wrong with the Normative Theory (and the Actual Practice) of Left Populism?' (2019) *Constellations* 26. In my view it is certainly true for Latin American populists from Peron, Morales and Correa through to Chavez and Maduro, but not necessarily for European left populist parties, such as Podemos, the Five Star Movement and Syriza. The last two did not even show serious illiberal pursuits while in power.

[67] R Brubaker, 'Why Populism?' (2017) 46 *Theor. Soc.* 357–85.

[68] The term 'false' populism was used by Isaiah Berlin defining 'the employment of populist ideas for undemocratic ends'. See I Berlin, *To Define Populism,* The Isaiah Berlin Virtual Library, 1968, The Isaiah Berlin Literary Trust 2013. Posted 14 October 2013. 6. berlin.wolf.ox.ac.uk/lists/bibliography/bib111bLSE.pdf.

[69] Concerning the use of populist rhetoric by Viktor Orbán and his government, see a more detailed description in G Halmai, 'Populism, Authoritarianism and Constitutionalism' (2019) 20 *German Law Journal* 296–313. Similarly, Gáspár Miklós Tamás argues that the Orbán government is 'an ingenious old-new form of flexible and non-murderous dictatorship, but why is it "populist"?', GM Tamás, '"The mystery of Populism" finally unveiled' (*openDemocracy*, 24 February 2017) www.opendemocracy.net/wfd/can-europe-make-it/g-m-tam-s/mystery-of-populism-finally-unveiled. Based on Hannah Arendt's republican conception, Camila Vergara also distinguishes populism from proto-totalitarianism, arguing that populism aims to increase the welfare of the plebeian masses, and therefore its relation with liberal democracy appears to be one of reform, while totalitarian movements, even if using populist rhetoric, want to destroy liberal democracy and constitutionalism altogether. See C Vergara, 'Populism as Plebeian Politics: Inequality, Domination, and Popular Empowerment' (2020) 28(2) *The Journal of Political Philosophy* 222–46.

question about whether it is the groundswell of popular discontent in Europe and the Americas that is really threatening democracy[70] in the negative. Paraphrasing James Carville's bon mot we should say: It's the authoritarianism, stupid, which is behind illiberal and populist reactions to COVID-19. Let us hope that after all the other crises we have faced, and now after this pandemic, we will not face 'the crisis of the crisis of capitalism'[71] but the restoration of capitalism, and that democracy with it will still be possible.

[70] S Hahn, 'The Populist Specter. Is the Groundswell of Popular Discontent in Europe and the Americas What's really Threatening Democracy?' (*The Nation*, 28 January–4 February 2019) www.thenation.com/article/archive/mounk-galston-deneen-eichengreen-the-populist-specter/.

[71] This is the main claim of the recent book by A Albanova, *Capitalism on Edge* (Columbia University Press, 2020).

16

Populism versus Democracy during a Pandemic: Some Preliminary Considerations

JAN-WERNER MÜLLER*

Plenty of observers have rushed to predict that the COVID-19 pandemic will seriously harm the political fortunes of populists, or even make populism the outbreak's first 'ideological casualty', as one Indian commentator put it.[1] Populists, these observers assert, by definition vilify experts; now we are all learning that the price of not listening to experts may well be our own life. Populists, it is often said, are the great simplifiers;[2] during the pandemic, we clearly needed experienced bureaucrats and leaders who could deal with a complex challenge (Francis Fukuyama, for instance, argued prominently – and reasonably enough – that a successful response to COVID-19 required state capacity, social trust, and leadership).[3]

Yet this valiant attempt to see a silver lining in this political moment is itself highly simplistic. Populism, I argue in this chapter, is not primarily characterised by hostility to scientists or experts more broadly – even if there is indeed, as I also show, a particular suspicion of professionals which populists tend to share with neoliberals. Populists in power might benefit from a rally-around-the-flag dynamic in the face of the pandemic; more importantly, they can still deploy their key strategy of claiming that they are the uniquely legitimate representatives of the people, and of dividing citizens against each other (and de facto blame minorities, as well as a supposedly illegitimate political opposition, for all sorts of problems, including the pandemic). Still, there are limits to this approach: as figures like Trump and Bolsonaro demonstrated conclusively, a virus cannot be defeated by

* I draw here extensively on my *What is Populism?* (Penguin, 2017) and *Democracy Rules* (Penguin, 2021), as well as the article 'How Populists Will Leverage the Coronavirus Pandemic' (2020) *World Politics Review*.

[1] www.dailypioneer.com/2020/columnists/populism-the-first-ideological-casualty-.html.

[2] R Dahrendorf, 'Acht Anmerkungen zum Populismus' (2003) 25 *Transit: Europäische Revue* 156–63.

[3] F Fukuyama, 'Pandemic and Political Order' ((*Foreign Affairs*, 9 June 2020), www.foreignaffairs.com/articles/world/2020-06-09/pandemic-and-political-order.

populist culture war; and in many instances, attempts to associate the pandemic with particular groups (or entire nations, for that matter) have not proven very successful. It's true that the virus drove and kept people apart – but the divisions that followed from the pandemic were not the kinds of divisions from which populists obviously profit.

This leaves the question what democratic politics in the face of a pandemic should look like. State responses cannot be dictated comprehensively by science as such; questions about priorities (Who gets a vaccine first?), distribution, both material (Who is being helped? Who is left to die as an industry?), and in terms of rights (rights restrictions for those refusing to be vaccinated?) need to be resolved through proper democratic processes. Neither parliamentary opposition nor broader societal contestation become illegitimate because of the challenges posed by the pandemic, contrary to what those lauding autocratic responses to COVID-19 might say.

In this chapter, I shall first outline my understanding of populism, which breaks with the conventional wisdom that populism is primarily a matter of opposing experts and advocating simplistic policies. Rather, I argue, populists put forward a claim to a monopoly of representing what populist leaders often refer to as 'the real people' or also 'the silent majority'; what matters (and is dangerous about them) is not 'anti-elitism' or an 'anti-science stance' but a fundamental political anti-pluralism. I shall also say a few words about the complicated relationship between populism and professionals, against whom populists do occasionally deploy supposed folk wisdom and common sense. In a second step, I shall then examine how populists have responded to the pandemic. It turns out that not all of them have tried to wage culture war in the name of the 'real people', and there are reasons to believe that the pandemic just isn't the kind of crisis that is favourable to populist political strategies (be it ones adopted by governments or by parties in opposition that clamour for freedom). In a last step, I ask how issues around the pandemic – to do with basic questions of justice, for instance – can be properly politicised (in contrast with a technocratic stance according to which there is a uniquely rational stance in dealing with the virus). In other words, how are we to imagine a democratic politics of the pandemic?[4] After all, that question is not simply answered by rejecting populist or authoritarian strategies.

I. Populism versus Professionalism?

Conventional wisdom has it that populism is about opposition to elites. But that understanding is superficial; it is also normatively problematic: after all, keeping a close eye on the powerful can just as well be a sign of good, vigilant citizenship.

[4] On this question, see also P Kahn and MP Maduro (eds), *Democracy in Times of Pandemic* (CUP, 2020).

Now, it is true that populist politicians, when in opposition, criticise governments (and other political parties). But they also do something else: they claim that they, and *only they*, represent what populists frequently call 'the real people' or also 'the silent majority'. This might not sound so bad; it is not immediately the same as, for instance, racism or a hatred of global institutions like the WHO, or, for that matter, an irrational suspicion of science. And yet such a claim to a monopoly of properly representing the people has two detrimental consequences for democracy: for one thing, populists declare all other contenders for power to be fundamentally illegitimate. This is never just a matter of differences over policies or even values; rather, other politicians are simply vilified as corrupt characters. What Trump said about his rival in the 2016 presidential election (and more or less repeated in 2020) was extreme, but it was not exceptional: all populists try to convince electorates that other politicians are 'crooked'.

Less obviously, populists also claim that all those citizens who do not support their vision of the 'real people' – and therefore tend not to opt for populists at the ballot box – might not properly belong to the people at all. For the most part, Trump did not reject criticisms with arguments; he simply labelled the critics 'Unamerican'. Erdoğan says about himself and his party: 'We are the people' and then turns to his critics with the question 'Who are you?' Viktor Orbán claimed that 'the nation' – equated with his own political party – cannot be in opposition; and Jaroslaw Kaczyński rails against Poles who he says have treason in their genes (because they happen to disagree with his politics). In short, populists claim a monopoly of legitimately representing the people, with the latter understood as a homogeneous entity with a unified will which the populist leader will simply implement. This explains why populists in power – when they have *enough* power – tend to take their countries in an authoritarian direction. That is not to equate populism and authoritarianism: populists attribute legitimacy to the will of the people, and hold that the people are a source of wisdom; other authoritarians – think of military-bureaucratic authoritarianism – can be thoroughly technocratic and be dismissive of the people as irrational or irresponsible).

Populists frequently invoke the unity of the people. But it is always unity on their terms. And these terms are political and, in the case of right-wing populists, distinctly cultural, if not outright ethnic. Already vulnerable minorities and opposition voices get vilified, as they do not conform to the symbolic construction of the people which populists put forward. Thus, dividing the people is the political business model of populists; culture war is not incidental, but an essential part of their strategy: whenever they can, they will try to reduce policy questions to questions of who really belongs to the people and who does not. Hence elections for them also ideally turn into an existential battle of *us versus them*; and this kind of polarisation can bring citizens to vote for populists even when they realise that such figures are engaged in damaging democracy.[5]

[5] MW Svolik, 'Polarization versus Democracy' (2019) 30 *Journal of Democracy* 20–32. As Svolik puts it, 'the political acumen of Chávez, Orbán, or Erdoğan lay in their ability to draw political battle

Note the implications of this analysis: populism is not a matter of policy content. If you tell me what you think about the Eurocrisis, about refugees, or about vaccines, for that matter, I cannot tell whether you are a populist or not (though I might be able to say whether you are a Eurosceptic, a nativist, or possibly a conspiracy theorist). What matters is the actual talk of leaders – for they themselves tell us whether they are populists or not; they either invoke a monopoly of representing the people and de facto rule out something like legitimate opposition to them, or they don't.[6] If they don't, plenty of terms characterising particular ideological stances might still apply to them: they might be nationalists, or nativists, without being populists; or they might criticise representative democracy as being captured by particular elites and advocate more participation in political decision-making by ordinary people – again, without thereby becoming populists in any analytically meaningful sense of the term.

Still, one might wonder if there is not at least somewhat of a link – something like an elective affinity, if you like – between populism and other more substantive political positions. After all, populists cannot just invoke 'the people' in the abstract – they must say something about who exactly the 'real people' are. For instance, it might not be entirely an accident that virtually all right-wing populists today are effectively ethnic nationalists (and, in the EU context, deep Eurosceptics, if not outright Euro-rejectionists).

In the same vein, one might wonder about an elective affinity between populism and a basic hostility to professional expertise or to really anyone who claims authority on the basis of education and licensing as a result of specialised training – think lawyers, doctors, and professors. Such figures tend to be maligned by right-wing culture warriors as 'condescending' – after all, they tell other people what to do, because they claim to know better. According to Nigel Farage, for instance, the World Health Organization is just another club of 'clever people' who want to 'bully us'; his practical advice has been to 'ignore' their advice on smoking.[7]

It is true that populist often extoll the folk wisdom of ordinary citizens and attribute a healthy 'common sense' to the people as such. But it's important to realise that this does not allow us to equate populism with 'anti-elitism' after all; it is

lines along societal cleavages that were only simmering when these leaders were first elected. Once they succeeded, elections confronted their supporters with the choice between their partisan interests on the one hand and democratic principles on the other'. For detailed evidence on whether voters are willing to act as a check on undemocratic behaviour by politicians from the party with which they identify, see MH Graham and MW Svolik, 'Democracy in America? Partisanship, Polarization, and the Robustness of Support for Democracy in the United States' (2020) 114 *American Political Science Review* 392–409. The authors observe that 'voters are about 50% more lenient toward violations of democratic principles by candidates from their own party'.

[6] Assessments of 'talk' are not subjective, as in: I cherry-pick a few quotes from leaders I dislike and thereby prove that they are dangerous populists. Studies by scholars such as K Hawkins and S Stokes have shown that populist leaders really do talk differently than 'normal' democratic politicians.

[7] twitter.com/Nigel_Farage/status/928730704510320640?ref_src=twsrc%5Etfw%7Ctwcamp%5Etweetembed%7Ctwterm%5E928730704510320640%7Ctwgr%5E%7Ctwcon%5Es1_&ref_url=https%3A%2F%2Fwww.thelondoneconomic.com%2Fpolitics%2Fflashback-to-when-nigel-farage-said-the-experts-have-got-it-wrong-on-smoking%2F02%2F11%2F.

indeed professionals in particular who become the target of populist rhetoric. And it's equally important to realise that the way for a systematic hostility to professionalism was paved by – for lack of a better term – neoliberalism. Let me explain.

Neoliberalism and populism can share a suspicion that professionals – be it academics, lawyers, doctors, or, even journalists – run a kind of closed shop through requiring specialised education and training.[8] Once inside their self-created system, professionals supposedly can relax; unlike those engaged in business, who are mercilessly exposed to the punishments meted out by objective market mechanisms, they are able to get away with a lax attitude towards their own 'products'. Margaret Thatcher evidently assumed that most professors (other than in the hard sciences) were just wasting taxpayers' money by sitting around drinking tea and spouting leftist nonsense. The turn toward simulating markets inside universities and the National Health Service – through a 'tyranny of metrics' (which resulted in the metric becoming the target), and a relentless 'audit culture' which would have given central planners in the Soviet Union the pleasure of instant recognition – was to make professionals compete, work properly, and, above all, become accountable to society at large, ie taxpayers.[9] The latter were assumed to think that the whole game of professionalism was probably always rigged, that 'liberal elites' simply reproduce themselves in a world where in fact there are no real standards.

When Donald Trump revealed his cabinet appointments, some observers pointed with glee to what they thought was an obvious contradiction: how could a supposed 'populist' surround himself with corporate bosses and Wall Street figures with a combined worth of 4.3 billion dollars – all epitomising the elite, after all? What such critics failed to see was precisely that these exceptional human beings, for the most part, weren't professionals: their success (and 'hard work') could be measured objectively, in dollars;[10] they were obviously competent and capable of implementing the real people's will – unlike professionals who would always end up distorting it, while lecturing everyone on how they simply knew better because, after all, they had more education.[11]

The point bears repeating: populists are not 'anti-elite' tout court; they target a particular education-based professional elite (including journalists who are accused of being unfair und unbalanced). With Trump, this was always obvious; but there are more subtle ways of denigrating professionals (and sending a message that there's nothing special about them): during the pandemic, Boris Johnson, shifting to a more and more presidential style of press conferences, insisted on

[8] I am not denying that there are plenty of elements of today's professional cultures and meritocracies that should be criticised; I am just denying that critique by populists is the right one. See for instance D Markovits, *The Meritocracy Trap: How America's Foundational Myth Feeds Inequality, Dismantles the Middle Class, and Devours the Elite* (Penguin Press, 2019).

[9] JZ Muller, *The Tyranny of Metrics* (Princeton University Press, 2018).

[10] As Trump put it at a rally in Iowa in June 2017: 'I love all people, rich or poor, but in those particular positions, I just don't want a poor person. Does that make sense?'.

[11] See also JC Williams, 'What So Many People Don't Get About the US Working Class', hbr.org/2016/11/what-so-many-people-dont-get-about-the-u-s-working-class.

first taking a question from 'Michelle in Cornwall', making it plain that any citizen would be as capable as journalists to ask the important questions (the question Michelle, a hotel owner, ended up asking was 'Please can we ask how tourism within the UK will be managed in the coming weeks?').[12]

Thus, there is indeed an elective affinity between populism and a suspicion of a particular kind of expertise against which supposed folk wisdom can be deployed. But such a strategy is not inevitable, and by no means all populists used it during the pandemic. It's a mistake to take figures like Trump and Bolsonaro as representative in this regard.

II. Populists in the Face of COVID-19

It is tempting to generalise about populists' response to the pandemic. But ultimately, there are too many variables in play to make generalisations plausible.[13] Much depended on whether populists were in government or opposition when the public health crisis started; much also depended on whether populist leaders had extensive government experience and hence could deploy state resources effectively or not; and also what larger political worldview they generally tended to offer to their supporters (remember that populism is not as such a comprehensive ideology);[14] less obviously, trends also varied during the first and the second wave.

Now, it's true that a number of populists used to dominating the news cycle were initially sidelined by the COVID-19 crisis. For instance, in spring 2020, little was heard from (or at least about) Matteo Salvini, the once supposedly inevitable next Prime Minister of Italy. As one perceptive Italian analyst, Teresa Coratella, put it at the time, 'Salvini is neither a minister nor someone the media would ask to explain Italy's strategy on Covid-19. His political megaphone has been confiscated by the Civil Protection Agency, the regional authorities, and the government.'[15] The German far-right party AfD declined in the polls, consumed by infighting instead of capitalising on any discontent with Germany's grand coalition government; its contributions to national debate consisted of things like one of its

[12] And the answer? 'You will come back, Michelle, we are going to make sure that the UK bounces back as strongly and as fast as we possibly can'.

[13] See also the empirical evidence by J Wondreys and C Mudde presented in 'Victims of the Pandemic? European Far-Right Parties and Covid-19', www.cambridge.org/core/services/aop-cambridge-core/content/view/638E1BEA8CF82CA068DBC46149BE9F42/S0090599220000938a.pdf/victims-of-the-pandemic-european-far-right-parties-and-covid-19.pdf, as well as G Katsambekis and Y Stavrakakis, 'Populism and the Pandemic: A Collaborative Report', populismus.gr/wp-content/uploads/2020/06/interventions-7-populism-pandemic-UPLOAD.pdf.

[14] On the notion of populism as a 'thin-centered ideology' see C Mudde and C R Kaltwasser, *Populism: A Very Short Introduction* (OUP, 2017).

[15] T Coratella, 'Whatever It Takes: Italy and the Covid-19 Crisis', March 2020, ecfr.eu/article/commentary_whatever_it_takes_italy_and_covid_19_crisis/.

deputies tweeting that Merkel in self-quarantine was a good start, but that she really should be locked up.[16] Not unreasonably, some observers began to ask the question whether all the policy issues which far-right populists appear to 'own' are not in fact luxury problems when statesmen and stateswomen focused on life-and-death decisions are needed in politics. Who has time to worry about a few dozen people wearing or not wearing burkas and niqabs, when all of us are ordered to put on face masks in public?

Less obviously, far-right populists in particular were often caught in a dilemma as the pandemic dragged on: initially, they had celebrated border closures and assertions of national sovereignty, along the lines of 'we always told you this is necessary and possible' (to keep out migrants) Orbán not only took advantage of COVID-19 to implement further autocratic measures, as Gábor Halmai demonstrates in his chapter in this volume; he also deployed the usual conspiracy theories according to which criticism of his government is only ever voiced by paid-up members of the George Soros International. But, less noted, he also expelled a group of Iranian students, and made a point of saying that his government is focused 'on saving the lives of the Hungarian people'; by contrast, the president of his neighbouring country, in a televised speech, addressed himself to 'Austrians' and 'those who live here'.[17] The Hungarian Prime Minister also strained to equate the virus and migrants: 'We are fighting a two-front war. One front is called migration, and the other one belongs to the coronavirus. There is a logical connection between the two, as both spread with movement.'[18] Meanwhile, Trump and his right-wing enablers were super-spreading a vicious language in which 'Chinese virus' and 'Wuhan virus' became obligatory terms (and a sign of loyalty to the boss). As on previous occasions, the rhetoric at the very top has had effects on the ground, as Asian-Americans were being assaulted ever more frequently. What the philosopher Kate Manne has called 'trickle-down aggression' is likely to be a lasting effect of the populist portrayal of COVID-19.[19]

Yet the emphasis on putting one's nation first eventually sat uneasily with the claim that the virus was in fact less dangerous than professionals (and 'liberal elites' more broadly) made it out to be. If the virus was a hoax, how could restrictions (including border closures) really be justified? In other words, what at least in some countries appeared as a more or less bottom-up libertarianism, often advocated in a polity's foundational constitutional commitments (US militias brandishing

[16] The relative decline of the AfD is all the more astonishing in light of the fact that it is the party that has consistently opposed lockdowns and the only party that is not in government at any level; hence also the one that bears no responsibility for the multiple failures of Germany since dealing rather successfully with the first wave.

[17] www.bundespraesident.at/aktuelles/detail/neues-miteinander.

[18] D Rohac, 'Hungary's prime minister is using the virus to make an authoritarian power grab' (*Washington Post*, 25 March 2020) www.washingtonpost.com/opinions/2020/03/25/hungarys-prime-minister-is-using-virus-make-an-authoritarian-power-grab/.

[19] K Manne, 'The Logic of Misogyny', bostonreview.net/forum/kate-manne-logic-misogyny.

the constitution; German *Querdenker* invoking the Basic Law) sat uneasily with a protectionism and statism long associated with far-right populists trying to push forms of welfare chauvinism.[20] To be sure, not all those clamouring for 'freedom' were populists – but plenty did also present themselves as the 'real people' and denounced governing elites as corrupt.

It is important – yet again – to resist the temptation of equating populism with either statism or libertarianism, just because at particular points leaders one might plausibly identify as populists are associated with such views. Populists can change their views on social and economic policy (who remembers today that Jean Marie Le Pen and Haider's Freedom party were pro-market and pro-EEC in the 1980s?). What they cannot change their mind about is the primacy of the will of the people; but that does not translate into a uniquely correct prescription for the size of the state. What's more, according to theorists like Carl Schmitt, there is a difference between the strong state and the large state. The latter is captured by special interests; the former remains autonomous and above social pluralism. The strong state can also take decisive action in an emergency and assert a primacy of the political – putting the political will of the people as such ahead of particular economic imperatives, for instance.[21]

This notion of a primacy of politics is not exclusive to populists. As Sheri Berman has argued, it also characterised Social Democrats and fascists in the twentieth century; both rejected the subordination of politics to economics (be it in the form of orthodox Marxism or neoclassical economics).[22] The more Social Democrats, as well the centre-right, aligned themselves with neoliberalism in the past decades, the easier it became for populists to present themselves as the only actors who retained some faith in politics. At least in theory, populists could also use the pandemic to demonstrate not just 'our nation first!' but also: *politique d'abord*! (to invoke a signature phrase of Charles Maurrass, the leader of the proto-fascist Action Française).

Arguably, a figure like Orbán tried this route; as did Boris Johnson, putting a venture capitalist in charge of procuring vaccines and adopting an ostentatious whatever-it-takes-economic-constraints-be-damned attitude (of course, like the US, he also ended up with a my-people-first stance, prohibiting the export of vaccines produced in the UK).[23] Others took a different path, however, shying

[20] See also O Nachtwey et al, 'Politische Soziologie der Corona-Proteste' (on file with author) The study finds that the protest movement against restrictions is very heterogeneous; a large number of protestors also clearly do not fit the profile often attributed to the electorate of far-right populist parties (at least German *Querdenker* have high levels of education, many are self-employed, many do not share views often associated with right-wing authoritarian dispositions; the situation is significantly different in Switzerland and Austria).

[21] See also EA Posner, 'The Executive Unbound, Pandemic Edition' (*LAWFARE*, 23 March 2020) www.lawfareblog.com/executive-unbound-pandemic-edition.

[22] S Berman, *The Primacy of Politics* (CUP, 2006).

[23] D Keating, 'How the EU's Naivete led to its Vaccine Debacle' (*New Statesman*, 24 March 2021) www.newstatesman.com/world/europe/2021/03/how-eu-s-naivety-led-its-vaccine-debacle.

away from strong state action, instead combining forms of libertarianism with populist culture war. Trump culturally re-coded wearing a mask as 'Unamerican', liberal, elitist, etc; those opposing his policies (or lack thereof) were deemed to be fearful, weak characters. Fox News and Rush Limbaugh framed the pandemic as a liberal conspiracy; Trump himself at one point called it a new hoax by the Democrats to damage him. He tweeted that the real people want to get back to work ASAP', whereas the 'LameStream Media' allegedly wanted to keep the country closed as long as possible in order to sabotage the re-election to which the reality TV President felt entitled.

The fact that both Trump and Bolsonaro appeared to survive the virus personally without any obvious major consequences for their health made it all the easier for them to present the pandemic as a matter of having a strong, non-corruptible character (and belonging to the real people), as opposed to medical knowledge or conduct oriented towards some sense of solidarity.[24] One might even say that their individual resurrection – produced Riefenstahl-like by Trump's team for TV – helped their strategy to turn COVID-19 into a national cultural drama disconnected from the more abstract truths of a rising number of deaths and devastating effects on the economy. The truth of the pandemic was revealed by the exemplary overcoming of all perils by the leader – not the statistics invoked by the Anthony Faucis of this world.

Analysts picked up not just on the prominent culture war antics of Trump and Bolsonaro; they also pointed out another, much more surprising commonality. These leaders precisely seemed not to do what diagnosticians of impeding authoritarianism in the US and Brazil would have predicted: take advantage of a crisis to grab powers and solidify their rule. If COVID-19 was the Reichstag fire, it seemed that Trump just sat there, Nero-like, and let it all burn without realising the golden opportunity for his own set of enabling laws. The result, according to legal scholars, was the opposite of the executive over-reach observed in other parts of the world: it was passivity and 'executive under-reach'.[25]

This is an intriguing interpretation. But it suffers from two problems: for one thing, Trump did display plenty of his authoritarian instincts; he simply had no plan and, at least on this occasion, not enough help from figures like Bill Barr who, otherwise, were willing to bend or even entirely reshape basic legal norms. Moreover, it's not quite true that the Trump administration did nothing; rather, it continued what it had been doing from day one: de-regulate and, in particular, try to reverse as many of Obama's executive orders as possible. Under the pretext of

[24] Of course, for Bolsonaro (whose middle name happens to be Messias), it was already the third coming; after all, he had survived a stabbing during the 2018 presidential campaign. A Netflix series producer who made up this story might have a hard time selling it.

[25] DE Pozen and KL Scheppele, 'Executive Underreach, in Pandemics and Otherwise' (2020) 114 *American Journal of International Law* 608–17, www.cambridge.org/core/journals/american-journal-of-international-law/article/abs/executive-underreach-in-pandemics-and-otherwise/1C63F88765300 02D489CB8E434BA4FA5#.

helping the economy, the US government allowed companies to pollute the country even more. Something similar happened in Brazil: Bolsonaro – hailed upon his election as a boon for business by the *Wall Street Journal* – made sure that even more of the Amazon rainforest could be devastated.

It would be satisfying, of course, if we had a simple answer to the question: was the pandemic good or bad for populists? But, as I've tried to show, the picture is much messier than many analysts initially expected.[26] Moreover – and this a more meaningful observation than the always available 'it's complicated': the pandemic did not ultimately lend itself so easily to the strategies of cultural division which populists practice. One could not clearly associate particular ethnic groups with the virus, even if the likes of Orbán and Modi tried (and even Trump to some degree: 'liberal cosmopolitan' states like California and New York were particularly blamed for the pandemic).[27] In short, one could not plausibly portray scientists as a homogeneous liberal elite bent on betraying the people, because in many countries scientists also disagreed (even if none agreed with Trump's recommendation that injecting disinfectant might be the answer to COVID-19).

III. Democratic, Non-Populist Politics for a Pandemic and a Post-Pandemic World

A pandemic is an emergency, but an emergency is not automatically an exception during which all democratic politics must stop. There are good reasons why an opposition should come on board with emergency measures, but, given how contestable policies also are (who gets a vaccine first? Who pays? How do we understand basic rights during a pandemic etc), it would be entirely unjustified if dissent became delegitimated in the name of some form of 'national unity', or if one pretended that only conspiracy theorists found it worthwhile to debate threats to the rule of law during an emergency.[28] On the contrary: a watchful opposition is likely to make a response to a pandemic go better (as opposed to autocracies where mistakes are hushed up). And citizens are more likely to accept policies when they have a sense that dissent could be properly articulated (and then still be rejected by a majority in a representative assembly); as always, when opposition can be represented within a political system, people are less likely to oppose the system as such.

[26] P Manow, 'COVID-19, Europa und der Populismus', paper on file with author. See also T Hale, N Angrist, B Kira, A Petherick, T Phillips and S Webster, 'Variation in Government Responses to COVID-19' (Blavatnik School of Government Working Paper 2020/032 Version 6.0, May 2020), www.bsg.ox.ac.uk/sites/default/files/2020-05/BSG-WP-2020-032-v6.0.pdf.

[27] Supposed mainstream politicians also tried, of course. Sebastian Kurz attempted to blame the second wave in Austria on people with Balkan roots; later on he put his faith into anti-Brussels rhetoric, when he blamed the EU's supposed 'vaccine bazaar' for under-supplying his compatriots with jabs.

[28] See also HM Heinig et al, 'Why Constitution Matters' (2020) 75 *Juristenzeitung* 861–72.

From this point of view, it is concerning that in many democracies, parliaments have effectively been sidelined. Sometimes, this has come down to procedural changes: for instance, time allotted for debate was drastically limited (as sitting days for parliament were cancelled in Australia, as one example);[29] on some occasions, effective dissent was articulated primarily by different executives, rather than on a national parliamentary stage (individual governors and premiers in federal systems such as Brazil and Germany, also often sidelining individual state parliaments).[30]

How dissent is articulated of course crucially depends on leaders of parties; after all, no conflict explains itself, no opposition is obvious; every political battle needs to be staged consciously (and responsibly).[31] Clearly, competence versus incompetence is one possible battle line, but it is not itself enough to generate a democratic form of politics, for, again, the problem of such a framing is an effective denial of the fact that there are always choices. 'Science' does not choose for us; 'competence' does not prescribe uniquely correct solutions; it will at best narrow the range of possible choices, but those responsible for collective choices still have to make them – and admit to them. The premier of Saxony claimed at one point that the government's policies were not unjust; instead, 'the virus is unjust'. But that is a form of obfuscation; every form of politics operates on the basis of an underlying theory of justice; what matters is the content of that theory and politician's willingness to avow it (and defend it against an opposition).

An opposition should offer alternatives, and, above all, hold a government strictly to account. It is often forgotten just how crucial it is for democracies properly to institutionalise the role of a loyal opposition (which means: loyal to the democratic system and its basic principles, not loyal to government policies). Concrete ways of doing this vary: a procedure whereby opposition leaders can reply immediately to ministers' speeches, giving the opposition a chance to dramatise differences and demonstrate an alternative; low thresholds for establishing committees of inquiry; opposition days, where the losers of an election set the agenda of parliament's business; even installing opposition figures as the chairs of important committees (where much of the real work of parliaments gets done). A government is authorised to have its way, but, at all stages, an opposition must have its say.[32]

[29] M Rizzi and T Tulich, 'The Australian Response to COVID-19: A Year in Review' (*VerfBlog*, 22 February 2021) verfassungsblog.de/the-australian-response-to-covid-19-a-year-in-review/.

[30] E Peluso N Meyer and T Bustamante, 'COVID-19 in Brazil: A Sick Constitutional Democracy' (*VerfBlog*, 22 February 2021) verfassungsblog.de/covid-19-in-brazil-a-sick-constitutional-democracy/, DOI: 10.17176/20210222-153853-0.

[31] The political theorist Nancy Rosenblum observes that conflicts 'do not spontaneously assume a form amenable to democratic debate and decision … someone must create the lines of division over social aims, security, and justice. Party rivalry is constitutive. It "stages the battle"'.

[32] I am riffing here on the nice formula 'the minority should have its say, and the majority should have its way' in the Venice Commission's Opinion On the Relationship between the Parliamentary Majority and the Opposition in a Democracy: A Checklist (2019), www.venice.coe.int/webforms/documents/default.aspx?pdffile=CDL-AD(2019)015-e.

Take a concrete example: New Zealand leader Jacinda Ardern proposed a plausible solution in the face of the country's lockdown and the temporary suspension of parliament: rather than having a grand coalition paper over all legitimate disagreement with the rhetoric of unconditional 'national unity', she suggested a select committee chaired by the leader of the opposition, which can hold the government to account.[33]

To prevent emergency measures from becoming permanent – especially once public attention has shifted elsewhere – Bruce Ackerman has argued for the ingenious mechanism of a 'super-majoritarian escalator': laws and decrees can be renewed periodically, but only if ever larger majorities agree to do so.[34] This would focus political debate on the question whether a return from the new to the old normal is possible. In particular, it would put the spotlight on basic rights protection (such as the attempt by the Trump administration and the Johnson government to claim powers to hold citizens in detention).

And professionalism? The COVID-19 crisis might lead us to a clear-eyed view of the value of professionalism (including professionals in politics like, say, Hillary Clinton). But it's also important to keep professionalism in its place. Professional advice should meaningfully constrain political choices, not determine them. Proper professionals, unlike a certain type of technocrat, do not promise that they know the uniquely correct solution to all policy problems.

The assumption that there is only one right way is perversely shared by populists and technocrats: populists claim that there is only one authentic popular will (to build a Wall, get Brexit done, or what have you), and that they are the only ones who know it -- and the only ones who can implement it. The technocratic stance – widely on display on the continent during the Eurocrisis – holds that there is only one rational answer to policy challenges, and that only technocrats can identify it. If you disagree with a populist, you are declared a traitor to the people; if you disagree with a technocrat, you'll be told politely that you are not smart enough.

The lesson is not that professionalism should replace democratic politics, or, for that matter, wide-spread participation by citizens – a conclusion drawn by unashamedly elitist liberals who have sought to reinstate professional gatekeepers everywhere. Citizens still know best what their problems are; professionals – in perfectly non-condescending ways – play a crucial role in addressing them. Or, as John Dewey put it, 'no government by experts in which the masses do not have the chance to inform the experts as to their needs can be anything but an oligarchy managed in the interests of the few'.

Then again, 'the masses informing the experts' and democratic contestation do not happen all by themselves – at least not in a structured way. It's true that the pandemic was like an X-ray: it exposed structural vulnerabilities (in public health, in protections for essential workers, etc) which had hardly been unknown,

[33] 'Special committee set-up as parliament is adjourned', www.rnz.co.nz/news/political/412520/special-committee-set-up-as-parliament-is-adjourned.

[34] B Ackerman, *Before the Next Attack* (Yale University Press, 2007).

but which arguably had never been so clearly visible. But seeing structural vulnerabilities does not always translate into fighting for change, and even cataclysmic experiences do not open 'new ages' in any obvious way (as Brecht observed in his poem about new ages, written during one of the watershed periods of the twentieth century, World War II). It will take political mobilisation for progressive interpretations to prevail (just think back to how to how the Tea Party managed to push a deeply inegalitarian framing of the financial crisis, while Obama's grassroots movement demobilised at the same time). It will matter whether the left, which in theory could benefit from a new emphasis on state capacities, can find an institutional form to mobilise citizens. After 2008, it experimented with different movements and parties based on digital platforms which would have made it easier to participate in politics (Podemos and France Insoumise are the obvious examples).[35] These had lasting influence in Southern Europe, but never managed in the end to reverse austerity policies.

It is largely forgotten that not only the financial crisis, but also 9/11 initially unleased an inflationary rhetoric of 'shared sacrifice', collective purpose, and an age of state responsibility replacing a frivolous period of individual hedonism.[36] Yet in the end those who benefited most were private contractors; instead of a collective purpose sustained by the citizenry, particular state tasks were outsourced to the likes of Blackwater.

Such a future of individual contracting (or, for that matter, individual nation-states contracting, strictly putting their people first) instead of anything like collective purpose is also entirely possible as a legacy of the present crisis. The very real suffering caused by COVID-19, rather than inspiring structural reform, might become part of the narratives circulating in a right-wing culture of grievances, carefully tended by populists who push polarisation and make majorities feel like minorities under siege.

[35] P Gerbaudo, *The Digital Party* (Pluto, 2020).
[36] DT Rodgers, *Age of Fracture* (Harvard University Press, 2011).

17

Conclusions: Pandemocracy – Governing for the People, without the People?

KONRAD LACHMAYER AND MATTHIAS C KETTEMANN*

I. Emergency Approaches in the Pandemic

A. An Unexpected Health Crisis in Europe

The COVID-19 crisis took European governments by surprise. This unpreparedness[1] was not, however, truly justified, since various epidemics had spread locally and globally within the last two decades.[2] Since the COVID-19 pandemic affected people around the globe to a different degree than previous pandemics, a more differentiated approach was required, but had not been elaborated in advance. Governments were forced to make rapid decisions in a complex and uncertain situation.[3] While European governments had faced many different crises in the last two decades,[4] a pandemic of this dimension and severity had not been experienced in Europe for a long time.[5] European governments were unprepared, both on the domestic front and on the transnational European level.

* We are grateful to the contributors of the country chapters for reviewing this comparative analysis.

[1] See M Poiares Maduro and PW Kahn, 'Introduction: A new beginning' in M Poiares Maduro and PW Kahn (eds), *Democracy in Times of Pandemic. Different Futures Imagined* (CUP, 2020) 1, 8.

[2] The WHO provides an overview of disease outbreaks news, www.who.int/emergencies/disease-outbreak-news.

[3] Frankenberg pleads for a learning law to overcome the challenges of the pandemic; see G Frankenberg, 'COVID-19 und der juristische Umgang mit Ungewissheit' (*Verfassungsblog*, on matters constitutional, 25 April 2020) verfassungsblog.de/covid-19-und-der-juristische-umgang-mit-ungewissheit/.

[4] In Europe, the first two decades of the 21st century were marked politically by terrorism, an economic crisis, a decline of the rule of law, challenges to principles-led, human rights-based migration governance and accelerated global warming. All these developments were characterised as crisis: security crisis, economic crisis, rule of law crisis, migration crisis and climate crisis. The COVID-19 pandemic is understood as a health crisis.

[5] The 1918 influenza pandemic (also known as Spanish flu) infected in four waves approx. 0.5 billion people; between 20–50 million people died globally. See eg L Spinney, *Pale Rider: The Spanish Flu of 1918 and How It Changed the World* (PublicAffairs, 2018).

It seems entirely justified to call the COVID-19 pandemic a public health emergency, which can be understood as 'something dangerous or serious […] that happened suddenly or unexpectedly and needs fast action in order to avoid harmful results'.[6] Faced with such an emergency situation, democratic governments had to decide not only how their measures could stop the emergency and deal with its effects, but also to what extent their measures would affect their country's constitutional and democratic framework. The latter consideration was sometimes treated with too little caution, as the chapters in this volume demonstrate.

B. A State of Emergency?

Not every emergency situation gives reason to call for a (constitutional or legislative) state of emergency. Temporary restrictions of human rights and the empowerment of the governments to act fast, efficiently and effectively could already fulfil substantive criteria of a state of emergency but could – depending on the respective legal order – also be handled in a regular normative framework. Such a substantive perspective cannot be placed on the same level as a formal declaration of a state of emergency by a government. Moreover, different countries and legal traditions have established different (legal) concepts of states of emergency. From an overall perspective, states of emergency can provide a constitutional framework to limit the transfer of power to the executive in times of emergency, but could also legitimise extensive executive powers while bypassing parliament. The analyses of different European democracies[7] in this volume demonstrate a wide range of approaches towards states of emergency.[8]

To understand the democratic dimension, it is necessary to clarify if a state of emergency has been declared (by parliaments or governments) and if this declaration has been in conformity with the constitutional framework of the respective country. As a precondition to this question, it is possible to distinguish between countries whose constitutions provide the possibility of a state of emergency and those whose constitutions do not.

i. *Constitutions without a State of Emergency Concept*

The Swedish, French and Italian constitutions do not provide for a constitutional state of emergency, at least not in relation to peacetime. In Sweden, a shift of legislative powers to the executive was discussed and later enacted, while in France

[6] Cambridge Dictionary, dictionary.cambridge.org/dictionary/english/emergency.

[7] In certain countries like Hungary democracy had already been under threat before the pandemic.

[8] All countries discussed in the volume have been affected significantly by the pandemic, some of them in the first wave, some in the second or third wave. The different countries represent different legal cultures and different constitutional traditions. The similarities and differences illustrate how constitutional culture affects the reaction of the different countries to the specific crisis.

a state of emergency was declared by Parliament; in Italy a state of emergency was declared (not through Parliament but) by resorting to a statutory source, ie Legislative Decree no. 1/2018.

The Swedish Constitution does not provide for a state of emergency in peacetime, but the introduction of such a concept was discussed. In Sweden, originating from situations that occurred in the 1970s, concerning an extra-legal state of emergency due to a debated principle of constitutional necessity, a debate has occurred on and off, mostly in literature.[9] This concept of constitutional necessity would legitimise the deviation from constitutional law without having an explicit constitutional foundation. Although the Swedish state has continually rejected the concept of constitutional necessity since the introduction of the 'new' Instrument of Government in 1974, the concept arises in discussions whenever a crisis has occurred. Nevertheless, it still seems unlikely that governmental arguments towards an application of constitutional necessity would have been accepted in the pandemic.[10]

The French Constitution does not provide for state of emergency concepts except in Article 16 (presidential exceptional powers in the event of other serious threats) and Article 36 (state of siege in the event of foreign war or armed insurrection, which implies a transfer of various powers from the civilian to the military authority). This is why Parliament intervened to enable the executive to act as a matter of urgency in the COVID-19 crisis.[11] The Members of Parliament could have relied on two existing legislative bases (a statutory law of 1955 and Article L.3131-1 of the Public Health Code) but, under pressure from the executive, they chose to create a new emergency regime.[12]

The Italian Constitution does not provide state of emergency concepts except the state of war. However, it includes a provision (Article 77 Italian Constitution[13]), which was drafted with a view to natural catastrophes but was then interpreted more broadly.[14] By relying on Legislative Decree No 1/2018 (ie, a statutory, not

[9] See J Reichel and J Dahlqvist, 'Swedish Constitutional Response to the Corona Crisis – The Odd One Out?' in this volume.

[10] ibid.

[11] In France, a state of emergency was declared based on the Act of Parliament, which introduced a fast-track procedure a new state of emergency system in a fast-track procedure. This ordinary statutory act was not referred to the constitutional judges. The specific Institutional Act suspended the deadlines for examining constitutional reviews. As the adoption of the Institutional Act did not consider appropriately the procedural framework laid down by the constitution, it clearly breached the constitution; the constitutional judges did not censure it, due to the 'specific circumstances' linked to the pandemic.

[12] See S Brunet, 'The Hyper-Executive State of Emergency in France' in this volume.

[13] Art 77 Italian Constitution: 'The Government may not, without delegation from the Houses, issue decrees having the force of ordinary law. When in extraordinary cases of necessity and urgency the Government adopts provisional measures having the force of law it must on the same day present them for conversion into law to the Houses that, even if dissolved, shall be especially summoned and shall assemble within five days. The decrees lose effect from their inception if they are not converted into law within sixty days from their publication. The Houses can however regulate through laws juridical relations arising out of decrees not converted'.

[14] Art 77 Italian Const is not explicitly circumscribed to natural catastrophes. Rather, in the mind of members of the Constituent Assembly, it should have been used to deal with these kinds of events.

constitutional source), a state of emergency was declared to confront the pandemic. After that, a set of decree laws deferring the adoption of rights-restrictive measures to decrees of the President of the Council of Ministers (ie, the head of the Italian government) were adopted. The decrees of the Presidents of the Council of Ministers were criticised for not meeting constitutional conditions to limit certain rights and freedoms.[15]

These examples show that, although a constitutional state of emergency did not exist, in times of crisis it depends on the bodies involved as well as the legal and political culture if the government is successful in introducing a new concept of state of emergency or not. While Sweden did not establish a state of emergency concept, the recurrent academic debate in Sweden about an extra-legal state of emergency illustrated the conceptual possibility. In Italy and France concrete concepts of state of emergency were established.

ii. Constitutions with a State of Emergency Concept

The UK, Hungarian, Swiss, German and Estonian Constitutions provide a state of emergency concept. While Hungary violated the constitutional framework by extending the concept of a state of emergency, in Switzerland the existing constitutional framework was active and the state of emergency was established in conformity with the constitution.[16] In between these two poles of constitutionality and unconstitutionality concerning the declaration of a state of emergency, the Estonian case can be understood as a declaration of a state of emergency which was formally correct, but contradicted the constitutional principle of parliamentary democracy. In contrast to the aforementioned countries regarding the declaration of a state of emergency, the German and the UK's government did not declare a constitutional state of emergency in the COVID-19 pandemic.

a. Violating the Constitution by Creating a (New) State of Emergency

The Hungarian constitution provides an emergency clause, which was not fulfilled by the COVID-19 pandemic. As the Hungarian Fundamental Law only refers to natural and industrial disasters, a human pandemic was not considered to be encompassed by the Hungarian Constitution.[17] In contrast to this constitutional

In practice, it was used to address a variety of circumstances, some of which did not even fit the concept of 'emergency'. See A Vedaschi, 'The Marginalisation of Parliament in Facing the Coronavirus Emergency: What about Democracy in Italy?' in this volume.

[15] See A Vedaschi, 'The Marginalisation of Parliament in Facing the Coronavirus Emergency: What about Democracy in Italy?' in this volume.

[16] Some constitutional scholars have argued that the measures aimed at addressing the (social and economic) consequences of the pandemic went beyond what Art 185(3) of the Swiss Constitution allows (eg, G Biaggini). See O Ammann and F Uhlmann, 'Switzerland: The (Missing) Role of Parliament in Times of Crisis' in this volume.

[17] See F Gárdos-Orosz and Z Szente, 'Using Emergency Powers in Hungary: Against the Pandemic and/or Democracy?' in this volume.

interpretation, the Hungarian Parliament enacted a Disaster Management Act in 2011, which can be considered as unconstitutional as it went beyond the definition of a disaster in the Hungarian Fundamental Law. As a first response to the COVID-19 crisis the Hungarian Parliament furthermore enacted an Authorisation Act in 2020, which also has to be seen as unconstitutional as the statutory act refrained from defining the legislative framework of the emergency powers of the government and delegated unlimited powers to the government.[18]

The Hungarian example illustrates that existing state of emergency concepts in a constitution or other provisions and procedures provided in a constitution do not prohibit the government and the parliament from breaching existing constitutional frameworks in times of crisis to strengthen their own power while claiming the need to do so. Many other countries in the COVID-19 crisis, however, proved that such a necessity to breach the constitutional framework did not exist. It was, therefore, merely a political smokescreen to argue in favour of a constitutional state of emergency.

b. Staying in Conformity with the Constitutionally Provided State of Emergency

An in-between situation could be observed in Estonia, where the government formally stayed in conformity with the constitutionally provided state of emergency, but did contradict the constitutional concept of parliamentary democracy. The Estonian government declared a state of emergency, which was formally in conformity with the Constitution and the Emergency Act. The declaration of the state of emergency, however, completely bypassed the Estonian Parliament and ignored the possibilities of involving it.[19]

Switzerland also made use of an intra-constitutional emergency concept. The Swiss Constitution provides an emergency clause (Article 185 Swiss Constitution),[20] which was activated in the COVID-19 pandemic.[21] It provided sufficient possibilities for the Swiss government to take appropriate measures; this, however, does not mean that all measures taken by the Swiss government have been necessary (especially in light of legislative competences and direct democracy).[22]

[18] ibid.

[19] See R Maruste, 'State of Emergency in Estonia' (*Verfassungsblog*, 17 May 2020) verfassungsblog.de/state-of-emergency-in-estonia/.

[20] There are actually two emergency clauses in the Swiss Constitution: Art 184(3) – which pertains to foreign affairs – and Art 185(3). In the COVID context, only the latter clause was relevant. See O Ammann and F Uhlmann, 'Switzerland: The (Missing) Role of Parliament in Times of Crisis' in this volume.

[21] See also F Uhlmann and O Ammann, 'Switzerland and the COVID-19 Pandemic: A Look Back and a Look Into the Future' (*Verfassungsblog*, 1 March 2021) verfassungsblog.de/switzerland-and-the-covid-19-pandemic-a-look-back-and-a-look-into-the-future/; F Uhlmann, 'Concentration of Powers in the Federal Executive: The Application of Emergency Powers in Switzerland' (*Verfassungsblog*, 30 April 2020) verfassungsblog.de/concentration-of-powers-in-the-federal-executive-the-application-of-emergency-powers-in-switzerland/.

[22] See O Ammann and F Uhlmann, 'Switzerland: The (Missing) Role of Parliament in Times of Crisis' in this volume.

These countries exemplify that constitutionally existing states of emergency might be activated in times of crisis, but that the constitutional frameworks usually do not provide crisis-based concepts of involving the parliaments in a way which is commensurate with upholding representative democracy. It still depends on the relevant statutory law and governmental decrees, which have to guarantee parliamentary involvement.

c. Not Using the Constitutionally Possible State of Emergency

The German Basic Law provides different forms of states of emergency,[23] but Germany did not formally declare a state of emergency.[24] Though not analysed in this volume, Austria can be mentioned as another example in this regard. Although the Austrian Constitution contains an emergency concept, the constitutional possibilities have not been considered to be practical or efficient with regard to a pandemic and were not activated by the Austrian government.[25] On the contrary, the reactions to the pandemic were taken within the regular constitutional framework. The UK government also did not declare a state of emergency, even though it used a wartime-style rhetoric. The Coronavirus Act did not exclude the government from the Human Rights Act;[26] the foundational approach was not to leave the constitutional framework and not to use the possibility of a state of emergency.

These countries proved that it was not necessary to activate a constitutional state of emergency in the COVID-19 pandemic. Although it might be argued that in different countries different constitutional pre-conditions exist to enable the same governmental measures, most of the relevant governmental measures could have been based on existing or newly enacted statutory health law.

d. Summary

In conclusion, besides the question as to whether a constitution provides a state of emergency, it seems highly relevant whether the respective country respects the existing constitutional framework. While Hungary, Italy and France breached the constitutional framework in the context of the declaration of a state of emergency, the Swedish, German and Swiss governmental reactions remained within the constitutional framework.

This, however, does not tell us anything about the constitutionality of the concrete measures taken on the basis of the declaration/non-declaration of a state of emergency. The Estonian case illustrates that formally correct procedures might

[23] See P Thielbörger, 'Germany – Federalism in Action' in this volume.

[24] ibid.

[25] See K Lachmayer, 'Austria: Rule of Law Lacking in Times of Crisis' (*Verfassungsblog*, 28 April 2020) verfassungsblog.de/rule-of-law-lacking-in-times-of-crisis/.

[26] See R Thomas, 'Virus Governance in the United Kingdom' in this volume.

still contradict the principle of representative democracy; debates in Sweden show us that the risk of breaching the constitutional framework can also exist even if no actual breach has occurred in the current situation.

C. Democratic Challenges

The discussions about a state of emergency illustrate how deeply the pandemic has affected the constitutional structures of democracy in European countries. Manifold democratic challenges can be identified. Most prominently, the shift towards the executive changed the interplay of the different institutional bodies, which significantly influenced the role of the parliaments and the people not only on a domestic level but also – from a neo-federalist perspective[27] – in the realm of European multi-level governance.

In that regard, the following considerations will focus on the role of the parliaments in the COVID-19 pandemic, especially their interplay with the respective governments (section II). Moreover, the multi-level dimension of democracy will be analysed with regard to international organisations, the European Union and federalism or decentralisation in times of the COVID-19 crisis (section III). This comparative analysis includes the countries (and respective chapters) presented in this volume: Germany, France, Italy, the United Kingdom, Hungary, Sweden and Switzerland.[28] The overall question to be addressed is to what extent domestic governments (re)acted for the people without participation of the people, especially their (parliamentary) representatives.

II. The Role of the Parliaments

A. Introduction

In emergency situations – regardless of the formal declaration of a state of emergency – a rapid response by a government is not only expected but also demanded (by the people). From a democratic perspective, it is relevant whether governmental measures are in conformity with the constitution and statutory law: if they are, the parliamentary oversight concerning the measures taken will tell us something about the relevance of democracy in times of crisis; if not, the method of involving the parliament indicates the degree to which the concept of a representative democracy is realised in times of crisis.

Different strategies of government can be observed and shall be distinguished. The range of approaches is very broad and can be distinguished by the depth of

[27] See www.federalism.eu/projects/overview/.

[28] Further references to other European countries will only be selective.

the involvement of the respective parliament. From bypassing the parliament or a one-stop involvement by obtaining a general approval by the parliament to the concretisation and therefore limitation of measures by the parliament, as well as the opposition towards governmental measures, a variety of responses could be observed in the COVID-19 pandemic. The chosen mixture of parliamentary involvement in each country gives us an impression of the resilience of representative democracy in times of such a health crisis.

B. Bypassing Parliament

A general bypassing of parliament could not be observed in the analysed European countries. The Hungarian government bypassed the Parliament on existing provisions of the Hungarian constitution and statutory law, which could not be applied, as the constitutional requirements were not fulfilled. At the end of March 2020, however, Parliament legitimised governmental action by an Act of Parliament (still not fulfilling the requirements of the constitutional framework).[29] In France too, Parliament retrospectively legitimised governmental action (Decree of 16 March introducing a general lockdown) by an Act of Parliament of 23 March 2020.[30] Elements of bypassing the parliament could also be observed in Italy concerning decrees of the head of the executive without parliamentary approval nor (at least in the first instance) information.[31] It seems that this only refers to exceptional cases and not to the regular procedure in the COVID-19 crisis in Italy.

Another example can be observed in the UK.[32] In a fast-track procedure, the UK Parliament approved a statute of more than 350 pages.[33] Further regulations based on secondary legislation were introduced based on this legal foundation. Significantly, the Westminster Parliament could not substantively debate these regulations. Although regulations by constitutional convention had to be laid before Parliament at least 21 days before entering into effect, in the COVID-19 crisis most of the regulations came into effect before being laid before Parliament. There were no means by which Parliament could amend regulations and parliamentary scrutiny remained unsatisfactory. Step by step, the Westminster Parliament was able to regain some power by having more time to debate and discuss secondary legislation.[34]

It seems deeply problematic when governments do not respect the role of the parliament in times of crisis. Parliaments have an important role in ensuring that

[29] See KL Scheppele and D Pozen, 'Executive Overreach and Underreach in the Pandemic' in Poiares Maduro and Kahn (n 1) 38, 40–43.

[30] See S Brunet, 'The Hyper-Executive State of Emergency in France' in this volume.

[31] A Vedaschi, 'The Marginalisation of Parliament in Facing the Coronavirus Emergency: What about Democracy in Italy?' in this volume.

[32] See R Thomas, 'Virus Governance in the United Kingdom' in this volume.

[33] ibid.

[34] ibid.

the legitimacy chain to the people remains intact. The cases illustrate that parliaments had to fight to be considered instead of governments attempting to involve them properly (even if the usual standards regarding the necessary timeframe could not be met).

C. Legitimising a General Transfer of Power by the Parliament

In Italy, measures adopted by the head of government through his own decrees were based on a set of decree laws. Decree laws have the same force as ordinary legislation, are adopted by the government as a whole (ie, the Council of Ministers) and need to be submitted to the Houses of Parliament, which, within 60 days, decide whether or not to convert them into permanent legislation. Yet these decree laws were very vague and left much to the discretion of decrees of the President of the Council of Ministers, which have a lower rank than law in the Italian hierarchy of legal sources; they are adopted by the sole head of government and are not scrutinised by Parliament. In March 2020, a further decree law obliged the President of the Council of Ministers to inform the two houses of Parliament before adopting rights-restrictive measures through his own decrees.[35] In some cases the information only took place ex post. In the latter case the houses could not vote on the resolution, but could only engage in an ex-post debate; possibilities of approval were quite limited.

In France, the new statutory law empowered the government to legislate by decree laws called ordinances.[36] The Senate limited the transferred measures at least to a certain extent, though these were still very broad. The government could govern through ordinances, which could derogate statutory law for the time of emergency.[37]

The Hungarian case also falls in the category of 'general legitimation of transfer of power' by the parliament. Parliament gave its consent to any emergency decree ex ante as long as governmental measures were necessary and proportionate to address the emergency. As a safeguard, the government regularly had to inform Parliament of the measures taken (ex post). The Hungarian Parliament could only withdraw the transfer of powers; the first state of emergency was not limited to a

[35] See A Vedaschi, 'The Marginalisation of Parliament in Facing the Coronavirus Emergency: What about Democracy in Italy?' in this volume.

[36] Article 38 of the French Constitution: 'In order to implement its programme, the Government may ask Parliament for authorization, for a limited period, to take measures by Ordinance that are normally the preserve of statute law. Ordinances shall be issued in the Council of Ministers, after consultation with the Conseil d'État. They shall come into force upon publication, but shall lapse in the event of failure to table before Parliament the Bill to ratify them by the date set by the Enabling Act. They may only be ratified in explicit terms. At the end of the period referred to in the first paragraph hereinabove Ordinances may be amended solely by an Act of Parliament in those areas governed by statute law'.

[37] See S Brunet, 'The Hyper-Executive State of Emergency in France' in this volume.

certain time period; only the second one was limited. Parliament did not approve or review any specific measure.[38]

A general legitimation of governmental emergency measures does not sufficiently specify the possible measures that can be taken by the government through legislation. It might even open up the possibility to enact governmental decrees or ordinances which violate or amend statutory law. The parliaments are usually only informed ex post and cannot change the enacted ordinances. Such a situation endangers the application of democratic principles. The necessity argument did not seem convincing as – at the very least – ex post review and rejection of governmental measures should be possible. Fast-track parliamentary procedures and the limitation of transfer of powers would – in contrast to this general legitimation concept – uphold certain standards of parliamentary democracy.

D. Legitimising the Particular Measures by Statutory Law

In Sweden, Parliament was not initially involved as the measures taken were based on the existing constitutional and statutory framework. Sweden has chosen a soft law approach, mainly in favour of non-binding measures.[39] Step by step, the Swedish Parliament amended relevant statutory law to allow the government to introduce stronger measures. Some amendments made in 2020 were never used by the government. However, the parliament eventually enacted a new statutory 'pandemic' law in 2021, which enabled further measures by the government.[40]

In the case of Switzerland, the government started with frenetic regulatory activity based on the existing constitutional framework to enact ordinances, but with the COVID-19 Act adopted in September 2020, Parliament created a regulatory framework for this specific situation.[41] This statutory act created not only the obligation to inform Parliament, but also the requirement to consult the relevant parliamentary committees before emergency ordinances are adopted or amended. However, no parliamentary veto right was introduced. The integration of Swiss Parliament remained limited and did not offer a full deliberation of the governmental measures.[42]

The German Parliament amended the relevant statutory law to grant more competences to the Federal Minister of Health, excluding the involvement of

[38] See F Gárdos-Orosz and Z Szente, 'Using Emergency Powers in Hungary: Against the Pandemic and/or Democracy?' in this volume.

[39] J Reichel and J Dahlqvist, 'Swedish Constitutional Response to the Corona Crisis – The Odd One Out' in this volume; see also H Wenander, 'Sweden: Non-binding Rules against the Pandemic – Formalism, Pragmatism and Some Legal Realism' (2021) 12 *European Journal of Risk Regulation* 127, 134–42.

[40] J Reichel and J Dahlqvist, 'Swedish Constitutional Response to the Corona Crisis – The Odd One Out?' in this volume.

[41] See O Ammann and F Uhlmann, 'Switzerland: The (Missing) Role of Parliament in Times of Crisis' in this volume.

[42] ibid.

the second chamber of Parliament. Statutory law, however, still legitimised only particular measures and not a general transfer of powers.

The limitation of governmental measures by parliamentary restrictions laid down in statutory law definitely contributes to accountable actions of government in times of crisis. This, however, as the examples illustrate, neither led to a full involvement of parliament nor guaranteed parliamentary scrutiny. It still led a reasonable approach in this time of crisis by involving the parliament at least in the explicit limitation of governmental measures, while at the same time rejecting a carte blanche for governmental actions.

E. Approving or Opposing Governmental Measures

The number of examples of parliaments having explicitly to approve certain governmental measures is limited, but a few could be identified. In Italy, there were certain possibilities for the Italian Parliament to exert influence.[43] The decrees of the President of the Council of Ministers had to be submitted to Parliament, which could engage in a debate about them, but had no legally binding tools to change the government's will. The French Senate limited the overall transfer of powers to certain listed measures. Thus, at least a certain parliamentary resistance could be identified in the Senate; an approval of certain governmental measures, however, was not included.[44] In Austria, the main committee of the parliament has to be involved when the government plans hard lockdowns.[45] Moreover, the second chamber of parliament, which is considered to be quite weak and can only postpone statutory bills for eight weeks, has become influential as statutory measures have to be enacted quickly and the government does not have a majority in the second chamber. The government, therefore, has to find compromises with opposition parties regarding the COVID-19 legislation.[46]

F. Reviewing/Surveying Measures

The review of governmental measures can create governmental accountability. There are no reasons not to involve parliament to critically review governmental activities in times of crisis, especially after the measures have been taken. On the contrary, the parliamentary involvement in surveying governmental

[43] A Vedaschi, 'The Marginalisation of Parliament in Facing the Coronavirus Emergency: What about Democracy in Italy?' in this volume.

[44] See S Brunet, 'The Hyper-Executive State of Emergency in France' in this volume.

[45] See K Lachmayer, 'Muddling through Mutation Times or the Return of Federalism in Austria: From Covid-19 Response to the Vaccination Campaign' (*Verfassungsblog*, 8 May 2021) verfassungsblog.de/muddling-through-mutation-times-or-the-return-of-federalism-in-austria/.

[46] ibid.

measures creates not only political debate on emergency activities but also an enormous potential for institutional learning.

Attempts to review or survey governmental measures existed at least in France and the UK. In France, Parliament started to investigate the governmental measures by committees of enquiry. But in June 2020, the President of the Republic started a fact-finding mission by experts on his own to relativise parliamentary activities; at the beginning of 2021, the democratic committee of enquiry of Parliament was dissolved by the governing majority.[47] Parliamentary scrutiny could be observed in the form of parliamentary committees in the UK. Given the nature of the emergency, they represented more of a retrospective accountability.[48]

G. The Limitations of Deliberations in Parliaments

A further challenge of parliamentary involvement concerned fast-track procedures of parliaments and the question whether parliaments should meet in person or online. Both developments raised the question whether the deliberative function of parliaments was upheld in times of crisis or if it was thwarted.

In all countries compared, acceleration of parliamentary procedures could be observed. In many cases, a proportionate timeframe for parliamentary deliberation was often not provided. One might distinguish between fast, faster and turbo legislation. How many hours or minutes should the parliament be involved or be able to debate? It becomes clear that parliaments had to take decisions too quickly without actually having enough time for debate. The problem intensified as the relevant statutory law concerned the transfer of powers from the parliament to government.

The other (much-debated) topic relates to the question whether members of parliament shall meet in person or only online. Meetings which only take place virtually limit the possibilities of direct parliamentary deliberations. Meetings in person, however, conflict with health requirements during the COVID-19 pandemic. Moreover, many constitutional and legislative frameworks did not provide specific regulations on the topic and had to be amended to enable new concepts.

The Swiss Parliament, for example, convened for an extraordinary session outside the regular parliamentary building in an exhibition centre in the capital.[49] This location enabled Parliament to stick to health recommendations and physical distancing, while complying with statutory law. Swiss scholars have highlighted that the establishment of virtual meetings would require further amendments and concrete determination by statutory law.[50]

[47] See S Brunet, 'The Hyper-Executive State of Emergency in France' in this volume.

[48] See R Thomas, 'Virus Governance in the United Kingdom' in this volume.

[49] See O Ammann and F Uhlmann, 'Switzerland: The (Missing) Role of Parliament in Times of Crisis' in this volume.

[50] ibid.

In Italy, remote voting was not introduced and thus all space available in Parliament was used to allow as many members of Parliament as possible to attend.[51] In other cases, only half of the members of each house could participate in person. Germany reduced the requirements for quora[52] and France introduced reduced formats for parliamentary sittings combined with proxy voting.[53] Although Estonia is renowned for its digitalised government, rules for remote voting in Parliament were missing.[54] In the UK, remote voting was introduced and then switched to a hybrid basis with a mixture of in-person and virtual participation.[55]

These examples illustrate a broad variety of approaches in dealing with physical distancing in parliamentary meetings and remote voting. It depends on the existing constitutional framework, the willingness to amend the regulatory framework and the approach to virtual meetings and remote voting in parliaments, which ranged from pragmatism to scepticism. It can be concluded that it depends on the respective political and legal culture if new forms of deliberation are accepted; the change of the way parliamentary debate takes place when using technological support can not be ignored.

H. Conclusion

Different forms of governmental engagement can be distinguished. The shift of power from the parliaments to the executive is not only a question of executive emergency powers, but also related to the self-understanding of parliaments and parliamentarism. In this regard, it is possible to identify different grades of engagement of parliaments in European democracies. The authors suggest distinguishing between confident parliaments, 'business as usual' parliaments, hesitant parliaments and obedient parliaments.

i. Confident Parliaments

During the developments of 2020 the UK Parliament became more confident and demanded increased parliamentary scrutiny.[56] With regard to the French Parliament, a certain ambivalence can be observed. On the one hand the French Parliament could even be understood as obedient[57] in transferring power to the

[51] See A Vedaschi, 'The Marginalisation of Parliament in Facing the Coronavirus Emergency: What about Democracy in Italy?' in this volume.
[52] See P Thielbörger, 'Germany – Federalism in Action' in this volume.
[53] See S Brunet, 'The Hyper-Executive State of Emergency in France' in this volume.
[54] Maruste (n 19).
[55] See R Thomas, 'Virus Governance in the United Kingdom' in this volume.
[56] ibid.
[57] See below.

French government, but on the other hand both the Senate and the opposition parties seem to be quite confident in opposing the enormous transfer of powers to the executive. Their options for succeeding in prohibiting this transfer of powers were quite limited, however.

ii. 'Business as Usual' Parliaments

The approach of the Swedish Parliament could be characterised as 'business as usual' (although some aspects of how the parliament works have been altered to fit the pandemic situation). While at the beginning of the pandemic in Sweden the government did not intervene in the legal framework and limited itself to a soft law approach, Parliament provided limited powers to the government as time went on.[58] This reflects a normal approach of legislation and representative democracy although the limiting of members of parliament actually present in person could challenge the notion of representative democracy. In Germany, Parliament also remained active and provided the necessary amendments. Only regarding parliamentary scrutiny it could be observed that Parliament was restricting itself.[59]

iii. Hesitant Parliaments

A good example of a hesitant parliament is the Italian one; although it had the possibilities to get involved (to a limited extent, ie only by debating forthcoming measures to be adopted by the President of the Council of Ministers), it did not always engage in thorough and in-depth discussion.[60] The Swiss Parliament did not appear to bear political responsibility for the measures taken during the pandemic.[61] The legislator legitimised the transfer of powers to the government to take the necessary emergency actions and did not oppose its limitation and restrictions. Although the Swiss Parliament was involved before certain governmental measures were taken, it was still hesitant to push for further involvement and to introduce deliberation on the governmental measures.

iv. Obedient Parliaments

The Hungarian Parliament can be understood as an obedient one since it did not involve itself in the relevant measures of the government but only created a general statutory (though unconstitutional) basis for governmental action.[62] In contrast

[58] J Reichel and J Dahlqvist, 'Swedish Constitutional Response to the Corona Crisis – The Odd One Out?' in this volume.

[59] See P Thielbörger, 'Germany – Federalism in Action' in this volume.

[60] See A Vedaschi, 'The Marginalisation of Parliament in Facing the Coronavirus Emergency: What about Democracy in Italy?' in this volume.

[61] See O Ammann and F Uhlmann, 'Switzerland: The (Missing) Role of Parliament in Times of Crisis' in this volume.

[62] See F Gárdos-Orosz and Z Szente, 'Using emergency powers in Hungary: against the pandemic and/or democracy?' in this volume.

to the formal possibilities to review and debate the proportionality of the measures, Parliament even enabled the transfer of decrees into statutory law by the Act on Transitional Rules.[63] The French Parliament can (partly) be understood as an obedient parliament as it enabled the huge transfer of powers to the executive and even stopped its own committees of enquiry from working.[64] This perspective, however, only reflects the governmental majority and not the position of the opposition parties.[65]

III. Multi-Level Democracy

A. The Re-Concentration of Power on the Domestic Level

The pandemic is not only affecting the nation states, but also international, supranational and sub-national governance. All levels of the multilevel governance have been challenged by this global pandemic. The effects of the pandemic on the democratic dimensions of rising governance networks are no less than those on the domestic level. The first observation regarding multi-level governance is that the domestic governments not only used emergency powers to obtain competences from the legislator (in a horizontal dimension), but also concentrated their power (in a vertical dimension) from other layers of the multi-level system of governance. Thus, international, European and sub-federal states and entities lost powers in favour of domestic governments. Such a centralisation of power on the domestic level would have required an even greater horizontal oversight and review by domestic parliaments, which – as described above – did not take place.

B. The Role of the WHO

The COVID-19 pandemic is a global crisis and the reaction of humanity to this global challenge has required an international response. The UN sub-organisation WHO (World Health Organisation) plays a significant role in addressing global pandemics. As analysed in this volume, the emergency committees of the WHO operated as a black-box and were thus lacking in transparency.[66] Wrong decision making (eg, concerning travel restrictions) or the influence of certain Member States on the decision-making illustrated the necessity to improve the transparency, objectivity and independence of this international organisation.[67] Democratic improvements could be achieved by stronger representation, public

[63] ibid.
[64] See S Brunet, 'The Hyper-Executive State of Emergency in France' in this volume.
[65] ibid.
[66] P Villareal, 'Pandemics, Expertise and Deliberation at the International Level' in this volume.
[67] ibid.

deliberation and transparency.[68] This also includes the need to incorporate legal expertise and to develop substantive justifications for decision-making in the expert committees of the WHO.

C. The Missing Competences of the European Union

The potential of the Union to manage the crisis was enormous. The transnational dimension of the health crisis favours transnational entities to coordinate measures and enable rapid and consistent action. The possible coordinative tasks start with information exchange, facility support, uniform sourcing strategies and the development of strategies for the freedom of movement or goods. The Union, however, suffered from a lack of competence in health policies, inertia in crisis management and the clear focus of the Member States on their own countries, ignoring European solidarity. It is significant and rather symbolic that in 2020 statistics on COVID-19 infection fatalities only concerned each Member State; a European statistic was not presented to the public.[69] The minor issues the Union was able to take on (eg, the management and procurement of vaccines) did not lead to satisfying results.[70] The effects of this lack of initiatives and competences[71] on the one hand and the lack of efficiency and effectiveness on the other hand did not strengthen European democracy. While at the same time the Union took action regarding authoritarian tendencies in Eastern Europe,[72] the institutions of the EU remained silent regarding constitutional violations of other Member States in the context of the COVID-19 pandemic. As a result of the lack of European legislation in the context of the pandemic, the role of the European Parliament was marginalised not only in approving measures, but also in reviewing violations of European law by the Member States in their responses to the COVID-19 crisis.

D. Struggles with Decentralisation and Federalism

While international and transnational organisations lost influence and power to domestic governments, sub-national entities were also under pressure (due to the measures of the federal/central governments). Although the United Kingdom

[68] ibid.

[69] But see eg ec.europa.eu/eurostat/web/covid-19/overview; ec.europa.eu/eurostat/statistics-explained/index.php?title=Weekly_death_statistics; www.ecdc.europa.eu/en/cases-2019-ncov-eueea. In the public of the Member States, European statistics did not play a significant role.

[70] A Naumann, 'The EU-Response to Fighting the Coronavirus – Coordination, Support, Action – Heeding its Citizens' Calls?' in this volume.

[71] ibid.

[72] See eg European Parliament resolution of 17 September 2020 on the proposal for a Council decision on the determination of a clear risk of a serious breach by the Republic of Poland of the rule of law; or 'MEPs express concerns over attacks on media in Poland, Hungary and Slovenia' www.europarl.europa.eu/news/en/press-room/20210304IPR99220/meps-express-concerns-over-attacks-on-media-in-poland-hungary-and-slovenia.

cannot be qualified as a (full) federal state, the devolutions of the last decades have transferred power to sub-national levels. In the pandemic, strong centralising tendencies could be observed in the UK government; the London-centric mindset of the central government revealed a structural weakness of governing the pandemic.[73] In France, centralism was already very strong in health policies before the crisis. During the crisis, it was up to the central state to enact measures and representatives of the central government were empowered to adopt more restrictive measures. Local autonomy was further weakened.[74]

In Germany, federalism influenced the particular form of crisis governance. The German example illustrated that federalist approaches can both assist and inhibit efforts to fight the pandemic effectively.[75] Only if the executive is balanced with cooperative federalism the federalist approach can create structural advantages.[76]

In both the British and German cases, the COVID-19 pandemic revealed many lessons to be learned to improve the respective federalist approach and calls for reform of the federal system. In other countries, like Switzerland and Austria, the role of federalism did not lead to a debate concerning reform of the federalist system. While in Switzerland the cantons have been quite active and the federal government intervened to create a more coherent approach,[77] the Austrian federal government has been dominant in health governance and also enacted ordinances which have been applicable only in certain regions.[78]

E. Conclusion

The reactions of the domestic governments regarding the COVID-19 pandemic can be understood as a backlash to multi-level governance in Europe.[79] While the domestic governments concentrated power on the national level, the weaknesses of the nation state approach became clearly visible. The potential of flexibility of local and regional solutions supported by cooperative federalism and the potential of international and transnational approaches to fight the pandemic are significant. The realisation of these potentials could not be observed and the effectiveness of the other layers of multi-level governance was missing. This also led to a degeneration of the democratic dimensions of multi-level governance.

[73] See R Thomas, 'Virus Governance in the United Kingdom' in this volume.

[74] See S Brunet, 'The Hyper-Executive State of Emergency in France' in this volume.

[75] See P Thielbörger, 'Germany – Federalism in Action' in this volume.

[76] ibid.

[77] See verfassungsblog.de/switzerland-and-the-covid-19-pandemic-a-look-back-and-a-look-into-the-future/ and O Ammann and F Uhlmann, 'Switzerland: The (Missing) Role of Parliament in Times of Crisis' in this volume.

[78] See Lachmayer (n 45).

[79] AJr Golia et al, 'Constitutions and Contagion – European Constitutional Systems and the COVID-19 Pandemic' (2021) *81ZaöRV/ HJIL* 147, 158 came to another conclusion: 'By contrast, the pandemic did not trigger a single common trend in relation to the vertical allocation of power, either towards centralisation of emergency governance at the national level or towards de-centralisation towards sub-national units.'

Democracy was thrown back to the national level of governance and, thus, especially to the parliaments, which – as analysed above[80] – were marginalised in the crisis by the domestic governments.

IV. Final Conclusions

The pandemic posed an enormous challenge to European democracies. Besides dealing with overcrowded hospitals, the unexpected death of hundreds of thousands of people and enormous economic consequences, one of the crucial challenges was the upholding of the democratic model during times of crisis. Although the shift of power towards the government seemed to be inevitable, the role of the parliaments in the COVID-19 pandemic revealed the state of affairs regarding democracy in Europe. The pandemic can be understood as an endurance test for democracies, which are already challenged by populism, illiberalism and authoritarianism in the upcoming third decade of the twenty-first century.[81]

Although most of the countries compared carried out measures that limited democracy in a disproportionate way, this analysis has illustrated that different reactions were possible to uphold democracy. Parliamentary debate can be organised in various ways, including a change of location and remote meetings. Most of the measures (though perhaps not in the first wave of the crisis) would have had enough time to be prepared and debated properly in parliament. Parliamentary approval and scrutiny could have been guaranteed to uphold representative democracy. In most of the countries, the crisis led to exorbitant governmental measures which infringed upon democracy without the required necessity being present. These limitations of democracy turned out to be too far-reaching and intrusive.

The missing element in European democracies was a lack of preparedness to guarantee democracy in a crisis mode. State of emergency concepts are used to focus on the empowerment of the government and not on the establishment of parliamentary modalities to uphold legislation and parliamentary scrutiny in extreme situations. Crisis legislation attempts to restrict rights to uphold public order instead of establishing differentiated structures to uphold the exercise of rights. The conclusion is therefore that the traditional government-based understanding of crises has to be overcome and a democracy-based concept of the state of emergency should be established. The enabling of a parliamentary mode of crisis would be able to stop the (old monarchic) belief that it is the government and not the people, the Parliament and the public, which is destined to participate in crisis governance. Cooperation between the different state powers and the relevant multi-level network should be what provides the relevant crisis governance to guarantee democracy and such an approach would also effectively counter the spread of populism and authoritarianism in the twenty-first century.

[80] See above.

[81] See G Halmai, 'The Pandemic and Illiberal Constitutional Theories' in this volume; J-W Müller, 'Populism versus Democracy during a Pandemic: Some Preliminary Considerations' in this volume.

INDEX

abuse of power 2, 33–45
accountability
death and dying 67
executive 44
France 210
Italy 3, 118, 124–5, 131–2
online platforms and disinformation 266
parliaments, role of 339
Sweden 3, 146–7, 153–4
United Kingdom 74, 83, 340
WHO's Emergency Committees 237, 239
Ackerman, Bruce 326
advanced purchase agreements (APAs) for vaccines 253–5, 257–8
Aeschi, Thomas 190
Agamben, Giorgio 20, 31, 50–1
anomia 17–19, 21–2, 23
apriority of rights 15–17
Ardern, Jacinda 326
Aristotle 14, 15–16
asylum seekers 165, 171, 222, 304
Athens, plague in 9–10
austerity measures 63–5, 74, 88
Austria 334, 339, 345
authoritarianism/autocracies
commissarial dictatorship and sovereign dictatorship, difference between 307
democracy 346
despotism 14, 28–30
dictatorship 51, 307
Hungary 155–6, 301, 303–6, 321
illiberalism 4, 301, 303–11
Poland 306
populism 317
states of emergency/exception 4, 303, 306–9
United States 323–4

Barr, Bill 323
Bar-Siman-Tov, I 43
Belarus, Revolution in Dignity in 302
Berlin, Isaiah 299
Berlusconi, Silvio 36
Berman, Sheri 322
biopolitics 48, 50–5, 67
Blair, Tony 72
blockchain 285, 294–6
Boccaccio, Giovanni 10
Bolsonaro, Jair 303, 315–16, 320, 323–4
border control 163, 165, 244, 321
Brady, Graham 82, 89
Brandeis, Louis 182, 293–4
Brazil 67, 301, 303, 315–16, 320, 323–4
Brexit 72–3, 75, 84
Brown, Gordon 90
Brubaker, Rogers 312
budgets
death and dying 2, 48, 54–6, 58, 60–4
European Union 249, 250–3, 256–9, 262, 305
France 210
Hungary, EU budget sanctions imposed on 305
national budgets 250–1, 256, 258–9, 262
Sweden 137
Burnham, Andy 88–9
Burri, Boris 188–9
Buzyn, Agnès 210

Camus, Albert 10
Caroni, Andrea 190, 193, 196–7
Carville, James 313
Castex, Jean 207
categorical imperative 24–5, 30–1
centralisation
decentralisation 109, 111, 150, 215, 344–5
democracy 343, 345–6
European Union 247, 255, 256–8, 260, 262
France 3, 201, 211, 215–16, 223, 345
Germany 105–6, 109, 111
sub-federal states, centralisation of power in 343
United Kingdom 2, 72, 84, 87–90, 344–5
Chan, Margaret 234
China 227, 236–8, 263, 273, 293, 301, 321
Cicero 9

Colombia, conflicts on right to health in 62–3
colonialism 51, 65, 67
competition and state aid 167
conspiracy theories 321, 323–4
constitutional courts
Colombia 62–3
France 217–19, 221
Germany 57–8, 96
Hungary 164–7, 169–70, 173, 177, 304
Italy 124, 130, 132
constitutions *see also* **constitutional courts**
France 119, 207–11, 214–18, 223, 331
Germany 2, 92, 96–8, 113–15, 334
Hungary 155–62, 164, 174–7, 304, 309, 332, 334, 336
illiberal constitutional theories 4, 299–313
India 60
Italy 118, 119–22, 127–9, 133, 332
politics and law, relationship between 18
South Africa 61
states of emergency/exception
states with concept 332–5
states without concept 330–2
sub-constitutional law 18
Sweden 3, 135–54, 334, 338
Switzerland 182, 196, 333, 334, 338
United Kingdom 2, 71–6, 90, 334, 336
contingency of good 15–17
Coratella, Teresa 320
corruption 14, 36–7, 312, 317, 322
courts, role of *see* **constitutional courts; judiciary/courts**
crime
corruption 14, 36–7, 312, 317, 322
France 210–11
Hungary 160–1
jury trials, suspension of 37
misconduct in public office 147
online platforms and disinformation 265
social media 301
Sweden 147
United States, postal voting in 38
culture wars 316, 317, 323–4
Cummings, Dominic 73

Daly, Tom 301
death and dying 47–67
biopolitics 48, 50–5, 67
budgetary decision-making 55–6, 58, 60–4
death, definition of 49
democracy 2, 47–67
dignity and autonomy of death and dying 57–8
economic dimension of death 55–7
economised timing of death 2, 48, 49–50, 52
enabling life 59–64
health, right to 2, 60–3, 67
health systems
distribution of resources 55–6, 58, 60–4
financing 55–6, 58
structure of 55
human rights 2, 48, 52–3, 57, 60–4, 67
international perspectives 65–6
legal thanatology 49–65
governing life and death 54–7
necro-law 65–6
pre-requisites 49–54
rationalisations of life and death 54–64
Thanato judgments 57–64
liberal democracies, role of death in 64–6
life expectancy 2, 48–9, 55–6, 61–4
life, right to 2, 48, 60, 67
lockdowns 53–4, 64–5
necropolitics 50–2
needs and necessities, sidelining of 53–4
prolonging life 49–50, 55–6, 64–5
rationalisations of life and death 48, 54–64
resources 49–50, 55–6, 58, 60–4
social rights 2, 56–7, 59, 61–4
taboo subject, death as 50
deaths and COVID-19 cases, number of
France 202
Germany 93–5
global deaths 33, 91
Hungary 174–5
United Kingdom 74, 82
democracy
biopolitics 48, 50–5, 67
budgetary law 2, 48, 54–5
centralisation of power 343, 345–6
citizen democracy 283
colonialism 51, 65, 67
death and dying 47–67
decentralisation 344–5
decision-making 2, 48, 55–6, 58, 60–7
equality rights 59–60
European Union 246, 251, 253–4, 260, 262, 344
France 210–16, 220, 223
Germany 96–103, 107, 109, 114
human rights 2, 48, 52–3, 57, 60–4, 67, 283, 296

Hungary 155–6, 159, 168–9, 176, 305
illiberalism 300–1, 310–13, 346
input and throughput 43
Italy 118–19, 124–32
legal thanatology 49–65
lockdowns 53–4, 64–5
multi-level democracy 343–6
parliaments, role of 56–7, 335–6, 338, 343, 346
populism 5, 315–27, 346
proportionality 54, 346
resources 49–50, 55–6, 58, 60–4
states of emergency/exception 5, 51, 52–4, 330, 335, 343, 346
sub-federal states, centralisation of power in 343
sub-national entities, pressure on 344–5
Sweden 136, 153–4
Switzerland 179–82, 186–7, 192, 194, 198, 333
WHO, role of 239–40, 343–4
demonstrations 80, 222, 263
deontology 14
despotism 14, 28–30
devolution in United Kingdom 2, 72, 83–8, 89, 344–5
Dewey, John 326
dictatorship 51, 307
digital human rights proportionality 283–96
blockchain 285, 294–6
democracy 283, 296
e-governance 285, 286, 289
e-public administration 285
e-state 4, 286–96
five caveats 286–95
governance, horizontal or vertical 291–3
non-coherence theory 288–9, 291, 293
privacy 284, 293–6
private domains 283–4, 291–2, 294
public domains 291–2, 294
QR codes 4, 283–4, 287–90, 293–6
rhetoric 286–9
social development 287
social media platforms 4, 283–92, 294, 296
terms of service/community standards 291–2
testing 283–4
tracing 283
travel status, monitoring 4, 293, 295
vaccines 4, 283–5, 287, 295
variance principle 287–8, 291
digital technology *see* **digital human rights proportionality; online platforms and disinformation**
discrimination 51, 59–60, 166–7, 194, 299
disinformation *see* **online platforms and disinformation**
distributive justice 55
division of powers 22–3, 37, 44, 96, 104, 114, 210
drones, police surveillance by 222
Durov, Pavel 278–9
Dworkin, Ronald 299
dying *see* **death and dying**
Dyzenhaus, David 306–9

Ebola crisis 235
economic dimension of death 55–7
economised timing of death 2, 48, 49–50, 52
e-governance 285, 286, 289
elections
executive 35
France 202, 216
Hungary 156, 160–2, 303–4
Poland 303, 309
re-election, mechanism for 40
elites
anti-elitism 315–22, 324
corruption 312
populism 315–22, 324
Ely, John Hart 40, 45
emergency measures *see* **states of emergency/exception; WHO's Emergency Committees authoritarianism** 4, 303, 306–9
emergency, definition of 121–2
Emergency Support Instrument (ESI) (EU) 246–7, 250–1, 253–61
Germany 2, 98–100, 108, 114, 120
Hungary 1, 155–78
illiberalism 299–303
Italy 117–24
self-entrenchment of executive 37–9
Switzerland 3, 181, 182–4, 333
United States 303
England, devolution in 84, 86–9
Epicurus 24
epidemic, definition of 48
e-public administration 285
equality rights and non-discrimination 51, 59–60, 166–7, 194, 299
equivalence, principle of 337

Erdoğan, Recep Tayyip 317
Erhard, Ludwig 92
ESF+ programme (EU) 252
e-state 4, 286–96
Estonia
  human rights online 283–96
  remote voting, lack of 341
  states of emergency/exception 332, 333, 334–5
EU4Health Programme (EU) 246–7, 250–3, 254, 256, 258, 260
European Union 1, 243–62
  advanced purchase agreements (APAs) for vaccines 253–5, 257–8
  border control 244
  Brexit 72–3, 75, 84
  budgets 261–2
    2021–27 249
    Emergency Support Instrument (ESI) 253, 257–8
    ESF+ programme 252
    EU4Health Programme 252, 258
    financial contributions from EU 258–9
    national budgets 250–1, 256, 258–9, 262
    sanctions 305
  centralisation 247, 255, 256–8, 260, 262
  citizens 243–4, 246–7, 250–1, 253–5, 261
  Civil Protection Mechanism 245, 253, 257
  competences in health 4, 243–52, 255–62, 344
    budget 258–9, 261–2
    conferral 249–50
    consensus 249–50
    creeping 248, 259
    explicit competences 247–9, 255–6, 258–61
    limited competences 247–9
    mechanism and concerns 249–50
    shared 247
  Conference on the Future of Europe 255, 262
  constitutional violations by Member States 344
  decision-making 245–6, 251, 254–9, 262
  democracy 246, 251, 253–4, 260, 262, 344
  Emergency Support Instrument (ESI) 246–7, 250–1, 253–61
    advanced purchase agreements (APAs) for vaccines 253–5, 257–8
    budget 253, 257–8
    democracy 251, 254
    European Commission 251, 257–8
    European Parliament, absence of duty to report to or notify 255
    Steering Group, Member State involvement through 254
    vaccines 253–4, 257
  ESF+ programme 252
  EU4Health Programme 246–7, 250–3, 254, 256
    budget 252, 258
    democratic legitimacy 253
    European Commission 251–3, 256
    Steering Group, Member State involvement through 252–3
    transparency 252, 260
  European Commission 256–61
    advanced purchase agreements (APAs) for vaccines 253–5, 257–8
    competition law and state aid 167
    democratic control 251
    Emergency Support Instrument (ESI) 251, 257–8
    EU4Health Programme 251–3, 256
    legitimisation 251
    online platforms and disinformation 280–1
    transparency 251, 260
    vaccine contracts, transparency of 260
  European Parliament 243–4, 246, 251–5, 258, 260, 344
  faster response, need for 4, 243–4, 259–60, 262, 344
  financing 246–7, 250–61
  free movement of goods 244, 262, 344
  free movement of people 244, 262, 344
  Germany 92, 106
  Global Health Summit 2021 255, 262
  harmonisation 4, 247–9
  Health Union, proposal for 255
  Hungary 167, 305
  joint procurement
    countermeasures 258, 260–1
    Emergency Support Instrument (ESI) 253
    EU4Health Programme 251–2
    Joint Procurement Agreement (JHA) 245–6, 253–4, 257–8
    vaccines 257–8
  media 243–4
  medical supplies, availability of 244, 246, 250–1

Member State involvement 252–3, 254, 260–1
multi-level governance 5, 335, 345–6
national budgets 250–1, 256, 258–9, 262
online platforms and disinformation 280–1
Parliament Survey 243–4, 246
policy areas 245
procurement
Commission 256
Emergency Support Instrument (ESI) 246–7, 250–1, 253–8
faster response, need for 260
joint procurement 245–6, 251–4, 257–8, 260–1
preventive procurement 244
vaccines 253–8, 261
RescEU reserve 245–6, 253
solidarity 244, 246, 249, 256, 261, 344
statistics 47–8, 344
subsidiarity 249, 251, 253, 258
Sweden 143
transparency 251–2, 255, 260, 262
vaccines 244, 246, 250–1, 253–8, 260–1, 344

Europol 279

exception, state of *see* **states of emergency/exception**

executive *see* **self-entrenchment of executive**
centralisation 343
criminal proceedings 210–11
democracy 343
electoral reform 35
France 3, 201–2, 204–11, 214, 219–20, 223, 336, 337, 340–3
Germany 2, 93–4, 98–101, 107–10, 113–14
Hungary 3, 155, 158, 160, 171–7
illiberalism 300–1, 303, 308–10
Italy 121–4, 128–32, 337, 339
judiciary, deference of 41–2
ministerial accountability 44
parliaments, role of 5, 337–43
France 204–14, 336, 337, 339–43
Germany 94, 100–1, 109–10, 114
Hungary 3, 158, 160, 171, 173, 175–7
Italy 2–3, 118, 125–31, 336, 339
political self-entrenchment 35–45
populism 323
public broadcasting to promote government, use of 35, 36
separation of powers 22–3, 37, 44
states of emergency/exception 19, 22–3, 52–3, 346
France 3, 201–2, 204–11, 214, 219–20, 223, 336, 337, 340
Italy 332
transfers of power 330–1
Sweden 3, 135, 137–40, 142, 144–8, 151–4, 330–1, 338, 342
Switzerland 342
United Kingdom 2, 71–2, 76–7, 79, 83
United States 303

experts *see* **technocrats and experts**

extremist groups 278–9

Facebook 263, 267–70, 280, 293
algorithms 269
amount of misinformation 269–70
anti-lockdown demonstrations, deletion of events for 263
automated moderation 268, 269
Data for Good programme 269
fact-checking 268–9, 280
financial support 280
Information Hub 268
literacy skills, improving media, digital and health 280
lockdowns 263, 269
terms of service/community standards 268
viral, likelihood of information becoming 270
working conditions 269, 281
YouTube 270

fact-checking 33, 268–9, 275, 280, 288

Farage, Nigel 318

fast-track procedures 2, 43, 77–8, 152–3, 203–4, 336, 338, 340

Fauci, Anthony 323

federalism 2, 92–9, 102–14, 180, 343–5

financial support
Emergency Support Instrument (ESI) (EU) 246–7, 250–1, 253–61
ESF+ programme (EU) 252
EU4Health Programme (EU) 246–7, 250–3, 254, 256, 258, 260
Facebook 280
Hungary 166–7
public subsidies to political parties 36
Twitter 273
United Kingdom, furlough and job retention support schemes in 73, 85, 88–9
United States 37–8
YouTube 276

Florence, epidemic in medieval 10
forgotten, right to be 294
Foucault, Michael 48, 50–1
France 201–23
accountability 210
asylum seekers 222
authorisation to legislate by Ordinance 208–9, 337
budgetary reforms 210
case law of administrative courts 221–2
centralisation 3, 201, 211, 215–16, 223, 345
crisis management and centralism 215–16
decentralisation/centralisation dialectic 215
minimalist differentiation 216
uniform policy throughout national territory 215–16
chronology 201–4
Citizens' Collective 223
commissions of enquiry 214, 340
Conseil constitutionnel 217–19, 221
Conseil d'Etat 209, 217, 221–2
Constitution 119, 207–11, 214–18, 223, 331
Cour de cassation 217
criminal proceedings against ministers 210–11
crisis management and centralism 215–16
curfews 203, 216, 222
cycle, freedom to 222
deaths and cases, number of 202
Defence Council 201, 205–6
democracy 210–16, 220, 223
demonstrations 222
discrimination 222
drones, police surveillance by 222
elections 202, 216
emergency bill 202–4, 213–14
ending state of emergency, regime for 205
executive 3–4, 204–11, 331, 336, 337
criticisms of policies 209–10
hyper-executive state of emergency 3, 201–23
management within the executive 204–11
Parliament, relationship with 204–14, 336, 337, 339–43
political control over government, restraints on 213–14
President 3, 201–2, 204–7, 214, 223, 340
Prime Minister 201–2, 205–7, 214, 218–20
experts, role of 131, 204–6, 223
extensions to state of emergency 203–4, 213–14
fact-finding missions 214, 340
French Revolution 29
human rights and freedoms, breach of 218–22, 223
hyper-presidentialism 206–7
Institutional Act 202–3, 217–18
legal framework 202
local bodies
centralised management 3, 201, 211, 215–16, 223
mayors 209, 215
prefects 209, 215–16
weakening of local democratic bodies 4, 216, 345
lockdowns 202–3, 207–8, 212, 215–17, 221–2, 336
masks, wearing 209, 210, 215
mayors 209, 215
media 206, 210
Minister of Health 201–2, 204–8, 212–13, 218–19
National Assembly 204–5
necessity principle 222
opposition 209, 214, 342–3
Parliament (Council of Ministers/Senate) 201–2, 204–14, 331
attempts to respond by Parliamentarians 214, 340
commissions of enquiry 214, 340
confident parliament, as 341–2
Defence Council 206
deprivation of power to create statutory laws 211–14
echo chamber, as 204–7
emergency bill 202–3
executive 204–14, 336, 337, 339–43
experts, role of 131, 204–6, 223
extension to state of emergency, authorisation of 213–14
fact-finding missions 214
hyper-presidentialism 206–7
marginalisation 204–7, 336, 337
obedient Parliament, as 343

oversight, insufficiently reinforced 213–14
political control over government, restraints on 213–14
President 201, 205
proxy voting 126, 341
transfer of power, legitimising 337
weakening of Parliament 211–14
parliamentary groups 201
policing powers 218–22
political control over government, restraints on 213–14
prefects 209, 215–16
President 201–2, 204–5, 223
Citizens' Collective 223
fact-finding mission 214, 340
hyper-presidentialism 206–7
isolation 206
powers 3, 201, 206–7
Prime Minister 206–7
Prime Minister 201–2, 205–7, 214
government requirements 220
Head of Government 207
list of powers 219–20
policing powers, extension of 218–19
President 206–7
regulatory power 206
proliferation of government measures 207–11
proportionality 212, 220, 222
proxy voting 126, 341
public gatherings 201, 220, 222
Public Health Code 207–8
regulation-making power 207–9
rule of law 4, 216–22, 223
Scientific Council 131, 204–5, 208, 214, 223
state-of-emergency regime 3, 201–23, 332, 334
declaration 208, 213–14, 219, 334
emergency bill 202–4, 213–14
ending state of emergency, regime for 205
extension 203–4, 213–14
human rights and freedoms, breach of 218–22
hyper-executive state of emergency in 3, 201–23
Institutional Act 202–3
legal basis 203, 207–8, 211–13
litigation 220–2
new legal basis for action 212–13
political control over government, restraints on 213–14
rule of law 216–22
senators, concerns of 219–20
statutory laws 211–13, 220, 336
Institutional Act 202–3, 217–18
legal basis 207–8, 211–12
regulation-making power 207–9
transparency 205–6
travel restrictions 202–3, 220, 221–2
uniform policy throughout national territory 215–16
vaccinations 204, 223
Frankfurter, Felix 42
Hungary 163
people, of 244, 262, 344
freedom 15–16, 21, 64–5 *see also* **free movement; freedom of expression**
Freedom House 39, 300–1
freedom of expression
censorship 301
Hungary 169–70
online human rights 283
online platforms and disinformation 264, 278–9, 280
Telegram instant messaging service 278–9, 280
Fukuyama, Francis 300, 315
fundamental rights *see* **human rights**

Gabriel, Markus 10
Gardbaum, S 35
Germany 1, 91–115 *see also* **Nazi Germany**
administrative federalism 97
Basic Law 91–3, 96–102, 108–9, 334
Bundesrat 97–8, 102–6, 107, 110, 112–13, 115
Bundestag 1, 47, 99–103, 108–10, 114
centralisation 105–6
Constitution 2, 92, 96–8, 113–15, 334
Constitutional Court 57–8, 96
constitutional regulations, clarifying 108–9
cooperative federalism 2, 97–8, 112–13, 345
coordinated and cooperative collective action 109
critical evaluation of legal regime for pandemics 105–9
curfews 94, 102
deaths and cases, number of 93–5
decentralisation 109, 111

decision-making 109–11
democracy 96–103, 107, 109, 114
economic and financial power 91–2
emergencies, rules on 2, 98–100, 108, 114, 120
European Union 92, 106
executive
decrees 93, 107
federalism 2, 98–9, 107–10, 113
Parliament, relationship with 94, 100–1, 109–10, 114, 342
federal courts, importance of 111
federalist structure 2, 92–9, 102–13, 345
complex federalism 107
enabler, federalism as 109–11
executive 2, 98–9, 107–10, 113
fragmentation 105–6
inhibitor, federalism as 105–9
fragmentation through federalism 105–6
fundamental rights 98, 101–2, 104, 107–9, 113–14
good faith 97
Infection Protection Act 102–10, 114
infectious diseases, challenges to legal regime of 102–10, 114
influence, proven ability to gain 110
Länder 92, 95, 96–100, 102–15
legal framework 95–105
legal reform, options for 111–15
legislative powers 96–7, 338–9
lockdowns 95, 106
Parliament
Bundesrat 97–8, 102–6, 107, 110, 112–13, 115
Bundestag 1, 47, 99–103, 108–10, 114
business as usual parliaments 342
disempowerment 106–7, 338–9
executive 94, 100–1, 109–10, 114, 342
future role 113–15
quora 341
role of 99–101
social distancing 126
political reform, options for 111–15
populism 320–1, 325
Prime Ministers Conferences 111, 113–14
proportionality 113
reform, legal and political 111–15
Robert Koch Institute (RKI) 105–6, 109–10
rule of law 92, 104
science 105, 109–10
separation of powers 96, 104, 114
social distancing 94, 104–5
social state (*Staatsqualität*) 91, 96
states of emergency/exception 99, 332, 334
statutory law
Basic Law 91–3, 96–102, 108–9, 334
Infection Protection Act 102–10, 114
legal framework 95–105
legislative powers 96–7, 338–9
test and trace 94
transparent decision-making 109–10, 113
vaccination strategy 94, 113
Gfeller, Katja 187, 191–2, 194, 198
Ginsburg, Tom 41, 300–1
Glaser, Andreas 187, 191–2, 194, 199
global financial crisis 2008 63–4
goodness 10–17
government *see* **executive**
Greece
lockdown 38
media, payments by executive to the 38–9, 42, 45
parliament, limited function of 43

H1N1 influenza epidemic in 2009 234–5
Haider, Jörg 322
Hale, Brenda 78
happiness 289–90
Harding, Dido 83
health, right to 2, 60–3, 67
health systems
death and dying 55–6, 58, 60–4
distribution of resources 55–6, 58, 60–4
non-citizens, exclusion from healthcare of 64, 66
structure 55
Hobbes, Thomas 28, 307
hospitals
Hungary 166, 173
military management 166, 173
wards as core paradigm of pandemic 53
housing, right to 61
Hoyle, Lindsey 80–1
human dignity 57–9, 101
human rights *see also* **digital human rights proportionality; social rights**
death and dying 2, 48, 52–3, 57, 60–4, 67
due diligence 266
European Convention on Human Rights (ECHR) 264–5
forgotten, right to be 294
France 218–22, 223
freedom of expression 264
Germany 98, 101–2, 104, 107–9, 113–14

health, right to 2, 60–3, 67
housing, right to 61
Hungary 156–66, 170, 174–7, 304, 309, 332–3, 336
illiberalism 299, 302
inhuman or degrading treatment 59
International Covenant on Civil and Political Rights (ICCPR) 264
Israel 302
Italy 3, 123–4, 129–32
life, right to 2, 48, 60, 62, 67
online platforms and disinformation 263–6
policing powers, extension of 219–20
proportionality 52–3
self-entrenchment of executive 34, 40, 45
social distancing 34
suspension or abolition 14, 330
Sweden 139, 141, 152
Switzerland 180
UN Guiding Principles on Business and Human Rights 265–6
United Kingdom 334
Universal Declaration of Human Rights 264

Hungary 1, 155–78
asylum seekers 165, 171, 304
Authorisation Act 160–2
constitutional concerns 161–2
first Act 160–2, 333, 336, 337–8
repeal 170–1
second Authorisation Act 175–6, 333, 337–8
autocratic, Hungarian regime as 155–6, 301, 303–6, 321
borders, control of 163, 165
budget sanctions imposed by EU 305
by-elections, suspension of 160–1
cardinal acts 157, 159
Chief Medical Officer 168, 172
companies, state control of 165, 172
competition and state aid 167
Constitution 155–8, 336
amendments 156
Authorisation Acts 161–2, 175–6
constitutional system 155–8
Fundamental Law 2011 156–8, 164, 304
special legal order 174
state of danger as unconstitutional 158–60, 177, 309, 332, 334
Constitutional Court 164–7, 169–70, 173, 177, 304
crisis management with government decrees 162–70
deaths, number of 174–5
democracy 155–6, 159, 168–9, 176, 305
Disaster Management Act 159–61, 175, 333
disclosure of public data 166
discriminatory measures 166–7
economic activities, financial advantages for 171
Economy Protection Action Plan 163, 166
effectiveness 162, 165, 169
Epidemic Fund 166–7
European Union 167, 305
executive 171–7
health crisis situation, introduction of concept of 172–5
National Assembly 3, 158, 160, 171, 173, 175–7, 336
self-empowerment 3, 155
subordination of National Assembly 3, 171, 173, 175–7
unlimited powers 155
expropriation of funds from municipalities 164
Fidesz 36, 156, 303–4
first Authorisation Act 160–2, 333, 336, 337–8
freedom of expression 169–70
Fundamental Law 2011 156–66, 170, 175–7, 304, 309, 332–3, 336
fundamental rights, restriction of 174
general elections 162, 303–4
health crisis situation, introduction of concept of 172–5, 177
hospital system, military management of 166, 173
illiberal regime, Hungary as a 4, 155–6, 301, 303–6, 308–9
immigration 174, 304
justice break 168
lockdowns and quarantine 173
management of legal consequences of the emergency situation 170–4
media 36, 169
National Assembly 158, 160–2
Authorisation Acts 160–2, 175–6, 333, 336–8
continuous operation 158, 162, 177
Disaster Management Act 159–61, 175, 333
executive 3, 158, 160, 171, 173, 175–7, 336

guarantees, lack of 161–2
obedient Parliament, as 342–3
state of danger, abolition of 170–1
suspension 43, 158, 176
transfer of power, legitimising 337–8
natural disaster, concept of 159–60, 166, 176, 332–3
necessity 162–4, 337
obstruction of the protection against the pandemic, crime of 160–1
policy aims, promotion of other 172–3
populism 155–6, 177–8, 317, 321–2
proportionality 160, 162–70, 173, 337, 343
public gatherings 163, 173
referendums, suspension of 160–1
rule of law 155, 164
scaremongering and freedom of speech 169–70
second Authorisation Act 175–6, 333, 337–8
second state of danger, declaration of 175
semi-authoritarian regime, Hungary as a 155–6, 177
social distancing 163
special economic zones, introduction of 164–5
special legal order, forms of 157–8, 173–8
state of danger 155, 157–65, 174–8, 303–6, 309, 332
abolition 170–1
asylum procedure 165, 304
Constitution 158–60, 169, 177, 309, 332, 334
declarations 157, 158–60, 305, 334
extension of scope 3, 161–2, 168, 176
second state of danger, declaration of 175–6
special legal order, as 157
termination 158, 170–2
transitional rules 171
statutory law
Authorisation Acts 160–2, 170–1, 175–6, 333, 336–8
cardinal acts 157, 159
crisis management with government decrees 162–70
Disaster Management Act 159–61, 175, 333
Fundamental Law 2011 156–66, 170, 175–7, 304, 309, 332–3, 336
guarantees 160–2
health crisis situation, introduction of concept of 172–5, 177
policy aims, promotion of other 172–3
suspension 157–8, 160
temporal effect of emergency decrees 3, 157–62, 168–9, 176, 304–5, 309, 337–8
tax breaks 166–7
temporal effect of emergency decrees 3, 157–62, 168–9, 176, 304–5, 309, 337–8
transitional rules 165, 171, 343
hygienic state 53–4

illiberalism 299–313
authoritarian use of emergency power, justification for 4, 303, 306–9
autocracies 301, 303–6, 310–11
categories of countries 301
checks and balances 299–300
commissarial dictatorship and sovereign dictatorship, difference between 307
common-good constitutionalism 309
constitutional theories 4, 299–313
democracy 300–1, 310–13, 346
emergency measures 299–303
equality 299
executive
overreach 303, 309–10
oversight, lack of 300–1
unbound 308–9
underreach 303
groups and movements, opposition from 302
homogeneity of the people 306–8
human rights 299, 302
Hungary 4, 155–6, 301, 303–6, 308–9
lockdowns 301
meritocracy 311–12
national sovereignty 302
political liberalism 299
populism 4, 302, 310–13
rule of law 299, 306–7
semi-liberal systems 302
social media 301
social trust 300
unskilled low-paid workers 311–12
immigration
asylum seekers 165, 171, 222, 304
border control 163, 165, 244, 321

deportation due to health situations of aliens, prohibition of 50
Hungary 165, 171, 174, 304, 321
impartiality, principle of 145
India 60–1, 303
information *see* **digital human rights proportionality; online platforms and disinformation**
inhuman or degrading treatment 59
inquiries 74, 131, 141, 148, 214, 325, 340
International Covenant on Civil and Political Rights (ICCPR) 264
international law 65–6, 264, 267 *see also* **WHO's Emergency Committees**
Internet *see* **digital human rights proportionality; online platforms and disinformation; social media**
Israel, state of emergency in 302
Italy 117–33
accountability 3, 118, 124–5, 131–2
administrative courts 130, 132
certainty of law 3, 118, 124, 132
Civil Protection Agency 320
comparative scenario 119–22, 126
Constituent Assembly 121–2, 133
Constitution 118, 119–22, 127–9, 133, 331–2
Constitutional Court 124, 130, 132
Council of Ministers 121–4, 128–32, 337, 339
head of the executive as dominus of the emergency 122–4
Parliament, relationship with 2–3, 118, 125–31, 336, 339
state of emergency, declaration of 122–3, 332
democracy 118–19, 124–32
early legal reactions 119–24
emergency, definition of 121–2
emergency measures 117–24
decrees of the President 123–4, 128–30, 132, 337, 339
general clause model 119
growing intensity model 120
macro-models 119–20
rationalised model 119–20
state of emergencies/exception 120, 122–3, 128
temporary measures converted to permanent measures 122
Five Star Movement 311
fragmented attitudes of institutions 3, 132
head of the executive 122–5, 131
human rights/personal freedoms 3, 123–4, 129–32
incoherent attitudes of institutions 3, 132–3
legal reactions to COVID-19 122–4
lockdown 118
majority and opposition forces, relationship between 3, 132–3
mass communication/media 36, 131
national disasters 122, 331–2
Parliament
Chamber of Deputies 118, 126–9
executive, relationship with 2–3, 118, 125–31, 336, 339
hesitant parliament, as 342
marginalisation of 2–3, 118, 125–9, 336, 337
remote voting 126–8, 341
Senate 118, 126–9
social distancing 126–8
suspension 126
political accountability 3, 125, 132
populism 320
remote voting 126–8, 341
representativeness 3, 124, 127, 132
scientific evidence 131
social distancing 125, 126–8
states of emergency/exception 120, 122–3, 128, 330–2
statutory law 117–24
decrees of the President of the Council of Ministers (DPCMs) 123–4, 128–30, 132
early legal reactions 119–24
legislative decrees 122–4, 128, 331–2
marginalisation of Parliament 125–9
Technical-Scientific Committee 131
temporary measures converted to permanent measures 122
transparency 3, 118, 124, 127, 131–2

Johnson, Boris 72–3, 75, 81, 84, 319–20, 322, 326
judicial review 40–2, 45, 83, 124, 143–4, 181
judiciary/courts *see also* **constitutional courts**
deference of judiciary 37, 41–2, 45
France 221–2
Germany 111
independent and impartial tribunals 14
India, Supreme Court in 60

Italy 130, 132
judicial review 40–2, 45, 83, 124, 143–4, 181
judiciary to emergency powers, deference of 37, 42, 45
jury trials, suspension of 37
online trials 37
self-entrenchment of executive 37, 40–3, 45
Sweden 140–4, 147
jury trials, suspension of 37

Kaczyński, Jarosław 317
Kant, Immanuel 15–16, 18–19, 24–30
Kelsen, Hans 21
Krastev, Ivan 302
Kurz, Sebastian 13

La Rue, Frank 264
law and politics, relationship between *see* **politics and law, relationship between**
lawlessness 9–10, 17–19
Le Pen, Jean Marie 322
leadership 300–1, 315–16, 318, 320, 322–3, 325
legal certainty 3, 118, 124, 132, 167–9
legal thanatology 49–65
economised timing of death 49–50
governing life and death 54–7
necro-law 65–6
pre-requisites 49–54
rationalisations of life and death 54–64
Thanato judgments 57–64
legality, principle of 3, 146
legislation *see* **statutory law**
legislature *see* **parliaments, role of**
Leonard, Mark 302
libertarianism 322–3
life expectancy 2, 48–9, 55–6, 61–4
life, right to 2, 48, 60, 62, 67
Limbaugh, Rush 323
local areas/regions
France 3, 4, 201, 209, 211, 215–16, 223, 345
Germany 92, 95, 96–100, 102–15
Hungary 164–5
illiberalism 304
Sweden 138, 140–2, 144–5, 147, 150
Switzerland 180, 182, 187, 345
United Kingdom 2, 72–3, 77, 83–8, 89, 344–5
lockdowns
anti-lockdown demonstrations, deletion of Facebook events for 263
Austria 339
democracy 53–4, 64–5
Facebook 263, 269
France 202–3, 207–8, 212, 215–17, 221–2, 336
general lockdowns 34
Germany 95, 106
Greece 38
Hungary 173, 301
Italy 118
New Zealand 326
online platforms and disinformation 280
partial lockdowns 34
prioritisation of different liberties in different countries 64–5
Sweden 135, 153
United Kingdom 73, 77–86, 89
Lucretius 9

Machiavelli, Niccolò 22
Macron, Emmanuel 201, 206, 223
Manne, Kate 321
masks, wearing 34, 77–8, 209, 210, 215, 323
Maurrass, Charles 322
May, Theresa 72, 82
Mbembe, Achille 51–2
media *see also* **social media**
corruption 36–7
European Union 243–4
France 206, 210
free airtime for political parties 36
Greece 38–9, 42, 45
Hungary 169
Italy 131
political bias 38–9
public broadcasting to promote government, use of 35, 36
self-entrenchment of executive 36–9, 43–4, 45
transparency 44
meritocracy 311–12
Merkel, Angela 92, 95, 114, 321
minorities, vilification of 317, 324, 327
misinformation *see* **digital human rights proportionality; online platforms and disinformation**
Modi, Narendra 303, 324
Mozes, Arnon 'Noni' 36–7

national sovereignty 302, 321
national unity 5, 324, 326
Nazi Germany 305–8
 authoritarian legalism 307
 concentration camps 51
 fundamental rights 96
 Night of the Long Knives 307
 racial homogeneity 308
 Weimar Constitution 306–7
necessity
 democracy 58, 346
 France 222
 human rights 222
 Hungary 162–4, 337
 parliaments, role of 338
 source of law, as 21–2, 24, 331
 states of emergency/exception 19, 26–8
 state of necessity 10–13, 16–19, 21–2
 Sweden 149, 152
necro-law 65–6
necropolitics 50–2
neoliberalism 50, 319, 322
nepotism 14
Nergelius, Joakim 151
Netanyahu, Benjamin 36–7
Netherlands 302
New Zealand 301, 326
Nietzsche, Friedrich 14
non-citizens, exclusion from healthcare of 64, 66
non-coherence theory 288–9, 291, 293
Nordhaus, WD 36
Northern Ireland, devolution in 84–6
Nozick, Robert 17
number of deaths and COVID-19 cases *see* **deaths and COVID-19 cases, number of**

Obama, Barack 323–4, 327
objectivity, principle of 3, 145, 152
online platforms and disinformation 263–82 *see also* **Facebook; Telegram instant messaging service; Twitter; YouTube**
 accountability 266
 algorithms 269, 274, 281
 automated moderation 263, 268, 269, 272, 277, 281–2
 criminals, misuse by 265
 dominant platforms 265, 267
 European Commission, recommendations of 280–1
 European Convention on Human Rights (ECHR) 264–5
 fact-checking 268–9, 275, 280
 freedom of expression 264, 278–9, 280
 human moderators 268–9, 272, 280
 human rights 263–6
 increase in traffic 270, 281
 intermediaries 265–6
  Council of Europe Recommendation 265, 266
  mergers 265
  Protest, Respect and Remedy framework (Ruggie Principles) 266
  social licences 266
  UN Guiding Principles on Business and Human Rights 265–6
 international law 264, 267
 lockdowns 280
 OECD, recommendations of 280
 opinions, freedom to hold 264
 private duties 263–7
 private ordering of coronavirus-related content 280–1
 private military contractors 267
 social networking 267, 277–8, 280
 state responsibilities 263–7
 transnational corporations 267
 transparency 280
 United States 263
 working conditions 269, 274, 281
opinions, freedom to hold 264
opposition
 Austria 339
 France 209, 214, 342–3
 Germany 112
 Greece 39
 Hungary 165, 176–7
 illiberalism 301, 304
 Italy 3, 132
 national unity 5
 populism 315–18, 320, 324–6
 self-entrenchment of executive 43–5
 Sweden 153
 United Kingdom 79, 81
Orbán, Viktor 36, 303–9, 317, 322, 324

pandemic, definition of 48
parliaments, role of 335–43 *see also* **remote sittings of Parliament**
 accountability 339
 biopolitics 54–5
 business as usual parliaments 342

confident parliaments 341–2
death and dying 56–7
decision-making 56–7
deliberations 340–1
democracy 56–7, 335–6, 338, 346
depth of involvement 335–6, 341, 342
European Parliament 243–4, 246, 251–5, 258, 260, 344
executive 5, 337–43
France 204–14, 336, 337, 339–43
Germany 94, 100–1, 109–10, 114
Hungary 3, 158, 160, 171, 173, 175–7
Italy 2–3, 118, 125–31, 336, 339
France 131, 201–14, 223, 336, 337, 340–1
Germany 1, 47, 97–110, 112–15, 126, 338–9, 341
Greece 43
hesitant parliaments 342
Hungary 3, 158–62, 170–1, 173, 175–7, 333, 336–8
input and throughput democracy, problems of 43
Italy 2–3, 118, 125–31, 336, 337, 339, 341
limiting functions 2, 34, 37, 43
necessity 338
obedient parliaments 342–3
oversight/scrutiny 335, 336–7, 339, 341–2
parliamentary sovereignty 140–4
populism 325
reviewing/surveying measures 339–40
scrutiny 2, 43–4, 53, 71, 77–83, 175–7, 182, 336, 339–42, 346
self-entrenchment of executive 43–5
states of emergency/exception 53, 343, 346
statutory law, legitimising particular measures by 338–9
suspension of Parliament 37, 43
Sweden 135, 137–53, 338, 342
Switzerland 180–98, 340
transfers of power to executive, legitimising general 337–8, 340, 341–2
United Kingdom 2, 43, 71–5, 77–84, 87, 336, 340–1
Patel, Priti 75–6
people
democracy 48
governing for the people 5, 329–46
homogeneity of the people 306–8
Italy 122
monopoly of representing the people 317–18, 326
populism 317–18, 326
self-entrenchment of executive 43–4
sovereignty of the people 44, 136, 140, 153
Sweden 136, 140, 153
will of the people 122
personality, right of 57–8
Philippe, Edouard 201, 207, 210
Pildes, Richard H 41
Poland 303, 306, 309, 317
police
drones, police surveillance by 222
Europol 279
France 218–22
police state 295
United Kingdom 78–9
politics and law, relationship between 10–31
abnegation of the law 13–19
apriority of right 15–17
contingency of good 15–17
creation of law 14, 17–18
despotism 14, 28–30
freedom 15–16, 21
goodness 10–17
irrational law 18–19
lawlessness 9–10, 17–19
necessity, state of 10–13, 16–19, 21–2, 24
positive law 17–19
primacy claims of politics 10–18, 21–2, 24, 31, 322
reason 14–19
self-entrenchment of executive 34–44
state of nature 19, 21, 28, 30
states of exception/emergency 2, 10, 18–31
Popper, Karl 299
populism 315–27
anti-elitism 315–22, 324
anti-science 315–17, 324–5
authoritarianism 317
border control 321
conspiracy theories 323
corruption 312
culture wars 316, 317, 323–4
democracy 5, 315–27, 346
experts/technocrats 315–19, 326
Germany 320–1, 325
Hungary 155–6, 177–8, 317, 321–2
illegitimacy of opposition 317
illiberalism 4, 302, 310–13
Italy 320
justice 316
leadership 315–16, 318, 320, 322–3, 325
libertarianism 322–3

masks, wearing 323
meritocracy 311–12
minorities, vilification of 317, 324, 327
monopoly of representing the people 317–18, 326
national unity 5, 324
opposition 315–18, 320, 324–6
Poland 317
primacy of politics 322
professionalism 316–20, 326
real people/silent majority rhetoric 5, 316–18, 322
simplistic policies 315–16
structural vulnerabilities 326–7
trickle-down aggression 321
United Kingdom 322–3, 326
United States 315–17, 320–4, 326
vaccines 316, 322–3
positive law 16–20, 25, 27–8
Posner, Eric 308
poverty 61
press *see* **media**
primacy claims of politics 10–18, 21–2, 24, 31, 322
privacy 284, 293–6
private sector 263–7, 280–1, 283–4, 291–2, 294
procurement (EU)
Commission 256
Emergency Support Instrument (ESI) 246–7, 250–1, 253–8
faster response, need for 260
joint procurement 245–6, 251–4, 257–8, 260–1
preventive procurement 244
vaccines 253–8, 261
professionalism 316–20, 326
prolonging life 49–50, 55–6, 64–5
proportionality *see also* **digital human rights proportionality**
assessment 289
deficit paradox 4, 283–6, 291, 296
democracy 54, 346
European Union 244
France 212, 220, 222
Germany 110, 113
human rights
online 4, 283–6, 289, 291, 294, 296
states of emergency/exception 52–3
Hungary 160, 162–70, 173, 337, 343
Italy 130
Sweden 141, 152
public gatherings, limits on
France 201, 220, 222
Hungary 163, 173
Sweden 137–9, 142, 151
public subsidies to political parties 36

QR codes 4, 283–4, 287–90, 293–6

Rawls, John 299
reason/rationality 14–19, 27–9, 301
referendums 160–1, 183, 187
regions *see* **local areas/regions**
remote learning 277
remote sittings of Parliament 43, 340–1, 346
Estonia 341
Italy 126–8, 341
Switzerland 189–99, 340
United Kingdom 74–5, 341
RescEU reserve 245–6, 253
resources 36, 40, 42, 49–50, 55–6, 58, 60–4
responsibility, principle of 137
rhetoric 286–9
Ruggie Principles (Protest, Respect and Remedy framework) 266
rule of law
abuse of power 43
France 4, 216–22, 223
Germany 92, 104
Hungary 155, 164
illiberalism 299, 306–7
states of emergency/exception 216–22
Sweden 148–9
United Kingdom 75–6, 82
Runciman, David 301
Russia, Telegram instant messaging service in 278–80
Rutte, Mark 302

Salvini, Matteo 320
Sandel, Michael 311
sanitary state 53–4
Schmid, Stefan G 190, 193, 196–7
Schmitt, Carl 12, 19, 21, 23, 27–8, 30, 50–3, 305–9, 322
science
anti-science 315–17, 324
death and dying 49, 54, 67
France 131, 204–5, 208, 214, 223
Germany 105, 109–10
Hungary, Chief Medical Officer in 168, 172
illiberalism 301

Italy 131
populism 315–17, 324–5
sanitary state 54
United Kingdom 80, 83
WHO's emergency committees 236, 237–8

Scotland, devolution in 72, 84–6

security
discipline, imposition of 53
international security 295
national security 295
security state 53

self-determination 57–8

self-entrenchment of executive 33–45
abuse of power 2, 33–45
agencies, government capture of independent 35
courts, role of 37, 40–3, 45
emergencies, self-entrenchment during 37–9
executive 35–45
Greece 38–9, 42–3, 45
human rights 34, 40, 45
illegitimate measures 36–7
judicial review 40–2, 45
legitimate measures 36
media, role of 36–9, 43–4, 45
opposition, role of 43, 45
ordinary conditions, political self-entrenchment during 35–7, 40
parliaments 2, 34, 37, 43–5
people 43–4
political self-entrenchment 34–44
press 36–7, 43–4
public broadcasting used to promote government 35, 36
public subsidies to political parties 36
re-election, mechanism of 40
resources, maladministration of state 36, 40, 42
United Kingdom 43
United States 37–8, 42, 45, 52

separation of powers 22–3, 37, 44, 96, 104, 114, 210

slavery 15–16, 50

social distancing 10, 34
Germany 94, 104–5
Hungary 163
Italy 125, 126–8
masks, wearing 34
Sweden 137–8, 142–3, 153
Switzerland 191
United Kingdom 74

social media
chilling effect 294
criminal sanctions 301
human rights 4, 283–92, 296
illiberalism 301
online platforms and disinformation 267, 277–8, 280
public entities 285
self-entrenchment of executive 44

social rights 2, 56–7, 59, 61–4

social state (*Staatsqualität*) 91, 96

social trust 3, 136, 150–3, 300

soft law 281, 342

solidarity 244, 246, 249, 256, 261, 344

sources of law 21–2, 24, 331

South Africa 61–2, 301

South Korea, Mers outbreak in 301

sovereignty
biopolitics 51
national sovereignty 302, 321
people, of the 44
theory of sovereignty 23

Sozialstaat principle 59

Spain 63–4, 120

Spanish flu 48

state aid 167

states of emergency/exception 19–31, 330–5
constitutions with a state of emergency concept 332–5
constitutions without a state of emergency concept 330–2
death and dying 51, 52–4
declarations 330–1, 332, 333–5
democracy 5, 51, 52–4, 330, 335, 343, 346
despotism, resistance against 28–30
dictatorships and democracies, moving between 51
Estonia 332, 333, 334–5
executive 19, 22–3, 52–3, 330–1, 346
France 3, 201–23, 332, 334
Germany 99, 332, 334
human rights 52–3, 218–22, 330
Hungary 3, 155, 157–65, 168, 170–8, 303–6, 309, 332, 334
illiberalism 4, 299–303, 306–9
Israel 302
Italy 120, 122–3, 128, 330–2
Kantian approach to the state of exception 24–30
lawlessness 9–10
necessity 19, 21–2, 24, 26–8, 331

paradoxical nature 19, 20–1
parliaments, role of 19, 22–3, 53, 343, 346
politics and law, relationship between 2, 10–31
positive law 20, 25, 27–8
reason, law of 27–8
rule of law 216–22
self-entrenchment of executive 37–9
sovereignty 23, 53
Sweden 147–8, 152–3
Switzerland 333
temporary measures as becoming permanent 34
United Kingdom 334
universalisable principles 24–7
war, as state of 53

state of nature 19, 21, 28, 30
statism 322
statutory law
France 207–8, 211–13, 220, 336
Germany 91–110, 114, 334, 338–9
Hungary 3, 156–77, 304–5, 309, 332–3, 336–8
Italy 117–30, 132, 331–2
legitimacy 338–9
Sweden 137–46, 148–54, 338, 342
Switzerland 179, 181–7, 198, 338
United Kingdom 2, 77–81, 83, 334, 336

Stringer, Graham 83
subsidiarity 137, 249, 251, 253, 258
Sumption, Jonathan 78–9
Sundström, G 150
surveillance 222, 229, 238–40, 284–5, 289, 301–2
Sweden 135–54
access to official documents 145
accountability 3, 146–7, 153–4
actors within norm-making procedures 141–3
administration, instruments to steer 146
administrative model, softness of 151–2
anticipatory statutorification 148–9, 154
budgets 137
businesses, measures targeted at 139–40
Chancellor of Justice 147
commission on Covid-19, appointment on 154
Committee on the Constitution 146–7, 152
Communicable Diseases Act of 2004 137–9, 148, 150
consensus-building in political culture 3, 136, 150–3
Constitution 3, 135–54, 338
constitutional committees 143
constitutionalism 150–3
Council of Legislation 139, 143–4, 152
courts 143–4, 147
Covid-19 Act 135–7, 139, 150–4
criminal charges for misconduct in public office 147
decentralisation 150
delegation 135, 137–40, 142, 144–6, 151–3
democracy 136, 153–4
disciplinary action against public officials 147
dualism with Swedish administrative model 144–5
equivalence, principle of 137
EU law 143
executive 330–1, 338
accountability 3, 146–7
command and control 144–6
commission on Covid-19, appointment on 154
Committee on the Constitution 146–8
delegation 135, 137, 142, 144–6, 151–3
norm-making powers to government, delegation of 138–40, 151
Riksdag 144–7, 152–3, 330–1, 338, 342
extraordinary measures in times of crises 147–9
fast-track legislation 152–3
fundamental rights 139, 141, 152
general governance in relation to communicable diseases 137–8
governance 137–8, 150–3
impartiality, principle of 145
informal and voluntary measures 135
Instrument of Government 136, 138–9, 140–53
judicial review 143–4
judiciary 140–4
legal responses 136–40
legality, principle of 3, 146
legislation 141–9, 151, 154, 338, 342
legislative institutions 135, 137–8, 140–53, 330–1, 338, 342
local areas/regions 138, 140–2, 144–5, 147, 150
lockdowns 135, 153
municipalities 144–5
necessity 149, 152
non-binding measures as binding 151–2, 153–4

norms and legislation 141–6, 151, 154
objectivity, principle of 3, 145, 152
parliamentary committees 139, 141–3
Parliamentary Ombudsman 139, 147
parliamentary sovereignty 140–4
peace or war 147–8
popular sovereignty, principle of 136, 140, 153
proportionality 141, 152
public authorities 145–7, 154
public gatherings, restrictions on 137–9, 142, 151
Public Health Agency (PHA), recommendations of 135, 137–40, 142, 147, 150–4
publication of measures 152
regions 138, 140, 142, 144–5
responsibility, principle of 137
Riksdag 135, 137–8, 140–53
  accountability of executive 147
  Corona-Riksdag 143, 153
  executive 144–7, 152–3, 330–1, 338, 342
  members present, reduction in number of 142–3, 153
  parliamentary committee to follow-up work of Riksdag 143
  parliamentary supremacy 153
  social distancing 142–3, 153
rule of law 148–9
social distancing 137–8, 142–3, 153
social trust 3, 136, 150–3
state of emergency 3, 147–8, 152–3, 330–1, 332
statutory law 338, 342
  anticipatory statutorification 148–9, 154
  Communicable Diseases Act of 2004 137–9, 148, 150
  Council of Legislation 139, 143–4, 152
  enacting legislation 141–2
  fast-track legislation 152–3
  institutions 140–4
  judiciary 140–4
  norms 141–6, 151, 154
temporary prohibitions 138–40
transparency 3, 145, 152
travel restrictions 137, 147, 151
voluntary measures 135, 137–8, 150–2
welfare policies 144–5, 150
Switzerland 179–99
  Administration Delegation 188–9
  cantons 180, 182, 187, 345
  Conference for Coordination 188
  Constitution 182, 196, 333, 334, 338
  Council of States 183, 185–6, 189–95
    extraordinary sessions 189–92
    meetings of the Councils 189–95
    President 190
    virtual meetings 189–90, 192–5, 198–9, 340
  Covid-19 Act of 25 September 2020 3, 181, 182–7, 198, 338
  delegation 185–7
  democracy 179–82, 186–7, 192, 194, 198, 333
  discriminatory effect of virtual meetings 194
  emergency ordinances and rulings (Verfügungen) of Federal Council 181, 182–4
  emergency parliamentary legislation 182–3
  Epidemics Act 183
  extraordinary epidemiological situations 179
  Federal Assembly 180–98
    adjustment to the pandemic 187–97
    Administration Delegation 188–92
    capacity to act 3, 181
    chambers 188
    coalitions 198
    Council of States 183, 185–6, 189–95
    Covid-19 Act of 25 September 2020 3, 181, 182–7
    emergency parliamentary legislation 182
    extraordinary sessions 189–92
    Federal Council 180–7
    functioning 3, 187–97
    hesitant parliament, as 342
    interruption of sessions 189–91, 195
    meetings of the Committees 195–7
    meetings of the Councils 189–95, 198–9
    MPs, protection of 190
    National Council 183, 185–6, 189–95
    non-professional legislature, as 181, 193
    Offices 188–97
    organs 187–9
    social distancing 191
    standing committees 189, 196
    supreme authority, as 181, 199
    virtual meetings 189–90, 192–5, 198–9, 340

Federal Council 180–7, 198
Conference for Coordination 188
Covid-19 Act of 25 September 2020 3, 181, 182–7
delegation 185–6
emergency ordinances and rulings (Verfügungen) 181, 182–4
Federal Assembly 180–7
intra-constitutional emergency powers 3, 180
Parliament, relationship with 180
regulatory activity 3, 179–80
Federal Epidemics Act 179
federalism 180, 345
Finance Delegation (FinDel) 187, 198–9
Government and Administration Organisation Act (GAOA) 184
independence and neutrality of Switzerland, safeguarding 182–3
intra-constitutional emergency powers 3, 180, 333
legal framework 182–4, 338
meetings of the Committees 195–7
meetings of the Councils 189–95, 198–9
municipal legislatures 182
National Council 183, 185–6, 189–95
extraordinary sessions 189–92
meetings of the Councils 189–95
President 190
virtual meetings 189–90, 192–4, 198–9
normal epidemiological situations 179
Ordinance on the Standstill of Deadlines for Federal Popular Votes 179
Parliament, role of 3, 179–99
parliamentary committees 185–6, 189, 195–7
phone meetings 193–6
Presiding College 188
referendums 183, 187
regulatory activity 3, 179–80, 338
social distancing 191
special epidemiological situations 179
standing committees 189, 196
states of emergency/exception 332, 333
statutory law 182–4, 338
Covid-19 Act of 25 September 2020 3, 181, 182–7, 198, 338
emergency ordinances and rulings (Verfügungen) of Federal Council 181, 182–4
emergency parliamentary legislation 182–3
Epidemics Act 183
Federal Epidemics Act 179
Government and Administration Organisation Act (GAOA) 184
Ordinance on the Standstill of Deadlines for Federal Popular Votes 179
virtual meetings 189–99, 340

tax 166–7
technocrats and experts
France 3, 131, 204–6, 223
policies, decisions on 42
populism 315–19, 326
self-entrenchment of executive 42
WHO's Emergency Committees 228, 230–6, 239–41
technology *see* **digital human rights proportionality; online platforms and disinformation**
Telegram instant messaging service 278–80
teleology 10–14, 17
terms of service/community standards 266, 268, 271, 276–8, 291–2
terrorism 51, 58, 279
testing 74, 83, 87–9, 94, 283–4
thanatology *see* **legal thanatology**
Thatcher, Margaret 319
Thucydides 9
tracing 74, 83, 87–9, 94, 283
transparency
European Union 251–2, 255, 260, 262
France 205–6
Germany 109–10, 113
Italy 3, 118, 124, 127, 131–2
media 44
online human rights 283
online platforms and disinformation 280
Sweden 3, 145, 152
WHO's Emergency Committees 237, 343–4
travel, measures concerning
France 202–3, 220, 221–2
monitoring travel status 4, 293, 295
online human rights 4, 293, 295
Sweden 137, 147, 151
WHO's Emergency Committees 236–8
Trump, Donald 37–8, 90, 303, 315–17, 319–21, 323–4, 326
Tusk, Donald 305
Twitter 263, 270–4, 280
access to reliable sources 270
automated filtering 263, 272

criteria for misinformation 271
employees, safety of 274
fact-checking 280
financial donations 273
increase in traffic 270
literacy skills, improving media, digital and health 280
public engagement, supporting 272–3
search prompt 271
sentiment analysis 273–4
terms of service/community standards 271
Twitter Developer Labs 273
working conditions 274, 281
zero tolerance 272

UN Guiding Principles on Business and Human Rights 265–6
United Kingdom 71–90
accountability 74, 83, 340
A-level results 73–4
asymmetrical quasi-federalism 84, 86
austerity measures, impact of 74, 88
Brexit 72–3, 75, 84
centralisation 72, 84, 87–90, 344–5
codification of the constitution 2, 76, 90
constitutional background 71–3
constitutional conventions 2, 71, 75–6, 336
constitutional record of Johnson's government 75–6
constitutional crisis 71, 75–6, 90
Coronavirus Act 2020 77–8, 334
deaths, number of 74, 82
devolved government 2, 72, 83–8, 89, 344–5
England
devolution in 84, 86–8
northern England, increase in cases in 88–9
executive 2, 71–2, 87
command and control structure 76–7
initiative, right of 72
Parliament 71, 77–81, 336, 340–1
scrutiny 2, 71, 77–83, 336, 340–1
self-entrenchment 37–8, 42, 45
fast-track legislation 2, 77–8, 336
furlough and job retention support schemes 73, 85, 88–9
good governance, undermining 75
guidance, use of 78
House of Commons Public Administration and Constitutional Affairs Committee 80
House of Lords 2
Human Rights Act 1998 334
judicial review 83
leadership, lack of 300
levelling up 73, 89
lockdowns 73, 77–86
devolution 85–6
legislation 77–80
Scotland 85
second lockdown 73, 81–3, 89
secondary legislation 77–83
tiered system of regional lockdowns 78, 88–9
Wales 85
London-centricism 72, 87, 89, 345
masks, requirement to wear 77–8
mayors in England 87
ministerial responsibility, doctrine of 75–6
NHS Test and Trace 74, 83, 87–9
Northern Ireland 84–6
Parliament
confident parliament, as 341
contempt of government for Parliament 81
democracy 2
England 87
hybrid system 74–5
limitation of function 43
prorogation 72–3, 75
remote voting 74–5, 341
scrutiny 2, 71, 77–83, 336, 340–1
secondary legislation 77–83, 336
select committees 83, 340
sovereignty 84
police 78–9
political background 71–3
political self-entrenchment of executive 37–8, 45
populism 322–3, 326
postal voting 38, 42, 45, 52, 45
public inquiry, need for 74
public protests 80
reform 2, 72, 90
regional devolution 87–8
relief package 37–8
remote voting 74–5, 341
rule of law 75–6, 82
science 80, 83
Scotland 84–6
Brexit 84
devolution 84
independence 72, 84

select committees 83, 340
social distancing 74
state capacity, lack of 300
states of emergency/exception 332, 334
statistics 48
statutory law 77–81
Coronavirus Act 2020 77–8, 334
fast-track legislation 2, 77–8, 336
Human Rights Act 1998 83
lockdowns 77–80
secondary legislation 77–83, 336
stimulus cheques, President's name on 37–8
territorial constitution, impact on 71, 72, 83–6
uncodified constitution 71–2
U-turns 73–4
vaccines 322–3
virus governance 71, 76–7, 79, 83–6
virus law 77–9
Wales 84–6
United States
authoritarianism 323–4
Chinese virus, references to 321
constitutional coup in Washington on 6 January 2021, attempted 90
emergency measures, lack of 303
executive underreach 303
jury trials, suspension of 37
leadership, lack of 300, 301
masks, wearing 323
online platforms and disinformation 263
populism 315–17, 320–4, 326
trickle-down aggression 321
Universal Declaration of Human Rights (UDHR) 264
universalisable principles 24–7

vaccines 4, 283–5, 287, 295
acceptance 285
advanced purchase agreements (APAs) 253–5, 257–8
European Union 244, 246, 250–1, 253–8, 260–1, 344
France 204, 223
Germany 94, 113
online human rights 4, 283–5, 287, 293, 295
QR codes 293
populism 316, 322–3
rejection 285
United Kingdom 322–3
YouTube, misinformation on 275–6
variance principle 287–8, 291
Véran, Olivier 210
Vermeule, Adrian 308–9
Versteeg, Milla 300–1
virtual meetings *see* **remote sittings of Parliament**
von der Leyen, Ursula 255
von Wyss, Moritz 193

Wales, devolution in 84–5
Walker, Charles 82
Warren, Samuel D 293–4
welfare state 63, 136, 144, 150, 250, 322
Wenander, Henrik 150
WHO's Emergency Committees 227–41
accountability 237, 239
ad hoc body, as 229–30, 232
advice 228–30, 236–7
allocation of powers 229–30
Articles on the Responsibility of International Organizations (ARIO) 239
black box metaphor 233–5, 236, 343
Chair 233
composition 228, 230–2
conflicts of interest 234
Constitution 228
declaration of an emergency 33, 119, 227–9, 233–6
deliberations 4, 228–9, 231–41
assessment 231–3
enhanced 239–41
input and output 231–3, 234–6, 239
democracy 239–40, 343–4
thick conception 239–40
thin conception 239–40
Director General
advice 228–30, 236–7
declaration of an emergency 228, 236
deference of 4, 229–30
election 239
input/output 234–6
powers 229–30
disclosure of names 235
experts 228, 230–3, 236, 239–41
fear-mongering and overreaction 227, 230
future of international deliberation in health emergencies 236–9
Geneva, meeting on 22–23 January 2020 in 227–8
geographical representation 232–3

independence 343
internal proceedings 230–1, 240–1
International Health Regulations (IHR) 228, 229–30, 232–8, 240–1
legal powers 229
mandate 229–31
meetings 227–8, 230–1
agendas 230
closed door 231, 234–5
public deliberations 231, 343–4
non-scientific considerations 238–9
opacity 234–5
political elements in decision-making 228
public deliberations 231, 343–4
recommendations 233, 236–9
representation 231–3, 239–40, 343–4
rules of procedure 240–1
Staff Regulations 239
technocracy 233–6
transparency 237, 343–4
travel restrictions 236–8
underfunding 65
unitary decisions 233
Zika epidemic 236

Wilhelm, Martin 191, 193, 196
working conditions in technology companies 269, 274, 281
World Health Organization (WHO) *see* **WHO's Emergency Committees**
Wuhan, China 227

YouTube 274–8, 280
algorithms 274
automated moderation 277
borderline content 276
Centre for Disease Control (CDC) 275
collaborative filtering 274
Depression and Anxiety Information Panels 275–6
Facebook 270
fact-checking 275, 280
fundraising 276
literacy skills, improving media, digital and health 280
Medical Misinformation Policy 275
monetising COVID-19 related content 276–7, 281
non-profit organisations and governments, free ad inventory for 275
promoted content 274
ranking 274
recommendation system 274
remote learning 277
removal, time for 277
terms of service/community standards 276, 277
vaccines, misinformation on 275–6
warning labels 275
working conditions 281

Zika epidemic 236
Zuckerburg, Mark 293

www.ingramcontent.com/pod-product-compliance
Ingram Content Group UK Ltd.
Pitfield, Milton Keynes, MK11 3LW, UK
UKHW020233290926
15470UKWH00002B/525

9 781509 946365